THE GROWING YEARS

Volume Two of *The Oxford History of the American People* opens with the election of George Washington as first President of the United States and the period of intense political creativity that followed. It moves across seventy years of explosive territorial expansion and increasing regional tension. It climaxes with the mammoth bloodletting of the War Between the States and the painful era of reconstruction and reconciliation that saw America bind up her wounds and turn to the promise and the problems of maturity. Here, in its triumphs and tragedies, is the epic of a nation and a people discovering their identity and their destiny.

"A splendid book!"—*The New York Times*

"Sparkling, living history, brimming with personality, bright with anecdote . . . the product of America's most fastidious historian. Professor Morison has not merely served up vivid, inspiring impressions. . . . He is precise; he is learned; he imparts to the general reader a knowledge of those dates and deeds, facts and figures, without which talk and writing of 'trends' is meaningless."
—*Saturday Review*

MENTOR

THE ROOTS OF AMERICA

(0451)

☐ **THE OXFORD HISTORY OF THE AMERICAN PEOPLE, Volume I: Prehistory to 1789 by Samuel Eliot Morison.** From the Pulitzer Prize-winning historian, the first of this magnificent three volume set covers the period of American history from the earliest Indian civilizations to the beginnings of George Washington's first administration. (621921—$3.95)

☐ **THE OXFORD HISTORY OF THE AMERICAN PEOPLE, Volume II: 1789 to 1877 by Samuel Eliot Morison.** The second volume opens with the election of George Washington as first President of the United States and extends through the troubled era of Reconstruction following the War Between the States. (624084—$4.95)

☐ **THE OXFORD HISTORY OF THE AMERICAN PEOPLE, Volume III: 1869 to the Death of John F. Kennedy 1963 by Samuel Eliot Morison.** This volume opens with America united after the carnage of the Civil War, through the Industrial Revolution, World Wars I and II, and closes with the death of the president who symbolized both the greatness of America and its continuing dilemmas. (624467—$4.50)*

☐ **KOSTER: Americans In Search of Their Past by Stuart Struever, Ph.D. and Felicia Antonelli Holton.** A lively narrative describing the ten-year archaeological dig in a cornfield in west central Illinois conducted in 1968 by the author. His find turned out to be a village dating back to 6,500 B.C. that shed light on settlements in prehistoric America. "Should have wide appeal; strongly recommended."—*Library Journal* (624351—$4.95)

*Prices slightly higher in Canada.

THE
OXFORD HISTORY
OF THE
AMERICAN PEOPLE

Volume Two, *1789-1877*

SAMUEL ELIOT MORISON

A MENTOR BOOK

NEW AMERICAN LIBRARY

NEW YORK AND SCARBOROUGH, ONTARIO

TO MY BELOVED WIFE

PRISCILLA BARTON MORISON

WHO HAS HELPED ME TO UNDERSTAND

THE MOVING FORCES IN THE HISTORY

OF OUR NATION

I find the great thing in this world is not so much where we stand, as in what direction we are moving. . . . We must sail sometimes with the wind and sometimes against it, — but we must sail, and not drift, nor lie at anchor.

Oliver Wendell Holmes *The Autocrat of the Breakfast Table* (1858)

The role of government and its relationship to the individual has been changed so radically that today government is involved in almost every aspect of our lives.

Political, economic and racial forces have developed which we have not yet learned to understand or control. If we are ever to master these forces, make certain that government will belong to the people, not the people to the government, and provide for the future better than the past, we must somehow learn from the experiences of the past.

Bernard Baruch, presenting his papers to Princeton University, at the age of 93. *The New York Times,* 11 May 1964

Preface

THIS BOOK, in a sense, is a legacy to my countrymen after studying, teaching, and writing the history of the United States for over half a century.

Prospective readers may well ask wherein it may differ in form and content from other American histories of similar length. Politics are not lacking; but my main ambition is to re-create for my readers American ways of living in bygone eras. Here you will find a great deal on social and economic development; horses, ships, popular sports, and pastimes; eating, drinking, and smoking habits. Pugilists will be found cheek-by-jowl with Presidents; rough-necks with reformers, artists with ambassadors. More, proportionally, than in other histories, will be found on sea power, on the colonial period in which basic American principles were established, on the American Indians, and the Caribbean. I am offering fresh, new accounts of the Civil War and the War of Independence. A brief account of the parallel history of Canada, so near and dear to us, yet so unknown in her historical development to most citizens of the United States, has been attempted.

Having lived through several critical eras, dwelt or sojourned in every section of our country, taken part in both world wars, met and talked with almost every President of the United States in the twentieth century, as well as with thousands of men and women active in various pursuits, I have reached some fairly definite opinions about our history. At the same time, I have tried when writing about great controversial issues, such as war and peace and the progressive movement, to relate fairly what each side was trying to accomplish.

Since this is not primarily a textbook, but a history written for my fellow citizens to read and enjoy, footnote references, bibliographies, and other "scholarly apparatus" have been suppressed. Readers may take a certain amount of erudition for granted! Of course nobody, much less myself, can possibly read every printed source and monograph on American history from the beginning through 1964. This is particularly true of social history, comprising ideally, though impossibly, all human activities. Consequently, I have depended for particular subjects on the information and advice of experts, some my colleagues or former pupils, many my friends, but others who were strangers; and it has been most gratifying to find people so generous with their special knowledge. Moreover, having learned from my naval experience the value of oral testimony by participants, I have sought out, talked with, and profited by conversations with many of the civilian and military leaders of the past fifty years. These, excepting a few who wish anonymity, are named in the following section on Acknowledgments.

For many years I have been interested in collecting the popular music of American history, from that of the Indians to the present. The Oxford University Press has given me the opportunity to use some appropriate tags and choruses of these at the ends of appropriate chapters, and more could have been added to the later chapters but for the reluctance of music publishers to part with copyrighted material.

The illustrations have been chosen as much for their artistic appeal as for illustrations in the strict sense. The late Dr. Harold Bowditch helped me to make the point that the English Colonies were not originally democratic, by selecting and delineating coats of arms of colonial founders to which they were entitled, and which they used on bookplates, silver, and in other ways.

One thing has deeply impressed me as I swept through the history of North America — the continuity of American habits, ways, and institutions over a period of three centuries. The seeds or roots of almost everything we have today may be discerned in the English, French, and Spanish colonies as early as 1660. Nobody has better expressed this fundamental unity of American history than George E. Woodberry in his poem "My Country."

> She from old fountains doth new judgment draw,
> Till, word by word, the ancient order swerves
> To the true course more nigh; in every age
> A little she creates, but more preserves.

SAMUEL ELIOT MORISON

44 Brimmer Street
Boston
Christmastide 1964

Preface to the New American Library Edition. The entire text has been reviewed and corrected, in the light of fresh information and of errata noted and sent in by readers. I hope they will continue to do just that! Renewed thanks are due to Miss Antha E. Card for collecting and collating these errata, and to Oxford University Press for its steady cooperation and consideration.

SAMUEL ELIOT MORISON

"Good Hope"
Northeast Harbor, Maine
July 1971

Acknowledgments

MY BELOVED WIFE Priscilla Barton Morison not only encouraged me to write this book but listened critically to the reading of draft chapters, and greatly contributed to my happiness and well being while the work was going on.

General acknowledgments are due to my secretaries during the period of writing, Diana G. Hadgis and Antha E. Card. Miss Card, especially, has helped me by repeatedly checking facts, and by research and suggestions.

To Dr. Sydney V. James, Jr., who for a year helped me by research on the Indians, the Jacksonian period, and other subjects.

To my daughters Emily M. Beck, editor of the latest edition of Bartlett's Familiar Quotations, for looking up and checking quotations, and to Catharine Morison Cooper for research on American music.

To the many naval and military officers and civilians who are mentioned in the prefaces of my earlier books, especially in the fifteen-volume *History of U. S. Naval Operations in World War II*.

To my colleagues at Harvard and other American universities, and at the Universities of Oxford, Paris, and Rome, from whom I have learned very, very much, through friendly conversation and correspondence.[1]

Special Subjects of Acknowledgment

AVIATION: Professors Secor D. Browne and Jerome C. Hunsaker of M.I.T., and Dr. J. Howard Means of Boston.

CANADA: Professor A. R. M. Lower of Queen's University, Professor John J. Conway, formerly of Harvard, and the Honorable William Phillips.

CATHOLIC CHURCH HISTORY: Professor Marshall Smelser of Notre Dame University and Monsignor George Casey of Lexington, Massachusetts.

COLONIAL PERIOD: Professors Edmund S. Morgan of Yale and

1. My Balzan lecture at Rome on "The Experiences and Principles of an Historian" is printed in *Vistas of History* (Knopf, 1964).

Carl Bridenbaugh of Brown; both Professors Schlesinger and the late Perry Miller of Harvard, and the Rev. Arthur Pierce Middleton of Brookfield Center, Connecticut.

CONSERVATION: Mr. Ernest C. Oberholtzer of Ranier, Minnesota, Mr. Edmund Hayes of Portland, Oregon, Mrs. Marguerite Owen of Washington, D.C., and Professor Arthur A. Maass of Harvard.

ECONOMICS, especially the Great Depression: Professors Edward S. Mason of Harvard, Joseph Stancliffe Davis of Stanford, and Adolf A. Berle of Columbia Universities.

FEDERAL CONVENTION: Professor Henry S. Commager of Amherst College.

HORSES AND SPORTS: Mrs. Thomas E. P. Rice of Boston, Mr. Franklin Reynolds of Mount Sterling, Kentucky, Dr. George C. Simpson of the Harvard Museum of Comparative Zoology, and Mr. Colin J. Steuart Thomas of Baltimore.

ILLUSTRATIONS: Addison Gallery of American Art, Andover; American Museum of Natural History; Archives of Canada; Mrs. Bern Anderson of Newport; Atkins Museum of Fine Arts, Kansas City; Mr. David W. Barton; Boston Athenaeum; Boston Museum of Fine Arts; British Museum; Mrs. Richard E. Byrd; Corcoran Gallery, Washington; Mrs. John Duer; the H. F. DuPont Winterthur Museum; Mrs. Frederica F. Emert; the Franklin D. Roosevelt Library; Harvard University; Historical Society of Pennsylvania; Professor M. A. de Wolfe Howe of the Harvard Law School; Mrs. Mabel Ingalls; the John Carter Brown Library; Johns Hopkins University; Karsh of Ottawa; Mrs. Fred C. Kelly; The Mariners Museum, Newport News; Maryland Historical Society; the National Archives and National Gallery of Art, Washington; New-York Historical Society; Pach Brothers of New York; Peabody Museum of Cambridge; Peabody Museum of Salem; Pennsylvania Academy of Fine Arts; Princeton University; the Syracuse Savings Bank; Tennessee Valley Authority; Virginia Chamber of Commerce; United States Navy.

IMMIGRATION: Professor Oscar Handlin of Harvard.

INDIANS AND PRIMITIVE MAN IN AMERICA: Mr. Leonard Ware of the Bureau of Indian Affairs, Department of the Interior; Professor J. Otis Brew of Harvard University and the late Samuel K. Lothrop, curator of Andean Archaeology in the Peabody Museum, Cambridge.

LATIN AMERICA: Professor Roland T. Ely of Rutgers; Colonel Robert D. Heinl Jr. USMC (Ret.); the Honorable Mauricio Obregón of Colombia; the Honorable Aaron S. Brown, American Ambassador to Nicaragua.

MARITIME: Mr. Marion V. Brewington of Peabody Museum, Salem; Professor K. Jack Bauer of Morris Harvey College, Charleston, West Virginia; Rear Admiral Ernest M. Eller, Mr. Jesse R. Thomas, and Mr. Donald R. Martin of the Navy Department; Mrs. John M. Bullard of New Bedford.

MEDICINE: Drs. Paul Dudley White, J. Howard Means, and Sidney Burwell of the Harvard Medical School; Dr. J. Whittington Gorham of New York.

MUSIC AND THE FINE ARTS: Mr. Erich Leinsdorf, conductor of the Boston Symphony Orchestra; Professor G. Wallace Woodworth of Harvard; Mr. George Biddle of New York; Mr. Joseph A. Coletti; the late Maxim Karolik; the several music publishers who have allowed me to quote snatches of their songs.

PSYCHOLOGY: Professor Erik H. Erikson of Harvard.

SUEZ AFFAIR: Marshal of the R.A.F. Sir John Slessor; the Honorable Winthrop Aldrich, former Ambassador to Great Britain.

TEXAS: the late Walter P. Webb and J. Frank Dobie of the University of Texas; Professor Allan Ashcroft of the Texas Agricultural and Mechanical University.

WITCHCRAFT: Miss Esther Forbes of Worcester.

Contents

List of Illustrations

Thomas Jefferson, by Houdon, c. 1785
Museum of Fine Arts, Boston

John Adams, by Mather Brown, 1785
Boston Athenaeum

President Washington Reviewing the Western Army at Fort Cumberland, 1795, by Frederick Kemmelmeyer
Collection of Edgar William and Bernice Chrysler Garbisch in National Gallery of Art, Washington, D.C.

"The Tory Editor and his Apes" Caricature, 1808
Courtesy of the New-York Historical Society, New York City

"America Guided by Wisdom," allegorical print by B. Tanner.
H. F. DuPont Winterthur Museum, Winterthur, Del.

President Andrew Jackson in 1829, by Thomas Sully
Historical Society of Pennsylvania

Anti-Jackson tokens and temporary money, 1832–37
Author's collection

Traveling by Coach, c. 1836, by George Tattersall
Tattersall, an English artist who traveled in western America 1836–42, made an album of sketches, now in the Karolik Collection. The coach is of the Concord type, built in Concord, N.H., and used all over the country. It has just rolled off a planked bridge and is beginning to get bogged down in the stump-studded road, a mere slash in the forest, as most American roads were at the time.
Museum of Fine Arts, Boston

Waiting for the Stage, by Richard Caton Woodville
Woodville, a Baltimorean who died at the age of thirty-one in 1856, studied in Europe and there did some of the best *genre* paintings of American life. Note the carpet bag, the spittoon, the Franklin stove, and the slate hanging by the bar for chalking up drinks.
In the collection of the Corcoran Gallery of Art, Washington, D.C.

List of Maps

MAPS BY VAUGHN GRAY

List of Songs

The first New York to Liverpool packet line, started in 1816. These ships kept a rigid schedule—three weeks out, six home—which required hard driving and notorious discipline; it was a boast to have survived it. Verse three brags: "Once there was a Black Ball ship that fourteen knots an hour could clip!"

Reprinted from *Songs of American Sailormen*, by Joanna C. Colcord. Copyright, 1938, by W. W. Norton & Co., Inc., New York. Reprinted by permission of the publisher.

A drinking song that cheered the "canawlers" on the long slow route from Albany to Buffalo.

From *Burl Ives Song Book*, 1953, Ballantine Books, New York. Reprinted by permission of Mrs. Helen Ives.

The black cotton loaders sang their own words to the long pull of "Lowlands," a British-derived capstan ballad, and soon it was taken up by chantymen on every sea.

Reprinted from *Songs of American Sailormen*, by Joanna C. Colcord. Copyright, 1938, by W. W. Norton & Co., Inc., New York. Reprinted by permission of the publisher.

Sung by Saints who made the long journey on foot, pulling their worldly goods in hand-carts.

From *Burl Ives Song Book*, 1953, Ballantine Books, New York. Reprinted by permission of Mrs. Helen Ives.

This English ballad of maidenhood exchanged for a soldier's love was a favorite of the United States Army in the Mexican War. The Mexicans who heard the soldiers sing it, called them "los Gringos," a nickname that sticks to this day.

From Alan Lomax *The Folk Songs of North America*, 1960, Doubleday, New York.

A song of the deep-sea whaler, to the tune of an Elizabethan ballad; this is verse 2.

From the recording "Songs of the Whaling Era," issued by the Whaling Museum of New Bedford, Mass.

Dan Emmett, a famous "pop" composer of the day, nostalgically penned this air one day in 1859 as a "walk-around" for a local minstrel show. It was appropriated by the Confederates, to the dismay of the Union composer.

From David Ewen *Songs of America*, 1947. Courtesy A. S. Barnes Co., New York.

Written for a recruiting rally in 1862 by G. F. Root, musical laureate of the Union.

From David Ewen *Songs of America*, 1947. Courtesy A. S. Barnes Co., New York.

By Julia Ward Howe, to the tune "John Brown's Body," which in turn had been lifted from a Southern hymn tune.

From David Ewen *Songs of America*, 1947. Courtesy A. S. Barnes Co., New York.

Walter Kitteredge, a New Hampshire ballad singer drafted in 1863, wrote this song that was sung by both sides in the war, and became a favorite at G.A.R. reunions.

From Olin Downes and Elie Siegmeister *Treasury of American Song*, 1940, New York.

THE
OXFORD HISTORY
OF THE
AMERICAN PEOPLE

I

Washington's First Administration

1789-1793

1. Organizing the Federal Government

WASHINGTON'S ADMINISTRATIONS were no less creative, and even more critical, than the six previous years. A proper organization of the new government could not be taken for granted. No federal or republican government had ever worked on so large a scale. The Dutch and Swiss Republics were federal, but covered no more area than a single state of the American Union; the unified Roman Republic was followed by an autocratic empire. But our new federal show opened with fair weather and before expectant spectators. Defeated Antifederalists were ready to "play ball," but they were so prone to cry "Foul!" at any hit close to the constitutional base line as to cramp the style of Federalist batters.

George Washington made so triumphant a progress from Mount Vernon to New York that a lesser man might have thought himself a god. But the President had no illusions about himself or the situation. He wrote to General Knox that he faced "an ocean of difficulties, without that competency of political skill, abilities, and inclinations which is necessary to manage the helm." Prospects seemed bright on the morning of 30 April 1789 when Washington, a fine figure of a man, stepped out onto the balcony of Federal Hall overlooking Wall

Street and took the oath: "I do solemnly swear that I will faithfully execute the office of President of the United States and will, to the best of my ability, preserve, protect, and defend the Constitution of the United States." But "an ocean of difficulties" did lie ahead. The Federal Constitution was so flexible and open to such varied interpretation that the solution of those difficulties it had been created to overcome depended more upon precedents created, traditions begun, and policy followed during the ensuing years than upon the actual words of the document. Gouverneur Morris wrote wisely when urging Washington to accept the presidency: "No constitution is the same on paper and in life. The exercise of authority depends on personal character. Your cool, steady temper is *indispensably necessary* to give firm and manly tone to the new government."

This new government had to create its own machinery. Every revolutionary regime of Europe and Asia, and most of those in Africa, took over a corps of officials, an administrative system, and a treasury; but the American Confederation left nothing but a dozen clerks with their pay in arrears, an empty treasury, and a burden of debt. The American army consisted of 672 officers and men; the navy had ceased to exist. No successful leader of a revolution has been so naked before the world as Washington was in 1789. There were no taxes or requisitions coming in, and no machinery for collecting taxes. The new Congress quickly imposed a customs tariff; but months elapsed before officials could be appointed to collect it, in a loose-jointed country 2000 miles long. Until a federal judiciary were set up, there would be no means of enforcing any federal law. The country itself was just beginning to experience the return of prosperity; but free capital was exceedingly scarce. Washington, reputed to be a man of great wealth, had to borrow $3000 to meet pressing debts and the expense of his removal to New York.

Fortunately, there were many saving elements. By 1790 a time of easy money had returned. Virginia and the Carolinas had recovered their prewar volume of exports. Crop failures in Europe profited the grain growers of the Middle states. The West Indies trade, mainstay of New England, was now almost normal, and new markets had been opened in China, India, and Russia. All this had been effected by individual enterprise before the new government came into operation; but the Federalists were quick to claim credit for the tide on which their ship was launched.

The federal government could count on good newspaper support, but also hostility; journals which had opposed ratification soon began sniping at Washington's administration, and later became out-and-out opponents. Antifederalists continued to regard the federal government with deep suspicion, despite Washington's essential simplicity and his appearing at his inauguration in brown homespun instead of English broadcloth or a military uniform. The excessive adulation poured on him by *The Gazette of the United States,* and his custom of driving about New York in a coach and six, like royal George, were regarded by some as very sinister. So were the fortnightly "levees" and more select "drawing rooms" by which the new President and his lady tried to solve one of the social problems that has bedeviled their successors. Aping the British court, hissed the Antifederalists! Everything that the Washingtons said was repeated; everything they did was watched. No subsequent President of the United States has lived in such a glare of publicity.

In describing himself as one who had inherited "inferior endowments from nature," Washington was too modest; but his superiority lay in character, not talents. He had the power of inspiring respect, but no gift of popularity. He was direct, not adroit; stubborn rather than flexible; slow to reach a decision rather than a man of quick perception. The mask of dignity and reserve that concealed his inner life came from humility, and stern self-control. A warm heart was revealed by innumerable kindly acts to his dependents and subordinates. Some men, especially unreconstructed Antifederalists such as Senator Maclay of Pennsylvania, found him dull and stiff; but the ladies never did. He talked with them charmingly and danced with gusto. Fifty years later there were dowagers in every town from Portsmouth to Savannah who cherished memories of presidential persiflage when he danced with them as young girls, on his tours of North and South.

In his inaugural address Washington hinted that Congress should promptly add a bill of rights to the Constitution, in order to appease the Antifederalists. Madison took the lead in the movement, and Jefferson wrote to him prophetically from Paris that the best argument for it was "the legal check which it puts into the hands of the judiciary." After much discussion in both houses, and a going-over by a committee composed of Madison, Ellsworth, Carroll, and Paterson, Congress approved twelve amendments on 25 September and submitted them to the states.

Although several leading Antifederalists continued to scream for a new Federal Convention and sneered at the bill of rights (William Grayson said they were "good for nothing," and Henry wanted an amendment hamstringing the taxing power), there is no doubt that they converted most of those who still opposed the Constitution. Virginia was only the eleventh among the states to ratify the bill of rights, on 15 December 1791; but eleven were sufficient to put Amendments I through X into effect.[1] But Massachusetts, whose convention had started this whole movement, never did ratify until the 150th anniversary of the bill of rights, when someone discovered the omission!

Virginian aristocrat that he was, in the proper sense of the word, Washington was more nationalist and less provincial than any other American of his generation. His army experience had given him intimate knowledge of men from all parts of the country and the ability to size them up, and get along with them. Like some of his ablest successors, he wisely used the qualities of able men while ignoring their faults. Thus, he could put up with Hamilton's insolence and Jefferson's indirectness, because he needed their virtues and capacities to help run the government.

Heads of departments had to be appointed by the President with the consent of the Senate, but Congress, in organizing executive departments, might have made their heads responsible to and removable by itself. Instead, it made the secretaries of state and of war responsible to the President alone, and subject to his direction within their legal competence. Moreover, when the first question of dismissal from office came up, the Senate admitted that the President could remove officials without its consent. The effect of this precedent was to make the entire administrative force and foreign service responsible to the chief executive, as he, by his independent tenure, was responsible to the people.

For heads of the three departments, there was no large field of choice, as the Confederation had given small scope for civil administration. For secretary of state someone with diplomatic experience was needed. Franklin was too old and feeble, John Adams had been elected Vice President, and John Jay had made enemies by negotiating an unfortunate treaty with Spain. So Washington's choice fell on Thomas Jefferson, who as minister to France had shown himself to be an excellent diplomat. Robert Morris declined the treasury department but suggested Alexander Hamilton, which fell in perfectly with Washington's inclinations. General Knox, Washington's reliable chief of artillery, continued as secretary of war, which he had been

---

[1] Two amendments submitted to the States but never ratified determined the size of the House of Representatives, and forbade congressmen and senators from raising their own salaries. Connecticut and Georgia also delayed ratification until 1941.

for the Confederation; Edmund Randolph, whose term as governor of Virginia had expired, was appointed attorney general.

The making of minor appointments turned out to be, as Washington feared, the "most difficult and delicate part of his duty." He wished to reward war service, but to avoid any suspicion of personal or sectional partiality. He appointed no prominent Antifederalists—since there were plenty of deserving Federalists available—and rather conspicuously refused office to Benjamin Franklin's progeny, who were somewhat disreputable. He scrutinized applications carefully, asked the advice of senators and representatives from the applicant's state, and sought out able men when none applied. The federal civil service began under principles of efficiency and honesty that were in sharp contrast to the jobbery and corruption in contemporary European governments, and even in some of the state governments.

A Vice President was created by the Federal Constitution in order to provide an acting chief magistrate in the event of the death or disability of the President, without the need of a special election. In order to give him something to do, he was made president of the Senate, with a casting vote in case of tie. John Adams, the first Vice President, received only 34 out of the 69 second votes of the presidential electors, the others going to a variety of favorite sons. It was generally felt that if the President were a Virginian the Vice President should be a New Englander; and John unquestionably was the most eminent New Englander for character, ability, and experience. His one fault was vanity. Unfortunately, during his residence in the Dutch Republic where every top government official was addressed as "His Highmightiness," Adams acquired the notion that no republic could be "respectable" without titles. Senator Maclay was shocked at Adams's referring to the President's inaugural address as "His Most Gracious Speech," and reminded the Senate that the removal of royal trappings was an object of the Revolution. The Vice President "expressed the greatest surprise that anything should be objected to on account of its being taken from the practice of that government under which we had lived so long and happily formerly; that he was for a dignified and respectable government"; but the phrase was struck out. Later a committee of the Senate reported that the President should be addressed as "His Highness the President of the United States of America and the Protector of the Rights of the Same." The House refused to agree; and Washington and his successors have remained plain "Mr. President."

Although this first Senate was friendly to the administration (about half the senators had been delegates to the Federal Convention), it early developed that club spirit which has been the bane of willful Presidents. "Senatorial courtesy," the practice of rejecting any nomination not approved by the senators from the nominee's own state, soon began. In the matter of treaties, however, the Senate's sense of its own dignity defeated its ambition. The Constitution grants the President power, "by and with the advice and consent of the Senate, to make treaties, provided two-thirds of the senators present concur." On one memorable occasion Washington appeared before the Senate with Secretary Knox to explain a negotiation pending with the Creek Indians. Hampered in freedom of debate by the august presence, the Senate voted to refer the papers in question to a select committee. The President declared, "This defeats every purpose of my coming here," and stalked out, irritated. On two other occasions Washington sent a message requesting senatorial advice on a current negotiation, but in later and more important matters he dispensed with advice until a treaty was ready for ratification. This practice has been followed by his successors.

"Impressed with a conviction that the due administration of justice is the firmest pillar of good government," wrote Washington in 1789, "I have considered the first arrangement of the judicial department as essential to the happiness of our country and the stability of its political system." The Constitution left this branch more vague than the other two. It defined the scope of federal judicial power, settled the mode of appointing judges, and fixed their tenure during good behavior. But Congress had to create and organize the federal courts, determine their procedure, and provide a bridge between state and federal jurisdiction.

All this was done by the Judiciary Act of 24 September 1789, the better part of which is still in force today. It provided for a Supreme Court consisting of a Chief Justice and five associates, for thirteen district courts, and three circuit courts. The problem of getting cases that involved jurisdictional disputes out of state courts and into federal courts, in order that the Constitution, laws, and treaties of the United States might indeed be "the supreme law of the land," was solved in the twenty-fifth section of this act. A final judgment in the highest court of a state, in any case involving a conflict between federal and state power, may be re-examined in the Supreme Court of the United States upon a writ of error. This section is as essential to the peaceful working of the federal system as the Constitution itself. Without it, every state judiciary could put its own construction on the Constitution, laws, and treaties of the Union.

John Jay having been appointed Chief Justice, the Supreme Court opened its first session at New York on 2 February 1790. The judges wore gowns of black and scarlet, but honored Jefferson's appeal to "discard the monstrous wig which makes the English judges look like rats peeping through bunches of oakum." Under Chief Justice Jay the federal judiciary assumed its place as the keystone to the federal arch. As early as 1791, in a case involving British debts, one of the circuit courts declared invalid a law of Connecticut which infringed Article VI of the treaty of peace. In 1792 a state law of Rhode Island was held unconstitutional, as impairing the obligation of contracts. The same year another circuit court refused to execute an act of Congress that required the federal courts to pass on veterans' pension claims on the ground that this was a non-judicial function, beyond the constitutional power of Congress to impose, or of the court to assert. Thus was asserted the power of judicial review over both state and federal laws. Later, and even in our time, judicial review has been vehemently attacked behind the cover of state rights and democracy; but in the early years of the Republic it went almost unchallenged.

Washington was unwilling to make any vital decision without taking the advice of people in whom he had confidence; hence the extra-constitutional cabinet. There had been talk in the Federal Convention of providing the President with a "council of state," but it went no further. Shortly after the Convention adjourned, Charles Pinckney wrote that the President was expected to call upon such heads of departments as Congress might create, for informal consultation; and that is what he did. The secretaries of state, war, and treasury, and the attorney general, began meeting at the President's house in 1791; two years later they met almost weekly. These officials were already known collectively as the President's cabinet; but not until 1907 was the cabinet officially recognized as such by law.

The American cabinet, unlike the British, has no connection with the legislature, and this lack of co-ordination between executive and legislature is one of the distinctive features of American federal government. It came as a reaction against George III's very intimate relations with the House of Commons. The Constitution guarded against executive control through "placemen" by disqualifying federal officials, whether civil or military, for membership in Congress, and by forbidding the appointment of members, during the term of their election, to an office created, or increased in profit, during that term. There was nothing, however, to prevent a cabinet official's appearing in person before either house. And the important section requiring the President to recommend measures to Congress, and to keep them informed as to "the state of the Union," reflected a desire that the executive should take the lead in legislation.

Washington had not the temperament to do this alone. He wanted a young and energetic man to give the impulse, and attend to his relations with the Congress. Fortunately, the right man, Alexander Hamilton, was appointed to the right office, the treasury. For the primary problems of Washington's first administration were fiscal.

2. Alexander Hamilton

If the character of Washington fortified the new government, the genius of his secretary of the treasury enabled it to function successfully. Alexander Hamilton was thirty-four years old in 1789 when Washington appointed him to the post.[1] As a student at King's College, he had brilliantly defended the rights of the colonies. At twenty-two he had earned a place on Washington's staff. At twenty-six he had published articles showing the defects of the Confederation, written a remarkable treatise on public finance, and as colonel of light infantry led the assault on a British redoubt at Yorktown. Admitted to the New York bar at the conclusion of peace, he quickly rose to eminence in the law. His contributions to *The Federalist* helped to obtain the ratification of a constitution in which he did not strongly believe. One of the greatest of Americans, he was the least American of his generation: a statesman rather of the type of the younger Pitt, whose innate love of order and system was strengthened by the lack of those qualities among his fellow citizens. Self-disciplined, Hamilton was eager to discipline his countrymen. He had a keen and quick perception of means, and a steady eye on remote ends. He produced bold plans and definite policies where others had cautious notions and vague principles. When Congress was thinking of what the people would say, Hamilton told it and the people what they ought to do. He had untiring energy, and accepted responsibility with gusto.

The treasury department was the creation of Congress, not

[1] Recent research has established that Hamilton was born in Nevis, 11 January 1755, not 1757 as had earlier been assumed.

of the Constitution; and the Organic Act of 1789, still in force, gave it so many duties as to make it the most important and powerful federal department for many years. The secretary had the duty "to digest and prepare plans for the improvement and management of the revenue and for the support of the public credit," as well as estimate of the same, "to receive, keep, and disburse the monies of the United States," to collect customs duties and excise taxes, to run the lighthouse service, set up aids to navigation, and start a land survey of the United States. Until 1792, when the post-office department was established by Congress, the treasury ran the mails. Other duties, such as providing medical care for seamen, were added by Congress from time to time, until, by the turn of the century, the treasury included over half the total federal civil service. This was little enough in comparison with the present horde of civil officials, although compared by jealous Jeffersonians to the "swarms of officers" sent by George III "to harass our people and eat up their substance."[1]

Hamilton's financial policy was determined by his conception of the governmental problem in 1789; and that, in turn, by his political philosophy. As he remarked in the Federal Convention, "All communities divide themselves into the few and the many. The first are the rich and well-born; the other the mass of the people . . . turbulent and changing, they seldom judge or determine right. Give therefore to the first class a distinct, permanent share in the Government." The Federal Constitution, leaving too many powers to the states, could only be made an instrument for good by "increasing the number of ligaments between the government and interests of individuals." The old families, merchant-shipowners, public creditors, and financiers must be made a loyal governing class by a straightforward policy favoring their interest. That was the object of Hamilton's domestic and foreign policy. His conscious purpose was to use that class to strengthen the federal government. He would clothe the Constitution with the sword of sovereignty and the armor of loyalty by giving the people who then controlled America's wealth a distinct interest in its permanence. The rest, he assumed, would go along, as they always had.

The House of Representatives called upon Hamilton, ten days after he took office, to prepare and report a plan for the "adequate support of public credit." The report was laid be-

[1] The treasury department, according to L. D. White, *The Federalists* (1948), in 1801 had 78 employees in the central offices, 1615 in the field services. The post-office department was run by the postmaster general and seven clerks, and the local postmasters numbered about 900.

fore the House at its next session, on 14 January 1790. Based
on the tried expedients of English finance, it was worthy of an
experienced minister of a long-established government.

Hamilton first laid down principles of public economy and
then adduced arguments in support of them. America must
have credit for government, industrial development, and commercial activity. Her future credit would depend on how she
met her present obligations. The United States debt, foreign
and domestic, "was the price of liberty. The faith of America
has been repeatedly pledged for it . . . Among ourselves, the
most enlightened friends of good government are those whose
expectations [of prompt payment] are the highest. To justify
and preserve their confidence; to promote the increasing re-
spectability of the American name; to answer the calls of
justice; to restore landed property to its due value; to furnish
new resources, both to agriculture and commerce; to cement
more closely the Union of the States; to add to their security
against foreign attack; to establish public order on the basis
of an upright and liberal policy; these are the great and invaluable ends to be secured by a proper and adequate provision,
at the present period, for the support of public credit."

Next, Hamilton made precise recommendations of ways
and means. The foreign debt and floating domestic debt, with
arrears of interest, should be funded[1] at par, and due provision should be made by import duties and excise taxes to pay
the interest and gradually repay the principal. The war debts
of the states should be assumed by the federal government in
order to bind state creditors to the national interest. A sinking
fund should be created in order to stabilize the price of government securities by buying them in whenever they fell
much below par. The want of banking facilities should be
filled by a Bank of the United States, on the model of the
Bank of England, but with the right to establish branches in
different parts of the country.

This daring policy could not have been carried out by
Hamilton alone. Every proposal was matured by the cool judgment of the President; and in both House and Senate he found
eager co-operation. Congress had already passed a customs
tariff, with tonnage duties discriminating in favor of American
shipping—essential parts of Hamilton's system. The foreign
and domestic debt was funded at par; the former was entirely

---

[1] To fund, in government finance, means to pay off one debt by creating
another; in this instance to issue 6 per cent bonds in exchange for various securities and certificates of indebtedness which had survived the
war.

paid off by the end of 1795, the latter, despite another war, in 1835. Most of the states' debts were assumed by Congress after a bitter struggle not unmixed with intrigue. The Bank of the United States was chartered, and its capital subscribed within four hours after the books were open. By August 1791 United States 6 per cents were selling above par in London and Amsterdam, and a wave of development and speculation had begun.

At the end of 1791, Hamilton presented to Congress a Report on Manufactures. Alone of his state papers, this report fell flat; yet it became an arsenal of protectionist arguments on both sides of the Atlantic. He wished the government to protect infant industries in order to increase national wealth, induce artisans to immigrate, cause machinery to be invented, and employ women and children. Hamilton's aim here, as with his funding system, was "to increase the number of ligaments between the government and the interest of individuals." He perceived that merchants and public creditors were too narrow a basis for a national governing class. He believed that manufactures might prosper in the South as well as in the North. The report was a distinct bid for Southern support over the heads of Jefferson and Madison. The South, however, regarded protection as another tax for Northern interests. Hamilton's argument would have been sound, had not Eli Whitney's invention of the cotton gin, the following year, made the culture of upland cotton a far more profitable employment for slave labor than manufactures.

Nobody in fact showed any enthusiasm for protection, because the Northern merchant-shipowners had a stake in free trade, and Congress took no action on the report. Twenty-five years later it was resurrected by the new manufacturing interest built up during the War of 1812, and never since have Hamilton's arguments been allowed to grow cold. They were imported into Germany by Friedrich List, into England by Joseph Chamberlain. Hamilton, far ahead of his time, grasped the nineteenth-century compromise between paternalism and laissez faire: protection to property interests valuable to the state; free competition for labor.

Hamilton's other plans were adopted. He turned dead paper into marketable securities, and provided for their redemption by taxes that the nation was well able to bear. He set standards of honesty and punctuality that were invaluable for a people with somewhat loose financial conceptions. His youthful country, so lately on the verge of bankruptcy, acquired a credit such as few nations of Europe enjoyed. Yet Hamilton failed to achieve his ultimate end of consolidating the Union. His measures, sound though they were, stimulated a dangerous opposition.

To understand wherein Hamilton failed, we have only to glance at the effect of his measures on two states: Massachusetts and Virginia. Massachusetts was the second state of the Union in population. Her premier interests were maritime; her fishing villages benefited by new bounties on dried codfish; her foreign trade and shipyards by the low tariff and the discriminating tonnage duties. Good businessmen themselves, the merchants knew the value of sound credit and honest finance. Their wartime gains were partly invested in government paper, worthless but for the funding system. Maritime prosperity, percolating from the coastal towns to the interior, raised the price of country produce and healed the wounds of Shays's Rebellion. Washington's foreign policy completed the process; and Boston, once the home of radical mobs, became safe for the new Federalist party. The "junto" of leaders from Essex County—Cabots, Higginsons, Lowells, and Jacksons—who had been to sea in their youth and viewed politics as from a quarterdeck, hailed Hamilton as their master. With them, in general, were the solid men of Rhode Island and Connecticut, of New York City and the seaports southward. Charleston, South Carolina, until 1800 was as solidly Federalist as Boston.

But the great mass of the American people was untouched, either in imagination or in pocket, by Hamilton's policy. It would have been otherwise had the public debt remained in the hands of its original possessors. But farmers, discharged soldiers, small shopkeepers, and the like who held government securities representing services rendered, goods supplied or money advanced during the war, had been forced to part with them at a ruinous discount during the hard times that followed. By 1789 the bulk of the public debt was in the hands of the "right people" at Philadelphia, New York, Charleston, and Boston; and the nation was taxed to pay off at par, securities which they had purchased at a few cents on the dollar.[1]

By the same economic test, a system that appeared sound and statesmanlike in Massachusetts seemed unwarranted and unconstitutional in Virginia. The Old Dominion was the most populous state in the Union, and easily the proudest. Although well provided with a long sea frontage, Virginia owned few seagoing ships; Yankees and foreigners carried her wheat and tobacco to market. Virginia planters knew little of business,

[1] In 1795 the federal government disbursed $309,500 in interest to citizens of Massachusetts as against $62,300 to natives of Virginia; $367,000 to New York as against $6800 to Georgia.

and less of finance. A gentleman inherited his debts with his plantation, and not infrequently bequeathed them to his eldest son; why then should debt trouble the United States? Why not pay it off at market value, as a gentleman compounds with his creditors? Most Virginians had sold their government I.O.U.'s at a loss; why should they be taxed to pay off the New York purchaser at par? Virginia had wiped off the larger part of her state debt; why should she be taxed to assume the debts of other states? Toward Hamilton's Bank of the United States, the opposition of the Virginia planters was as natural and spontaneous as that of the English Tories, a century before, toward the Bank of England; they felt that it was a scheme to make monied men richer and depress the landed interest. The confusing paraphernalia of Hamilton's system seemed to portend colossal taxation as in England, jobbery and corruption as in England; perhaps monarchy as in England.

Patrick Henry drafted a remonstrance against the federal assumption of state debts which the Virginia assembly adopted. Therein, on 23 December 1790, were expressed the misgivings of plain folk throughout the country, as well as those of the Virginia gentry:

> In an agricultural country like this . . . to erect, and concentrate, and perpetuate a large monied interest, is a measure which your memorialists apprehend must in the course of human events produce one or other of two evils, the prostration of agriculture at the feet of commerce, or a change in the present form of federal government, fatal to the existence of American liberty . . . Your memorialists can find no clause in the constitution authorizing Congress to assume the debts of the States.

A vision of future civil war flashed across Hamilton's mind as he read this remonstrance. "This is the first symptom," he wrote, "of a spirit which must either be killed, or will kill the Constitution of the United States."

Hamilton was making new enemies for the administration. The Federalists of 1790 were no longer the Federalists of 1788. But Virginia could hardly form an opposition party without aid from some of her citizens highly placed in the federal government. Washington, national in his outlook, and convinced that Hamilton's policy was honest and right, signed every bill based on his recommendations. Richard Henry Lee, elected to the Senate as an Antifederalist, became a convert to Hamilton's views. Thomas Jefferson, secretary of state, and James Madison, leader of the House of Representatives, wavered—but found the Virginia candle stronger than the Hamiltonian star.

The breach between Jefferson and Hamilton was not personal. The Republican and Federalist parties that they helped to found were not mere projections of rival personalities; only in a limited sense were they a division between democracy and aristocracy, or between radicalism and conservatism. They were the political expressions of a deep-lying antagonism between two great sectional interests—the planting-slaveholding interest which was mainly rural-Southern, anc' the mercantile-shipping-financial interest of seaport cities from Salem to Charleston. These interests, a century older than Washington's administration, found in the federal government a stake worth fighting for; and in Hamilton and Jefferson they found natural leaders. American political history until 1865 is largely the story of these rival interests, capitalist and agrarian, Northern and Southern, contending for the control of the federal government—using government to help themselves and starve their rivals, undermining each other's vote, interfering with each other's laboring force, bidding for Western support, gambling with petty wars, and finally staking everything on civil war. Principle also divided the parties, particularly in their infancy; but principles were both changed and exchanged, whilst Massachusetts and Virginia remained the intellectual foci after they ceased to be the economic nuclei of the two systems.

3. Thomas Jefferson and the Opposition

When Thomas Jefferson returned to Virginia in November 1789, he was surprised to learn of his nomination to the department of state; only Washington's urgency persuaded him to accept. He had no intention of founding a political party. "If I could not go to heaven but with a party, I would not go there at all," he wrote that very year. But, beneath his bland exterior Jefferson was ambitious for the highest office, and the presidency (if not heaven) could be attained only through a party, which he was the first to lead.

Jefferson, twelve years older than Hamilton, had had much more experience. As the author of the Declaration of Independence and *Notes on Virginia*, he was famous in both continents. As United States minister to France he had become a consulting attorney on revolution. Science, literature, and the fine arts interested Jefferson as much as they had Franklin; and he was the first American architect of his generation. His Virginia mansion "Monticello," superbly situated on a hilltop facing the Blue Ridge, was admirably designed and landscaped. "Bremo," the mansion that he built for a friend in Fluvanna County, is one of the most beautiful country houses in America; and for the University of Virginia he designed a beautiful and symmetrical group of buildings. Jefferson wrote upon Neo-Platonism, the pronunciation of Greek, the Anglo-Saxon language, the future of steam engines, archaeology; even on theology. In France he had assiduously promoted American business interests. But on one subject he was as ignorant as any Virginia planter, yet as self-confident as a French economist. That was Hamilton's specialty, finance.

Hamilton's political theories had more validity for the future America than for the simple country with whose common mind and condition Jefferson's ideas agreed. Yet if America has outgrown Jefferson's principles, she is still indebted to them for the ideals that she has preserved in an industrial society. Hamilton wished to concentrate power; Jefferson to diffuse power. Hamilton feared anarchy and thought in terms of order; Jefferson feared tyranny and thought in terms of liberty. Hamilton believed republican government could only succeed if directed by a governing elite; Jefferson that a republic must be based on an agrarian democracy. The people, according to Jefferson, were the safest and most virtuous, though not always the most wise, depository of power, and education would perfect their wisdom. Hamilton would diversify American economic life, encouraging shipping and creating manufactures by legislative enactment; Jefferson would have America remain a nation of farmers. All those differences in temper, theory, and policy were bracketed by two opposed conceptions of what America was and might be. Jefferson inherited the idealistic conception of the new world to which the French *philosophes* paid homage—a republic of mild laws and equal opportunity, asylum to the oppressed and beacon-light of freedom, renouncing wealth and power to preserve simplicity and equality. To Hamilton, this was sentimental nonsense. Having assimilated the traditions of the New York gentry into which he had married, Hamilton believed that the only choice for America lay between a stratified society on the English model and a squalid "mobocracy." Jefferson, who knew Europe, wished America to be as unlike it as possible; Hamilton, who had never left America, wished to make his country a new Europe.

Their appearances were as much of a contrast as their habits of mind. Hamilton's neat, lithe, dapper figure, and air of brisk energy, went with his tight, compact, disciplined brain. Yet Hamilton's written style was heavy; he could not have composed a state paper such as the Declaration of Independence. Jefferson's mind in comparison was somewhat untidy, constantly gathering new facts and making fresh syntheses. "His whole figure has a loose, shackling air," wrote friendly Senator Maclay in 1790. "I looked for gravity, but a laxity of manner seemed shed about him." His sandy hair, hazel eyes, and ill-fitting, much-worn clothes played up this impression of careless ease; whilst Hamilton radiated energy as well as charm. Women found him irresistible, but they did not care much for Jefferson; he wooed them or wrote to them in the stilted phrases of eighteenth-century literature.

Jefferson approved payment of the domestic and foreign debt at par, but not the assumption of the state debts. Nevertheless, he arranged with Hamilton a deal by which the capital was transferred from New York to Philadelphia in 1790 for ten years, pending removal to the new federal city of Washington on the Potomac.[1] Jefferson persuaded two Virginia congressmen to vote for assumption, and Hamilton rounded up Yankee votes for the Potomac capital. As late as November of 1790, Jefferson regarded the pending Virginia remonstrance against assumption as a mere afterclap of Antifederalism. But from the date of Hamilton's report recommending a national bank (13 December 1790), Jefferson's attitude toward him and his policies began to change. To George Mason, on 7 February 1791, he mentioned a "sect" high in office who believed the British constitution to be the goal of perfection; and intimated that Congress was under the control of "stock-jobbers."

Madison, principal architect of the Federal Constitution, and fellow author with Hamilton of *The Federalist*, opposed the bank bill in the House on the ground that the chartering of such an institution transcended the powers of Congress. The President called for opinions on that point from his cabinet. Jefferson declared that the congressional power "to make all laws necessary and proper" for executing its delegated powers did not include laws merely convenient for such purposes. A national bank was not strictly necessary—the existing state bank at Philadelphia could be used for government funds. It was a clear case, he thought, for the presidential veto.

Hamilton replied with a nationalistic, "loose construction" interpretation of the Constitution:

[1] Congress adjourned at New York 12 August 1790 and met next at Congress Hall, Philadelphia, on 6 December.

Every power vested in a government is in its nature sovereign, and includes by force of the term, a right to employ all the means requisite . . . to the attainment of the
ends of such power . . . If the end be clearly compre-
hended within any of the specified powers, and if the
measure have an obvious relation to that end, and is not
forbidden by any particular provision of the Constitution,
it may safely be deemed to come within the compass of
the national authority.

Congress, he pointed out, had already acted upon that theory
in providing lighthouses, necessary and proper to the regulation of commerce. A bank has a similar relation to the specified powers of collecting taxes, paying salaries, and servicing
the debt. This opinion satisfied the President. He signed the
bank bill; but it was not until 1819 that Chief Justice Marshall's opinion in the case of *McCullough* v. *Maryland* read the
doctrine of implied powers into the Constitution.

Jefferson was neither silenced nor convinced. The Federal
Constitution, from his point of view, now also Madison's, was
being perverted into a consolidated, national government,
building up through financial favors a corrupt control of Congress with an "ultimate object" of introducing monarchy. That
belief remained a fixed tenet of Jefferson for the rest of his
life. Completely innocent as Hamilton was of any such intention, he had laid himself open to suspicion. For Hamilton,
although he knew that monarchy would never do for America,
often expressed his admiration for it, and avowed his belief
that corruption was a necessary engine of government. Complicated projects in federal finance he arrogantly refused to
explain to those (Jefferson among others) who did not understand them.

The suspicions of plain people were deepened by the brisk
speculation in lands, bank stock, and government funds that
began in 1790. No sooner did Hamilton's financial reports
appear than Northern speculators began combing the countryside for depreciated government paper which they anticipated
would be redeemed at par. William Duer, Hamilton's first
assistant secretary, and Henry Knox, secretary of war, floated
the Scioto Company, a colossal speculation in Ohio lands.
Duer and Macomb, an associate of Hamilton's father-in-law,
formed a blind pool to speculate in government bonds; an
operation which produced a financial flurry in New York and
landed Duer in jail. Hamilton sincerely deprecated all this,

and his own hands were clean—but some of the speculators were very close to him.

Political parties were in bad odor at the end of the eighteenth century. No provision for party government had been made in the Constitution. Washington hoped to get along without one, and when organized opposition began to appear, nobody knew what to do about it. Should Jefferson resign as secretary of state, leaving Hamilton in control of the cabinet? Was it proper for a minister to oppose policies that the President had accepted? Washington, believing that every month and year the government endured was so much gained for stability, endeavored to keep the smoldering fires from bursting forth, preaching charity to Jefferson and forbearance to Hamilton. He entreated both men to remain in office, and both consented. But Jefferson, believing Hamilton's policy to be dangerous, used every means short of open opposition to check it; whilst Hamilton, when Jefferson's management of foreign affairs appeared to be mischievous, spared no effort to thwart him, even going over his head to the British minister at Philadelphia.

The most important step toward forming a nationwide opposition party was for Virginia malcontents to come to an understanding with Antifederalists and other discontented elements in the North. This was effected in the course of a summer visit by Jefferson and Madison to New York in 1791— which they called "botanizing." New York politics were still largely determined by family connections and hunger for the sweets of office. One faction was led by Governor George Clinton, whose political lieutenant, Colonel Aaron Burr, had discovered the value of a city benevolent society called the "Sons of St. Tammany." But the old aristocratic faction, including the Schuylers into which Alexander Hamilton had married, having supported the Constitution in 1788, obtained all federal appointments in New York; no plums went to the Clintons. We may be certain that promises were made on both sides in the course of this "botanizing" tour. It was then that the visitors from Virginia persuaded Philip Freneau, Madison's Princeton classmate and the poet of the Revolution, to come to Philadelphia and start an opposition newspaper. The inducement was a job in Jefferson's department as "translating clerk"—although Freneau knew no foreign language but French, and not much of that.

This alliance set the pattern of the Jeffersonian Republican party and its successors. Until 1964 the "solid South," Tammany Hall, and other big-city political machines have been the principal supporters of the Democratic party.

4. Washington's Foreign Policy

Washington's foreign policy may be summed up in three words: peace, union, and justice. Peace, to give the country time to recover from the Revolutionary War, and to permit the slow work of national integration to continue. But justice could not be done, nor the Federal Union maintained, without a vigorous foreign policy.

It was certain that Westerners would not long remain in the Union unless Washington could secure the navigation of the Mississippi; that the support of the trading classes would be lost if their commerce were not protected; that there would be a demand for war with Britain if the Northwest posts were not surrendered. The federal government had to satisfy all parts of the country that their essential interests were being promoted. To obtain these ends peaceably would require years of patient and skillful diplomacy. But Washington seemed to have absorbed in his person all the patience and serenity in America. War clouds were hanging over Europe, and if they broke it would be difficult to prevent their deluging the new world as well as the old.

Jefferson and Hamilton agreed with Washington's objects, but disagreed as to means. The polestar of Jefferson's policy was to cement commercial and diplomatic ties with France. And his love for France had been strengthened by the revolution, whose early and hopeful stages he had observed. Jefferson hated England, because English society, government, and manners were of a kind that he wished his country to avoid, and he believed it to be Hamilton's object to make the United States a transatlantic copy of the mother country.

Hamilton believed that the essential interests of Great Britain and the United States were complementary, not competitive. He never attempted to graft the British constitution onto the federal one, but believed that Americans had many political lessons to learn of their mother country. England, for him, had found the just balance between liberty and order. Her friendship would be wholesome for a young nation which needed above all things integration and stability. Hamilton, partly French in blood, liked individual Frenchmen, who in turn found him more *sympathique* than Jefferson; but on the French Revolution, Hamilton saw eye to eye with Edmund Burke, whose *Considerations* on that great upheaval are an arsenal of conservative arguments to this day. It was most disconcerting, just when there seemed some hope of America settling down, to have her favorite nation blow up and invite everyone else to follow her example.

Hamilton knew that Anglo-American commerce was valuable for England, but vital for America—and he knew that England knew it. Three-quarters of the foreign commerce of the United States was with Great Britain. Ninety per cent of American imports came from Britain, and Hamilton planned to finance his new fiscal system with customs duties, the only large source of revenue then open to the federal government. England could better afford to play the game of commercial retaliation than America; and retaliate she would if Congress began it. Commercial warfare, even if it did not lead to hot war, would destroy every calculation on which Hamilton's funding scheme was based; would "cut out credit by the roots." Without credit, Hamilton could see the federal government's becoming impotent as the Confederation, and the Federal Constitution discarded as another failure. Not on sentimental Anglophilism, but on this keen perception of the essential facts in relation to his domestic policy, was Hamilton's foreign policy based.

At Hamilton's suggestion the first Tariff Act, of 1789, levied higher duties on foreign than on American vessels, but placed English and French vessels in the same class. The effect was threefold. The British government perceived that Washington's administration was friendly, and American shipping recovered more than its fair share of the Anglo-American carrying trade. France complained of being placed in the same category as Britain in spite of her repeated favors to America. The French minister to the United States advised his government to press for the recovery of Louisiana from Spain, to keep America in hand. Within three years the French Republic acted upon this pregnant suggestion, and in 1800 Bonaparte put it through.

Britain's retention of the seven Northwest posts was serious. In 1791, when Parliament set off Upper Canada (the future Ontario) from Quebec, the seat of the new provincial government was placed at Fort Niagara on the United States side of the border, suggesting that Canada intended to hold that place forever. Posts on the Great Lakes, especially Detroit, enabled Canadian fur traders to preserve influence over the Indians of the American Northwest Territory, with whom Congress on 1 June 1789 concluded the first of 371 formal treaties with Indian nations. It became the firm belief of American frontiersmen that British garrisons incited the Indians to harass the American frontier. That was untrue; but the British did supply the redskins with arms and ammunition for hunting "game," which could be and occasionally was human.

Washington and Congress were as deeply concerned over

Indian as over European relations. In a number of presidential messages and congressional laws, certain basic principles for dealing with the Indians, inherited from the old colonial system, were laid down: (1) The Indians' lands should be guaranteed to them by solemn treaties, and land purchases therefrom prohibited, except by the federal government; (2) promotion of federally regulated and controlled Indian trade; (3) white people to be punished for abusing Indians, and they for attacking whites; (4) Indians living on their own lands not to be taxed or considered citizens of the United States, to govern themselves by tribal law but to be welcomed as citizens if they chose to settle among white people. As early as the treaty of 7 August 1790 with the Creek nation, the United States was to furnish "useful domestic animals and implements of husbandry," in the hope that they would become "herdsmen and cultivators instead of remaining hunters." Few of these highminded principles, except the exemption from taxation, were enforced in practice, owing to the weakness of the federal government and the rapacity of frontiersmen; in them we may discern the ambiguity that has been characteristic of our Indian relations from the seventeenth century almost to this day. Protect their rights, yes; but pressure them into becoming good Christian farmers, just like us.

The President, it must be admitted, first broke his own principles by attempting, without Indian consent, to build a fort at the principal village of the Maumee, in order to counteract British influence. This task was entrusted to General Arthur St. Clair, governor of the Northwest Territory. At the head of some 2000 troops, including the entire regular army, St. Clair jumped off from Fort Washington at the site of Cincinnati in the fall of 1791. On 4 November, when only a few miles short of his destination (the site of Fort Wayne, Indiana) his force was surprised and routed by the Indians, and suffered over 900 casualties. Washington, who from his experience under Braddock had warned St. Clair to "beware of surprise," burst into one of his rare explosions of wrath when he heard the bad news. He did not attempt to gloss it over. Knowing (what some of his successors have forgotten) that it pays to be candid with the American people, the President communicated the devastating facts to Congress. The House established a precedent in ordering an inquiry; but, more honest than some twentieth-century investigating committees, did not try to pin the blame on anyone.

In comparison with the nearby Indian menace, Algerian pirates attracted little attention in Congress, but gave Washington's administration almost as much trouble. Seamen taken

prisoner by Barbary corsairs, who had discovered that the
Stars and Stripes carried no naval protection, were still lan-
guishing in the dungeons of Algiers or chained to the thwarts
of the Dey's war galleys; and it was only under the protection
of the Portuguese navy patrolling the Strait of Gibraltar, that
American vessels were able to sail to and from Lisbon and
Cadiz. Jefferson reported the facts to Congress, leaving it to
choose "between war, tribute and ransom." The Senate piously
resolved that a naval force was the answer, but did nothing to
provide one; and the matter dragged along until 1792, when
survivors of the American sailors captured seven years earlier
sent Congress a petition threatening that if something were
not done for them promptly they would be forced to abandon
Christ and country and turn Moslem. This horrid prospect
moved Congress to appropriate $54,000 for ransoming the
captives at $2000 a head, and for a tribute treaty with Algiers.
John Paul Jones, charged with carrying out this ignominious
mission, died before he could undertake it. So the American
prisoners stayed in jail or on board the galleys for several
years more.

"Tranquillity has smoothed the surface," wrote a congressman after the Bill of Rights was adopted; but "faction glows
within like a coalpit." Washington was eager to retire in 1793.
Both Hamilton and Jefferson urged him to accept another
term; the one because the President had constantly supported
his measures, the other because he wanted more time to nurse
an opposition party. Washington consented, reluctantly. Again
he received the unanimous vote of the electoral college, and
John Adams was re-elected Vice President, but by a reduced
margin. First fruits of the Virginia-New York alliance were
gathered when those two states and North Carolina threw
their second electoral votes to George Clinton.

Americans have long argued and will continue to argue
over the respective merits of Hamilton and Jefferson. The
Republic was fortunate to have the services of both; for in a
sense they were complementary. Hamilton, the man of action,
grasping political and economic realities, promoted basic policies which enabled the new nation to attain unity and strength;
and the best tribute to those principles is that when Jefferson
became President, he accepted them as the basis of federal
power. Jefferson's theories make a seductive appeal to all
democrats and liberals, and he managed to impress an image
of himself which makes him the protagonist of American
idealism. He was probably right in resisting Hamilton's plan
to base government on an aristocracy of wealth and talents,
but no country can afford to disregard talents, and wealth has

been a greater factor in the federal equation during the last half-century than ever it was under the Federalists. Jefferson's foreign policy of disentanglement from European affairs suited the new nation far better than Hamilton's desire to be junior partner to Great Britain.

These opposing principles of foreign policy were now to come to a test, for Washington's second term opened in March 1793 in the shadow of a European war, which precipitated all floating elements of political dissension into two national parties: the Federalists led by Hamilton, and the Republicans led by Jefferson. These parties held the national stage for a generation; and with few intervals the two-party system has lasted to this day.

HAIL COLUMBIA

Firm, u-nit-ed let us be, Ral-'ying round our lib-er-ty, As a band of broth-ers join'd Peace and safe-ty we shall find.

II

Broils with England and France

1793-1801

1. *The French Revolution and American Politics*

EVENTS OF THE FRENCH REVOLUTION, beginning with the capture of the Bastille on 14 July 1789, were followed in America with the keenest interest and, up to a point, with universal sympathy. The French Constituent Assembly, in which Lafayette and Tom Paine were playing leading roles, abolished titles of nobility and other special privileges, and adopted a bill of rights modeled on those of the American states. Edmund Burke's *Considerations* on the course of events in France, by the most beloved English friend to the American Revolution, shook many leading Americans including Washington, Adams, and Hamilton, out of their complacency; and Tom Paine's answer to Burke, *The Age of Reason*, confirmed them as counter-revolutionaries. For, as the title indicated, the French intended to replace rule of law by rule of reason —their own reason; that was what put their revolution on the skids. But Jefferson wrote an introduction for the Philadelphia *The Age of Reason*, with a sneer at Hamilton.

Events moved so fast in France that it was difficult to figure out what really was going on, and news arrived so infrequently that it was three months before Americans heard that France had become a republic and was fighting Austria and Prussia.

Early in the new year 1793 the French decree of a "war of all peoples against all kings" reached America. Enthusiasm then became almost hysterical. Even Puritan Boston held a civic feast in French style. A procession of "citizens eight deep" escorted a roasted ox labeled "Peace Offering to Liberty and Equality," together with 1600 loaves of bread and two hogsheads of punch, to a spot rechristened Liberty Square. As the punch fell lower in the hogsheads, the ardor of the citizens rose; and if anyone had been so tactless as to suggest that all was not well in France, he would probably have been ducked in the Frog Pond.

For three months there was no news from Europe. Then, in April 1793, one month after Washington's second inauguration at Philadelphia, came word that brought war to the Delaware Capes and made the French Revolution an issue in American politics. France had declared war on Great Britain and Spain; Louis XVI, our good friend, had been guillotined; the Girondin party was in power, and Citizen Genet was coming over as minister plenipotentiary of the French Republic.

A cabinet meeting was promptly held at Philadelphia. Hamilton, loathing the French Revolution, wished to declare the alliance of 1778, which required us to defend the French Antilles, suspended by the change. Jefferson considered the cause of France "the most sacred cause that ever man was engaged in," but was eager to keep America out of the war; Washington still wished the French well, but thought of his own country first. Accordingly, on 22 April 1793, the President issued a neutrality proclamation declaring the "disposition of the United States" to "pursue a conduct friendly and impartial toward the belligerent powers," and warning citizens that "aiding or abetting hostilities" or carrying contraband would render them liable to prosecution in the federal courts. Congress implemented the proclamation by passing a Neutrality Act next session. Whether these could be enforced, when the great majority of Americans were eager to help France, was another matter.

In the meantime Citizen Genet, quaintest of many curious diplomats sent by European governments to the United States, had landed at Charleston, South Carolina. Before presenting his credentials he presumed to fit out privateers against British commerce and to recruit soldiers. His progress to Philadelphia was a continual ovation, in comparison with which the President's formal and dignified reception seemed cold and unfriendly. But the minister needed more than that to cool his revolutionary ardor.

Genet's instructions ordered him to use the United States as

a base for privateering on the ocean and filibustering Spanish
Florida and Louisiana, with the addition of Canada to the
American Union as bait. Several land speculators like George
Rogers Clark, who had corruptly obtained from the Georgia
legislature an immense land grant on the Mississippi near the
mouth of the Yazoo, eagerly accepted commissions from
Genet as officers in a "French army of the Mississippi." The
minister expected to finance these unneutral enterprises from
advances on the American debt to France. Hamilton naturally
refused to anticipate installments, and Genet's warriors had to
return empty-handed to their frontier farms.

The popular reception of Genet turned his head. "I live in
a round of parties," he wrote to his government. "Old man
Washington can't forgive my success." Like many later heroes,
he mistook the applause of curious crowds for approval.
When he found he could not move the American government,
he conceived the notion of turning it out. His progress through
the states was marked by founding Jacobin clubs, corresponding roughly to the Communist cells of our own time. Jefferson,
who at first welcomed Genet as a fillip to the opposition, concluded after a few weeks that he was likely to become a Jonah,
and supported Washington in requesting his recall. Robes-
pierre gladly consented, and in return asked for the recall of
Gouverneur Morris, whose intrigues in Paris had been more
frivolous than Genet's in Philadelphia, though hardly as mischievous. A new French minister arrived in the United States
early in 1794 with an order to send his predecessor home
under arrest. Instead of returning to feed the guillotine, Genet
married the daughter of Governor Clinton and settled down
to the life of a country gentleman on the Hudson.

That year, 1794, saw the crystallization of unstable political
elements into national parties. European issues are apt to
reach America without shadings, all black and white. Thus the
French Revolution seemed to some a clean-cut contest between monarchy and republicanism, oppression and liberty;
to others it was a fresh breaking-out of the eternal strife between anarchy and order, atheism and religion, poverty and
prosperity. Americans of the first way of thinking joined the
Republican party; others, the Federalist. Sectional and economic groups were polar to the completed parties; but in the
reverse order to general expectation. Formerly democratic
New England, especially the seaports, became the headquarters of the pro-British Federalists; whilst the landed interest,
particularly in slaveholding communities, was swept by Gallo-
mania.

The explanation is largely social and economic. In New England the clergy had been worrying over the younger generation: students preferred to read Voltaire and Gibbon rather than Jonathan Edwards. Tom Paine's scurrilous *Age of Reason* caused the sincerely religious to repudiate the party that supported France. Paine himself, by a nasty attack on Washington, identified Jeffersonianism with Jacobinism in the mind of the average Northerner. But the planters of Virginia seem to have been immune to religious panic and so certain of the loyalty of their own slaves that the massacre of white people in Haiti when "liberty, equality and fraternity" were applied in that French colony did not alarm them. Virginia's opposition to British capital and sea power was part of her hatred for Northern capital and Hamiltonian finance schemes. The writings of the French *philosophes* and *économistes* enabled country gentlemen to rationalize their instincts that land was the unique source of wealth, that trade and finance were parasites. Chief local philosopher was Colonel John Taylor "of Caroline" a Virginia county. His pamphlets declared that every dollar made by merchants came out of the farmer's pocket, that England through her disregard of "true economic principles" was a "sinking nation," and that trade with her was draining America of her wealth. These absurd notions became doctrine in the South; and it took them long to die.

To the merchant-shipowners, on the contrary, British capital was an indispensable credit instrument necessary for American trade with Britain. Like Hamilton, they did not care to risk a quarrel with the power that could give or withhold. British spoliations on neutral trade might annoy American shipowners, but the British admiralty gave compensation whilst the French Republic did not. During the entire period of the Anglo-French war, as in 1914–17 and 1939–41, there was no time when American shipowners could not make immense profits by accepting British regulations, whilst the French privateers' attacks on neutral commerce, like those of the German submarines, were a net loss.

Around these two poles American opinion crystallized in 1793–95. You were either for the Republicans and France, or for the Federalists and Britain. Emotion for a principle, and for the kind of country you wanted America to be, joined interest and policy. This was not Britain and France corrupting American opinion, but Americans seeking both practical and ideological support in Europe. "Each party will use foreign influence as it needs, to dominate," predicted Volney, a French scholar traveling in America. The Republicans (ancestors of the Democrats of today)[1] and the Federalists (of whom the present Republicans are residuary legatees) supported the Federal Constitution, although each accused the other of trying to subvert it. Their basic principles, to 1815, were agrarianism and the French Revolution against capitalism and Britain. If the one in 1794 stood for state rights, and the other for a strong federal government, it was only because the one was out and the other in. Each party attempted to undercut the other on its home field by appealing to some local interest contrary to the dominant one. Thus, in Virginia the wheat-growing Shenandoah valley, which hated the slave-owning aristocracy, remained Federalist; whilst the South Carolina back country, which hated Charleston, went Republican. Jefferson reached out to the underdog in New England, where Baptists and other sects of inferior status generally went Republican, as did poor fishing ports such as Marblehead, jealous of Federalist Salem. These are early illustrations of a side to American politics so puzzling to outsiders—the fact that national parties are always to a great extent local. Thousands of votes in every presidential election are dictated by state issues, local rivalries, and racial or religious feuds.

Polar also to the economic and section cleavage was the ideological. Jefferson believed that a government could be based on, and its official policy dictated by, "reason," as the French Republic was attempting to do, with dire results. John Adams and Edmund Burke, who warned France that this would happen, believed, as John Dickinson had said, "Let Experience be our guide. Reason may mislead us." And long has it continued to mislead people—notably the Communists. Over a century after Jefferson's day, Elihu Root said, "The great difficulty in the application of pure reason to practical affairs is that never . . . does the reasoner get all the premises which should affect the conclusions; so it frequently happens that the practical man . . . who feels the effect of conditions which the reasoner overlooks, goes right, while the superior intelligence of the reasoning man goes wrong."

Jefferson was no pure reasoner, and Hamilton no pure empiricist; but the one wished to make a fresh start based on reason; and the other, to build on tried ways and habits. In their approach to life and its problems, these two typified

---

[1] Jefferson began referring to his friends as "the Republicans" in 1791, in order to imply that all others were monarchists; the Hamiltonians kept the name Federalist in order to imply that all others were Anti-federal. Their favorite names for the Republicans were "Jacobins" or "Democrats." The latter name, sometimes used by the Northern wing of the Republican party, was distasteful to the Southerners. Jefferson tried calling the Federalists "monocrats" but it did not catch on.

Goethe's dichotomy: the spirit that creates and the spirit that denies; the hope that man is perfectible and the belief that he is irremediably stupid and evil. We shall find these two poles constant while our political globe spins. There was no clean-cut difference between the two parties that Hamilton and Jefferson organized. The Republicans had the greater share of optimism, and the Federalists of pessimism; but each had something to give the country, and both were equally guilty of appealing to men's fears and appetites. Jefferson's "botanical excursion" of 1791 began the substitution of expediency for idealism; whilst the character of Washington, the genius of Hamilton, and the intellect of Marshall transcended reaction by maintaining principles of national integrity and international justice that were vital to an enduring Union.

2. *The Crucial Year 1794*

If Victor Hugo's "1793," year of the Reign of Terror, was crucial in the French Revolution, 1794 was the most critical in America's federal experiment. The Supreme Court suffered a setback, but the executive won a signal victory in putting down a rebellion of Western "moonshiners" against Federal "revenooers." Outrages by Barbary corsairs induced Congress to re-establish the United States Navy. A new governor of Upper Canada tried to cash in on St. Clair's defeat by converting the Northwest Territory into an Indian satellite state, but General Wayne avenged St. Clair at the Fallen Timbers. The United States teetered on the brink of war with England, but Washington sent Jay to negotiate at London; and his treaty, viciously attacked by the Republicans as a base capitulation, not only prevented war but swung open the gate to the West.

The setback was a refusal of the State of Georgia to obey a decision of the Supreme Court of the United States, in a suit to recover debts, brought by a citizen of another state. Not only did Georgia get away with virtual nullification; the other states became so alarmed at the prospect of being forced by the Supreme Court to pay old war claims, that Congress passed (5 March 1799), and the states ratified, Amendment XI to the Constitution, forbidding the federal judiciary to entertain any suit brought against a state of the Union by a citizen of another state or nation. Thus the states recovered a traditional royal prerogative, to be sued only with their consent.

Congress's act of 1791 levying a moderate excise tax on distilleries seemed as unjust and tyrannical to mountain men as the British Stamp Act had to all Americans. In the Appalachians and beyond, distilling was a practical method of using surplus corn. Whisky could bear the cost of transportation and kegs of it were even used as currency. Congress modified the law so that there was less snooping, and opposition quieted down except in Washington County, the westernmost part of Pennsylvania. There a frontier lawyer named David Bradford and old Herman Husband, who had led the North Carolina Regulators before the war, organized resistance to the law. Covenants were signed never to pay the tax, law-abiding distillers were terrorized, federal marshals at Pittsburgh were roughly handled, a mass meeting appointed a "committee of safety," and citizens were conjured to rise and fight for their spirituous liberties. But for the moderating influence of Hugh H. Brackenridge and Albert Gallatin, a recent immigrant from Geneva, Washington County might have seceded from Pennsylvania and the Union. This movement became jocularly known as the Whisky Rebellion.

Governor Thomas Mifflin of Pennsylvania, now a Jeffersonian Republican, refused to do anything to enforce the law lest it hurt his popularity. But President Washington and his secretary of the treasury accepted this challenge as a test whether the federal government could really enforce the law without the help of the states. Congress had been given power "to provide for calling forth the militia to execute the laws of the Union." Congress so authorized the President, and on 7 August 1794 he called out 15,000 militiamen from four states. Most of them responded. The President, accompanied by Generals Daniel Morgan and Henry Lee, and Alexander Hamilton in uniform, led them in a stiff hike over the Alleghenies. Upon the approach of the army, most of the rebel leaders fled and the rank and file quit. Two ringleaders were caught and convicted of treason, but pardoned by the President.

This was a severe but successful test of the new government in its domestic relations. Henceforth, persons and interests who had a grievance against the federal government had to carry at least one state and evolve the doctrine of state rights as a defense. That form of resistance was supposedly ended in 1865; yet, almost a century later, it has been possible for several states to defy Congress and the Supreme Court on the racial question.

Washington's cool, serene temper had all it could do to quench a hot demand for war with England. In her war against the French Republic, England applied her ancient doctrine that enemy property on the high seas was good prize, even if in a neutral vessel. France and the United States, as the weaker sea powers, contended for the principle "Free ships make free goods"; meaning that a neutral flag protected enemy property except contraband of war, arms, and munitions. Britain now declared good prize any neutral ship carrying provisions to the French West Indies. When this order in council of 6 November 1793 reached British naval officers abroad, the Caribbean was swarming with small American vessels eager to profit by neutral trade. A number of them were captured and roughly treated in British vice-admiralty courts, since naval officers were eager for prize money and judges took a cut on condemnations. News of these captures brought consternation to the American trading community, backbone of the Federalist party. Even Hamilton was exasperated. Congress began war preparations and clapped an embargo on the seaports. In the midst of the crisis, news leaked into American newspapers of a truculent speech by Lord Dorchester to an Indian delegation, encouraging them to look for British aid in driving the Yankees across the Ohio river for good and all.

In Congress the opposition party was not prepared for war, but demanded commercial retaliation which would certainly have led to war, as it did in 1812 when Jefferson and Madison tried it, and in 1941 when Franklin D. Roosevelt tried it. A timely gesture of friendship from the British foreign minister prevented matters from going farther. He revoked the provision-capture order. In April 1794, shortly after this news reached Philadelphia, Washington nominated Chief Justice Jay envoy extraordinary to Great Britain. "My objects are, to prevent a war," he wrote, "if justice can be obtained." Jay's nomination was confirmed by the Senate on 19 April. "The day is a good omen," said John Adams. His casting vote as Vice President defeated a bill to suspend commercial intercourse with Great Britain, and the embargo on exports was allowed to lapse because the French minister wanted it so, in order to get food to France. An enormous convoy of American provision ships sailed from the Chesapeake under escort of French men-of-war, which Admiral Lord Howe defeated on "the Glorious First of June" 1794, thus winning the fame that he had sought in vain during the War of Independence. But the convoy of over a hundred sail slipped safely into Brest in time to relieve a famine which followed the Reign of Terror.

A main object of Jay's mission was to obtain British evacuation of the Northwest posts. General St. Clair's defeat had encouraged both the Indians and the government to retain them, and in 1792 the governor of Canada proposed that the entire territory between the Great Lakes and the Ohio river, together with a strip of New York and Vermont, be erected into a satellite Indian state. Although the British government did not take this up, it informed the United States government that the Northwest posts would be retained, whether or not America paid her contested debts, and Lieutenant Governor Simcoe of Upper Canada set up a new garrison at the rapids of the Maumee river about 100 miles southwest of Detroit.

The United States Army, reorganized after St. Clair's defeat and recruited to 2000 men, was now placed under the command of Major General Anthony Wayne. In the fall of 1793 he established winter quarters at the site of Greenville, Ohio. "Mad Anthony," as his men called Wayne for his reckless courage, really had a cool head. His communications were assured by six fortified posts, and by constant vigilance. An admirable disciplinarian, he trained his troops in the tactics of forest warfare, and the redskins gave them plenty of practice. Several hundred Kentucky mounted riflemen joined him in the spring of 1794.

Simcoe strengthened his new fort on the Maumee and bent all his energy to mobilizing the Indians. Provisions, blankets, muskets, powder and ball, and vermilion warpaint were dispensed from Canadian depots and arsenals. When the oak leaves were fully out, completing nature's ambush, the Indians attacked. Wayne beat them off and took the offensive. Advancing cautiously through the hardwood forest and protected by a screen of scouts, he debouched into the Erie plain, the Indians' granary. Along the Maumee and the Glaize there were log cabins, fruit trees, and cornfields. In the midst of these savage gardens, Wayne built Fort Defiance, a stockade with blockhouse bastions. There he offered peace once more, and again it was rejected. The Indians retreated to the vicinity of the new British fort and took cover behind a natural stockade of fallen trees. There were 1500 to 2000 of them: Miami under Chief Little Turtle; Black Wolf with his Shawnee; the "three fires" of the Ottawa, Chippewa, and Potawotomi under Blue Jacket; Sauk and Fox from Lake Superior; a few Iroquois diehards, and 70 white Canadian rangers under an old Loyalist. On 20 August Wayne marched forth to meet them. A squadron of dragoons charged on the Indians' left flank. Both the American captains were picked off, but a lieutenant took command, and the troopers, jumping their horses over the fallen timber as in a steeplechase, burst in on the redskins and gave them cold steel. The infantry and riflemen then poured in a volley of hot stuff and charged with bayonets before the Indians had time to reload. In forty minutes it was all over. The Battle of the Fallen Timbers sent all tribesmen from distant parts scampering home and enabled Wayne to destroy the Indian villages, lay waste their cornfields, and build Fort Wayne at the forks of the Maumee. His army returned to Greenville, to await envoys of peace.

On 16 June 1795 a peace conference was summoned in a forest clearing at Greenville. Delegates of tribes between the Great Lakes, the Mississippi, and the Ohio assembled to the number of 1130. The conferences lasted for six weeks. The patience of General Wayne was rewarded on 3 August 1795 with the Treaty of Greenville, between the assembled tribes and the "Fifteen Fires" of the States. The Indians ceded the southeastern corner of the Northwest Territory together with several enclaves such as Vincennes, Detroit, and the site of Chicago, in return for annuities to the value of some $10,000.

So ended almost twenty years of fighting: the last phase of the War of Independence. Peace came to the border from the Genesee country to the Mississippi. Pioneers began to swarm up the valleys of the Scioto and the Muskingum; but within ten years their greed for land made the Treaty of Greenville a scrap of paper.

This same year 1794 witnessed an overdue rebirth of the United States Navy, with Barbary corsairs acting as midwives. By February, 126 American sailors were enslaved at Algiers, and more were coming in weekly. A navy, rather than an indefinite payment of tribute, was the obvious remedy. Despite Republican opposition (Senators Maclay and Monroe accusing the Federalists of wanting patronage, not protection), Congress passed and the President signed a law authorizing the building of six warships, and a modest establishment of 54 officers and 2000 ratings. In accordance with this law, Joseph Humphreys designed the first three frigates of the new navy: U.S.S. *Constitution, United States,* and *Constellation.* But, as the limited appropriation made it impossible to complete these ships within three years, Washington had to buy peace with Algiers in 1796 and ransom the prisoners at a cost of almost a million dollars.

3. Jay's Treaty and the Election of 1796

Jay's treaty, signed in London on 19 November 1794, obtained the prime objects of his mission—a promise to evacuate the Northwest posts by 1796, and a limited right of American vessels to trade with the British West Indies. It preserved the peace, secured America's territorial integrity, and established a basis for Western expansion. Other unsettled questions were referred to mixed commissions, one of which made a beginning of settling the Maine-New Brunswick boundary. Some £600,000 was eventually paid by the United States in satisfaction of prewar debts, and £1,317,000 by Great Britain for illegal captures of American ships.

Yet, when the terms of this treaty were printed in Philadelphia (2 November 1795), a howl of rage went up that Jay had betrayed his country. This clamor was completely unjustified. Jay had refused even to discuss the proposed Indian satellite state. He resisted a British demand to rectify the frontier in the Northwest so as to give Canada a corridor to the site of St. Paul, and which would eventually have made lat. 45° N instead of 49° N the international boundary. He declined to make any concessions on the navigation of the Mississippi. He procured the desired evacuation of the posts. A good part of the rage against the treaty was due to the French "party line" being repeated by Republican newspapers; for it prevented a war which the French government wanted. A bare two-thirds majority for the treaty was obtained in the Senate, and Washington ratified it in 25 June 1795—a wise and brave act which made him the target for vicious party attacks. Six months later, the House of Representatives threatened to nullify the treaty by withholding supply for the mixed commissions, and a powerful speech by Fisher Ames just prevented the mischief.

All Northwest posts were evacuated before the end of the year. Lord Shelburne, who had been responsible for the treaty line so long withheld, wrote to Major William Jackson in 1797, "I cannot express to you the satisfaction I have felt in seeing the forts given up. . . . The deed is done, and a strong foundation laid for eternal amity between England and America. General Washington's conduct is above all praise. He has left a noble example to sovereigns and nations, present and to come."

Jay's treaty also gave America the unexpected dividend of a settlement with Spain that included the right of transit at New Orleans. Baron de Carondelet, governor of Louisiana, endeavoring to establish an Indian satellite state in the Southwest, built a new fort on United States territory at Chickasaw Bluffs (Memphis) and persuaded the Creek and Cherokee nations to denounce their earlier treaties with the United States. Thomas Pinckney, whom Washington sent to Madrid, found the Spanish government in a favorable frame of mind because it suspected that Jay's treaty included a secret Anglo-

American alliance, and feared losing Louisiana to American filibusters. Accordingly, in the Treaty of San Lorenzo (27 October 1795), His Catholic Majesty conceded the right to navigate the lower Mississippi, and the transit rights at New Orleans so ardently desired by the West. Spain then evacuated her posts on the east bank of the Mississippi, north of the southern boundary of the United States, which now had full control of her own territory.

When Jefferson retired from the department of state on the last day of 1793, Washington appointed in his place Edmund Randolph, whom his acidulous kinsman John Randolph of Roanoke compared to "the chameleon on the aspen, always trembling, always changing." Officially approving Washington's policy, he secretly worked against it; and his downfall was brought about through an indiscretion of Citizen Fauchet. A giveaway dispatch from this envoy of the French Republic to his government was captured at sea by the British, who passed it along to Washington. It referred to certain "precious confessions" by Randolph and hinted that the secretary had asked him for money at the time of the Whisky Rebellion. "Thus, a few thousand dollars would have decided between war and peace! So the consciences of the so-called American patriots already have their price!" observed Fauchet. Washington, like a Roman father, confronted Randolph with this dispatch in a cabinet meeting and demanded an explanation. Randolph promptly resigned. What really passed between him and Fauchet will never be known; the most probable explanation is that he tried to obtain secret service money from the French to procure evidence implicating England in the Whisky Rebellion.

Randolph's disgrace ended Washington's attempt to govern with a bipartisan cabinet. The premier secretaryship was now conferred on Timothy Pickering, a New England Federalist of the most pronounced type, a Puritan who hated the French Republic as the incarnation of evil. Hamilton, who had resigned from the treasury department after the Whisky Rebellion, had been replaced by the first auditor of the treasury, Oliver Wolcott, and James McHenry became secretary of war. All three were disciples of Hamilton.

Washington had made the mistake of appointing James Monroe, a pronounced Anglophobe, to the Paris legation while Jay was negotiating in London; and he made a greater mistake by recalling Monroe in 1796 when he was doing his best to appease the injured feelings of the French government. The Executive Directory of France, now regarding America as a British satellite, suspended diplomatic relations but retained its minister in Philadelphia as a political agent in the presidential election.

This situation Washington thankfully left to a successor. By refusing to stand for a third term he established the two-term tradition in American politics, which became constitutional in 1951 by virtue of Amendment XXII. Through correspondence and private consultation the Republicans decided to support Jefferson and Aaron Burr for President and Vice President; the Federalists, John Adams and Thomas Pinckney. Jay's treaty was the central issue of the campaign, to which the French minister contributed a political pamphlet, together with much intrigue. The result was a narrow Federalist victory. Adams obtained the presidency with 71 votes in the electoral college. Jefferson's 68 votes made him Vice President by the constitutional method that was changed by Amendment XII in 1804.

"I now compare myself," wrote Washington on 2 March 1797, "to the wearied traveler who seeks a resting place, and is bending his body to lean thereon. But to be suffered to do *this* in peace is too much to be endured by *some*." During his last year in office the President was assailed with a virulence such as few of his successors have suffered. Jefferson, in a letter to Filippo Mazzei, an Italian friend, which found its way into print, referred to "men who were Samsons in the field and Solomons in the Council," whose heads had been "shorn by the harlot England." Everyone knew that he meant Washington, Hamilton, and Adams. The Philadelphia *Aurora*, on the morrow of Washington's retirement, proclaimed that "this day ought to be a Jubilee in the United States . . . for the man who is the source of all the misfortunes of our country, is this day reduced to a level with his fellow citizens."

Six months previously, on 17 September 1796, Washington summed up his political experience in a farewell address of permanent value. An eloquent plea for union is followed by a pointed exposition of disruptive tendencies. Politicians, he said, misrepresent "the opinions and aims of other districts" in order to acquire influence within their own; pressure groups are formed to override or control the constitutional authorities; the "baneful effects of the spirit of party" hamstring a President's efforts to promote the national interest. As to foreign policy, the Father of his Country enjoined citizens to "Observe good faith and justice towards all nations; cultivate peace and harmony with all. . . . The Nation which indulges towards another an habitual hatred or an habitual fondness is in some degree a slave."

Washington's famous doctrine of isolation is contained in the following sentences:

> Europe has a set of primary interests, which to us have none, or a very remote relation. Hence she must be engaged in frequent controversies, the causes of which are essentially foreign to our concerns. . . . Our detached and distant situation invites us to pursue a different course. . . . 'Tis our true policy to steer clear of permanent alliances, with any portion of the foreign world. . . . Taking care always to keep ourselves, by suitable establishments, on a respectable defensive posture, we may safely trust to temporary alliances for extraordinary emergencies.

This farewell address fell on deaf ears in a Europe that was ringing with the exploits of a new hero, General Bonaparte. But there it was written, for whomsoever cared to read, that a new power in the West considered herself outside the European system. Nor was it much heeded in America, where the leading politicians believed that the dearest interests of their respective parties were bound up with England or with France.

Washington's services in time of peace have never been adequately appreciated. His unique place in history rests not only on his superb leadership in war, and on his wise administration of the federal government; but even more on his integrity, good judgment, and magnanimity. As Samuel T. Coleridge, one of his many English admirers, wrote shortly after Washington's death:

> Tranquil and firm he moved with one pace in one path, and neither vaulted nor tottered. . . . Among a people eminently querulous and already impregnated with the germs of discordant parties, he directed the executive power firmly and unostentatiously. He had no vain conceit of being himself all; and did those things only which he only could do.

4. John Adams and the Naval War with France

John Adams, now sixty-one years old, was "always honest, often great, but sometimes mad," remarked Franklin. Even after eight years' experience as Vice President, he was by temperament unsuited for the presidency. He did know more than any other American, even Madison, about political science; but as an administrator he was uneasy. He did not attract personal loyalty and had few close friends in the political

world; that probably explains his initial error of continuing
Washington's entire cabinet in office. The three key members,
Pickering, Wolcott, and McHenry, devoted to Hamilton, secretly referred every major question to him in New York,
acted on his recommendations, and persuaded the President to
adopt them. Thus Hamilton, whom Adams distrusted, really
ran his administration until 1799 when he discovered what
was going on and sent the triumvirate packing.

Adams paid less attention to his duties than any of his successors. Whilst Washington was absent from the seat of government 181 days in eight years, Adams stayed away for 385
days in four years. He did so mainly because he loved his
home and farm at Quincy, but partly because both he and his
excellent wife disliked Philadelphia society which insulted
them (so Abigail felt) by continuing to celebrate George's
birthday instead of John's. And when the federal government
moved to the District of Columbia in 1800, life in the uncompleted White House was too much like camping out for an
aging couple who liked comfort.

Adams's attitude toward his predecessor may be gathered
from a remark he made while being painted by Gilbert Stuart:
"Washington got the reputation of being a great man," he told
the painter, "because he kept his mouth shut." That was one
thing John could never do. But the foreign situation he faced
in 1797 was more difficult than Washington's. Jay's treaty had
embroiled the United States with the aggressive and subversive French Directory, and American Republicans seemed
determined to follow the French party line, no matter what.
They even advised the next French move, to let privateers
loose against the American merchant fleet. The ensuing
French spoliations on commerce made those of Britain in
1793 seem mild in comparison. Red-bonneted ruffians who
represented France in the West Indies made an open traffic of
blank letters of marque. Frenchmen at Charleston secretly
armed American vessels to prey upon American commerce
under the authority of forged commissions. In June 1797 the
secretary of state reported that more than 300 American vessels had been captured under the color of French authority.

The Directory refused to receive Monroe's successor at
Paris, and its official language toward the United States became truculent and threatening. President Adams declared
that he would submit to no indignities but hoped to maintain
Washington's policy of neutrality. Following the Jay precedent, he made another effort to obtain justice through diplomacy. In order to satisfy the Republicans that he was not seeking a quarrel, Adams appointed a Jeffersonian, Elbridge

Gerry; and in order to keep Gerry out of mischief, joined with him in the mission two sound Federalists, John Marshall and Charles Cotesworth Pinckney.

The first year of Adams's administration passed without news from the mission. In the meantime, the party cleavage deepened. The Republicans, refusing to believe that the French government had changed character since 1792, stoutly defended the spoliations as a natural answer to Jay's treaty, and opposed every effort of the Federalists to build up national defense. Congress now hastened to complete the three frigates under construction. But, when the *United States* was launched at Philadelphia in 1797, with such speed that she smacked the opposite shore, and at Boston the *Constitution* stuck on the ways, Jeffersonian papers shouted with glee and expressed the hope that these fine ships would never get to sea. Philip Freneau, the kept poet of the party, even published a poem to that effect: "O frigate *Constitution!* Stay on shore!"

To the Federalists, on the other hand, France had become just such a menace to American independence as certain communist powers became in 1946. The European situation was a small-scale portent of the world situation of our own era, when the free world has had to defend itself both against the Nazis and the Reds. For the French Republic had invented the political strategy that Hitler and Stalin imitated: an ideological offensive implemented by armies and the replacing of established governments by puppet regimes. Thus, Holland became the Batavian Republic in 1795, and the Cisalpine, Parthenopean, and Helvetian Republics followed. United Ireland received encouragement from Paris, and in 1798 British radicals were toasting the day when a French army would proclaim Tom Paine president of an English Republic. Would America's turn come next?

The Western world was being divided into countries which had made terms with France, and those which had not; and by 1797 Britain, the United States, and Russia were the only three important ones who had not. "If England will persevere," wrote Senator George Cabot, "she will save Europe and save us; if she yields, all will be lost. . . . She is now the only barrier between us and the deathly embraces of universal irreligion, immorality and plunder." Better to fight France by England's side, rather than be forced to fight her alone later.

So reasoned the Federalists—as Democrats and others did in 1917 and 1941. Fears of a French invasion were not unreasonable, since we now know that French designs on Canada, the West, and Florida were definite and dangerous. General George Rogers Clark and other prominent Westerners were on the payroll of the French Republic, which was pressuring Spain to cede Florida and Louisiana to France. That would have semicircled the United States with French territory and thrust her western boundary back to the Appalachians. General Victor Collot in 1796 traveled down the Ohio and the Mississippi to select strong points for this scheme Quebec inhabitants were being worked on by secret agents to declare a Canadian Republic under French protection Rela tions were renewed with Genet's unpaid warriors; and Milfort, a halfbreed chief of the Creek nation, was commissioned a French brigadier general.

The American mission arrived in Paris at an unpropitious moment, in October 1797, after Bonaparte had beaten Austria, and the Directory was at the height of power and arrogance. The Directors, at least one of whom had a pecuniary interest in privateering, felt they could with impunity continue "a little clandestine war" against the United States. A comic, if one-sided, bit of bargaining ensued. Talleyrand, the French minister of foreign affairs, sent some hangers-on (referred to in the dispatches as X, Y, and Z) to play on the fears of the American envoys, and sound their pockets. A bribe of some $250,-000 for the minister, and a loan of $10 million as compensation for President Adams's "insults," were the prerequisites to negotiation. Pressed for an alternative, Monsieur Y hinted at the power of the French party in America, and lightly touched upon the fate of recalcitrant European states. Gerry was alarmed by these suggestions, but Pinckney and Marshall were unshaken. "Our case is different from that of the minor nations of Europe," the Virginian informed Monsieur Y. "They were unable to maintain their independence, and did not expect to do so. America is a great, and, so far as concerns her self-defence, a powerful nation." After several months of fruitless palaver, Marshall and Pinckney took their leave. Gerry, fatuously believing his presence necessary to avert war, remained for a time in Paris.

The envoys' dispatches, recording in detail their strange experiences, reached America early in 1798, and were sent to Congress by the President. These "X Y Z despatches" were printed; and the public was deeply moved by its first-hand view of French diplomacy. On Republicans the effect was stupefying. "Trimmers dropt off from the party like windfalls from an apple tree in September," wrote Fisher Ames. Jefferson "thought it his duty to be silent." Loyal addresses poured in on President and Congress, indignation meetings were held, reams of patriotic poetry (including one national anthem that has endured—Joseph Hopkinson's *Hail Columbia!*) were produced, and "Millions for Defense, but Not One Cent for Tribute" became the slogan.

President Adams and the Federalists adopted a policy of armed neutrality, expecting a declaration of war by France to unite all honest men to their standard. Congress created a navy department, a vast improvement over having the navy treated as an adjunct to the army. Under the new secretary, Benjamin Stoddert, and the senior naval officer Commodore John Barry, the United States Navy became an efficient fighting force. Congress also revived the Marine Corps. Frigates *United States, Constitution,* and *Constellation* were fitted for sea; *President, Congress,* and *Chesapeake* were completed; five more frigates were built by groups of merchants and sold to the government; many smaller vessels were purchased and converted; navy yards were purchased, and an ambitious program of naval construction undertaken. Privateers were fitted out, and both they and the warships were authorized to capture French armed vessels wherever found. But they were not allowed to take unarmed merchant ships, as in a declared war. Since almost every French ship that they encountered was armed, that prohibition did not matter.

By the close of 1798 there were fourteen American men-of-war at sea, and some two hundred merchant vessels had taken out letters of marque and reprisal. By arrangement with Great Britain, her navy protected American transatlantic shipping, and the United States Navy took care of the merchant ships of both nations in the Caribbean. Organized in four task forces of three to ten ships each, it combed the Caribbean from Caracas to Cuba, and from the Straits of Florida to the Gulf of Paria, sweeping French picaroons out of those waters, protecting property worth millions of dollars from spoliation On 9 February 1799 the navy received its first battle test off Nevis, where U.S.S. *Constellation* (Commodore Thomas Truxtun) fought for an hour and, owing to superior gunnery, captured the crack French frigate *L'Insurgente.* A year later, off Guadeloupe, *Constellation* (38 guns) chased *Vengeance* (54 guns) all day, brought her to action at eight in the evening, and fought her within pistol shot until one in the morning. The French commander struck his colors twice during the action but Truxtun did not perceive it in the smoke and darkness, and the *Vengeance* managed to escape. Frigate *Boston* (28 guns, Captain Little) had a terrific fight with the French corvette *Le Berceau* (24 guns) in the open ocean on 12 October 1800, and captured her. The only United States ship to be defeated during this war was schooner *Retaliation* (14 guns), by two frigates which together mounted 80 guns.

The effect of this quasi-war on the United States Army was less happy. In 1798, when its total strength amounted to only 3500 officers and men, Congress ordered the immediate enlistment of 10,000 more; and the creation, on paper, of a "provisional army" of 50,000. George Washington, who wholeheartedly supported the Adams administration, accepted an appointment as lieutenant general to command this new army, and insisted on Hamilton receiving the senior major generalship, so that he could command in the field. President Adams growled over these preparations, which he considered excessive, and postponed active recruiting until the spring of 1799, when most of the anti-French fire had died down By that time the British navy, by bottling up Bonaparte's army in Egypt, had rendered France incapable of invading America. Consequently, only about 3000 men, whom Washington described as "the riff-raff of the country and the scape-gallows of the large cities," could be persuaded to enlist in the new army, and the provisional force existed only on paper. But one permanent benefit was derived from this army which never fought. The secretary of war promoted the formation of a school for gunners and sappers. West Point was selected as the location, and on his last day of office President Adams appointed the first faculty of the United States Military Academy.

In the congressional elections of 1798–99 the Federalists won a strong majority, destined to be their last. Jefferson and his party appeared to be discredited by their excuses for French aggression and for treating the exploits of the United States Navy with sneers and jeers But time was preparing the Republicans' revenge. A rift appeared in the Federalist party between the President and Hamilton, and into this rift Talleyrand insinuated a wedge.

A difference in objective caused the trouble. Adams's was to protect American commerce and force the French Republic to respect our flag. He was willing to accept war if declared by France, but hoped to avoid it; and most Federalists agreed. Hamilton and the New England Federalist leaders regarded the French imbroglio not as an affair to be wound up but as an occasion to be improved. It was to be a starting point for spirited measures that would strengthen the federal government, discipline the American people, and "crush the French canker that feeds on our vitals." Talleyrand, although annoyed by the exposure of his venality to the amused laughter of all Europe, refused to play into their hands, as Jefferson assured him a declaration of war would do. "The maintenance of republican principles," added the Vice President, "depends entirely on French prudence." Talleyrand cared nothing for republican principles, but he respected the new United States Navy. Accordingly, he used every available channel to communicate peaceful intentions to America. Any minister the President might send would be received, and no questions asked. The French embargo on American vessels was lifted, letters of marque issued in the West Indies were annulled, and French officials were ordered to respect neutral ships and property. An official explanation of the X Y Z episode was issued, in a tone of injured dignity. The American ministers, it appeared, had been imposed upon by charlatans. The Directory had intended to treat with the Americans, but they shut themselves up in their hotel and went off in a huff before they could be received. For just such a cue the discomfited opposition had been waiting in America. It became the Republican party line that the X Y Z affair was a hoax by Federalist warmongers.

French conciliatory advances were treated by the bent-on-war Federalists as insincere. In the President's absence the cabinet, advised as usual by Hamilton, decided to continue war preparations and to declare war on France as soon as Congress convened. Hamilton had the outlines of a grandiose plan. Since Spain was a French ally he, as senior major general, would lead the new American army overland, and with naval support would capture New Orleans and the Floridas. If that worked well, the next operation would be an invasion of Mexico while the British, in concert with the South American patriot Miranda, liberated New Granada. Anglo-American friendship would be cemented by dividing the spoils of Spanish America, Hamilton would return laurel-crowned at the head of his victorious legion, to become the first citizen of America as Napoleon Bonaparte was already the first citizen of France.

President Adams now made a decision which knocked these ambitions on the head. Without consulting a single person, on 18 March 1799 he nominated a new minister to France. The strongly Federalist Senate would have rejected the nomination, but dared not meet the Republican charge of prolonging hostilities after the President had initiated peace. So it compromised by asking for a commission of three instead of a single envoy, to which the President consented; but while Adams enjoyed one of his prolonged vacations at Quincy, Secretary Pickering held up the mission. In October 1799 the President hastened back to Philadelphia and hustled the peace commission on board an American frigate. It reached Paris in time to deal with Bonaparte, who had kicked out the Directory and set himself up as First Consul. For seven months the negotiations dragged, while Napoleon crossed the Alps to thrash the Austrians again. He would admit no liability for the French spoliations, unless the United States recognized the treaties of 1778, which Congress had denounced at the height of anti-Gallican feeling. No alliance, no money! The American mission, fearing to bring home a renewed entangling alliance, signed on 30 September 1800 a mere commercial convention, each party reserving its rights as to treaties and indemnities. Captured French warships had to be returned, but not captured privateers.

On the very next day, 1 October 1800, France secretly obtained the retrocession of Louisiana from Spain. Hamilton would have been proved right, after all, had not Napoleon tossed Louisiana to Jefferson in 1803.

Substantial gains to the nation from this quasi-war were protection of American commerce, and the virtual rebirth of the United States Navy. Fifty-four American warships were afloat at the end of hostilities, as compared with about ten at the beginning; and they had captured ninety-three French armed vessels. An officers' corps and thousands of seamen and marines received training that would bear fruit later. The total cost of operating the navy in this war was only $6 million. Unfortunately, peace with France and the election of Jefferson caused the navy to be radically reduced.

5. Federalist Intolerance and the Election of 1800–1801

While organizing defense and drumming up war enthusiasm, the Federalists did not neglect enemies at home. The Naturalization, Alien, and Sedition Acts of 1798 were aimed at domestic disaffection as much as foreign danger. These laws provoked the first organized state rights movement under the Constitution, and promoted the election of Jefferson to the presidency. They afford a striking instance of political intolerance. But provocation was not lacking.

The events of the 1790's sent many radical Europeans to America; and one who came earlier, Albert Gallatin, was now the Republican minority leader in Congress. Dr. Priestley, accused of trying "to decompose both Church and State" with his chemical formulas, had found refuge in Pennsylvania after a "patriotic mob" had gutted his house in England. There he was joined by another English radical, Thomas Cooper, who edited a violently Republican newspaper; both men were very much "wanted" by the Federalists. Adet, the French minister who worked for Jefferson in the election of 1796, was also a chemist by profession, and the French botanist Michaux did espionage for his government. By French consular estimates, there were 25,000 French refugees in the United States in 1798. Many were aristocratic *émigrés,* but most were proscribed Jacobins who wished to stand in well with the Directory. Refugees from the Irish rebellion of 1798 were also pouring in. A Federalist congressman wrote that in a journey through Pennsylvania he had seen very many Irishmen who, with few exceptions, were "United Irishmen, Free Masons, and the most God-provoking Democrats this side of Hell." Thus, as has happened twice in the twentieth century, the fear of political refugees engaging in treasonable activities against the United States, produced legislation against them. The Naturalization Act of 1798 extended the required period of residence for citizenship from five to fourteen years. The Alien Act, passed for two years only, gave the President power to expel suspected foreigners by executive decree. Adams, although frequently urged by Pickering to sign warrants for expulsion, did so only in the case of two Irish journalists, but over a dozen shiploads of Frenchmen left the country in anticipation of trouble.

For the Sedition Act of 1798 there was a legitimate need. There being no common law of the United States, the federal courts required statutory authority before taking cognizance of conspiracies against the government, or libels on high officials. One section of the new law, however, made it a misdemeanor punishable by fine or imprisonment to speak or write against President or Congress "with the intent to defame" or to bring them "into contempt or disrepute." The act made proof of the truth of the libel a sufficient defense, and required a jury trial, which was more than similar laws did in European countries. But the Sedition Act was foolishly enforced, so as to confound political opposition with sedition. About twenty-five men were arrested and ten convicted, including one member of Congress and several Republican editors who were silenced by heavy fines or jail sentences. David Brown, a wandering "apostle of sedition" who persuaded the Jacobins of a Massachusetts village to erect a liberty pole (French version of the liberty tree), got the longest sentence, four years in jail. All this seems mild in comparison with the killings and torturings that nowadays are inflicted on critics of petty tyrants the world over, but it was too strong meat for American taste in 1800.

Two startling protests by state legislatures: the Virginia resolves drafted by Madison, and those of Kentucky drafted by Jefferson, rallied the opposition. Both declared the Alien and Sedition Acts unconstitutional. As to the Alien Act, there is no getting around the fact that the power of expelling aliens belongs to the federal government, not to the states. The Sedition Act, however, stands in a different light; for Amendment I of the Constitution forbids Congress to pass any law abridging the freedom of speech, or of the press. Federalist lawyers, like many American lawyers of late, attempted to extract all meaning from this clause by assuming that freedom of the press meant freedom merely from censorship; or by asserting that it was not meant to apply in time of war. A much more drastic sedition law (the Espionage Act) was passed in 1917 and enforced by sentences far more severe than those of 1798. But the American Revolution was too near in 1798 for an American government to punish opinion with impunity.

The "compact" or "state rights" theory embodied in the Virginia and Kentucky resolves is significant. Kentucky declared that whenever Congress palpably transcends its powers, as in the Sedition Act, each state "has an equal right to judge for itself, as well of infractions as of the mode and measure of redress." She calls upon her "co-states" to "concur . . . in declaring these acts" void, and to unite "in requesting their repeal." Virginia hinted at "interposing" state authority between the persecuted citizen and his government.

Both state legislatures had their eyes on the coming presidential election and were really engaged in lighting a fiery cross to rally the Republican clans. Yet the principles of the Virginia and Kentucky resolves of 1798 became a platform to all later movements in state rights. Within ten years the New England Federalists were flinging them back at Jefferson and Madison; to the Southern particularists of a later generation they became an indispensable gloss on the Constitution.

In any true federal government there will be conflicts between powers of the nation and powers of the states. A minority party, or minority sectional combination, if ridden too hard or too proud to be ridden at all, will try to escape the consequences of a minority position by raising the banner of state rights. In American history the doctrine of state rights has not been a cause, but an effect of this condition. Almost every man in public life between 1798 and 1860 spurned it when his section was in the saddle, and embraced it when his constituents deemed themselves oppressed. Almost every state in turn declared its absolute sovereignty, only to denounce as treasonable similar declarations by other states. The Virginia doctrine of "interposition" has been invoked by the states of Alabama and Mississippi as recently as 1962 to justify illegal exclusion of Blacks from public schools and colleges.

The "Federalist Reign of Terror,"[1] as the Republicans called the second half of Adams's administration, alarmed a nation which had strong notions of personal liberty. Vice President Jefferson, however, remained hopeful and serene. Strong in his faith that the people would "recover their true sight," he presided impeccably over the Senate, writing letters far and wide to his political lieutenants, and enjoying the spectacle of Federalists hanging themselves on their own ropes. "Hold on then, like a good and faithful seaman," he wrote a discouraged congressman, "till our brother sailors can rouse from their intoxication and right the vessel." But it was John Adams who drove the drunken sailors from the quarterdeck, only to bring the ship into port for Thomas Jefferson.

If the French had been so obliging as to land even a party of saboteurs on American soil, the election of 1800 might have gone very differently. But, as time went on and no enemy appeared, the patriotic fervor of 1798 damped down. In the meantime, unwise sedition prosecutions and the direct tax were having their effect. There was even a flare-up in Pennsylvania, the "Fries Rebellion," a minor Whisky Insurrection in Bucks County. When federal assessors invaded this rural paradise to survey houses and lands for the direct tax on real estate, they were attacked by irate housewives with broomsticks and boiling water, and a popular auctioneer named David Fries put himself at the head of a rabble which drummed the officials out of the county. Fries, arrested by troops of the regular army, was tried for treason, found guilty, and sentenced to death in 1799, but pardoned by President Adams.

Presidential candidates for the election of 1800 were selected by party caucuses in Congress. The Republicans respected the original understanding between Virginia and New York by supporting Jefferson and Aaron Burr; Federalists renominated John Adams, with Charles Cotesworth Pinckney of the X Y Z mission for Vice President. The Hamiltonian faction then intrigued to bring in Pinckney over Adams's head, by persuading one or two presidential electors to vote for the South Carolinian. Adams undoubtedly gained popularity by his peace move, but the "high Federalists" threw it

[1] The use of this term by the opposition is understandable, but for historians to apply it is unpardonable, after the real reigns of terror that the world has survived. In Adams's administration nobody was hanged, nobody sent before a firing squad, nobody tortured; the writ of habeas corpus was not suspended, the rule of law operated, public discussion remained free. Only a few persons obnoxious to the Federalists were imprisoned for short periods.

away by their publicly expressed rage at having no war declared.

Neither in this, nor in any presidential or state election prior to the Jacksonian era, did candidates make speeches or issue statements. They were supposed to play coy, obeying a call to service from their country, saving their energies for the task of government. Electioneering was done by newspapers, pamphlets, and occasional public meetings. Even so, the politicians managed to make the campaign of 1800 very scurrilous. Jefferson was accused of being a Jacobin, an atheist, and a French agent; Adams was asserted to be an autocrat and a slavish admirer of the British monarchy. The Jonathan Robbins affair was typical. Thomas Nash, an Irish boatswain in the Royal Navy, had led a successful mutiny and killed an officer. Two years later, having changed his name to Jonathan Robbins, he indiscreetly boasted at Charleston of these exploits. On the British consul's application, in accordance with Jay's treaty, President Adams granted Nash's extradition to Jamaica, where he was tried, found guilty, and hanged. Nash and his lawyers claimed that he was a native-born citizen of Danbury, Connecticut; the Republicans played him up as a victim to Federalist tyranny; and his alleged martyrdom was the subject of a popular ballad, *Robbins's Lament,* one stanza of which, at least, is worth rescuing from the old songbooks:

> To his blood-thirsty foes, given up as a prey,
> When his claims were refuséd, he cry'd,
> "Tis thus" (his tobacco quid throwing away,)
> "Tis thus many brave men have died."

The Republicans in Congress forced an investigation, in the course of which it was proved that nobody named Robbins had ever lived in Danbury, and that Nash had confessed the crime before his execution. But the harm had been done. Jefferson, who was in a position to know, wrote that this false story "affected the popular mind more" than any "circumstance" in ten years—more even than the sedition prosecutions and the heavy taxes.

It was a close election. Seventy-three Republican and 65 Federalist electors were chosen. As no Republican elector dared throw away his second vote, Jefferson and Burr tied for first place. Until the Twelfth Amendment to the Constitution (1804) removed the possibility of a tie between two candidates on the same ticket, the House of Representatives, voting by states, had to make the final choice, a majority of one state being necessary for election. Federalists in the House saw an opportunity to thwart their enemies by voting for Burr, a cynical and pliant politician whom they preferred to a "dangerous Jacobin." But Burr refused to promise them anything, whilst Jefferson promised not to scuttle the new navy or dismiss Federalists from subordinate offices. Party division was so close that during 35 ballots, one all-night session, and until 17 February 1801, the House was deadlocked. There was talk of preventing an election, and of civil war. Virginia militia were preparing to march on Washington, D.C., where the federal government had finally settled in the summer of 1800. Finally, three Federalists cast blank ballots, permitting Jefferson to be elected President by a majority of two states.

This presidential election cannot fairly be called a popular verdict, since over half the electors were chosen by state legislatures. But in congressional elections the Republicans obtained an emphatic majority, and most of the newly elected senators were Republicans. This meant that the Federalists lost every branch of government except the judiciary, which Jefferson soon attempted to purge by impeachment.

So passed into minority the party that contained more talent and virtue, with less political common sense, than any of its successors. The Federalists went down with colors flying, content "that in the fall of laws a loyal man should die"; but their usefulness had gone. It had been their task to tame the wild forces set loose by the American Revolution, to integrate discordant elements, to lead an inchoate nation to enduring union. And they succeeded to a remarkable degree. But their chosen basis, an oligarchy of wealth and talent, was not sufficiently broad or deep. Neither their patience nor their vision was adequate for their task. Their old-world precepts of vigor, energy, and suppression had become fixed ideas, enclosing them in a network of delusion that set them in antagonism to deep-rooted popular feelings. The expanding forces of American life enveloped and overwhelmed them.

III

Jefferson's Administrations

1801-1809

1. The "Revolution of 1800"

THOMAS JEFFERSON, having proclaimed the proper goal of government to be preservation of "life, liberty and the pursuit of happiness," was now President of the one country in which there was reasonable likelihood of reaching those objectives. What did his followers expect, and his opponents fear? And what did he think about it?

Jefferson believed that his election saved the country from militarism and monarchy; that his mission was to get the ship of state on an even keel of peace and republican simplicity. But there never had been any danger of monarchy—that was just the Republican "big lie" about the Federalists, repeated so often that Jefferson came to believe it himself. And John Adams, if anyone, saved the country from militarism. In the other camp, the Federalists were victims of their own lies about Jefferson. Everyone who knew him personally believed that there was little or nothing to fear, but the New England parsons and local Federalist editors who had been denouncing Jefferson as an "atheist," "Jacobin," and the like, expected America under him to become a French satellite—guillotines, conscription and all. Now, when nothing of that kind happened, they hardly knew what to say. At the same time, thousands of plain people throughout the country felt that with Jefferson's election the federal government had been returned to them. Dr. Nathaniel Ames of Dedham, Fisher Ames's Republican brother, saluted the dawn of the nineteenth century as inaugurating "the irresistible propagation of the Rights of Man, the eradication of hierarchy, oppression, superstition, and tyranny all over the world."

Actually, the election of 1800—brought more change in men than in measures. Jefferson liquidated the misnamed "reign of terror" by letting victims of the Sedition Act out of jail, completing army demobilization, and dismantling most of the navy. But, in essence, his inauguration meant a transfer of the center of federal power from the Boston-Hartford-Philadelphia axis to the New York-Richmond-Raleigh axis. And as for "monarchy," it was Jefferson who founded the "Virginia Dynasty" which reigned for almost a third of a century. He was succeeded by his close friend and secretary of state, James Madison of Virginia; he, after two presidential terms, by his secretary of state and Jefferson's friend James Monroe of Virginia; and Monroe, after two terms, by his secretary of state John Quincy Adams who had been allied with this dynasty for twenty years. But when Andrew Jackson, whom Jefferson regarded as a menace, won the presidency in 1829, the dynastic pattern was broken and a mild revolution did occur.

Thomas Jefferson was no social democrat but a slave-holding country gentleman of exquisite taste, lively curiosity, and a belief in the perfectibility of man. His kind really belonged to the eighteenth rather than the nineteenth century. A Christian but no churchman, he had the serenity of one to whom now and then the Spirit has not disdained to speak. He held the hearts of plain people without speech-making, military service, or pretending to be anything he was not. The secret of his power lay in the fact that he appealed to and expressed America's idealism, simplicity, and hopeful outlook, rather than the material and imperial ambitions which Hamilton represented. Jefferson's political object, as he wrote in a letter of 1802, was to prove that Americans were ripe for "a government founded not on the fears and follies of man, but in his reason; on the predominance of his social over his dissocial passions."

The government that he took over answered this description better than any of its European contemporaries; but it is questionable whether Jefferson led it any further toward perfection than Washington and Adams had done. In order to gain support he was forced to give men offices; he acquired an empire in Louisiana, which Hamilton had dreamed of conquering by arms, but it was no less an empire for that. In the midst of Napoleonic wars, Jefferson attempted to carry to its logical conclusion the neutrality policy that he had supported as Washington's secretary of state in 1793. And he aspired to an almost Chinese isolation—social and economic as well as political.

Jefferson's first inaugural address was eighteenth-century idealism rubbed through the sieve of practical politics. Instead of denouncing his opponents as villains or heretics, he invited them to join the true republican church: "We are all Republicans—we are all Federalists. If there be any among us who would wish to dissolve this Union, or to change its republican form, let them stand undisturbed as monuments of the safety with which error of opinion may be tolerated where reason is left free to combat it." This government, "the world's best hope," must not be abandoned "on the theoretic and visionary fear" that it is not strong enough. "Sometimes it is said that man cannot be trusted with the government of himself. Can he then be trusted with the government of others?" The only thing "necessary to close the circle of our felicities" is "a wise and frugal government, which shall restrain men from injuring one another, shall leave them otherwise free to regulate their own pursuits of industry and improvement, and shall not take from the mouth of labor the bread it has earned."

If a government of that nature was ever attainable, the time and place were in the simple, rural America at the turn of the nineteenth century. And if the net result of Jefferson's and Madison's administrations was to bring Hamilton's dream of a warlike and industrial nation nearer fulfillment, that was due to world forces beyond their control.

Jefferson could well afford to be frugal because his administration opened during a brief truce in the European wars, Indians on the frontier were quiet, and the American public had not yet got the habit of looking to Washington for pensions, bounties, and handouts. Washington, D.C., was a perfect scenario for an experiment in republican simplicity. The federal city had been laid out according to plans of a French engineer, Major Pierre L'Enfant who (to the subsequent confusion of motor traffic) imposed a series of avenues radiating from circles on a grid of numbered and lettered streets. Jefferson himself, when secretary of state, had determined the sites for the Capitol and the White House after L'Enfant quit in a huff. William Thornton, a West Indies physician turned architect, won a competition for the design of the Capitol; and by 1801 the north wing, containing the "old" Senate chamber (now the "old" Supreme Court), was ready for occupancy.[1] The city itself was little more than a scattering of new buildings between a forest and the Potomac and Anacostia rivers. Pennsylvania Avenue, studded with stumps and alder bushes, led from the Capitol through a morass to the White House, for whose design Dublin-born James Hoban received a fee of $500 and a city lot. Two miles further west lay Georgetown, a comfortable little Maryland town that afforded officials an agreeable change from each other's society. The red clay soil of the District became dust in dry weather and liquid cement in every rain, after which swarms of mosquitoes spread malaria. Several fine groves of tulip trees were the only features of natural beauty within the city site; Jefferson's one recorded wish for despotic power was to save these trees from the inhabitants, who proceeded to fell them for firewood. Except for scornful Federalists and a complaining diplomatic corps (one of whom named the capital "The City of Magnificent Distances") everyone made light of the difficulties and looked forward to some magic transmutation of this backwoods settlement into a new republican Rome. It was a city of great expectations, much like Brasilia, the new capital of our sister republic to the south.

Washington, therefore, was a fit setting for an experiment in frugal government. Members of Congress, forced to leave their wives at home and live in boardinghouses, finished the public business as quickly as possible. The President, a widower, was free to establish a new code of republican etiquette. Every morning the White House was open to all comers. Invitations to dine were issued in the name of "Mr. Jefferson" instead of "The President of the United States." White House dinners were well prepared by a French chef, and Jefferson's wine bill for one year was $2800; but his attempt to abolish precedence of diners, leaving each guest to choose his own chair, resulted in so much pushing and shoving among wives of officials that a protocol had to be drawn up. And Washington has never been able to get rid of protocol.

Jefferson's inaugural pledge to pay the public debt, and preserve "the general government in its whole constitutional vigor" caused Hamilton to predict "that the new president will not lend himself to dangerous innovations, but in essential

---

[1] The south wing was completed in 1803–9 under the superintendency of Benjamin H. Latrobe, a recent immigrant from England. These two wings, with the rotunda between, were the entire Capitol until 1851, when work was begun on the present House and Senate wings and the great dome.

points will tread in the steps of his predecessors." That, in the main, was what Jefferson did. He took over the Federalist administrative machine, but fed a slightly different material into it.

Madison became secretary of state. For the treasury he chose Albert Gallatin, an offshoot of aristocratic Geneva who had risen to leadership in Congress. Gallatin had already proved himself in the Pennsylvania assembly to be a "wizard of finance," a branch of statesmanship in which Jefferson was woefully deficient. He agreed with the President in wishing to pay the national debt as quickly as possible. Gallatin would even have retained the excise on whisky, which his former constituents had resisted; but Jefferson insisted on removing that detested relic of federalism, and so made his name immortal in the mountains. Although "executive influence" over Congress had been a party cry of the Republicans when in opposition, Gallatin worked as cozily with the Republican majorities in Congress as Hamilton had with the Federalists, and he managed to reduce the national debt from $80 million to $45 million in ten years.

Under Washington and Adams, Congress had often appropriated lump sums to the different departments to spend at their discretion. The Republicans always opposed this practice as violating the sacred principle of separation of powers. Jefferson and Gallatin, with unusual self-denial, now recommended a change, but Congress moved very slowly toward the modern practice and slight detail was applied to the three basic appropriations for army, navy, and the civil list. The navy, for instance, was granted lump sums for pay, provisions, repairs, and maintenance of yards and docks, giving it a discretion that the navy department now regards somewhat wistfully, when its budget is over a hundred times as great.

Jefferson's remark, "We are all republicans—we are all federalists," caused no little dismay in his own camp. Commodore James Nicholson, Gallatin's father-in-law, asked if enemies were to be kept "in office to trample on us." William B. Giles, the loud-mouthed bully of the Virginia delegation, reminded the President that "a pretty general purgation of office, has been one of the benefits expected by the friends of the new order of things." No one seriously charged the federal civil service with inefficiency or corruption, but it was almost completely Federalist, since Washington and Adams never knowingly appointed an Antifederalist or a Republican. Offices were regarded as proper rewards for public service, and Jefferson's followers were hungry. There was then no such thing as a retirement pension, and Jefferson complained that officials seldom die, and never resign. He had to create vacancies by the presidential prerogative of removal. There was no general purge, only a mild bloodletting; but even that did not square with the bland professions of the inaugural discourse. It was a good instance of what Hamilton called Jefferson's "ineradicable duplicity"—seeming to say one thing while meaning another. But neither Jefferson nor his three immediate successors tried to buy votes in Congress with patronage; and Jefferson's appointments, in the main, were excellent.

Other features of the Federalist establishment were retained, such as discriminatory tonnage duties, fishing bounties, and the mixed commissions set up under Jay's treaty. The army was reduced by a "chaste reformation," as Jefferson called it, from 4000 to 2500 men; but Congress in 1802 enlarged President Adams's school for army gunners and sappers at West Point to create the Military Academy. The Republican press having viciously attacked the navy as a sink of waste and corruption, and a vile imitation of England's, Jefferson, who knew nothing about ships, felt he must cut it down radically. An act of the last Federalist Congress allowed the President to reduce by about two-thirds the respectable navy that had been built up during the hostilities with France. Jefferson not only did that, selling naval vessels to become merchantmen, but stopped new construction, discharged every naval constructor, and had most of the retained frigates dismantled to save expense. Naturally they disintegrated; wooden ships cannot be "put up in mothballs" like modern steel warships. Yet, paradoxically, the most brilliant achievements of Jefferson's first administration were in war and diplomacy!

The only Federalist creation that Jefferson really tried to destroy was the judiciary, where the Federalists had invited attack. In January 1801 President Adams made his most fortunate appointment, that of John Marshall as Chief Justice of the United States. Toward Marshall his kinsman Jefferson entertained an implacable hatred because he had shown him up and broken the sentimental French bubble in the X Y Z affair. The last Federalist Congress passed a new judiciary act (February 1801) creating sixteen circuit courts to relieve Supreme Court justices of the arduous duty of riding circuit. Had President Adams left it to Jefferson to make the new appointments, the law might have stood; but he filled up every newly established judicial office by "midnight appointments" on the evening of 3 March. Consequently, Jefferson hammered at Congress until he got this law replaced by a new judiciary act which added one more justice to the Supreme Court but abolished the new circuit courts and required all federal judges to resume their wide-ranging horseback exercise. A peculiar item in this act postponed the next session of the Supreme Court to February 1803.

At that session Chief Justice Marshall defied the executive in the case of *Marbury* v. *Madison*. William Marbury was one of forty-two justices of the peace for the District of Columbia, included among President Adams's "midnight appointments." Madison, the new secretary of state, refused to deliver his commission to Marbury, who then sued him for it before the Supreme Court. By a legal twist, which the Jeffersonians considered mere chicanery, the Chief Justice managed to deliver an opinion which has become classic, on the superiority of the Constitution over acts of Congress: "The particular phraseology of the Constitution of the United States confirms and strengthens the principle, supposed to be essential to all written constitutions, that a law repugnant to the Constitution is void; and that *courts,* as well as other departments, are bound by that instrument."

Jefferson now incited some of his henchmen in the House to move against certain federal judges. A district judge who had become intemperate to the point of insanity was removed by impeachment. The next victim was to be Justice Samuel Chase of the Supreme Court, a signer of the Declaration of Independence, who on the bench had made himself peculiarly obnoxious to the Republicans, predicting that under Jefferson "our republican constitution will sink into a mobocracy, the worst of all possible governments." The House of Representatives presented him for impeachment on several counts of malfeasance and misfeasance in office. Strange to relate, after all that had been said about the danger of following British precedents, the Senate was fitted up in imitation of the House of Lords at the impeachment of Warren Hastings. Vice President Burr, who a few months earlier had killed Alexander Hamilton in a duel, presided; and the eloquent John Randolph of Roanoke prosecuted. There was no evidence to substantiate the serious charges against Justice Chase, although his manners on the bench were bad; and when it came to a vote on 1 March 1805 the impeachment failed.

Had Chase been found guilty on the flimsy evidence presented, there is good reason to believe that the entire Supreme Court would have been impeached and purged. As it was, this trial proved to be the highwater mark of Jefferson's radicalism. Under Chief Justice Marshall conservatism rallied, and from the Supreme Court there developed a subtle offensive of ideas —the supremacy of the nation, the rule of law, and the sanctity of property.

2. *Pirates Punished and an Empire Acquired*

By the time Jefferson became President, almost $2 million, one-fifth of the annual revenue, had been paid to the Moslem states of Morocco, Algiers, Tunis, and Tripoli, either to ransom prisoners or in return for permitting American merchant ships to sail the Mediterranean. Jefferson, after reducing the navy somewhat further than the Act of 3 March 1801 permitted, looked around for profitable employment of warships remaining afloat. He found it against the bashaw of Tripoli who, feeling he was not receiving enough tribute money, declared war on the United States in May 1801. This naval war dribbled along in desultory fashion until 1804, when Commodore Edward Preble appeared off Tripoli in command of a respectable task force, U.S.S. *Constitution* flagship, and dished out a series of bombardments. Before his arrival, frigate *Philadelphia* had grounded on a reef off Tripoli, from which the enemy floated her free. The bashaw imprisoned Captain Bainbridge and his crew, and would have equipped the frigate for his own navy had not Lieutenant Stephen Decatur, in captured schooner *Intrepid,* entered the harbor at night, boarded and captured *Philadelphia* and, after setting fire to her, made a safe getaway. Decatur performed other dashing feats in this war, but the most extraordinary exploit in it was that of a former army officer named William Eaton, American consul at Tunis.

Eaton, who had acquired a deep disgust for the pirate prince of Tripoli, and believed that blockade and bombardment would never defeat him, persuaded the American naval commander on the Mediterranean station to espouse the cause of a pretender to the Tripolitan "throne," then in exile in Egypt. At Alexandria he collected a force composed of sixteen members of the United States Navy and Marine Corps, forty Greeks, a squadron of Arab cavalry, a hundred nondescripts, and a fleet of camels. Under his command this motley expeditionary force marched over 500 miles across the Libyan desert, the terrain made famous in World War II by the exploits of Rommel and Montgomery, to Derna. Eaton then led an attack on that town, in which three American man-of-war brigs co-operated, and captured it. His exploit led to a favorable treaty with Tripoli, negotiated by the captured Captain Bainbridge. Eaton's efforts went for nought, he and the rival bashaw were repudiated, and he became an embittered enemy of the Jefferson administration.

While Tripoli was being taught a lesson, the boundary of the United States advanced to the Rocky Mountains. Louisiana, comprising all territory between the Mississippi and the Rockies, had been in Spanish possession since 1769. Less than one per cent of it was settled. The Creoles, numbering with their slaves about 40,000 in 1800, were concentrated on both banks of the lower Mississippi. There were a few garrisons and trading posts on the west bank of the river up to St. Louis, and a few more on the Red river; the rest was in undisputed Indian possession. Sugar cane and cotton had recently been introduced from the West Indies, and the commercial importance of the Mississippi river to the American West was greater than ever.

The retrocession of this great province from Spain to France, by a secret treaty on 1 October 1800, completed the policy of successive French governments to replace the loss of Canada by a more profitable base in North America. Bonaparte, as soon as his hands were free in Europe, proposed to make France the first power in the New World as in the Old. As it was inconvenient to take immediate possession of Louisiana, he kept the treaty secret until late in 1801, when another event revealed its implications. Bonaparte dispatched an expeditionary force to Hispaniola with orders to suppress Toussaint L'Ouverture's black republic and then take possession of New Orleans and Louisiana. The prospect of a veteran French army at America's back door was very unpleasant. On 18 April 1802 Jefferson wrote to the American minister at Paris, "The day that France takes possession of New Orleans . . . we must marry ourselves to the British fleet and nation." He was ready to adopt Washington's formula of "temporary alliances for extraordinary emergencies."

Late in 1802 the Spanish governor of Louisiana withdrew the right of transit at New Orleans from American traders. The West exploded with indignation, and the Federalists, delighted at an opportunity to divide Jefferson from his Western admirers, fanned the flame and clamored for war. Jefferson remained serene and imperturbable. His annual message, in December 1802, breathed platitudes of peace, friendship, and economy. In the meantime, some of his friends pushed through Congress an appropriation of $2 million for "expenses in relation to the intercourse between the United States and foreign nations." And in March 1803 the President commissioned James Monroe as envoy extraordinary to France, with an interesting set of instructions to himself and to the resident minister Robert Livingston.

First they were to offer anything up to $10 million for New Orleans and the Floridas. That would give the United States the whole left bank of the Mississippi, and the Gulf coast. If

LOUISIANA PURCHASE
AND EXPLORATIONS
IN THE WEST
Scale of Miles
0   100   200   300   400   500

France refused, $7.5 million should be offered for the Island
of New Orleans alone. Failing there, they must press for a
perpetual guarantee of the right of transit. If that were refused, Monroe and Livingston were ordered to "open a confidential communication with ministers of the British government," with a view to "candid understanding, and a closer
connection with Great Britain."

Livingston began the negotiations before Monroe sailed,
and at first made little progress. Fortunately for us, Bonaparte,
who was about to renew war with England and make himself
emperor, was becoming disgusted with the Hispaniola campaign. Troops had been poured into that island to the number
of 35,000, and yellow fever swept away those that the Haitians
did not kill. Without Hispaniola, Louisiana lost half its value
to France; and when war came, Louisiana, for want of French
sea power to keep up communications, would be Britain's for
the plucking. So, why not sell it to the United States?

On 11 April 1803, the day that France broke diplomatic

relations with England, Talleyrand suddenly remarked to Livingston, "What will you give for the *whole* of Louisiana?" Livingston gasped that he supposed the United States would not object to paying $4 million. "Too low!" said Talleyrand. "Reflect and see me tomorrow." Napoleon had already determined to sell the whole. On 30 April 1803 the treaty of cession was signed; $12 million was paid for the province of Louisiana as acquired by France from Spain, and the United States assumed the claims of citizens against France for the naval spoliations of 1797–98. Inhabitants of Louisiana were guaranteed the rights of American citizens, and eventual admission to the Union.

The Louisiana purchase turned out to be the greatest bargain in American history; but in 1803 it seemed likely that the United States was paying $12 million for a scrap of paper. Her title was defective on several points. The province was still in the hands of Spain. Bonaparte had promised never to dispose of Louisiana to a third power. The French constitution allowed no alienation of national territory without a vote of the legislature. The boundaries were indefinite; how far north Louisiana extended, and whether it included West Florida or Texas, or neither, was uncertain. Finally, according to the "strict construction" of the Virginia Republicans, the treaty itself was unconstitutional! If the federal government, as Jefferson had always claimed, possessed no power not expressly granted, the President had no right to increase the national domain by treaty, much less to promise incorporation in the Union to people outside its original limits.

Jefferson's constitutional scruples vanished when a letter arrived from Livingston, urging immediate ratification before Napoleon changed his mind. The President's friends furnished him with some good Hamiltonian arguments, and the treaty was ratified by the Senate. On 30 November 1803 Louisiana was formally handed over by the Spanish governor to a French prefect, who promptly established the *code Napoléon*, and as many other French institutions as he could think up. Three weeks later he transferred it to the United States.

Even before the purchase, Jefferson had ordered Meriwether Lewis and William Clark, officers of the regular army, to conduct an overland exploring expedition in the hope of finding a water route from the headwaters of the Missouri river to the Pacific. Lewis and Clark left St. Louis 14 May 1804 with thirty-two soldiers and ten civilians, embarked in a 55-foot keel boat and two "periaguas." These, propelled by sails and oars, took them up the Missouri into North Dakota, where they wintered among the Mandan near the site of Bismarck, and the following spring pushed on into Montana. A fleet of dugout canoes, built above the Great Falls, took them to the foothills of the Rocky Mountains in what is now Idaho. Here their interpreter Sacajawea made friendly contact with the Shoshone, who furnished horses for the men, and women to tote the baggage. Crossing the Lemhi pass over the Rockies, the expedition moved north down the Bitter Root valley and in the Nez Percé country reached a branch of the westward-flowing Snake. In newly built boats they rowed downstream to the Columbia, reaching tidewater on 7 November 1805. There, within sound of the Pacific breakers, the party built Fort Clatsop. Lewis and Clark expected to hail a ship and sail home, since through the coastal Indians' use of such elegant phrases as "son-of-a-pitch" they guessed that Yankee fur traders had been frequenting this region.

Months passed with no ship, so the leaders decided to return overland. Lewis and half the party took the shorter route to the Great Falls, while the other half cut overland from the forks of the Missouri to the Yellowstone, and floated down to its junction with the Missouri at the site of Fort Union. There the leaders met, and the expedition reached St. Louis 23 September 1806 intact, having avoided fights with the Indians.

Jefferson was delighted with Lewis and Clark's reports, their conduct toward the natives, and the specimens that they brought to Washington; and their journals are still a valuable source of information on the Far West in the early nineteenth century.

"Never was there an administration more brilliant than that of Mr. Jefferson up to this period," said John Randolph in later years. "We were indeed in the 'full tide of successful experiment.' Taxes repealed; the public debt amply provided for, both principal and interest; sinecures abolished; Louisiana acquired; public confidence unbounded."

3. Plots and Conspiracies

Jefferson yearned to convert New England from her perverse conservatism. He appreciated the danger of attempting to govern a loose federal union by a sectional party, and hoped by moderation to persuade the Yankees that their mercantile and shipping interests were safe in Republican hands. Gains in the congressional elections of 1802–3 showed that he was succeeding; but the Federalist leaders grew bitter and desperate as their power waned.

To the clergy and party leaders of New England, Jefferson's

victory was a triumph of democracy, which to them meant terror, atheism, and free love. "The principles of democracy are everywhere what they have been in France," wrote Fisher Ames. "Our country is too big for union, too sordid for patriotism, too democratic for liberty." New England was yet pure; but the barricades to her virtue were falling. "And must we with folded hands wait the result?" asked Senator Pickering of Massachusetts. "The principles of our Revolution point to the remedy—a separation."

Thus Virginians like John Taylor had reasoned in 1798 when Virginia was hag-ridden by the Federalists. Jefferson then had calmed them with a promise of victory, but no such hope could console New England Federalists for the Louisiana purchase. Their minority was dwindling, and they knew it. Ohio, admitted to the Union in 1803, looked to Virginia for guidance, although largely settled by Yankees. In all probability the new states to be formed from Louisiana would follow the same light. New England Federalists reasoned that the annexation of that vast province, upsetting the balance of power within the Union, absolved all original states from their allegiance. Before 1803 was out, Timothy Pickering, Roger Griswold, and other leaders in Massachusetts and Connecticut began to plan a Northern Confederacy of New England and New York, "exempt from the corrupt and corrupting influence and oppression of the aristocratic democrats of the South." New England conservatives in 1804, like Southern conservatives in 1861, assumed that a political boundary could protect them from ideas.

Knowledge of this conspiracy was confined to a very few Federalists, and the British minister at Washington in whom they confided. Hamilton would have none of it. Intrigue was repulsive to his character, and reasoning such as Pickering's to his intellect. Secession was a futile cure for democracy, he pointed out, since the democratic "poison" was already present in every Northern state.

The conspirators then turned to Aaron Burr. He had carried New York for Jefferson in 1800, and without that state's vote Jefferson could not have been elected. Once safe in office, Jefferson ignored Burr in distributing New York patronage, and his party dropped Burr from the presidential ticket in 1804 in favor of George Clinton. The Vice President then decided to contest the governorship of New York with the regular Republican candidate. In return for Federalist aid in this election he agreed, if successful, to swing New York into the Northern Confederacy and become its president. Hamilton, on hearing of this deal, advised his friends to vote against

Burr, and defeated him. The Federalist conspiracy then dissolved. How remote its chance of success the election of 1804 proved; Jefferson and Clinton carried all New England except Connecticut, and every other state except Delaware.

Burr was a ruined politician at the age of forty-eight, but far from finished. He had broken with the Republicans and failed the Federalists. Hamilton was responsible. This was not the first time that Hamilton had crossed his path, but it must be the last. In June 1804, six weeks after the New York election, Burr wrote to his enemy, demanding retraction of a slur upon his character reported in the press. Hamilton refused, Burr challenged him to a duel, Hamilton accepted. He had no business to accept, for he did not believe in dueling and he did not need to prove his courage. But Hamilton expected the Jefferson regime to end in anarchy like the French Republic. America would then demand a Bonaparte, and he intended to fill that role; but no one suspected of cowardice could do that. So Hamilton went to his doom, resolved to prove his courage, yet not kill; to throw away his fire in the hope that his adversary would miss and honor be satisfied. Aaron Burr, in the duel on 11 July 1804 under the Palisades, took deliberate aim and hit Hamilton just below his chest. Death relieved him after thirty hours of intense suffering.

So perished one of the greatest men of the age, for his little faith in the government he had helped to form, and in the people he had served so well.

Before leaving Washington at the expiration of his term as Vice President (4 March 1805), Burr approached the British minister with an offer to detach Louisiana from the Union for half a million dollars and the loan of a naval force. The minister thought well of the offer and urged his government to buy, but received no reply. Britain was not interested in promoting American secession. Burr then proceeded to the headwaters of the Ohio, and sailed down-river in a luxury flatboat, stopping over to visit prominent people and to promote some project—a different one to each. The Westerners, duellers themselves, were charmed by the polished gentleman from New York. Harmon Blennerhasset, a romantic Irish *émigré*, was fascinated by a plan to conquer Mexico and make Burr emperor, and himself grand chamberlain. In Tennessee, Burr met and won the friendship of Andrew Jackson, who proposed getting him into the Senate if he would make his home in Tennessee. James Wilkinson, an old friend of Burr, still in Spanish pay while federal governor of Louisiana Territory and commanding general of the United States Army, had already, in Washington, discussed with him a secret project. They would "liberate" Mexico from Spain, and at the same time make Louisiana an independent republic, which Mississippi Territory would surely decide to join. At New Orleans Burr got in touch with Creoles who disliked being annexed to the United States, and with American filibusters who were eager to invade Mexico. The Catholic bishop of New Orleans and the Mother Superior of the Ursuline convent gave Burr their support and blessing. Returning overland to Washington, Burr obtained $2500 from the Spanish minister, ostensibly to promote the independence of Louisiana and the West.

In the summer of 1806 the former Vice President established his headquarters at Lexington, Kentucky, and began active recruiting for his expedition. His public pretext was to take up a dubious claim to 400,000 acres of land in western Louisiana which he had purchased. Evidence is strong that Burr intended to wait at Natchez until his supporters at New Orleans had declared the independence of Louisiana, and offered him the presidency; he would then build up his army and on some pretext invade Mexico. By the end of the year, Burr and Blennerhasset, commanding an advance guard in ten flatboats, had reached the mouth of the Cumberland river. At this juncture General Wilkinson, deciding that Burr was worth more to betray than to befriend, wrote a lurid letter to President Jefferson denouncing "a deep, dark, wicked, and widespread conspiracy" on Burr's part to dismember the Union. Jefferson issued a proclamation offering a reward for Burr's arrest. He was apprehended and brought to Richmond for trial on the charge of treason against the United States.

The President left no stone unturned to obtain a conviction. Chief Justice Marshall presided at the trial and took care that the constitutional definition of treason, "levying war against the United States or adhering to their enemies," with the safeguard of "two witnesses to the same overt act," was strictly observed. Hence it followed that the mere gathering of forces with intent to promote secession was not treason if the expedition collapsed. Burr was acquitted. Regretting, no doubt, that he had not killed Jefferson instead of Hamilton, he sought exile in Europe. Wilkinson, a traitor to every cause he embraced, retained his command and the confidence of the President.

This was the most formidable secession conspiracy prior to 1860, one which probably would have succeeded had not Wilkinson ratted on Burr. Not adventurers only but hundreds of respectable people in many parts of the country were behind Burr, although most of these supporters, including Andrew Jackson, were duped by the public explanation that he intended a mere filibustering expedition.

Burr continued his schemes in Europe. His charm was such that he obtained money from influential people in England and France for wild schemes such as restoring Canada to France, and enlisting unemployed sailors during Jefferson's embargo to march on Washington and set himself up as dictator. By some means he obtained a passport and returned to the United States in 1812, built up a law business in New York, and, at the age of seventy-seven, married the beautiful widow Jumel, who used to boast that she was the only woman in the world who had slept with both George Washington and Napoleon Bonaparte. After he had run through her property she divorced him, shortly before his death in 1836.

4. Foreign Complications and the Embargo

The acquittal of Justice Chase, and of Aaron Burr, marked a turning point in Jefferson's fortune and popularity. His second term, which began on 4 March 1805, was compared by Bible readers to Pharaoh's dream of the seven lean kine that ate up the seven fat kine. Many old Virginia Republicans felt that Jefferson had deserted his own principles with the acquisition of Louisiana; as he certainly did when, in his second inaugural address, he recommended spending federal money on roads and other internal improvements. As John Randolph put it, Jefferson spelled Federalism backward for four years, and now began spelling it forward again, by adopting policies that he had formerly condemned. The President began to rely for support in Congress on Republicans from the Northern states, who for the most part were a sad lot, interested mainly in patronage. Randolph called one of them, Barnabas Bidwell of Massachusetts (who later fled to Canada to escape the consequences of stealing public money), "The President's clerk of the water-closet."

To do Jefferson justice, he built up the federal government (what Randolph meant by "spelling Federalism forward") to cope with the European situation. Peace in Europe had been the condition of his earlier success; but there was to be no peace in Europe for many years. By the end of 1805 Napoleon had become supreme on land, and Britain on the ocean. Each sought to strangle or starve the other by continental or maritime blockade. Washington and Adams dealt with one belligerent at a time; Jefferson was confronted with both at once. A clever diplomat might conceivably have played off one country against another, with an armed force as stake in the game. But neither Jefferson nor Madison could grasp the realities of Napoleonic Europe, and the President began a further reduction of the United States Navy even before concluding peace with Tripoli.

During Mediterranean hostilities, American naval officers had felt the need of small gunboats for use in shoal water and light wind. Jefferson snapped at this suggestion for more than it was worth, "believing," as he wrote, "that gunboats are the only *water* defence which can be useful to us, and protect us from the ruinous folly of a navy." Gunboats were cheap, they could be hauled out when not in use, and contracts for their construction by numerous small shipbuilders could be used to reward the faithful.[1] Congress did provide a useful class of 119-foot sloops of war (*Hornet* and *Wasp*) and 80-foot brigs (*Nautilus, Vixen, Viper*). But instead of the frigates that the leading naval officers wanted, Congress caused 69 gunboats to be built by 1807. None sailed to Europe in time for the Tripolitan war; not one proved useful in the next war. These little vessels, averaging 60 feet in length and costing about $10,000 each, were equipped with a battery of one or two guns, which in foul weather had to be stowed below to prevent the vessel's capsizing. When one gunboat, torn from her moorings by a spring tide and heavy gale, was deposited in a cornfield, a Federalist wit offered the toast: "Gunboat No. 3: If our gunboats are no use on the water, may they at least be the best on earth!"

For two years Jefferson's principal foreign problems were connected with British sea power. For the Royal Navy in 1805 resumed its disagreeable practice of impressing sailors from American vessels on the high seas. Britain never claimed the right to impress native-born Americans; but until other means were found to recruit the Royal Navy, she insisted on impressing the king's subjects from foreign vessels wherever encountered. As Britain did not then recognize expatriation— nor did the United States—American naturalization was no protection to British-born seamen. And it was notorious that the comparatively high wages in the United States Navy and merchant marine stimulated desertion from the Royal Navy; the *Constitution* in 1807 carried 149 British subjects and 29 other foreigners in her crew of 419.

British frigates began operating off New York in 1805, stop-

[1] For instance, Matthew Lyon, hero of the first fist-fight in Congress, jailed under the Sedition Act, and returned to Congress in time to cast the vote of his state for Jefferson, was given a contract for five gunboats at Eddyville, Ky., on the Cumberland river.

ping every passing vessel and stripping her of seamen whom the captain supposed to be British subjects. American merchants and shipowners, making big profits in neutral trade, remained silent under these indignities until Sir William Scott announced in the *Essex* case the doctrine of continuous voyages. This meant that the voyage of a neutral ship from an enemy port, calling at a neutral country and then going on to another enemy port, was in effect one continuous voyage, which rendered both ship and cargo good prize. The United States enforced the same principle against blockade runners during the Civil War.

James Madison, secretary of state, now sent a set of unrealistic instructions to James Monroe and William Pinkney, joint ministers to Great Britain: England must stop impressment, scrap the continuous voyage doctrine, and pay for confiscations under the *Essex* decision. Monroe and Pinkney soon realized that without a strong navy to back them up, these demands were a joke. So, at the end of 1806, they accepted the best terms they could get. Britain offered to moderate her maritime practices without abandoning any principle, and to improve the situation of American commerce without granting complete reciprocity. But this smelled so of Jay's hated treaty against which the Republicans had screamed "Treason!" that Jefferson did not even submit the Monroe-Pinkney treaty to the Senate.

In June 1807 there occurred an impressment outrage that brought the two countries to the verge of war. A British squadron, stationed within the Capes of the Chesapeake to blockade two French warships which were being repaired at Annapolis, was losing men by desertion. The officers had reason to believe that many had enlisted in the United States Navy, which was true. On 22 June U.S.S. *Chesapeake,* flying the broad pennant of Commodore James Barron, got under way from Norfolk, and among her crew were a number of these deserters. Ten miles outside the Capes, H.M.S. *Leopard* drew alongside and demanded the right to examine *Chesapeake*'s crew and impress deserters and, when Barron refused, poured three broadsides into the American warship and rendered her helpless. Barron's crew was then mustered by *Leopard*'s officers, who impressed a British-born deserter, an American Negro, an Indian, and a native of Maryland.

News of this insult to the flag brought the first united expression of American feeling since 1798. Even the Federalists, who hitherto defended every move of the British, went along. If Jefferson had summoned Congress to a special session, he could have had war at the drop of a hat, and a more popular and successful war than the one finally declared in 1812. But Jefferson's serenity was undisturbed. He instructed Monroe to demand apology and reparation in London, and ordered British warships out of American territorial waters. When Congress met in late October, the President obtained an appropriation of $850,000 for building 188 more gunboats, and ordered three of the largest vessels of the seagoing navy to be hauled out. No suggestion of war, or war preparations.

For Jefferson imagined he could strangle England by economic sanctions. For years he had been wanting an opportunity to try commercial exclusion as a substitute for war. The moment had arrived. A private word to the faithful in Congress, and in one day, 22 December 1807, it passed the Embargo Act. American or other vessels were forbidden to sail foreign; all exports from the United States whether by sea or land were prohibited; certain specified articles of British manufacture were refused entrance. The embargo went into effect immediately; and for fourteen months all American ships that were not already abroad, and could not escape, lay in port or went coasting.

From what particular egg in Jefferson's clutch of theories this chick was hatched it is difficult to say. Probably he was merely carrying out a favorite Republican theory that American trade was so vital to Great Britain that she would collapse if it were stopped. But the embargo was not directed against England alone. Napoleon had issued drastic decrees against neutral trade, confiscating any neutral ship which had touched at a British port. The Republicans defended the embargo as a protection to American shipowners, who wanted no part of it. For they were thriving on trade with England under a system of licensing and inspection far less rigorous than the methods adopted by the United States and her allies in both world wars.

There were plenty of leaks in the embargo. Smuggling of British goods and American products went on over the Canadian frontier, on the Great Lakes, and from Spanish Florida. But there was much suffering in the seaports. Unemployed seamen and shipwrights emigrated in large numbers to the British provinces. The great shipowners who already had fleets abroad survived the embargo well enough; but many others were ruined, and certain small seaports such as Newburyport and New Haven never recovered their earlier prosperity. Agricultural produce fell, and the interior had to live on its own fat; but cotton, tobacco, and wheat could bear storage better than ships. Consequently, the embargo bore most heavily on New England and New York; and it was there that its political effects were felt by the administration.

One of these leaks became legendary. John Jacob Astor, who had branched out from fur trading to the China trade, managed to get his 427-ton ship *Beaver* out and home through the embargo by playing a trick on Jefferson. A character describing himself as "The Honorable Punqua Wingchong, a Chinese mandarin," requested permission to charter a ship to return from New York to China, "where the affairs of his family and particularly the funeral obsequies of his grandfather, require his solemn attention." Jefferson, thinking this might strengthen American relations with China, ordered Gallatin, who knew John Jacob Astor, to issue the necessary papers. Gallatin not only did so but allowed Hon. Punqua to take numerous "attendants" and $45,000 worth of specie or merchandise, and permitted the *Beaver* to bring a return cargo from China. As it turned out, the alleged mandarin was a petty clerk in Astor's employ, the cargoes were Astor's speculations; and the *Beaver*, returning to New York crammed with China goods while the embargo was still in effect, put her owner well on his way to becoming the richest man in America.

As a successful diplomatic weapon, commercial retaliation requires an unusual combination of circumstances, such as actually occurred four years later, but not in 1808. The embargo created a shortage of provisions in the French islands and of colonial produce in France; but Napoleon, tongue in cheek, confiscated every American vessel that arrived at a French port, on the ground that he was enforcing Jefferson's wishes. British shipowners were delighted with Jefferson's policy. When the American minister in London offered to lift the embargo if Britain would withdraw her antineutral orders, George Canning replied that His Majesty's government "would gladly have facilitated its removal as a measure of inconvenient restriction upon the American people." As John Quincy Adams once remarked, Canning "had a little too much wit for a minister of state."

Jefferson's mistake was the Federalists' opportunity. Their strength had been dwindling steadily; in 1807 every state government except Connecticut had gone Republican. Senator Pickering, the secession conspirator of 1804, rallied Yankee opinion in a public letter, asserting that the embargo was dictated by Napoleon and adopted by Jefferson in hope of helping him and impoverishing New England. Northern Republicans were restive under a measure that turned their constituents Federalist; and in New York City the embargo produced a schism in the Republican party. When Madison was nominated for the presidential succession by a congressional caucus, the New York legislature placed George Clinton in nomination as an anti-embargo Republican. In Virginia, a group of dissident Republicans nominated Monroe, disaffected by Jefferson's treatment of his English draft treaty. If a union could have been effected between this faction and the Federalists, Madison might have been defeated; as it was, the Federalist candidate carried little but New England, and Madison was elected President by a comfortable majority.

Jefferson intended to maintain the embargo until the British orders or the French decrees were repealed. In January 1809 Congress passed a Force Act, permitting federal officials without warrant to seize goods under suspicion of foreign destination, and protecting them from legal liability for their actions. George III and Lord North had been tender in comparison! The New England people, now in their second winter of privation, began to look to their state governments for protection, and by this time every state government in New England was Federalist. The state legislatures hurled back in the teeth of Jefferson and Madison the doctrines of the Kentucky and Virginia resolves of 1798. A proposal to summon a New England convention for nullification of the embargo was under serious discussion in February 1809. But by that time the embargo had been in force fourteen months, the Northern Republicans revolted, and Jefferson was shaken by a battery of resolutions from New England town meetings, some threatening secession. A bill for the repeal of the embargo was rushed through Congress, and on 1 March 1809 Jefferson signed it. Three days later his term ended, and he retired to Monticello.

The embargo was intended to be the crowning glory of Jefferson's second administration, as Louisiana had been of his first. It proved to be his greatest mistake. It altered the policy of Britain or of Napoleon not by one hair, it failed to protect the American merchant marine, and it convinced many good people that the Virginia Dynasty was bound to the Napoleonic. Pro-British leanings of the Federalist party were confirmed and strengthened; and whatever President Madison might do, he would never have such united support as Jefferson had enjoyed in 1807.

Of all ironies in American history, the career and influence of Thomas Jefferson are the greatest. This Virginia aristocrat and slave-owner proclaimed the "self-evident" truth "that all men are created equal." In so doing he undermined and overthrew both Tories and Federalists, who believed that man was created highly unequal and that the best, not the most, should govern. The Federalists, but for Jefferson—and their own folly—might have continued for another generation to direct the government along conservative and national lines; might even have settled the slavery question without war, which Jefferson's disciples were unable to do. His Southern supporters accepted Jefferson's principles with the reservation that they applied only to white men, and used them mainly as a stick to beat the Federalists and win power. But the Northerners whom Jefferson converted to his views took him seriously and literally. They came to believe that political equality meant all Americans, no matter what race or color; that democracy meant rule of the majority, not by a cultivated minority of merchants and landowners. Long did the art of politicians ignore or muffle this ambiguity; but when the issue became really acute in 1860–61, the society which Jefferson loved, and which still worshipped his name, repudiated both his basic principles; and in so doing was overthrown by the society which had taken those principles to heart. If Jefferson anticipated the end product of his "glittering generalities," he was a humbug; if not, he lacked intelligence.

Still, the gift of prophecy is given to few men. We should judge Jefferson by his acts rather than his words; and still more by what he refrained from doing when he had the power. Of all revolutionists (taking him at his own word that he was one), Jefferson was the most tolerant. He never "brayed humanity in a mortar to bring the savor from the bruised root."[1] Accustomed as we now are to revolutionary leaders imposing their policies by rigid tyranny and cruel oppression, we may take inspiration from one who deliberately preferred the slow process of reason to the short way of force. By his forbearance, even more than by his acts, Jefferson kept alive the flame of liberty that Napoleon had almost snuffed out in Europe.

[1] Robinson Jeffers, *Apology for Bad Dreams.*

IV

The Second War with Great Britain

1809-1815

1. *Diplomacy and Drift*

JAMES MADISON must be accounted a great statesman, owing to his labors on the Federal Constitution, but he was a very poor politician; and we have learned by experience that to be a successful President one has to be a good politician. Slight in stature and unimpressive in personality, eager to please but always looking puzzled, as if people were too much for him, "Jemmy" Madison had few intimate friends, and among the people at large he inspired little affection and no enthusiasm. He had a talent for writing logical diplomatic notes; but logic was of little use in dealing with Europeans locked in a deadly struggle. Negative in his dealings with Congress, he allowed Jefferson's personal "strings" for influencing House and Senate to rot from disuse. And he was stubborn to the point of stupidity.

Yet, within six weeks of his inauguration on 4 March 1809, Madison was being greeted as a great peacemaker. Congress, when repealing Jefferson's embargo, substituted a non-intercourse act aimed at both Britain and France, with the promise that the President would restore commercial relations with either nation, if and when it repealed its decrees injuring American commerce. Madison, almost too eager to reach an understanding with England, arranged a treaty with Erskine, the British minister in Washington, by virtue of which His Majesty's government would rescind its orders in council against neutral shipping, and the United States would resume normal trading relations with Britain but maintain non-intercourse with France. Touchy subjects such as impressment and the *Chesapeake* affair were postponed.

Had this draft been accepted by George Canning, the British foreign minister, there would have been no second war with England. But Canning brutally and inexplicably repudiated both Erskine and the treaty, and Anglo-American relations returned to a state of mutual recrimination. The Congress that assembled in December 1809 had no idea what to do, and received no lead from Madison. On 16 April 1810 it voted to reduce both the army and the navy, weak as they already were. And on 1 May it passed the so-called Macon's Bill No. 2, reversing the principle of the Non-Intercourse Act of 1809. This law restored intercourse with both Britain and France, but promised to the first power which recognized neutral rights, to stop trading with its enemy. American shipping soon engaged in making profits under British licenses, and merchant tonnage reached figures that were not attained for another twenty years.

Madison took advantage of this interlude in commercial warfare to take a bite of West Florida. The Republican administrations claimed it to be part of Louisiana, but forbore to insist while there was hope of inducing the Spanish government to recognize the claim. In 1810 the Spanish empire appeared to be breaking up. Accordingly, the inhabitants of that portion of West Florida bordering on the Mississippi "self-determined" for the United States, seized Baton Rouge, and were incorporated by presidential proclamation into the Territory of Orleans, which two years later became the State of Louisiana. In May 1812 a second bite was taken when the district between the Pearl and Perdido rivers was annexed by Act of Congress to Mississippi Territory.

Napoleon found time between campaigns, and divorcing Josephine and marrying Marie Louise, to cast his eye over Macon's Act and observe an opportunity to incorporate the United States in his continental system. That system was strikingly similar to Hitler's scheme for bringing England to her knees without winning control of the sea. It meant getting the European continent under his control, in order to impoverish the country which he, like Hitler, considered "a nation of shopkeepers." America could help this strategy by adding a sea-power component, as she actually did in 1812, too late to help Napoleon.

For five years Napoleon had treated American shipping harshly and arbitrarily. In the summer of 1810 our merchant-men in the Bay of Naples were seized by his command and sold. But on the same day Napoleon's foreign minister informed the American minister to France that "His Majesty loves the Americans," and as proof of his solicitude had declared that his decrees against neutral shipping after 1 November would be revoked, "it being understood that the English are to revoke their orders in council."

John Quincy Adams, then minister to Russia, warned Madison that this note was "a trap to catch us into a war with England." But the guileless President snapped at the bait. By proclamation on 2 November 1810 he announced that France had rescinded her antineutral system and that non-intercourse would be revived against Britain, if in three months' time she did not repeal her orders in council. Almost every mail, for the next two years, brought news of fresh seizures and scuttlings of American vessels by French port authorities, warships, and privateers. But Madison, having taken his stand, obstinately insisted that "the national faith was pledged to France." On 2 March 1811 he forbade intercourse with Great Britain, under authority of Macon's Act. That was a diplomatic victory for Napoleon; it brought the United States within his continental system. And at this, the third attempt, economic sanctions really worked on England, but too late to preserve the peace.

The winter of 1811–12 was the bitterest that the English people experienced between the Great Plague and 1940–41. Napoleon's continental system had now closed all western Europe except Portugal to British goods. American non-intercourse shut off the only important market still open except Russia, which Napoleon was about to try to force into his cordon. A crop failure drove up the price of wheat, warehouses were crammed with goods for which there was no market, factories were closing, workmen rioting. Deputations from the manufacturing cities besought Parliament to repeal the orders in council, hoping to recover their American market.

During these critical months several accidents postponed the repeal too long to maintain peace with America. On 16 May 1811 there took place an off-the-record fight between U.S. frigate *President* and H.M. corvette *Little Belt*, the results of which seemed to prove that the United States Navy was not to be feared. The American legation at London was vacant, except for a silly young chargé d'affaires, when the conciliatory Lord Castlereagh entered the foreign office. Spencer Perceval, the prime minister, was assassinated just after he had made up his mind to repeal the orders in council, and the business of finding a successor brought another and fatal delay. Finally on 16 June 1812 Castlereagh announced that the orders in council would be suspended immediately. If there had been a transatlantic cable, this would not have been too late. For Congress, without word of the concession, declared war against Great Britain two days later.

2. War Fever Rises

Congress so acted in response to a message from President Madison recommending war with Britain on four grounds—impressment of seamen, repeated violations of American territorial waters by the Royal Navy, declaring an enemy coast blockaded when it was not blockaded in fact, and the orders in council against neutral trade. Yet eight senators, a large majority of the congressmen from the New England states, and a majority in both houses from New York, New Jersey, and Maryland voted against the declaration of war; whilst representatives of the inland and Western states from Vermont to Tennessee, and of the states from Virginia south, were almost solid for war. New England, where three-quarters of American shipping was owned, and which supplied more than that proportion of American seamen, wanted no war and agitated against it to the brink of treason; whilst back-country congressmen who had never smelt salt water (unless in the Potomac) and whose constituents would as soon have thought of flying to the moon as enlisting in the United States Navy, screamed for "Free Trade and Sailors' Rights." And, still more curious, one-quarter of the Republicans abstained.

What is the explanation?

In the first place, a new generation of Americans which had grown to maturity since the Revolution was "feeling its oats." Nearly half the inept House that passed Macon's Act No. 2 failed of re-election in 1810–11, and new members became leaders. There were thirty-four-year-old Henry Clay and Richard M. Johnson from Kentucky, young Felix Grundy and the aged but bellicose John Sevier from Tennessee; Peter B. Porter, also in his thirties, from Buffalo, New York, and twenty-nine-year-old John C. Calhoun from the back country of South Carolina. These men, collectively dubbed the "war hawks" by John Randolph, combined with other new members to brush aside old Nathaniel Macon and elect Henry Clay speaker of the House; and Clay named his friends chairmen of the important committees. The war hawks wished to scuttle diplomacy and economic sanctions and declare war against

Great Britain, using arguments that reminded old hands of the Hamiltonian reasons for war with France in 1798. They passed a bill to raise a regular army of 25,000 but did nothing for the navy; it was still Republican doctrine that navies were evil. Some of the war hawks wished also to declare war on France, but Madison used his influence to stop that. Stubbornly, against cumulative evidence of Napoleon's bad faith, the President insisted that France had repealed her antineutral decrees.

The war hawks were disgusted with the wordy diplomacy of Madison and his secretary of state Monroe; they felt that national honor demanded a fight. In vain the Federalist minority urged that if we must fight someone, we should fight France, since Napoleon had become the Number 1 enemy to the free world and an autocrat. But the war hawks had very good reasons for wanting to fight England, if they must fight someone. War with Great Britain, if successful, would conquer Canada, end the Indian menace on the western frontier and throw open more forest land for settlement by United States pioneers. These motives were open and avowed. John Randolph of Roanoke, leader of the old-fashioned "pure" Republicans who wished to keep the peace, poured his scorn on this "cant of patriotism," this "agrarian cupidity," this chanting "like the whippoorwill, but one monotonous tone—Canada! Canada! Canada! Not a syllable about Halifax, which unquestionably should be our great object in a war for maritime security." Land-hungry pioneers of the Old Northwest coveted the fertile, wooded peninsula of Upper Canada between Lakes Huron, Erie, and Ontario. Actually, several thousand emigrants from the United States had already infiltrated this country. They lived easy under the "British yoke," but the war hawks in Congress expected them to "rise as one man" and rally to the Stars and Stripes.

And there was the Indian question. The Treaty of Greenville (1795) put the Northwest Indians on the defensive. Jefferson professed benevolent principles toward them, but coveted their lands in order to encourage western migration and keep the United States agricultural. He looked forward to removing all Indians across the Mississippi. Such a policy could be squared with humanity and justice only by protecting the red men from the whites during the process; and that was not done. Although the Indians faithfully fulfilled their treaty stipulations, white pioneers in the Northwest committed the most wanton and cruel murders of them, for which it was almost impossible to obtain a conviction from a pioneer jury. From time to time a few hungry and desperate chiefs were rounded up by government officials and plied with oratory and whisky until they signed a treaty alienating the hunting grounds of their tribe; sometimes of other nations as well. Jefferson encouraged this process, and William Henry Harrison, superintendent of the Northwest Indians and governor of Indiana Territory, pushed it so successfully that between 1795 and 1809 the Indians parted with some 48 million acres.

The process then came to a temporary halt, owing largely to the formation of an Indian league or confederacy by two really noble savages, the twin brothers Tecumseh and Tenskwatawa, sons of a Shawnee chief. The former, a lithe, handsome, and stately warrior, had been one of those who defeated St. Clair in 1791; Tenskwatawa, better known as The Prophet, was a half-blind medicine man. These undertook the task of saving their people. They sought to reform their habits, stop the alienation of their land, keep them apart from the whites, and weld all tribes on United States soil into a confederacy. It was a movement of regeneration and defense; a menace indeed to the expansion of the West, but in no sense to its existence. The Indians had so decreased in the last decade that scarcely 4000 warriors were counted in the space between the Lakes, the Mississippi, and the Ohio. Opposed to them were at least 100,000 white men of fighting age in the Ohio valley.

For a time the partnership of warrior and priest was irresistible. The Prophet kindled a religious revival among the tribes of the Northwest and even induced them to give up intoxicating liquor. All intercourse with white men, except for trade, ceased; rum and whisky were refused with disdain. In 1808 the two leaders, forced from their old settlement by the palefaces, established headquarters at a great clearing in Indiana where Tippecanoe creek empties into the Wabash river. The entire frontier was alarmed; Indian prohibitionists were something new to backwoods experience.

Governor Harrison met the situation with an act that Tecumseh could only regard as a challenge. Rounding up a few score survivors of tribes whom he frankly described as "the most depraved wretches on earth," the governor obtained from them several enormous tracts, to the amount of some three million acres, cutting into the heart of Tecumseh's country up both banks of the Wabash. This deprived Tecumseh of his remaining hunting grounds and brought the white border within fifty miles of the Tippecanoe.

With justice, Tecumseh declared this treaty null and void. He called on the British authorities at Amherstburg in November 1810, and declared that he was ready for war; but Canada was not. More Western nations joined his confederacy, and in

July 1811, assuring Governor Harrison that his object was defensive, he journeyed south to obtain the allegiance of the Creek nation. Harrison decided to force the issue. With the tacit approval of the war department, he collected about 1100 soldiers, marched up the Wabash valley and encamped hard by Tecumseh's village. The Prophet allowed himself to be maneuvered into battle by a few reckless young braves, who raised the war-whoop and pierced the first line of American tents. The engagement then became general, the Americans were almost surrounded; but after two hours' fighting Harrison drove the Indians into a swamp and destroyed their village. The general brought his army safely back to Vincennes and was hailed throughout the West as their savior. This Battle of Tippecanoe (7 November 1811) elected him President, thirty years later.

Throughout the West it was believed that Britain was behind Tecumseh's confederacy. That was not true; the confederacy would have been formed if there had been no white men in Canada. After Tippecanoe, however, the new governor general, Sir George Prevost, decided that war with the United States was inevitable, and his agents welcomed Tecumseh with his warriors at Amherstburg in June 1812.

These events explain why Western and many other patriots were keen for war with England. It would, they hoped, absorb Canada and wipe out the assumed source of Indian troubles. The Carolinians and Georgians went along because they hoped to do the same to the troublesome Creek nation and Spanish Florida, Spain being an ally of England. John Sevier, in the long debate on Madison's war message, said that "fire and sword" should be carried into the Creek country where "British emissaries" were supposed to be lurking, and that Florida should be annexed along with Canada. Henry Clay boasted, "The militia of Kentucky are alone competent to place Montreal and Upper Canada at your feet."

Shortly after the declaration of war, the Republican organ of Boston printed a gallant exhortation to the local citizenry:

> Since war is the word, let us strain every nerve
> To save our America, her glory increase;
> So, shoulder your firelock, your country preserve,
> For the hotter the war, boys, the quicker the peace.

But New England, now that an end had come to Indian raids on her frontier, showed very little sympathy with other frontiers.

3. *The War of 1812: Aggressive Phase*

Everyone knew, well before the declaration of 18 June 1812, that this war for "Free Trade and Sailors' Rights" would be fought largely on land, preferably in Canada. That made strategic sense, just as England's attacking Napoleon in Spain made sense; Canada was the only part of the British Empire that Americans could get at dryshod. But Canada was a very long, strung-out country, and a good deal depended on where she was attacked.

The population of British North America was less than half a million; that of the United States, by the census of 1810, seven and a quarter million. In the States, by the time the war broke out, the regular army had been recruited to about 7000 officers and men. There were fewer than 5000 British regulars in North America at that time, and little chance that Britain, heavily engaged in the Peninsular campaign, could spare reinforcements. Upper Canada (Ontario) had been, as we have seen, largely settled from the States, and the French Canadians in Quebec were not expected to do much to help Britain. The former American Loyalists who had peopled the Maritimes were ready to fight for King George, but the war never swung their way.

Canada, however, could count on Tecumseh's braves, and the war was far from popular in the United States. Not only Federalists but old-school Republicans were against it. Congress adjourned 6 July 1812 without making any provision to increase the navy, whose total strength until the spring of 1813 was six frigates, three sloops-of-war, and seven smaller vessels, not counting the fleet of completely useless gunboats. To refuse to increase one's naval force in a war with the world's greatest sea power for "Free Trade and Sailors' Rights" seemed gross hypocrisy to the Federalists. And the President, instead of trying to rally them to the flag, drove them to fury by publishing, three months before his war message, the purchased letters of a British spy in an attempt to incriminate them as British agents. This attempt backfired. At the time the letters came out the Massachusetts state government was Republican, as a result of the first "gerrymander" signed by Governor Gerry; but in the spring elections the Bay State went Federalist again. The lower house issued a manifesto urging the country to "organize a peace party" and "let there be no volunteers." The new governor, as well as his colleagues in Rhode Island and Connecticut, refused to call state militia into national service, and Federalist merchants refused to subscribe to war bonds or fit out privateers.

Although New England was the most solid section against the war, merchant-shipowners everywhere disliked it. At Baltimore the plant of a Federalist newspaper which came out for peace was demolished by a mob. The friends of Alexander C. Hanson, the editor, lodged for safety in the city jail, were dragged out of it by a waterfront mob led by a Frenchman, and beaten to a pulp. Hanson and General Henry Lee were badly injured, and General J. M. Lingan was killed. Federalists throughout the country shuddered over this episode, recalling as it did the cowardly massacres of prisoners in the French Revolution; and it turned Maryland Federalist for the duration.

Robert Smith, a former secretary of state, issued a public address against the war; Chief Justice Marshall wrote to him that he was mortified at his country's base submission to Napoleon; that the only party division henceforth should be between the friends of peace and the advocates of war. That was indeed the division in the presidential election of 1812. The Federalists supported De Witt Clinton, who had been placed in nomination by an antiwar faction of the New York Republicans and carried every state north of the Potomac except two. But Madison was re-elected.

The administration's military strategy was as stupid as its diplomacy. The settled portions of Canada (excluding the Maritimes) may be compared to a tree, of which the St. Lawrence river was the trunk, the Great Lakes and their tributaries the branches, and the sea lanes to England the roots. Britain had conquered Canada in 1759–60 by grasping the roots and grappling the trunk. Madison had no proper navy to attempt the former; but he might well have tried to hew the trunk by a sharp stroke at Montreal or Quebec. Instead, he attempted several feeble and unsystematic loppings at the branches.

Three weeks before war was declared, Governor William Hull of Michigan Territory, a sixty-year-old veteran of the War of Independence, was given a brigadier's commission. In command of 1500 troops, he was ordered to march to Detroit from Dayton, Ohio, cutting his own road through the wilderness, and thence to invade Upper Canada. Hull begged the war department first to obtain control of Lake Erie, in order to secure his communications and hamper those of General Isaac Brock, the British commander in Upper Canada. But nothing was done. Hull led his force, now stiffened by a regiment of regulars, to Detroit, and on 12 July crossed the river.

The Canadian inhabitants of that thinly settled area were little impressed by the general's proclamation offering them liberty under the American flag, and their militia gave a good account of itself.

In the meantime, a small military encounter in the far Northwest made Hull's situation precarious. The commander of the British post at St. Joseph's on the Sault forced the American garrison at Michilimackinac to surrender (17 July). General Hull then fell back on Detroit, and ordered the American commander at Fort Dearborn (Chicago) to come to his assistance; but the Indians captured a part of that small force and massacred the rest. General Brock, having transported to Detroit the few troops he could spare from the Niagara front, paraded them in sight of General Hull and summoned him to surrender. A broad hint in Brock's note, that the Indians would be beyond his control the moment fighting began, completely unnerved the elderly general. Dreading a general massacre, deserted by some of his militia, cut off from his base, Hull surrendered his army on 16 August 1812.

So ended the first invasion of Canada. The effective military frontier of the United States was thrown back to the Wabash and the Ohio.

Major General Samuel Hopkins, another veteran of Hull's vintage, was now ordered to lead 4000 Kentucky militiamen, mobilized at Vincennes, on a punitive expedition against the Indians who had massacred the Fort Dearborn garrison. Henry Clay boasted he could conquer Canada with Kentucky militia alone; declared that his problem was to quench, rather than blow up, the ardor of his native state. In this instance, ardor cooled so quickly that after five days the Kentucky militia became mutinous and unmanageable. A council of officers advised the general to retreat. Hopkins made the militia an eloquent address, asking for 500 volunteers to press forward. Not one man offered himself.

One week after Hull's surrender, General Brock was back at Niagara, eager to attack his enemy on the New York side of the Niagara river. Governor Prevost restrained him, letting the Americans take the initiative on 13 October 1812. Captain John E. Wool led a small detachment of regulars across the river, to an attack on Queenston heights, and General Brock was killed; but the tide of battle soon turned. Several thousand New York militia under General Stephen Van Rensselaer who were there to support Wool, refused to budge. They had turned out to defend their homes, not to invade Canada. In vain the patroon exhorted them. They calmly watched their countrymen on the other bank being enveloped and forced to surrender.

Command of the American troops on the Niagara front was now given to a curious character named Alexander Smyth, known as "Apocalypse Smyth" because he wrote an explanation of the Book of Revelation. He owed his briga-dier's commission to a reputation in the Virginia House of Delegates for oratory, a gift which he proceeded to employ in speeches to his army. These orations were studded with such gems as, "Be strong! Be brave! and let the ruffian power of the British king cease on this continent!" On a sleety November evening Smyth tumbled his army into boats to cross the Niag-ara, consoling them for spending the night embarked with this message: "Hearts of War! Tomorrow will be memorable in the annals of the United States!" But on the morrow, not lik-ing the looks of the Canadians on the further bank, Smyth called off the campaign. The soldiers joyfully discharged their muskets in every direction, showing a preference for the gen-eral's tent as a target. Smyth followed Hull and Van Rens-selaer into retirement and got himself elected to Congress, where he continued to bray for many years.

There still remained a considerable force at Plattsburg on Lake Champlain, under the immediate command of Major General Henry Dearborn, a sixty-two-year-old veteran of Bunker Hill. He was supposed to strike the Canadian trunk at Montreal. On 19 November he marched his troops twenty miles north of Plattsburg. The militia then refused to go fur-ther, and Dearborn marched them back to Plattsburg.

On the ocean there is a different story to tell. The United States Navy was vastly outnumbered, but the Royal Navy was so deeply engaged in war with France that it could spare only one ship of the line, seven frigates, and a number of smaller warships to operate off the American coast. The pride of the United States Navy were frigates *Constitution, United States,* and *President,* designed to outclass all other two-deckers and outrun ships of the line. They threw a heavier broadside than the British frigates, and were so heavily timbered and planked as to deserve the name "Old Ironsides"; yet with such fine, clean lines and great spread of canvas that they could outsail anything afloat. The crews were volunteers; and the officers, young and tried by experience against France and Tripoli, were burning to avenge the *Chesapeake.* On the other hand, the compatriots of Nelson, conquerors at Cape St. Vincent, Trafalgar, and the Nile, were the spoiled children of victory, confident of beating any vessel not more than twice their size. Hence, when U.S.S. *Constitution,* Captain Isaac Hull, knocked

H.M.S. *Guerrière* helpless in two hours and a half on 19 August 1812, and on 29 December, under Captain Bainbridge, reduced H.M. frigate *Java* to a useless hulk; when sloop-of-war *Wasp* mastered H.M.S. *Frolic* in 43 minutes on 17 October, and U.S.S. *Hornet*, Captain James Lawrence, in a hot fight off the Demerara river, sank H.M.S. *Peacock* in fifteen minutes; and when frigate *United States*, Captain Stephen Decatur, entered New London harbor with H.M. frigate *Macedonian* as prize on 4 December 1812, there was amazement and indignation in England, and rejoicing in the United States.

The moral value of these victories to the American people, following disaster on the Canadian border, was beyond calculation. They even converted Jeffersonian Republicans from their anti-navy doctrine, as may be read in a report of the House committee on naval affairs on 27 November 1812. "It is a bright attribute in the history of the tar," it says, "that he has never destroyed the rights of the nation. Thus, aided by economy and fortified by republican principle, your committee think they ought strongly to recommend that the fostering care of the nation be extended to the Naval Establishment." Congress accordingly made generous appropriations to increase the navy by four ships-of-the-line and six heavy frigates. "Frigates and seventy-fours," sighed Thomas Jefferson, "are a sacrifice we must make, heavy as it is, to the prejudices of a part of our citizens." None of this new construction got to sea during the war; but after Madison had obtained a competent secretary of the navy, William Jones of Philadelphia, important reforms were effected in naval administration.

Unfortunately, the military value of these naval victories was slight. Most of the American men-of-war that put into harbor during the winter of 1812–13 never got out again. The British blockaded Delaware Bay and Chesapeake Bay from the fall of 1812, extended the blockade in the spring of 1813 to New York and the seaports south of Norfolk, and to New England in the spring of 1814. This blockade stifled the operations of the small American high-seas fleet. Frigate *United States* and her prize *Macedonian* stayed in New London harbor for the duration. Frigate *President*, after crossing the Atlantic and capturing twelve small prizes, put into New York in the fall of 1813, and Captain Decatur lost her when trying to elude the blockading squadron. Captain Lawrence of unlucky *Chesapeake*, with a green and mutinous crew, unwisely accepted a challenge from Captain Broke of H.M.S. *Shannon* and sortied from Boston to defeat and glorious death on 1 June 1813. U.S.S. *Essex* eluded the blockade, rounded Cape Horn, and, after clearing British privateers from the South

Pacific, was captured (28 March 1814) by two British frigates off the coast of Chile. *Constitution* entered Boston for repairs after sinking *Java,* and never got out until December 1814. Under Captain Charles Stewart she again distinguished herself by capturing *Cyane* and *Levant* off the African coast on 20 February 1815—almost two months after peace had been signed.

Thus, the situation at sea for the United States in 1813–14 was much as it had been during the War of Independence in 1779–80, but with no help from France; the British were able to move troops by water at will. And their base at Halifax was almost as effective as their loyalist base had been at New York.

During 1813 the Royal Navy was too busy in Europe to lay anything better than hit-and-run raids on the Atlantic seaboard. Randolph of Roanoke, in one of his imprecatory orations against the war, declared, "Go march to Canada! Leave the broad bosom of the Chesapeake and her hundred tributary rivers unprotected!" Which is exactly what happened. From Bermuda a powerful raiding force under Admiral John Borlase Warren, with Rear Admiral Sir George Cockburn second in command, was sent to spread terror and destruction in Chesapeake Bay. It was prevented from attacking Norfolk by a navy- and militia-manned battery on Craney Island, which drove off the landing force and sank the admiral's barge. Cockburn, a tough and ruthless old salt, then devastated the country around Lynnhaven Bay, sailed to the upper part of the Chesapeake, and within one week in April–May 1813 raided Havre de Grace, destroyed a cannon foundry up the Susquehanna and a munitions store on the Elk, and two villages on the Sassafras river; all without the loss of a man on either side. During the rest of the year, Warren and Cockburn cruised around Chesapeake Bay and off the Delaware Capes, landing frequently to burn buildings and replenish provisions.

In the meantime naval history was being made on the Great Lakes. Hull's surrender at Detroit convinced President Madison that command of the Lakes was essential. The Canadian authorities naturally determined to retain the supremacy they already enjoyed. It was comparatively easy for them to bring in more guns and fresh supplies up the St. Lawrence river to Lake Ontario. The Americans surmounted greater difficulties through the energy and resourcefulness of Captain Isaac Chauncey, with headquarters at Sackets Harbor on Lake Ontario, and Captain Oliver H. Perry, with headquarters at Presqu'ile (Erie), Pennsylvania. Here the Americans had a logistic advantage, since Pittsburgh, not far from Erie, was already a manufacturing town. And an American raid on York (Toronto) obtained some valuable cannon for this fresh-water United States Navy. Captain Perry managed to construct a fleet of stout little vessels during the winter of 1812–13.

General Harrison, victor of Tippecanoe, advanced from the Ohio river toward Detroit in three divisions, during the winter of 1812–13. British General Proctor did not wait for them to unite, but beat two separately at Frenchtown on the Raisin river (22 January 1813) and Fort Meigs at the rapids of the Maumee (5 May). Harrison then decided to await a naval decision on Lake Erie. Perry got his fleet over the Presqu'ile bar on 4 August and sought out the British Lake squadron. He found it on 10 September at Put In Bay among the islands at the western end of the lake. A strange naval battle ensued between vessels hastily built of green wood, manned largely by militiamen, blacks, frontier scouts, and Canadian canal men. The fight was a matter of banging away until one or the other fleet gave up; and it was the British who quit. Perry's laconic report "We have met the enemy, and they are ours," was literally true.

General Proctor's prudent strategy would have been to fall back on the Niagara front. But Tecumseh induced his ally to make a stand at an Indian village near the center of the Ontario peninsula. Thither Harrison pursued him, after reoccupying Detroit. The Battle of the Thames or Moravian Town (5 October 1813) was a victory for the Kentucky mounted riflemen. Tecumseh was killed, Proctor fled, the Indian confederacy broke up, and the American military frontier in the Northwest was re-established. This victory helped to advance the political ambitions of the "Hero of Tippecanoe," and Colonel Johnson's claim that he personally had slain Tecumseh made him Vice President of the United States.

On Lake Ontario and the Niagara front there were no decisive battles in 1813. On 27 April Captain Chauncey and General Dearborn raided York, the capital of Upper Canada. A large powder magazine exploded while the Americans were advancing upon the village, killing General Zebulon M. Pike and about 300 men. As a result of this incident, and indiscipline, the American troops got out of hand after the British had surrendered the town, and burned two brick parliament houses, the governor's residence, and other buildings. But, as Sir James Yeo now had a strong naval force on Lake Ontario, the Americans had to evacuate York.

The next attempted American invasion of Upper Canada was a probe at Hamilton on Lake Ontario. General Vincent stopped it at Stony Creek (6 June 1813) and captured two

THE WAR OF 1812-1814

Principal roads   ✗ *Battle sites.*

Scale of Miles
0   50   100

NIAGARA BORDER

L. Ontario
Ft. George
May 1813 ✗ Ft. Niagara
           Lewiston
Queenston
Oct. 1812 ✗
                NIARA FALLS
Lundy Lane ✗ Ft. Schlosser
Chippewa
July 1814 ✗   U.S.
           GRAND
CANADA
July 1814 ✗ ✗ Black Rock
Ft. Erie   Buffalo
Scale of Miles
0   10
           L. Erie

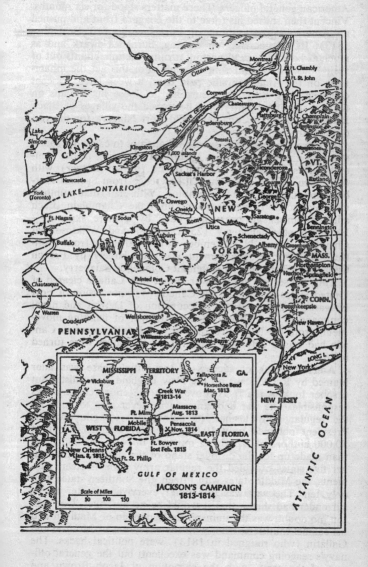

MONTREAL
Ft. Chambly
Ft. St. John
Ottawa R.
Cornwall
Rouses Point
Chateaugay
Plattsburg
Champlain
CANADA
Lake Simcoe
Kingston
1,000 Islands
Ogdensburg
Russell
Ticonderoga
VT.
St. Lawre. R.
Sackett's Harbor
G. George
Rutland
Newcastle
LAKE ONTARIO
Ft. Oswego
L. Oneida
NEW
Saratoga
York (Toronto)
Ft. Niagara
Sodus
Rome
Utica
Mohawk R.
Bennington
Buffalo
Leicester
Genesee R.
Auburn
Schenectady
Albany
YORK
MASS.
L. Chautauqua
Painted Post
Northampton
Springfield
Warren
Coudersport
Wellsborough
CONN.
Poughkeepsie
PENNSYLVANIA
Wilkes-Barre
New Haven
LONG I.
New York
NEW JERSEY

MISSISSIPPI TERRITORY
Tallapoosa R.
GA.
Vicksburg
Creek War 1813-14
Horseshoe Bend Mar. 1813
Ft. Mims
Massacre Aug. 1813
Pearl R.
WEST FLORIDA
Mobile
Pensacola Nov. 1814
EAST FLORIDA
LA.
New Orleans Jan. 8, 1815
Ft. Bowyer lost Feb. 1815
Ft. St. Philip
GULF OF MEXICO
Scale of Miles
0   50   100   150
JACKSON'S CAMPAIGN 1813-1814

ATLANTIC OCEAN

American general officers. There matters stood for six months. Vincent then shifted his force to the Niagara front and pushed an American garrison out of Fort George (10 December 1813). Its commander, on retiring, burned Newark and as much as he could of Queenston, turning the inhabitants out of their houses on a cold winter's night. For this act the inhabitants on the American side paid dear, a week later. Vincent captured Fort Niagara by surprise, let loose his Indians on the surrounding country, and destroyed the villages of Black Rock and Buffalo. Canadians held Fort Niagara for the rest of the war.

In the meantime, an unsuccessful attempt to carry out sound strategy, a pincer attack on Montreal, was being made. General James Wilkinson (Aaron Burr's former partner) with 8000 men floated down the St. Lawrence from Sackets Harbor; and General Wade Hampton, with half that number, marched north from Plattsburg on Lake Champlain. Each allowed himself to be turned back by a mere skirmish—Hampton at Chateaugay (25 October) and Wilkinson at Chrysler's Farm (11 November 1813), 70 miles from Montreal. The former engagement was won largely by French Canadian militia under Lieutenant Colonel de Salaberry.

Thus the second year of war closed with Canada cleared of United States troops, and the Canadians in possession of Fort Niagara; whilst American reoccupation of Detroit and naval command of Lake Erie ended the danger of flanking movements from the Northwest. So far, the British forces in Canada had waged defensive warfare; but the tables were turned in 1814.

American lack of success in the initial phase was later blamed by Republicans on the New England Federalists. But a sober look at the facts proves that the entire country was responsible. The war department was never able to build up the regular army to half its authorized strength, and the President obtained only 10,000 one-year volunteers out of 50,000 authorized. The loyal minority in New England more than made up for the disloyal stand of the state governments; her five states provided the regular army with nineteen regiments, the Middle states with fifteen, the Southern states with only ten. The war was unpopular everywhere, after Hull's surrender had shown that it would be no pushover. One reason, no doubt, was the uninspiring leadership of Madison and his cabinet ministers, who, with the exception of Monroe and Gallatin (who resigned in 1813), were political hacks. The navy's seagoing command was excellent; but the general officers of the army, with the exception of Jacob Brown and

Andrew Jackson, who only came into the picture in 1813, were the worst military leaders of any war in which the United States has ever been engaged. Jackson had been eager for service at the start, and it was typical of the way this war was run, that Madison refused him a federal commission because he had supported Monroe for President in 1808.

4. The War of 1812: Defensive Phase

After Napoleon's abdication on April 1814, Britain was able to provide Canada with an adequate army to carry the war into the United States, and to extend and intensify the naval blockade of the Atlantic coast. The war office planned to invade the United States from three points successively: Niagara, Lake Champlain, and New Orleans, and simultaneously to raid the Chesapeake.

On the Niagara front America took the initiative before British reinforcements arrived. The army had learned much from two years of adversity. Incompetent officers had been weeded out, and promising young men were promoted; more reliance was placed on regulars, less on militia. On 3 July 1814 General Jacob Brown floated his army of about 5000 men across the Niagara river and forced Fort Erie to capitulate. On the 5th, his subordinate Winfield Scott was about to hold a holiday parade when three regiments of British regulars broke up the celebration and the Battle of Chippewa was joined. This was a European-style stand-up fight in open country. Both lines advanced in close order, stopping alternately to load and fire; the British broke when they were about 60 paces away. On 25 July, hard by Niagara Falls, occurred the Battle of Lundy's Lane, the most stubbornly contested fight of the war. Fighting was begun in the late afternoon by Winfield Scott's brigade, which crossed bayonets with the enemy four times before being reinforced by General Brown's brigade. The battle continued until midnight. General Brown ordered Colonel James Miller to capture the artillery which protected the enemy's position. "I'll try, Sir," said the colonel, and did; his infantrymen rushed the British guns and bayoneted the cannoneers in the act of loading. Both American generals were badly wounded, and the casualties were very heavy for a battle of that era: 43 to 45 per cent. The British later recovered their guns, but these actions prevented an invasion of the United States from the Niagara front and gave the United States Army a new pride and character. British officers who had fought in the Peninsular War said they had never seen anything to equal Colonel Miller's charge.

By mid-August General Sir George Prevost commanded some 10,000 British veterans encamped near Montreal, ready to invade the United States by the classic route of Lake Champlain and the Hudson. It was the strongest, best disciplined, and most completely equipped army that had ever been sent to North America. Prospects were very bleak for the United States, particularly as the war department had lately transferred most of the regulars from Plattsburg to Niagara. Early in September, Sir George moved down the western shore of Lake Champlain, synchronizing his movements with that of a fresh-water flotilla, and forcing the Americans back to a strong position behind the river that empties into Plattsburg Bay. There they were protected by a line of forts, and by the American lake squadron, Captain Thomas Macdonough, anchored inside the entrance.

Prevost's army reached Plattsburg on 6 September 1814. Facing him were only 1500 American regulars and a few thousand militia. The American forts were formidable, and Prevost wished to secure control of the lake before advancing further. Early in the morning of 11 September the British fleet hove to off Cumberland Head. There followed a murderous engagement. Small vessels, without bulwarks to protect their crews, anchored side by side at pistol range, attempted to pound each other to pieces. After British flagship *Confiance* had silenced the starboard battery of American flagship *Saratoga* and killed one-fifth of her crew, Captain Macdonough "wound ship"—turned *Saratoga* completely around while at anchor—brought his port battery to bear and forced H.M.S. *Confiance* and three other vessels to surrender. The British commodore lost his life, and Prevost was so discouraged by the loss of the fleet that he retreated to Canada. "Macdonough's Victory," the naval Battle of Plattsburg, proved to be decisive. But it was not the last battle of the war.

In June 1814 a British expeditionary force was mounted at Bordeaux to make a diversion in the Chesapeake. The campaign that followed reflected little credit to the one side, and considerable disgrace to the other. General Robert Ross, commander of the land forces, was instructed by Admiral Cochrane "to destroy and lay waste such towns and districts upon the coast" as he might find assailable. A fleet of Jeffersonian gunboats, retreating up the Patuxent river, led Ross's army from Chesapeake Bay to the back door of Washington. For five days the British army marched along the banks of the Patuxent, approaching the capital of the United States without seeing an enemy or firing a shot. In the meantime, Washington was in a fever of preparation. About 7000 militia, all that turned out of 95,000 summoned, were placed under an unusually incompetent general and hurried to a strong position behind the village of Bladensburg, five miles from the capital. After the militia had suffered only 66 casualties, they broke and ran, leaving Commodore Joshua Barney with 400 seamen and some 120 marines to resist the enemy. They battled stoutly for two hours, after which Ross entered Washington unopposed (24 August). Some of the officers arrived in time to eat a dinner at the White House that had been prepared for President and Mrs. Madison.

All public buildings of the capital were deliberately burned, partly in retaliation for the American burning of York and Newark, partly to impress the administration with the uselessness of further resistance. General Ross personally superintended the piling up of furniture in the White House before it was given to the flames, and Admiral Sir George Cockburn gave orders to burn the department buildings; but the troops, under good discipline, were not allowed to indulge in looting or destruction of private property.

This was a dark period for Madison's fugitive administration. Discouraging news only had arrived from the peace commission at Ghent. Sir George Prevost was expected to march south again; and a new British expeditionary force was on its way to New Orleans. The last war loan had failed, and all banks south of New England had suspended specie payments. John Jacob Astor, who had received many favors from the government since his "mandarin" hoax, combined with two Philadelphia bankers to buy the unsubscribed part of the federal loan at 80, paying in such depreciated bank notes that they really got the bonds for 40 cents on the dollar.

Fortunately the destruction of Washington illustrated the strategic truth that hit-and-run raids accomplish nothing except to amuse the aggressors and infuriate the victims. On the night of 25–26 August 1814 the British army withdrew to its transports, and proceeded to the next objective, Baltimore. Here the inhabitants were prepared, and Maryland militia showed a very different spirit from that of their Virginia countrymen. Naval bombardment of Fort McHenry accomplished nothing for the British, but gave us a stirring national anthem. Francis Scott Key, a prisoner on board one of the bombarding vessels, gained his inspiration for "The Star Spangled Banner" from seeing the flag still flying over Fort McHenry "by the dawn's early light." General Ross was killed at the head of a landing party (12 September), and that ended the Chesapeake campaign.

Before the third British expeditionary force reached New

Orleans, the West had produced a great military leader, General Andrew Jackson. He had emigrated to Tennessee as a young man, grown up with that state, represented it in the United States Senate, and as commander of its militia had been winning laurels in warfare against the "Red Sticks," the Upper Creeks.

That Indian nation endeavored to remain neutral, but Tecumseh's emissaries stirred up the younger braves. The result was a series of raids on the frontier and the capture of Fort Mims above Mobile, together with some 260 white scalps. This news found Andrew Jackson in bed at Nashville, recovering from a pistol shot received in a street brawl with Thomas H. Benton, the future senator from Missouri. Within a month, Jackson at the head of 2500 militia and a band of Choctaw and Lower Creek auxiliaries was in the Upper Creek country. Five engagements, fought between November 1813 and January 1814, accomplished little; and the Tennessee militia showed the same disposition to panic as their brethren on the Canadian border. But after Jackson had executed a few militiamen to encourage the others, the spring campaign of 1814 went very well. At the Tohopeka or Horseshoe Bend of the Tallapoosa river (27 March 1814), the military power of the Creek nation was broken; they left 557 warriors dead on the battlefield, and Jackson lost only 26 of his men and 23 Indian allies. This campaign deprived the British of a powerful ally. And a subsequent treaty with the Upper Creeks opened about two-thirds of Alabama, the heart of the future cotton kingdom, to white settlement and Negro slavery.

In early August, a small British force landed at Pensacola in Spanish Florida. Its leader, an impetuous Irishman named Edward Nicholls, proceeded to organize and drill Creek refugees, and the "maroons," blacks who had escaped from the United States, with a view to renewing the war in that quarter. Jackson invaded Florida on his own authority and crushed this diversion by capturing Pensacola on 7 November 1814.

The most formidable British expedition of this war was already under way. The Cochrane-Ross force which had captured Washington and been repulsed before Baltimore, retired for refit and rendezvous at Negril Bay, Jamaica. There this assault force of 3000 men, now under command of Major General Sir Edward Pakenham, was reinforced by fresh troops from England and a fleet under Admiral Cochrane, consisting of 6 ships of the line, 14 frigates, dozens of smaller ships, and 11 transports capable of carrying 7450 troops. The objective was to occupy New Orleans and as much Gulf territory as possible, to be used as bargaining pawns in the peace. Louisiana was to be encouraged to secede from the United States, and either annex herself to the Spanish empire or become a British satellite state.

To meet this threat Jackson had about 5000 men, three-quarters of them militia; and for naval support, two 15-gun sloops-of-war at New Orleans, and seven gunboats on Lake Borgne. And he made the bad guess that the British would attack Mobile first. He wished all naval forces to be moved to Mobile Bay, which their senior officer refused to do, recalling what had happened to Commodore Hopkins at Charleston in 1780. The two sloops remained at New Orleans (and later lent Jackson's army valuable gunfire support), while the gunboats were drawn up across Lake Borgne, by which the British elected to approach the back door of New Orleans. These 5-gun craft, under Lieutenant Ap Catesby Jones, were overwhelmed and sunk by an advance force of British in 40 armed boats, on 14 December. Only then did General Jackson realize that New Orleans was the British objective.

The boating of an amphibious force in that era took days instead of hours, so that it was not until 23 December that the British assault force could be floated up the bayou that almost connects Lake Borgne with the Mississippi. It then occupied the Villeré plantation on the left (north) bank of the great river, only a few miles from the city. Up to that moment it looked as if General Jackson were in a class with Hull and Smyth; and he might have been, if Pakenham had promptly advanced on New Orleans. But delay was fatal to anyone facing Andrew Jackson. This lank, long-haired general in his "well-worn leather cap, a short Spanish cloak of old blue cloth, and great unpolished boots whose vast tops swayed uneasily around his bony knees," was master of the situation the moment an enemy was in sight.

In a sharp night attack on the British, 23–24 December, Jackson checked their advance, then retired to the Maccarty plantation five miles below New Orleans, and entrenched. In an artillery duel on New Year's Day 1815, the British were again repulsed. While General Pakenham waited a week for reinforcements, Jackson strengthened his main position behind a canal and high mud breastworks, reinforced by sugar barrels.

At dawn 8 January began the main Battle of New Orleans. On the south bank of the river the Kentucky militia "ingloriously fled" before a British brigade which included a regiment of West Indies blacks. This gave the enemy a chance to attack the main American army on the north bank, from the rear. But General Pakenham threw away the chance. Instead, he chose, at 6:00 a.m., to direct a foolhardy frontal assault of some 5300 men in close column formation, against Jackson's 3500 men on the parapet, so well protected that the British, without ladders or fascines, could not get at them. The result was more of a massacre than a battle. General Pakenham and over 2000 of all ranks were killed, wounded, or missing; the second and third generals in line of command were fatally wounded. Only 13 Americans were killed and 58 wounded before the attacking columns melted. For ten days the two armies maintained their respective positions. Then the only surviving British general officer withdrew the army to its transports.

This Battle of New Orleans had no military value since peace had already been signed at Ghent on Christmas Eve; but it made a future President of the United States, and in folklore wiped out all previous American defeats, ending the "Second War of Independence" in a blaze of glory.

5. Disaffection and Peace

One of the many anomalies in this war was bitter opposition by the New England states, despite the fact that war built up their economy. Since the British blockade was not extended to the New England coast until May 1814, that section of the country traded freely with the enemy in the Maritime Provinces and Quebec, and legitimate foreign trade passed through New England seaports, whence it was distributed to the Middle states and the South by ox wagons and sleds. Permanently important for New England was the stimulus to manufacturing; by 1815 half a million spindles were in operation.

Although this war enriched New England, the Federalists claimed that their section was being ruined. Their leaders, and many followers too, got themselves into just such a state of emotional frustration over Republican "Jacobins" and "that Little Man in the Palace," as Republican leaders did in the 1930's about "dangerous radicals" and "that man in the White House."[1] Federalist press and pamphlets spread the notion that the real objects of the war were to help Napoleon, and to lay open Eastern seaports to devastation by the Royal Navy while the American army pranced into Upper Canada. Allied victories in Europe were celebrated, and a vote of thanks to a naval hero was rejected in the Massachusetts legislature as

[1] The White House was generally called "The Palace" until around 1820.

"not becoming a moral and religious people." However justified these stern Puritans may have been in refusing to support a war of conquest against a kindred people, there was no excuse for stiffening this attitude after Napoleon had been disposed of and the character of the war had changed. It was now a matter of defending national integrity against an overwhelming land and sea power.

For some years there had been talk of holding a New England convention to make a concerted protest against Republican policy. Events of the summer of 1814 conspired to bring it about. Massachusetts was thrown upon her own resources for defense, with no protection from Washington. The British occupied Maine east of the Penobscot, and the Royal Navy raided various parts of the coast. This was largely the fault of Federalist governors in refusing to place state militia under the war department, for fear that they would be marched off to Canada; but New England was past reasoning on such matters. On 6 October 1814 Massachusetts summoned a New England Convention at Hartford, for the express purpose of conferring upon "their public grievances and concerns," upon "defence against the enemy . . . and also to take measures, if they shall think proper, for procuring a convention of delegates from all the United States, in order to revise the Constitution thereof."

This language showed a compromise between the moderate and the extreme Federalists. The former, led by Harrison Gray Otis, were not disunionists, but wished to take advantage of the situation to obtain concessions for their section. Alarmed at the rising tide of secession sentiment, they hoped the Convention would act as a safety valve to let it off; and their desire to concert defensive measures against the enemy was sincere. But the violent wing of the Federalist party, led by Timothy Pickering and John Lowell, had other objects in view. It was their belief that the British invasion of New Orleans would succeed and that Aaron Burr's secession plot for Louisiana and the West would then bear fruit. They wished the Hartford Convention to draft a new Federal constitution, with clauses to protect New England interests, and present it as to the original Thirteen States only. If these accepted, well and good; if not, New England would make a separate peace and go it alone. In answering echo, the London *Times* declared on 26 December, "New England allied with Old England would form a dignified and manly union well deserving the name of Peace."

The New England Convention, representing mainly Massachusetts, Rhode Island, and Connecticut, with scattered delegates from New Hampshire and Vermont, met in secret session at Hartford on 15 December 1814. Fortunately the moderates gained control and issued a calm and statesmanlike report on 5 January 1815. An element of their caution was the strength of the Republican party in New England; the Federalists controlled all five states, but only by small majorities, and there would certainly have been civil war had the extremists put through an ordinance of secession. Madison's administration and the war were severely arraigned by the Hartford Convention; "but to attempt upon every abuse of power to change the Constitution, would be to perpetuate the evils of revolution." Secession was squarely faced, and ruled out as inexpedient and unnecessary since the causes of New England's calamities were not deep and permanent but the result of bad administration, and of partisanship in the European war. A suggestion was thrown out that the administration permit this section to assume their own defense, applying to that purpose the federal taxes collected within their borders. A few constitutional amendments were proposed. But there was no threat of a separate peace.

Secession agitation in New England now calmed down. Presently the good news from Ghent and New Orleans put Madison's administration on a high horse, and made New England the scapegoat for government mismanagement of the war. A stigma of unpatriotism, from which it never recovered, was attached to the Federalist party. Yet no stigma was attached to the doctrine of state rights; and within a few years it was revived by states like Virginia, which had denounced the Hartford Convention as treasonable.

Peace negotiations began almost as soon as the war did, but time was wasted over an attempted mediation by the emperor of Russia. When Lord Castlereagh finally offered to treat directly with the United States, Madison replied favorably (January 1814) and Ghent in Belgium was selected as the place of negotiation. By the time the American commissioners arrived there in June, the British government was in no hurry for peace. It shortly expected news of decisive victories on the Canadian border, which would place it in position to dictate instead of negotiate.

To the astonishment and distress of the American peace commissioners (John Quincy Adams, Albert Gallatin, Henry Clay, Jonathan Russell, and James A. Bayard), their opposite numbers were instructed to admit neither impressment nor neutral rights even as subjects of discussion. The United States must abandon all claims to the Newfoundland fisheries, the northeastern boundary must be revised to provide a direct

British road between St. John, N.B., and Quebec; and the northwest boundary must also be rectified to give Canada access to the upper Mississippi. Finally, the old project of an Indian satellite state north of the Ohio river was revived. Adams, an experienced diplomat, expected the negotiations to terminate on this point, and prepared to go home. Henry Clay, untrained in diplomacy but an expert poker player, was confident the British would recede, as they did. On 16 September, the British commissioners were instructed to drop the Indian project. The next obstacle was a British proposal to settle the boundary on the basis of what each side held when the war was over, which would mean the cession of eastern Maine and of any territory that Generals Prevost and Pakenham might conquer. The Americans refused to entertain any other basis than the 1783 boundary. This deadlock was broken in mid-October by news of the British repulses at Baltimore and on Lake Champlain, which the London *Times* described as a "lamentable event to the civilized world." But to the American peace commission the news from Plattsburg had "the effect of a reprieve from execution."

The British premier now turned to the Duke of Wellington, since Napoleon had been temporarily disposed of. The Iron Duke was invited, on 4 November, to take over the top command in America, with full powers "to make peace, or to continue the war with renewed vigor." He promptly replied in terms that showed a sound grasp of strategy. "That which appears to me to be wanting in America is not a general, or general officers and troops, but a naval superiority on the Lakes," he wrote. "The question is, whether we can acquire this. If we can't, I shall do you but little good in America, and I shall go there only to prove the truth of Prevost's defence; and to sign a peace which might as well be signed now. I think you have no right from the state of the war to demand any concession of territory from America."

Thus, Macdonough's victory at Plattsburg proved to be the decisive action.

By this time, the British public was sick of war, and the ministry was eager to wind it up and conclude peace all around. So, in the end, nothing much was said about anything in the Treaty of Ghent, signed on Christmas Eve 1814. Both sides agreed to disagree on everything important except the conclusion of hostilities and restoring prewar boundaries. Nothing was said about Madison's declared reason for the war —impressment and neutral rights. Yet the treaty did bear good fruit. Four boundary commissions were created to settle the boundary between Canada and the United States. Claims, commercial relations, naval forces on the Lakes, and the Oregon question were postponed to future negotiations. And, before the next maritime war broke out, impressment had been given up as a means of manning the Royal Navy.

So ended a futile and unnecessary war which might have been prevented by a little more imagination on the one side, and a broader vision on the other. At least it was a cheap one, in terms of money and casualties; only 1877 American soldiers and sailors were killed in action. On relations between the two governments, however, the war had a good effect. The fighters and the diplomats learned to respect one another. The United States was never again denied the treatment due to an independent nation, and Americans began to grasp the basic fact that whatever Canada's future, she would never join the United States. At the same time, Jackson's incursion into Florida indicated that the Spanish empire in North America was ready to fall apart.

Internally, the conduct of this conflict offered many lessons in how not to fight a war and how not to organize and lead armies. Practically none of these were heeded. The myth of "citizen soldiery" being a sufficient defense, and of self-taught

THE CONSTITUTION AND THE GUERRIERE

It oft-times has been told—how the Brit-ish sea-men
bold— Could— flog the tars of France so neat and
han—dy O! But they ne-ver found their
match till the Yan-kees did them catch, Oh, the
Yan-kee boys for fight-ing are the dan'-dy O!

generals being superior to West Pointers, persisted for a century. But the gallant record of the navy wrought a change of public opinion toward that fighting force. Most of the wartime fleet was maintained after peace, and within three months of the Treaty of Ghent it found profitable employment in punishing three Barbary States for piracy.

V

Good Feelings and Bad

1815-1823

1. *A Nationalist Era*

AN "ERA OF GOOD FEELINGS," as contemporaries called it, followed the second war with England and the quarter-century
of struggle between Federalists and Republicans. Relations
with Great Britain became friendly, and a permanent basis for
peace with Canada was furnished through partial disarmament. President Madison and his party adopted the nationalism of Washington and Hamilton as if they had been born to
it, and Federalist enmity did not long survive Republican
conversion. A Congress in which Republicans were dominant
resurrected Hamilton's Report on Manufactures, passed the
first protective tariff, and in the same year, 1816, chartered a
second Bank of the United States, on the model of Hamilton's.
James Monroe, legitimate heir of the Virginia dynasty, succeeded to the Presidency in 1817 almost unopposed, and in
1821 he obtained every electoral vote but one; two years later,
with unanimous approval, he issued a momentous declaration
of American foreign policy.

The United States was tired of party and sectional strife, as
Europe was weary of war and revolution. New forces were
transforming the country, and while this readjustment was
taking place, Americans acquiesced in nationalism. That is

the key to the Era of Good Feelings. Manufacturing was displacing shipping as the premier interest of New England and Pennsylvania. Society and politics were being democratized in New York. Virginia was declining as an agricultural state, but finding no other interest than slave-breeding to take the place of tobacco. King Cotton's domain was advancing from South Carolina and Georgia into the new Gulf states. The Northwest, rapidly expanding in population and influence, was acquiring new wants and aspirations. A series of sharp and bitter sectional conflicts brought out the underlying antagonism, and by 1830 sections had again become articulate, defining the stand they were to take until the Civil War. It became a major problem of politics to form combinations and alliances between sections whose interests were complementary, in the hope of achieving their common wants through the federal government; the task of statesmanship was to reconcile rival interests and sections through national party organizations.

These new interests brought a change in the attitude of different parts of the country toward the Constitution, reversing the similar change that had taken place during Jefferson's administration. As soon as nationalist legislation, in appearance at least, began to cramp the economic life of certain states and sections, their public men adopted the state rights theories of New England Federalists, which they in turn had taken over from Jefferson. Daniel Webster, who in 1814 warned Congress that Massachusetts would nullify a conscription law, by 1830 was intoning hymns to the Union. John C. Calhoun, leader of the war hawks of 1812 and promoter of nationalist legislation thereafter, began in 1828 to write textbooks on state rights. Of prominent American publicists and statesmen whose careers bridged the War of 1812, only five were consistent, and three were Virginians. John Taylor went on writing, and John Randolph talking, as if nothing had happened since 1791. Henry Clay and John Quincy Adams hewed to the nationalist line that they had long followed, and Chief Justice Marshall intensified the nationalism that he had learned from Washington.

Except for the Monroe Doctrine, Marshall's Supreme Court opinions were the only enduring feature of the new nationalism of 1815. The first, *McCulloch* v. *Maryland,* defended the constitutionality of the new Bank of the United States against the State of Maryland, which, in taxing the bank's Baltimore branch, denied the power of Congress to charter it. Marshall met this argument with an historical survey of the origin of the Constitution, and concluded: "The government of the Union . . . is emphatically and truly a government of the people. In form and substance it emanates from them. Its powers are granted by them, and are to be exercised directly on them, and for their benefit." Here is the classic definition of national sovereignty, undercutting the ground of state rights. On a second point, that the power to charter corporations is not expressly granted to Congress by the Constitution, and cannot be inferred from the "necessary and proper" clause, Marshall remarked:

> The government of the Union, though limited in its powers, is supreme within its sphere of action . . . We admit, as all must admit, that the powers of the government are limited, and that its limits are not to be transscended. But we think the sound construction of the Constitution must allow to the national legislature that discretion, with respect to the means by which the powers it confers are to be carried into execution, which will enable that body to perform the high duties assigned to it, in the manner most beneficial to the people. Let the end be legitimate, let it be within the scope of the Constitution, and all means which are appropriate, which are plainly adapted to that end, which are not prohibited, but consist with the letter of the spirit of the Constitution, are constitutional.

"A deadly blow has been struck at the Sovereignty of the States," declared a Baltimore newspaper in printing this opinion. Pennsylvania proposed a constitutional amendment prohibiting Congress from erecting a "moneyed institution" outside the District of Columbia; Ohio, Indiana, and Illinois concurred. The legislature of South Carolina, on the contrary, declared that "Congress is constitutionally vested with the right to incorporate a bank," and "they apprehend no danger from the exercise of the powers which the people of the United States have confided to Congress." South Carolina would not speak this language much longer; Pennsylvania and the Old Northwest would shortly speak no other.

The Supreme Court was not deterred by local opposition, or influenced by public opinion, as long as Marshall was Chief Justice. To mention only four cases: in *Martin* v. *Hunter's Lessee* (1817) and *Cohens* v. *Virginia* (1821) the Court reasserted its right to review any final judgment of a state supreme court that affected treaties or laws of the United States. In *Martin* v. *Mott* (1827) the Court denied to a state the right to withhold militia from national service when demanded by the President. In *Gibbons* v. *Ogden* (1824) it not only smashed a state-chartered monopoly of steamboat traffic but mapped out the course that Congress followed in regulating interstate commerce.

Henry Clay and John C. Calhoun were the nationalist leaders in Congress during the Era of Good Feelings. Both feared growing sectionalism. Their formula, which Clay christened the "American System," was a protective tariff for manufacturers, a home market, and better transportation for the farmers. "Let us," said Calhoun in 1817, "bind the Republic together with a perfect system of roads and canals." And, he added, a protective tariff "would form a new and most powerful cement." It was a propitious moment. "Infant" industries, some of them born during the war, were crying for protection, from which almost every section of the country expected to benefit. Pittsburgh, a center for the iron deposits of the Alleghenies, was eager to sell its charcoal-smelted pigs and bars in the coastal region, in place of British and Swedish iron. In Kentucky there was a new industry of weaving local hemp into cotton bagging, menaced by the Scots jute industry. All Western centers wanted roads and canals. Vermont and Ohio shepherds demanded protection against English wool; the grain producers of central New York, excluded from England by the corn laws, were attracted by the "home market" argument that manufactures increase local purchases of farm produce. Even this early, vineyards which would eventually rival those of Europe were being planted in New York. Congressmen from states which a generation later preferred secession to protection, eagerly voted for the tariff of 1816; maritime New Englanders, destined to pocket great benefits from protection, voted against it.

Internal improvements, meaning roads and canals, were the complement to protection. Immediately after the War of 1812, people eager to exploit the lands conquered from Tecumseh and the Creek nation, began a new westward movement. Between 1810 and 1820 the population of states and territories west of the Appalachians more than doubled. Four new states —Indiana (1816), Mississippi (1817), Illinois (1818), and Alabama (1819)—were admitted to the Union. Steam traffic increased on the Western rivers. In 1817 a steamboat chugged up the Mississippi to Cincinnati; within two years 60 light-draught stern-wheelers, of the type familiar to readers of Mark Twain, were plying between New Orleans and Louisville. Their freight charges to the upper Ohio valley were less than half the cost of wagon transport thither from Philadelphia and Baltimore. For selfish reasons, Eastern cities would not promote the Western desire for federal roads and canals.

Pennsylvania built her own roads, and later her own canals, and New York in 1817 began the construction of the Erie Canal, which was destined to make New York City outstrip all rival seaports.

Clay and Calhoun persuaded Congress to build a national road from old Fort Cumberland to Wheeling in western Virginia.[1] Connected with Baltimore by a state road, this "national pike" became the most important westward route for emigrants, who traveled on foot, on horseback, and in Conestoga wagons. Congress proposed in 1817 to earmark certain federal revenues for bolder projects of the same sort. President Madison so far had accepted every item in the nationalist program, but here he drew the line and vetoed that internal improvements bill.

2. Western Panic and Missouri Compromise

The usual postwar panic and depression, caused by too great optimism and overextension of credit, began in 1819. The Bank of the United States, which might have put a brake on inflation, was second to none in the scramble for profits. Late in 1818 the directors took overdue steps to curtail credit. Branches were ordered to accept no bills but their own, to present all state bank notes for payment at once, and to renew no personal notes or mortgages. The result was to hasten the inevitable panic; and in 1819 it broke. Many state banks collapsed, and enormous amounts of Western real estate were foreclosed by the B.U.S. At this juncture came the decision in *McCulloch* v. *Maryland,* forbidding states to tax the "monster," as Westerners began to call it. "All the flourishing cities of the West are mortgaged to this money power," declared Senator Benton of Missouri. "They may be devoured by it at any moment. They are in the jaws of the Monster. A lump of butter in the mouth of a dog—one gulp, one swallow, and all is gone!"

Would the panic and the McCulloch case turn the West against nationalism, and some new leader arise to plot secession? Or would West and South shake hands, control the federal government by votes, and turn it against the "money power"? Or would North and West combine? That was anyone's guess.

[1] The National or Cumberland road was later pushed across Ohio and Indiana to Vandalia, Illinois, by successive appropriations between 1822 and 1838; but the federal government relinquished each section, upon its completion, to the state within which it lay. It is now part of national route 40.

Up to 1820 the basic law for the sale of public land was that of 1796. This required alternate townships to be sold in blocks of eight sections, intervening townships in single sections (640 acres), all at auction for an upset price of two dollars an acre, which could be paid by installments within three years. The only important change in this law, in 1800, was to lower the unit of sale to a quarter-section. When Ohio, first state to be hewn out of the national domain, was admitted to the Union in 1803, two important precedents were adopted: the federal government retained all ungranted land within the new state's borders, but donated one section of each township still unsold to a state education fund. Under the Act of 1796, the United States sold, to 1 July 1820, 19.4 million acres for $47.7 million; but some 5.7 million acres were recovered for non-payment of installments, especially during the depression. By the Public Land Act of 1820 credit was stopped, the upset price was lowered to $1.25 an acre, and the minimum unit of sale to 80 acres. This made it easier for a poor man to acquire land, but the West was not satisfied. The panic of 1819 was brief and mild in the East, but hard times lasted in the West until 1824, affording an ideal culture-bed for state rights.

While debt and deflation were producing preliminary symptoms of a vertical cleavage between East and West, the question of slavery extension threatened to cut the Union horizontally into North and South. Ever since the Federal Convention of 1787 there had been a tacit political balance between these two sections, along the old Mason and Dixon's line and the Ohio river. This boundary divided slave-holding states and territories from those in which slavery had been abolished, or was in process of extinction. In 1789 North and South were approximately equal in numbers, but in 1820 the Northern or free states had a population of 5,152,000 with 105 members in the House; whilst the Southern or slave states had 4,485,000 people with 81 congressmen. An even balance had been maintained in the Senate, by the admission of free and slave states alternately, and after the admission of Alabama in 1819 there were eleven of each.

Congress had done nothing to disturb slavery in the territory of the Louisiana purchase, where it existed by French law, and Louisiana entered the Union in 1812 as a slave state. During the westward rush after the war, several thousand slave-owners with their human property moved into the Territory of Upper Louisiana. There they established corn and cotton plantations in the rich bottom lands of the lower Missouri river, or on the west bank of the Mississippi near the old fur-trading town of St. Louis. Thus, when the people of this region claimed admission to the Union as the State of Missouri, slavery was permitted by their proposed state constitution.

In February 1819, a bill admitting Missouri as a state came before the House of Representatives. To the surprise and indignation of Southern members, James Tallmadge of New York offered an amendment prohibiting the further introduction of slaves into Missouri, and requiring that all children subsequently born therein of slave parents should be free at the age of twenty-five. Thus amended, the bill passed the House, but was lost in the Senate.

After Congress adjourned in March, the question of slavery or freedom in Missouri went to the people. In state legislatures, in the newspapers, and in popular mass meetings it was discussed and agitated—not so much as a moral question but as one of sectional power and prestige, yet no less bitterly for that. Northerners had long been dissatisfied with the "federal ratio" which gave the slave states, it was estimated, twenty seats in Congress and twenty electoral votes, based on enumerating human chattels, who could not vote. Northern leaders regarded the admission of Missouri, which lay almost wholly north of the then dividing line between freedom and slavery, as an aggressive move toward increasing the voting power of the South. Southerners were not yet prepared to defend the rightfulness of slavery, but asserted their right to carry their property across the Mississippi. Both sides uttered threats of secession. Surviving Federalist politicians and Republicans of the Middle states saw an opportunity to create a solid North; to "snatch the sceptre from Virginia," as Harrison Gray Otis put it. Thomas Jefferson, who reverted to sectional and pro-slavery feelings as he grew older, was outraged over what he regarded as an attempted revival of Federalism.

When Congress took up the question again in January 1820, fear of a Federalist renaissance caused enough Northern Republicans to defect from antislavery to pass a compromise measure. Missouri was admitted as a slave-holding state, but slavery was prohibited in the territory of the United States north of Missouri's southern boundary, latitude 36° 30'. At the same time, Maine, which had just detached herself from Massachusetts, was admitted to the Union, making twelve free and twelve slave states. This was the famous Missouri Compromise, which put the question of slavery extension at rest for almost a generation. It was a fair solution. The South obtained her immediate object, with the prospect of Arkansas and Florida entering as slave states in the near future; the

North secured the greater expanse of unsettled territory, and maintained the principle of 1787, that Congress could keep slavery out of the Territories if it chose.

Angry passions quickly subsided, the sectional alignment dissolved, and politics resumed their delusive tranquillity. But for a moment the veil had been lifted, and some saw the bloody prospect ahead. "This momentous question, like a fire bell in the night, awakened and filled me with terror," wrote Jefferson. "I considered it at once as the knell of the Union." And John Quincy Adams recorded in his diary, "I take it for granted that the present question is a mere preamble—a title-page to a great, tragic volume."

3. Anglo-American Adjustments

In 1815 there seemed slight hope of a lasting Anglo-American peace. John Quincy Adams considered the treaty that he had negotiated a mere truce because "nothing was adjusted, nothing was settled." Canada's long and vague boundary, rival fur and fishing interests, and fresh-water navies, provided so many points of friction that a leading English banker with American investments wished his government would give Canada back to the Indians. It "was fit for nothing but to breed quarrels."

A good beginning was made by an Anglo-American commercial treaty in 1815, which ended discriminating duties in Britain against United States ships, and vice versa. But the postwar attitude in Britain toward America was defiant, even truculent. Governing classes in England no longer regarded America as a jest, but as a menace to British institutions. That uneasy feeling was largely responsible for sneering strictures upon American life, character, and letters with which English literature abounded during the generation following 1815; an attitude which prevented the common ties of blood and language from having their natural effect.

The three statesmen who did most to preserve peace were President Madison, his successor President Monroe, and Lord Castlereagh, who had done his best, though too late, to prevent the War of 1812. Castlereagh was the first British statesman since Shelburne to regard friendship with America as a permanent interest. His policy was to treat the United States in every respect as an equal, "to smooth all asperities between the two nations, and to unite them in sentiments of good will as well as of substantial interest, with each other." Madison and Monroe met him halfway, but not John Quincy Adams.

He, too, hoped to preserve the peace, but he had a suspicious nature. Harsh and irascible in personal intercourse, Adams made a poor diplomat and as Monroe's secretary of state his notes needed pruning and softening by the now kindly and mellow President. But Adams's perception was abnormally keen, and he alone of contemporaries in either hemisphere foresaw America's future place in the world.

The Treaty of Ghent provided that the contracting parties "use their best endeavors" to abolish the African slave trade. Congress had outlawed the traffic in 1808, and in 1820 declared it to be piracy, punishable by death. But the United States refused to enter any international agreement for joint suppression, because, owing to recent memories of impressment, Adams refused to allow American ships to be searched for slaves by British men-of-war. A squadron of the United States Navy was maintained off the African coast, to watch for slavers flying the American flag; but plenty of enslaved blacks got by under the flag of freedom, into Cuba or the Southern states.

Disarmament on the Great Lakes was the first and most lasting fruit of Anglo-American diplomacy after the war. Peace found each side "armed to the teeth" on the Lakes, especially on Lake Ontario, and building more ships. Two American and two British 74s were on the stocks; and at Kingston, Ontario, a fresh-water battleship designed to carry 110 guns was nearing completion. The Canadians, apprehensive of further American aggression, frustrated in their hope of an Indian satellite state to give them control of the Lakes, expected the British treasury to complete this building program.

It is a national trait to prepare for war only when war comes; and when war is over to disarm. Congress in February 1815 authorized the President to sell or haul out each unit of the Lake fleet not necessary for enforcing the revenue laws, which he promptly did. At the same time the army was reduced to 10,000, and in 1820 to 6000 officers and men. During the summer and fall of 1815 there occurred several "right of search" incidents on the Lakes, and from London came a disquieting rumor that the British government had decided to complete its naval construction program. President Madison then made a momentous proposal. On 16 November 1815 he instructed Adams (then minister to Great Britain) to point out that if each side began competitive building on the Lakes, "vast expense will be incurred and the danger of collision augmented in like degree." He therefore authorized Adams to propose a limitation of naval forces on the Lakes, to "demonstrate their pacific policy." Considering that only fifteen months before President Madison had been a refugee from devastated Washington, this was a rare example of magnanimity.

Castlereagh, after sounding the British cabinet, transferred the formal negotiation to Washington, and on 28 and 29 April 1817 an agreement was effected by an exchange of notes between Charles Bagot, the British minister, and Richard Rush, acting secretary of state. This agreement which the Senate approved, though not a formal treaty, limited the naval force of each country on the Lakes to four single-gun vessels of 100 tons each; one on Lake Ontario, one on Lake Champlain, and two on the upper Lakes; and forbade further naval construction on any of the Lakes. The Rush-Bagot agreement is still in force, modified as to details by mutual agreement, in order to meet newer types of warships.[1]

Disarmament, to be successful, must be a symptom of underlying friendliness, as happened here; though not immediately. The development of mutual respect and good will have been the main forces in keeping this long boundary undefended and unfortified.

First, one had to settle the boundary. Only a scant 200 miles of the easternmost section, from the Bay of Fundy north, had been determined. Several joint commissions for this purpose were provided in the Treaty of Ghent. The first ran the eastern end of the boundary between Eastport, Maine, and Campobello, New Brunswick. The second commission was unable to discover what the treaty of 1783 meant by the "highlands between the St. Lawrence and the Atlantic Ocean." So this major part of the northeastern boundary was referred to the arbitrament of the king of the Netherlands who, pleading similar inability to locate nonexistent highlands, recommended a compromise that the United States refused to accept. The matter was then postponed to the Webster-Ashburton negotiation of 1842. A third joint commission drew the long part of the boundary from latitude 45° up the St. Lawrence and through the Great Lakes, to the Sault Ste. Marie between Huron and Superior; Webster and Ashburton continued it as far as the Lake of the Woods.

[1] In 1838 both sides began to replace sailing revenue cutters by steamers; U.S.S. *Michigan*, an iron paddle-wheel gunboat completed in 1844, remained in commission until 1926. In 1939, when the U.S. Navy had five ships on the Lake, only one armed and the newest 34 years old, it was agreed by exchange of notes with the Canadian foreign minister that both navies could build vessels on the Lakes for oceanic service and maintain a few ships armed with 4-inch guns for training naval reserves. This was extended in 1946 to allow any warships to be sent to the Lakes for training purposes.

At that point the international frontier had been left hanging in mid-air by the treaty of 1783. No line could be drawn "from the Lake of the Woods westerly to the Mississippi," because the source of the Mississippi lay to the eastward and southward of that lake. This problem was dealt with in a fresh Anglo-American treaty of 1818; it extended the boundary along 49° N, latitude of the Lake of the Woods, to the "Stony Mountains."

West of the Rockies, between Spanish California and Russian Alaska, lay a region vaguely known as Oregon. Britain had challenged Spain's exclusive claim to this territory in 1790, but Captain Gray's discovery of the Columbia river mouth in 1792 gave the United States a claim. No real settlements had yet been made, but the Canadian Northwest Company (absorbed by the Hudson's Bay Company in 1821) and J. J. Astor's American Fur Company established trading posts near the mouth of the Columbia. During the War of 1812 the Canadian company purchased Astoria. America's rights were recognized by the Treaty of Ghent, but no agreement could be reached in 1818 as to partition. So Oregon was left open for ten years to the vessels and nationals of the two powers. Before the period ended, the United States had extinguished the claims of Russia and Spain, and in 1827 the agreement for joint Anglo-American occupation was renewed. A final partition was effected in 1846.

The Newfoundland fisheries question was also dealt with in 1818. Although the broad provisions of the treaty of 1783 were not renewed, American fishermen were conceded the right to take, dry, and cure fish, and obtain wood and water, within the three-mile limit on definite parts of the Newfoundland and Labrador coasts. Unfortunately, since diplomats had very slight knowledge of codfishing, certain privileges which American fishermen considered essential, such as purchasing bait, were not accorded; and the efforts of the Newfoundland government strictly to enforce the treaty produced a series of brawls and an almost continual diplomatic controversy until 1910. The Hague tribunal then gave an arbitral decision which put that question to sleep.

The dreary subject of American trade with the British West Indies still caused friction, despite the fact that this line of commerce was becoming less and less important. It remained for Andrew Jackson's administration to settle that question. But there was no bar to American sailing vessels in other parts of the world. They went everywhere. Edward Trelawny, Shelley's friend, describes a visit that he and the poet made to the waterfront of Leghorn in 1822. Ships of almost every nation were at the docks. The two friends first visited a Greek coaster, so ill-kept that Shelley said she suggested hell rather than Hellenism. They then boarded an American clipper schooner, of so graceful a model that they thought a poet must have designed her. Let Trelawny describe the visit, and what the Yankee mate said:

> I said we wished to build a boat after her model. "Then I calculate you must go to Baltimore or Boston to get one; there is no one on this side the water who can do the job. We have our freight all ready, and are homeward-bound; we have elegant accommodation, and you will be across before your young friend's beard is ripe for a razor. Come down, and take an observation of the state cabin." It was about seven and a half feet by five; "plenty of room to live or die comfortably in," he observed, and then pressed us to have a chaw of real old Virginian cake, *i.e.* tobacco, and a cool drink of peach brandy. . . . I seduced Shelley into drinking a wine-glass of weak grog, the first and last he ever drank. The Yankee would not let us go until we had drunk, under the star-spangled banner, to the memory of Washington, and the prosperity of the American commonwealth. "As a warrior and statesman," said Shelley, "he was righteous in all he did, unlike all who lived before or since; he never used his power but for the benefit of his fellow-creatures."
>
> "Stranger," said the Yankee, "truer words were never spoken; there is dry rot in all the main timbers of the Old World, and none of you will do any good till you are docked, refitted, and annexed to the New."

Those Yankee ships took no back wind from anyone. Lord Byron, sailing near the Dardanelles in H.M.S. *Salsette,* was on deck when the frigate almost fouled an American trader. Captain Walter Bathurst RN hailed her "and with the dignity of a lord, asked him where he came from, and the name of his ship." Byron was delighted with the reply: "You copper-bottomed sarpent, I guess you'll know when I've reported you to Congress!"

On the southeastern border, Anglo-American peace was gravely endangered. Florida was still a Spanish province, but Spanish authority was little exercised beyond the three fortified posts of Pensacola, St. Marks, and St. Augustine. There a situation developed not unlike that of 1811 in the Northwest. There was meddling with the Indians on the American side of

the boundary, not by Spaniards but by individual British traders. The Seminole were cultivated by an elderly Scot named
Arbuthnot, who owned a trading schooner named *Chance*. He
gained the Indians' friendship, became their informal protector, and suggested the dangerous notion that Andrew Jackson's
treaty of 1814 with the Upper Creeks was voided by the
Treaty of Ghent. And Arbuthnot's companion, a young adventurer named Ambrister, joined a group of Seminoles and
maroons on the Suwannee river, under a chief called Bowlegs.
Independent of English activities, frontier hostilities broke out
in the fall of 1817, owing largely to Indian resentment of the
United States Army's pretension to hunt runaway slaves on
the Spanish side of the border. In the course of these brawls,
some white settlers on the American side were scalped, and a
detachment of forty officers and men on their way to reinforce
Fort Scott were ambushed on the Apalachicola river and killed.
General Andrew Jackson and a force of Tennessee militia,
under federal orders, now burst into Spanish Florida like
avenging demons, marched into St. Marks (7 April 1818) and
hauled down the Spanish flag. Jackson arrested Arbuthnot,
and had the two Seminole chiefs, who had refuged there,
hanged. Next he pushed through a gloomy forest festooned
with Spanish moss to surprise Bowlegs at the Suwannee river.
The Indians escaped to the Everglades. Jackson, furious and
baffled, learned the cause of their escape when Ambrister
blundered into his camp with a letter from Arbuthnot warning
Bowlegs of Jackson's approach, and offering him ten kegs of
gunpowder. The general promptly set up a court-martial to
try Arbuthnot for espionage and Ambrister for actively leading Indians in war against the United States. Both were found
guilty and executed.

The Seminoles' power was broken for the time being, but
Jackson was not through. After another quick march through
the jungle, Pensacola was taken (25 May), the Spanish governor
ejected, and the fortress garrisoned with Americans. Jackson
then returned to Tennessee, acclaimed a hero by Westerners.
But in Washington, senators thought of Roman history and
trembled; Henry Clay reminded Congress that "it was in the
provinces that were laid the seeds of the ambitious projects
that overturned the liberties of Rome." Calhoun, the secretary
of war, and an excellent one (it was he who revived the moribund military academy at West Point by appointing Major
Sylvanus Thayer superintendent in 1817), wanted the aggressive general to be court-martialed, or at least reprimanded.
John Quincy Adams alone of the cabinet ministers took the

ground that Jackson's acts were justified by the incompetence of Spanish authority to police its own territory, and Adams had his way.

When the news reached London, the press rang with denunciation of the "ruffian" who had murdered two "peaceful British traders." Public opinion demanded instant apology and reparation, or war. "The firmness of Lord Castlereagh under the emergency," wrote the American minister, Richard Rush, was the main reason why no war occurred. Unmoved by public clamor, the foreign secretary calmly examined the documents from Washington, and decided that the "unfortunate sufferers" had been engaged in such practices "as to have deprived them of any claim on their own government for interference."

There was no need to repeat Jackson's warning. His invasion of Florida convinced Madrid that this province, which it had neglected for three centuries, had better be sold before it was seized. Accordingly, Spain ceded all her lands east of the Mississippi, together with her claims to the Oregon country, in return for $5 million on 22 February 1819. In addition, the boundary between the United States and Mexico, which lasted until 1846, was determined.

Castlereagh's life ended in September 1822. He did more for Anglo-American friendship than any other statesman of the century. George Canning, his successor, was spoiling for another round with the same adversary he had beaten in 1809. Five new American nations had come into existence. Let them be linked up with British America, and the United States stew in their vaunted isolation!

4. The Monroe Doctrine

There were only two independent nations in the New World in 1815, the United States and Haiti. The next seven years saw an eruption of new republics in South America, a revolution comparable only to what has happened in Africa since 1957. An unstable situation, rich in possibilities of trouble, had been created. Anything might happen—armed intervention by the European Holy Alliance, new balance of power, an Anglo-American entente, or a Pan-American alliance. Out of the confusion of voices came one clear note: the Monroe Doctrine, to which the policy of the United States respecting Latin America has ever since been tuned, although redefined from time to time to meet new conditions or Latin American susceptibilities.

The Latin American nations, excepting Brazil,[1] acquired their independence under unfortunate circumstances which rendered almost impossible their union on the United States model. Spanish America began to enjoy preparation for self-government in the enlightened reign of Carlos III (1759–88). Then the French Revolution spoiled everything; and Ferdinand VII, the monarch restored in 1814, was such an imbecile that the colonies had to strike for independence. Since there had been no prior movement for colonial union, as in North America, all Spanish provinces became *de facto* independent, their commerce was thrown open to the world and their intellect to modern ideas. Ferdinand demanded unconditional submission from all South American leaders, which they refused. The king, however, had an army and a fleet. By 1816 he had reduced all the *de facto* states but La Plata (the Argentine) and had restored the Spanish colonial system. José de San Martín kept the revolutionary flame alive in a remote province of La Plata, among a population not unlike the North American frontiersmen. In January 1817 he began his famous march across the Andes with 3500 men, to defeat a royalist army at Chacabuco on the Pacific slope. Chile now organized as a republic under Bernardo O'Higgins, son of an Irish officer in the Spanish service. In the meantime, Simón Bolívar had spread revolution up the Orinoco valley and created the Republic of Great Colombia, comprising the present Colombia, Panama, Ecuador, and Venezuela.

Recognition of their independence at Washington was naturally expected by the new republics. Henry Clay, in an oration describing the "glorious spectacle of eighteen millions of people struggling to burst their chains and be free," gave the lead to North American opinion. Yet Clay's eloquence had slight effect on Monroe's administration, especially on John Quincy Adams, who "wished well" to the new republics, but saw "no prospect that they would establish free or liberal institutions of government. Arbitrary power, military and ecclesiastical, was stamped upon their habits, and upon all their institutions. Civil dissension was infused into all their seminal principles."

This attitude, together with fear of offending Spain while the Florida treaty was pending, explains the cautious policy of Monroe's administration toward the Latin Americans. Their independence was desired as an additional bulwark for American isolation, but not with sufficient ardor to risk a European

[1] Portugal may be said to have seceded from Brazil, rather than the contrary; after Portugal had gone liberal, a senior branch of the House of Braganza continued to rule in Brazil, 1822–89.

war. Monroe and Adams did not entertain the remotest idea of forming a Pan-American league with the United States at the head. As long as Europe did not actively intervene, they were content to stand aside and let Spain fight it out with her former colonies; but they would certainly oppose any general European attempt to interfere. So Gallatin, now American minister at Paris, informed the French foreign minister in June 1823.

Castlereagh, and after him Canning, were at one with the American government in that feeling, but at variance in every other aspect of policy toward Latin America. British exports to South America in 1822 surpassed those to the United States. British commercial houses were established in South American ports, mining concessions were obtained by British subjects in several countries, and loans of the new republics were floated in London.

In 1821, events in Spanish America began to march with a rapidity that forced the North American hand. The Argentine and Chile, having established their independence, went to the aid of Peru, San Martín leading an army, the Chilean navy co-operating under Admiral Cochrane. Bolívar, at the same time, was rolling up Spanish armies westward from the Orinoco, consolidating liberated territory in the Great Colombian Republic. In 1822, when Bolívar and San Martín met in Guayaquil, only one Spanish army was left in the field, and that surrendered after the battle of Ayacucho. A mutiny in the Spanish garrison at Vera Cruz forced the Spanish viceroy to accept a provisional treaty for the independence of Mexico, including Central America. Thus, by the autumn of 1822, continental America from Great Lakes to Cape Horn was independent, and all except Mexico and Brazil were republican. Europeans retained control only in Belize, Bolivia, and the Guianas.

In his message of 8 March 1822, President Monroe declared that the new governments of La Plata, Chile, Peru, Colombia, and Mexico were "in the full enjoyment of their independence," of which there was "not the most remote prospect of their being deprived," and that they had "a claim to recognition by other powers." Congress then appropriated money to defray the expenses of "such missions to the independent nations on the American continent as the President might deem proper." Diplomatic relations were shortly after established with these five nations.

France invaded Spain in 1823, with the object of delivering Ferdinand VII from a liberal constitution that he had been forced to accept. It was a matter of common talk that a

Franco-Spanish expeditionary force to South America would follow this military promenade. The possibility that this, too, would succeed, made the British government apprehensive. So it happened that on 16 August 1823, Canning at the foreign office put a question to Richard Rush, the American minister at London, that started wheels revolving in the United States. What did Mr. Rush think his government would say to going hand in hand with England to bar France from South America? Rush's dispatches embodying the conversation arrived in Washington in October 1823. President Monroe sent copies to Jefferson and Madison. The covering letter stated his own opinion that Canning's overture should be accepted.

Jefferson, then eighty years old, was in placid retirement at Monticello. Horace and Tacitus, he wrote to the President, were so much more interesting than the newspapers that he was out of touch with public affairs. But this question of cooperation with Great Britain was "the most momentous which has ever been offered to my contemplation since that of Independence. . . . America, North and South, has a set of interests distinct from those of Europe, and peculiarly her own. . . . One nation, most of all, could disturb us in this pursuit; she now offers to lead, aid and accompany us in it. . . . With her then, we should most sedulously cherish a cordial friendship." And Madison, from Montpelier, gave similar advice, adding that he was in favor of an additional Anglo-American declaration to support Greek independence.

Three white-haired statesmen, each on his Virginia hilltop (for Monroe was now at Oak Hill), pondering a vital question of foreign policy: what a delightful aroma of antique republicanism! Hard-boiled Adams, however, came up with a different idea. Strongly nationalist, ever suspicious of England, at the next cabinet meeting in Washington (7 November 1823) he declared, "It would be more candid, as well as more dignified, to avow our principles explicitly to Great Britain and France, than to come in as a cockboat in the wake of the British man-of-war." For Adams, moreover, the big question transcended Latin America. Russia in 1821 claimed that Alaska extended to latitude 51° N, well within the Oregon country, and closed to foreigners the waters thence to Bering Strait. Adams believed that colonial establishments were immoral and destined to fall, and that the New World should now be considered closed to further colonization by European powers. On 17 July 1823 he told the Russian minister so, explicitly. Then, in October, the Russian minister at Washington communicated to Adams a note that contained remarks on "expiring republicanism" which were as offensive to the American government then as were Khrushchev's remarks about "burying" us, over a century later.

As Adams saw it, his government had been challenged on four points, which could be answered at once: (1) the proposal of Anglo-American co-operation; (2) rumored European intervention in Latin America; (3) Russian extension of her colonial establishments, and (4) the czar's denunciation of republican principles. "I remarked," Adams wrote of the cabinet meeting of 7 November, "that the communications lately received from the Russian Minister afforded, as I thought, a very suitable and convenient opportunity for us to take our stand against the Holy Alliance, and at the same time to decline the overture of Great Britain."

Monroe agreed in principle, but vacillated between doing nothing in fear of the Holy Alliance, and carrying the war into Turkey, to aid the Greeks. Their struggle for independence had aroused immense interest, because the Greek language and literature were then basic in the education of American gentlemen. South Carolina petitioned Congress to acknowledge Greek independence; Albert Gallatin proposed to lend Greece a fleet; William Cullen Bryant wrote *The Greek Partisan;* the martyrs of Chios and the exploits of Ypsilanti were commemorated in the names of frontier hamlets; classic colonnades were added to modest farm-houses. All this struck a chord in Monroe's kindly heart; in his annual message to Congress of 1822 he remarked, "The mention of Greece fills the mind with the most exalted sentiments and arouses in our bosoms the best feelings of which our nature is susceptible." In the first draft of his epoch-making message, the President proposed to acknowledge the independence of Greece, and to ask Congress to provide for a diplomatic mission to Athens. Against this meddling in European affairs Adams argued vehemently. He wished "to make an *American* cause and adhere inflexibly to that."

In the end Adams had his own way. Monroe consented to omit all but a pious wish for the success of Greece, but he forced Adams to delete a high-pitched exposition of republican principles. The passages on foreign relations in Monroe's annual message of 2 December 1823, although written in more concise language than Adams would have used, expressed the basic conception of his secretary of state. We may summarize this original Monroe Doctrine in the President's own words:

1. Positive principles: (a) "The American continents, by the free and independent condition which they have assumed and maintain, are henceforth not to be considered as subjects for future colonization by any European powers." (b) "The

political system of the allied powers is essentially different . . . from that of America . . . We should consider any attempt on their part to extend their system to any portion of this hemisphere as dangerous to our peace and safety."

2. Negative principles: (a) "With the existing colonies or dependencies of any European power we have not interfered and shall not interfere." (b) "In the wars of the European powers in matters relating to themselves we have never taken any part, nor does it comport with our policy so to do."

Therein is the whole of President Monroe's doctrine, whatever later developments may be included under the name of the Monroe Doctrine. Critics of Monroe have pointed out that his message was a mere declaration, which in itself could not prevent an intervention which had already been given up; that in view of the exclusive power of Congress to declare war, a mere presidential announcement could not guarantee Latin American independence. That may be true, but is irrelevant. What Adams was trying to do, and what he and Monroe accomplished, was to raise a standard of American foreign policy for all the world to see; and to plant it so firmly in the

HUNTERS OF KENTUCKY

You've heard, I s'pose, how New Or-leans is
There's girls of ev'-ry hue, it seems, from

fam'd for wealth and beau-ty, So Pack-en-ham he
snow-y white to soot-y.

made his brags, if he in fight was luck-y, He'd

have their girls and cot-ton bags, In spite of old Ken-tuck-y.

Oh, Ken-tuck-y! the hunt-ers of Ken-tuck-y.

national consciousness that no later President would dare to pull it down.

By this time the Era of Good Feelings was over. When the year 1824 dawned, no fewer than five candidates who claimed to represent the Jeffersonian tradition were jockeying for the presidency. John Quincy Adams who, more than any other man, was responsible for the Monroe Doctrine, won; but his presidential administration was the unhappiest in history for the incumbent.

VI

Second Adams and First Jackson Administrations

1825-1833

1. *A Minority President*

AMERICA WAS FAR MORE INTERESTED in the coming presidential election of 1824 than in the Monroe Doctrine or the Holy Alliance. The Jeffersonian Republican party was breaking up into factions, and it was anyone's guess how they would divide or blend to make new parties. Three members of President Monroe's cabinet and two others aspired to the succession. John Quincy Adams, secretary of state, qualified by faithful and efficient public service for thirty years, wanted it. William H. Crawford of Georgia, secretary of the treasury, wanted it very much, and thought that he should have it since his nomination by a congressional caucus made him officially the party candidate; but this hardly counted, since the caucus was attended by only one-quarter of the Republican senators and congressmen. Henry Clay, speaker of the House, placed in nomination by the legislature of his native Kentucky, once said that he would "rather be right than be president," but now he wanted to be President. As advocate of the "American System" he made a wide appeal, and his charming personality made him everyone's second choice. But Clay had a Western rival, General Andrew Jackson, senator from Tennessee, whose legislature nominated him for the presidency. John C. Calhoun, secretary of war, was the favorite son of South Carolina; but after Jackson's strength in the Southwest became evident, Calhoun consented to be nominated for the vice presidency, expecting to be next in line for the top.

The presidential campaign of 1824 was quiet and seemly. All four candidates stood for about the same thing, none electioneered actively, and the newspapers were decent. But no one obtained a majority in the electoral college. The framers of the Constitution expected this situation to occur more often than not; but it has never happened again in a century and a half.

Adams carried New England, received 26 of New York's 36 votes, and picked up a few elsewhere, making a total of 84. Crawford carried only Virginia and his native Georgia, but obtained a few scattered electoral votes which put him ahead of Henry Clay for third place; and, according to the Constitution, only the first three could be candidates for the final election by the House. Jackson showed surprising strength. He ran away with Pennsylvania, New Jersey, the Carolinas, and most of the South and West, with a total of 99, still short of a majority but an impressive plurality; and in states where electors were chosen by the voters he had three votes to Clay's one. Politicians all asked each other, what did this mean? They would soon learn.

The election of a President now had to be made by the House of Representatives, voting by states, a majority of states being necessary for choice. So when Congress convened in January 1825, the corridors of the Capitol, and the streets, barrooms, and boardinghouses of Washington became scenes of personal conferences, sly offers, and noncommittal replies, as backers of Jackson and Adams tried to work up a majority for their respective candidates. Crawford, who had suffered a paralytic stroke, was no longer considered. Jackson had eleven states in the bag, but needed two more. Adams had seven states, and needed six more. Clay, no longer a candidate himself, controlled the votes of three states; and, after it was half understood, half promised that if Adams were elected Clay would be secretary of state, he threw all three for the New Englander. James Buchanan of Pennsylvania had already tried to make a similar deal between Clay and Jackson but failed. Adams still needed three more. Missouri and Illinois, which had voted for Jackson, were now represented each by one congressman, who were "conciliated" (Jackson men said "bought") by Adams. Doubtful Maryland members who still called themselves Federalists were assured that Adams, if elected, would not take revenge on that dying party for what it had done to him and his father. And so it happened that on 9 February 1825 the House on its first ballot elected John Quincy Adams President of the United States, by a majority of one state.

It was a barren victory, although perfectly legal and constitutional. The cry "We was robbed!" at once went up from the Jackson forces, and active electioneering for 1828 began.

John Quincy Adams had shown signal ability in political finagling, but he was a lonely, inarticulate person unable to express his burning love of country in any manner to kindle the popular imagination. Short, thick-set, with a massive bald head and rheumy eyes, his port was stern and his manners unconciliatory. His concessions were ungraceful, and his refusals were harsh. A lonely walk before dawn, or an early morning swim in summer, fitted him for the day's toil, which he concluded by writing his perennial diary. Even in his own New England Adams was respected rather than loved, and other sections resented his election over favorite sons. Senator Benton of Missouri, with a wild plunge into what he believed to be Greek, said it violated the *demos krateo* principle. When Adams defiantly gave Clay the state department, the cry "Corrupt bargain!" was raised; Randolph of Roanoke called it "the combination unheard of till then, of the puritan with the blackleg." There followed a duel between Randolph and Clay; fortunately both were bad shots.

Woodrow Wilson, another stern President elected by a minority, built up a personal following by appointments as well as oratory. But Adams was no orator, and he refused to make appointments to cultivate the support of journalists; and in that day, before highly developed ward politics (not to speak of radio and TV) newspapers could make or break a President. Although Crawford had opened the way to the spoils system in the four-year tenure-of-office act of 1820, Adams would have none of it; he reappointed men who had worked against him, and, when vacancies occurred, appointed Jackson men to prove his public virtue. That was the road to political suicide.

President Adams's major mistake was to trim his sails to nationalism after the wind had changed, and to refuse to come about. A sentence in his first annual message: "The great object of the institution of civil government is the improvement of those who are parties to the social compact," is the keynote of his domestic policy. To "slumber in indolence" would be "to cast away the bounties of Providence and doom ourselves to perpetual inferiority." He would use the ample federal revenue to increase the navy, build national roads and canals, send out scientific expeditions, establish institutions of learning and research, and make Washington the national cultural center. All these things were to come; Adams was a true prophet; but he urged them in the midst of a state rights reaction. If, asked the cotton states, we admit federal powers of this scope, will not some future administration claim the power to emancipate slaves?

In foreign affairs, the outstanding conflict in Adams's administration was the pulling and hauling between him and George Canning, the British foreign minister, for the favor of new Latin American republics. We had got the jump on England with the Monroe Doctrine; Canning made the next move by recognizing all the new republics early in 1825. The United States had already recognized six of them, but they accepted that as a right from a sister republic; from the king of Great Britain it was an honor, an accolade. Canning wrote jubilantly, "Spanish America is free, and if we do not mismanage our affairs sadly, she is English, and *novus saeculorum nascitur ordo*," a new era is born—quoting the very motto on the Great Seal of the United States.

President Adams's policy toward Latin America was honest and cautious. He wished to obtain commercial treaties on the basis of most-favored-nation, to encourage the new nations to observe republican principles and live at peace among themselves, and to discourage them from provoking Spain by attacking the *sempre fidel isla* of Cuba.

Mexico, largest and most conservative of the new republics, having many points of possible friction with the United States and a pressing need for capital and markets that England could best supply, was the most promising ground for British influence. President Adams appointed as the first United States minister to Mexico Joel R. Poinsett, an accomplished gentleman from South Carolina who spoke fluent Spanish, had visited Mexico, and written a short book about it. He appeared to be the ideal choice, but made a mess of his mission for want of judgment and superfluity of zeal, that quality fatal to diplomatists. The Republican party in Mexico, eager to establish York rite Masonic lodges in opposition to Scottish rite lodges then being used by the British and the monarchists, persuaded Poinsett to obtain York rite charters for new lodges. All Mexico became divided into *Escoceses* and *Yorkinos;* civil war broke out, and Poinsett's name became the rallying point for one party and the target for the other. The Scots won, and Poinsett was recalled under a cloud. But his mission was not wholly fruitless, for he brought home cuttings of the scarlet flower which botanists named *Poinsettia pulcherrima* after him.

At the Panama Congress of 1826, Canning scored again. Bolívar the Liberator summoned this meeting to promote the unity of Latin America and to work out a common policy toward Spain. He disliked the United States and intended to leave her out, but to invite England in the hope that she might become leader of a Latin American league. Mexico and Colombia, however, invited President Adams to send delegates, and he accepted. He hoped to convince the new republics of North American friendship, to dissuade them from "liberating" Cuba and Puerto Rico, and to adopt his favorite principles of most-favored-nation and freedom of the seas. To cover the cost of sending delegates, he appealed for an appropriation to Congress, where vehement opposition developed. Jackson supporters regarded the Panama Congress as a gala performance invented by Henry Clay to dazzle the public mind and enhance the administration's prestige. Congress finally voted the money and the Senate confirmed the President's appointments, but too late for the two American delegates to arrive in time. The Congress accomplished nothing, to be sure; but the British delegate who attended made the United States, in comparison, appear coldly indifferent. Fortunately this dangerous rivalry, which might have made Central America the Balkans of the New World, ended with the death of Canning in 1827.

Many things recommended by President Adams were thus rudely rejected by Congress but adopted years later. For instance, he wanted, as a beginning to making Washington a cultural center, a national astronomical observatory; and, hoping to give it constitutional grounds, he described observatories as "lighthouses of the sky." That phrase was kicked about in Congress as if uttered by a halfwit. He recommended the establishment of a naval academy, and that touched off old Jeffersonian prejudices. Representative Lemuel Sawyer of North Carolina predicted that the glamour of a naval education would "produce degeneracy and corruption of the public morality and change our simple Republican habits"; Senator William Smith of South Carolina, after pointing out that neither Julius Caesar nor Lord Nelson attended a naval academy, predicted that American bluejackets "would look with contempt upon trifling or effeminate leaders," such as a naval school might produce. Not until the eve of the Mexican War did Congress create the United States Naval Academy at Annapolis.

Watchers from afar can discern the shadow of things to come in 1826, midway in President Adams's term of office. The Erie Canal, completed the previous year, made New York the Empire State and New York City the world's most populous urban center. Yet the doom of the canal as a principal means of heavy transportation was sounded in 1826 by a little horse-drawn line, first railroad in the United States, built near the home of the Adamses in Quincy; and shortly the Baltimore & Ohio steam railway would be chartered. In 1826 J. Fenimore Cooper published *The Last of the Mohicans*, which strengthened the "noble red man" theme in literature, without helping the Indians. The same year an obscure preacher named Charles G. Finney was conducting a religious revival in the Mohawk valley which eventually fed the anti-slavery movement. In 1826 Josiah Holbrook founded the American lyceum, a scheme for "the public diffusion of knowledge" through lectures by experts in scientific and cultural subjects; this fathered the Chautauquas, forums, and adult education movements. The American Home Missionary Society was organized in 1826 to carry the gospel to the frontier and the immigrant. George Bancroft, destined to become America's favorite historian, spoke on the Fourth of July in favor of "a determined, uncompromising democracy." And on that same Glorious Fourth, there occurred an event which for a moment fused the jarring factions of American life into one great, loving family.

The lives of Thomas Jefferson and John Adams, the one eighty-three and the other ninety years old, were flickering to a close. Could they live until the Fourth, fiftieth anniversary of the adoption of that great Declaration for which they were jointly responsible? All America was praying that they would. As midnight of 3–4 July approached, Jefferson at Monticello returned to consciousness for the last time. He murmured to a kinsman at his bedside, "This is the Fourth?" The young man nodded assent, Jefferson heaved a sigh of content that proved to be his last utterance, and at noon breathed his last. At that moment the house of John Adams at Quincy was shaken by the blasts of saluting cannon, and watchers by his bedside could hear the roar of approval in the town square when an orator flung out the sentiment given to him by the old gentleman—"Independence forever!" The dying patriot seemed trying to speak; and his granddaughter who bent her ear close, caught between gasps the whispered words, "Thomas

—Jefferson—still—surv—." He lingered until the tide turned, and crossed the bar at sunset.

Forgotten for a time were party struggles and rivalries of other days. Americans thought of Saul and Jonathan, "Lovely and pleasant in their lives; and in their death they were not divided; they were swifter than eagles, they were stronger than lions."

2. Election of 1828

John Quincy Adams's campaign for re-election began even before he was inaugurated President, and there was little let-up during the next four years. The election of 1828 was simpler than that of 1824 because there were only two candidates. Just as the Jeffersonian and Hamilton factions of 1791 were the nuclei of the Republican and Federalist parties, so the Jackson-Calhoun and Adams-Clay factions of 1823–28 were developing into the Democratic and Whig parties that occupied the political stage until the eve of the Civil War.

National political parties in the United States are generally of local origin, and never completely lose their basic character as a bundle of local factions and interests. In this instance, the impulse for the election of Jackson came largely from state politicians seeking national power. During the Era of Good Feelings, the Republican party within each state was breaking up into conservative and democratic factions. Generally speaking, the democratic group wished to level down such political inequalities as still remained, especially property qualifications for the franchise, thus diluting the electorate with elements susceptible to a more emotional appeal than those of the Jeffersonian school. Another effect was to breed a new litter of professional politicians, among whom enjoyment of state office and patronage created a brisk appetite for the more luscious emoluments of federal power. The best of these men represented some genuine aspiration toward equality, the worst were mere demagogues; but at the head of them were able men of lowly origin but ingratiating form and phrase, such as Martin Van Buren of New York and James Buchanan of Pennsylvania. Their political strategy was to join hands with democratic factions in other states, under some national figure who would reflect glory on themselves and lead them to victory. Adams, stiff and scrupulous, was no leader for such as these; Calhoun, the Carolina highbrow, was little better; and Clay's lot was now cast with the President. General Jackson, hero of New Orleans and subjugator of the Creek nation, was a man who could be counted on to reward friends and punish enemies, a heaven-sent leader for this new democracy.

It did not matter that there was no national issue or popular grievance; the politicians would see to that, and principles could be attended to after victory. Adams must be discredited. The "corrupt bargain" charge, engineered by Buchanan, was the opening gun of the Jackson campaign. Next came the attack on Adams's motives for promoting the Panama Congress. Pro-Jackson men won a majority in mid-term congressional elections. Investigations of alleged presidential corruption were started but not pushed home, so that the victim had no chance to clear himself. Van Buren admits in his *Autobiography*, "Adams was an honest man, not only incorruptible himself, but an enemy to venality in every department of the public service." Yet Van Buren was the first to prefer charges of outrageous corruption against the President. The South, now in full tide of reaction against nationalism, was assured that Jackson would defend state rights. The West's loyalty to Henry Clay was impaired by Adams's professed intention to administer the public lands on business principles, rather than squander them on shiftless squatters. Richard Rush, who became Adams's secretary of the treasury after his return from London, reported that the low price of government land was a "bounty in favor of agricultural pursuits." That sort of talk won no votes in the West. Adams counted on income from the sale of public land to finance far-reaching plans for exploring expeditions and scientific research. The West cared for none of that, but cheap land it must have.

This election of 1828 was the first presidential one that really smelled. The most absurd lies were spread. Adams had furnished the White House at his own expense with a billiard table and a set of chessmen; in the mouth of a Jackson orator these became "gaming tables and gambling furniture" purchased from public funds. He was even accused of playing pimp to the emperor of Russia. Newspapers that supported Adams, however, were not idle; there was a "coffin hand-bill" on the shooting of six militiamen by Jackson for insubordination; and the general's frontier brawls and alleged premarital relations with Mrs. Jackson were described in detail. Altogether, it was the most degrading presidential election the United States had ever experienced. Worse, however, were to come.

Jackson polled 56 per cent of the popular vote, carried the Southern and Western states, Pennsylvania, and most of New York, winning 178 electoral votes to Adams's 83. Virginia held her aristocratic nose and voted for Jackson, believing him the lesser evil; South Carolina voted for him as a state rights man, which she soon had reason to regret. But in the last instance it was classes rather than sections that elected Jackson: The Southern hunters and backwoods farmers whom he had led to glory, and the Northern democracy, tired of respectable, gentlemanly promotions from cabinet to White House. They cared little for policies, but much for personality, and they voted for Jackson because he was their sort of man. After all, the most sophisticated among us have often no better reason for voting as we do than had the American democracy of 1828, in exalting a man of their own sort; ill-educated, intolerant, yet professing the immortal principles of the Declaration of Independence and, though a state rights man, completely devoted to the Union. Nor was the democracy disappointed.

John Quincy Adams never understood why he was spurned by the country he loved with silent passion, rejected by the people he had served so faithfully. In the four sad months between election and the end of his term, there kept running through his head the refrain of an old song he had first heard at the court of Versailles: *Richard O mon Roi, l'univers t'abandonne*—"The whole wide world has abandoned thee."

Yet this was not the end for Adams. The noblest part of his long career lay ahead.

3. Jacksonian Democracy

We are now in an age of great political figures. Adams, Clay, Webster, Van Buren, and Calhoun were statesmen of whom any age or country could be proud; and the man who towered above them in popularity and gave his name to an era was Major General Andrew Jackson. "Old Hickory" as he was nicknamed by the press, "The Gineral," as his intimates called him, "reigned," as his enemies called his occupancy of the White House, for two terms. He practically appointed his successor, Martin Van Buren; and, after one term of Whig opposition, democracy returned to the saddle in the person of James K. Polk, "Young Hickory," who was followed by Zachary Taylor, a tired old general who died in office, and a colorless vice president. Then came two Democratic Presidents who had been spoon-fed by Jackson—Franklin Pierce and James Buchanan. And that brings us to the great American tragedy.

Thus, Andrew Jackson and the brand of democracy associated with him dominated the political scene from 1828 to the Civil War. And they set a pattern of American politics which, with surprisingly few changes, has persisted into the second half of the twentieth century. People with long memories frequently compared Franklin D. Roosevelt and Harry Truman to Andrew Jackson, and both Presidents regarded this as a compliment. So, what was Jacksonian Democracy, and what manner of man was Andrew Jackson?

Jacksonian Democracy was the upsurge of a new generation of recently enfranchised voters against a somewhat ossified Jeffersonian Republican party. It was a national movement in that it opposed disunion and knew no geographical limits; Jackson men in Maine and Louisiana uttered the same clichés in spell-binding oratory and deplored the same largely imaginary sins of their opponents. But it was antinational in rejecting Henry Clay's "American System." That is, it wanted roads, canals, and (in a few years) railroads to be chartered and aided by the states, but no federal government messing into them or sharing the expected profits. Jacksonian Democracy believed in equality only for white men; it was far less charitable toward the Indian and the black than its "aristocratic" opponents. It was not "leveling" in the European sense, having no desire to pull down men of wealth to a common level; but it wanted a fair chance for every man to rise. In the states, Jackson Democrats sometimes, but not invariably, favored free public education and a somewhat cautious humanitarianism, but dissociated themselves from most of the "isms" of the period, such as abolition, feminism, and Mormonism. In general, they shared that contempt for intellect which is one of the unlovely traits of democracy everywhere. There was no contact between the political democracy of Jackson and the philosophical democracy of such men as Emerson; and the efforts of a few intellectuals (such as Theodore Sedgwick III and Robert Rantoul, Jr.) to bridge the gap were ineffective. Of the greater literary figures of this era, only Nathaniel Hawthorne and, in a half-hearted way, James Fenimore Cooper were Democrats, and President Jackson could not have cared less. His attitude toward literature may be gauged by a letter he wrote late in life to President Polk, urging that his old crony Amos Kendall be appointed to the Madrid legation, then held by an eminent American author. "There can be no delicacy in recalling Erwin," he wrote; "he is only fit to write a book and scarcely that." He could not even remember Washington Irving's correct name! The jackass as symbol of the Democratic party was first used by the Whigs as a satire on the supposed ignorance of Old Hickory, and it is significant that the party not only joyfully accepted this emblem but has retained it to this day.

With that bland inconsistency so characteristic of politicians, Jackson cultivated the old Federalists, whom Adams had always kept at arm's length, and even won over the sons of Alexander Hamilton. Alexis de Tocqueville, an observant young Frenchman who toured the United States in 1831, had a talk with Charles Carroll of Carrollton, last survivor of the signers of the Declaration of Independence. He then reflected, "This race of men is disappearing, after providing America with her greatest men. With them is lost the tradition of cultivated manners. The people become educated, knowledge extends, a middling ability becomes common. Outstanding talents and great characters are more rare. Society is less brilliant and more prosperous." But there was a good side to all this. The common man gained active participation in government at all but the highest levels, and public education was provided for his children—if he were white and free.

One amusing sign of the times was a new appetite for political and military titles. Before Jackson came to Washington, nobody thought of addressing officials under the President as anything but plain "Mr." But from now on, every man had to be "Senator" this, "Mr. Secretary" or "Governor" that; or, if he had nothing better, his rank in the state militia. As W. S. Gilbert parodied this phenomenon,

> When every one is somebodee
> Then no one's anybody.

Jacksonian Democracy catered to mediocrity, diluted politics with the incompetent and the corrupt, and made conditions increasingly unpleasant for gentlemen in public life. The party caucus, the stump speech, the herding and mass-voting of drunks and helpless immigrants by city bosses, became standard practices in Jackson's time, although curious students can find a few earlier instances. But there was nothing low or vulgar about Jackson himself; he was one of nature's gentlemen. And although we think of him as peculiarly and exclusively American, his friend Martin Van Buren, when minister to Great Britain, found Jackson's likeness in the "Iron Duke," Wellington.

"Old Hickory," rough-hewn out of live-oak, accustomed to command and to be obeyed, quick to anger and slow to forgive, had a fine sense of honor, and a gallant attitude toward "the fair," as he called the other sex. Born on the Carolina frontier in 1767 to immigrant parents from Northern Ireland, he had risen to be a successful lawyer in Tennessee and acquired lands, slaves, and blooded horses. But he had none of the touchiness about slavery that was common among the Southern politicians of his era. He had sufficient knowledge of the Bible and Shakespeare to write good, forcible English and to express himself well. Jackson was no champion of the poor, or even of the "common man"; but they loved him because he proved that a man born in a log cabin could become rich, win battles, and be elected President of the United States. Incidentally, once Jackson was in, it became difficult for anyone *not* born in a log cabin to reach the presidency.

The President-elect, sixty-two years old, was an impressive figure. Six feet one in height and weighing 145 pounds, slim and straight as a ramrod, his lean, strong face lit up by hawklike eyes and surmounted by a mane of thick gray hair, he could never melt unseen into a crowd, as J. Q. Adams did all too easily. Leaving his Hermitage near Nashville in deep mourning because his beloved wife Rachel had lately died, he traveled by steamboat to Pittsburgh and thence by horseback over the Alleghenies to Washington. At the capital, where he put up at Gadsby's Indian Queen Tavern near the northwest corner of Pennsylvania Avenue and 6th Street, he became the center of attention, while Adams quietly and sadly prepared to move out of the White House. On the day of inauguration Washington (population about 18,000) was crowded to suffocation with an estimated 10,000 visitors, some of whom had come from very distant parts to see their idol. Jackson could have had an imposing parade of military companies and Old Hickory clubs, but he declined all such honors, and in republican simplicity walked with a few friends the half mile from Gadsby's to the Capitol. After taking the oath of office, administered by Chief Justice Marshall, and delivering his inaugural address, he mounted his saddle horse and rode to the White House. An informal and unplanned inaugural parade, people in carriages, wagons, and carts, mounted and on foot, followed the President up Pennsylvania Avenue, parked their horses in Lafayette Square, and surged into the White House almost on his coattails. No police arrangements had been made, and the press of well wishers forced the President to escape by a rear window and take refuge in Gadsby's. Glasses were broken and trodden under foot, punch was spilled, and damask chairs soiled by muddy boots. Conservatives shuddered over what they feared to be the opening scene of another French Revolution; the pastor of the Unitarian church preached a sermon on Luke xix.41, Jesus "beheld the city and wept over it." But the

Jacksonian Revolution, if it may so be called, was marked neither by class war nor persecution of "aristocrats"; the only victims of mobs were unpopular minorities, such as blacks, abolitionists, Catholics, and Mormons. Washington's and Jefferson's principles of toleration declined as the power of the common man rose.

No President of the United States suffered from so many continued and painful illnesses as Jackson, and his pain was augmented by never ending sorrow for his wife. At the time of his inauguration he carried in his body two bullets which poisoned his system. He suffered from headaches, chronic dysentery, nephritis, and bronchiectasis. In the eight years of office he had at least two severe pulmonary hemorrhages and several attacks of dropsy. Numerous doctors, including the celebrated Philadelphia surgeon Philip S. Physick, who had saved the life of Chief Justice Marshall by a bladder operation, did their best for "Old Hickory," and a stout will and iron constitution pulled him through.

4. The Spoils System and the Cabinet

A simple way of thinking—everything black or white—and a habit of command are keynotes to Jackson's policy, which he well summed up in a short note to Van Buren in 1830, after vetoing the Maysville Road bill:

> The people expected reform, retrenchment and economy in the administration of this Government. . . . The great object of Congress, *it would seem,* is to make mine one of the most extravagant administrations since the commencement of this Government. This must not be; The Federal Constitution must be obeyed, state rights preserved, our national debt *must be paid, direct taxes and loans avoided,* and the Federal union preserved. These are the objects I have in view, and regardless of all consequences, will carry into effect.

Note the emphasis on reform. The pro-Jackson editors and politicians, by persistent lying about the "extravagance and corruption" of the honest, efficient, and economical Adams administration, had persuaded both President and people that his first task was to "cleanse the Augean stables" of accumulated filth; in other words, to fire enough office-holders to make way for deserving Democrats. Rotation in office and the spoils system had long been in vogue in New York, Pennsylvania, and other Northern states. Many members of the civil service came out for Jackson in time to save their jobs, but others did not. Jackson removed only 252 out of 612 presidential appointees and, like Warren Hastings, was "surprised at his own moderation." Even this 40 per cent purge entailed much hardship, as there were then no pensions for aged or retired civil officials, many of whom had been appointed for charitable reasons. A few cases of overdrawn or careless accounts by earlier appointees were unearthed and held up to public scorn; but these were nothing in comparison with the scandals created by Jackson appointees. The most notorious was Samuel Swartwout, a participant in the Burr conspiracy who became a speculator in New York and worked hard to elect Jackson. Rewarded with the juiciest plum at the President's disposal, the collectorship of the port of New York, he managed in less than ten years of office to steal more than a million dollars of public money.

It is a fair statement that Jackson introduced the spoils system into the federal government, and that he never regretted it. His theory, stated in his first annual message, was that "the duties of all public offices" were so "plain and simple" that any man of average intelligence was qualified; and that more would be lost by continuing men in office than could be gained by experience. Naturally, when the Whigs won in 1840 they threw the Jackson men out, and when the Democrats came back under Polk, they threw the Whigs out; and so on. The consequences were more power to party organizations, diminishing prestige of the federal civil service, and decreasing efficiency. This sort of thing became so engrained in the American political system that, despite repeated reform legislation, it still continues. As recently as 1959 Senator Herbert H. Lehman of New York "called for the eradication of the spoils system in politics," especially the removal of the judiciary from "the control of party bosses."

Jackson's first cabinet was a collection of mediocrities, with the exception of Martin Van Buren, secretary of state. Noteworthy was the lack of anyone from Virginia or New England, the first time that had occurred. Jackson's choices registered, rather neatly, the rise of the Western and Middle states' democracy to federal power, and a brush-off to the Virginia Dynasty and the Yankees. But he had to call on them in the end.

For two years the simple political issue of the Jackson administration was, who would be the next President? For Jackson, like many others in that exalted office, had let it be known that he intended to retire after one term. Vice President Calhoun was the heir presumptive. There had been some sort of gentlemen's agreement to that effect between his followers and Jackson's that if Calhoun, fifteen years younger than the general, should accept the vice presidency, Jackson would go all out for him in 1832. But Old Hickory was already beginning to feel cool toward Calhoun, and his appointment of Martin Van Buren as secretary of state, instead of the man whom Calhoun wanted, showed how the wind blew. Van Buren was much too astute to ask the President for an official accolade. He simply allowed events to take their course, and came out on top as he always knew he would.

An ill wind that helped to waft "Little Van" into the White House and blow Calhoun back to South Carolina, arose over the wife of Secretary Eaton. Born Peggy O'Neale, daughter of the principal tavern keeper at the Georgetown end of Washington, she was a luscious brunette with a perfect figure and a come-hither look in her blue eyes that drove the young men of Washington wild, and some of the old ones too. Married at an early age to a purser in the navy, she became during his long absences at sea the mistress of her father's star boarder, John H. Eaton, bachelor senator from Tennessee. At least so "all Washington," except Jackson, believed. Eaton bought the tavern when Papa O'Neale went broke, in order to continue this pleasant arrangement, and persuaded the navy department to give the purser plenty of sea duty. About the time of the presidential election, the complaisant husband, caught short in his accounts, died or committed suicide—nobody knew which; and shortly after the news arrived, on New Year's Day 1829, his bonny widow, now thirty-two years old, married Eaton. All except the President-elect tried to stop it, but Jackson practically commanded him to marry her in order (as he thought) to stop the gossip and make her an honest woman. And Jackson appointed Eaton his war secretary.

Mrs. Calhoun refused to receive the "hussy," and the other cabinet wives followed suit. They declined to call, and at official receptions or White House dinners, refused to speak. Neither would the ladies of the diplomatic corps or the wives of most of the senators and congressmen. Van Buren, however, was a widower, and Charles Vaughan the British minister and Baron Krudener the Russian minister were bachelors. They could afford to show the lady marked attention, which was not difficult since she had wit as well as beauty. The crisis came at a Jackson birthday ball in January 1830. All the secretaries' ladies ignored Peggy and tempers rose so high that cabinet meetings had to be postponed. But the President refused to surrender. He actually held a cabinet meeting re Mrs. Eaton, whom he pronounced "as chaste as a virgin."

Henry Clay, hearing this, quipped "Age cannot wither nor time stale her infinite virginity!"

This "Eaton malaria" as the gossips called it was catching, and no laughing matter for the Jackson men. It was not only making a breach between the administration and respectable society, but making a fool of the President. The opposition was jubilant; for if the American people can once be got to laugh at instead of with a national figure, it is all up with him.

Still, there was use to be made of the affair by Van Buren. The sly fox from New York was wrapping himself around the heart of the old hero. It was "Little Van" who bound up the wounds of disappointed office-seekers and directed the negotiations which brought prestige to the administration. His tiny figure could be seen riding horseback beside the tall President on his daily constitutionals. Many a time they must have discussed the Eaton affair. That gave Van Buren the opportunity gently and discreetly to eliminate one possible anti-Peggy plotter after another, until Jackson inevitably reached the conclusion that Calhoun had put up his wife to start the snubbing.

At the same time, the President was moving toward a breach with Calhoun on other grounds. From our present point of view, American politicians of that period were highly vindictive. Jackson's hostility to Adams stemmed in part from the assumption that in President Monroe's cabinet he had been the one who wanted him recalled and court-martialed for his unauthorized invasion of Spanish territory. William H. Crawford, one of the defeated candidates of 1824, was the real mischief-maker in that case, and this. Animated by an implacable hatred of Calhoun, he caused letters to be placed in the "right" hands to prove that the South Carolinian was the cabinet member who had wanted the general punished. Jackson demanded an explanation. Calhoun was really out on a limb, since for years he had encouraged Jackson to believe that he had been the general's ardent supporter in Monroe's cabinet. He answered with a lengthy and unconvincing letter which the President endorsed: "This is full evidence of the duplicity and insincerity of the man."

These two controversies, Peggy Eaton's virtue and the Vice President's lack of candor, trivial and personal as they were, combined to deprive Calhoun of his expected succession, with dire results. Once it was clear that Jackson would never support him, Calhoun embraced the separatist doctrine that his native state was assuming. And Van Buren stepped into his shoes. "Little Van" used to point out the spot on the Tenallytown road where, after Jackson had sounded off about the

Calhoun men in the cabinet, he, Van Buren, offered to resign; how Jackson wouldn't hear of it, but was finally brought to see that if the secretary of state resigned, the small fry would have to follow, and that the President could then reconstruct his cabinet. This was done, and the whole lot resigned except the postmaster general, who had offended nobody. Van Buren was nominated minister to the Court of St. James's and exercised that function very capably for seven months, when the Senate by a majority of one (Calhoun's casting vote) rejected his nomination. Eaton was consoled by an appointment as American minister to Spain.

Thus, in 1830–31, Jackson's cabinet was completely reconstructed. Edward Livingston of Louisiana, a capable lawyer who had been on the general's staff at the Battle of New Orleans, became secretary of state; Louis McLane received the treasury; General Lewis Cass, a rising Democratic politician of Michigan, stepped into the war department; Levi Woodbury, who had helped swing New Hampshire into the Democratic column, became secretary of the navy; and Roger B. Taney, later a great chief justice of the United States, succeeded an obscure attorney general. With a strong and distinguished cabinet, "Eaton malaria" cured, "Calhoun the traitor" eliminated for the time being, Andrew Jackson decided to run for a second term.

VII

Nullification and the Bank War

1833-1837

1. *The Tariff, the South, and Calhoun*

AFTER ANDREW JACKSON had been in the saddle about two years, riding nowhere in particular, events began to give him direction. He had become President with no other policy than "reform," by which he meant reviving the republican simplicity of Jefferson's first term. But by the time he left office, republican simplicity was out, never to return. The country had moved, and the new Democratic party moved with it.

The two vital issues of Jackson's presidency were nullification and the Bank of the United States. Neither figured in the campaign of 1828, neither had been anticipated, and Jackson did not ask for them. They were presented to him in a form that one of his wishy-washy successors might have evaded but that he, brave and conscientious, chose to face. And it was the manner in which he faced these issues that gave Jackson his place in history. But for them, he might have gone down as one of several military men who made undistinguished chief magistrates.

The first issue with which Jackson had to deal was South Carolina. That state evolved politically between 1820 and 1830 (as Massachusetts between 1790 and 1812) from ardent nationalism to a state of economic flux in which everything bad was blamed on the federal government. The protective tariff of 1816 was largely the work of two South Carolinians, Lowndes and Calhoun. Although national in outlook, they expected their state to share the benefit. Their state had water power and cotton; so why not cotton mills? And was it wise for planters to be so dependent on outside markets for selling cotton? The next few years disproved these expectations. Competent managers were rare in the South, and Yankee mill superintendents were unable to handle slave labor, which could be employed with more immediate profit in growing cotton. Thus, the benefits of a protective tariff appeared to be going to Northern manufacturers, whilst Southern planters bore the burden of higher prices for consumer goods. As tariff schedules rose by successive acts of Congress, and the country as a whole grew richer, South Carolina remained stationary in population and declined in wealth. Many of her more enterprising planters emigrated to the newly opened black belts of Alabama and Mississippi, where their bumper crops enriched Mobile and New Orleans instead of swelling the exports of Charleston. And, as the area of cotton growing increased, the price declined. Soon it reached a point so low that planters on worn-out land in the older states were impoverished.

Actually, the protective tariff merely aggravated a situation for which the wasteful, land-destroying system of cotton culture was responsible, but the South Carolina planters could not see it. By 1825 there had been created among them just that atmosphere of pride, poverty, and resentment which, in our time, has favored the growth of Arab nationalism. In South Carolina this took the form of a local state rights party, propagating a doctrine that the protective tariff and "internal improvements" were wicked devices for taxing the South for the benefit of the North. The New England Federalists had taken the same line not long before, but that ended in talk at Hartford. Charleston, however, lay ten degrees of latitude south of Boston, and the South Carolina aristocracy was beginning to squirm over race relations. Behind all the heat and fury was the fear lest nationalism, in any form, lead to congressional tampering with slavery. Jackson saw that, and so did Calhoun.

Northern manufacturers were not satisfied with the tariff of 1824, and in 1828 when J. Q. Adams was still President, a new bill was passed. It was a politicians' tariff, drafted with an eye on the presidential election. Pro-Jackson congressmen wished to present their candidate to the South as a free trader, and to the North as a protectionist; they therefore introduced a bill with higher duties on raw materials than on manufactures, hoping that New England votes would help defeat it, and Adams be blamed. As Webster said, "Its enemies spiced it with whatever they thought would help render it distasteful; its friends took it, drugged as it was."

In July 1828, two months after this "tariff of abominations" passed Congress, William Huskisson made a speech in the British House of Commons the object of which, he later admitted, "was to alarm the Southern States in respect to the means within our power, of drawing from other countries the articles with which we are now supplied principally from those States." And, he added, if the tariff be not lowered, "it will expedite an event inevitable, I think, at no distant period— the separation of the Southern States." That speech probably found more readers in South Carolina than in England. Senator McDuffie cleverly popularized the British free trader's views in the "forty-bale theory." The protective tariff, according to him, so decreased English purchasing power for American cotton, and enhanced the price of consumers' goods to the South, that forty out of every hundred bales of cotton there produced were, in effect, stolen by Northern manufacturers. John Randolph went back even further, asserting again and again that the capital which built up manufactures in the North had been plundered from the South through Alexander Hamilton's financial measures. Progress in the North was not due to skill, thrift, or know-how, but to battening on the South. Harriet Martineau observed a few years later, in the course of her sojourn at Charleston, "The high spirit of South Carolina is of that kind which accompanies fallen, or inferior fortunes . . . When they see the flourishing villages of New England they cry, 'We pay for all this!' " At a great anti-tariff meeting in Columbia, S.C., in 1827, President Thomas Cooper of South Carolina College asked, "Is it worth our while to continue this Union of States, where the North demands to be our masters and we are required to be their tributaries?"

Calhoun, aloof in the vice presidential office, was not indifferent to this local turmoil. He had always been alive to the danger of disunion in a country so rapidly expanding. Like Hamilton, Adams, and Clay, he had sought to prevent disintegration by the cement of national legislation. Now he admitted his mistake. Protection, instead of a binding force, had proved an instrument of class and sectional plunder. So he came up with the doctrine of nullification.

First set forth in a document called the Exposition of 1828, it was approved that summer by the legislature of South Carolina. Nullification was based on two postulates: the common assertion that the Federal Constitution was a compact between states, and the theory of indestructible sovereignty. If the Constitution was established, not by the American people but by thirteen sovereign states, they must still be sovereign in 1828; and as such, each had the right to judge when its "agent," the federal government, exceeded its powers. A state convention, the immediate organ of state sovereignty, may then determine whether a given act of Congress be constitutional or not; and, in the latter event, take measures to prevent enforcement within state limits.

Such was the doctrine of nullification. It was not wholly new or original. The Kentucky and Virginia resolves of 1798 asserted the same state sovereignty; but the remedies which they demanded against the Sedition Act were a collective "interposition," followed by nullification of the law by all the states. Nullification by a single state, disobeying the laws of the Union while claiming its privileges, was a different matter. As the aged Madison declared, "For this preposterous and anarchical pretension there is not a shadow of countenance in the Constitution."

Calhoun was a tiresome person. One wearies of his dry, humorless, logical writings as of the Noble Roman pose of his portraits, hand resting on heart, handsome features, and glaring eyes. But we must admit his intelligence and his sincerity. His political switch was not entirely caused by thwarted ambition. Confronted, like John Adams in 1775, with an accepted constitutional theory that supported what he considered tyranny, he sought a new one to preserve liberty, within the existing body politic. The South, constantly growing away from the rest of the country—or, if you will, left behind by it— could not afford to remain in the Union unless some constitutional check were applied to majority rule. So Calhoun sought in the Federal Constitution an implicit theory to provide that check, and discovered nullification. But, unless the other side would yield, the only possible result, as in 1776, must be disunion. And Calhoun's conception of liberty, which he held more dear than union, was the liberty of the slave-owner to the full product of his slave's labor, and his right to full protection by the federal government. He admitted in 1830 that "the real cause of the present unhappy state of things" was "the peculiar domestic institution of the Southern States."

Calhoun's authorship of the Exposition of 1828 was secret, since as Vice President he was supposed to be loyal to the administration. He advised South Carolina to stay quiet, hoping that Jackson would insist upon a reduction of the tariff. But, as months stretched into years and the "tariff of abominations" remained on the statute books, it became clear to the South-

erners that they could obtain no reduction without Western
votes. And Western votes against nationalism could only be
purchased by conceding something that the West wanted more
than protection.

2. *The West and Daniel Webster*

The West, as we have seen, looked to Jackson to reform
certain features of the national land system. The poorer public
lands, unsalable at the minimum price of $1.25 per acre, made
large blocks of untaxable wilderness between settled areas. To
remedy this, Senator Benton of Missouri proposed a device
called "graduation," which was the bargain-basement principle, reducing the price of unsold public land after a given
period. Frontiersmen who squatted on the public domain before it was placed on sale disliked having their illegal holdings
sold to outsiders. The squatters, better men with fist or rifle
than the settlers who bought the lands they occupied, could
usually make the latter pay handsomely for "improvements,"
and move further West. Prospective buyers were sometimes
frightened away by squatter eloquence, of which this is a
specimen: "My name, sir, is Simeon Cragin. I own fourteen
claims, and if any man jumps one of them, I will shoot him
down at once, sir. I am a gentleman, sir, and a scholar. I was
educated at Bangor, have been in the United States Army, and
served my country faithfully—am the discover of the Wopsey
—can ride a grizzly bear, or whip any *human* that ever crossed
the Mississippi, and if you dare to jump one of my claims, die
you must!" But the Westerners preferred, or politicians thought
they preferred, to legalize their position by a pre-emption act,
giving them an option to purchase at a minimum price the
quarter-section (160 acres) where they had squatted, whenever it was offered for sale by the government.

Older communities, both North and South, were opposed to
encouraging westward migration, since by making labor scarce,
it supposedly kept up wages; but if tariff schedules were to be
maintained, some way must be found to get rid of the surplus
revenue coming in from public lands. In order to catch Western votes for protection, Henry Clay proposed a clever scheme
known as "distribution." The proceeds from land sales would
be distributed among the states for use in public works and
education, giving a special bonus to those states wherein the
lands lay.

This was all a game of balance between North, South, and
West, each section offering to compromise a secondary interest,
in order to get votes for a primary interest. The South would

permit the West to plunder the public domain in return for reduction of the tariff. The North offered the sop of "pre-emption" and the bait of "distribution" in order to maintain protection. On the outcome of this sectional balance depended the alignment of parties in the future; even of the Civil War itself. Was it to be North and West against South, or South and West against North and East?

On 29 December 1829 Senator Foot of Connecticut pro-posed that Congress inquire into the expediency of putting a brake on the sale of public lands. Senator Benton of Missouri denounced this as a barefaced attempt of Eastern capitalists to keep laborers from settling "the blooming regions of the West." He summoned the gallant South to the rescue of the Western Dulcinea, and Senator Hayne of South Carolina was the first to play Don Quixote. One after another the giants of the Senate rushed into the fray, and there took place one of those classic debates that America used to love—speeches hours long, each consuming a whole day's session, yet de-livered from mere scraps of notes held in the palm of the hand, and every word reported in the newspapers; one of those contests of eloquence that seemed to typify the manliness and shrewdness of the nation.

As the debate progressed, less was said about the public land, more on the subject of whether North or South was the West's best friend, and most of all on constitutional theory. The acme came on 26 January 1830, when Daniel Webster replied for the second time to Robert Y. Hayne. Webster was the most commanding figure in the Senate, a swarthy Olympian with a crag-like face, and eyes that seemed to glow like dull coals under a precipice of brows. It has been said that no man was ever so great as Daniel Webster looked. His mag-nificent presence and deep, melodious voice gave distinction to the most common platitudes; but his orations were seldom commonplace. He carried to perfection the dramatic, rotund style of oratory that America then loved. The South Caro-linian's attack on the patriotism of New England, and his bold challenge to the Union, called forth all Webster's intel-lectual power. His reply is the greatest recorded American oration, thrilling to read even today in cold print, when the issues with which it deals are long since settled by men who followed in 1861 the standard that Webster raised in 1830.

Imagine, then, the small semicircular senate chamber in the Capitol, the gallery and every bit of floor space behind the desks of the forty-eight senators packed with visitors; Vice President Calhoun in the chair, his handsome, mobile face gazing into that of the orator, and reflecting every point; Daniel Webster, in bluetailed coat with brass buttons and buff waistcoat getting under way slowly and deliberately like a man-of-war, then clapping on sail after sail until he moved with seemingly effortless speed and power. Hour after hour the speech flowed on, always in good taste and temper, relieving the high tone and tension with a happy allusion or turn of phrase that provoked laughter, thrilling his audience with rich imagery, crushing his opponents with a barrage of facts, passing from defense of his state and section to a devastating criticism of the "South Carolina doctrine," and concluding with an immortal peroration on the Union:

I have not allowed myself, Sir, to look beyond the Union, to see what might lie hidden in the dark recess behind. I have not coolly weighed the chances of preserving liberty when the bonds that unite us together shall be broken asunder. I have not accustomed myself to hang over the precipice of disunion, to see whether, with my short sight, I can fathom the depth of the abyss below; nor could I regard him as a safe counselor in the affairs of this government, whose thoughts should be mainly bent on considering, not how the Union may be best preserved, but how tolerable might be the condition of the people when it should be broken up and destroyed. While the Union lasts we have high, exciting, gratifying prospects spread out before us, for us and our children. Beyond that I seek not to penetrate the veil. God grant that in my day at least that curtain may not rise! God grant that on my vision never may be opened what lies behind! When my eyes shall be turned to behold for the last time the sun in heaven, may I not see him shining on the broken and dishonored fragments of a once glorious Union; on States dissevered, discordant, belligerent; on a land rent with civil feuds, or drenched, it may be, in fraternal blood! Let their last feeble and lingering glance rather behold the gorgeous ensign of the republic, now known and honored throughout the earth, still full high advanced, its arms and trophies streaming in their original lustre, not a stripe erased or polluted, nor a single star obscured, bearing for its motto, no such miserable interrogatory as "What is all this worth?" nor those other words of delusion and folly, "Liberty first and Union afterwards"; but everywhere, spread all over in characters of living light, blazing on all its ample folds, as they float over the sea and over the land, and in every wind under the whole heavens, that other sentiment, dear to every true American heart,—Liberty *and* Union, now and forever, one and inseparable!

That peroration, declaimed from thousands of school platforms by the lads of the coming generation, established in the hearts of the Northern and Western people an emotional, almost religious conception of the Union. It became something that men were willing to fight for. One of its earliest readers was a dreamy youth on the Indiana frontier named Abraham Lincoln.

Time only could reveal the full import of Webster's reply to Hayne; but it went home instantly to the honest old patriot in the White House. Jackson counted himself a state rights man, but he never doubted the sovereignty of the nation. State rights could never justify disobedience to the laws of the Union. Calhoun and the nullification group, at a dinner on the anniversary of Jefferson's birthday in 1830, foolishly attempted to trap Jackson into endorsing their cause. The formal toasts were worded to prove a connection between nullification and Republican orthodoxy. Jackson sat silently through them, but when his turn came, the old soldier rose to his full height, fixed his eye on Calhoun, and flung out a challenge:

"Our Federal Union—it *must* be preserved!"

Calhoun may, as Van Buren asserts, have drunk the toast with trembling hand; but he took up the challenge with another:

"The Union—next to our liberty, the most dear!"

3. *Nullification Attempted*

For two years after that famous dinner, the South Carolina nullifiers were held in check by the unionists of their own state, and by Calhoun's reluctance to break with the President and lose hope of reducing the tariff. As time went on the Carolinian hotheads grew hotter, and the rise of abolition sentiment inflamed them still more. Henry Clay forced their hands in 1832. With the aid of Western votes, attracted by "distribution," Clay pushed a new tariff bill through Congress on 14 July, and Jackson signed it. Some of the abominations of the 1828 tariff were removed, but high duties on iron and textiles were maintained; and the new law had an air of permanence which acted upon South Carolina as a challenge.

In the state election that autumn, the state rights party, the "pinks of chivalry and fire-and-brimstone eaters," carried all before them. The new legislature summoned a convention, which on 24 November 1832 declared in the name of the sovereign people of South Carolina that the tariff act was "unauthorized by the Constitution of the United States, null, void, and no law, nor binding upon this State, its officers or citizens." This ordinance of nullification forbade federal officers to collect customs duties within the state after 1 February 1833, and threatened instant secession if the federal government attempted to blockade Charleston or to use force.

President Jackson took precautions to maintain the law of the land. Forts Moultrie and Sumter were reinforced, revenue cutters were ordered to collect duties if customs officials were resisted, and close touch was maintained with the South Carolina unionists. On 10 December he issued a ringing proclamation to the people of South Carolina. Their nullification ordinance, he said, was founded on the strange proposition that a state might retain her place in the Union and yet be bound only by those laws that she might choose to obey. He then faced the "right of secession" which Calhoun inferred from the compact method of forming the Constitution: "Whether it be formed by compact between the States, or in any other manner," he said, "it is a government in which all the people are represented, which operates directly on the people individually, not upon the States. Each State having parted with so many powers as to constitute, jointly with the other States, a single nation, cannot possess any right to secede, because such secession does not break a league but destroys the unity of a nation." Such was the doctrine upon which Abraham Lincoln acted in 1861.

South Carolina could not be cowed by proclamation. Her legislature hurled defiance at "King Jackson" and raised a volunteer force to defend the state from "invasion." The President, encouraged by loyal addresses that poured in from all parts, wished to throw an army into South Carolina at the first show of resistance to customs officers. But could he afford to? It was no question of suppressing a mere local insurrection, as Washington had done in 1794, but of coercing a state of the Union. Virginia regarded nullification as a caricature of her resolves of 1798, Georgia "abhorred the doctrine," and Alabama denounced it as "unsound in theory and dangerous in practice"; but Georgia had made the dangerous proposal of a Southern Convention. Thus, Jackson's friends feared that coercion would disrupt their party; and the nullifiers did not want bloodshed, but to reduce the tariff. Within three weeks

of the President's proclamation, the House committee of ways
and means proposed to lower the duties. Concession and compulsion went hand in hand. On the same day (2 March 1833)
Jackson signed a force bill, authorizing him to use the army
and navy to collect customs duties if judicial process were
obstructed; and Clay's compromise tariff, providing a gradual
scaling down of schedules until they reached 20 per cent
ad valorem in ten years' time. The South Carolina convention
then reassembled and repealed the nullification ordinance.

Each party marched from the field with colors flying, claiming victory. Both seemed to have derived fresh strength from
the contest. The Union was strengthened by Jackson's firm
stand, but South Carolina had proved that a single determined
state could force her will on Congress. Jackson would have
preferred to have conceded nothing until Calhoun and his
party had passed under the Caudine forks; for beyond nullification he saw secession. The "next pretext," he predicted,
"will be the Negro, or slavery question." He counted on Calhoun, whom he now described as "one of the most base,
hypocritical and unprincipled villains in the United States," to
bring that up later.

4. Jackson, Re-elected, Fights the Bank

In the midst of these alarums and excursions came the
presidential election of 1832, memorable in the history of
political organization. Jackson men from all parts of the
Union, now organized as the Democratic party, sent delegates
to a national convention at Baltimore. It resolved that a two-
thirds majority was necessary for nomination, a rule which
Democratic national conventions did not abandon until 1936.
The 1832 convention renominated Jackson for the presidency
by acclamation, and Van Buren for the vice presidency with
somewhat less enthusiasm. The opposition, organized as the
National Republican party (for which the name Whig, of
happy memory, was shortly substituted), nominated Henry
Clay. And there was a third party in the field, the Anti-Masons.

That a party of so strange a title should contend for national power was of social rather than political significance.
Americans of the nineteenth century were so in love with the
methods of democracy, that no sooner did a few earnest men
capture a bit of what they took to be eternal truth, than they
proceeded to organize it politically. If local success proved the
scent good, it brought politicians hotfoot to the hunt, that
they might partake of the kill or lead off the field in pursuit
of bigger game. The Anti-Mason party arose in 1826 out of the

disappearance of a New York bricklayer named Morgan, who had divulged the secrets of his masonic lodge. A corpse was found floating in the Niagara river. It could not be proved to be Morgan's; but, as a politician said, it was "good enough Morgan until after election." Both the event and the free-masons' efforts to hush it up revived an old prejudice against secret societies. Several young politicians such as William H. Seward, Thurlow Weed, and Thaddeus Stevens threw them-selves into the Anti-Masonic movement, which became strong enough to elect a couple of state governors. In 1831 it held a national convention and nominated presidential candidates, who took thousands of Northern votes away from Clay. In a few years' time this party faded out; but the sort of people who were attracted by it easily took up with others such as the Liberty party, the Free-Soil, the Know-Nothing and, finally, the Republican party.

This presidential election decided the case of Andrew Jack-son v. the Bank of the United States. Since 1819 the B.U.S. had been well managed. In the Eastern states it had become a necessary part of business mechanism; Pennsylvania Demo-crats and Carolina nullifiers had no quarrel with it and even Calhoun had no constitutional qualms on the subject.[1] But the Bank was still unpopular in the West because it kept local banks within bounds by presenting their notes promptly for payment, thus reducing the amount of paper credit for specu-lation. Jackson shared this prejudice, together with a vague feeling that the "money power" was an enemy to democracy. As the B.U.S. charter would expire in 1836, if not earlier renewed by Congress, Jackson's opinion was of some impor-tance. "I do not dislike your bank more than all banks," he informed Nicholas Biddle, president of the B.U.S., "but ever since I read the history of the South Sea Bubble, I have been afraid of banks." What he wanted was a bank of deposit attached to the treasury department under officials appointed by himself.

Biddle was no mean antagonist. Precursor of a race of ener-getic and autocratic financiers, he had the same dislike of democracy that Jackson had of banking, but was anxious to keep his bank out of politics. Unfortunately, his social and business relations were largely with Jackson's opponents. Daniel Webster was at the same time a bank director, its lead-ing counsel, its debtor to the sum of many thousand dollars,

---

[1] In January 1832 the bank stock was distributed as follows (in round numbers): New York, 31,000; Pennsylvania, 51,000; Maryland, 34,000; South Carolina, 40,000; New England, 15,000; the West, 3000; Europe, 84,000.

and senator from Massachusetts. Congressmen were often paid their salaries by the Bank in advance of the annual appropriation bill, without interest charges. Journalists like James Gordon Bennett, the Scots-born father of the American yellow press, obtained loans on very favorable terms in return for favorable publicity in their columns.

Henry Clay was responsible for the financial war. He insisted on making the rechartering of the B.U.S. a major issue in the campaign of 1832; a most inadvisable move, as it aroused Jackson's pugnacity. Congress, led by Clay, passed a recharter bill on 3 July 1832, and most of Calhoun's partisans voted for it. Jackson vetoed it, with a message that smacked of demagoguery. The bank recharter was not only an unconstitutional invasion of state rights; it would continue a monopoly and exclusive privilege, the profits of which must come "out of the earnings of the American people," in favor of foreign stockholders and "a few hundred of our own citizens, chiefly of the richest class." He could not permit the "prostitution of our Government to the advancement of the few at the expense of the many." The logic of this veto message was defective, but as a popular appeal it was irresistible, and it helped to re-elect Jackson, together with a House of Representatives upon which he could depend. Nicholas Biddle took up the challenge. "This worthy President," he boasted, "thinks that because he has scalped Indians and imprisoned judges, he is to have his own way with the Bank. He is mistaken."

So the fight was on. Instead of waiting for the Bank to die a natural death in 1836, Jackson decided at once to deprive it of government deposits. One secretary, McLane, had to be "kicked upstairs" from the treasury to the state department, and his successor dismissed, before another, Levi Woodbury, could be found to obey orders. Government receipts were then (1833) deposited in local banks—the so-called "pet banks"—which Jackson believed to be safer than the expiring "monster."

This financial war came in the midst of a period of speculative activity, coincident with improved transportation, a brisk demand for cotton, and heavy westward migration. The death of the B.U.S., with its wholesome policy of keeping local banks in line, took off the last brake. The currency was already chaotic, when an Act of 1834 made matters worse by establishing the coinage ratio of 16 to 1 between silver and gold, which drove silver from the country. Yet the treasury's main embarrassment was a surplus! After January 1835, when the national debt was completely paid off, the tariff and public land sales began to bring in more money than the federal government could use in those frugal days before foreign aid, cold wars, welfare, and price supports. Jackson considered this a great triumph, but surplus proved to be a greater curse than deficit.

From Jackson's veto of the Maysville road bill, it was evident he could never be induced to spend the surplus on internal improvements. So Clay, fearing lest Jackson blow it in, got through Congress a "distribution" scheme in 1836. About $28 million was theoretically lent, but really given by the treasury to state governments. Some states used the money for public works, others turned it into educational funds, many of which were badly invested and fed the speculative movement. Jackson countered with a severe astringent, the "specie circular" of 1836, ordering the treasury to receive nothing but hard money for public lands. For he had always hated "folding" money, and many of his supporters believed that metallic coinage would cure all the country's financial ills.

Shortly after, the panic of 1837 burst upon the country, and the federal surplus disappeared overnight. Short-term treasury notes tided over the crisis, but the whole of Van Buren's administration (1837–41) was spent in seeking a substitute for the B.U.S. None comparable with it for service and efficiency was found until 1913, when the Federal Reserve system was adopted.

Jackson's war on the bank was not wholly personal, but an aspect of that fundamental hostility to monopoly and special privilege which the colonists had brought from England, and which had broken out in the Boston Tea Party. It would break out again in the populist and progressive movements, and in the New Deal. But rarely to this day has a bank in the United States been permitted to have branches outside the locality or county where it is established. In every other Western country the important banks are nationwide or (as in the case of the Bank of Nova Scotia) spread throughout the British Commonwealth.

After the lapse of over a century, it is clear that although democracy won the battle with the Bank, it lost the war. The bankers of New York City, almost splitting their sides laughing over the discomfiture of rivals on Chestnut Street, Philadelphia, promptly picked up the pieces of the B.U.S. and on Wall Street constructed a vastly bigger money power than anything ever dreamed of by Mr. Biddle. Poor farmers, mechanics, and frontiersmen gained nothing by this bank war; the net result was to move the financial capital of the United States from Philadelphia to New York.

VIII

Foreign Affairs and Removal of the Indians

1830-1838

1. *Peace with England, Fight with France?*

ANDREW JACKSON was unpredictable. One would suppose
him to have been the sort of person who would enjoy "twisting
the British lion's tail," but he inaugurated the most friendly
period of Anglo-American relations in the nineteenth century.
When in 1830 Louis Philippe, who as an exile had toured
widely in America, was made king of the French liberal elements, led by Lafayette, one would suppose that Franco-Amer-
ican relations would reach an all-time high; but the contrary
happened. In view of Jackson's strong republican sentiments,
it was assumed that he would maintain the Monroe Doctrine
and cultivate the new republic of Latin America. But he and
Van Buren never invoked or even mentioned the Monroe Doctrine, regarding it apparently as an Adams shirt to be discarded;
and their Latin American policy gravely offended Argentina
and Mexico.

Jackson and Van Buren entertained the most friendly feelings toward the British and reversed the policy of Adams and
Clay who, even after the Rush-Bagot agreements, had been
querulous and complaining. Minor issues on which Clay would
have written waspish notes to the British government, were

now settled as man to man between Sir Charles Vaughan and Van Buren, with an "assist" from Peggy Eaton, whom they both admired. Adams had made stiff and impossible demands in respect to the West Indies; Van Buren made haste to accept British concessions, removing all restrictions there upon American produce and ships—much to the dismay of Canada's Maritime Provinces. It was not Jackson's fault that Dutch arbitration in 1831 of the Maine-New Brunswick boundary question was not accepted. The State of Maine insisted that no treaty could deprive her of territory without her consent—precisely what Georgia was contending respecting the Cherokee. The President, consistent with his attitude in that case, refused to press the Dutch compromise, which allotted the United States a greater share of the disputed territory than Webster later obtained from Lord Ashburton.

Jackson's dealings with Great Britain were in marked contrast to his handling of a controversy with France. He and the "Citizen King" bristled at each other like a couple of gamecocks, and war was narrowly averted. The dispute was over claims. The United States demanded about $23 million for French depredations on American ships and property during the Napoleonic wars. France had a smaller claim for supplies furnished to the United Colonies at the beginning of the Revolution. Adams and Clay had worked on these claims for twelve years with no success. Old Senator Samuel Smith, uncle of Madame Jerome Bonaparte, reminded Van Buren of what Ben Franklin did not need to be told: "It is not well-written notes—that can succeed in France; it is sociability, intercourse, pleasantry—in fine what the French call 'les maniers.' The man must make himself acceptable to the ladies as well as to the gentlemen."

William Cabell Rives, Jackson's minister to France, followed this advice to such good purpose as to negotiate a treaty on 4 July 1831 by which France promised to pay the United States $5 million, less $300,000 for French claims against the United States. In return, Rives agreed to reduce American customs duties on French wines by about one-third. This treaty was ratified in France and unanimously approved by the United States Senate; and the House, disregarding complaints from New York vintners, duly knocked down the wine duties. So, when the first payment of a million dollars fell due, the treasury hopefully wrote a draft on the French minister of finance for that sum.

Alas, that check bounced! The French government refused to honor it because the Chamber of Deputies had not yet appropriated the money; and the United States Treasury had the further mortification of having to pay Nicholas Biddle's B.U.S. 15 per cent damages on the "rubber" draft. Jackson was furious with the Bank and still more so with Louis Philippe. Nevertheless, he appointed the best possible man, secretary of state Edward Livingston, to relieve Rives as American minister at Paris. Livingston, although his "maniers" were better than his predecessor's, could get nowhere; the French legislature repeatedly stalled. Jackson, in his annual message of December 1834, recommended that Congress pass "a law authorizing reprisals upon French property," if the debt were not paid at the next session.

At that era there was nothing unusual in this procedure— France herself had recently done it vis-à-vis Portugal—but for the United States to threaten France was denounced as barbaric, Red Indian diplomacy. A French fleet was dispatched to the West Indies; Jackson alerted the United States Navy; ministers to both countries were recalled; mass meetings were held in seaboard cities to back up the President. John Quincy Adams came out strongly in his favor; only Calhoun made snide remarks to the effect that if war came it would be Jackson's fault.

The French legislature now voted the money, with the proviso that nothing should be paid until the king had received *des explications satisfaisantes* of the President's message of 1834. This demand for "satisfactory explanations" sounded so like the preliminaries to a duel, of which Jackson had plenty of experience, that he flew into a passion. He disclaimed any intention to insult France, but refused to "explain" his threat of reprisals. Matters were at a deadlock and the two countries on the brink of war when the British foreign secretary, Lord Palmerston, miraculously mediated. "Pam" had a reputation as quarrelsome as Jackson's but he did not wish to see England's ally involved in an unprofitable war with the United States. A formula was found that satisfied wounded honor on both sides, and the treaty was executed some five years after it had been signed.

An important though unseen element in preventing war was the United States Navy. The French minister of marine warned the foreign office that his navy, with heavy commitments in the Mediterranean, would find it difficult to operate profitably against the United States. The American West Indies Squadron might well capture Guadeloupe and Martinique before France could come to their assistance.

2. The Navy and Latin American Relations

Andrew Jackson was land-minded rather than sea-minded. His calls on Congress to build shore installations and coast-defense forts, which created more jobs than did shipbuilding, were better heeded than his recommendations to lay down new warships. But he used the navy, as his predecessors had done, to protect American commerce on the high seas, especially in the Pacific, where whaling ships from New England had become very active. Sloop-of-war *Vincennes* made the first voyage around the world by any American warship in 1829–31, presenting letters from the President to King Kamehameha III of Hawaii and showing the flag at Guam, Macao, and Capetown. On a subsequent cruise she called at the Fijis, the Marquesas, and Tahiti (affording Queen Pomaré an inter-island cruise), rescued American merchant seamen held prisoner by the king of Babelthuap in the Palaus, and burned a Samoan village where American whalers had been murdered.

President Jackson would stand for no more "nonsense" on the part of Orientals, than of the French. Upon complaint that ship *Friendship* of Salem had been ambushed and plundered and her crew slaughtered by the sultan of Quallah Battoo on the coast of Sumatra, the President sent U.S. frigate *Potomac* to retaliate. She did that very successfuly, in a one-ship amphibious operation of 1832. But Sumatra had not yet been taken over by the Dutch, and another local sultan, at Mukkee, had to be given the same treatment before American ships could trade safely with Indonesia. A Yankee pioneer in Far Eastern trade and diplomacy named Edmund Roberts, appointed "special agent of the United States" and embarked in sloop-of-war *Peacock*, negotiated treaties with the king of Siam and the sultan of Muscat in 1833.

The most important official overseas project in this era was an exploring expedition. This brainchild of John Quincy Adams, turned down by the congresses of his administration, was picked up by Senator Southard of New Jersey in 1836 and supported by memorials from men interested in the China trade. Van Buren's literary secretary of the navy, James K. Paulding, got the expedition off to sea in the summer of 1838. Under command of Captain Charles Wilkes USN, it comprised three warships (*Vincennes*, flag) and three auxiliaries, with surveyors, botanists, geologists, and other scientists. In a cruise lasting four years, the Wilkes expedition sailed as far north as Alaska and as far south as Antarctica (where Wilkes Land records the visit), made charts of Polynesia and Micronesia (which we used when invading Tarawa in 1943), and prepared other data of inestimable value to commerce and science.

Another naval incident of the period had unhappy consequences for relations with Latin America. Spanish claims to the Falkland Islands in the South Atlantic, off the southern tip of Argentina, had been ceded in 1771 to England. She had never bothered to take possession, but the islands were frequented by ships from Stonington, Connecticut, whose crews slaughtered, for the skins, the great herds of seal that bred there. Around 1820 the Argentine Republic put in a claim for the Falklands and appointed as governor Louis Vernet, who imported cattle and *gauchos* and established a flourishing ranch. As the American seal-skinners showed a propensity to slay and eat his cattle, Vernet caused two of their vessels to be seized, plundered, and sent to Buenos Aires. Jackson's secretary of the navy, Levi Woodbury, then ordered sloop-of-war *Lexington*, Captain Silas Duncan, to sail to the Falklands and protect American interests. Duncan did this very effectively by rounding up the not unwilling *gauchos*, long unpaid and heartily sick of the Falklands, and sailing them 1000 miles to Buenos Aires and Montevideo.

Unknown to Secretary Woodbury, the British government had decided to take possession of the Falklands, and did so without opposition in 1833 since nobody was there—thanks to Captain Duncan. The Argentine government protested both to Britain and the United States, alleging that but for Captain Duncan the "invaders" would have been driven off by Vernet's forty cowboys. Naturally the Monroe Doctrine was invoked and the argument made that it was a mere sham if Britain were allowed to get away with the Falklands. The United States maintained the view that these islands were legally a British colony with which, as the Doctrine expressly stated, we "shall not interfere"; and that Duncan's act was a suppression of piracy. But the Duncan incident has never been forgotten or forgiven at Buenos Aires.

"Van Buren observed to me," wrote Sir Charles Vaughan to the British foreign secretary in 1830, "that the present administration of the United States was not disposed to assume the high tone in their relations with the States of Spanish America which had been assumed by President Adams and Mr. Clay." This resolution was not observed with respect to Mexico, since Jackson wanted Texas. To further this end, he replaced Poinsett as minister to Mexico by an old crony, Colonel Anthony Butler, a vain and ignorant swindler who thought that if he greased the right palms in Mexico City he could buy anything. Jackson finally got wind of Butler's behavior and recalled him. The Texas Revolution, toward which Jackson's neutrality was benevolent, now broke out and succeeded. That gave a new and bad twist to United States-Mexican relations.

3. Removal of the Eastern Indians

An American journalist who had spent several years in India, and whose small children had come to love the Indians, came home in 1958. Shortly thereafter he found the boys crying as they watched a TV "Western" because, as one moaned, "They're killing *Indians!*" Papa had to explain that these were not Indians of India but Red Indians, and that to kill them was part of the American Way of Life.

The only extenuation of American policy toward the natives of North America is that it continued an old-world process of one race or people pushing a weaker one out of an area that it wanted. Almost every European today is a descendant of Asiatic intruders into Europe; almost every North African the descendant of Arab intruders. "The country is a land for cattle," said the children of Reuben to Moses when they saw the land of Gilead, "and thy servants have cattle; wherefore, said they, if we have found grace in thy sight, let this land be given unto thy servants for a possession." In the United States, as elsewhere in the nineteenth century, this process of conquest and expansion took the form of a relatively highly developed civilization pushing out a backward people who could not or would not be absorbed, and who were too few in number and weak in technique long to resist. But some of the Indians put up a very good fight.

The problem of United States-Indian relations, which for many years had involved international rivalries, became localized after the Florida treaty was ratified in 1821. "Foreign interference" could no longer be used as an excuse for abusing the Indians. And there was no more need to placate them to prevent their siding with the British, French, or Spanish.

Efforts to maintain Indian reservations within the Eastern states were generally unsuccessful, although a few small ones, such as that of the Abnaki in Oldtown, Maine, and the Tuscarora reservation near Niagara Falls, still endure, menaced or sliced away by the bulldozer. Conditions for a reservation's lasting were a partial adoption by Indians of the American Way of Life, and a strong government service to protect them from the white man's trickery and alcohol. But, for fifty years after American independence, the Indians did not wish to conform, many federal agents were political hacks, government trading posts were unable to compete with unauthorized private traders who supplied the Indians with liquor, and frontiersmen everywhere coveted the Indians' land.

Monroe's administration bowed to demands of the West by adopting a removal policy. Plans for concentrating the tribes west of the Mississippi now began to take shape, and piecemeal removal began in the 1820's from the Old Northwest and the lower South, to segments of what had been the domains of the Caddo, the Quapaw, and the Osage. Tribesmen with well-developed farms, especially influential halfbreeds, were given the choice of removal, or staying put and becoming American citizens. Those who preferred to leave, exchanged their property for new lands in the West and were promised payment for travel expenses and the value of improvements on their relinquished property. The assent of the Indians was often merely nominal; federal commissioners bribed important chiefs and, if necessary, got them drunk enough to sign anything. "Persuasion" often took the form of urging the Indians to sell improvements for cash with which to pay off debts to white traders. This removal policy slowed down during the administration of John Quincy Adams, whose attitude toward the Indians was humane and paternal, but picked up momentum and was carried to a successful conclusion (from the white point of view) under Jackson. The President, having negotiated several removal treaties during his military career, knew very well the hardships involved, but regarded this as the only possible way to save the Indians from extinction. They were faced with the irresistible force of a white expansion which the Democrats had no intention of checking.

Soon after Jackson's inauguration, Georgia, Alabama, and Mississippi asserted jurisdiction over Indian reservations, in contemptuous disregard of federal treaties, and even set up county governments to be put in operation as soon as the rightful owners of the soil were expelled. Congress then passed an Indian Removal Act (1830), appropriating half a million dollars for this purpose. The President was authorized to grant lands in the unorganized part of the Louisiana Purchase in exchange for those relinquished in the East, to protect the Indians in their new reservations, to pay expenses of removal and one year's subsistence, and compensate them for improvements on the relinquished land.

The liquidation of Indian reservations in the Old Northwest was largely accomplished between 1829 and 1843. Mixed bands of Shawnee, Delaware, Wyandot, and others were persuaded to accept new reservations west of Missouri. Their numbers were drastically reduced by disease on the journey. Theft by federal officials of what was due to the Indians, and funeral rites for those who died en route, exhausted their resources long before this "trail of tears," as it was aptly called by later writers sympathetic to the Indians, came to an end. Many groups were unable to make the journey in one season and suffered intensely at improvised winter quarters. A cholera epidemic broke out in 1832; measles took hundreds of lives. Further trials awaited the survivors, especially those who hoped to till the soil; the cost of equipment reduced them to penury or debt long before they could raise a crop or draw upon tribal annuities. Money from the sale of improvements at the old village ordinarily went into the expenses of travel, if it did not stick in the pockets of federal agents.

At one point during these removals, hostilities broke out. Black Hawk, chief of the Sauk and Fox, who had fought on the British side in 1812, tried to retain his ancient tribal seat at the mouth of Rock river, Illinois, opposite Davenport, Iowa. White squatters encroached on the village and enclosed the Indians' cornfields. After the governor of Illinois had threatened him, Black Hawk agreed that after crossing the Mississippi for his annual winter hunt, he would never return. But his people, threatened by hostile Sioux, ran out of food. Hoping to find a vacant prairie in which to plant a corn crop, Black Hawk recrossed the Mississippi in the spring of 1832 with about 1000 members of his tribe. The governor of Illinois, assuming this to be a hostile expedition, called out the militia (Abraham Lincoln commanding a company) and pursued the starving Indians up the Rock river into the Wisconsin wilderness. It was a disgraceful frontier frolic, stained by wanton massacre of Indians, including women and children. The only redeeming feature was the chivalrous consideration of Black Hawk by Lieutenant Jefferson Davis of the regular army, when the captured chief was placed in his charge; forty years later, Davis referred to Black Hawk's rear-guard action at Wisconsin Heights as the most gallant fight he had ever witnessed. Black Hawk subsequently visited the "Great White Father" in Washington and was presented with a sword and a medal by President Jackson. But he lost his tribal lands.

The four great Indian nations of the Old Southwest, the Chickasaw, Creek, Choctaw, and Cherokee, were Jackson's particular problem. In 1830 the Choctaw of Mississippi signed a treaty providing for their removal within three years. As with others, this migration brought death, suffering, and poverty. In 1832 a treaty was signed with the Creek nation to wind up their large reservation in Alabama. Some members kept in-

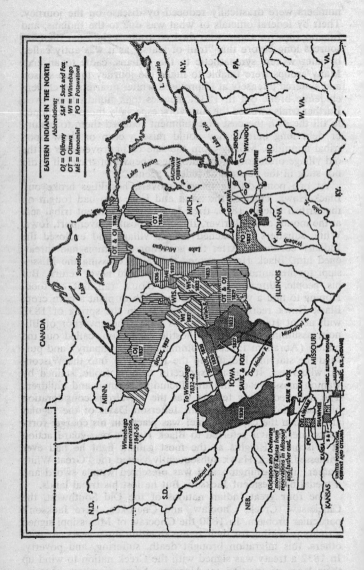

EASTERN INDIANS IN THE NORTH

Abbreviations:

Oj = Ojibwa   S&F = Sauk and Fox
OT = Ottawa   WI = Winnebago
Mé = Menomini   PO = Potawatomi

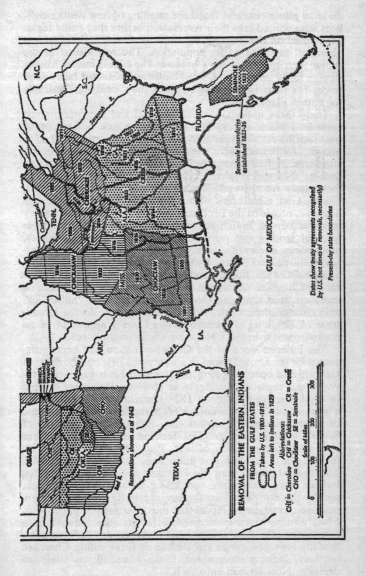
REMOVAL OF THE EASTERN INDIANS FROM THE GULF STATES

dividual allotments and faced the cunning of new white neighbors who poured into their reservation before they could leave. Many died on the journey. By 1860 the Creek nation had lost about 40 per cent of its population. The rest settled in the Indian Territory, near the Choctaw. The Chickasaw of Mississippi, a fairly small group, fared better and obtained fairly good prices for their improvements, since their land was desirable for cotton plantations.

These three nations were agricultural and sedentary; some even held black slaves. The Cherokee, whose nation spread over northwest Georgia into Alabama and around Chickamauga, Tennessee, were even more advanced, by European standards. It had always been a white grievance against the Indians that they rejected "civilization." The Cherokee, unfortunately for themselves, took the palefaces at their word. George Gist, a halfbreed whose Indian name was anglicized as Sequoya, provided the necessary spark. Convinced that literacy was the key to Indian survival, Sequoya invented a simple form of writing and printing the Cherokee language; Bibles, other books, and even a weekly newspaper, *The Cherokee Phoenix,* were printed. These Indians welcomed Christian missionaries, built roads, houses, and churches, adopted a constitution for the Cherokee nation and elected a legislature. They became more civilized than the Georgia "crackers" and "hill-billies" who coveted their lands. Nor, for that matter, do the inhabitants of Faulkner's Yoknapatawpha County appear to be an improvement over the Chickasaw whom they replaced.

The independence of the Cherokee nation had been guaranteed by the United States in a treaty of 1791, but the State of Georgia had been chopping away at their lands for over thirty years, and regarded the treaty as obsolete. Discovery of gold in the Cherokee country in 1828 brought this controversy to a head, and a rough class of whites to the spot. Here was a case of federal supremacy against state rights, as clear as that of South Carolina; but President Jackson let Georgia have her own way. His secretary of war, Peggy Eaton's husband, informed the Cherokee that they were mere tenants at will. The federal troops sent by President Adams to protect the Indians were withdrawn, and Major Ethan Allen Hitchcock, sent by the war department to investigate frauds against them, made so devastating a report that the department suppressed it. Chief Justice Marshall decided, in a test case brought by a missionary (the Reverend Samuel C. Worcester of Vermont), that the laws of Georgia rightly had no force within Cherokee territory. Jackson commented, "John Marshall has made his decision. Now let him enforce it."

As Georgia held a lottery to dispose of their lands, and no friends in power appeared to help them, the Cherokee were forced to accept removal. Agents of the Indian administration negotiated a treaty with a small minority of the chiefs in 1835, but most of them refused to attend the negotiations, and few departed within the three-year limit set by the treaty. A protest to President Van Buren, signed by 15,665 Indians, was blandly ignored. So, in 1838, regular troops under General Winfield Scott rounded up the Cherokee and started them on the long trail to Indian Territory. This journey cost them one-quarter of their number, but the remainder reorganized their national government, prospered, and have retained their language and alphabet to the present day. Several hundred diehards in the Great Smokies, who resisted removal, were eventually given the Qualla reservation in North Carolina.

A similar controversy with the Seminole of Florida ended in war. A tricky treaty of removal, negotiated in 1832 with a few chiefs, was repudiated by the greater portion of the tribe, led by a brave chieftain named Osceola. Secure in the fastnesses of the Everglades, Osceola baffled the United States Army for years, and was only captured by treachery at a truce conference. Many Seminoles were rounded up and sent west, but others kept up the fight until 1842. By that time they had cost the United States some $20 million and 1500 lives. A few thousand remained in the Everglades. Their descendants, known as the Miccosukee Seminoles, are the only occupants of some 200,000 acres of swampland north of the Tamiami trail. They live, like their ancestors, by hunting, fishing, and a little agriculture. Never having made peace with the United States, they are currently threatened by drainage and development projects, and a "progress" which they do not want.

The only Western statesman to denounce these shabby and dishonorable proceedings was Henry Clay. His speech in the Senate on 14 February 1835 is the more praiseworthy because the Indians had no votes, and because his Kentucky constituents cared nothing for them. He quoted the long list of treaties guaranteeing to the Cherokee their lands, and the still longer list of acts of the State of Georgia which violated not only these treaties, but the most elementary principles of justice and decency. He drew tears from the eyes of the senators, but they did nothing for the Cherokee except to expedite their removal.

President Jackson seems to have kept a good conscience about all this, and several friends of the Indians, such as Lewis Cass and Thomas L. McKenney, head of the war department's bureau of Indian affairs, supported removal as the only alternative to extermination. Jackson's rationale of Indian removal appears in his Farewell Address of March 1837: "The states which had so long been retarded in their improvement by the Indian tribes residing in the midst of them are at length relieved from the evil, and this unhappy race—the original dwellers in our land—are now placed in a situation where we may well hope that they will share in the blessings of civilization." Lewis Cass went the general one better, piously invoking the theory that God intended the earth to be cultivated. Cherokee cultivation evidently did not count.

By the end of Van Buren's presidential term, it was assumed, at least by the Democrats, that the Indian question had been solved. All important Eastern tribes—those who, in Jackson's phrase, had "retarded improvement" (i.e. resisted white land grabbers) had been provided for behind a barrier that ran from Lake Superior through Wisconsin and Iowa Territories, thence along the western boundaries of Missouri and Arkansas to the Red river on the Texas border. Behind this line the tribes were guaranteed possession "as long as grass grows and water runs"; and thence most of them were eventually ousted, when the tide of white settlement lapped around them and slaughtered their game. But, in a sense, the removal policy was justified by the later history of the "five civilized Indian Nations"—Creek, Cherokee, Choctaw, Chickasaw, and Seminole —in Oklahoma. Removal gave them the necessary respite to recover their morale, and until the Civil War they succeeded in keeping white men out.

Looking backward, it is now evident that, in view of the irresistible push of the westward movement, Indian removal was the lesser evil. It had to be, but the process was carried out with unnecessary hardship to the victims.

In many instances missionaries and other individuals managed to protect the Indians. The Ojibway or Chippewa had a reservation along the Bad river of Wisconsin, which was taken under the protection of the Reverend L. H. Wheeler, a Protestant missionary at La Pointe. When, in 1850, white pioneers began lobbying Congress to remove these Indians west of the Mississippi and acquire their lands, Wheeler visited the proposed site of the resettlement and reported that it would be a deed of mercy to shoot every Ojibway rather than send them there. Congress reconsidered, and in 1854 guaranteed these Indians three small reservations on the south shore of Lake Superior, which they still hold. Other tribes were not so fortunate. Between 1853 and 1856 the United States negotiated no fewer than fifty-two treaties, mostly with nations in the Mississippi valley or west of the great river, by virtue of which it added 174 million more acres to the public domain.

Remnants of the Six Nations who had been guaranteed possession of reservations in New York State, by treaties concluded as far back as 1784, have been fighting a losing battle. Chief Red Jacket of the Seneca long managed to preserve the integrity of his people in their reservation, which is now covered by the city of Buffalo. After his death in 1830, a group of New York speculators known as the Ogden Land Company began an intensive drive to get possession of the Seneca reservation. By bribing greedy individuals to act as "chiefs" and sign away land, this company managed to rob the tribe of almost their entire heritage. President Van Buren, to his credit, denounced the subsequent "treaty" as a steal, but it passed the Senate, by the casting vote of Vice President Johnson, the reputed slayer of Tecumseh.

As recently as 1960, the Tuscarora, in the sacred name of progress, lost a case to preserve their reservation against the Niagara Power Project's bulldozers. They carried the case to the Supreme Court of the United States, which decided against them. Mr. Justice Black, in his dissenting opinion, in which Chief Justice Warren and Justice Douglas joined, said: "The record does not leave the impression that the lands of their reservation are the most fertile, the landscape the most beautiful or their homes the most splendid specimens of architecture. But this is their home—their ancestral home. There they, their children and their forebears were born. They, too, have their memories and their loves. Some things are worth more than money and the costs of a new enterprise. I regret that this court is the governmental agency that breaks faith with this dependent people. Great nations like great men, should keep their word."[1]

Thus, unjust treatment of the Indians was not confined to the Jackson era, or to the South, or to the Democrats. Some day an American historian of Indian blood may pen a devastating indictment of the United States.

4. Conclusion on Jackson

The fourth of March 1837 marked the passing of a vital personality and the arrival of Number Two in a new presidential dynasty. Up Pennsylvania Avenue wound a military

[1] *Federal Power Commission and New York Power Authority* v. *Tuscarora Indian Nation.*

procession, escorting a small phaeton (built from the wood of U.S.S. *Constitution*) drawn by four gray horses. The President, though emaciated by illness and feeling his seventy years, sat erect with his white hair bared to the sunshine, the old indomitable spirit flashing from his eyes. Beside him, and a head lower, sat Martin Van Buren with the bland aspect of a cat who had swallowed the canary. Chief Justice Taney administered the inaugural oath and there followed a more seemly reception at the White House than that of 1829. Andrew Jackson then returned by easy stages to his home in Tennessee. He was not expected to live long, but he survived another eight years and continued to dictate party decisions and appointments. The Hermitage became a sort of Mecca where Democratic aspirants had to do homage.

President Jackson had so many limitations that it is doubtful whether he should be included in the ranks of the really great Presidents. His approach to problems was too personal and instinctive, his choice of men, at times, lamentably mistaken; and, unlike the Roosevelts, he had little perception of underlying popular movements, or of the ferment that was going on in the United States. His modern counterpart for pugnacity, chivalry, and capacity for quick but correct decisions is Harry Truman. But one cannot help but love old Jackson. His simplicity and forthrightness, his refusal to equivocate or compromise, his gentleness where women were concerned, are admirable. And he dealt swiftly and severely with the one disruptive movement whose significance he did perceive. In 1861 men of good will were saying, "O for one hour of Andrew Jackson!"

Of all the Presidents, only Lincoln and the second Roosevelt have made as great an appeal as Jackson to the popular imagination. In his person he proved that the average American of sound character and common sense could win, and was fit to administer, the powerful office of the presidency. He left a mass of unsolved problems for his successors, and the ground swell of the slavery question was beginning to break along the political coast. Yet he is, and always should be, a popular hero; so with Vachel Lindsay let us sing:

> A natural king with a raven wing;
> Cold no more, weary no more—
> Old, old, old, old Andrew Jackson.

IX

Van Buren and Our Northern Neighbors

1837-1858

1. *Democrats, Whigs, and the Panic of 1837*

MARTIN VAN BUREN, nominated unanimously at Jackson's behest, and elected by 170 votes out of 294, made a shrewd, able, and dignified President. After, to a great extent, inventing the game of democratic politics in New York, he had obtained a firm grip on the federal administration as Vice President, and learned about foreign affairs both as secretary of state and minister to Great Britain. After seeing his predecessor off by the new Baltimore & Ohio Railway—first presidential patronage of a railroad—Van Buren announced his cabinet appointments. He kept John Forsyth as secretary of state, gave the unlucky but capable Poinsett the war department, and appropriately left in office Jackson's wire-pulling crony Amos Kendall as postmaster general. Democratic (and some Republican) Presidents seem to require one of these "twilight personages" on whom they can rely—Woodrow Wilson's Colonel House, Franklin D. Roosevelt's Harry Hopkins, and Dwight Eisenhower's Sherman Adams are recent examples. Amos Kendall, "A puny, sickly-looking man with a weak voice, a wheezing cough, narrow and stooping shoulders, a sallow complexion, slovenly dress and a seedy appearance generally," could never have been a leader himself; but he en-

joyed the power of being the leader's confidential adviser, and
for two Presidents he acted as sifter of patronage demands
and liaison to the press.

One of the strangest characters ever to serve as Vice President was Richard M. Johnson, congressman from Kentucky,
a favorite of Jackson's, and his errand boy during the Peggy
Eaton affair. Colonel Johnson was a hero of the War of 1812,
and claimed to have killed Tecumseh at the Battle of the
Thames. Since William H. Harrison, one of the several Whig
candidates for the presidency, was campaigning as the Hero of
Tippecanoe, Johnson's friends countered with:

> Rumpsey dumpsey, rumpsey dumpsey,
> Colonel Johnson killed Tecumseh!

But this slogan, never surpassed for electioneering imbecility,
failed to give him a majority in the electoral college. So the
election of Vice President had to be made by the Senate, voting by states according to Amendment XII of the Constitution;
the only time that has happened. Johnson was then elected.

The Whig party, on the losing end, was a regrouping, under
a new name, of Republican factions which refused to follow
Jackson, and of surviving Federalists. It inherited from Jefferson a humanitarian attitude toward the poor and helpless; and
from Hamilton, a tender regard for finance, commerce, and
manufacturing. If the Democrats had the "best principles," as
Ralph Waldo Emerson wrote, the Whigs had the "best men,"
with Clay of Kentucky, Webster and Everett of Massachusetts,
John Bell and Hugh L. White of Tennessee, Reverdy Johnson
of Maryland, Hugh S. Legaré and James L. Petigru of South
Carolina, and a dozen others of intelligence and integrity. Had
they not been overwhelmed by the rising tide of democracy,
these men might have saved the Union. But the Whigs, with
too many prima donnas jostling one another for the big spot,
could not agree upon one candidate in 1836, so the election
became a tryout of "favorite sons." General Harrison won the
most electoral votes; and when the *Boston Atlas,* which affected
to carry the whole Eastern business world on its shoulders,
came out solemnly for his nomination in 1840, all other con-
tenders withdrew.

The "Little Magician" (as people called Van Buren) might
turn political dross into precious metal, but he was unable to
cope with the panic of 1837. It was blamed on the Democrats,
as panics always are on the party in power. Speculation was
the basic cause. The boom in Western land, manufacturing,

transportation, banking and all other business enterprises that began about 1825, resulted in overextension of credit, to which Jackson unwittingly contributed by withdrawing government deposits from the conservative B.U.S. in favor of "pet banks," which used them to promote further speculation. In pursuance of Jackson's specie circular, millions in hard money were withdrawn from deposit banks to pay for purchases of government land in the West; at the same time, the price of cotton fell by one-half, and the wheat crop of 1836 failed. The same thing, in a smaller way, was happening in Europe; and American enterprises were then largely dependent on European capital. Thus, when continental Europe put pressure on English banks, they demanded the repayment of their short-term loans to American enterprises. Demands for gold from English creditors reached the banks at the very time they were depleted to pay for Western lands; and the failure of three English banking houses early in 1837 precipitated the crisis, much as the Austrian Kreditanstalt failure precipitated the crash of 1931.

Van Buren was no sooner seated in the White House than American mercantile houses and banks began to fail, and there were riots in New York over the high cost of flour. In May, after almost every bank in the country had suspended specie payments, and the government had lost $9 million through the collapse of pet banks, the President summoned Congress for a special session. In the meantime, there was widespread suffering; less probably than in later depressions, because the majority of Americans were farmers, and industrial workers in many cases could return to a parental farm. On the other hand, there was no social security or government assistance of any kind for the desperate other than town and county poorhouses. Cold and hungry people in the cities had to depend on private charity for fuel and food. And a promising labor movement collapsed; the estimated 300,000 trade unionists of 1837, about half the total number of skilled workers, could no longer pay their dues.

The special session of Congress accomplished nothing except to authorize a large issue of temporary treasury notes, which began a new national debt. As a permanent fiscal measure, Van Buren proposed an independent treasury, essentially a government bank; but that was too much for state banking interests to swallow, and an alliance of conservative Democrats with the Whigs prevented it from becoming law until 1840. Thus, the next presidential election was held in the midst of a depression, which has always meant woe for the party in power.

2. *The Log Cabin Campaign of 1840*

"Little Van" deserved re-election, and he might have been re-elected had he chosen to play politics with the Canadian rebellion, which we shall consider presently. He lost his own state, where sympathy with the Canadian rebels was strongest, by only 13,293 out of 441,139 votes; and New York's 42 electoral votes would have gone far toward giving him the decision.

The reason why the 1840 campaign became the jolliest and most idiotic presidential contest in our history is that the Whigs beat the Democrats by their own methods. They adopted no platform, nominated a military hero, ignored real issues, and appealed to the emotions rather than the brains of voters. Expectations of profit and patronage were employed to "get out the vote," and the people were given a big show. Democratic politicians, even Jackson himself, now complained of Whig demagoguery.

Who were the Whigs in 1840? The only really accurate answer is, everyone who was not a Democrat. Everyone, that is, except a few rabid abolitionists at one end of the political spectrum, and sullen nullifiers at the other. The party included people hard-hit by the depression and the war on the Bank, old-fashioned state-righters offended by Jackson's nationalist stand; New England and Middle-state Yankees who disliked all Democrats, factory owners who wanted more protection, and Westerners who had discovered that Clay's "distribution" and "pre-emption" did more for them than Jackson's and Van Buren's promises. Yet Clay, the logical candidate and the most fit man living to be President, did not get the nomination. For Henry had made many enemies; whilst old General Harrison, the Hero of Tippecanoe, had proved to be a good vote-getter and could be "built up." Harrison was not politically inexperienced, having served as congressman and senator from Indiana, but he was not associated with any particular measures. As American minister to Colombia (appointed by Adams and recalled by Jackson) he had incurred the enmity of Bolívar by lecturing the Liberator on the duties of a republican president. But that did not hurt him with the North American public.

Harrison's nomination set the pattern that Jackson's had begun—a nationally known figure, uncommitted on controversial issues. The Whig convention even appointed a committee to supervise the general's correspondence lest he write something incautious and be quoted! In order to capture the

state rights vote in the South, the convention, to its members'
subsequent regret, nominated a very positive and rambunctious
character, John Tyler. This old-fashioned Virginia Republican
resigned his seat in the Senate rather than vote to expunge a
resolution of censure on Jackson, as the state legislature had
instructed him to do. That made him a hero to the Whigs, but
failed to change his views or even make him a Whig. He had
just turned fifty years of age, whilst Harrison was already
pushing seventy.

For principle the Whigs substituted mass enthusiasm. "Tippecanoe and Tyler Too!" was the slogan. Van Buren, unfortunately for himself, had acquired luxurious tastes on his
brief diplomatic mission and transferred them to the White
House; this gave the Whigs a chance to repeat Jackson's tactics
against Adams. Charles Ogle, a Pennsylvania congressman
otherwise unknown to fame, made a famous and widely circulated speech on "The Royal Splendor of the President's
Palace." Maine lumberjacks, Buckeye farmers, and Cajans in
the bayou country were shocked to learn that under Little
Van the White House had become a palace "as splendid as
that of the Caesars"; that the President doused his whiskers
with French *eau de cologne,* slept in a Louis XV bedstead,
sipped *soupe à la reine* with a gold spoon, ate *paté de foie gras*
from a silver plate, and rode abroad in a gilded British-made
coach, wearing a haughty sneer on his aristocratic countenance.
What a contrast to old hero Harrison, Cincinnatus of the West,
the plain dirt farmer of North Bend, Ohio!

> No ruffled shirt, no silken hose,
> No airs does Tip display;
> But like "the pith of worth" he goes
> In homespun "hodden-grey."

> Upon his board there ne'er appeared
> The costly "sparkling wine,"
> But plain hard cider such as cheered
> In days of old lang syne.

What really turned the tide, however, was the unlucky sneer
of a Democratic journalist in Baltimore to the effect that if Old
Tip were given a barrel of hard cider and a pension of $2000
he would prefer his log cabin to the White House. It then
became the log-cabin, hard-cider campaign. There were log-
cabin badges and log-cabin songs, a *Log Cabin* newspaper and
log-cabin clubs, big log cabins where the thirsty were regaled
with hard cider that jealous Democrats alleged to be stiffened

with whisky; little log cabins borne on floats in procession, with latchstring out, cider barrel by the door, coonskin nailed up beside, and real smoke coming out of the chimney, while lusty voices bawled:

> Let Van from his coolers of silver drink wine,
>   And lounge on his cushioned settee;
> Our man on his buckeye bench can recline,
>   Content with hard cider is he.
> Then a shout from each freeman—a shout from each State,
>   To the plain, honest husbandman true,
> And this be our motto—the motto of Fate—
>   "Hurrah for Old Tippecanoe!"

In vain the Democrats worked a counter-line of campaign lies, to the effect that Harrison was an abolitionist and a "Hartford Convention Federalist"; in vain did "Rumpsey-dumpsey" Johnson try to take the curse off dandy Van by clowning in a red jacket he claimed to have stripped off Tecumseh. In vain James Buchanan, in his nasal Pennsylvania twang, stuffily "endeavored, without giving personal offense, to carry the war into Africa."

In those days some states, notably Maine (which continued the practice until 1958), held their elections in late summer; and from the 1840 Maine election, which Edward Kent the Whig candidate for governor won easily, it was clear that a landslide had started. After the Maine returns were in, it became the custom for one Whig, meeting another on the street, to ask: "How did old Maine went?" To which the other would answer: "She went hell bent for Governor Kent!" And, together with sympathetic bystanders, they roared the chorus,

> And Tippecanoe and Tyler too!

By mid-November it was clear that "Tip and Ty" had won. They carried Clay's Kentucky, Jackson's Tennessee, and the entire West except Illinois and Missouri which were salvaged for Little Van by the stentorian voice and bad grammar of "Old Bullion" Benton. They carried all the populous Middle states all New England except Isaac Hill's bailiwick New Hampshire, and the solid South except Virginia and South Carolina. The result was 234 electoral votes against 60. But the popular vote was very close—Harrison 1,269,763; Van Buren 1,126,137. A few thousand votes in New York, Pennsylvania, and Ohio could have turned the tide.

General Harrison, an honest, simple old soldier, was expected by Whig politicians to place himself in the hands of such men as Clay and Webster. The latter had the impudence to offer him a ready-made inaugural address of his own composition. But the general had already compiled from schoolboy memories of Plutarch a turgid address of which he was very proud. With some difficulty he was persuaded to let Webster revise it. After one day's work the "god-like Daniel" arrived late to a dinner party, looking so haggard that his hostess was alarmed. She hoped that nothing had happened? "Madam," replied Webster, "you would think something had happened, if you knew what I have done. I have killed seventeen Roman proconsuls as dead as smelts!"

The fourth of March 1841 was the coldest inauguration day in history. The old soldier disdained the protection of hat or overcoat, and his expurgated address took an hour and forty minutes to deliver. John Quincy Adams, who had supported Tip and Ty somewhat wryly, remarked in his diary, "Harrison comes in upon a hurricane; God grant he may not go out upon a wreck!" Worse than that, he went out in a hearse. In the damp, unheated White House the cold that Harrison caught at the inauguration developed into pneumonia, complicated by congestion of the liver. The doctors, after blistering and "cupping" him, administered violent emetics and cathartics; then switched to opium, camphor, and brandy; finally, in desperation, administered Indian medicine men's remedies such as crude petroleum and snakeweed. These finished him—Tecumseh's revenge, perhaps! On 4 April 1841, the hero of Tippecanoe gave up the ghost. John Tyler succeeded to his office, and title, too.

Tyler declared Sunday, 14 May, a day of national fasting and prayer in honor of the departed President. This gave the ministers a chance to preach hortatory sermons, no fewer than 138 of which were printed. The death of Harrison, after only one month in office, was assumed to be a divine castigation for national sins. There was complete disagreement, however, as to what sins the Almighty intended to rebuke. Immorality and sabbath-breaking were the choices of most; but some Northern preachers thought that the Lord was delivering a warning to free the slaves, whilst the Reverend Mr. Gadsden of St. Philip's, Charleston, believed that "current wild notions of equality" and "organized movements to break down distinctions among men" had aroused the divine wrath.

It was soon demonstrated that lust for office was the only binding force in the Whig party. Henry Clay expected to be "mayor of the palace" as well as leader of the Senate; but Tyler was an obstinate man with a mind of his own. Clay's im-

mediate object was to charter a new Bank of the United States.
Tyler believed it to be his mission to assert Virginia state rights
principles of 1798, and to strip the federal government of its
"usurped" powers. He took over Harrison's cabinet, carried
through a purgation of the civil service that Harrison had
begun, and signed a "distribution pre-emption" bill of Clay's
to discharge the party's debt to the West. This law gave the
squatters what they had long wanted, the right to pre-empt a
quarter-section of public land at the minimum price. Tyler
accepted an upward revision of tariff schedules as a measure
necessary to raise revenue, but vetoed all bills for internal
improvements and harbor works, and refused to accept any
fiscal device that bore the remotest resemblance to the B.U.S.
of detestable memory. Clay's bill for a new national bank was
returned with the President's veto, as was a second bill specially drafted to meet his constitutional scruples.

From that date, 9 September 1841, there was open warfare
between Tyler and Clay. Four days later the entire cabinet,
excepting Webster, resigned and the President was practically
read out of the Whig party. Here was Calhoun's chance to
count in the sectional balance of power. For three years
(1841–43) he played a waiting game, intriguing to obtain
the Democratic nomination for the presidency in 1844. Webster left the cabinet in 1843; and the following March Calhoun
became secretary of state.

This meant that Tyler had gone over to the Democrats, and
that Calhoun had returned to the fold. Calhoun's purpose was
to "reform" the Democratic party on the basis of state rights;
to adopt the formula which he believed to be necessary to
preserve the Union. The formula at bottom was a theoretic
cover for the main purpose of his devoted followers, to perpetuate slavery where it existed, and extend it into regions
where it was not. Calhoun tipped the internal balance of the
Democratic party very definitely southward; the defection of
Tyler inclined the internal balance of the Whig party no less
definitely northward.

The important question of which side the West would take
was decided when the Democrats nominated James K. Polk
for the presidency in 1844, on a platform of westward expansion, which proved to be an even more potent appeal to the
voters than "Tippecanoe and Tyler too." But it was ominous
that in the same platform the Democrats neglected to reaffirm
their faith, as had been their wont, in the principles of the
Declaration of Independence.

The same declining faith in "the right of the people to alter
or to abolish" a government which has become destructive of

"inalienable rights," became evident in the attitude of the Tyler administration, and the American public generally, toward the so-called Dorr Rebellion in Rhode Island. That state was still using its seventeenth-century charter, unamendable by due process, as a constitution. Landed property was still a requirement for voting, and the apportionment of seats in the legislature virtually disfranchised Providence and other rising cities. Thomas H. Dorr, a young Harvard graduate and manufacturer who for years had been agitating political reforms which the legislatures rejected, organized the People's Party, which called a constitutional convention in 1841 without the legislature's permission. This convention drafted a new constitution embodying manhood suffrage and reapportionment which, submitted to popular vote, was ratified by a huge majority. Dorr was elected governor in April 1842 and a new slate of state officials was chosen. But another state government, elected under the colonial charter, defied Dorr's. President Tyler, appealed to by both, declared that only the old government was legal and that he would support it by force if necessary—a somewhat startling conclusion for a man who had supported South Carolina's nullification. Encouraged by this promise, the old government issued warrants for the arrest of Dorr, who was actually convicted of treason to Rhode Island and sentenced to life imprisonment at hard labor. But the old government was frightened by the threat of civil war into calling a new constitutional convention which extended the franchise to all native-born white citizens. This was adopted by popular vote before the end of the year. Governor Dorr was pardoned, but the Supreme Court of the United States, in the case of *Luther* v. *Borden,* branded his entire movement as an extralegal rebellion.

The effect of that decision, to this day, has been to deny constitutional reform in certain states, including Massachusetts, unless by permission of the government which needs to be reformed.

3. *Canada Boils Over*

During the quarter-century from 1815 to 1840 the development of British North America ran parallel to that of the United States in some respects, and in others was dissimilar as if on a separate continent. It is fascinating to follow Canadian history during this period because it indicates what might have happened to the Thirteen Colonies if the American Revolution had ended in a suppressed rebellion.

Canada, as we may for short call the whole of British North

America, although it had no union until 1867, consisted in 1825 of six settled provinces: Newfoundland, the three Maritimes (Prince Edward Island, Nova Scotia, and New Brunswick); Lower Canada, which at the time of federation became the Province of Quebec; and Upper Canada, which at the same time became the Province of Ontario.[1] The Hudson's Bay Company continued to own the watershed around the bay of that name, and with the Northwest Company divided control of all western Canada to the Pacific. In these vast regions the natives still hunted and fished with no European contacts other than a few trappers and missionaries.

The five provinces south of Newfoundland received a large stream of immigrants from Great Britain and Ireland, and the Ontario peninsula, thrusting down between New York, Pennsylvania, and Michigan, attracted a good share of westward-moving pioneers from the United States. Canada was increasing about as fast as her big neighbor. Of the three most populous provinces, Nova Scotia counted 202,600 people in 1838; Quebec, 625,000 in 1841; and Ontario in the same year, 455,700; about the same as Michigan, Indiana, and Maryland respectively. The total population of British North America in 1840, about 1,450,000, was roughly the same as that of the white population in the Thirteen Colonies around 1765. Apart from the Indians, who were not counted in this enumeration, the Canadians were practically all white; the few hundred African slaves owned by the French in Quebec, and those brought in by American Loyalists, were all liberated in 1833.

Relations between Canada and the United States during this period may be described as warily friendly. The strong Loyalist element in the population tended to be anti-American, and everyone remembered the aggressive War of 1812. But the Rush-Bagot agreement for naval disarmament on the Great Lakes was faithfully maintained, and prevented border incidents—up to a point. That point was reached in 1837 when the political lid blew off in Quebec and Ontario; the lack of armed forces on the border then became a handicap to enforcing neutrality laws. There was nothing in the Rush-Bagot agreement, however, against building forts. During this period the British government strengthened the citadels at Halifax and Quebec, built a new strongpoint at Kingston, near old Fort Frontenac; and kept more than 5000 regular troops in Canada.

Although Canada had enjoyed since 1791 a measure of representative government in the shape of a lower house elected on a fairly broad franchise, the British government had

[1] The later names Quebec and Ontario are used here for the sake of clarity.

ample means of control in order to defeat inconvenient expressions of popular will. As in the royal provinces among the Old Thirteen before 1775, the crown appointed and removed at pleasure the governor, most of the high officials, the judges, and a legislative council which acted as upper house of the legislature. The governor not only could veto a bill; he could send any act of the legislature to England for disallowance. Moreover, the governor and other high officials were paid out of crown revenue instead of being dependent on the lower house, as the royal governors in the Old Thirteen had been. In other words, the British government had the same set-up in the Canadian provinces that Lord North was aiming for in Massachusetts Bay in 1774: an element of authority strong enough to keep popular movements in check.

Each province was in fact ruled by a local Tory oligarchy which supported the governor. In Quebec it was the "château clique" led by Chief Justice Jonathan Sewall, son of an old Massachusetts Tory; in Ontario it was the "family compact," led by Archdeacon Strachan of the Anglican Church and John Beverley Robinson, of Virginia and New York loyalist background. The result was a feeling of frustration on the part of a large number, perhaps a majority, of the voters. They saw the United States advancing rapidly in power and wealth, with representative government responsible to the people. This proved that democracy worked, for aught the Tories might say. But every attempt to express popular wants was quashed by the ruling oligarchy. A serious blow-up resulted.

In Quebec, the dominant French population had few aspirations toward progress. Their ideal was to preserve *l'ancien régime* as of 1760; but the Scots merchants of the château clique wanted improvement and development. Paradoxically, it was a Canadian gentleman of the old regime, Louis-Joseph Papineau, speaker of the assembly since 1815, who combined with John Neilson, a sturdy Scots liberal, and Edmund B. O'Callaghan, an emotional Irishman, to agitate for responsible government in Quebec. Papineau, a student of the French and American revolutions, appeared to be leading Quebec in their footsteps, with himself in the combined roles of Samuel Adams and Mirabeau. A cholera epidemic of 1832 was blamed on the British; the same year there was a "Montreal massacre" to parallel the Boston massacre of 1770; patriotic demands were incorporated in ninety-two resolutions (the mystic Massachusetts number); non-importation agreements followed, and patriots ostentatiously wore homespun. The government rejected Papineau's minimum proposal, to let the voters choose the legislative council. Young men began organizing as *Fils de la liberté,* the countryside armed secretly and displayed the tricolor, and called extralegal conventions. One of some 5000 people met at Saint-Charles on 23–24 October 1837, rallying around a liberty pole topped by the Phrygian liberty cap. It looked as if the "Spirit of '76" had entered Canada.

But the same combustible materials were not present in Canada as in the earlier Boston. As the Canadian historian Creighton well says, "The radicals in both provinces sought to persuade a people whose grandfathers had rejected the gospel of Thomas Jefferson, to accept the revised version of Andrew Jackson. They tried to induce the Canadians to re-enact the American Revolution sixty years after their ancestors had failed to take part in the original performance."

Papineau's fatal error, in contrast to Sam Adams's cultivation of the Protestant clergy, was to alienate Catholic priests by anticlerical outbursts. After the Bishop of Montreal had pronounced against him, few French Canadians would follow his lead. Warrants were issued for the arrest of O'Callaghan and Papineau. At Saint-Denis and Saint-Charles on the Richelieu river, cast for the roles of Lexington and Concord, a few armed men defied British regulars. But the repeat performance ended then and there. The "rebels" did "disperse," and their leaders fled to Vermont. And at Saint-Eustache north of Montreal, a loyal rabble chased the patriots into a church and then smoked them out. The entire rebellion would have ended as a farce but for refugees in the United States.

President Van Buren issued a neutrality proclamation on 5 January 1838, and the governors of New York and Vermont forbade citizens to help refugee rebels. Nevertheless, between December and February there took place three or four raids on Quebec by bands of Canadian patriots who had organized on American soil. The most serious, led by two Quebec physicians, Robert Nelson and Cyrille Coté, crossed Lake Champlain, invaded Canada from Vermont, and issued a declaration of independence. There was no response; no "embattled farmers" flocked to the tricolored banner. The rebels retreated to Plattsburg, where General Wool disarmed them. Nelson maintained a republican government of Quebec in exile, with a secret society of refugees and American sympathizers called the *Frères Chasseurs,* or Hunters' Lodges. Those at one time had an estimated 50,000 members, but only 3000, of whom barely one-third were armed, accompanied "President" Nelson to a grand encampment at Napierville, P.Q., in November 1838. Loyal volunteers and regular British troops dispersed them and took 750 prisoners, of whom 99 were sentenced to death for treason, and a dozen were executed.

In Ontario, the uprising came much nearer success. Here the social rift was religious rather than racial. Methodists, Presbyterians, and Baptists, mostly recent immigrants from the British Isles and the United States, were pressing for a share of public money from the dominant old-Tory Anglicans and North of Ireland Presbyterians, and for an overhaul of the public land system. The provincial government, not wanting a rowdy West of the American type, reserved one-seventh of every 640-acre township for the crown, and one-seventh for the church; these reserves obstructed roads, retarded settlement, and were generally a nuisance. In addition, there were immense private grants to government favorites, untaxed but held for future profit, like the proprietary lands in provincial Pennsylvania. Rural Ontario was full of poor people from Britain who had hoped to better their condition by emigration but found themselves as poor as ever, together with a substantial middle class of whom a witty Irishman remarked, "All had money, but few of them had any sinse, and none of them knew how to work." Outside the "family compact" and snug little groups of officials and professional men in towns like Kingston and Toronto, Ontario was a scene of frustration and blighted hopes.

The principal leaders of opposition in Ontario, fundamentally conservative men who wanted only a fair deal, were Egerton Ryerson, son of a New Jersey Loyalist who founded a Methodist newspaper in 1829; William Lyon Mackenzie, a fiery Scots journalist, editor of a newspaper published in Toronto and mayor of that city; and Marshall S. Bidwell, son of Jefferson's "clerk of the water-closet" who had fled to Ontario when the Federalists found his accounts to be $10,000 short. Five times Mackenzie was elected to the assembly, five times he was ejected from that body for a supposed libel on the government, a procedure recalling that of the House of Commons with Jack Wilkes in the 1770's. On the sixth re-election, Mackenzie was allowed to keep his seat and became the opposition leader, with a program of political and land reform which was more moderate and constructive than Papineau's ninety-two resolutions. The Ontario reform party was largely inspired by American example, especially that of New York. Mackenzie aimed to give the people more control over their provincial and local governments, and to unlock the land reserves; but he too became anticlerical, which lost him the support of the Methodists and Orangemen.

The explosion occurred in Ontario at the same time as in Quebec, but for different reasons. It was precipitated by the appointment as lieutenant governor of Upper Canada of a stupid retired soldier named Francis Head, apparently by mistake—the colonial office in London thought it was appointing his gifted cousin Sir Edmund Head. The new governor, after a brief flirtation with the reformers, decided that they were a pack of traitors, and embarked on a policy of autocracy and repression. He vetoed all bills for roads, schools, and public works, dissolved the assembly dominated by Mackenzie, and orated for the Tories in a new election. With the aid of the Orangemen, who provided strong-arm work at the polls similar to what their Catholic fellow countrymen were doing in New York, Head won a majority of seats.

Mackenzie, defeated in his Ottawa constituency, now took the road to rebellion, drafted a declaration of independence on 31 July 1836, armed and drilled thousands of settlers, and set a date, 7 December 1837, for the patriots to capture Toronto. The panic of 1837, in the meantime, had hit Ontario. It was not so severe as in the United States, because the "family compact" had checked speculation and inflation. Nevertheless, it created unemployment and discontent, which the rebels exploited. Under Mackenzie's vacillating and incompetent leadership, the rebels were defeated in their march on Toronto by one volley delivered by a loyal sheriff and 27 militiamen from behind a rail fence. The embattled farmers of York County duly rallied on 7 December, several hundred strong, but were routed by loyal militia in a field outside the town. Mackenzie then fled to Buffalo and set up a "Republican Government of Upper Canada" at Navy Island in the Niagara river but on the Canadian side of the border. He made active preparations, with the aid of the Hunters' Lodges and American sympathizers, to invade Ontario from three points at once.

Here is where the United States almost became involved. American sympathies, naturally, were for the rebels; it was expected that "history would repeat itself" (which it never does), and that the Canadian provinces would be freed from British tyranny by Mackenzie's and Nelson's patriots.

President Van Buren, friendly to the British empire and anxious to avoid trouble, endeavored to maintain strict neutrality. On the long, unfortified boundary his means were few and feeble, whilst the state governments of New York and Vermont were weak in will and not much stronger in means. Hence Mackenzie and his followers were able to obtain money, supplies, and recruits in the United States to invade Canada. It was a scandalous situation; within a year (1837–38) some dozen to fifteen raids on Canada were launched from American soil. Some of them, to be sure, were only two men in a rowboat, but all defied the neutrality laws.

After Mackenzie had recruited 200 or 300 "liberators" at Buffalo among unemployed bargees, lake sailors, and stevedores, President Van Buren sent thither a force of regulars under General Winfield Scott. Rebel headquarters on Navy Island were supplied from the New York shore by the small American paddle steamer *Caroline*. On the night of 29 December 1837, as she lay at her wharf on the United States side, a picked band of Canadian volunteers performed the hazardous feat of rowing across the Niagara river where its current rushes toward the falls, capturing the *Caroline*, and sinking her. In the brawl an American named Durfee was killed. It was a violation of neutrality analogous to that of General Jackson's in Florida; but New York was not a Spanish province, and England now had a pugnacious foreign minister, Lord Palmerston.

This affair created a tremendous uproar along the border; the Rochester *Democrat* called for revenge "not by simpering diplomacy but by blood." Van Buren, however, relied on diplomacy, both internal and external. He protested to Palmerston about the "outrage," but also prosecuted Mackenzie and "General" Rensselaer Van Rensselaer of his American volunteers. He jailed them both, sent more troops to the border, and kept General Scott's men busy disarming volunteers. But the President was unable to prevent the Hunters' Lodges from organizing an attack on Prescott, across the St. Lawrence, in November 1838. That was the last serious raid. The Hunters surrendered to Canadian troops, and a number of them were hanged.

In the meantime, another danger point had developed in the disputed territory on the Maine-New Brunswick frontier. Canadian lumberjacks entered the region claimed by the United States on the Aroostook river in 1838 and seized a protesting state senator from Maine. The governors of New Brunswick and Maine called out the militia, but this " 'Roostook War," as it was called, ended in bloody noses and mutual invective. General Scott arranged a truce in March 1839; and three years later Daniel Webster and Lord Ashburton concluded the treaty that settled this troublesome boundary question.

But there was no peace for Van Buren. In November 1840, before the President could persuade Palmerston to admit that the attack on the *Caroline* had been deliberate and official, a Canadian named McLeod boasted in a New York barroom that he had killed Durfee, the American in the affray. McLeod was promptly arrested and indicted for murder. Palmerston demanded his immediate release. The execution of McLeod, so he informed the British minister at Washington, "would produce war, war immediate and frightful in its character, because it would be a war of retaliation and vengeance." By the time this barroom boaster came to trial at Utica, Tyler was President and Daniel Webster, secretary of state. Although anxious as Van Buren to preserve the peace, they were equally hampered by the limitations of federal government. Governor Seward of New York insisted that his state's justice should take its course, and Webster could do no more than provide counsel for the prisoner. Fortunately, McLeod sober managed to find an alibi for McLeod drunk, and was acquitted.

Nova Scotia, which was not subjected to the religious and racial stresses of the Canadas, obtained responsible government in 1848 without a rebellion. This peaceful solution came about largely through the statesmanship of her native son Joseph Howe, son of a Boston Loyalist. The governments of New Brunswick and Prince Edward Island underwent a similar peaceful evolution.

The outcome of the Canadian rebellion was happy for both countries. Queen Victoria appointed the young and energetic Earl of Durham commissioner for British North America, with power to suspend provincial legislatures and the duty to make recommendations. "Radical Jack," as he was called, arrived at Quebec in May 1838. He adopted a policy of clemency toward captured rebels, traveled about the settled regions of the Canadas, sent his brother-in-law Charles Grey to talk to President Van Buren; and, although forced to resign in the fall, owing to the English political situation, wrote his "Report on the Affairs of British North America." This Durham Report, one of the finest state papers in the English language, laid down the principles which have guided British colonial policy ever since. He advised a union of Upper and Lower Canada as a step toward federation of all Canada. He made many recommendations in advance of his time (such as the Canadian Pacific Railway); he cited devastating statistics on the land reserves, and recommended that the American public land system be adopted. But the crux of his advice was to give Canada responsible government in the English sense; i.e. a ministry responsible to an elective assembly. His union of the two Canadas was immediately adopted, but that turned out to be a false step, as the French of Quebec hated it. But his federation and responsible government projects bore fruit in the British North America Act of 1867, which brought the Dominion of Canada into existence.

Thus the rebellions of 1837–38, tragi-comic failures though they were, started the British government on a course of colonial reform, because Durham and the British liberals learned the right lessons from them.

TIPPECANOE AND TYLER TOO

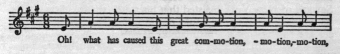

Oh! what has caused this great com-mo-tion, - mo-tion,-mo-tion,

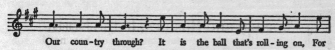

Our coun-try through? It is the ball that's roll-ing on, For

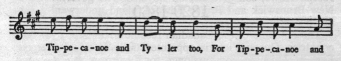

Tip-pe-ca-noe and Ty-ler too, For Tip-pe-.ca-noe and

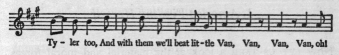

Ty-ler too, And with them we'll beat lit-tle Van, Van, Van, Van, oh!

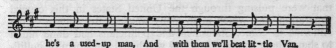

he's a used-up man, And with them we'll beat lit-tle Van.

X

Society and Business in the North

1820-1860

1. *America Finding Herself*

Now LET US TAKE a look at the material and moral forces that were pulsing through the United States in this crucial generation, and which in so many ways set the pattern of the America to come. Statesmen and politicians had done much to shape those forces. They had weathered the storm of nullification and created two national parties, both pledged to preserve the Union. Yet, despite their efforts, North and South were pulling apart. Both were progressing, but divergently. Northern society was being transformed by the industrial revolution, cheap transportation, and educational, humanitarian, and migratory movements. These, to some extent, touched the Border slave states; but the lower South lay almost wholly outside such influences, and adjusted itself to a slave and cotton economy. By 1850 two distinct civilizations had been evolved, as different in material basis and outlook on life as England and Spain are today. Only the common language and religion, the common political institutions, and the devoted efforts of elder statesmen, prevented them from flying apart in 1850.

In appearance the North had not much changed in fifty years. Harriet Martineau, an intelligent Englishwoman who traveled through the country in 1836, was never out of sight of the woods, except for a short time in the Illinois prairies. A new feature in the Northern landscape was the factory village, built near river rapids or falls, containing from two to ten mills plainly built of wood, brick, or stone, pretentious mansions of the owners or superintendents, and hundreds of operatives' houses, exactly alike. Georgian architecture had given place to the neo-classic. Public buildings were being constructed of gray granite, and the wealthier farmers and country lawyers masked their wooden houses with a classic colonnade and pediment. In the Middle West the white painted farmhouse was beginning to predominate; but in new settlements, log cabins and untidy clearings full of stumps dominated the landscape.

American scenery now began to be appreciated for its contrasts of mountain with valley, sand beach or rocky coast with island-studded sea, gorges and cataracts. Every foreign visitor had to see Niagara Falls, the Hudson river, and the Natural Bridge of Virginia. Big wooden hotels with long, covered piazzas were being put up at places like Saratoga Springs, Niagara Falls, Newport, and Nahant, to accommodate sightseers and provide for the brief vacations of professional and business men and the longer ones of their wives. Country houses imitated from Italian villas or the "Gothic" cottages of England multiplied near the larger cities, portending a new class of city-bred gentleman farmer.

As at the time of the American Revolution, liberal elements in Europe looked to America with admiration and hope. The aged Madame de Staël told young George Ticknor, "Vous êtes l'avant garde du genre humain, vous êtes l'avenir du monde." Ten years later Goethe, who loved to talk with any American who came to Weimar, wrote a poem to the United States:

> America, thou hast it better
> Than our old continent; . . .
> Within, naught restrains thee
> From a livelier era;
> No useless memories
> Of unforgotten strife.
> Face thy future with happiness!

And Achille Murat, liberal offspring of the Napoleonic dynasty, wrote home from Florida in 1826, "You should see the calm, majestic advance of this Republic. You can form no idea of it, you who have only known Liberty amid the tempest and under attack by subversive parties. Here her principles are imperishably established both in minds and in hearts. The people are unanimous in support of the government."

True enough, and what's more, republicanism and democracy did work, and the resources of a new country, exploited by the people under laws of their own making and breaking, had brought a degree of comfort and security to the common man that his forebears in Europe had never known. It is not surprising that Americans were full of bounce and bluster, contemptuous of Old-World monarchies. They had many unpleasant habits, particularly in connection with tobacco. "Spitting and swearing are nearly out of fashion in Philadelphia," says the writer of *A Pleasant Peregrination in Pennsylvania* (1836); "at this moment we cannot recall more than two or three gentlemen who would think of such a thing as spitting on the carpet of a lady's drawing room." Obeisance was not to be had of the white American at any price; but those who addressed him as an equal discovered a natural civility and kindness that took the place of manners. Intercourse between man and man (providing both were white and not too recent immigrants) was easy because there was no assumption of social superiority on the one side, or acknowledged inferiority on the other.[1] It was not so much the freedom, simplicity, and good humor of the people that endeared them to Harriet Martineau as the "sweet temper diffused like sunshine over the land," and "the practice of forbearance requisite in a republic."

Forbearance the Americans carried to excess in their uncritical attitude toward their own books, customs, institutions, and abuses. Almost every foreign traveler of the period remarked the patience of Americans under the afflictions of contemporary travel, denounced their deference to majority opinion, and deplored their fear of expressing unpopular views. This meant that Americans were becoming less independent and more gregarious, deference to the opinions of others being a condition of social intercourse on a democratic level. Yet so complex was the American character that the excess of one quality was balanced by the reverse. Intolerance appeared in the persecution of unpopular groups such as blacks, immigrants, abolitionists, and Catholics; and in hot resentment of unfavorable criticism. But we find these unattractive qualities in some of the countries that have become

[1] One aspect of this attitude that has disappeared was dislike of uniforms. The first New York City police force in 1844 struck at wearing a uniform blue coat as servile. Railroad conductors and postmen refused to wear uniforms until some time after the Civil War; academic gowns were revived about the same time.

independent since World War II, as also in those with ancient traditions.

Nor was distinction wanting in a country that produced in one generation Clay, Jackson, Calhoun, and Webster; Poe, Bryant, and Washington Irving; and in the next, Emerson, Longfellow, Whitman, Lee, and Lincoln. There was merely a lack of those differences in dress, manner, and mode of living by which Europeans were accustomed to recognize the distinguished person. Clerks dressed almost as well as their employers, and factory girls copied the latest Paris fashions. Scarcity of good servants, since Americans regarded domestic service as a badge of inferiority, made it impossible for all but the wealthiest to keep up a large establishment. Young married couples in the cities often had to live in a hotel or boardinghouse for lack of "help" to perform the heavy domestic tasks that modern gadgets have to some extent superseded.

It was America's busy age, or one of them. Eighteenth-century travelers scolded Americans for their indolence; nineteenth-century travelers criticized their activity. Each Northern community was an anthill, intensely active within and constantly exchanging with other hills. Every man worked, or at least made a semblance of it; the few who wished to be idle and could afford it, fled to Europe and dabbled in the arts or pursued some pallid branch of scholarship—the type of American expatriate immortalized by Henry James. Nothing struck European travelers more forcibly than the total want of public parks and pleasure resorts, of games and sports, or of simple pleasures like country walking. For the Northern American had not learned how to employ leisure. His pleasure came from doing; and as almost everyone worked for long hours six days a week, and (except in New Orleans) the Puritan sabbath prevailed, there was not much time for recreation, and very few holidays other than Thanksgiving (still confined to the Yankee area), Christmas, and the Glorious Fourth. Farmers enjoyed county fairs with their agricultural exhibits, trotting races, and sideshows. Country boys found time for shooting and fishing; Henry Thoreau in *Walden* remarked, "Almost every New England boy among my contemporaries shouldered a fowling-piece between the ages of ten and fourteen, and his hunting and fishing grounds were not limited, like the preserves of an English nobleman." But the average adult American regarded games as a waste of time. Oliver Wendell Holmes described the college students of 1832 as "soft-muscled, pasty-complectioned youth." Francis Parkman found it difficult to find a friend to go camping with him in the northern wilderness, and his classmates thought him odd to follow the Oregon trail. As early as 1840 there were informal sculling and 6- to 8-oar rowing races on the Schuylkill and in the Eastern harbors, and by college crews; rowing was the only competitive sport to be organized before the Civil War.

Country gentlemen both North and South, and many plain farmers too, took a deep interest in horse breeding, and horse racing was the most popular sport of this era. A memorable event on the turf was the running race on 27 May 1823 at Union Park, Long Island. Colonel William R. Johnson, the "Napoleon of the Turf," brought north from Virginia and Kentucky five horses to challenge nine-year-old Eclipse, descendant both of Diomed and Messenger, for the thoroughbred crown. Some 60,000 people viewed this race, in which four-year-old Sir Henry, by Sir Archie out of a daughter of Diomed, won the first four-mile heat, but lost the next two and the championship to Eclipse. At least $200,000 changed hands on this intersectional race, which was several times repeated in the next twenty years. Even more popular than running races were the harness races, trotters driven from a spindly sulky (four-wheeled at this era), a sport exclusively North American. Justin Morgan's breed dominated the trotting world, especially after it was crossed with that of the New York stallion Hambletonian, a famous name in American equine annals. He was foaled in 1849 in Orange County, New York, by Abdallah, grandson of Messenger, out of a lame mare. A farm hand bought Hambletonian and his dam for $125, and in 24 years made $300,000 in stud fees. Hambletonian blood revitalized the American quarter horse and is now considered the leading family in Standard Bred.[1] And the Morgan breed was still prominent. Ethan Allen, foaled in 1849, a descendant of Justin Morgan, won countless trotting races in the 1850's and reduced the mile record to 2:25½ in 1858. As early as 1856 there were 38 trotting courses of national repute in the Northern states, and five in the South; and every agricultural fair included a one-mile track where local sports tried the paces of their horses. "Never was such horseflesh as in those days on Long Island or in the City," wrote Walt Whitman. "Folks look'd for spirit and mettle in a nag, not tame speed merely." In this era, too, we have the first American sporting books, by "Frank Forester" (H. W. Herbert) of New Jersey. His *Warwick Woodlands*, *Field Sports*, and *Horse and Horsemanship* have become classics.

[1] Greyhound, who established a trotting harness record of 1:55¼ for the mile in 1938, came from four generations of Hambletonians, as did Adios Butler, who lowered the pacing record to 1:54⅗ in 1960.

The only completely professional sports of this era were cock-fighting and boxing. The *New York Herald* of 1850 devoted only two inches of small print, on an average, to "Sporting Intelligence," mostly local harness races and to such contests as: "A Rat Match, at no. 72 Prince Street will take place at 9 o'clock This Evening, for $50 a side, between Mr. Tibley's dog and John Walker's to kill 25 Rats each, against time." Boxing matches, a traditional Anglo-American sport, were also reported, but the "manly art" took a black eye in 1842 when two welterweights, Chris Lilly and Tom McCoy, fought 120 rounds with bare knuckles to a finish which involved the death of McCoy.

Respectable forms of public entertainment were the theater, the concert, and grand opera. There were choral societies in the larger cities, and German immigrants carried their love for Bach and Beethoven to the frontier; but apart from folk ballads, sentimental songs, and minstrel shows there was little native music.

Most famous of ballad singers were the Hutchinson quintet from New Hampshire, who toured the North and West for over thirty years. The Hutchinsons "packed 'em in" to hear jolly and sentimental songs, some of their own composition, and many with a definite antislavery slant. Every principal city had a stock company, and traveling companies brought theater to the smallest towns. Edwin Forrest of Philadelphia, William Warren of Boston, Junius Brutus Booth of Maryland and his sons Edwin and John Wilkes (the assassin) were the most famous American actors of this era. Charlotte Cushman, who graced the boards for forty years from 1835, was one of the most powerful actresses in tragic and melodramatic roles that America has ever produced. They frequently toured England; and the best English actors of the day, such as Charles Matthews, Edmund Kean, and William Macready, played to crowded houses in America. Cultural exchanges of this sort were not always happy. Kean was egged off the stage in Boston in 1825; Macready's friends countered by hissing Forrest's performance of *Macbeth* in London; and when Macready returned to New York in 1849 to act *Macbeth*, Forrest's partisans, mustered by "Captain Rynders" the Tammany brave, mobbed the theater, broke all the windows, battled a militia company, and the riot ended only after 22 people had been killed and the Astor Place Opera House completely gutted.

Although small-town "opry houses" seldom entertained grand opera, that art was imported. A company from Havana played Italian opera, including Verdi's *Ernani* and Bellini's *Norma* to crowded houses at the gas-lighted Howard Athenaeum in Boston for six consecutive weeks in the spring of 1847. Owing to old Puritan prejudice, almost every theater in New England was disguised under the name of "Museum" or "Athenaeum." So, too, was Phineas T. Barnum's American Museum of New York, a collection of oddities, freaks, fakes, and midgets, including the famous "General Tom Thumb." Barnum was the impresario for the concert tour of Jenny Lind, "The Swedish Nightingale," in 1850.

Another form of entertainment was the panorama, a painting on continuous strips of cloth arranged around a circular auditorium. John Rowson Smith, a painter of theatrical scenery in Philadelphia, made a panorama of Burning Moscow which, accompanied by bells, cannon shots, and explosions, thrilled audiences throughout the country. John Banvard traveled up and down the Mississippi to paint a panorama of the Father of Waters which was shown all over the United States and Great Britain. Benjamin Russell, a self-taught painter of New Bedford, sailed around the world in a whaleship between 1841 and 1845, making notes; and the quarter-mile panorama which he and a local house painter produced on muslin not only has considerable artistic merit but is a precious document for the ships and seaports of that era. During the infancy of photography, panoramas had an enormous vogue and were never wholly superseded until colored moving pictures were invented.

American cooking at this period was generally bad, and the diet worse. Senator Beveridge of Indiana once described to me the breakfasting habits of the people in his native village before the Civil War. Shortly after dawn the men might be seen issuing from their cabins and houses, converging on the village butcher's, where each purchased a beefsteak cut from an animal slaughtered the previous evening. Coming and going, they stopped at the village store for a dram of corn whisky. Returning, their wives prepared a breakfast of black coffee, fried beefsteak, and hot cornbread.

This regimen, and lack of outdoor exercise, made the "females" of this period somewhat "delicate"; and the robust constitutions of frontiersmen were undermined by fevers and agues, particularly in the river bottoms or alluvial plains of the Mississippi and its tributaries. "We was sick every fall regular," reminisced the mother of President Garfield. Medicine was still relatively primitive, and a lad who wanted a good medical education had to go to Austria or France, where Louis Pasteur was beginning the experiments which founded the science of bacteriology. Nobody knew how to cure tuberculosis, diphtheria, or a dozen other diseases; cholera, typhus, and yellow fever killed thousands of adults, and puerperal fever thousands of mothers every year, but nobody knew what to do about them. Dr. Oliver Wendell Holmes did indeed anticipate bacteriology by his paper on the causes of puerperal fever in 1843, but some obstetricians considered him "jejeune." A few other Americans at this period made notable contributions to medical knowledge. Dr. William W. Gerhard of Philadelphia made a careful study of cerebral meningitis in 1834 and, three years later, first distinguished typhus from typhoid fever; but he could not cure either. In searching for some better anesthetic than the old method of getting the patient dead drunk, Dr. Crawford W. Long of Georgia in 1842 and Dr. William T. G. Morton of Massachusetts in 1846, successfully applied ether, with gratifying effects on the alleviation of human suffering. On the whole, the quality of American physicians declined after 1830, owing to small, inefficient private schools of medicine supplanting the old apprentice system of training, and a complete lack of medical regulation, despite the efforts of the American Medical Association, founded in 1847.

Since America has become as famous for plumbing as for liberty, it is astonishing to find how little progress had been made in sanitary engineering before the Civil War. The lack of city water systems, and a crude system of sewers were responsible. Philadelphia, generally reckoned the cleanest North American city, set up the Fairmount waterworks, pumping water from the Schuylkill river through wooden pipes bored out of solid logs, as early as 1801; it was gradually improved to a point when, in 1830, six million gallons could be delivered daily. Low-lying New Orleans followed, of necessity, in 1833. But New York City did not complete her Croton aqueduct until 1842, and prior to the present century the principal city reservoir was on the site of the Public Library at Fifth Avenue and 42nd Street. Boston tapped Lake Cochituate, whose water was introduced with a great display of fountains in the Frog Pond in 1848. Until a town or city obtained municipal water, residents drew their supplies for cooking and drinking from wells in their back yards (cozily adjacent to the privies), or from rainwater cisterns which were breeding places for mosquitoes, or patronized tank wagons which peddled country water from door to door. Boston's four-story Tremont House, built in 1829 of native granite in the Greek revival style, with columns, capitals, and other details faithfully copied from James Stuart's *Antiquities of Attica*, had numerous public rooms and private parlors, 170 guest rooms, and eight "bathing rooms" in the basement, supplied with cold water only from rainwater cisterns. The Tremont House's rival for

"America's best hotel" was the Astor House in City Hall Square in New York, built in 1836. This had 309 guest rooms and was the first building to have running water laid on above the ground floor. Chicago, owing to difficulty of drainage, had practically no plumbing until 1861. In towns and cities, waste water from baths and sinks was commonly discharged into adjacent street gutters.

The worst pests in this era of cesspools, manure piles, and the like were flies, mosquitoes, and other insect life. Although "wire cloth" had been made since the end of the previous century, and housewives used sieves made of it, not until after the Civil War did the better houses get window screens. Cotton mosquito net was commonly draped over four-poster beds in summer, but the only way to keep flies from the food was to cover everything and wave a fan over the table.

The humble watercloset, which European humorists consider an emblem of American civilization, came in slowly, and only where city water and sewerage made it possible. Boston, with a population of 165,000 in 1857, had only 6500 W.C.s of which eight, in the basement of the Tremont House, served 200 to 300 guests. New York City had 10,384 W.C.s but only 1361 set bathtubs in 1855, when the population was 630,000. At that time, very few American bathrooms had hot water laid on. The standard bathtub was a wooden box lined with copper or zinc, filled with water brought up in buckets from the kitchen stove.

Central heating was rare, even in the cities. About a million "parlor stoves" in thousands of different designs were manufactured in 1860; but many large houses were still heated by wood or coal in open fireplaces, inadequate to keep interior plumbing from freezing in zero weather. Foreigners traveling in America, who now complain of being roasted by steam heat in winter and chilled by air-conditioning in summer, in those days could never keep warm in winter or cool in summer. Cooking stoves were being improved, but all used coal and wood fuel. Illuminating gas was fairly common by 1860—337 cities and towns in the North and 44 in the South had it piped in from central plants using coal fuel. Whale-oil lamps and tallow or spermaceti candles were universally used in country districts, and in many city houses as well, since the gas was both smelly and dangerous. Successful drilling of mineral oil wells in Pennsylvania, starting in 1859, led to a brisk development of kerosene for lighting purposes.

All in all, the United States was a pretty crude country in 1850 by present standards, or European standards of that era.

Yet, with all their drawbacks, the Northern and Western states were a land where dreams of youth came true; where the vast majority of men were doing what they wished to do, without restraint by class or administration. "We were hardly conscious of the existence of a government," wrote a Scandinavian immigrant in New York. The fun of building, inventing, creating, in an atmosphere where one man's success did not mean another's failure, gave American life that peculiar gusto that Walt Whitman caught in his poetry. Half the population were engaged in realizing the ambition of frustrated peasant ancestors for a farm of their very own, clear of rent. The other half, having achieved the farm, had tired of it; and like the boy who loses interest in his completed toy boat, had turned to some other occupation or taken up pioneering again.

2. Land and Sea Transportation

The westward movement recovered momentum after the hard times of 1837–41. New Englanders, who a generation before had settled the interior of New York and Ohio, now pressed into the smaller prairies of Indiana and Illinois, where the tough sod taxed their strength but repaid it with bountiful crops of grain; where shoulder-high prairie grass afforded rich pasturage for cattle, and groves of buckeye, oak, walnut, and hickory furnished wood and timber. A favorite objective for Yankee settlement was southern Michigan, a rolling country of "oak openings," where stately trees stood well spaced as in a park. Others were hewing farms from the forests of southern Wisconsin, and venturing across the Mississippi into land vacated by Black Hawk's warriors—to Minnesota and

Ioway, Ioway, that's where the tall corn grows!

German immigrants, and the old pioneer stock from Pennsylvania and Kentucky swelled the stream.

Improved transportation was the first condition of this quickening life. Canals, roads, and railroads not only took people west but connected them with markets when they got there. In 1826, when Charles Vaughan made a trip on the newly opened Erie Canal, the country on each side of it between Utica and Rochester had been cleared to a width of not more than one mile. Yet only next year the governor of Georgia was complaining that wheat from central New York was being sold at Savannah more cheaply than wheat from central Georgia. By bringing the Great Lakes within reach of a metro-

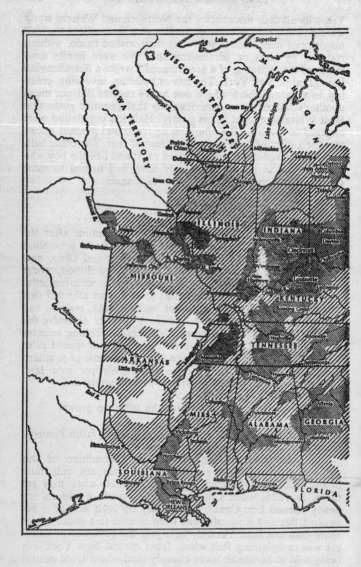

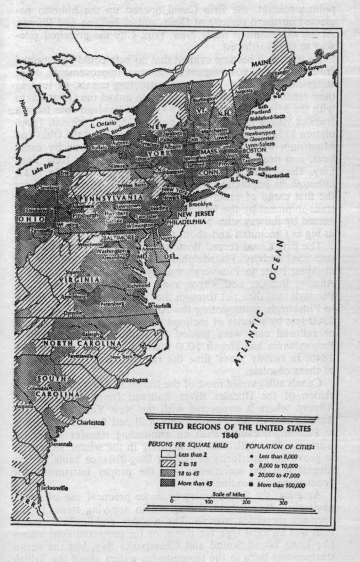

SETTLED REGIONS OF THE UNITED STATES
1840

PERSONS PER SQUARE MILE:

☐ Less than 2
▨ 2 to 18
▦ 18 to 45
▨ More than 45

POPULATION OF CITIES:

· Less than 8,000
◎ 8,000 to 10,000
● 20,000 to 47,000
⬤ More than 100,000

Scale of Miles
0   100   200   300

politan market, the Erie Canal opened up the hitherto neglected northern regions of Ohio, and of Indiana and Illinois.
At the same time it made New York City the principal gateway to the Northwest.

As soon as it became evident that no help could be expected
from the federal government for internal improvements, other
states followed New York in constructing canals, or lending
their credit to canal corporations. Ohio linked the Great Lakes
with the Mississippi valley in 1833–34. Cleveland rose from a
frontier village to a great lake port by 1850; Cincinnati (population 115,000 in 1850) sent pickled pork down the Ohio and
Mississippi by flatboat and steamer, shipped flour by canal
boat, and drove cattle on the hoof 1000 miles to New York
City. Three hundred lake vessels arrived at Chicago in 1833,
although its population was then only 350. Three years later
the first cargo of grain from Chicago arrived at Buffalo for
trans-shipment by the Erie Canal. In 1856 Chicago was connected by railway with New York, and by 1860 it was almost
as big as Cincinnati and about to pass St. Louis.

The Erie Canal forced Boston, Philadelphia, and Baltimore
into rival activity. Philadelphia was shocked to find that her
cheapest route to Pittsburgh was by way of New York City,
Albany, Buffalo, and wagon road or canal from Lake Erie.
Pennsylvania then put through the "portage" system of canals
to Pittsburgh, surmounting the Alleghenies at an elevation of
2300 feet by a series of inclined planes, up which canal boats
or railroad cars were hauled by stationary steam engines.
Pennsylvania had almost 1000 miles of canal in operation by
1840. In twenty years' time the railroads had rendered most
of them obsolete.

Canals still carried most of the freight in 1850, but the completion of the Hudson River Railroad from New York to
Albany, where it connected with the New York Central for
Buffalo, and of the Pennsylvania Railroad from Philadelphia
to Pittsburgh, caused such an astounding transfer of freight
from canals to railroads, particularly in the winter season, as
to prove the superiority of rail for long-distance hauls, and to
suggest that the locomotive was the proper instrument for
penetrating the continent.

America, the first country to make practical use of steam
navigation, lagged behind England in applying steam to the
deep-sea merchant marine. The wooden paddlewheel steamboat was an ideal type for rivers, or for protected tidal waters
like Long Island Sound and Chesapeake Bay, but the ocean
steamer was born in the tempestuous waters about the British
Isles. American shipbuilders concentrated their skill and en-

ergy on sailing vessels, which largely captured the freight and passenger traffic between Liverpool and New York. "The reason will be evident to anyone who will walk through the docks at Liverpool," wrote an Englishman in 1824. "He will see the American ships, long, sharp built, beautifully painted and rigged, and remarkable for their fine appearance and white canvas. He will see the English vessels, short, round and dirty, resembling great black tubs." The former were the flash packets of the American marine, the famous Swallow Tail and Black Ball liners, that were driven by their dandy captains, bucko mates, and Liverpool Irish crews, across the Western Ocean, winter and summer, blow high blow low, in little more than half the average time taken by the British vessels.

THE BLACK BALL LINE

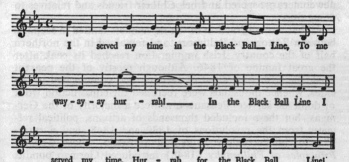

I served my time in the Black Ball Line, To me way-ay-ay hur - rah! In the Black Ball Line I served my time, Hur - rah for the Black Ball Line!

3. *Immigration*

Canal and railway construction created a demand for cheap labor, and made it easier for people to reach the West. During the decade of the 1820's only 129,000 "alien passengers" entered the United States from foreign countries; in the 1830's the number swelled to 540,000, of whom 44 per cent were Irish, 30 per cent German, and 15 per cent English; this figure was almost tripled for the 1840's, and rose to 2,814,554 for the 1850's. Roughly half of the immigrants from 1840 were Irish, with Germans a close second.[1]

Liverpool, Le Havre, and Hamburg were the principal ports

[1] To appreciate what this influx meant, the total population of the United States in millions was 9.6 in 1820, 12.9 in 1830, 17 in 1840, 23.2 in 1850, and 31.5 in 1860. The number of immigrants arriving in the 1930's was only 699,315, when the total population rose to 131.7 million.

of embarkation. European governments attempted without much success to mitigate the hardships of the passage by requiring a minimum of space, rations, and decent treatment on shipboard. Congress did not legislate on the subject until 1855; prior to that neither the federal nor the state governments attempted to protect the immigrant. Many arrived penniless, having exhausted their savings on the journey; and those who did not, often fell prey to waterfront sharpers. But, as soon as they recovered their shore legs, the immigrants were well able to defend themselves. As early as 1835 we hear of Irishmen driving the Whigs from the polls in New York, and putting the mayor and sheriff's posse to flight with showers of "Irish confetti"—brickbats. Despite the dark picture of suffering, homesickness, and difficult adjustment painted in those days by Charles Dickens, and in ours by Oscar Handlin, most of the newcomers prospered and helped their friends and relatives to come over.

All but a small fraction of the newcomers landed in seaports between Boston and Baltimore, and remained in the northern half of the country. Irish immigration reached its peak after the great famine of 1846. Although mostly of the peasant class, the Irish were tired of farming and congregated in the cities, whence thousands were recruited for construction work or domestic service. Peasants also were a majority of the Germans, but these included thousands of artisans, political refugees from the revolutions of 1830 and 1848, and a sprinkling of intellectuals such as Johann Stallo, whose *General Principles of Philosophy* (1848) introduced German pundits to American readers. German colonies were formed in the cities, especially New York, Baltimore, Cincinnati, and St. Louis; Milwaukee was a German town by 1850. But the greater number bought Western land as soon as they could earn the wherewithal, especially in Wisconsin and Missouri, which Friederich Münch hoped to make a new Germany for exiled liberals.

A few hundred refugees from the abortive Polish revolution of 1830–31 arrived in 1834, the aged Albert Gallatin headed a committee to take care of them, and Congress voted them a township from the public lands in Illinois. This attempt to start a "little Poland" in the Middle West was thwarted, partly by the hostility of nearby squatters, partly by dissensions among the Poles themselves. But this settlement did start Polish emigration to America; "Big Mike" Goldwasser, grandfather of Senator Barry Goldwater, was one who came over in 1848.

Sloop *Restaurationen,* which sailed from Stavanger in 1825

with 53 pilgrims from the northern kingdoms, was the Scandinavian *Mayflower*. Her passengers, bound for western New York, were precursors of many thousands who before the Civil War settled among the forests and lakes of Wisconsin and Minnesota, similar to those of their native land; and many more followed.

Almost every immigrant of the period 1820–60 came from northern Europe. They were naturalized, and those in the cities became Jackson Democrats, largely because the politicians of that party were the first to cultivate them, to see that they got jobs, and to help them when in trouble. This wave of immigration enhanced the wealth and progress of the country, yet encountered bitter opposition, as did Asiatics half a century later. Sudden influxes of foreigners with strange ways and attitudes always do that, everywhere. In part, the antagonism was religious, since most of the Irish and many of the Germans were Roman Catholics. In part it was due to the widespread belief among native Americans that the immigrants were paupers. It is true that European authorities, in order to relieve their taxpayers, paid for thousands of their poor to go to the United States, and some of these became public charges the moment they landed. The greater number of immigrants, however, only wanted an opportunity to work; but their need for work was so desperate that they cut wages at a time when native-born mechanics were trying to raise their standard of living through the labor unions. Natives often refused to work with the newcomers. In the depression of 1837–40, wages for common laborers fell to between 50 and 75 cents a day. "A dollar a day is a white man's pay" was an ideal rather than a fact. The only people who took much interest in the immigrants were the contractors who used their labor, the politicians who wanted their votes, and the priests who preferred ghetto-like isolation for their flocks as protection from Protestant influence. Irish immigrants of the first generation comprised 34 per cent of all voters in New York City in 1855. Yet they added surprisingly little to American economic life, and almost nothing to American intellectual life. The reform movements of the age met the determined opposition of the Irish Catholic population of the cities. Their hostility to abolitionists and hatred of free blacks became proverbial; and as the Democratic party swung into that attitude, Irish loyalty to the party of Jackson became firmer. German immigrants, even though a majority were Catholics, took the same position as native Americans on all reform issues except Prohibition. The German refused to give up his beer; instead, he made Milwaukee famous.

Protestant Irish fitted easily into American communities because they were free from the influence of the Catholic clergy, most of whose leaders had been afraid of liberalism since the French Revolution. The Irish-American press not only reflected this hostility, but expressed it in the angry tones of Dublin journalism. Orestes Brownson, a New England reformer who became a Catholic convert, attempted to acquaint Irish Catholics with the main currents of American thought but gave it up in despair. Father Isaac Hecker, converted like Brownson after a brief flirtation with transcendentalism, made a successful bridge to the German immigrants; but he became posthumously the center of a conflict within the church, in which his ideas, very similar to those of Pope John XXIII, were repudiated by Leo XIII.

Ugly racial and religious riots arose in the Eastern cities at least once every decade. These were not only the result of inherited "no popery," but also of Irish provocation. The American states had accorded to Catholic immigrants complete religious and political liberty, far more than Spain and several other Catholic countries have accorded Protestants to this day. Native-born Americans disliked having their heads broken by the "bhoys" when they attempted to vote Whig in the cities, and resented Catholic agitation against the use of the King James Bible in the public schools. The Irish, on the other hand, resented having Protestant-slanted textbooks crammed down their children's throats, and regarded as Protestant bigotry the understandable reluctance of employers to give "genteel" jobs to newly arrived uncouth peasants.

In 1843, nativist resentment against immigrants, mostly Irish in the East and German in the West, boiled over into politics. A short-lived "American Republican party" was founded, pledged to obtain a new naturalization law requiring a residence of 21 years. In the midst of this agitation occurred the worst religious riot of the century in the "City of Brotherly Love."

The Philadelphia school board in 1843 conceded the Catholic bishop's reasonable request that pupils of his faith be allowed to use the Douay version of the Bible, and be exempted from other religious exercises. This sparked a campaign of vilification—"The Pope reigns in Philadelphia," etc.—by local anti-Catholics and their weekly newspaper. In the spring municipal election of 1844, "American Republican" voters were assaulted and driven from the polls in Irish Catholic districts. This and other incidents aroused the "Americans," who around 1 May provocatively held mass meetings in the heart of Kensington, the principal Irish district. They were driven out with clubs, stones, and shots, one of which killed a Protestant boy. The "Americans" rallied, advanced armed into Kensington, and burned down about thirty houses, together with St. Michael's and St. Augustine's churches. Some 200 Irish families were rendered homeless, militia had to be called out to restore order, and rioting again flared when the "Americans" staged an anti-Catholic parade. A third Catholic church was then attacked, and bluejackets from U.S.S. *Princeton* helped the militia to defend the church and disperse the rioters. Order finally was restored, but casualties in the two sets of riots amounted to 30 killed and 150 wounded.

These riots had the effect of discrediting the "American Republicans" as "church burners," and the movement went underground, except in Baltimore. That lusty, growing city, which had acquired a sinister reputation for mobbing as early as 1812, was dominated on the low level by white native American workmen, who were equally hostile to blacks and to the Irish, and intimidated Irish Catholics from voting. Edgar Allan Poe died a victim of Baltimore political practices. Arriving from Richmond by steamer just before the fall election of 1849, in a state of advanced inebriation, he was seized and hustled into one of the "coops," where local Whig politicians kept down-and-outs "on ice" for repeated voting. He was rescued after five days' detention, but in such condition that he died in a hospital.

4. Manufacturing

New methods of transportation not only helped to people the North and West; by extending the domestic market they hastened industrialization, and attracted rural boys and girls to urban communities. Between 1820 and 1850 the combined population of New York, Philadelphia, Baltimore, and Boston rose from 343,000 to 1,162,000. During the 1840's the population of the United States went up 36 per cent, but the growth of towns and cities of 8000 or more people showed a phenomenal 90 per cent increase. Measured by numbers, the urban movement was stronger than westward migration; and its effect on the American character has been equally important.

The factory system for cotton spinning and weaving became firmly established in New England as a result of the War of 1812. In Europe, textile machinery destroyed domestic industries in which the worker owned his tools and implements; but in America there was so little domestic weaving that the factory was introduced without friction. By 1840 there were

1200 cotton factories in the United States, operating 2,250,000 spindles, two-thirds of them in New England. Ring or frame spinning had been invented, power looms were being manufactured in large numbers, and even exported.

Francis C. Lowell, inventor of the first American power loom, was a man of social vision. At Robert Owen's model town in Scotland, he learned to run a factory without degrading labor. Farmers' daughters were attracted to the new factory city of Lowell, Massachusetts, by relatively high wages; the scruples of their parents were overcome by the provision of strictly chaperoned boardinghouses. For a generation the Lowell factory girls, with their neat dresses, correct deportment, and literary weekly, were one of the wonders of America. Never, unforunately, were they typical of America; but, owing to wide opportunities in a rapidly developing country, no permanent proletariat was created. Factory girls left the mills to marry after three or four years, and child laborers elsewhere usually managed to find some other occupation by the time they reached their majority.

Woolen manufactures developed more slowly, and although protected by higher tariff schedules than those of cotton, were less successful in capturing the domestic market. Lawrence, Massachusetts, a woolen counterpart to Lowell, was established on the same river in 1845. Rhode Island, with Woonsocket and Pawtucket, became another important textile center. By 1850 there were over 1500 woolen mills in the Northern states; most of them small, individually owned establishments with a few sets of machinery, employing country people of the neighborhood, and producing blankets, flannel, and coarse worsteds.

In England the industrial revolution depended largely on coal and iron, but not in the United States. Textile and other mills were operated largely by water power, and the iron industry developed very slowly. Suitable coal for coking was not found east of the Appalachians, and Pennsylvanian ironmasters were more skillful in obtaining tariff protection than in improving their methods. Cort's puddling process, invented in 1783, was not introduced to America until 1830, and then on a small scale. Even Pittsburgh, "the Birmingham of America," used charcoal for smelting prior to 1840, rather than the bituminous coal which was plentiful in the neighborhood. American production of pig iron, only 54,000 tons in 1810, increased tenfold in 40 years; but by 1850 Great Britain's production was almost 3 million tons, and the United States was importing iron and steel to almost twice the value of the domestic product. Almost every waterfall in Connecticut was harnessed to a small factory for making machine tools, fire-arms, furniture (the famous Hitchcock chairs), wooden clocks, and all manner of oddments. Connecticut tin ware and wooden ware were carried by Yankee peddlers far and wide; and one of the standard jokes of this era was the Yankee peddler who sold wooden nutmegs and basswood hams to unsuspecting Southerners.

Most American industries developed locally, as a result of some person's enterprise, but others were imported directly from Europe. The pottery towns of England, for instance, sent scores of entrepreneurs and thousands of potters to various towns of the Middle West, where clay suitable for making domestic crockery was found. Viticulture was begun by Nicholas Longworth of Cincinnati, who after much experimentation settled on the native Catawba grape as a base; and by 1830 wine making had become a leading industry of south-western Ohio. Although Longworth and his compeers never succeeded in making America a nation of wine drinkers, their enterprise extended profitably into central New York, and eventually to California. And the introduction of American *porte-greffes,* grafted vine stalks, rescued European vineyards from the devastation of the phylloxera rot in the last third of the century.

The most important American industry that remained in the domestic stage until after the Civil War was boot and shoe making, for which no machine process of any importance had been invented. In New England it was a winter occupation of farmers and fishermen who, when the harvest was gathered or the vessel hauled out for the winter, formed a "crew" to make shoes in a neighborhood workshop, from stock put out by some local merchant. Every man was master of his own time, and had something to fall back on when demand slackened; there was no clatter of machinery to drown discussion. A boy was often hired to read to the workers. It was said that "Every Lynn shoemaker was fit to be a United States Senator"; and Henry Wilson, "the cordwainer of Natick," became Vice President.

XI

The Empire State, Citadel of Democracy

1820-1860

1. *New York State and City in Mid-Century*

THE DEMOCRATIC PARTY's solidarity from 1828 to 1860 to a great extent was the work of the New York wing. From Martin Van Buren's upstate machine the "Albany Regency," and Tammany Hall in New York City, emanated the political methods and tactics that were copied by both parties throughout the Union, as well as the objectives that held Democrats together. In New York, too, lived most of the few intellectuals who supported the party with brain and pen.

The "Empire State"—a sobriquet which at this time replaced the plain old "York State"—was justly so called. With 1,372,812 inhabitants in 1820, New York, which had been one of the smaller states at the time of the Revolution, reached first place. And she held that distinction through all subsequent censuses, although probably passed by California in 1964. In 1880 New York was the first state to count more than 5 million inhabitants; in 1920, first to have more than 10 million; in 1951, first to reach 15 million; and in 1960, still first with 16.8 million. Between 1830 and 1860 New York contained about one-seventh of the population of the United States, which made her electoral vote top prize in a presidential contest. And a galaxy of brilliant politicians exploited this advantage to the full.

New York City, first in the United States since 1820, grew even faster than the state, partly because of the Western commerce that came to it via river and railroad, but also through the skill of its financiers and merchants in handling Southern and European trade. President Jackson, in his war on the Bank of the United States, was not trying to build up Wall Street at the expense of Chestnut Street, Philadelphia; but that is precisely what he accomplished. An ambitious state program of public works created thousands of jobs and attracted hordes of immigrants, especially Irish. There were 343,000 Irish-born in New York State in 1850, thrice the number of the next nationality, the Germans. Most of them stayed in or near the city, but many settled along the line of the Erie Canal, for the digging of which they supplied much of the labor.

The city's increase in population was phenomenal; there has been nothing like it since, even in California. It passed the 100,000 mark about 1815; 300,000 in 1840; and in 1850 counted 515,547 souls, to which should be added 96,838 living in Brooklyn. The 1960 population was 7,781,984. New York City was a bustling metropolis with no distinction except that of its magnificent site and harbor. The masts of square-riggers at the wharves topped the highest buildings, except a few church steeples; City Hall was the finest structure; shops and office buildings with cast-iron fronts and frames, precursors of the steel skyscraper, were just beginning to rise, and A. T. Stewart's, the first big department store, was opened in 1845 on Broadway between Read and Chambers Streets. At the time the city had only one restaurant, Delmonico's at 2 South William Street, but plenty of "eating-houses." Visiting foreigners admired the monuments of Baltimore, the rows of imposing stone public buildings in Philadelphia, the lush gardens of New Orleans, and the literary society of Boston; but they found nothing to praise in New York except the bustle.

The built-up part of Manhattan extended only to 14th Street in 1820, and to 42nd Street in 1850. Everything north of 44th Street was then country; Edgar Allan Poe and his wife boarded with a farmer at Broadway and 84th Street in 1844 and lived in a cottage at the rural village of Fordham in 1846. Central Park was laid out in 1856, just in time to save that rocky central spine of Manhattan for the people. Downtown New York had no public parks, only a few open squares restricted to residents.

Fortunes were being accumulated by the Astors and others simply by holding on to real estate in a growing city; and also by the bankers, merchants, and shipbuilders. The New York Yacht Club, founded in 1844, put on a "voyage" to Newport under Commodore Stevens that year. New York society was easygoing and flexible in comparison with the top social circles of Boston, Philadelphia, Baltimore, and Charleston. As a cultural center, however, the city fell short of her competitors, largely for want of institutions of higher education. Columbia University, the only college in the city until 1831 when New York University was founded, graduated on an average only 24 bachelors of arts each year between 1835 and the Civil War; N.Y.U. added a bare 21 to the list, and Fordham a few more after 1841. New York businessmen, unlike those of other cities, did not send their sons to college. The boys went straight into business from school or read law by the apprentice system in a lawyer's office, or attended a medical school or theological seminary. People raising money for New England and Western colleges never bothered to apply to the rich men of New York; it was no use.

An integral part of the American political picture from 1820 to the present has been the "foreign vote," that of recent immigrants and their children. After manhood suffrage went into effect in New York in 1827, Tammany Hall developed a system of recruiting aliens, in contrast to the indifferent or hostile attitude of Federalists and Whigs. Immigrants, especially the Irish, were met at the dock, assisted in finding jobs, and rushed through naturalization, sometimes in a few days, although five years were required by federal law. Chief hatchet man of "The Wigwam" (Tammany Hall) was "Captain" Isaiah Rynders, a former New Orleans gambler of uncertain origin. His henchmen were mostly Irish—John Morrissey, a popular prizefighter; "Honest John" Kelly, "Slippery Dick" Connolly, and "Mike" Walsh.

Saloons and volunteer fire companies, social organizations such as the "chowder and marching clubs," were organized by Democratic politicians. By 1855 over 300 of the city's 1100 policemen were Irish. The immigrants were slow to obtain clerical positions for want of education (New York's schools were unable to keep up with the flow of newcomers); and not until after the Civil War were any appreciable number of them elected alderman or state assemblyman. Immigrants in general gave their votes for the satisfaction of immediate needs—shelter, jobs, relief, and friendship. An alliance between urban politicians, the underworld of gambling and prostitution, and the foreign vote was already cemented in 1850.

In New York State at large, especially along the colonial

highway of the Hudson river and in western Long Island, descendants of Dutch colonists were still the ruling class, socially and financially. Martin Van Buren, though not of the elite, attracted a large part of it, including the Livingstons and Roosevelts, into his party. But in the great seaport and the interior, the Yankees, as Washington Irving wrote in his delightful *Knickerbocker's History*, were still disproving the ancient adage that a rolling stone gathers no moss. Merchants and shipowners, with a keen scent for new opportunities, deserted decaying seaports of New England for New York City. Farmers for whom the hills of New Hampshire and Vermont offered little attraction, flocked into the Mohawk valley to provide a body of thrifty husbandmen and a top layer of ambitious citizens eager for a chance to get rich from a country store or bank, handling produce, selling land, floating stock of a canal or turnpike company. These were the men who broke the rural, semi-feudal pattern of the Dutch patroons. As early as 1840 one-quarter of the population of the state, and two-thirds in New York City, were engaged in trades and manufacturing; mostly in small, widely scattered establishments run by water power.

Albany was the upstate metropolis as well as the capital; Rochester, Schenectady, Syracuse, Utica, and Buffalo had not yet caught up. A few miles from Albany lay Saratoga Springs, the leading American spa, with enormous firetrap hotels where for a modest room-and-board of two dollars a day you could meet everybody who was anybody. Into Albany poured Hudson river steamboats and schooners, the railway that became (under Commodore Vanderbilt's manipulation in the 1850's) the New York Central, and the Western Railroad from Boston which eventually the N.Y.C. swallowed. Westward-bound passengers crossed the Hudson by horsepower ferry in summer or sleigh in winter, and there entrained on a railroad which, with several changes, took them to Buffalo, the gateway through which freight and people streamed westward. By 1845 almost 100,000 westward-bound people were passing annually through Buffalo.

Upstate New York, owing to the predominantly New England population, was well provided with secondary academies and colleges. As people pushed up the Mohawk valley, Protestant sects saw to it that they obtained the proper facilities. Union College at Schenectady (Presbyterian) came early under the presidency of a celebrated academic czar, the Reverend Eliphalet Nott, who outlasted all critics and hung up an all-time record of 62 years for a college presidential term.

Hamilton College (Congregationalist) at Clinton was founded in 1812; Hobart (Episcopalian) at Geneva in 1822, Colgate (Baptist) at Hamilton in 1835, the University of Rochester (Baptist) in 1850. These were denominational colleges of the familiar New England pattern, which in time developed into non-sectarian universities. New York's most original contribution to higher education was Rensselaer Polytechnic Institute, founded at Troy in 1824. This was the precursor of M.I.T., California Tech, and a host of engineering and technical universities. It was at Rensselaer that Amos Eaton, an expert botanist and geologist who had studied under Benjamin Silliman at Yale, initiated scientific training by individual laboratory work and field trips.

2. The Albany Regency and National Party Organization

Martin Van Buren was not only responsible for bringing order, discipline, and cohesion to the forces that followed the Jackson banner; he may be considered the principal architect of the modern American political party. When he entered the United States Senate in 1821 he left control of New York politics in charge of a coterie of his friends who were first known as the "Holy Alliance," and then as the "Albany Regency." With uncanny instinct for a winner, Van Buren won them for Andrew Jackson in 1824, and they became the backbone of the new Democratic party.

All members of the "Regency" were transplanted New Englanders; the most important being William L. Marcy who, when defending Van Buren in the United States Senate, added to our political vocabulary by stating that he could see "nothing wrong in the rule that to the victor belongs the spoils of the enemy." John A. Dix, Silas Wright "the Cato of the Senate," a confidant of Van Buren as Van had been of Jackson; Benjamin Franklin Butler, Van Buren's law partner,[1] and Samuel A. Talcott, editor of the Regency's mouthpiece, the Albany *Argus,* were also of New England origin. These were not faceless local "pols," but well-educated, public-spirited men of character. Their views on social and economic questions varied between left center and extreme right, but they agreed that the Democratic party in New York must be a united center party. This they effected by a system of rewards and

[1] Jackson's attorney general and secretary of war, not to be confused with the Civil War general and Massachusetts politician (1818–93) of the same name.

punishments, through control of the state senate and so (under the constitution of 1821) of appointive offices. They extended their organization into every town and county, which afforded them an unparalleled political intelligence service. By supporting winning presidential candidates in 1828, 1832, and 1836, they got a stranglehold on the federal patronage as well. Van Buren and his friends, regarding themselves as champions of "the people" against "special interests," advocated making former appointive offices elective since they could select the candidates in party conventions. They honestly believed that "the people," to prevail against organized wealth, must be led by bosses and kept in line by the spoils system.

The Albany Regency was embarrassed by Jackson's war on the Bank of the United States, which upstate Democrats interpreted as a war on all paper-issuing banks, and insistence on hard-money currency. That did not suit the city financiers at all; they were delighted with Jackson's downing the Philadelphia bank, but a prohibition on issuing bank notes would have spoiled the juicy prospect of making Wall Street the nation's financial center. Democratic politicians, fearing lest their new friends the city bankers go Whig, resisted the upstate hard-money program. The result was a temporary schism in Democratic ranks. And in 1835 there was a radical rebellion in the usually solid Tammany organization over the subject of "monopolies," as the dissidents called chartered turnpikes, railroads, banks, and manufacturing corporations. The rebels had the majority in a nominating caucus but the regulars turned off the gas. Undaunted, the rebels found candles, struck a light with a new brand of safety match called "locofoco," and continued the meeting. They organized as the Equal Rights party, won the support of the *Evening Post* while editor Bryant was in Europe, and drew up their own slate of candidates. Playing the political game according to the accepted rules, they dickered with Whigs and other possible allies for mutual exchange of endorsements. That was one reason why the thirty-seven-year-old Whig candidate William H. Seward was elected governor in 1838. But the "Locofocos," as their rivals named them, really wished to control the Democratic party in order to establish hard money, abolish charter privileges, and enforce strict accountability of representatives to their constituents. Believing they were in line with national Democratic policies, they sought to organize on a statewide basis, taking in a local third party called the Workingmen's, which wanted free schools and other reforms.

Despite these internal stresses between doctrinaire radicals and the expedient, anything-to-win politicians, the New York

Democratic party held together well enough to give Van Buren the state's electoral votes for president in 1837. After his election the President, by a judicious use of patronage, pulled the dissidents back into regularity, undercut the Locofocos, and apparently restored the former solidarity. But in 1842 the Democrats split again over the issue of expanding the state canal network by public loans. The two wings of the party, the conservative "Hunkers" and the radical "Barnburners" (as the Locofocos were now called) became clearly defined. In 1845 the latter, disappointed because President Polk gave none of them a cabinet office, moved toward the Free-Soil opposition, which attained national importance in 1848.

The Albany Regency's political system in New York spread throughout the Union, although issues differed from state to state. Party organization in the Jackson era settled into a pattern that has changed little since. In contrast to its British prototype, which exists normally on the one level for electing members of Parliament, the American party existed in three layers, federal, state, and municipal. Analysis of the Whig and Democratic parties and their successors reveals a bundle of local, sectional, and class interests. Their cross sections, instead of displaying a few simple colors, were a jigsaw puzzle of radicalism and conservatism, nationalism and state rights, personal loyalties and local issues. Party strategy was directed toward accumulating as many bundles as possible, and statesmanship was the art of finding some person or principle common to all factions that would make them sink their differences and in union find strength.

Constitutional developments in the states were quickly reflected in the national party organizations. State constitutional changes between 1830 and 1850, in most instances effected by constitutional conventions and popular referendums, tended toward government of, for, and by the people. Religious tests and property qualifications for office were swept away, and manhood suffrage adopted. The newer state constitutions, beginning with that of Mississippi in 1832, transferred many offices from the appointive to the elective class. County officials such as sheriffs and justices of the peace, heads of executive departments such as state treasurer and attorney general, even judges of the higher courts, were henceforth elected by the people; and the democratic principle of rotation limited both the number and the length of their terms. As the urban movement gathered volume, new municipalities with elective mayors and bicameral city councils were established. Political partisanship extended down from the federal to the state and municipal governments: a good Democrat would no more think of voting for a Whig governor or a Whig sheriff than for a Whig congressman or President. Federal, state, and local politics were so closely articulated that the misconduct of a state treasurer might turn a presidential election, and the attitude of a President on the tariff or the public lands might embarrass his party's candidates for municipal office. State legislatures consumed much time in drafting resolutions on federal subjects outside their competence, for the purpose of attracting voters and influencing Congress.

The convention method of nominating candidates for elective office, if not invented by the Albany Regency, was perfected by it, spread nationwide, and was adopted by the Whigs. Local caucuses sent delegates to county conventions which nominated candidates for county offices and elected the delegates to state conventions for nominating state candidates, and to district conventions for nominating congressional candidates. State conventions chose delegates to the quadrennial national convention for nominating presidential candidates and drafting the platform. Few but professional politicians managed to survive these successive winnowings. Every state had its captains of tens, hundreds, and thousands working for the party every day in the year, and looking for reward to the spoils of victory. Annual or biennial state and local elections kept interest from flagging during a presidential term, and were regarded as portents of the next general election. Innumerable local rallies, often synchronized with an anniversary, a county fair, or a barbecue, gave the leaders an occasion for inspiring the faithful, "spellbinding" the doubtful, and confounding the enemy. Steamboats and railways now carried political orators long distances without undue expenditure of time, enabling them to speak in many parts of the country. In 1840, for instance, Senator Rives of Virginia addressed a vast outdoor gathering at Auburn, New York, for three and a half hours, after which Legaré of South Carolina carried on for two and a half hours more. Clay addressed 12,000 men in a tobacco factory, Webster stumped from Vermont to Virginia, attracting audiences of 15,000. On one occasion, so many favorite sons preceded Webster at an evening rally that he did not come on until 2:00 a.m.; he talked for over an hour, "and you could have heard a pin drop," the audience was so entranced. Seargent Prentiss, whom many regarded as the greatest American orator, in the same campaign made speeches in Portland, New Orleans, Chicago, and fifty other places.

This was a good system for socially democratic regions where politics still offered the most attractive career to talented and ambitious men, and where the people, for want of other diversions, took a keen interest in government. Men like Abraham Lincoln rose through the caucus and convention to heights that they could hardly have attained otherwise. But in the cities and manufacturing districts of the North, and wherever social inequality prevailed, property went in search of political power and the politicians in search of property. The multiplicity of elective offices and the spoils system led to corruption. The rough-and-tumble of politics repelled good men from public life, and the civil service was degraded in America when it was improving in England. As Emerson jotted in his Journal in 1845 after the election of Polk, the Whigs, "The real life and strength of the American people, find themselves paralyzed and defeated everywhere by the hordes of ignorant and deceivable natives and the armies of foreign voters who fill Pennsylvania, New York and New Orleans. . . . The creators of wealth, and conscientious, rational and responsible persons, . . . find themselves degraded into observers, and violently turned out of all share in the actions and counsels of the nation." Yet these political methods, insofar as they aroused the active interest of the average voter and stimulated party loyalty, strengthened the Federal Union. They brought humble men forward and rewarded ability.

3. The Anti-Rent War

Most political parties start radical but turn conservative after they reach power. This principle is well illustrated by the Democratic party in New York. It took a popular rebellion and a constitutional convention to bring about a reform which should have been dealt with in the early years of the Republic.

Rensselaerswyck and Livingston Manor on the Hudson, covering respectively 24 by 48 miles and 10 by 18 miles of good agricultural land, as well as smaller manors like Scarsdale, Pelham, and Fordham which covered most of Westchester County, were the principal targets. Land in these manors was not held by the occupants in absolute ownership but by perpetual lease from the lord of the manor, in return for a bewildering variety of feudal dues. These were more irksome than onerous—such as ten bushels of wheat per 100 acres, one day's labor of a man and yoke of oxen and, inevitably, "four fat hens." (One wonders what the Van Rensselaers and Livingstons did with so many hens, lacking deep freeze.) The really burdensome thing to the tenant was "quarter money." This meant that if he sold out, at least 25 per cent of the sum he received went to the landlord. And the tenant paid state and local taxes, and for all improvements to his farm. From time to time popular discontent with these outmoded charges broke out in local riots; but the influence of the old families was still so pervasive that nothing was done about it until the death of Stephen Van Rensselaer, "the last patroon," in 1839. That sparked off a rebellion. As a contemporary ballad puts it,

> A great revolution has happened of late,
> And the pride-fallen landlord laments his sad fate;
> The cry has gone out through the nine counties o'er,
> Our landlord is falling to rise nevermore.

Since America became independent, Van Rensselaer had let out the hitherto untilled part of his enormous domain to thousands of immigrants from New England and elsewhere, on the same old feudal terms. But he had been so easygoing about collecting the rent that at the time of his death the tenants owed his estate some hundreds of thousands of dollars and about a million fat hens; and when the patroon's sons tried to collect, trouble arose. Farmers in the western, hilly part of Albany County forcibly resisted the serving of writs. Governor Seward called out the militia and put down the embattled farmers by force. He did appoint a commission to look into the whole matter; but before it reported, the "anti-rent war," as these disturbances were called, broke out in the Livingston and other manors.

These affairs usually took the form of men crudely disguised as Indians[1] who tarred, feathered, or otherwise maltreated sheriffs when trying to serve writs for overdue rent. The New York legislature, on recommendation of Seward's Democratic successor Governor Silas Wright, passed a law punishing men who appeared in disguise carrying arms. After a body of 200 "Injins" in Delaware County had opened fire on a sheriff's posse and killed one of his deputies, the governor declared that county to be in "a state of insurrection." Sixty of the rebels were imprisoned, and two of them convicted of murder. Next, a convention of anti-rent delegates from eleven counties was held at Berne, birthplace of the movement; a weekly paper, *The Anti-Renter,* was published at Albany; ballads were written and songbooks published, and candidates for the state assembly were required to declare themselves pro- or

[1] J. Fenimore Cooper sneers at these "Injins" and vents his indignation over the anti-rent movement in his novel *The Redskins.*

anti-rent. The issue was thus forced into politics; but the politicians cannily passed the buck to the state constitutional convention of 1846.

This convention, to which a majority of Democrats, but no leading politician, was elected, drafted a new and democratic constitution. All judges were to be popularly elected for definite terms, white adult male suffrage was adopted, one-year terms for assemblymen and two years for state senators were set. On the anti-rent question, the bill of rights was augmented by declaring "feudal tenures of every description with all their incidents to be abolished"; and, "no lease or grant of agricultural land for a longer period than twelve years" should thereafter be legal.

Actually, the system was already on the way out, because the anti-rent agitation had forced most landlords to cancel or modify their leases. But the constitutional convention of 1846 put a seal on the process, leaving the Province of Quebec the only place in North America where feudal dues and services persisted. Henceforth the Van Rensselaers and Livingstons had to raise their own poultry.

The New York Whigs, despite their respect for vested rights, showed more sympathy for the anti-renters than did the Democrats. Walt Whitman, editor of the Democratic *Brooklyn Eagle*, denounced the anti-renters as a "violent faction which had disgraced the state." The Whig candidate for governor, said Walt, was counting on the spirit of rebellion to win. "Let the people judge," he added smugly, "whether the Indians shall again raise their fiendish cries." The Whigs won, nevertheless. The reason for this party line is clear. Democratic politicians, who once had been radical, were now trying to shake off the curse. Since the Whigs liked to accuse them of flirting with various "isms," they were eager to appear respectable and conservative, so that the Democratic party could pose as the nationwide defender of the Union and of property. In this aim they were very successful until a fire that they were unable to quench—antislavery—blew them apart.

In the Democratic state convention of 1847 a so-called "cornerstone resolution" expressing "uncompromising hostility" to slavery extension was adopted. That really split the party, causing the formation of the Free-Soilers, whose presidential nomination was accepted by Van Buren, smarting from his defeat by "dark horse" Polk. David Dudley Field, who drafted this cornerstone resolution, was one of the party's reformers. Almost singlehanded he carried on against the New York bench and bar (notably against Chancellor Kent) a campaign for codification of the common law. This reform, which Daniel Webster called "the wildest and weakest argument of the age," was conceived as a protection of the people from lawyers. Field's code of civil procedure, rejected by New York, was adopted in whole or part by 24 states; and since (as has well been said), substantive law has been "gradually secreted in the interstices of procedure," Field may be considered one of the great law reformers of the century.

4. *The Intellectuals*

In New York State, American democracy found most of its intellectual supporters. Van Buren appointed as secretary of the navy James Kirke Paulding, who had done more than anyone except Washington Irving to make popular the traditions and folkways of the old Dutch. Although Irving never pretended to be a Democrat, President Jackson gave him his first diplomatic appointment, secretary of the American legation in London, where he was already famous for his *Sketch Book* and *Life of Columbus*. Irving met Van Buren in London, and they became lifelong friends; in return for the author's introducing him to English country life, Van Buren took him on a two-week tour of the Hudson valley in 1833, to gather more Dutch legends. But Irving "ratted" on the Democrats after he had become a country gentleman near Tarrytown, and accepted an appointment by President Tyler as minister to Spain. Nominally a Democrat, J. Fenimore Cooper, after returning from Europe in 1833, devoted himself to berating democratic aspects of American life. He continued to produce novels, but became as stodgy and contemptuous of the American scene as Irving.

The most fruitful of President Van Buren's diplomatic ventures was to send John Lloyd Stephens, a New York lawyer and Tammany Hall orator, on a somewhat hazy mission to the Federal Republic of Central America. Intrigued by previous hints from Europeans of jungle-covered ruins, Stephens traveled in company with an English artist named Frederick Catherwood, to sketch them. The *Incidents of Travel in Central America, Chiapas, and Yucatán*, which they published jointly in 1841, introduced Palenque, Chichen Itzá, Copan, Uxmal, and other forgotten Mayan cities to an astonished world, and founded the science of American archaeology.

Nathaniel P. Willis, who wrote, "The shadows lay along Broadway, 'Twas near the twilight tide," was one of thirty or more poets who lived in New York City. They formed little self-conscious coteries, oases of culture in a desert of commerce, meeting at a bookshop on the corner of Broadway and Pine Street. The most famous, Fitz-Greene Halleck, is remembered for his lyric "Marco Bozzaris." But he also wrote mildly amusing satires on city politics and society. Halleck and his pals would have been greatly astonished to learn that the fame of one whom they never recognized as a poet has outlasted them all. This was Clement C. Moore, professor of Hebrew and Greek at the General Theological Seminary, forever famous for the poem that he tossed off at Christmastide 1821:

> 'Twas the night before Christmas, and all through the
> house . . .

Santa Claus, hitherto a tutelary deity of the New York Dutch, reached every child in America through that poem. Moore's other claim to fame is his success in procuring a Columbia College professorship in Italian for Lorenzo da Ponte, a talented scamp from Venezia, who in his youth had written the librettos for Mozart's *Le Nozze di Figaro, Don Giovanni,* and *Cosi Fan Tutte.* Da Ponte may claim to have been the herald of Italian culture in North America; he taught the first classes on Dante at Columbia, promoted Italian opera, and, supported by other Italian immigrants who had made money, built the first opera house in New York in 1833. It was a dismal failure, and Da Ponte died poor and forgotten in 1838, wishing he had cast his lot in Athenian Paris rather than Boeotian New York.

All these people were on the fringe, as it were, of democratic culture in New York City. The core consisted of a series of literary periodicals of which the most notable was *The Literary World,* edited by Evert Augustus Duyckinck. He held a salon at 10 Clinton Place, where American writers whom he appreciated were welcomed and distinguished foreigners were entertained. Duyckinck, a fastidious gentleman, edited the best anthology of American literature published in the nineteeth century, and contributed to *The Democratic Review.* John Louis O'Sullivan, the editor of that monthly, coined the phrase "manifest destiny" in 1845, founded the "Young America" movement, and dedicated his periodical "to strike the hitherto silent string of the democratic genius of the age and the country." He and his contributors, whose names are now known only to graduate students writing dissertations on American literature, were a pretty sad lot. They were always shouting for a national literature free from contamination by decadent Europe; but whenever a writer of national scope appeared, such as Emerson, they failed to recognize him. They objected to Parkman's *Oregon Trail* because his Indians did not resemble Cooper's Indians, and sneered at Melville's *White Jacket* as manufactured for the English market by a traitor to his country.

The Whigs, too, had their organ, *The American Review,* which in 1845 thus challenged the Democrats: "If they want something really native, let them consider the Ethiopian Minstrels; let them hold up as the national symbol, Jim Crow." This really went home, for the minstrel show was a native folk art which blossomed in New York City out of African dancing, singing, and banjo-playing. After a New York "ham" actor named Thomas Rice had made an astounding success with his character "Jim Crow," Edwin P. Christy in 1842 put on the first full evening of his "Virginia Minstrels" in a pattern that endured into the twentieth century. In the first act the performers, most of them white men in blackface, sat in a semicircle around the interlocutor, a dignified colored gentleman in dress suit who acted both as master of ceremonies and butt for the jokes of the end men—"Mistah Tambo" who banged a tambourine, and "Mistah Bones" who rattled castanets. Besides repartee and horseplay, the cast played banjo melodies and sang comic or sentimental songs. The second act, known as the olio, included a "hoe-down" dance, comic parodies of grand opera, and a "walk-around," in which the players one by one took the center of the stage for individual songs or dances while the rest clapped time to the music. Minstrel shows were immensely popular. Christy's played continuously in New York City for nine years and made a triumphal tour of England; in the 1850's ten theaters were presenting minstrel shows in New York alone.

The Democratic literati despised the minstrel show as unworthy of "Young America"; but, though unable to comprehend Melville's *Mardi* or *Moby-Dick,* they inadvertently helped to launch him on a literary career. When Louis McLane accepted the London legation in 1845 to help President Polk solve the Oregon question, he was given as first secretary a young man from Albany named Gansevoort Melville, who was looked upon as the coming Democratic orator to rival Webster; and it was Gansevoort who sold *Typee,* the first book by his younger brother Herman, to a London publisher. Herman roamed the seas to very good purpose, when he might have been picking political plums in New York; and his masterpiece, *Moby-Dick,* came out in 1851. No second edition was needed for over sixty years, and *Billy Budd,* now the basis for a movie, two plays, and an opera, he could never get published. He showed no interest in politics and received his first political appointment, that of a customs inspector on the New York wharves, after the Civil War.

William Cullen Bryant, whose position as America's greatest poet was disputed only by Poe (and in the next two decades by Longfellow), maintained a loose connection between the Democratic party and the intellectuals by virtue of his long editorship of the New York *Evening Post*. Bryant supported the workers' right to strike at a time when judges called strikes conspiracies, and endeavored to counteract Democracy's pro-slavery tendencies. He followed Van Buren into the Free-Soil party, returned to the fold with Franklin Pierce, but went Republican with Frémont. President Pierce obtained for his Bowdoin College classmate Nathaniel Hawthorne, in return for writing the campaign biography, two custom house jobs, the meager income from which enabled the "Locofoco surveyor," as he humorously described himself, to write *The Scarlet Letter*.

Almost every member of the Democratic literary coterie enjoyed at one period or another a clerkship in the New York Custom House, as reward for hewing to the party line. Thus the party "took care" of its intellectuals. But the attempt of these literati to create a democratic literature was a dismal failure; and when Walt Whitman, who had taken their admonitions to heart, published his first book, he got nothing from them but contumely.

Walt could have occurred nowhere else but in New York. He edited or contributed to twelve or fifteen different newspapers and magazines; he wandered through the streets of "the Manhatoes" and along the then deserted beaches of "Paumanok" (Long Island); he rubbed shoulders with wildcat journalists, reformers, Tammany braves, Irish workingmen, saloon keepers, ferryboat sailors, drunks, and bawds. Especially he loved the theater, for which this was a golden era in New York City;[1] and at Da Ponte's opera house he became fairly intoxicated with the "vocalism of sun-bright Italy." Walt's genius, applied to this hotchpot of experience, produced his *Leaves of Grass* (1855). After losing his job on the *Eagle* for refusing to follow the party line in 1848, Whitman became independent of clique or party; but always, after his brief attack on the anti-renters, on the side of "liberdad" and the "comerados" of equality and fraternity. For word pictures of mid-century New York there is nothing to compare with the poetry and prose of Walt Whitman. Take this, for instance, on the ferry boats between Brooklyn and Manhattan:

[1] See Chapter X, above.

The river bay scenery, all about New York island, any time of a fine day—the hurrying, splashing sea tides—the changing panorama of steamers, all sizes, often a string of big ones outward bound to distant ports—the myriads of white-sailed schooners, sloops, skiffs, and the marvelously beautiful yachts—the majestic Sound boats as they rounded the Battery and came along toward 5, afternoon, eastward bound—the prospect off toward Staten Island, or down the Narrows, or the other way up the Hudson—what refreshment of spirit such sights and experiences gave me years ago (and many a time since).

5. *The Hudson River School of Painting*

Although the *Democratic Review* literati were pitifully unsuccessful in making New York the literary center of the nation, New York City, with no help from them, became the North American center of the fine arts. Colonel John Trumbull of Connecticut, painter of the famous "Declaration of Independence" and "Battle of Bunker Hill," established a pathetic little American Academy of Fine Arts in City Hall Square around 1817. This, after his death in 1843, was absorbed by the National Academy of Design founded by Trumbull's rival Samuel F. B. Morse. Thomas Sully remained faithful to Philadelphia, but other portait painters, such as John Wesley Jarvis, came to New York where merchants and bankers were eager to immortalize their features in oil at $100 a head. As there were not enough of them to support an artist, Jarvis, like Sully, toured the South every winter, doing six portaits a week with the aid of an assistant. There was a sufficient number of American artists by 1834 to provide material for William Dunlap of New York to publish his *History of the Rise and Progress of the Arts of Design in the United States*. That book accomplished for early American fine arts what Vasari did for *cinquecento* Florence.

Hitherto the few American artists who went beyond portraits painted "edifying" scenes from the Bible and ancient history; anything but what they could see in their own country. But there presently arose in New York the Hudson River School of artists, first to paint American scenery with its violent contrasts, wild cataracts, brilliant autumn scenery, and long white beaches. Their instigators were Thomas Cole and Asher B. Durand.

Durand, an engraver from New Jersey, became teacher of painting at the National Academy of Design. Around 1825–30 he formed a "Sketch Club" with other local artists and the poet Bryant, who had already struck a keynote for the future in his *Thanatopsis:*—"Go forth, under the open sky, and list to Nature's teachings." Thomas Cole, English-born, emigrated to Philadelphia in order to see the "romantic" American scenery for which Shelley had yearned in vain. After years as an itinerant painter, doing portraits at $5 and $10 a head, he came to New York in 1825, visited the Catskills, and became a devotee of Hudson valley scenery. Cole persuaded Durand to drop the heroics and historicals and paint landscape. He too fell in love with American scenery and the Hudson River School was born.

Of other members of this school, one may name Frederick E. Church (Cole's favorite pupil) of Hartford; Christopher P. Cranch, who had connections with the New England transcendentalists; and George Inness of New Jersey, who studied for several years in France. Most of these men had studios in New York but traveled in search of subjects as far east as Mount Desert Island, Maine, and as far west as California. There were dozens of artists of this school, many of their names now unknown; but their paintings are now eagerly sought by galleries and collectors. From them it was but a step to Winslow Homer (who had his first drawing lessons at the National Academy of Design in the 1850's) and the great American painters of the second half of the century. But the spark came from Cole, Durand, and Bryant in New York.

Two New York organizations which did excellent missionary work for the fine arts were the Apollo Association, which became the American Art Union; and the International Art Union, founded in 1848, which acquired over 5000 subscribers in two years, imported annually over a hundred paintings, and sent them on a traveling exhibition to the principal American cities, including Chicago, Charleston, and New Orleans. After that they were raffled off to the subscribers. The American Art Union published a bulletin, the first American periodical devoted to the fine arts, and held annual exhibits of the work of American artists.

While the Hudson River School limned the wilder beauties of American scenery, Andrew Jackson Downing of Newburgh on the Hudson, son of a nurseryman from Lexington, Massachusetts, cultivated landscape architecture and the building of country estates. His *Treatise on Landscape Gardening* (1841) led to his being employed by President Fillmore to lay out the grounds of the Capitol, the White House, and the Smithsonian in Washington. His *Architecture for Country Houses* (1850) dictated the designs of gentlemen's country residences for the next twenty or thirty years, long after he had perished in one of those tragic and not infrequent burnings of Hudson river steamboats.

Thus New York City, in spite of the absorption of leading citizens in politics and business, and the futility of its literati, became a real cultural center, and remained the principal center of the fine arts in America for another thirty or forty years.

All this proved to the satisfaction of Americans and the astonishment of foreigners that the finer things of life could be attained in a democratic medium, even though the general trend of democracy was toward uniformity and mediocrity.

THE ERIE CANAL

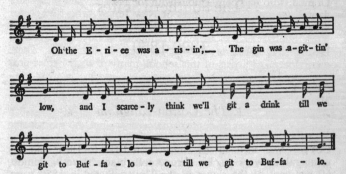

Oh the E - ri - ee was a - ris - in', __ The gin was a - git - tin' low, and I scarce - ly think we'll git a drink till we git to Buf - fa - lo - o, till we git to Buf - fa - lo.

XII

The Southern States

1820-1850

1. *The Cotton Kingdom*

COTTON WAS KING in the South from 1815 to 1861; and the principal bulwark of his throne was black slavery. Almost 60 per cent of the slaves in the United States in 1850 were employed in growing cotton. In 1820 the cotton crop of 160 million pounds was the most valuable Southern interest. As more and more people in the Western world discarded woolen and linen clothes and took to wearing cotton, the South doubled its production by 1830. By 1850 the crop exceeded a billion pounds, and that of 1860, almost 2.3 billion, and accounted for two-thirds of the total exports of the United States. This enormous growth was not caused by any radical improvement in method, but by rapid expansion of the cotton-growing area to at least tenfold what it had been when the cotton gin was introduced. Cotton planting advanced from South Carolina and Georgia across the "black belts" (so called from the color of the soil) and Indian cessions of the Gulf states, occupied the Mississippi valley up to Memphis, pushed up the Red river of Louisiana to Indian Territory, and passed the boundary of Mexico into Texas. On the march King Cotton acquired new subjects: monied immigrants from the North, or ambitious dirt farmers who purchased a slave or two on credit, and with good luck became magnates. In every region fit for cotton, the richest lands were absorbed by plantations during the first generation of settlement. Hunter folk moved westward and poor whites closed in on the gullied hillsides and abandoned fields. Some of the best minds of the South endeavored to arrest this process by scientific methods of agriculture; but as long as good land remained plentiful and cheap, whether within the United States or adjacent under the feeble sovereignty of Mexico, the cotton growers preferred their old ways.

On a first-class plantation, with improved implements, healthy blacks, strong mules, and a competent overseer, ten acres of cotton or corn could be cultivated per able-bodied field hand. On rich soil, with a proper division of labor, five bales (2000 pounds) or more of cotton per field hand could be produced; but a more nearly average figure, in the Carolina and Georgia piedmont, would be 1200 pounds. The average annual price of upland cotton at Liverpool fluctuated between 11 and 19 cents a pound from 1820 to 1840, fell to 8 cents in 1845–48, rose to 14 cents in 1850, and averaged about 12 cents until the Civil War. A planter was lucky to get half the Liverpool price for himself; the rest was consumed by transportation, brokerage, and interest on advances. One of the puzzles of the old Southern economy was its dependence on New York for money to move the cotton crop to market. Southerners frequently threatened to establish shipping lines and banks of their own; but the capital that might have done these things was poured into more land and more slaves.

Sugar planters of Louisiana and tobacco growers of Virginia and Kentucky were allies of the cotton kingdom. Border slave states acted as tributary provinces, supplying labor, food, and mules. Northern centers of banking, shipping, and manufacturing profited as the cotton kingdom prospered. North Carolina, where little cotton was grown, remained an enclave of antique republicanism in the new monarchy; western Virginia and the mountainous regions of Kentucky and Tennessee were Northern salients. Virginia, with a surplus of labor, could maintain her economy only through hiring out the surplus to tobacco factories and ironworks or selling it to the lower South. The economic decrepitude of the Old Dominion was a spiritual loss to the nation. Once she had led American progressive thought and statesmanship; now she devoted herself to sustaining a hopeless cause.

Kentucky had the most varied agriculture of any slave state, and largely replaced Virginia as the home of the American Thoroughbred. The blue-grass country around Lexington, where limestone soil promoted bone and stamina, and nearby parts of Tennessee, were ideal for breeding blood horses. General Jackson started his stud as far back as 1806, and on his deathbed confessed that he regretted only two things: that no horse of his had ever beaten a Diomed filly named Haynie's Maria—and that he had not hanged John C. Calhoun! Boston, a chestnut sired by Timoleon, son of Sir Archie, foaled in 1833, reigned king of the turf for nine years; he won 35 out of 38 two-, three- and four-mile races which he contested as far north as Long Island and as far south as Georgia, winning purses of $50,000 for his owners. Boston at stud produced blood-bay Lexington, the most famous American Thoroughbred prior to Man O'War, and a chestnut named Lecompte. These two sons of the same sire contested a race at New Orleans in 1854, the most brilliant event in prewar annals of the American turf. Lexington won, covering the four miles in 7:19¾, a record unbroken for 40 years. The Kentuckians "came back from New Orleans with a boatload of money," and Lexington, who had now gone blind, continued for 21 seasons to sire the fastest-running horses of the next generation.

The human thoroughbred of the plantation regime was the Southern gentleman. Although few in number, he ruled the older Southern states by virtue of his personality even more than his property, and governed them honorably and efficiently. States like Mississippi, which engaged in wildcat banking enterprises and repudiated debts, were under the control of middle-class and poorer planters, not the gentry. Discriminately hospitable, invariably gracious to women, endowed with a high sense of personal honor and civic virtue, the Southern aristocrat, had he not succumbed to democratic pressure, might have kept his beloved Southland from suffering one of the worst debacles in modern history. His way of life, as related in postwar memoirs and fluffed up by novelists, makes a sentimental appeal to a democratic age just as, in Europe, people like to read about France of the old regime or Victorian England.

Of this class, only a small fraction were descended from the colonial aristocracy. Washington's type appeared undiminished in his Lee kinsmen, the old Huguenot families of South Carolina had a large share in promoting Southern culture, and wealthy descendants of the French creoles of Louisiana were fairly numerous. But the mass of the wealthier planters, by 1860, were self-made men like Jefferson Davis, whose parents had lived in log cabins. If not well educated themselves, their sons and daughters would be.

One of the really great gentlemen of the lower South was

John Hampden Randolph, who in 1841 purchased a plantation in Iberville Parish, Louisiana, for $30,000—the down payment being only $863. For several years he planted cotton, but by the time the debt was paid he turned to sugar, increased his land holdings to several thousand acres, and his labor force from 23 to 195 slaves. He maintained a resident physician to care for their health, employed white Arkansans to help process the sugar, and hired Irish immigrants to dig the drainage ditches. For his children's education he employed a Northern college graduate as tutor as well as itinerant music and dancing masters. The older boys entered the University of Virginia or Rensselaer Polytechnic, and the girls attended a fashionable school in Baltimore. In 1858 Randolph built the fifty-one-room mansion Nottoway which has successfully weathered a century. After the Civil War, with free black labor, his plantation proved to be more profitable than it had been with slaves, a thing that no Southerner before 1860 would have thought possible.

The average upper-class cotton or sugar plantation was not nearly as splendid as Randolph's. The mansion house, seated on rising ground, was usually a well-proportioned wooden building with a columned portico that gave dignity to the front elevation and afforded shade to the ground floor and first story. The rooms were high-studded and simply furnished. There were plenty of flowers and masses of native flowering shrubs and creepers, in which the Southland was rich. Simplicity rather than ostentation was the dominant note in the Southern gentleman's life. His recreations were largely field sports, but he enjoyed little leisure. On a Virginia plantation visited by Frederick Law Olmsted, not ten consecutive minutes elapsed, even during dinner, when the owner was not interrupted by a servant. He had to lock his stables every night as the alternative to finding his horses hagridden in the morning. Even if an overseer were employed to direct the field force, the owner's wife had to keep linen, silver, food, and household supplies under lock and key, serve out supplies with economy, and admonition with tact; had to bind up wounds and nurse the sick. Mrs. Ann R. Page of Virginia devoted her life to the welfare of her slaves, and when the property had to be divided after her husband's death, she prayed that none might fall into alien hands. Yet even Mrs. Page had to put up with late meals, tasks unfinished, and orders forgotten—to say nothing of the cockroaches, centipedes, and other insect life against which the Southern housewife waged perpetual war.

Such a life was a continuous exercise of tact, self-control, and firmness; yet the condition of unlimited power over a race with exasperating habits was a constant temptation to passion. The Southern gentleman had the same conflicting character as an old regime Russian or Hungarian landlord. He could tolerate an amount of shirking and evasion that would drive any Northern or British employer frantic; but to cross his will, question his authority, or impugn his honor was to ask for serious trouble. The descendants of "Cavaliers" were so afraid of being thought afraid that they were apt to see insult where none was intended, and to respond in a manner that forced a fight. Governor John L. Wilson of South Carolina published a textbook on dueling in 1838, but most disputes between white men were settled by less honorable forms of conflict. Alexander H. Stephens, future vice president of the Confederacy, was unable to take part in a political campaign because he had been disabled by stabs received in an "affray" with Judge Cone. Items in the press such as the following are revealing:

The Hon. Edward P. Pitts, late state senator from Accomac Co., Va., was attacked by John C. Wise Esq. at a public vendue on December 27 last and horsewhipped by him. Mr. Wise was inflamed by a remark made by Pitts at a political meeting during a recent campaign, at which the Hon. James W. Custis knocked Mr. Wise off the stand, while speaking, for some disrespectful remark.

Although the gentry gave the tone to Southern white society, there were relatively few of them, probably not more than 15,000 families. The typical Southerner was a farmer who owned his land and buildings, and with his own labor and that of half a dozen slaves cultivated the cash crop—sugar, tobacco, or cotton—which seemed most profitable. He also raised cattle, swine, and a large part of his own food; and there were several hundred thousand Southern families who owned no slaves. These were the backbone of the country, who proved so difficult for Union armies to defeat. Small slave-owners and non-slave-holding yeomen lived in a double log cabin or bare frame house without conveniences, on a diet largely of "hog and hominy," read no literature but the Bible and a weekly paper, enjoyed no diversions but hunting, fishing, and visits to the county seat. Such people belonged to the governing class in Alabama, Mississippi, and Arkansas.

About half the cotton crop was made by those who owned from one to half a dozen slaves. Mark Twain describes "one of those little one-horse cotton plantations" in *Huckleberry Finn:*

A rail fence around a two-acre yard . . . big double log house for the white folks—hewed logs, with the chinks stopped up with mud or mortar, and these mud-stripes had been white-washed some time or another; round-log kitchen, with a big, broad, open but roofed passage joining it to the house; log smoke-house back of the kitchen; three little log nigger-cabins in a row t'other side the smoke-house . . . outside of the fence a garden and a water-melon patch; then the cotton fields begin; and after the fields, the woods.

Below these yeomen farmers came a class known as "pore white trash," "crackers," "peckerwoods," and other opprobrious nicknames. These dwellers on numerous antebellum "tobacco roads" constituted less than 10 per cent of the white population. They appear to have been largely frontiersmen stranded on worn-out land by the westward march of the cotton kingdom. A sallow, undernourished, and illiterate class, envious of successful white men and bitter haters of the black, their only pride was their color. Twentieth-century biologists, notably Charles W. Stiles, discovered that the principal causes of the poor whites' indolence were improper diet and the hookworm, which they contracted by going barefoot. Very different were the mountain men, the "hillbillies" who lived in the secluded valleys and on the steep slopes of the Appalachians and the Ozarks. These were a proud, upstanding, and independent people, expert hunters and fishermen, almost completely isolated from the rest of the South, which knew them only when they drove ox teams to market to sell moonshine whisky that they made in illicit stills, and the pork that they cured from acorn-fed pigs.

The white urban population of the South was small; fewer than 8 per cent lived in towns of over 4000 inhabitants. And small-town dwellers were so closely integrated with the plantation aristocracy as to exercise no liberal influence on public opinion, as the burghers of European towns had on feudal society. James L. Petigru, the leading lawyer of Charleston, "engaged in the ordinary and legitimate proceeding of investing his professional profits in a plantation and negroes," according to his contemporary biographer. "It was the approved Carolina custom in closing every kind of career. No matter how one might begin, as lawyer, physician, clergyman, mechanic, or merchant, he ended, if prosperous, as proprietor of a rice or cotton plantation."

2. Slavery and the Slave

Although cotton growing was the most profitable employment for slaves, slave labor was an uneconomical method of growing cotton. Once entangled in the system, no planter could escape it, and few wished to. Slaves were the only available labor for large-scale production, and slaves cost only $15 to $60 a year (according to various estimates), to keep; but the purchase absorbed a large amount of capital. The most expensive, a "prime field hand" 18 to 25 years old, was worth $500 in 1832 and $1300 just before the panic of 1837. The price of this class of slave reached $1800 on the eve of the Civil War. Black women on cotton plantations were such poor breeders that the labor supply had to be replenished by purchase, and the land was always wearing out; hence the profits that on a Northern farm would have been put into better buildings and equipment, in the South went into more land and more slaves. Even planters opulent in nominal wealth found it difficult to keep out of debt, and probably a majority of them depended on loans from cotton factors to carry them between crops.

What did the black himself think of this system? Here we have inferences that are poles apart. On the one hand (as stated by Jefferson Davis in his reply to Lincoln's Emancipation Proclamation), these "several millions of human beings of an inferior race" were "peaceful and contented laborers in their sphere." The pampered domestic servant, the happy, carefree, banjo-playing "darkey," theme of countless post-Civil War novels, were all that many upper-class travelers saw of the South's "peculiar institution," as her statesmen like to call it. On the other hand, it is the fashion for black intellectuals to describe their forebears as the most oppressed and exploited labor force in modern history, held down by fear and force, constantly striving for escape from slavery. It has often been said that the black understands the white man much better than the other way around; but it is also possible that the colored intellectual of the 1960's knows less about the plantation black of the 1840's than did many white masters of that era.

It should not be forgotten that the African slave trade began among the Negroes themselves in Africa; that to be reduced to slavery was a common expectation in the Dark Continent, and that victims of the system who were shipped to America, provided they survived the passage, were better off than those who remained in bondage in Africa;[1] better off, in fact, than many thousand poor workers and peasants in Europe. John Randolph's slave valet who accompanied his master to Ireland in 1827, "looked with horror upon the mud hovels and miserable food" of the Irish peasantry. But these "white slaves," as the

---

[1] Compare Saint-Exupéry's account in Wind, Sand and Stars (1939) of an old and useless slave being turned out into the desert by his Moslem master to die of starvation, around 1928.

scornful Virginian called them, could emigrate to America as free men; their sons could become congressmen and bishops, and their grandsons, governors and even President; whilst the great majority of blacks in America were slaves, and their children were born into bondage, despite the proud statement in the Declaration of Independence, "All men are created equal." And their descendants are still struggling for equality.

The black was expedient. He accepted his slave status because he had to, and got as much fun out of life as he could, consoled by belief in a Heaven where no color line would be drawn. When converted to Christianity, he observed the parallel between his own bondage and that of the Israelites, and derived his most poignant spiritual hymns from the Book of Exodus. Owing to his capacity for hard work, in addition to his adaptive qualities and cheerful spirit, the African made an excellent slave. He did not mope and die, like the Indians enslaved by the colonists, and his color prevented him from infiltrating his master's society as the Greeks and Asiatics enslaved by the Romans had done. Between him and his "white folks" there often developed mutual affection; and for the Southland itself he acquired so firm a love that it was long after the Civil War before any appreciable number would move to other places where they could enjoy more opportunity and encounter less prejudice.

Southern blacks as a whole cannot fairly be described by sweeping generalizations. There were social gradations among them even before they landed. The social gap between a colored Virginian majordomo, whose ancestors had been American for two centuries, and a "Gullah" (Angola) African recently smuggled into South Carolina, was equal to that between prince and pauper in the Old World. Domestic slaves, the favored class, became completely assimilated to American civilization. Many an aged butler or nurse enjoyed a position similar to that of the household slaves one encounters in Greek and Roman literature. Blacks had an uncanny flair for recognizing "quality" or lack of it; their observations on the characters of young men who courted master's daughters were freely offered and often respected.

Field hands constituted the majority of slaves. A third and intermediate class were slaves who learned a trade such as carpenter, millwright, blacksmith, or barber; many of these were hired out by their masters and some were allowed to purchase their freedom out of their wages, but state laws made that increasingly difficult. Free blacks were anathema to the whites; their "very virtues became objects of suspicion, and the instinct of [white] self-preservation would nip in the bud the first development of superior intellect," wrote in 1828 William Black-ford, a public-spirited Virginian.

In the decade of the 1840's, slaves increased more than twice as fast as free blacks. In antiquity, the Roman usually freed a talented slave, and in any case his progeny were free. But America offered no legal escape to the talented or intellectual slave. It subjected a writer like Frederick Douglass or a born leader of men like Booker T. Washington to the caprice of a white owner who might be his inferior in every respect. And one drop of African blood made a person a black. Thirteen per cent of all blacks in the United States in 1860 were mulattoes. The beautiful octoroons of New Orleans, equal in their profession to the most talented courtesans of old France, were bought and sold like field hands—but at far higher prices, and for a different purpose.

Whilst the average Englishman or free-state American disliked the black as such, Southern slave-owners understood and loved him as a slave; Southern gentlefolk still love him "in his place." There was no physical repulsion from color in the South. White children were suckled by black "mammies" and played with their children. In a stagecoach or railroad car, as a squeamish English visitor observed, "A lady makes no objection to ride next a fat Negro woman, even when the thermometer is at ninety degrees; provided always that her fellow travellers understand she is her property." In the treatment of field hands, there was an immense difference between one plantation and another. Olmsted passed a plantation in central Mississippi owned by a "very religious" lady who had the reputation of working her slaves from 3:30 every weekday morning until 9:00 at night, and alternately catechizing and whipping them every Sunday. A few days earlier, however, he had stayed with the jolly owner of twenty slaves who had "not been licked in five year," who taught one another to read, languidly swung master's hoes, and shared his dinner "right out of the same frying-pan." In every part of the South the small slave-owner worked side by side with his men in the field, and treated them like his own children, as indeed they sometimes were. But if he rose to planter's estate, that sort of thing became *infra dig.*

Flogging with a rawhide or blacksnake whip was the usual method of punishing slaves. Imprisonment lost the master their time, and short rations impaired their health. Most Southern towns had a public flogger with a regular tariff for laying on the number of lashes prescribed by the culprit's owner. Although the laws forbade cruelty, a master or overseer was not often brought to book for it, since even a free black's testimony was not received against a white man, and the feeling rose that for prestige reasons the white must be right. Severity pushed too far was apt to maim a slave or force him to run away, thus destroying or losing a valuable piece of property. Yet the most civilized communities today need societies for the prevention of cruelty to children and animals. It was an old plantation maxim, "Never threaten a Negro, or he will run." Consequently, little time elapsed between detection and a punishment which was not softened by reflection. Instances of sadistic cruelty to slaves are so numerous in the records that they cannot be dismissed as mere abolitionist propaganda. These were extreme cases; no doubt the majority of masters were kind and humane; but should not a system be judged by the extremes that it tolerates? May we not judge Hitler's regime by the gas chambers, or Stalin's by purges, forced-labor camps, and firing squads?

The feature of slavery that most outraged human sympathy was the separation of families by private sale or auction. The laws of two states forbade this, but only for children under ten. It was often asserted that blacks had very slight family attachment; that Whittier's "Farewell of a Virginia Slave Mother," with its haunting refrain:

> Gone, gone,—sold and gone
> To the rice-swamps dank and lone,

was mere abolitionist cant. Yet, when a young Northerner asked Randolph of Roanoke, who had listened to the speeches of English and American statesmen, to name the greatest orator he had ever heard, the old Virginian snapped out: "A slave. She was a mother, and her rostrum was the auction-block."

The years 1822–32 are a watershed in the history of Southern ideas about slavery. Before that, the general attitude of the planter class was to apologize for slavery as a bad system they could not get rid of. Beginning around 1822 there was a gradual tightening up of the "black codes" in the slave states to keep the blacks in order, and the defiant adoption of a theory that slavery was not only the one possible means of keeping blacks subordinated, but a positive good in itself, sanctioned by the Bible.

The starting point for this change of sentiment was Denmark Vesey's insurrection at Charleston in 1822, the first serious one in the United States since colonial days. Vesey was a free black who enlisted slaves in an attempt to capture the city of Charleston, although what he intended to do if he succeeded is a mystery. Betrayed by one of the conspirators, who could not bear to kill a kind master, Vesey's revolt was nipped in the bud and thirty-seven blacks were executed for participation. A system of control was then adopted in the lower South and gradually spread to Virginia and the border states. Blacks were forbidden to assemble or circulate after curfew, and nightly road patrols were set up. Whites were forbidden to teach slaves to read and write in every Southern state except Maryland, Kentucky, and Tennessee.

On the assumption that the majority of slaves were happy and contented, Vesey's and subsequent insurrections were blamed on outside agitators—as, after the two world wars, domestic discontents were blamed on communist agitation. In accordance with this theory, free colored sailors on Northern or European ships calling at Charleston or Savannah were by law haled ashore and confined to the local calaboose until the ship sailed. Justice William Johnson of the Supreme Court, a native of Charleston, ruled that this was unconstitutional,[1] but gave no relief to the imprisoned black plaintiff, and South Carolina successfully defied his dictum. A distinguished Massachusetts lawyer and former member of Congress sent to Charleston in 1844 to try to get the law relaxed (it being inconvenient for a shipmaster to have his colored cook impounded while in port), was accused by the South Carolina legislature of attempting to incite a slave insurrection, threatened with violence, and hustled on board ship.

A very serious insurrection took place in tidewater Virginia in 1831. A pious slave named Nat Turner enlisted a number of others who ran wild in August and killed 57 whites before they were rounded up, with the help of regular troops from Fortress Monroe and sailors from the navy. Between 40 and 100 blacks were killed, and Turner was hanged. This outbreak was blamed by Southern opinion on William Lloyd Garrison's new abolitionist newspaper *The Liberator*, although there is not the slightest evidence that even one copy of it had reached the Southern black. Harrison Gray Otis, mayor of Boston where *The Liberator* was published, received an appeal from General Washington's niece, Mrs. Lawrence Lewis of Woodlawn, to suppress the paper. She gave an eloquent description of the terror created in Virginia:—"It is like a smothered volcano—we know not when, or where, the flame will burst forth, but we know that death in the most repulsive forms awaits us." Otis answered that he had no power to suppress the journal, and that in his opinion any attempt to do so would drive moderate men "to make common cause with the fanatics." In a letter to a friend in Philadelphia he observed that nothing could satisfy the Southerners. "The force of opinion in favor of emancipation through-

---

[1] *Elkison* v. *Deliesseline* (*U.S. Federal Cases*, No. 4366, p. 493).

out the world must blow upon them like a perpetual tradewind, and keep them in a constant state of agitation and discomfort."

That is exactly what happened. Sentiment for the abolition of slavery was not brewed in the "obscure hole" (as Otis described it) where Garrison printed his "incendiary" sheet. Abolition had already gone far in England, where slave revolts in the West Indies had an effect contrary to that in the United States, creating a feeling that slavery must go, and soon. Under the leadership of Wilberforce and Clarkson, Parliament in 1833 passed an act emancipating all slaves in the British colonies, with compensation to their owners. The Second Republic did the same for the French Antilles in 1848. The Spanish American republics, starting with Argentina (1813), Central America (1824), and Mexico (1829), abolished slavery shortly after they became independent; and by the time President Ramón Castilla issued his emancipation proclamation for Peru in 1854, slavery was legal in the New World only in the Spanish and Dutch islands, the United States, and Brazil. Nevertheless the white South refused to admit that anything had to be done about it in the United States. Rufus King in 1825, Otis in 1832, Henry Clay in 1849, proposed gradual compensated emancipation financed by the sale of public lands, and removing the freedmen. These and other suggestions of the sort received only abuse in the South. Lincoln, as late as 1862, presented a gradual emancipation plan to the representatives of loyal slave states, with the bait of an appropriation of $100 million, but they would have none of it.

Every scheme for gradual emancipation, to be acceptable even in the border states, had to include a return of the freed slaves to Africa. This had been going on, in a small way, since 1817 when the American Colonization Society was founded. That society, supported largely by private contributions in Maryland, Virginia, and Kentucky, by 1855 had returned to Africa only 3600 blacks. But its efforts had one concrete result, the Republic of Liberia which became independent in 1857 with a constitution patterned on that of the United States. Liberia attracted very little voluntary emigration, since the American blacks had assimilated the civilization of their white masters and did not wish to return to Africa; and the return of hundreds of thousands of them to Africa against their will would have been disastrous to them and ruinous in cost. Any practical scheme of compensated emancipation would have left the blacks on the spot, as had happened in the Northern states and British West Indies; and that was unacceptable to the white South.

Although there were no slave insurrections comparable to Nat Turner's during the next 30 years, it was the strict patrol and control system which prevented anything getting started. But a number of spontaneous and unsuccessful strikes for freedom were recorded in the Southern press. In 1845, for instance, about 75 unarmed slaves from southeastern Maryland attempted to fight their way through to Pennsylvania and freedom. They were rounded up about 20 miles north of Washington and shot, hanged, or sold "down the river." However docile the majority of slaves may have been, unrest was so widespread as to keep the master class in a constant state of apprehension. And evidence is wanting that any of these outbreaks was caused by Northern abolitionist influence.[1]

The cold war between pro- and antislavery was waged largely between white extremists on both sides. For thirty years the politicians of both political parties tried to ignore or suppress this conflict, or find some way to compromise. They failed utterly and completely, and emancipation was achieved the hard way, and in the worst way.

3. The Literature of Chivalry

A Southern chivalry tradition arose during the generation following 1820. Readers of Walter Scott's *Ivanhoe* and the flood of imitative literature that followed found a romantic mirror of their life and ideals. William A. Caruthers's novel *The Cavaliers of Virginia* (1832) set the tradition. Michel Chevalier, in his *Lettres sur l'Amérique du Nord* (1836) asserted that Northerners were descended from Cromwell's Roundheads, and Southerners from King Charles's Cavaliers; this explained their differences in a manner very comforting to the South. Every owner of two blacks, however dubious his origin or squalid his ex-

---

[1] It is sometimes said that Virginia was within an ace of emancipation in 1831–32 when Garrison's intemperate attitude stiffened the slaveholders and defeated the movement. What actually happened is this: The Nat Turner insurrection aroused public opinion in two opposite directions: abolition, and a more stringent slave code. Some members of the old liberal families combined with western Virginians in the state legislature of 1831–32 to push for the principle of gradual emancipation. A committee to which petitions in that sense had been referred, reported that action thereon was inexpedient. W. B. Preston, a westerner, then moved, "It is expedient to adopt some legislative amendment for the abolition of slavery." This motion was defeated, 73 to 58; the ayes coming almost exclusively from members from the Shenandoah valley and the western counties. Subsequently, in January 1832, a bill was brought in for the colonization in Africa of free Blacks, and of such as might subsequently be freed by their owners. This passed the House, but was lost by a single vote in the Senate. The assumption that this defeat was due to Garrison finds no support in contemporary reports of the debates.

istence, became a "cavalier," entitled to despise the low-bred shopkeepers, artisans, and clerks of the North. The rage to establish *Mayflower* or Knickerbocker ancestry in the North, fifty years later, was a compensation of the same sort for old families being crowded by immigrants.

To comprehend the Southern planter, we must remember that his social system was on the defensive against the rest of the civilized world. His common sense, too, made him indifferent or hostile to the multiple "isms" which were trying to put all crooked ways straight in England and the Northern states. Just as New England in 1800 refused every quickening current from France or Virginia lest it bear the seeds of Jacobinism, so the South, a generation later, rejected literature and philosophy which might conceal abolition. The enthusiasm for compulsory free popular education that swept over the North hardly got under way in the South prior to the 1850's, when Calvin H. Wiley of North Carolina and William L. Yancey of Alabama began improvements that were interrupted by the Civil War. At that time, the percentage of illiteracy among native-born Southern whites was about 20 per cent, compared with 0.42 per cent among native-born New Englanders. The University of Virginia, which Jefferson had intended to be the crown of a free public school system, became instead the seminary of a privileged class. At a time when Bryant, Emerson, Longfellow, and Whittier were redeeming Northern materialism with cheerful song, Southern silence was broken only by the gloomy and romantic notes of Edgar Allan Poe. Stephen C. Foster, who attuned the beauty and pathos of the Old South to the human heart in "Uncle Ned," "Old Black Joe," and "My Old Kentucky Home," was a Pennsylvanian.

The intellectual barrenness of the antebellum South has been ascribed by her apologists to the want of urban centers where creative spirits could meet and talk, whence literature and the arts have usually sprung. There were at least five urban centers in the slave states bigger than Athens, Jerusalem, or Florence at their prime, yet none seemed capable of supporting a literary, artistic, or scientific group. William Gilmore Simms of Charleston, the most distinguished Southern man of letters, had to publish in New York the ten romances that he wrote between 1834 and 1842, including *The Yemassee*, one of the best American historical novels; and at a time when Northern men of letters had become shining figures in their communities, Simms went unrecognized in his. He wrote in 1858, "All that I have done has been poured to waste in Charleston." And his biographer wrote that a Southerner "had to think in certain grooves." These grooves were glorification of the Southern way of life, and defense of slavery. The abolition agitation, instead of making converts in the South, engendered a closing of minds. Not immediately, however; at least not in Virginia. In 1832 the Richmond *Enquirer* could still call slavery "a dark and growing evil"; but twenty-three years later, when it was still darker and still growing, the same newspaper was calling for a revival of the African slave trade.

Public criticism of slavery was suppressed in the South by the force of public opinion, even where laws were lacking. Mails from the North and England were examined and "purified" of any matter which might suggest to the slaves that they were not the world's happiest working people. Ministers, teachers, professional men, and politicians who would not bow down to mumbo-jumbo were eliminated. Laws were even passed against criticism outside the South of Southern institutions, and a price was placed on the heads of prominent abolitionists. Bishop Moore of Virginia, in conversation with Dr. Daubeny of Oxford, "spoke of the certainty of an abolitionist being lynched, not indeed as a thing he approved, but without any expression of moral indignation."

Yet who are we, having lately weathered a hurricane of unreasoning intolerance, to scorn the antebellum South? Southern whites were not by nature less tolerant than their Northern counterparts whose attitude toward Catholics, Mormons, and other minorities we have had occasion to notice. The presence of slavery subjected Southern white people to a constant emotional pressure which led them to do many wrong and foolish things. And the result of their efforts to smother discussion is the strongest warning in all American history against attempts to suppress free speech.

A positive proslavery theory of society, corresponding to the political doctrine of state rights, was provided by Thomas R. Dew, a bright young Virginian who returned from study in Germany to a chair at William and Mary College. In a pamphlet of 1832 he argued that slavery had been the fertilizer of classical culture, that the Hebrew prophets and St. Paul admitted its moral validity, that civilization required the many to work and the few to think. George Fitzhugh, in a tract entitled, *Cannibals All!* argued that the black was something less than human; and in his *Sociology for the South* provided a new set of principles to replace the "glittering generalities" of a century of enlightenment. John C. Calhoun gave proslavery doctrine the sanction of his name and character, and so cunningly combined it with the American prepossessions that slavery appeared no longer the antithesis but an essential condition of democracy.

Calhoun began with the axiom that no wealthy or civilized society could exist unless one portion of the community lived upon the labor of another. White labor, class-conscious in England and enfranchised in the Northern states, threatened property and civilization. Social stability could not be maintained where labor was free. It was too late to re-establish serfdom in Europe or extend it to the North; but a beneficent providence had brought to the South a race created by God to be hewers of wood and drawers of water for His chosen people. In return, kind masters provided for all reasonable wants of their slaves and saved them from the fear of misery and destitution that haunted the white proletariat. The masters, themselves, relieved from manual labor and sordid competition, would attain that intellectual and spiritual eminence of which the founders of the Republic had dreamed. "Many in the South once believed that slavery was a moral and political evil. That folly and delusion are gone. We see it now in its true light, and regard it as the most safe and stable basis for free institutions in the world."

This nonsense became orthodox in the South by 1850; but how wide or deep it really went we shall never know. It was not accepted by the great Virginians who fought so valiantly for the Confederacy.[1] There was no place in the system for the poor whites, from one of whom, Hinton R. Helper, came *The Impending Crisis* (1857), a prophecy of disaster which was suppressed. Calhoun, more humane than his doctrine, refused privately to condone the domestic slave trade, although he might publicly threaten that the South would secede rather than allow it to be excluded from Washington. Many non-slaveholding, illiterate whites disliked slavery, but they agreed with the planters that it would never do to emancipate the black, and fought bravely to maintain an institution that bore more heavily upon them than upon any other class.

4. Science and Religion

Scientific culture in the South followed in general the genial eighteenth-century tradition, exemplified by Jefferson, of liberally educated gentlemen pursuing natural science for their

[1] Robert E. Lee emancipated the few slaves he inherited from his mother, and owned no others. Stonewall Jackson purchased two slaves at their own request, and allowed them to earn their freedom. J. E. Johnston and A. P. Hill never owned slaves and disliked slavery. J. E. B. Stuart owned but two slaves, and disposed of them, long before the war. M. F. Maury, who called slavery a "curse," never owned but one, a family servant.

own amusement and edification. The South had many amateur botanists, mineralogists, and geologists who were intent on finding out more about the nature that they loved. John James Audubon, America's most popular naturalist, born in French Saint-Domingue, lived for a time in Louisiana and Kentucky. He ranged America from the Labrador to Texas in search of material; but he had to journey to London and Edinburgh to find a publisher for his famous *Birds of America*. Upon his return to America in 1831, Audubon met at Charleston the Reverend John Bachman, who helped him write *The Quadrupeds of North America*, his second classic. He was entertained by Dr. Edmund Ravenel, who had already become the leading American authority on shells, both living and fossil; and he may have met the Doctor's young cousin Henry W. Ravenel, who in 1853 would start publishing the first American work on fungi. A nearby Georgia planter, Louis Le Conte, maintained a botanical garden at his plantation, where his two famous sons John and Joseph were born. Edmund Ruffin published a work on soil chemistry in 1832 and kept up a continual agitation for better methods, which did much to bring back to fruitfulness the "old fields" of tidewater Virginia; but he was also a violent agitator for secession. Commander Matthew Fontaine Maury USN, also of Virginia, became the world's greatest oceanographer, charting the ocean winds and currents, and publishing *The Physical Geography of the Sea* (1855) which helped navigators to cut down the time and increase the safety of ocean voyages. This scientific achievement was the fairest cultural flower of the South before the Civil War.

Organized religion, which had declined in the South when that section was liberal and antislavery, recovered after it became conservative and proslavery. The influence of the evangelical sects increased in proportion as their ministers claimed arguments for slavery in the Bible. The Catholic and Episcopalian churches remained neutral on the subject, and stationary in numbers. Thomas Jefferson, dying, saluted the rising sun of Unitarianism as destined to enlighten the South; but it sent only a few feeble rays beyond Baltimore. Horace Holley, the gifted young Unitarian who had made of Transylvania University in Kentucky a Southern Oxford, was driven from his post by Jackson Democrats and Presbyterians. Thomas Cooper, a chemist who had taken refuge in the South from persecutions under the Federalist Sedition Act, was forced to resign both from the University of Virginia and the College of South Carolina, as a Unitarian.

For a time the Protestant churches were a bond of union between North and South; but when in 1842 the Methodist

Church insisted that a Southern bishop emancipate his slaves, the Southerners seceded and formed the Methodist Church South on a proslavery basis. The Baptists followed, and doubled their membership in fifteen years. While these Southern evangelicals defended slavery, they banned card-playing and dancing; by 1860 the neo-puritanism of the age was more prevalent in Alabama and Mississippi than in Massachusetts and Connecticut.

One religious manifestation that drew both sections and races together was the revival, or camp meeting, as it was generally called, because no one building was big enough to hold the crowds. These were equally popular with middle-class and poor whites, and with the blacks. The camp meeting and the "spirituals" that went with it gave people who led drab lives an outlet for their emotions. Despite all the fun poked at them by sophisticated sects, they did much to elevate the moral and religious tone of thousands of rural communities.

The years following 1831 were crucial for the future relations of the two major sections. In the United States the peaceful process of slave emancipation stopped with New Jersey's law of 1804. Why did not Americans follow the example of Britain's emancipation of 1833? One reason, doubtless, was the invention of the cotton gin, which made the cultivation of upland cotton by slaves immensely profitable. We can make that concession to economics; yet slavery seemed no less necessary to maintain the sugar industry of the West Indies. The difference in part was constitutional. The West Indian planter had no representatives in Parliament, where the abolitionists, gathering public opinion like a snowball, proved to be irresistible. Yet there was another factor in causing the South to dig in her heels and resist emancipation to the death—Jacksonian Democracy.

The old Federalist and Jeffersonian leaders in the South were well-educated and thoughtful men, in close touch with English and European currents of thought. They looked forward to eventual emancipation of the slaves, and might have put it across, at least in Virginia and the border states, but for the horrible example of the massacres that followed emancipation in Haiti. If they and their kind had been left in control of the Southern press, the legislatures and the congressional delegation, it is possible that gradual compensated emancipation would have been worked out. But the growth of democracy and the rise of the common man overwhelmed the old governing aristocracy (most of whose survivors went Whig) with a tide of provincial, ill-educated politicians who catered to the prejudices of the middle-class and poor whites. Only a minority of the middle class, as we have seen, were slave-owners; but for the most part they were "nigger haters" who did not imagine it possible to keep blacks in order except as slaves. This new race of Southern politicians, instead of preparing the South to face inevitable emancipation and seek a peaceful way out, flattered people into a fatal belief in the righteousness of slavery and their own ability to protect the "peculiar institution" perpetually. Southern policy then came to be based on two principles which were assumed to have divine sanction: (1) Blacks are an inferior race and must be kept subordinate, like children who cannot take care of themselves. (2) The only way to do this is to keep them in a slave status.

The second axiom was blown up at Appomattox. But the first, after the lapse of another century, is still believed by middle- and lower-class whites whom democracy has brought into power. And, at the time of writing, this dominant white South is displaying exactly the same ostrich-like attitude toward the world-wide movement for equality as its ancestors did toward the world-wide movement for emancipation.

MOBILE BAY

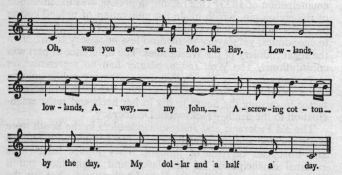

Oh, was you ev-er in Mo-bile Bay, Low-lands, low-lands, A-way,— my John,— A-screw-ing cot-ton by the day, My dol-lar and a half a day.

XIII

Ferment and Culture in the North

1820-1850

1. *Reformers and Revivalists*

"THE ANCIENT MANNERS were giving way. There grew a certain tenderness on the people, not before remarked," wrote Emerson of his America. "It seemed a war between intellect and affection; a crack in Nature, which split every church in Christendom. . . . The key to the period appeared to be that the mind had become aware of itself. . . . The young men were born with knives in their brain."

One of the young men was Thomas H. Gallaudet, son of a Philadelphia merchant, who studied the education of deaf-mutes under Abbé Sicard in Paris and, before he was thirty, established the first American school for the deaf at Hartford, Connecticut. Samuel Gridley Howe of Boston fought for Greek independence in his early twenties and returned with Michael Anagnos, one of his comrades in arms, to found the Perkins Institute for the Blind, a searchlight for those deprived of sight. Elihu Burritt, the "learned blacksmith" of New Britain, Connecticut, in his early thirties threw himself heart and soul into the peace movement and organized a series of international peace congresses which were completely ineffective; but his efforts in a less ambitious field, the exchange of what he called "friendly addresses" between people and municipalities in the British Isles and America, certainly helped to prevent war between the two countries. Neal Dow, a prominent Maine businessman with Quaker antecedents, started a brisk campaign against "demon rum," which had tangible effects on the drinking habits of the people, and persuaded thirteen states to pass laws prohibiting alcohol by 1857. These are but a few examples of what the young men were accomplishing.

Young women, too, were "born with knives in their brain." It was the age of the Women's Rights movement. This, like others, had its lunatic fringe, but included a number of sensible women reformers such as Elizabeth C. Stanton and Lucretia Mott, who in 1848 launched the women's suffrage movement at Seneca Falls, New York. Carried forward by the eloquence of Lucy Stone and the energy of Susan B. Anthony, this finally bore fruit in Amendment XIX to the Constitution (1920). One of Miss Stanton's early converts, Amelia Bloomer the dress reformer, should not be blamed for the baggy gym pants formerly associated with her name; her "bloomers" were well-cut slacks, adopted by thousands of women for housework, although only the bravest could face the jeers and insults to which wearers of them were subjected in public.

Most remarkable of all was Dorothea Lynde Dix, a New England gentlewoman who, after teaching for several years in a fashionable girls' school, at the age of thirty-three began a lifelong crusade in favor of intelligent and humane treatment of the mentally afflicted. Most of these unfortunates were then treated as criminals, "chained, naked, beaten with rods and lashed into obedience," as she described their plight in her memorial of 1843 to the Massachusetts legislature. This beautiful young woman, naturally timid and diffident, visited every part of the United States investigating conditions and lobbying to better them. She persuaded Congress to establish St. Elizabeth's Hospital. She was the first New England reformer to penetrate the South, where chivalry gave her a hearing; and, at her urging, public hospitals for the insane were established in nine Southern states between 1845 and 1852. Off then she went to Europe, where the situation was almost equally appalling. Dorothea enlisted the support of Queen Victoria, and in Rome told Pope Pius IX that the local insane asylum was "a scandal and disgrace"; the Pope listened to her, and even did something about it.

The great breeding ground of mid-century "isms" was not New England itself, but the area peopled by Yankees in the rolling hills of central New York and along the Erie Canal. These folk were so susceptible to religious revivals and Pentecostal beliefs that their region was called "The Burned-over District." There antimasonry began and the temperance movement gathered strength. Joseph Smith published The Book of Mormon at Palmyra, New York, in 1830, and there converted Brigham Young. Charles G. Finney, probably the greatest American evangelist, stumped up and down the state bringing souls to Christ. William Miller, a veteran of the War of 1812, worked out at Hampton, New York, the theory that the second coming of Christ would take place on 22 October 1843. He founded the Millerite or Adventist sect which persuaded thousands to sell their goods and, clothed in suitable robes, await the Second Coming on roofs, hilltops, and haystacks, which they believed would shorten their ascent to Heaven. Mother Ann Lee at New Lebanon, New York, and Jemima Wilkinson at Jerusalem, New York, attempted to sublimate the sexual urges of mankind by founding celibate Shaker and "Universal Friend" communities. John H. Noyes, on the contrary, sought perfection as well as catharsis in sexual indulgence at his Oneida Community, which ended as an arts-and-crafts organization. Spirits from the other world seeking means to communicate with this, appropriately chose Rochester, New York, the burned-over metropolis, where the Fix sisters' spirit-rappings and table-turnings had the whole country agog in 1848. From their performances issued the cult of Spiritism, which within ten years had sixty-seven newspapers and periodicals devoted to culling messages from "angel spheres." And from central New York a vast swarm of Yankee "isms" descended on the West like a flight of grasshoppers.

2. Abolition, Antislavery, and Utopia

Southern chivalry was no protection to lady abolitionists. The Grimké sisters, Sarah and Angelina, pretty blonde daughters of a wealthy Charleston lawyer, grew up hating slavery, but had to leave home and confine their work to the North. And that was no easy matter in the early years of the abolition movement. Advocates of black emancipation were attacked furiously in the free states. Whether in city or country, in New England, New York or the Middle West, devoted men and women addressing an abolition meeting were assailed by rotten eggs and stones, and their voices were drowned by tin horns, drums, and sleigh-bells. Charles Stuart, son of a British army officer who, after observing slavery in Jamaica, hoped to destroy it in the United States, was whipped out of Plainfield, Connecticut, by angry farmers. A philanthropist who built a school for black children in a Maine village found it one day in the middle of a swamp, hauled there by local ox teams. Elijah Lovejoy, who persisted in printing an abolitionist paper at Alton, Illinois, had his press twice thrown into the river, and he was murdered by a mob in 1837. Philadelphia abolitionists held a protest meeting in Pennsylvania Hall, which they and their reformer friends had just built; but a mob burned it down. All that summer there were outbursts of mob violence against Blacks in the City of Brotherly Love; in 1842 a particularly bad one, when many homes of black residents were burned.

Philadelphia was far from unique in violence. On 21 October 1835 William Lloyd Garrison was paraded around Boston with a rope around his neck, by what was called a "broadcloth mob"; and on the same day delegates who met at Utica to organize an antislavery society were dispersed by a mob of "very respectable gentlemen" led by a congressman and a judge. Yet the abolition movement grew, and made converts at every mobbing:—of Gerrit Smith, for instance, at the Utica affair; of Wendell Phillips in Boston; of Cassius M. Clay, a cousin of Henry Clay, in Kentucky. By 1840 the membership of the abolition and antislavery societies in the Northern states was over 150,000. The pen of John G. Whittier was already consecrated to the movement, and presently James Russell Lowell would lend his gift of biting satire.

The abolitionists were not single-minded; they supported many other reforms as well. Their general starting point was the Puritan conscience, stirred up by an evangelical preacher. They made slight appeal to politicians of either national party (although the Northern ones, in the end, had to pay them some attention) or to financiers, manufacturers, and others who were making money. They had no support from any immigrant group except, shortly before the Civil War, from the rural Germans. But they slowly captured the native farmers and middle classes by appealing to their Jeffersonian liberalism, and making them reflect that if monarchical England could do it, the Land of the Free could and should liberate its slaves.

Theodore Dwight Weld, the most effective abolitionist, was typical for his many reform interests. A Connecticut boy who attended Hamilton College, New York, he was converted to evangelical Christianity by Finney. He then became interested in a "Society for Promoting Manual Labor in Literary Institutions," which proposed to cure the physical flabbiness of college students by making them do their own chores and learn an honest trade. A great bear of a man himself, Weld was capable of cowing a mob or whipping an assailant, which he often had to do. He took up with another Yankee reformer, the Reverend Sylvester Graham, who was waging a one-man war against white bread, for which he was mobbed by the bakers of Boston.[1] The South was wont to charge abolitionists with knowing nothing of slavery at first hand; but Weld really studied it, traveling to the Gulf of Mexico in 1831–32, and observing social conditions very closely. On that trip he recruited James G. Birney, an upstanding young blood of Kentucky who owned a big plantation in Alabama, and Birney became the first antislavery candidate for President of the United States, polling 3000 votes in 1840.

Weld and two wealthy New York City merchants, Arthur and Lewis Tappan, organized the American Anti-Slavery Society in 1833. Weld then tried teaching at Lane Seminary, Cincinnati, so close to the slave area and so dependent on Southern trade that the trustees forbade discussion of slavery by the students. He and his student converts—many of them Southerners—seceded to Oberlin, which became the first college in the United States to admit both women and blacks. In the meantime the Grimké sisters, after many hesitations, had taken the public platform for abolition; and Angelina, the younger and comelier, was wooed and won by Theodore Weld.

In the South, everyone not for slavery was called an abolitionist, but opponents of slavery in the North were divided into a number of sects. At the extreme left was William Lloyd Garrison the Boston firebrand, who demanded emancipation immediate and uncompensated, or else secession of the free states from the Union. In the center were Theodore Weld, the Tappans, and their friends, who demanded a beginning of emancipation, compensated or otherwise, and who became an expert pressure group for their cause. Their weekly journal *The Emancipator* had the largest circulation of any antislavery paper; on its staff were Elizur Wright and the poet Whittier. Weld wrote *Slavery As It Is,* concentrating on the inhumanity of the system through telling extracts from Southern newspapers; over 100,000 copies were sold the first year. He also brought out a careful study, *Emancipation in the British West Indies* (1838), to prove that it did work well there and to assure Southern whites that British masters' throats had not been cut by the freed slaves.

Abolitionists took every opportunity to bring test cases into the courts. As a matter of interstate comity, slaveholders had always been allowed to bring slaves with them in and out of the

---

[1] Hence the name graham bread. Sylvester Graham was also responsible for the regimen of cold showers and sleeping with wide-open windows in zero weather, which took about 50 years to become popular, and another 50 years to be proved the cause of pulmonary disorders.

free states; but this became difficult after the Nancy Jackson case. She was a young domestic owned by a Presbyterian parson in Georgia. When he moved to Hartford, Connecticut, he brought her along and kept her there for two years. Weld brought suit to show cause why Nancy should be kept in bondage in a free state, and freed she was in 1837 in a decision which became a precedent.

The most famous case involving slavery, until eclipsed by Dred Scott's, was that of the *Amistad* in 1839. She was a Spanish slave ship carrying 53 newly imported Africans who were being moved from Havana to another Cuban port. Under the leadership of an upstanding black named Cinqué, they mutinied and killed captain and crew. Then, ignorant of navigation, they had to rely on a white man whom they spared to sail the ship. He stealthily steered north, the *Amistad* was picked up off Long Island by a United States warship, taken into New Haven, and with her cargo placed in charge of the federal marshal. Then what a legal hassle! Spain demanded that the slaves be given up to be tried for piracy, and President Van Buren attempted to do so but did not quite dare. Lewis Tappan and Roger Sherman Baldwin, a Connecticut abolitionist, undertook to free them by legal process, and the case was appealed to the Supreme Court. John Quincy Adams, persuaded to act as their attorney, argued that the Africans be freed, on the ground that the slave trade was illegal both by American and Spanish law, and that mankind had a natural right to freedom. The court, with a majority of Southerners, was so impressed by the old statesman's eloquence that it ordered Cinqué and the other blacks set free, and they were returned to Africa. The ironic epilogue is that Cinqué, once home, set himself up as a slave trader.

At the right wing of the emancipators were people who spurned the name abolitionist (just as socialists hate to be confused with communists), and called themselves antislavery men. They opposed the extension of slavery into more United States territory, but did not propose to interfere with slavery in the states. The antislavery wing included many evangelists such as Finney, who warned "Brother Weld," his proselyte, that extremist sentiment would "roll a wave of blood over the land." Similarly, Francis Wayland, president of Brown University, warned the abolitionists that their agitation had "rendered any open and calm decision of this subject in the slaveholding states utterly impossible"; that abolition "would be a great calamity were it to terminate by violence, or without previous moral and social preparation." Emerson took a similar position. But most of these moderate antislavery men were eventually forced by Southern intransigence into more radical views.

The South made tactical errors in combating abolition. It assumed that every antislavery person was a firebrand, an inciter of black insurrection. Southern legislatures passed laws making it increasingly difficult for masters to liberate slaves, or for free blacks to exist. And by frantic attempts to suppress discussion of the subject, and to buttress, protect, and expand slavery, the spokesmen of the South ended in convincing the North that every man's liberty was at stake. Birney, one of the first to see this aspect of the problem, wrote from Kentucky to Gerrit Smith in 1835, "It has now become absolutely necessary that slavery should cease in order that freedom may be preserved in any portion of the land." William Jay, son of the Chief Justice, pointed out the next year, "We commenced the present struggle to obtain the freedom of the slave; *we are compelled to continue it to preserve our own.*"

Excepting that lonely fanatic John Brown, no abolitionist attempted to incite a slave insurrection, but many took part in a conspiracy of evasion. The "grapevine telegraph" carried news south of an "underground railroad" to liberty. Slaves who had the courage to strike for freedom would take cover in woods or swamps near their master's plantation until the hue and cry was over, then follow the North Star to the free states. The most dangerous part of the escape route was in the South itself, where slaves helped one another. Harriet Tubman, an illiterate field hand, not only escaped herself, but returned repeatedly and guided more than 300 slaves from bondage to freedom, taking some as far as Canada. In the Northern states, fugitives were transferred from one abolitionist or free black household to another, sometimes driven in a Friend's carriage, disguised in women's clothes and wearing a deep Quaker bonnet.

Efforts have recently been made to pooh-pooh the underground as a myth, and it never rescued more than a tiny fraction of the slave population. But it was real enough to the blacks whom it helped, and to the masters whom it robbed. Here, for instance, is what Moncure D. Conway, a young antislavery Virginian, observed at a Concord home in 1853:

I found the Thoreaus agitated by the arrival of a coloured fugitive from Virginia, who had come to their door at daybreak. Thoreau took me to a room where his excellent sister Sophia was ministering to the fugitive, who recognized me as one he had seen. . . . I observed the tender and lowly devotion of Thoreau to the African. He now and then drew near to the trembling man, and with a cheerful voice bade him feel at home, and have no fear that any power should again wrong him. That whole day he mounted guard over the fugitive, for it was a slave-hunting time. Next day the fugitive was got off to Canada.

By a federal law, any master or his agent who caught a runaway in a free state could forcibly repatriate him after swearing to his identity before a magistrate. Owing to the employment of professional slave-catchers who were not particular about identification, the kidnapping of free Northern Blacks became so frequent that Pennsylvania in 1825 and other states later passed personal liberty laws to protect their free colored citizens. Local resentment against kidnapping fed public opinion against the return of genuine fugitives, and the tightening up of the personal liberty laws which made a runaway's identity almost impossible to establish. A fugitive was forcibly rescued from his captors in Boston in 1843, and his freedom purchased by popular subscription. The abolitionists for the first time voiced a popular sentiment when Whittier declared:

No slave-hunt in our borders—no pirate on our strand!
No fetters in the Bay State—no slave upon our land!

Southerners played into the abolitionists' hands not only by stifling criticism of slavery when they had the power, but by demanding its suppression in places where they had no power. Thousands of Northerners who were indifferent to slavery valued freedom of speech, of the press, and of petition. In 1835 the abolitionists began sending petitions to Congress to abolish slavery and the slave trade in the District of Columbia, over which Congress had exclusive jurisdiction, and which had become a shipping point for slaves from Virginia and Maryland to the cotton states. Even from the windows of the Capitol one could see coffles of chained Africans marching by, guarded by armed men. Slave auctions were frequently held in the District. Why, as Henry Clay inquired, should members be continually "outraged" by scenes "so inexcusable and detestable"? The answer was that members from slave states felt that Washington was a strategic outpost, a prestige point to be held at all costs. John C. Calhoun, now back in the Senate, declared that any intermeddling with slavery in Washington would be "a foul slander on nearly one-half the States of the Union." All such petitions were rejected unread and forgotten; but that was not enough for the Southern members. In 1836, at their behest, the House voted the first of the so-called "gag resolutions," declaring that all petitions or papers "relating in any way" to slavery or the abolition thereof, should be "laid on the table."

John Quincy Adams, now a congressman from Massachusetts, was no abolitionist, but the gag rule awakened ancestral memories of royal tyranny; a thing to be resisted in its prime, like taxation without representation. He denounced it as "a direct violation of the Constitution of the United States, of the rules of the House, and the rights of my constituents." The gag actually stimulated abolitionists to greater efforts. During the session of 1837–38, tens of thousands of petitions on the forbidden subject were sent to Congress. The flood continued unchecked until it reached this Congressional dam. Session after session, Adams fought against the gag, using his knowledge of parliamentary practice and rich resource in harsh and bitter eloquence. Theodore Weld came to Washington to participate, and from one of his letters to his wife we have a lively description of a debate when the seventy-five-year-old Adams defended himself and clawed his assailants, like a bear at bay:

Old Nestor lifted up his voice like a trumpet; till slaveholding, slave trading and slave breeding absolutely quailed and howled under his dissecting knife. Mr. Adams had said the day before that he should present some petitions that would set them in a blaze, so I took care to be in the house at the time, and such a scene I never witnessed. Lord Morpeth, the English abolitionist of whom you have heard, was present and sat within a few feet of Mr. Adams, his fine intelligent face beaming with delight as the old man breasted the storm and dealt his blows upon the head of the monster. Wise of Virginia, Rayner of North Carolina, W. C. Johnson of Maryland, and scores more of slaveholders, striving constantly to stop him by starting questions of order and by every now and then screaming at the top of their voices: "That is false!" "I demand, Mr. Speaker, that you shut the mouth of that old harlequin!" A perfect uproar like Babel would burst forth every two or three minutes as Mr. Adams with his bold surgery would smite his cleaver into the very bones. At least half of the slaveholding members of the house left their seats and gathered in the quarter of the Hall where Mr. Adams stood. Whenever any of them broke out upon him, Mr. Adams would say, "I see where the shoe pinches, Mr.

Speaker, it will pinch *more* yet!" "If before I get through every slaveholder, slave trader and slave breeder on this floor does not get materials for bitter reflection it shall be no fault of mine."

Every attempt short of personal violence was made to silence, to censure, or to expel Adams; but the tough old Puritan persisted. Public opinion in the Northern states finally forced their representatives to support him, and in 1844 the gag rule was repealed. It made no difference to the salves, but the eight-year controversy had educated opinion on both sides of the cold war as nothing else could. The South learned that she needed more weight in the councils of the nation by annexing Texas certainly, Cuba probably, and Mexico perhaps; that slavery's banners must fly not only over the Capitol but on the high seas and even in the free states, where discussion of the subject must be stifled. The North began to see that the price of union would be surrender all along the line to the "slaveocracy," as Adams called it, and that this surrender would involve rights for which their fathers fought.

That same curious reversal of values which argues that resistance to Hitler was the cause of the Second World War, or that unilateral disarmament or our part will exorcise the communist menace, has been applied to the whole antislavery movement. The abolitionists, we are told, were nasty, power-hungry men and sex-starved women seeking notoriety; everything would have worked out all right and slavery have died a "natural death" if they had been shut up. But it is perfectly clear that slavery was too firmly rooted in Southern society to die otherwise than by violence. The abolitionists are also accused of hypocrisy because they did so little for free blacks in the free states. Actually, they did a great deal, such as getting public schools legally desegregated; but, sharing the laissez-faire philosophy of that era, they assumed that the black, once free, could compete on equal terms with white people. Time has proved them wrong in this confident expectation, but the antislavery people were right in concentrating on freedom as the essential first step.

Abolition was an irresistible power in a world awakening to new concepts of humanity. It could no more be kept down in Boston and Indianapolis than in London and Paris. Orators such as Weld, Garrison, the Grimkés, Charles Sumner, and Wendell Phillips, spoke with voices to which America was obliged to listen. "They were members of a family of minds that had appeared in all the Western countries, in Italy, in Germany, in France, to defend the religion of liberty, poets militant, intellectual men who were glad to fight and die for their beliefs, figures that were appearing in flesh and blood on battlefields and barricades in Europe. Brothers of Mazzini, heirs of William Tell, men of the world themselves and men of culture, they roused the indifferent minds of the thinking masses and made the American antislavery movement a part of the great world-struggle of darkness and light."[1]

The abolitionists, as we can now see, expended so much compassion on the slave that they had no pity left for the owner who was equally involved in the system and could see no way to get rid of it. But in view of Southern resistance to any form of gradual, compensated emancipation, and of Southern insistence on acquiring more territory and more federal protection for slavery, violence was the only way left. Yet the freedmen were not really free in 1865, nor are most of their descendants really free in 1965. Slavery was but one aspect of a race and color problem that is still far from solution here, or anywhere. In America particularly, the grapes of wrath have not yet yielded all their bitter vintage.

The American artisan now began to question the value of his vote. Jacksonian Democracy killed Monster Bank, but supplied no bread. As they were searching for the root of the trouble, American laborers were approached by earnest idealists, each with his peculiar vision of a new society in which people might lead free and happy lives. Robert Owen in 1845 summoned a "World Convention to Emancipate the Human Race from Ignorance, Poverty, Division, Sin and Misery." Instead of trying to assimilate and humanize the new industrial order, these well-meaning people dissipated their energy in efforts to escape it.

Almost every known panacea was applied, with the same meager results as in Europe. Josiah Warren, the first American anarchist, devised a system of "time stores" and "labor notes," which were no cure. The typical experiment of the period was a community. Brook Farm, the transcendentalist group so happily described in Hawthorne's *Blithedale Romance,* was one of forty Fourierite phalanxes in the Northern states, of which Owen's New Harmony, Indiana, was the most long-lived and successful. The one at Ripon, Wisconsin, was almost too successful—its land became so valuable that the brethren decided to sell out and become individual farmers. These communities solved no problem, but for a time they gave friendship and a sense of "belonging" to thousands of sanguine souls. The one

[1] Van Wyck Brooks, *The Flowering of New England,* pp. 393–4.

positive gain was the co-operative movement, which emerged phoenix-like from the ruins of little producers' and consumers' co-operatives set up by labor unions during the depression of 1837–40.

Horace Greeley kept the columns of his New York *Tribune* hospitable to all these movements; but his best advice to the worker was, "Go West, young man, go West!" Here was a point of contact with national politics. Public land at $200 the quarter-section was not for those who needed it most, but for those who had the price, or for squatters who defied all comers to dislodge them. George Henry Evans and Horace Greeley insisted that every man had the same natural right to a piece of land as to air and sunlight. "Equality, inalienability, indivisibility" were Evans's three points: a free homestead from the public domain to every settler, limitation of individual holdings, no alienation of the homestead, voluntary or otherwise. "Vote yourself a farm" was his slogan. The first free homestead bill was introduced in 1846 by Andrew Johnson of Tennessee. Northern Whigs and Southern Democrats combined to defeat it. In 1851 an agrarian law limiting inheritance of land to 320 acres passed a second reading in the Wisconsin legislature, but did not become law, for the Western farmer was a land speculator by nature.

In the field of labor relations, a landmark is the decision by Lemuel Shaw, Chief Justice of Massachusetts, in the case of *Commonwealth* v. *Hunt* (1842), that a trade union was a lawful organization whose members were not collectively responsible for illegal acts committed by individuals, and that a strike for a closed shop was legal.

All this ferment was little reflected in legislative acts. A typical first child labor law was that of Massachusetts in 1836, which forbade the employment of children under fifteen in *incorporated* factories, *unless* they had attended school at least three months the year before. Jefferson had so firmly grounded his ideal of a simple agrarian society that Americans did not know how to check the abuses that arose in the new industrial order. Farmers could see no reason why factory operatives should work shorter hours than they did; reformers were much too busy with diet, demon rum, and their dark brethren to look into child labor in the cotton mills; evangelicals were generally persuaded that if everyone would come to Jesus, everything would work out all right.

It must have been a stimulating if somewhat exhausting experience to live among those young men and women "with knives in their brain." As Wordsworth wrote of the French

Revolution, so we may say of America between 1820 and 1850:

> Bliss was it in that dawn to be alive,
> But to be young was very heaven.

3. The Renaissance of New England

Just as the Virginia galaxy of political theorists flickered to its close, the same revolutionary spirit that inspired them ignited a new constellation in a higher latitude. The year 1836, when Emerson published his *Essay on Nature,* may be taken as opening a period in American literary culture, corresponding to 1775 in American politics.

Transcendentalism is the name generally given to this spirit in the Northern states between 1820 and 1860. It may be defined as an intellectual overtone to democracy, a belief in the divinity of human nature. It appeared in some men as intense individualism, in others as a passionate sympathy for the poor and oppressed. It gave to Hawthorne his perception of the beauty and tragedy of life, to Walt Whitman his robust joy in living. Transcendentalism inspired many of the American men of letters who flourished between 1820 and 1860; and almost every aspect of it may be found in Emerson, who embodied the essence of it, a belief in the soul's inherent power to grasp the truth. Historically speaking, transcendentalism was an attempt to make Americans worthy of their independence, and elevate them to a new stature among the mortals.

It may have been mere accident that this outburst of intellectual activity occurred largely within a fifty-mile radius of Boston during a single generation. Transcendentalism has been called the inevitable flowering of the Puritan spirit. But Puritanism does not necessarily bear blossoms, and the fruit thereof is often gnarled and bitter. In New England, however, the soil was conserved by a bedrock of character, mellowed by two centuries of cultivation, and prepared by Unitarianism. New England Federalism checked the flow of sap, fearful lest it feed flowers of Jacobin red. There was just time for a gorgeous show of blossom and a harvest of wine-red fruit, between this late frost and the early autumn blight of the Civil War.

Unitarianism and her sister Universalism took a great weight off the soul of New England. Yet something was lacking in Unitarianism. Faith in the essential goodness of human nature might be a theological counterpart to democracy; but it failed to supply the note of mysticism that democrats, no less than subjects of a monarchical state, seek in religion. The historical function of Unitarianism in America was to liberate the minds of the well-to-do and to provide a church for rationalists. Unitarianism became prolific in men of letters and reformers, but did not extend far from the New England settlements, or even deep within them. Holmes's "One-Hoss Shay" was a symbol of the sudden crumbling of Calvinism; but that happened only in eastern Massachusetts. Congregationalists, Presbyterians, Methodists, and Baptists howled down the Unitarians as atheists and maintained their hold on the native-born masses. Most immigrants remained loyal to Catholicism and other old-country faiths. The reform movements that we have described were inspired by evangelical sects rather than by liberal religion. But the influence of liberalism went far beyond those who embraced it as a faith.

The Reverend Theodore Parker began as a Unitarian, but, as Lowell wrote in his *Fable for Critics,* "from their orthodox kind of dissent he dissented." Parker became a fiery preacher for prison reform, the rights of factory workers, and the slave; Lincoln remembered and treasured his definition of democracy as "the government of all, by all, for all." His scholarship in law, philosophy, and German literature was impeccable. When he died in Florence in 1860, Parker was mourned by Emerson as "my brave brother," whose "place cannot be supplied."

Ralph Waldo Emerson in 1832, at the age of twenty-nine, laid down his pastoral office in the Unitarian church because it no longer interested him. In his next four years of reading and travel he found God again in nature, and settled down a "lay preacher to the world" in a Concord which harbored during one generation Emerson, Hawthorne, Thoreau, and the Alcotts. The atmosphere of the placid village is preserved in *Little Men* and *Little Women,* which Louisa Alcott wrote in order to maintain her transcendental father and family after the failure of his "Fruitlands" community. And at the same time Nathaniel Hawthorne was writing tragedies of New England life that penetrate to the core of all human life.

If Jefferson was the prophet of democracy and Jackson its hero, Emerson was its high priest. Like Jefferson, he believed ardently in the perfectibility of man, but the philosopher knew what the soldier and the statesman never learned, that free institutions could not liberate men not themselves free. His task was to induce Americans to cleanse their minds of hatred and prejudice, to make them think out the consequences of democracy instead of merely repeating its catchwords, and to seek the same eminence in spirit that they had reached in material things.

Henry Thoreau, whose *Week on the Concord and Merrimack Rivers* came out in 1849, was the best classical scholar of the Concord group, and the most independent of classic modes of thought. Concord for him was a microcosm of the world. His revolt was directed against a society so confident and vigorous that it could afford to ignore him. His genius was little appreciated in his own country until the twentieth century. W. H. Hudson called Thoreau's *Walden* (1854) "the one golden book in any century of best books." Marcel Proust hailed Thoreau as a brother; and in France, Germany, Holland, Scandinavia, South America, and Russia, his works were translated. Tolstoy in 1901 sent a "Message to the American People," inquiring why they paid so little attention to the voices of Emerson, Thoreau, and Theodore Parker. On the Orient Thoreau has had an even greater impact. Mahatma Gandhi was inspired by the *Essay on Civil Disobedience;* Pandit Nehru sponsored translations of *Walden* into the principal languages of India. When bumbling county commissioners in 1959 tried to turn the shores of Walden Pond into a beach resort protests world-wide halted the desecration.

In Hawthorne, Emerson, and Thoreau, in half-Yankee Herman Melville, and in Emily Dickinson of the next generation, the New England that had slowly matured since the seventeenth century justified herself. Excellence is the binding quality of these five. Longfellow, Bryant, Poe, and Whitman wrote bad poetry as well as good; Cooper, Irving, and the New York Democratic group were responsible for much wretched, pretentious prose; but every word that the three Concordians, Melville, and Dickinson wrote, whether published in their lifetimes or later, is a treasure. They had this too in common, that they recognized no law save that of their own nature. They obeyed Sir Philip Sidney's injunction, echoed by Longfellow in his *Voices of the Night:* "Look in thy heart and write."

If Walt Whitman was the poet of democracy, Longfellow was democracy's favorite poet. The American people, when they read poetry, wished to be lifted out of themselves by verses that rhymed or scanned into a world of romance and beauty. Hawthorne, Whittier, and Longfellow felt that craving themselves, deriving many themes from American folklore and colonial history: Hawthorne's *Scarlet Letter,* his masterpiece; Whittier's "Skipper Ireson's Ride": Longfellow's "Song of Hiawatha" and "Evangeline." Longfellow, "poet of the mellow twilight of the past," as Whitman called him, "poet of all sympathetic gentleness—and universal poet of woman and young people"—had an influence on his generation second only to

Emerson's. And no poem had a greater effect in creating that love of the Union which made young men fight to preserve it, than the peroration to Longfellow's "Building of the Ship":

> Thou, too, sail on, O Ship of State!
> Sail on, O Union, strong and great!
> Humanity with all its fears,
> With all the hopes of future years,
> Is hanging breathless on thy fate!

Energy was a binding quality of New England men of letters—excepting Hawthorne, who always "lived like a ghost," and shy Emily of Amherst. These writers were in a sense provincial, but they were intensely aware of what was going on in the world. Whittier and Lowell were energetic editors; George Ticknor, Longfellow, and Lowell taught college students; and Dr. Oliver Wendell Holmes, "The Autocrat of the Breakfast Table," lectured at the Harvard Medical School. Emerson toured the lyceums of the North and West; but he was a philosopher who founded no cult and gathered no disciples, since what he said came from no wish to bring men to himself, but to themselves.

In the art of painting, Gilbert Stuart monopolized the field until his death in 1828. He was succeeded as portraitist of merchants, statesmen, and current belles by Chester Harding, a New York State country boy who, after painting eighty portraits in six months, made a triumphant tour of England. Alvan Fisher, who set up a studio in Boston as early as the War of 1812, began to paint American landscapes even earlier than did the Hudson River School and, unlike them, depicted country scenes such as corn husking, punging, children swinging, and barn interiors. Fitz-Hugh Lane of Gloucester, crippled in early life so that he could not be a sailor, more than compensated by painting ships, harbors, and coastal scenes.

Whilst these artists lived aloof from the New England intellectuals, the sculptors were in the mainstream. They did live in Italy during the greater part of their careers; not, however, as escapists but for the good reason that in America it was difficult to find a young girl to pose nude, and impossible to have plaster statues executed in marble or bronze. Fortunately for the American sculptors, it had become fashionable to augment family portraits by portrait busts, and for public buildings to be adorned with statues of celebrities (usually in Roman togas), and battle groups, pioneers, and Indians. First among American sculptors were three remarkable Greenough brothers of Boston, Horatio, Henry, and Richard. Horatio, after graduating from Harvard, went to Rome to study sculpture under Thorwaldsen, and later settled in Florence, where he became the center of an artistic-literary circle. In 1833 he obtained a commission for the heroic statue of Washington at the Capitol, which after many vicissitudes has found a resting place in the new Smithsonian. In 1843 he published *American Architecture,* in which he had the wit to declare that nothing constructed in the New World gave a better example of a practical design producing true beauty, than did the square-rigged sailing ship. Henry and Richard Greenough joined their brother in Florence; Richard made an equestrian statue of Washington for West Point and also executed classic subjects such as "Circe" and "The Carthaginian girl," which Henry James scornfully but not unjustly said were characterized by a "senseless fluency."

Hiram Powers, son of a Vermont farmer, self-educated in Ohio, made busts of statesmen in Washington, which attracted such admiration that friends subscribed to send him to Florence to study under Horatio Greenough. There he executed the most famous piece of American statuary of that era, "The Greek Slave," to which Mrs. Browning dedicated a sonnet. The first nude statue to be exhibited in America, it aroused hostility as well as admiration, but served to make the country sculpture-conscious and shattered a Puritan prejudice against the nude in art.

Parallel to the career of Powers was that of Thomas Crawford, a poor Irish boy of New York City whose artistic ability so impressed his employer, a maker of gravestones, that he sent him in 1835 to study with Thorwaldsen in Rome. There, after almost starving to death, he attracted the interest of Charles Sumner who found him the money to complete "Orpheus," his first great group of statuary. This made Crawford famous, orders flowed in from all parts of America, and in 1849 he won a competition for the equestrian statue of Washington at Richmond. In the 1850's he executed the sculptures on "The Past and Present of America" for the Capitol at Washington; and his death in Rome at the age of thirty-four, in 1857, was regarded as a national calamity.

Youngest of the New England sculptors who made a career in Italy was William Wetmore Story. For ten years after graduating from Harvard he labored in the legal groove set by his father, Justice Joseph Story, but yearned to be a sculptor; and to Italy he went in 1847. His statue "Cleopatra," described by

Hawthorne in *The Marble Faun*, made his fame. He also won distinction as a poet and descriptive writer, and in Rome he resided, center of an artistic circle, until his death in 1895.

4. Popular and Higher Education

The most tangible social gain during this period of ferment was in education. Since the War of Independence, education had been left largely to private initiative and benevolence. Secondary academies and colleges had been founded, and in this the South was ahead of the North. But almost all these institutions charged fees. Elementary education was then the most neglected branch. Most of the Northern states had some sort of public primary school system, but only in New England was it free and open to all. In some instances a child had to be taught his letters before he was admitted to one of these schools, and in others only parents pleading poverty were exempted from paying fees. In addition, the Quakers and other philanthropic bodies maintained charity schools for the poor, which had the effect of fastening a stigma on free schools. In New York City, around 1820, nearly half the children went uneducated because their parents were too poor to pay fees, or too proud or indifferent to accept charity.

Opposition to free public education came from the people of property, who thought it intolerable that they should be taxed to support common schools to which they would not dream of sending their children. To this argument the poor replied with votes, and reformers with the tempting argument that education was insurance against radicalism.

In New England the first problem was to make efficient the colonial system of free elementary schools, maintained by townships and taught by birch-wielding pedagogues or muscular college students during their vacations. Horace Mann sought efficient methods in Europe, and found them in Germany. Victor Cousin's report on Prussian education, which he had translated, became widely known in the United States and was adapted to American needs when, in 1837, Horace Mann became chairman of the new Massachusetts board of education. He and his colleagues combined enthusiasm with an intellectual balance that brought permanent results. Under their influence the first American teachers' college was established in 1839. After a struggle with the older teachers, who insisted that mental discipline would be lost if studies were made attractive, the elementary school ceased to be a place of terror for the young; but there was no "permissiveness"—children still had to learn the fundamentals. Boston set the pace in free public

Thomas Jefferson, by Houdon, *c.* 1785.

JOHN ADAMS, by
Mather Brown,
1785.

President Washington reviewing the Western Army at Fort Cumberland, 1795, by Frederick Kemmelmeyer. Riding behind him are Generals Morgan and Henry Lee, and Colonel Alexander Hamilton.

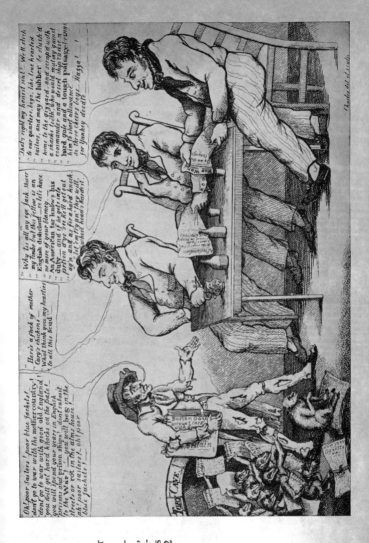

"The Tory Editor and his Apes."

Caricature by William Charles, 1808, illustrating American sailors as dressed in 1812 period.

"AMERICA GUIDED BY WISDOM." Allegorical print by B. Tanner, published in England about 1800.

Minerva points to the shield, upheld by the Genius of America. At her feet is a Horn of Plenty, symbolizing Prosperity. General Washington's statue is placed in front of the triumphal arch, "indicating the progress of the liberal arts." At the left, Mercury, representing Commerce, stands on "bales of American Manufactures," and points to the ships as a lesson in "the advantage of encouraging and protecting Navigation," for the benefit of Ceres, who holds wheat sheaves. Behind her is a beehive, symbolizing Industry, a plow, flail, and harrow for Husbandry, and a "female spinning," to indicate another useful occupation.

PRESIDENT ANDREW JACKSON in 1829, by Thomas Sully.

ANTI-JACKSON TOKENS AND TEMPORARY MONEY, 1832-37.
Obverse and reverse of a pro-Bank token.

Obverse: Jackson removing the deposits; *reverse:* first appearance
of the Democratic donkey. The "LL.D." alludes to Jackson's
being granted that degree by Harvard.

One cent tokens. The building is the Merchants' Exchange in
New York.

Traveling by Coach, *c.* 1836, by George Tatershall.

Waiting for the Stage, by Richard Caton Woodville.

Flying Cloud

TWO AMERICAN CLIPPER SHIPS

Young America

Blue Sulphur Springs, Greenbrier, Virginia. From a lithograph by Ritchie and Dunnavant of Richmond, 1859.

Penn Steam Marble Mantel Factory, Philadelphia, *c.* 1859.

ABRAHAM LINCOLN.
Brady photograph taken during the campaign of 1860.

LIEUT. GEN.
ULYSSES S. GRANT

MAJ. GEN.
WILLIAM
TECUMSEH
SHERMAN

MAJ. GEN. GEORGE
H. THOMAS, USA

LIEUT. GEN.
THOMAS J.
JACKSON, CSA

CAPTAIN OLIVER
WENDELL HOLMES, JR.
USA

LIEUTENANT
RANDOLPH BARTON
CSA

TWO YOUNG OFFICERS IN THE WAR, AND FIFTY YEARS LATER.

JUSTICE OLIVER WENDELL HOLMES *(left)*, and RANDOLPH BARTON,
Esq., president of the Maryland Bar Association, about 1920.

high schools (English High School 1821, Girls' High School 1828); and Massachusetts in 1852 passed a truancy law that had teeth. The argument against compulsory school attendance, which time and experience gradually overcame, now sounds odd; it was then compared with compulsory church attendance, infringing on the rights of parents to the use of all their children's time.

Outside New England, public schools generally were supported by interest on a fund set up out of the proceeds of the sale of public lands, or earmarked taxes, administered by a specially appointed state board. The Board of Regents of the University of New York, which still has oversight of all public education in the Empire State, is a survival of this system. In Pennsylvania there was a terrific fight for free schools, because not only the well-to-do but the Germans did not want them, fearing the loss of their language and culture. The Pennsylvania public school law of 1834, although optional in the school districts, was bitterly attacked, and the eloquence of Thaddeus Stevens is credited with preventing its repeal the following year. By 1837, about 42 per cent of the children in the Keystone State were in free schools.

Ohio was well provided with free public elementary schools by 1830, and six years later the state sent Calvin E. Stowe, professor of Biblical literature in Lane Theological Seminary at Cincinnati (better known as husband of the author of *Uncle Tom's Cabin*), to Europe to investigate public school systems. His *Report on Elementary Instruction in Europe* had an influence only less than the reports of Horace Mann, and among other things was responsible for dividing Ohio public education into elementary, grammar, and high school grades. By 1850 the modern system of grades one through twelve had been adopted in every place where there were enough pupils.

Indiana adopted a free public school system by a narrow majority in 1848. Several years passed before it was enforced, and court decisions adverse to the right of local authorities to raise taxes for their maintenance, in the 1850's, closed most of the high schools that had been started and almost wrecked the system. Illinois used its state educational fund to subsidize private schools. Orville H. Browning, a Whig friend of Abraham Lincoln, pleaded in the state assembly for a public school law in 1843, alleging the benefits conferred on Connecticut by her public schools; to which a Democratic member replied that taxing one class for the benefit of another was unjust, and Connecticut had inundated the West with clock peddlers and others who lived by their wits! A statewide public school law, passed by representatives of the northern part of the state against the opposition of the river counties, was not adopted until 1855.

Many years elapsed before free blacks of the North derived any benefit from free public education. In Philadelphia, the controller of public schools opened the first school for colored children in 1822, apologizing to the public for doing something for "this friendless and degraded portion of society." In northern New England, where blacks were few, they were admitted to the public schools without question; but in urban centers both reformers and blacks themselves favored separate schools to give the children more congenial companionship. The move against segregation began with the antislavery agitation of the 1830's. Massachusetts in 1855 was the first state to enforce integration of all colors, races, and religions in her public schools. None of the feared consequences, still used as arguments against integration, occurred. Other Northern states where there was a considerable colored population followed very slowly; segregation was not legally ended in New York City schools until 1900.

By 1850, then, there had been formulated and, to some extent established, the basic principles of American education: (1) that free public primary and secondary schools should be available for all children; (2) that teachers should be given professional training; (3) that all children be required to attend school up to a certain age, but not necessarily the free public school; religious and other bodies having complete liberty to establish their own educational systems at their own cost. These privileges as yet were only imperfectly extended to women, and even less to blacks. Quality had not been sacrificed to quantity; yet the public elementary schools of 1850 were generally superior to the private schools thirty years earlier, and the public high schools, small according to twentieth-century standards and mostly taught by a few scholarly and enthusiastic men and women, gave a far better training in the fundamentals of mathematics, the classics, modern languages, and history than do most of the bloated and diluted central high schools of today.

The Old Northwest in general, and Ohio in particular, were as prolific in founding colleges at this period as New York State. New settlers were eager to reproduce institutions of higher education, and their motives were largely religious. The Methodists were very energetic, opening instruction of college grade at De Pauw (1837), Ohio Wesleyan (1841), Illinois Wesleyan (1850), Lawrence (1847), and Northwestern University (1855). Presbyterians were responsible for Muskingum (1837) and Knox (1842); the Disciples of Christ for

Antioch (1853). Congregationalists from Yale founded Western Reserve (1826), Wabash (1832), Oberlin (1833), Beloit (1846), and Ripon (1855). Baptist colleges included Denison (1837). Shurtleff (1831). Bucknell (1846), and the first University of Chicago (1859), of which Stephen A. Douglas was a founder. German Lutherans founded Wittenberg (1845); the Episcopalians, Kenyon (1824), and the Catholics, with help from Europe, St. Xavier in Cincinnati (1831) and Notre Dame (1842).

In New England there were founded Amherst College (1821, Congregational), to preserve country boys from the wickedness of Harvard; Trinity (Episcopalian, 1823), located in Hartford for the same reason respecting Yale; Colby (1818, Baptist); Wesleyan (1831, Methodist), and Holy Cross (1843, Catholic). In 1835 Wheaton Female Seminary, now Wheaton College, was founded at Norton, Massachusetts. A temporary member of the teaching staff was Mary Lyon, who in 1836 established the first American women's college, Mount Holyoke. But few opportunities for women in higher education were offered before 1880.

It was typical of America that nobody thought founding a new college in the same town where one already existed; local and sectarian feelings were too strong to follow the example of Oxford and Cambridge. By 1840, over 150 small denominational colleges, each located as far distant as possible from the others, were in existence. The driving impulse for secondary and higher education in the United States prior to the Civil War, and a principal motive to this day, has been religious, not secular; and these slenderly endowed sectarian colleges educated the whole man and maintained a standard of excellence in the liberal arts that has seldom been attained in wealthy, tax-supported state universities.

The older colonial and early federal colleges were now being transformed into proper universities by adding faculties of law, medicine, theology, and science to the original arts and letters. George Ticknor and others who followed postgraduate studies in Germany persuaded Harvard to make the course for the bachelor's degree more flexible and varied, to establish professorial chairs, and make a greater use of lectures. But the idea of a university being a center for scholarly and scientific research lay far in the future. Michigan established a state university in 1837, Missouri two years later, and the University of Wisconsin was founded at Madison in 1849 at a wilderness site crossed by Black Hawk's warriors only fifteen years before.

Adults were not neglected in this educational awakening. In all cities and larger towns, mechanics' institutes provided vocational courses and night schools. Free public libraries, supported by taxation, were generally established, the first being that of Peterborough, New Hampshire, in 1833. In towns and even villages the lyceum offered popular lectures, scientific demonstrations, debates, and entertainment. Under their influence, Americans of the Northern states acquired the habit of attending lectures. Reading was furthered by mechanical improvements in printing, which made possible the penny press. The New York *Tribune*, Baltimore *Sun*, and Philadelphia *Ledger* started as penny newspapers in the 'forties. These, and the mildly sensational New York *Herald* of James Gordon Bennett, were journals of information, with abundant domestic and foreign news and serialized English novels. Under Horace Greeley's editorship, the *Tribune* became a liberal power of the first magnitude. English visitors of the period invariably remarked, and usually deplored, the fact that shop clerks, mechanics, and even common laborers subscribed to daily newspapers.

5. *Science and Technology*

American science, like everything else, now became specialized. Benjamin Franklin had made stoves and lightning rods as well as pursuing original research in electricity. But it was typical of our era that Joseph Henry, who discovered the electromagnet, handed over to Samuel F. B. Morse the problem of adapting it to the telegraph.

Joseph Henry, son of a Scots day laborer in Albany, began to experiment with electricity in 1826 when, at the age of twenty-nine, he was appointed professor of natural philosophy in the local academy which he had attended. After inventing the electromagnet, he devised means to increase the intensity of attraction produced by the same source of current, and by reversing the current he produced a rudimentary motor which he regarded as "a philosophical toy." His studies of induced currents, begun independently of his English contemporary Michael Faraday, who first announced the discovery, led Henry to discover step-up and step-down transformers, formulate theories of intensity (voltage) and quantity (amperage) of currents, and make some of the earliest observations of oscillating energy discharged by electricity in a spiral coil. Outside that field he worked on solar radiation and capillary action of liquids.

Henry came as near to being a "pure" scientist as any American prior to the 1870's. The stress in the United States always had been on "useful knowledge"—the declared purpose of the eighteenth-century American Philosophical Society and the American Academy of Arts and Sciences. Tocqueville devoted a chapter of his *Democracy in America* (1835) to the subject, "Why Americans Prefer the Practice Rather than the Theory of Science." He pointed out that there were few calm spots in America for meditation, which is necessary for the cultivation of pure science; democracy wanted results and American scientists were afraid of losing themselves in abstractions. The sapient Frenchman observed that in a democratic society short-cuts to wealth, labor-saving gadgets, and inventions which add to the comfort or pleasure of life, "seem the most magnificent effort of human intelligence." And this on the whole remained true of America until after World War II. Almost all the great and fruitful scientific ideas were hatched in Europe; but the widest applications of them to common life, or to destruction in war, were made in America. "Mind, acting through the *useful* arts, is the vital principle of modern civilized society," pontificated Edward Everett in 1857. "The mechanician, not the magician, is now the master of life." Everett was premature; but in due time the scientist occupied a position in American society analogous to that of the medicine man among the Indians.

The machine-tool industry with interchangeable parts was already entrenched in the Naugatuck valley of Connecticut by 1836, the year that Samuel Colt patented the revolving pistol, "equalizer" of the frontier. Charles Goodyear in 1844 patented the vulcanization of rubber, which eventually enabled all America to roll or fly. Two years later, Elias Howe invented the sewing machine, which took the making of clothes out of the home and tailor's shop into the factory. Cyrus McCormick of Virginia in 1834 invented the reaper, which made possible prairie farming on a grand scale. More spectacular and far-reaching was Samuel F. B. Morse's invention of the electric telegraph in 1832. Morse worked it out while teaching painting and sculpture at New York University. His friends in Congress got him an appropriation of $30,000 in 1843 to establish between Baltimore and Washington the first telegraph line, built by Ezra Cornell who later founded Cornell University. The first message sent over this line in dots and dashes on 24 May 1844 between Morse himself and a friend in Baltimore, was "What hath God wrought!"

John Goffe Rand, an assistant to Morse, invented in 1841, to hold paints, the collapsible metal tube, the use of which has extended to thousands of other products. At the Crystal Palace Exposition in London in 1851, the cheap clocks, reapers, ranges, machine-made buckets, and other "Yankee notions" exhibited by Americans gave notice that the tide of invention had risen higher in the United States than in the Old World. The preserving of food by canning was invented in time to be put to limited use in the Civil War.

Noteworthy was the popularity of science on lyceum platforms. One of the greatest teachers and scientists of the era was Benjamin Silliman, for 51 years professor of chemistry and natural history at Yale. It was he, more than any other, who grafted the new natural science onto the old liberal education. His popular lectures on geology and chemistry, delivered all the way from New England to New Orleans and St. Louis, were as important in spreading knowledge of the fast-growing body of natural science, as Emerson's for thought and literature. *The American Journal of Science and Arts* which Silliman founded in 1818 became a leading vehicle of information. In 1847 at the age of sixty-eight when, according to modern ideas, he should have retired, Silliman founded the Sheffield Scientific School of Yale University. The central idea was to supplement lectures and readings in the current topics of scientific education (mainly physics, chemistry, geology, and mineralogy) by laboratory research as the core of a college scientific department. At the same time, Amos Eaton at Rensselaer Polytechnic was using the Erie Canal as a practical training ground for civil engineering, even setting up a traveling summer school on a canal boat.

At Amherst College one of Silliman's lifelong friends, the Reverend Edward Hitchcock, made his mark as a professor of geology and natural theology. As promoter and director of the first state geological survey to be completed, he set standards which made his advice and assistance sought for similar projects, North and South. He published a popular textbook on geology and exhibited to a wondering public the footprints left by dinosaurs in sandstone along the Connecticut river.

In 1848, when Louis Agassiz from Switzerland accepted the chair of natural history at the Lawrence Scientific School (Harvard's bid to equal Yale's "Sheff"), the Cambridge college began to rival Yale in science. Agassiz, renowned as paleontologist and propounder of the glacier theory, became a famous personality and helped to bring government aid to scientific investigation. Asa Gray, who had taken a chair at Harvard a few years earlier, wrote a *Manual of the Botany of the Northern United States* (1848) which became a classic. And he became America's first great exponent of Darwin's theory of evolution. All leading American scientists of this period were devout men, presenting scientific discoveries as unfolding the wonderful works of God. It was otherwise with the later disciples of Darwin and Huxley, who repudiated the Biblical account of creation.

Organized religion, however, was partly responsible for the slow development of astronomy in America as compared with other Western countries or even Russia. To probe the starry firmament with a telescope was considered mildly blasphemous; Democrats defeated President Adams's suggestion of a government observatory. Nevertheless, Professor Denison Olmsted of Yale studied the Leonids, the great meteoric shower of 1833, which the superstitious thought heralded the world's end, and proved that they were particles from comets passing through the earth's atmosphere. Harvard College, stimulated by Benjamin Peirce, built an observatory for its 15-inch refracting telescope (as big as any then in the world), which was imported and assembled in 1847. The work of this observatory was largely practical, such as plotting the latitude and longitude of places on earth, and the orbits of planets and the visible stars, and computing the annual *American Nautical Almanac*. Through the new telescope William C. Bond and a Boston daguerreotypist made the first stellar photograph in 1850.

Why did Congress never establish a national university at Washington as every President of the United States through John Quincy Adams recommended? State rights and the distaste of older colleges for competition are the probable answer. The nearest thing to the "national institution of learning" which the Father of his Country hoped for, was the Smithsonian Institution, founded by a bequest of £100,000 to the United States in 1835 "for the increase and diffusion of knowledge among men," by an English man of science, James Smithson. President Jackson ignored it; several senators, including Calhoun, declared it to be unconstitutional; but John Quincy Adams finally argued Congress into accepting it.

Then came a ten-year wrangle over what to do with Smithson's bounty. Congress incorporated the Smithsonian Institution and set up a Board of Regents who first met in 1846. They persuaded Joseph Henry to leave his chair of natural philosophy at Princeton to be the first director; and, as such, he made the Smithsonian the first institution for pure scientific research in the New World. Originally he was required by law to promote practically every branch of knowledge. He persuaded Congress and the regents to slough off several arts and sciences to other institutions in the District of Columbia such as the Corcoran Gallery of Fine Arts, the Congressional Library, the Weather Bureau, and the Bureau of Standards, leaving a central core of scientific research that has functioned admirably. Samuel P. Langley, secretary of the Smithsonian, wrote *Experiments in Aërodynamics* (1891) which became the take-off for heavier-than-air aviation.

American archaeology and ethnology languished, despite the good start given by Stephens's books on Central America. In 1847 George Catlin's remarkable collection of life portraits of American Indians, which had been displayed in the Louvre to the admiration of French critics, was offered for sale to the Smithsonian. Congress refused to appropriate the money, one senator remarking that he would rather acquire portraits of American citizens murdered by the Indians. But eventually the collection became one of the glories of the National Museum.

XIV

Pacific Empire Beckons

1766-1860

1. *Oregon and the "Mountainy Men"*

Lieutenant Jonathan Carver, on a Western journey in 1766-67, learned from Cree and Sioux Indians that the sources of the four biggest rivers in North America lay close together. These were the St. Lawrence, the Mississippi, the Red river of the North, and a great westward-flowing stream which they called the Oregon. William Cullen Bryant picked up that euphonious name and ensured its place on the map of North America in his *Thanatopsis* (1817):

> Where rolls the Oregon, and hears no sound
> Save his own dashings.

That concept of a "Great River of the West" flowing majestically to the Pacific long dominated geographic thought and Western ambitions.

Shortly after the end of the War of 1812, Great Britain and the United States agreed to a joint occupation of the Oregon country, which included the present states of Oregon, Washington, Idaho, and the province of British Columbia. John Quincy Adams, one of those

Stern men with empires in their brains
Who saw in vision their young Ishmael strain
In each hard hand a vassal ocean's mane

kept the American claim to the Oregon country alive through decades of national indifference. His diplomacy persuaded Spain to limit her claims to the present northern boundary of California, and Russia to limit hers to latitude 54° 40' North, the present southern tip of Alaska. But the Yankee fur trade dwindled, while the Hudson's Bay Company in 1824 set up a great trading "factory" at Fort Vancouver on the Columbia river opposite the site of Portland. Four times did Adams, as secretary of state and President, offer to divide Oregon with Canada by extending the northern boundary of the United States along latitude 49° to the Pacific. Four times England refused, demanding everything north of the Columbia. Adams declined to make that concession because he envisaged a naval base and trading city on Puget Sound. He wished to open a window to the Pacific, and shorten the sea route to China. That was the ancient dream of Columbus; again the reality surpassed the dream.

In the meantime, the west coast from San Diego to Queen Charlotte Island was being visited by Boston fur traders and "hide droghers." Many of these vessels also traded with Hawaii, where the American Board of Foreign Missions had established a native Congregational church in 1820 under the Reverend Hiram Bingham. California belonged to Mexico and to the Roman Catholic church, but Bingham kept urging his Boston backers to do something about the free-for-all Oregon country. This appealed to an odd Yankee named Hall J. Kelley, who in 1830 founded "The American Society for Encouraging the Settlement of the Oregon Territory." Kelley stirred up Nathaniel J. Wyeth, whose zest for oceanic trade had been whetted by successfully exporting ice from Fresh Pond, Cambridge, to South America.

Since even seagoing Yankees could not send large numbers of settlers to Oregon by the 200-day voyage around Cape Horn, they would have to come overland. And that leads us to the third element which contributed to the securing of Oregon, the fur traders and trappers of the Great Plains and Rocky Mountains. These "mountainy men" were indispensable to land-trailing immigrants. Once the pioneers had crossed the Great Plains, which covered the present states of Oklahoma, Kansas, Nebraska, the Dakotas, most of Montana, and large parts of Wyoming and Colorado, the mountainy men guided them across the Rocky Mountains to the Snake and Columbia rivers, which floated them to the Pacific.

The smooth or gently rolling surface of the Great Plains, rising gradually or by step-like escarpments to an elevation of 6000 feet, was covered with a carpet of grass which grew rank and thick in the eastern parts, but gave way to tufts of short buffalo grass and sagebrush in the parched High Plains. An occasional rocky dome, butte, or mesa made a welcome landmark, like a lighthouse to a mariner. The Platte and Missouri rivers, with their short tributaries, cut deep gashes in the soil and watered a thin line of willow, cotton wood, and wild plum trees. A short summer of blistering heat, with fierce thunderstorms and frequent cyclones, followed hard on a long winter of bitter northwest winds and heavy snow. Over this area roamed the Kansa, Pawnee, Sioux, Cheyenne, Blackfoot, Crow, Arapaho, and other tribes. Countless herds of buffalo grazed on the plains and supplied the redskins with every necessity of life: meat for immediate use, or, dried and pounded into pemmican, for winter subsistence; skins for clothing, harness, vessels, and the tipi or tent; sinews for thread, cordage, and bowstrings; bone for arrowheads and implements; peltry to sell to the traders; even fuel. These Indians had long since domesticated the wild mustang, offspring of those set free by Spaniards in Texas, and had become expert at killing buffalo with bow and arrow while riding bareback.

The Plains Indians seldom practiced agriculture or other primitive arts, but they were fine physical specimens; and in warfare, once they had learned the use of the rifle, much more formidable than the Eastern tribes who had slowly yielded to the white man. Tribe warred with tribe, and a highly developed sign language was the only means of intertribal communication. The effective unit was the band or village of a few hundred souls, which might be seen in the course of its wanderings encamped by a watercourse with tipis erected; or pouring over the plain, women and children leading dogs and packhorses with their trailing travois, while gaily dressed braves loped ahead on horseback. They lived only for the day, recognized no rights of property, robbed or killed anyone if they thought they could get away with it, inflicted cruelty without a qualm, and endured torture without flinching.

The "mountainy men" who, save for an occasional soldier or explorer, were the only whites to penetrate this region prior to 1832, were for the most part as savage and ruthless as Indians—they had to be, to survive. The thing that brought them into the High Plains and Rockies was beaver—that industrious little animal whose fur had kept the Pilgrim colony alive and made the Iroquois Confederacy arbiters of international rivalry. Beaver fur was more in demand than ever, to make the extravagantly tall hats then worn by gentlemen, while less valuable furs went into felt hats for the common people. Mountainy men, buckskin-clad, lean, bearded, and usually very dirty, were of all races and origins. Many had Indian wives, a valuable asset for a white trapper not only as a drudge, but because her Indian relatives were bound to avenge him if he were "rubbed out," a phrase first used here. Some were lone operators, others employees of General William Ashley's Rocky Mountain Fur Company or other less important companies. Annually an autumn rendezvous between trappers and buyers was set on the upper Platte, the Sweetwater, the Big Horn, or in the Teton Mountains farther west. Supplies and trading goods were sent thither from St. Louis in the spring floods, at first by 50-foot keel boats towed by 15 to 20 men trudging along the bank, and in shoal water by "bull boats" made of buffalo hide stretched on a wicker frame. To this rendezvous converged Indians and mountainy men, with their women and their season's take of beaver, "hairy banknotes" which they swapped for raw alcohol from the Cincinnati distilleries, and for arms and munitions, coffee, sugar, tobacco, and blankets. After this "blowout," as they called it, had lasted a few days or a couple of weeks and the liquor had been drunk and the goods gambled away, the mountainy men, poor as before, staggered off into the wilderness to get ready for next year's trapping. When the beaver hibernated they too holed up with their wives, trapped again as soon as the ice melted, and in the fall attended another rendezvous. By 1840 they had almost exterminated beaver in the Rockies; but in their hunting had discovered and mentally mapped every stream and mountain in that region. Jed Smith in 1823 discovered the South Pass of the Rockies in Wyoming, a wide valley of rolling hills that takes one to the transcontinental divide by easy gradients, and which later became the most practical route for wagons. Without such men as guides, most of the emigrants to the Oregon country, Utah, and California would have perished.

Among these guides were the Sublettes who guided Wyeth on his first transcontinental journey; James Bridger, first white man to report the Great Salt Lake; "Kit" Carson and Thomas Fitzpatrick, who indicated a path to the misnamed "pathfinder" Frémont; Henry Chatillon, who guided Francis Parkman over the Oregon Trail. These men could neither read nor write but they were simple-minded, courageous nature's gentlemen, carrying in their heads an encyclopedic knowledge of Indians and the West. Bridger in 1843 established as a way station Fort Bridger, Wyoming, where the Oregon trail swings south to avoid the Yellowstone Mountains, and where his hospitality saved thousands of emigrants' lives. Fitzpatrick's influence with the Plains Indians was largely responsible for the important treaties of Fort Laramie (1851) and Fort Atkinson (1853) which kept them quiet while the transcontinental movement was at its height. Carson became a valuable army scout in the Mexican War and managed the Navajo during the Civil War.

2. Pioneers and the Oregon Trail

So much for the background: trappers swarming over the Great Plains and into the Rockies, missionaries trying to whip up interest in settling the Oregon country, and a Hudson's Bay trading post on the lower Columbia. If Nathaniel Wyeth the Cambridge iceman needed another stimulus, he got it when trading brig *Owhyhee* of Boston returned from the Northwest Coast in 1831, carrying the first shipment of pickled Columbia river salmon. The fish sold readily, but President Jackson's treasury department made the importer pay duty on it as "foreign-caught fish." Clearly it was time to prove that Oregon was part of the United States.

Wyeth raised capital to put a Yankee pincer on Oregon, and recruited 24 men and boys for the overland route. He constructed three vehicles that he called "amphibia"—ancestors of the World War II "dukws"—which could be drawn on wheels or sailed on the water. On 1 March 1832 he dispatched brig *Ida*, loaded with trade goods for the projected colony, around Cape Horn. Wyeth's own party proceeded by railway, road, and river steamboat to St. Louis. There William Sublette offered to guide him to a trappers' rendezvous provided he dropped the amphibia, and Wyeth accepted. Sublette's brother Milton eventually took over and guided the emigrants to the Snake river, whence Wyeth with a dozen men and boys pressed on. By mid-September they were in the wooded country that the French had named Boisé, and saw their first forests of tall Western conifers. At Fort Walla Walla, a Hudson's Bay Company outpost, he hired a boat to take him down the Columbia, carrying around the Dalles, and on 29 October 1832, 233 days from Boston and 190 from St. Louis, he reached Fort Vancouver. There he learned that brig *Ida* had been lost at sea, and his plans for a colony were ruined. So Wyeth returned overland, joining Captain Bonneville en route.

Wyeth's backers, who still had faith in him and in Oregon, now put up the money for a second trip, in 1834. Again he dispatched a brig around the Horn, laden with supplies and hundreds of knocked-down barrels which he hoped to fill with pickled salmon for the Boston market. With him on the overland journey were Thomas Nuttall and John K. Townsend, ornithologists, the Reverend Jason Lee, and four other missionaries who had been recruited to convert the Flathead Indians. This party made Fort Vancouver on 15 September 1834—160 days from St. Louis. Another failure. The fur company refused to accept Wyeth's trade goods, the ship arrived too late for the salmon fishing; and in 1836, at the age of thirty-four, Wyeth returned empty-handed to Boston and went back into the ice business.

Yet, from the long view, Wyeth's project did more than any other to win Oregon for the United States. The ornithologists helped to make that country known. Jason Lee and his fellow missionaries settled in the Willamette valley near the present Salem, Oregon, and combined with former employees of the Hudson's Bay Company to raise wheat and cattle. Lee's backers published a periodical called *The Oregonian and Indians' Advocate*, packed with luscious sales-talk on the Oregon country.

One could hardly exaggerate the beauty of this country. The majestic Columbia river, teeming with salmon, breaks through the Cascade range, where snowcapped peaks (Hood, St. Helens, Adams, Rainier) soar like serene white souls above virgin fir forests. Here are the fertile valleys of the Clackamas, the Willamette, and the Umatilla, ripe for grain fields and orchards, and a mild, moist climate more like Old England's than New England's. And the continent is rimmed by an ironbound coast, with an occasional sand beach on which the long Pacific surges eternally tumble and roar.

Fort Vancouver offered a market for all the grain and livestock the settlers could raise; the difficulties were in getting there, and settling the question of what flag you were under when you arrived. Presidents Jackson, Van Buren, Harrison, and Tyler paid no attention to Oregon. Nothing was done to extend American law to this region, or to settle the question of sovereignty. Nevertheless, Lee and his neighbors, following the same instinct for self-government that had produced the Mayflower Compact and the State of Franklin, called a meeting at Champoeg in the Willamette valley and drew up a compact for governing Oregon country on 5 July 1843. The laws of Iowa were adopted, and arrangements were made to settle land titles, that fruitful subject of frontier disputes.

In the meantime the American Board of Foreign Missions had sent religious and medical missionaries to the eastern part of the Oregon country, especially the future state of Idaho. In response to a plea from four Flatheads who had visited St. Louis, the Board sent out young Dr. Marcus Whitman with his twenty-year-old bride in the spring of 1836. It took them five months from St. Louis to reach Fort Walla Walla. Narcissa Whitman, first white woman to pass the Rockies, had to discard one article after another from their hand-drawn cart; even her bridal trunk.

This Whitman party and others that soon followed, established missions to the Cayuse Indians, to the Nez Percé, and to the Flathead, this last near the site of Spokane. For a decade these missions flourished and part of the New Testament was printed in Nez Percé. But the Cayuse became estranged when tough characters of the heavy migration of 1845–47 harassed them and brought in measles. Owing to an unfounded rumor that Dr. Whitman's measles medicine was poison, he and most of the mission group were massacred in November 1847. This provoked the first of Oregon's Indian conflicts, the Cayuse War, in which 250 armed men punished the guilty Indians.

Nor did the Catholic church neglect this mission field; by 1847 there were fourteen Jesuit missionaries in the Northwest. Father Pierre-Jean de Smet from the Catholic University of St. Louis, "Blackrobe" to the Indians, founded the Sacré Coeur Mission in the Coeur d'Alene country.

In 1842 "Oregon fever" struck the frontier folk of Iowa, Missouri, Illinois, and Kentucky. By temperament and tradition these were backwoodsmen who had no use for treeless prairies or arid high plains; they wanted wood, water, and game, which the Oregon country had in abundance, and to slough off the fevers and agues that afflicted them in the lowlands bordering the Mississippi. Independence, Missouri, was their jumping-off place. "Prairie schooners," as the canvas-covered Conestoga wagons were nicknamed, assembled there in May when the grass of the plains was fresh and green. Parties were organized, a captain appointed, an experienced mountaineer engaged as guide; and with blowing of bugles and cracking of long whips, the caravan, 100 wagons strong with a herd of cattle on the hoof, moved up the west bank of the Missouri. At Fort Leavenworth, bastion of the Indian

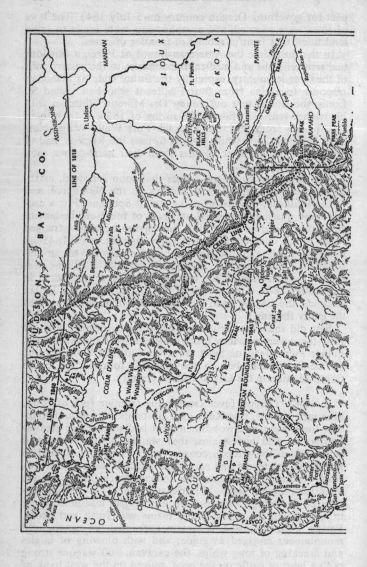

trapper, the emigrant broke contact with their line, and its

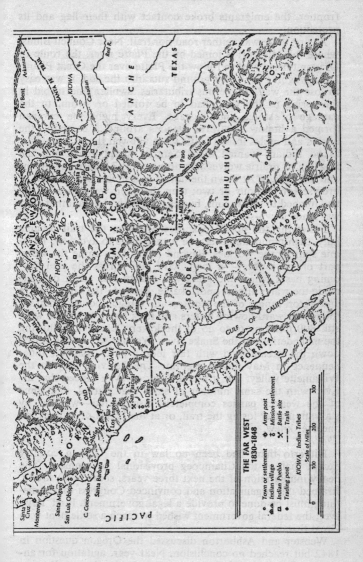

**THE FAR WEST
1830-1848**

o	Town or settlement
⚔	Army post
†	Mission settlement
×	Battle site
□	Indian Pueblo
	Trails
○	Indian village
	Trading post

KIOWA   *Indian Tribes*

Scale of Miles

0   100   200   300

frontier, the emigrants broke contact with their flag and its protection.

At first there was neither road nor trail. Near Council Bluffs, where the Missouri is joined by the Platte river, the route to Oregon turned west to follow the Platte over the Great Plains. Until wagon wheels had ground ruts into the sod, it was easy to lose the way. Numerous tributaries, swollen and turbid in the spring of the year, had to be forded or swum, to the damage of stores and baggage. Every night the caravan formed a hollow square of wagons around a campfire, the horses and mules inside; cattle were allowed to graze outside, as no Indians wanted them. Sentries stood guard and the howling of prairie wolves was drowned by a chorus of hymns and old ballads. At dawn the horses and mules were let out to browse for an hour or two; then the oxen were rounded up and hitched to the wagons, bugles blew gaily, and another start was made down-sun.

Following the north fork of the Platte, the trail became hilly, then mountainous as one turned aside to avoid the Laramie spur of the Rockies. Beyond South Pass came the worst part of the journey—a long, hard pull across the arid Wyoming basin where the grass was scanty and alkali deposits made the water almost undrinkable. Between the Gros Ventre and Teton ranges of the Rockies the Oregon-bound emigrant found westward-flowing waters and took heart; but there were still 800 miles more to go to the lower Columbia, following the meanderings of the Snake river. Wagons were often rafted down the stream; and with fair luck a party that left Independence in May might celebrate Thanksgiving Day in the Willamette valley. But it was a lucky caravan indeed that arrived with the same number of souls that started, and some of the weaker parties completely disappeared—whether by starvation after losing the trail, or at the hands of Indians, no one ever knew.

Hitherto there had been no law in the Oregon country except that of the Champoeg provisional government. The heavy immigration of the next three years, some 5000 strong, strained this organization and convinced Congress that something must be done to provide a legal government. First, however, the federal government wished to reach a settlement with Great Britain.

Webster and Ashburton discussed the Oregon question in 1842 but reached no conclusion. Next year, agitation for annexing the whole of Oregon up to the border of Russian Alaska, 54° 40′ N, started in the Western states. President

Tyler opened negotiations on the subject in 1844, repeating the proposal formerly made by J. Q. Adams, to divide the territory along latitude 49°. Lord Aberdeen, like his predecessors, refused to lower the Union Jack from the right bank of the Columbia.

If the question were decided by actual occupation, that British claim was fair. Over 700 British subjects but only half a dozen American citizens had settled north of the Columbia. The United States, however, could afford to wait. A decline in the fur trade was making Fort Vancouver unprofitable, and the increasing number of American immigrants threatened its security. The Hudson's Bay Company abandoned this fort in 1845 and erected a new post at Victoria on Vancouver Island.

By this time an expansionist, James K. Polk, had become President of the United States. The Democratic platform called for "re-occupation of Oregon, re-annexation of Texas." In his annual message of December 1845 Polk asserted that the American title up to latitude 54° 40′ N was "clear and unquestionable." He asked for authority to terminate the joint occupation agreement of 1818, and Congress gave it. Polk never intended to risk war over Oregon, since he expected shortly to be fighting Mexico for California. So, when Lord Aberdeen proposed to extend the international boundary along latitude 49° N to Puget Sound, thence to the ocean through Juan de Fuca Strait, leaving Vancouver Island to Canada, Polk accepted. He submitted this offer to his cabinet on 6 June 1846, when the war with Mexico was but three weeks old, and to the Senate immediately after. It was during this debate that a Western expansionist coined the slogan, "Fifty-four Forty or Fight!" Nevertheless, the Senate on 15 June consented to a treaty accepting Aberdeen's boundary. It took five months for the news to reach the settlements on the Willamette.

Thus Canada, as well as the United States, obtained an outlet to the Pacific. Except for a minor controversy over the islands of Puget Sound, this western end of the lengthy frontier between Canada and the United States gave no further trouble.

3. The Mormons

The Church of Jesus Christ of the Latter-day Saints, commonly called the Mormons, was responsible for settling Utah.

Joseph Smith came of a New England family which, after ten moves in less than twenty years, settled at Palmyra, New York, in the midst of the "burned-over district." An Angel of the Lord, so Joseph claimed, showed him the hiding place of inscribed gold plates, together with a pair of magic spectacles which enabled him to read the characters. The resulting Book of Mormon, first printed in 1830, described the history of allegedly lost tribes of Israel (the Indians), whom the Saints were commanded to redeem from paganism. Joseph Smith, a shrewd, able Yankee, organized his church as a co-operative theocracy, all power emanating from himself as "Prophet." The hostility of "gentile" neighbors forced the Saints to remove first to Kirtland, Ohio, then to Missouri; and again, in 1839, to a place in Illinois which the Prophet named Nauvoo. There Smith received a "revelation" in favor of polygamy.

In Illinois the Mormons were courted by both political parties and Nauvoo was given a city charter. But the settlement grew so rapidly—faster, even, than Chicago—that the Illinois "gentiles" (as the Mormons called other Christians) became alarmed, and a group of them in 1844 murdered Smith. Brigham Young, who succeeded to the Prophet's mantle and took over five of his twenty-seven widows, directed retaliation on the gentiles by a corps of "avenging angels," and for two years terror reigned in western Illinois. It was clearly time for another move.

Yet the Mormons had made an astonishing gain in numbers. Their missionaries had been raking in converts from the Northern states since 1831; and in 1840, when Brigham Young visited Liverpool, England became one of their principal harvest fields. Thousands of poor workers and tenant farmers were charmed by the prospect of decent living and the promise of heavenly "thrones, kingdoms, principalities and powers." Almost 4000 English converts reached Nauvoo between 1840 and 1846, and 40 or 50 churches of Latter-day Saints in the old country contributed modest tithes to the Prophet's bulging treasury.

Under their new Moses, Brigham Young, a ruthless autocrat but a leader of energy and vision, the Mormons abandoned Nauvoo in 1846 and began their great westward journey, several thousand strong. After wintering near Council Bluffs, Brigham Young pushed ahead with a pioneer band along a new trail on the north bank of the Platte. In July 1847 he reached the promised land, the basin of the Great Salt Lake. By the end of 1848, 5000 people had arrived in the future State of Utah, which Brigham Young called Deseret.

This new Canaan was an inhospitable land. Young chose it in the hope that his Saints would no longer be molested by gentiles, and because it was Mexican territory; but the Mexican War changed that. Arid wastes, where salt and alkali deposits glistened among sagebrush thickets, sloped down from the Rocky Mountains to the Great Salt Lake, desolate as another Dead Sea. But in the mountains lay natural reservoirs of rain and snow, the means of quickening life.

For such unfamiliar conditions the experience of English-speaking pioneers was inadequate, but the community sense of the Mormons proved competent to cope with them. Brigham Young caused irrigation canals and ditches to be dug, appointed committees to control water for the public benefit, discarding the common-law doctrine of riparian rights. He set up a system of small farms, intensively cultivated and carefully fertilized. He forbade speculation in land, but respected private property and accumulated a large fortune for himself. He kept the Indians quiet by a judicious mixture of firmness and justice. He repressed heresy and schism with a heavy hand. He organized foreign and domestic missions and financed both transatlantic and transcontinental immigration. By means of a complicated hierarchy he controlled both civil and spiritual affairs with Yankee shrewdness, rough humor, and substantial justice, holding himself responsible only to God.

For ten years there was intermittent want and starvation in Deseret, and the gold rush of 1849 to California caused unrest. Brigham Young announced in the Tabernacle at Salt Lake City, "If you Elders of Israel want to go to the gold mines, go and be damned!" The wiser Saints found it more profitable to sell corn and potatoes to passing Argonauts. Yearly the community grew in numbers and wealth, a polygamous theocracy within a monogamous and democratic nation. Congress organized Deseret as Utah Territory in 1850, and President Fillmore appointed Brigham Young territorial governor. Federal judges were driven from Utah when they refused to do his will; and when President Buchanan in 1857–58 sent an army of regulars under Colonel Albert Sidney Johnston to support a new territorial governor, the United States forces, defeated by Young's scorched-earth strategy, obtained only nominal submission. In the Civil War, Utah was practically neutral. After the Civil War, Utah and the Mormons profited by prosperity and the influx of new elements. Polygamy, forbidden by federal law in 1862, gradually died out. The Latter-day Saints brought comfort, happiness, and self-respect to thousands of humble folk; and Brigham Young must be included among the most successful commonwealth builders of the English-speaking world.

THE MORMON HAND-CART SONG

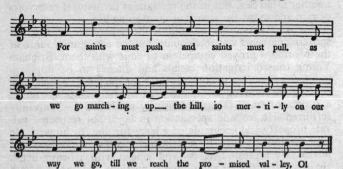

For saints must push and saints must pull, as we go march-ing up— the hill, so mer-ri-ly on our way we go, till we reach the pro-mised val-ley, O!

XV

Texas and the Mexican War

1820-1848

1. *The Lone Star Republic*

LONG BEFORE the Oregon question was settled, even before it arose, another problem of power and expansion was rising in the Southwest. While one column of pioneers deployed into the prairies of Illinois and Iowa, and another was preparing to wind over the Oregon Trail, a third from Louisiana and the Mississippi valley had crossed into Mexican territory and taken possession of the coastal plain of Texas. Expansion in that direction was no simple matter of endurance or of driving back redskins. In Texas the English-speaking pioneer came into contact with a proud and ancient civilization, represented by the Republic of Mexico. Who could tell whether Mexico might develop the same expansive force as the United States?

In 1820 Upper California (the present state of California), New Mexico (including Arizona), and Texas, frontier provinces of Mexico as of New Spain, spread out toward the United States and were attached to the parent trunk by the frailest of stems. Explored as early as the sixteenth century by the Spaniards, they had been thinly colonized after a long interval, and in the Roman rather than the English sense. Missions had been planted among the Indians as centers of civilization and exploitation; frontier garrisons were established to

311

protect the fathers in their work; and such few colonists as could be persuaded to venture so far were generously endowed by the Spanish government with lands and Indian serfs. Although a constant drain on the mother country, these frontier provinces were maintained mostly as protection against westward-pushing Anglo-Americans. The new Republic of Mexico, weak, distracted, and lacking expansive energy, knew not how to use them, but was too proud to dispose of them. Garrisons were withdrawn, the missions secularized, and the Indians allowed to relapse into their old folkways.

Santa Fe, capital and only town of New Mexico, was the gateway to a country of marvels and enchantments, shimmering plains with no vegetation but strange cacti, mesas striped with ochre and vermilion, aboriginal cliff dwellings, and the stupendous canyon of the Colorado river. Annually from 1824, an armed caravan of American traders assembled at Independence, Missouri, and followed the Sante Fe trail with pack mule and wagon through the country of the Osage and Comanche to this lonely emporium, returning with silver and peltry.

In 1823 a wedge of North Americans thrust across Mexico's borders into Texas. That province, 750 miles long from the Sabine river to El Paso, and of equal depth from the tip of the "panhandle" to the mouth of the Rio Grande, is larger than France and almost as varied in climate and natural resources. The pioneers found moist gulf plains studded with cane-brakes, and cold, arid plateaus; dense forests of pine and hardwood; prairies of a deep, black, waxy loam perfect for cotton growing, and others of lighter soil, adapted for grain; sagebrush and yucca deserts; and the Llano Estacado or High Plains where roamed immense herds of buffalo and mustang. Texas had never formed part of Louisiana, and the American claim to it, renounced in the Florida Treaty of 1819, was based on nothing better than the supposition that Napoleon was about to seize it before he decided to sell Louisiana to the United States. Nevertheless, no sooner had President Monroe agreed upon the Sabine and Red rivers as the southwestern boundary of the United States, than he was attacked for giving away something for nothing. Presidents Adams and Jackson, as we have seen, pressed the Mexican government to sell Texas. The first offer was received as an insult and the repetition created resentment.

Inexplicably, Mexico encouraged emigration from the United States to Texas. An important grant was given in 1821 to Moses Austin of Connecticut, successively dry-goods merchant in Philadelphia and Richmond, owner of the Chiswell lead mines in Virginia, pioneer lead miner in Missouri, and banker in St. Louis. He died six months after obtaining this Texan grant, but the Mexican Congress confirmed it to his son in 1823. This gave Stephen F. Austin the privilege of settling 300 American families in one of the most fertile regions of Texas; later, the number was increased. Each family received free 177 acres of rich tillage, together with 13,000 acres of prairie pasture, Austin taking a bonus of 65,000 acres. By 1834 Austin's colony comprised 20,000 white colonists and 2000 slaves, outnumbering the native Mexicans in Texas four to one. Austin, a grave and gentle young man, chose recruits for his colony with care, and ruled it with autocratic power until 1829. In social structure it resembled an English proprietary colony like Maryland; and Texas was more law-abiding and better governed than any nineteenth-century American frontier.

Although antislavery by preference, Austin found himself in the same dilemma as every colonist with capital: the choice between pioneer poverty and using some form of forced labor. There were no Indians who could be made peons, and the soil offered such rich opportunities for cotton and sugar culture that Southern planters would not come unless permitted to bring slaves, and could not prosper without them. The Mexican Congress in 1831 declared slavery abolished throughout the Republic. But Austin was always able to obtain some "explanation" of the decree which allowed his people to hold slaves in fact, if not by law. Similarly, it was a condition of his grant that all settlers should be Roman Catholics, but very few were.

Many factors pulled Texas away from Mexico. Austin and the older American *empresarios* tried to be good Mexicans; but it was difficult to respect a government in constant turmoil and revolution. The North American colonist admired the horsemanship of his Mexican neighbor, adopted his saddle and trappings and some of his vocabulary; but his general attitude toward him was condescending. There was trouble about the tariff, representation, immigration, and with Mexican army garrisons. And in the early 1830's Austin's law-abiding pioneers began to be outnumbered by men of another type—swashbucklers like Sam Houston of Tennessee, a former subordinate of General Jackson; David G. Burnet of Ohio, who had followed Miranda to Caracas in 1806; Branch T. Archer "of stalwart form and Cato-like look," who had fled from Virginia after a successful duel; the Bowie brothers of Louisiana, slave smugglers who designed the long knife that bears their name; Davy Crockett, a professional backwoodsman; others of restless ambition and pungent personality, who had left their country for their country's good.

President Santa Anna's proclamation in 1835 of a unified constitution, which made a clean sweep of state rights, caused the secession of Texas. The North American settlers set up a provisional government and expelled the Mexican garrison from San Antonio de Bexar. Santa Anna with 3000 men then crossed the Rio Grande and besieged the Alamo, the fortress of San Antonio, garrisoned by fewer than 200 Texans. They refused to retreat or to surrender. On 6 March 1836 Santa Anna assaulted the Alamo, captured it after every Texan had been killed or wounded, and killed the wounded.

Already a convention elected by North American colonists had proclaimed the independent Republic of Texas, elected Burnet president, and adopted a flag. Santa Anna's army advanced eastward, settlers and President Burnet fleeing before him; but Generalissimo Sam Houston managed to keep an army together and awaited the Mexicans in a grove of live oak by the ferry of the San Jacinto river, not far from the site of the city that bears his name. On 21 April, shouting "Remember the Alamo!" the Texas cavalry led by a gallant Georgian with the conquering name of Mirabeau Buonaparte Lamar, attacked Santa Anna's army. Infantry followed and put the Mexicans to flight, taking the general prisoner. The Texans ratified their new constitution, legalized slavery, elected Sam Houston president, and sent an envoy to Washington to demand annexation to the United States or recognition as an independent republic.

Enthusiasm over the defense of the Alamo, as well as liberal land offers, drew hundreds of North American adventurers into the Texas army. President Jackson made no attempt to prevent this unneutral aid, but on questions of recognition and annexation his attitude was diplomatically correct. Only on his last full day of office (3 March 1837), after Congress had approved, did he recognize the Lone Star Republic.

Texas would have preferred outright annexation, but that was a year of agitation in Congress over the domestic slave trade and the gag resolution. On 23 May 1836 Calhoun remarked in the Senate that "there were powerful reasons why Texas should be a part of this Union. The Southern States, owning a slave population, were deeply interested in preventing that country from having the power to annoy them." The same year a Quaker abolitionist named Benjamin Lundy, who had been to Texas, brought out a pamphlet called *The War in*

Texas; a Crusade against the Government set on foot by Slaveholders. His theory was simple: the Texas revolution was a conspiracy to gain new territory for slave-grown cotton. This appealed to that widespread Northern sentiment opposed to the political dominance of the South and to the extension of slavery. Everyone realized that the annexation of Texas would affect the balance of power between North and South. On 1 November 1837 the Vermont legislature "solemnly protested" against the admission of any state "whose constitution tolerates domestic slavery." That, naturally, aroused a contrary feeling in the South. Calhoun solemnly announced that any attempt to exclude a state on account of its "peculiar institution" would be a virtual dissolution of the Union.

The slave states were beginning to realize that they had got the thin end of the Missouri Compromise of 1820, prohibiting slavery in territories north of 36° 30′. Arkansas and Michigan had just been admitted to the Union, making thirteen free and thirteen slave states. Florida was the only slave territory left; but three free territories—Wisconsin, Iowa, and Minnesota— would be demanding admission shortly, and more would follow if the Indian barrier to the Great Plains were broken. The Alabama legislature, on Christmas Day 1837, resolved: "It needs but a glance at the map to satisfy the most superficial observer that an overbalance is produced by the extreme northeast, which as regards territory would be happily corrected and counterbalanced by the annexation of Texas." It might be carved into several slave states, a New Slavonia to balance New England.

A resolution for the annexation of Texas was promptly introduced in Congress. President Van Buren, engaged at the time in delicate negotiations with Mexico and anxious to keep slavery out of politics, used his influence against the resolution, which was finally smothered by a speech of J. Q. Adams that took three weeks to deliver in July 1838.

The politicians were content to let so explosive a question rest. In the meantime, thousands of petty planters, ruined by the panic of 1837, left their debts at home and started life anew across the Sabine.

2. President Tyler Annexes Texas

Texas built a navy, accumulated a national debt, and received British and French recognition. The Lone Star Republic now belonged to the family of nations, but for how long? Her white population was barely 50,000, and Mexico had 6 or 7 million people. Texan finances were even shakier than Mexico's—a debt of $7 million, and currency that depreciated to the vanishing point. Mexico made no attempt to reconquer Texas except for a fantastic raid in 1842. Next year Charles Elliot, British minister to Texas, negotiated a truce; but at any turn of the political wheel in Mexico City the truce might be denounced and hostilities renewed. Political conditions in Texas were chaotic. President Mirabeau Buonaparte Lamar aimed to annex New Mexico, California, and the northern tier of Mexican states to the new republic, and himself led an expedition against Santa Fe, which the Mexicans easily defeated. Sam Houston, who succeeded Lamar after that imperialist incursion, felt that Texas needed protection and security, not enlargement. He preferred annexation to the United States, but if the United States refused, the best bet would be a dual mediation by Britain and France to obtain Mexican recognition of Texas independence, and a guarantee to maintain it.

Lord Aberdeen in the foreign office toyed with the idea; Louis-Philippe, the French king, still smarting from his bout with President Jackson, was ready to go along. For here was a ready-made wedge between the United States and Latin America, and an independent source of supply for cotton, sugar, and tobacco. There was little doubt of Texan acceptance if the offer were made in time; but this mediation scheme required the consent of Mexico, and no Mexican cabinet dared accept Texan independence. More sense of reality and less of prestige at Mexico City in 1844 might have changed the entire course of American expansion.

Amid the cross-currents of notes, suggestions, and conversations between London, Paris, Washington, Austin, and Mexico City, another fact stands out clearly: the fear of Southern statesmen that Texas might abolish slavery. Duff Green, Calhoun's journalist son-in-law, picked up in London the alarming gossip that Aberdeen had agreed to guarantee Texan independence if the Lone Star Republic would do just that; he would even lend money to compensate Texas slaveholders, as England had done for her West Indian subjects. The prospect of Texas becoming a refuge for fugitive slaves from the Gulf states, even a springboard for abolition propaganda, alarmed Southern leaders to the point of panic. Abel P. Upshur, President Tyler's secretary of state, at once began negotiating a treaty of annexation with the Texas minister at Washington, and informed him that the English abolition project was inadmissible.

At this juncture a fatal accident on a United States warship influenced political history. Captain Robert F. Stockton had persuaded Congress to build U.S.S. *Princeton,* a 950-ton auxiliary screw frigate. Her architect was John Ericsson, a young Swedish engineer who had invented the propeller, and whom Stockton had persuaded to visit the United States. Equally revolutionary was *Princeton's* main battery, consisting of two smooth-bore 12-inch wrought-iron guns, one called "Oregon" which Ericsson had brought from England; the other "Peacemaker," designed by Stockton and cast in an American foundry. Both were tested successfully; but on a gala excursion down the Potomac on 28 February 1844, with President Tyler, cabinet ministers, diplomats, senators, and numerous ladies on board, Peacemaker burst. Secretary Upshur, navy secretary Gilmer, and a New York state senator were killed; Senator Thomas H. Benton and nineteen others were severely wounded.

The explosion virtually threw into President Tyler's arms the fair Julia Gardiner, daughter of the slaughtered state senator; she became the second Mrs. Tyler and mistress of the White House. And the loss of the two secretaries gave the President an opportunity to reconstruct his cabinet, without a single Northerner or even a Whig. John C. Calhoun returned to power as secretary of state. Tyler's compass needle no longer vacillated; it pointed southwest, to Texas.

Calhoun was appointed for two main purposes, to get Texas into the Union and to obtain for Tyler the Democratic nomination for the presidency in 1844. Like several later Vice Presidents who have succeeded through death, "Tyler too" dearly wanted to be elected President "in his own right." Calhoun accepted the state department because he hoped to be the blacksmith to link Texas with Oregon, forging a chain of South and West, and so reach the coveted presidency.

Lord Aberdeen, as soon as the gossip about his intention to emancipate slaves in Texas reached London, sent a dignified denial to Secretary Calhoun: "Great Britain desires, and is constantly exerting herself to procure, the general abolition of slavery throughout the world. But the means which she has adopted, and will continue to adopt, for this humane and virtuous purpose, are open and undisguised." Calhoun replied by reading the British government a lesson on the beauties of slavery. He also observed that the "threatened danger" to the "safety and prosperity of the Union" justified American annexation of Texas. In other words, the mere prospect of abolition in a neighboring republic was sufficient reason to absorb it.

To Northern Whigs there seemed to be no more danger to the United States in leaving Texas independent than in

Canada remaining British; the only things threatened were slavery, and the dominance of the Democratic party. Four Northern state legislatures, and those of Delaware and Maryland, all under Whig control, resolved that the annexation of a foreign country was unconstitutional and "an alarming encroachment upon the rights of the freemen of the Union." On the other hand, six Southern state legislatures, together with Democratic Maine, New Hampshire, and Illinois, memorialized Congress for annexation; and the extremist party in South Carolina made the fantastic proposal that, if annexation failed, the Southern states should secede and join the Republic of Texas.

A second annexation treaty, which Calhoun negotiated with some difficulty (since Sam Houston was playing coy and beginning to think that Texas would be a better theater for his talents than the United States Senate), failed to obtain ratification. But Tyler had another card up his sleeve. After the presidential election of 1844 he recommended that Texas be admitted to the Union by joint resolution of both houses, which did not require a two-thirds vote. This deed of questionable constitutionality was done on 28 February 1845. President Tyler on his last day of office had the satisfaction of sending a courier to inform President Houston that only the consent of the Lone Star Republic was necessary to make Texas the twenty-eighth state of the Union. That she gave promptly.

This indecent haste to annex Texas, in marked contrast to the administration's indifference to Oregon, was occasioned by fear on the part of influential Southern editors and politicians that the Republic of Texas would abolish slavery.

President Tyler was regarded by Whigs as a renegade, and the Democrats would have none of him. Yet, on the whole, Tyler was a good second-rate President. To his credit are the Maine boundary negotiations with England, and a reorganization and partial rebuilding of the navy. Socially, his administration was brilliant. Slim, gracious, and handsome, he and his charming young wife led capital society. He was the last Virginian in the White House. But by the end of his term he had incurred the dislike or hatred of Whigs and Democrats alike; and the country roared with laughter over his literally missing the boat—the day steamer from Washington to Norfolk—on the day after Polk's inauguration. It took so long to organize the ex-presidential cavalcade that by the time it arrived at the wharf, the steamboat had cast off. Someone shouted, "Hold on —the President is coming!" To which the skipper, a stout Whig, replied, "Tyler be damned—let him stay!" And the ex-President had to wait for the night boat.

3. President Polk and the Road to War

While Tyler and Calhoun were plotting to pull Texas into the Union, wiser men were trying to keep the subject out of politics. Martin Van Buren, who expected to receive the next Democratic presidential nomination, discussed Texas in 1842 with Henry Clay, equally confident of being the Whig choice. Each agreed to publish a letter opposing the immediate annexation of Texas, and did so; Van Buren predicting that to rush the affair would mean war with Mexico, Clay declaring that he would welcome Texas only if she could be annexed "without dishonor, without war, with the common consent of the Union, and upon just and fair terms."

These praiseworthy efforts to preserve the peace lost Van Buren the nomination and Clay the election. For "manifest destiny" was in the air. When the Democratic nominating convention met at Baltimore in May 1844, a majority wanted Van Buren. But the Southern and expansionist delegates, led by Robert J. Walker of Mississippi, put over the two-thirds rule,[1] which Little Van had not votes enough to surmount. After playing around with several candidates (even old "Rumpsey-dumpsey" Johnson), the expansionists trotted out the first "dark horse" in presidential history. His name, new to most of the country, was James K. Polk.

By holding firmly to "Old Hickory's" coattails, Polk had become speaker of the house and governor of Tennessee; now, with support of the aged and ailing Jackson, he won the presidential nomination. To appease Northern Democrats, "Reoccupation of Oregon" was given equal honors on the platform with "Re-annexation of Texas"; but Oregon was a minor factor in the campaign. Clay, now sixty-seven years old, received the Whig nomination by acclamation. He had recently made a triumphal progress through the South, speaking to "vast concourses of people," and felt confident of election. But his letter on Texas offended the annexationists, and enough antislavery Whigs voted for Birney, the abolitionist candidate in New York, to give Polk a slight edge in that state, whose electoral vote proved decisive. The popular vote was very close—1,337,000 for Polk; 1,299,000 for Clay.

Nobody really knows why Americans vote the way they do, and often they don't understand it themselves. But, in this instance, a growing conviction of America's "manifest destiny" to expand west to the Pacific and south to at least the Rio Grande brought victory to obscure Polk over radiant

[1] First adopted in 1836, but not used in 1840; after this it continued in Democratic national conventions until 1936.

Clay. America was on the move, and anyone who objected, be he Mexican, European, or Whig, had better get out of the way! The prospect of acquiring Texas, Oregon, and California appealed to simple folk who were recovering confidence after the hard times of 1837–41. They wanted all three, and Polk got them. If *vox populi* be *vox dei*, Polk was the Almighty's choice; and the Almighty must have willed a good, stiff blood-letting for America. Had Henry Clay become President in 1845, he would undoubtedly have managed to placate Mexico; and with no Mexican War there would have been no Civil War, at least not in 1861.

But would Clay have acquired California?

California! The very name connoted mystery and romance. It had been given to a mythical kingdom "near the terrestrial paradise," in a Spanish novel of chivalry written in the lifetime of Columbus. President Polk did not read novels, but he wanted California much as Don Quixote wooed Dulcinea, without ever having seen her, and knowing very little about her. The future Golden State, with forests of giant pines and sequoias, broad valleys suited for wheat, and narrow vales where the vine flourishes, extensive grazing grounds, mountains abounding in superb scenery and mineral wealth, was then a Mexican province, ripe for the picking. Barely 6000 white men lived there; and the Indians, a strangely feeble lot, were not to be feared. Oregon had been well advertised for years, but in 1845 almost nothing was known in the United States about California, except two descriptions—R. H. Dana's *Two Years Before the Mast,* and J. C. Frémont's *Report of the Exploring Expedition to . . . Oregon and North California.*

When Mexico opened her trade to foreigners, ships which rounded the Horn both ways began a profitable exchange of consumer goods from Boston for California hides, and several hundred New Englanders settled there, speaking Spanish with a down-east twang and marrying California heiresses. Dana wrote an unforgettable description of ships anchored off Santa Barbara, swaying in the long Pacific swell, sailors "droghing" hides on their heads out to the ship's longboat, hurling them over the cliff near San Juan Capistrano, in contrast to the relaxed life of the Spanish Californians, soon to be over-whelmed by energetic *Yanquis.*

About this time John C. Frémont, a twenty-eight-year-old second lieutenant in the United States Army's topographical corps, wooed and won sixteen-year-old Jessie, daughter of Senator Thomas H. Benton of Missouri. Papa Benton, equally devoted to daughter, hard money, and Western expansion, conceived the plan of sending his son-in-law exploring, with competent guides to take care of him. On his second trip, Frémont struck political pay dirt. Turning south from Oregon into the future Nevada and then into the Sacramento valley, he passed through central and southern California and returned via Santa Fe. His *Report* of this journey (largely written by Jessie), published in the fall of 1845, gave Washington its first detailed knowledge of the rich, luscious possibilities of California and the feeble bonds by which Mexico held that romantic land. And it made Frémont a presidential candidate.

Even though President Polk knew little about California except what Frémont related, he wished desperately to acquire it for the United States because he feared lest England or France get it first. First he tried to buy it, but Mexico refused to sell. Next, he tried to stir up revolution in California. When that failed to come off on time, he baited Mexico into a war with the United States in which California was the big pile of blue chips.

The country knew hardly more of James K. Polk than Polk knew of California. A stiff, angular person not yet fifty years of age, he already looked like an old man. Sharp gray eyes and a prim mouth set off a sad, lean face. Secretive, unhumorous, and prejudiced; to him, Whigs, Englishmen, abolitionists, and even many Democrats were villains. But Polk dominated a cabinet of able men, half of them his seniors; and in a single term he accomplished all his aims—to reduce the tariff (which a Whig congress had jacked up again in 1842), to re-establish Van Buren's independent treasury which the Whigs had destroyed, to settle the Oregon question, and to acquire California. All this with the handicap of chronic ill health, which the situation of the White House on the edge of "foggy bottom" made worse. Those swamps bordering the Potomac were breeding grounds of mosquitoes and flies which (completely undetected by science) carried the germs of malaria, dysentery, and typhoid to Presidents and garbage collectors alike; and the White House as yet was innocent of plumbing, or even a fixed bathtub.

Polk's apprehensions about California were not unfounded, in an era when England and France were picking up Pacific empires in New Zealand and the Marquesas, and King Kamehameha III of Hawaii even offered to place the Islands under the protection of Queen Victoria. She was not interested; but her Admiralty had an eye on San Francisco Bay, and there was talk of canceling Mexico's debt to Britain in exchange for

California. Polk would have preferred to buy California from Mexico, rather than take it, but similar propositions respecting Texas had been turned down.

Any chance of Mexico's selling California was spoiled by the surprising attempt of Commodore Thomas Ap Catesby Jones to beat the gun. He was at Callao in 1842, in command of the Pacific Squadron, when he read in the newspapers a peppery note from the Mexican government to President Tyler, from which he assumed that war with Mexico was inevitable. He set sail, arrived off Monterey on 19 October and forced the astonished Mexican governor to surrender to him. Then, upon receiving later newspapers which showed that no war had been declared, Commodore Jones returned Monterey to the Mexicans and sailed away. This premature "conquest of California" by Ap Catesby Jones occurred before Polk became President, but it convinced Mexican officials that North Americans were aggressive men of bad faith.

In October 1845 Polk's secretary of war wrote a significant dispatch to the American consul at Monterey, suggesting that the Californians follow the Texans' example. "If the people should desire to unite their destiny with ours, they would be received as brethren. . . . Their true policy for the present is to let events take their course, unless an attempt should be made to transfer them without their consent either to Great Britain or France." And Frémont was on his way to California with a third exploring expedition designed to support any revolt that might erupt.

Shortly after Polk entered office, Mexico protested against the annexation of Texas and broke diplomatic relations with the United States. In July 1845, after Texas had formally accepted annexation, Polk ordered a detachment of the regular army under General Zachary Taylor to take position on the Nueces river, the southwestern border of Texas, to protect the new state against possible Mexican assault. Polk's apologists make much of the sophistry that as soon as Taylor crossed the Sabine river into Texas he was invading Mexico from the Mexican point of view, hence war was inevitable. This argument makes no allowance for Latin disinclination to acknowledge a disagreeable *fait accompli*. In 1845 Spain was still technically at war with most of Spanish America, although there had been no hostilities between them for over twenty years; but no Latin American state would have thought itself thereby justified in attacking Cuba. If Polk had been content with Texas and had not reached for California, there is no reason to suppose that Mexico would have initiated hostilities, although she would long have delayed acknowledging the loss of Texas.

While Polk was priming revolt in California, he made another attempt to buy it, in exchange for writing off claims. These claims were for repudiated bonds, revoked concessions and damage to American property during the civil wars that broke out every few months. Hitherto, America had been forbearing, in comparison with the French government which sent a squadron to collect by bombarding San Juan de Ulúa in 1838. Mexico and the United States in 1843 ratified a convention by virtue of which Mexico was to pay about $4.5 million in twenty quarterly installments. After three installments, Mexico suspended payment—as several states of the Union had done on their bonds—but did not repudiate the debt, as Michigan and Mississippi had done with theirs. Torn by civil dissension and virtually bankrupt, she could then do no better.

Here was the President's opportunity. On 10 November 1845 he commissioned John Slidell minister to Mexico, with instructions to assume unpaid claims of American citizens against Mexico, in return for Mexican recognition of the Rio Grande as the southern boundary of the United States. Another $5 million was to be offered for the cession of New Mexico, and "money would be no object" for California. This was a sincere offer from a practical man who hoped to put through a business deal with a government that lacked business sense. Slidell was refused reception by President Herrera. Then, General Paredes raised the standard of rebellion on the ground that Herrera was proposing a treasonable bargain with the United States! His revolution succeeded, as most Mexican revolutions did; and by New Year's Day 1846 the government was in the hands of a military faction spoiling for a fight with the United States.

Polk did not give them long to wait. On 13 January 1846, the day after he received word of Herrera's refusal to receive Slidell, but before he knew of the Paredes revolution, Polk ordered General Taylor to cross the Nueces river and occupy the left bank of the Rio Grande del Norte. That was an act of war, since the Nueces had been the southern boundary of Texas for a century. The barren region between it and the Rio Grande, east of longitude 100°, belonged to the State of Tamaulipas. The authority of the Lone Star Republic had never been exercised beyond the Nueces. One of the best exposés of the falseness of Polk's claim that both banks of the Rio Grande were American soil was made by a freshman congressman from Illinois named Abraham Lincoln.

4. Glory and Conquest

General Taylor on 23 March 1846 occupied the left bank of the Rio Grande, his guns bearing on the Mexican town of Matamoras. The Mexican general there in command ordered him back to the Nueces. Taylor replied by blockading Matamoras. The Paredes government had made no military dispositions threatening Texas or occupying the disputed territory. But more than Mexican caution was needed to stop Polk now.

On 12 March 1846 the Mexican foreign minister informed Slidell definitely that he would not be received, that Mexico still regarded the annexation of Texas as just cause of war, which would be inevitable if the United States persisted in its present course of adding injury to insult. Having thus asserted his own and his country's dignity, the minister intimated a willingness to negotiate with a commissioner *ad hoc* the question of the annexation of Texas. This distinction without a difference, dear to the Latin American mind, was dismissed by Polk as insincere and treacherous. On 25 April he began to prepare a message to Congress urging war on the sole grounds of Slidell's rejection and the unpaid claims—which amounted to exactly $3,208,314.96 when adjudicated by a United States commission in 1851. On the evening of Saturday, 9 May, dispatches from General Taylor gave the President a more plausible *casus belli*. On 25 April, Taylor having blockaded Matamoras, a Mexican force crossed the Rio Grande, engaged in a cavalry skirmish with a troop of United States dragoons and inflicted several casualties. Polk promptly called a cabinet meeting. All agreed that a war message, with documents proving the "wrongs and injuries" the United States had suffered from Mexico, should be laid before Congress on Monday. All day Sunday, except for two hours spent at church, Polk labored with his secretaries preparing the war message. "It was a day of great anxiety to me," wrote the President in his diary, "and I regretted the necessity which had existed to make it necessary for me to spend the Sabbath in the manner I have."

At noon on Monday 11 May 1846 the war message was sent to Congress. "The cup of forbearance has been exhausted," declared the President. "After reiterated menaces, Mexico has passed the boundary of the United States, has invaded our territory and shed American blood upon the American soil." Congress then declared, "By act of the Republic of Mexico, a state of war exists between that Government and the United States."

That evening, Secretary Buchanan almost upset the presidential war chariot. He proposed to send a circular letter to American ministers and consuls stating, "In going to war we did not do so with a view to acquire either California or New Mexico or any other portion of the Mexican territory." The President remarked coldly that California was our own business, and ordered him to cut it out. This completes the proof that Polk baited Mexico into war over the Texas boundary question in order to get California, after concluding that Mexico would not sell California.

In the Mississippi valley this war was popular. Texas and states bordering on the Mississippi furnished 49,000 volunteers, eager to "revel in the halls of the Montezumas," but in the older states there was little enthusiasm and much opposition; the original Thirteen sent only 13,000 volunteers. Most of the elder statesmen of the South were content with Texas; Calhoun's clear vision foresaw that the conquest of more territory would upset the sectional balance and revive the question of slavery in the territories. The Whig party opposed, but voted for war credits and supplies in the hope that the Democrats would make a mess of the war, which they did. Antislavery men and abolitionists regarded the war as a conspiracy for more slave territory.

> They just want this Californy
> So's to lug new slave-states in
> To abuse ye, an' to scorn ye,
> An' to plunder ye like sin.

Thus James Russell Lowell castigated the Mexican War, in his *Biglow Papers*. The legislature of Massachusetts declared it to be a war to strengthen the "slave power," a war against the free states, unconstitutional, insupportable by honest men, to be concluded without delay, and to be followed by "all constitutional efforts for the abolition of slavery within the United States." But that was all talk; even the Northern "conscience Whigs," as the antislavery wing of the party was called, flinched before actually obstructing the war; remembering what had happened to the Federalists after the War of 1812.

Henry Thoreau made his private protest against the war by refusing to pay the state poll tax. After he had spent a night in the Concord lock-up, his aunt paid the tax and he went back to his cabin on Walden Pond. It sounds petty and futile, as one tells it. Yet, the ripples from that Concord pebble, like the shot of 19 April 1775, went around the world. Thoreau's *Essay on Civil Disobedience*, which he wrote to justify his action, became the best known work of American literature to the peoples of Asia and Africa struggling to be free, and it has earned the honor of being suppressed in communist countries.

Americans expected a quick and easy victory, for which 20,000 volunteers, in addition to the regular army of 7500, would suffice. In Europe, however, many doubted whether the United States could beat Mexico. Disparity in population and resources was admitted, but it was no greater than in the War of 1812, when the American offensive against Canada failed. Could soft, untrained American volunteers cope with the hard-bitten, wiry Mexicans? Mexico was confident enough. An officer boasted that his cavalry could break lines of infantry with the lasso. There was wild talk of breaking into Louisiana, arming the slaves, loosing the Comanche and Sioux on the American frontier. And the unsettled Oregon question suggested that Mexico might soon have a powerful ally.

But Polk was too smart for them there. As we have seen, he compromised on Oregon in the treaty of 15 June 1846.

California, the President's main objective, became the scene of amusing if confusing conflicts. Frémont, supposedly on another exploring expedition, rushed about distractedly. A few dozen American settlers in the Sacramento valley pulled off the "Bear Flag Revolt" on 14 June 1846, taking possession of Sonoma and hoisting a white flag with a bear painted on it. Commodore Sloat of the Pacific Squadron, having heard of the outbreak of hostilities, hoisted the Stars and Stripes at Monterey on 7 July and declared California annexed to the United States. Spanish-speaking Californians, not relishing these proceedings, rose in arms, reoccupied Monterey, and tangled with Colonel Kearny, who had led 150 troopers overland from Independence by the Santa Fe trail. But by the end of 1846 California was completely in the hands of the North Americans.

In the Rio Grande theater of war, General Taylor won two minor engagements but refused to move forward until he received reinforcements and supplies, since Polk originally assumed that he ought to live off the country! After a few men and some munitions had been sent, Taylor advanced and captured the town of Monterrey (Nuevo Leon) after a three-day battle (21–23 September 1846). Polk was not too pleased with this victory. "Old Rough and Ready" Taylor, an outspoken soldier of the Jackson breed, was becoming dangerously popular and was writing letters to the newspapers. When a general starts doing that, you may be certain that he has designs on the presidency. To bypass him, Polk executed the brilliant stroke of creating Thomas H. Benton, sixty-four-year-old senator from Missouri, lieutenant general in command of the United States Army. Unfortunately for Mexico, Congress refused to create this new grade. The President then turned to Major General Winfield Scott of the regular army, a Whig indeed but a dandy swashbuckler whose airs and foibles were unlikely to make him popular. Scott's plan to win the war by marching on Mexico City from Vera Cruz, earlier rejected by the Washington strategists, was now adopted. Taylor, starved of reinforcements and supplies, could not move beyond Monterrey, but the navy enabled Scott to strike from Vera Cruz.

Congress was within an ace of abolishing "undemocratic" West Point when war was declared, and the army was as unprepared for war as in 1812. But the United States Navy performed efficiently on 9 March 1847, landing within 24 hours General Scott's entire army of 12,000 men with artillery, horses, vehicles, and supplies on a beach three miles from Vera Cruz, using 65 "surf boats" shipped in the holds of transports. Siege guns manned by sailors and marines were then sited to bombard Vera Cruz, which surrendered on 27 March.

General Scott fought a brilliant campaign. With little more than half the troops he asked for, hampered by jealous subordinates and volunteer officers who had been appointed for political reasons, thwarted by the administration's incompetence, often forced to live off the country and to fight with captured ammunition, he yet accomplished his ends. Scott's army marched to Mexico City along the road Hernando Cortés had followed three centuries earlier. In two weeks' time it reached the fortified pass of Cerro Gordo. Captain Robert E. Lee found a way to outflank the Mexicans by a mountain slope, a brilliant operation in which Captain George B. McClellan and Lieutenant Ulysses S. Grant also took part. The army pushed on to Puebla and remained there for three months, receiving replacements for volunteers whose terms of enlistment had expired. On 10 August the army reached the continental divide, 10,000 feet above sea level, with the beautiful valley of Mexico below and the towers of Mexico City rising through the mist. A stiff battle was fought at Churubusco on 20 August, the American forces losing 177 killed or missing and 879 wounded, or about one in seven. Most of these casualties were inflicted by artillery of the San Patricio battalion, a Mexican outfit made up of Irish and other deserters from the United States Army. But 3000 Mexican prisoners (including eight generals) were captured, and the enemy was overwhelmed.

In the meantime, President Polk had provided Mexico with a new president. General Santa Anna, in exile at Havana, persuaded Polk that, once in possession of the Mexican government, he would sign the sort of treaty that the President wanted. He was then allowed to pass through the lines, enter Mexico City in triumph in September 1846, and assumed the presidency. General Taylor beat him badly at Buena Vista (22–23 February 1847) near Monterrey, a picture-book battle on a sun-soaked plain. That battle made two American Presidents—Taylor and his son-in-law Colonel Jefferson Davis who distinguished himself by so disposing his regiment (uniformed in red shirts, white pants, and slouch hats) as to break up a Mexican cavalry charge. Santa Anna then raised more troops and marched south to oppose Scott's advance from Cerro Gordo.

General Scott did not push on to the capital after his Churubusco victory of 20 August, because he did not wish to drive Santa Anna to desperation. Instead, he accorded Mexico an armistice. Polk had attached to the American army as peace commissioner Nicholas Trist, chief clerk of the department of state. Trist's instructions were to obtain the Rio Grande boundary for Texas, together with New Mexico, California, and the right of transit across the Isthmus of Tehuantepec, one of the proposed interocean canal routes. Mexican officials raised such a row on hearing these terms that Santa Anna decided to try another throw of the dice with Scott. The American army, refreshed by a fortnight among the orchards and orange groves of the valley of Mexico, marched to a blood bath at Molina del Rey (8 September), and five days later stormed its last obstacle, the fortified hill of Chapultepec, which was heroically defended by the boy cadets of the Mexican military school. On pushed Scott's troops, taking cover under the arches of the aqueducts, Lieutenants Raphael Semmes and U. S. Grant mounting howitzers on roofs and belfries. At dawn 17 September a white flag came out from Mexico City.

Mexicans crowded windows and rooftops of the city while a vanguard of battered, mud-stained doughboys[1] and marines, led by Brigadier General Quitman who had lost a boot in the latest fight, swung into the main plaza. There the conquerors gazed with wonder on the great baroque cathedral and the lofty pink-walled palace, the "Halls of the Montezumas." Presently a clatter of hoofs was heard on the stone-paved streets; and as the weary veterans snapped into "Atten-*shun!* Present—*arms!* General Scott, splendidly uniformed and superbly mounted, escorted by a squadron of dragoons with gleaming swords, dashed into the plaza.

[1] This term for infantrymen began in the Mexican War and lasted until World War II, when it was replaced by "GI."

Santa Anna abdicated, and months elapsed before any Mexican government was willing to negotiate. In the meantime, Trist had been recalled by Polk, who held him responsible for the broken armistice. Instead of obeying orders, he remained, and by dint of his remarkable ability to deal with Mexicans, negotiated the Treaty of Guadalupe Hidalgo (2 February 1848). Mexico ceded Texas with the Rio Grande boundary, New Mexico (including Arizona), and Upper California (including San Diego) to the United States. The victor assumed the unpaid claims and paid $15 million to boot—three-fifths of the amount Slidell had been instructed to offer for the same territory in 1846.

In the meantime Democratic expansionists, intoxicated with success, were beginning to demand the whole of Mexico. Polk set his face sternly against this. He sent Trist's treaty to the Senate, which ratified it after the usual bitter debate. Then the President did his best to humiliate Scott who had won the war, and Trist who had won the peace. He relieved the former by a Democratic major general, and dismissed the latter from the department of state.

The United States at minimal cost—1721 killed in battle or died of wounds; 11,550 deaths from "other causes," mainly disease—had rounded out her continental area, excepting Alaska. It remained to be seen whether these valuable acquisitions would be added to "Freedom's airy," or provide "bigger pens to cram with slaves."

GREEN GROWS THE LAUREL

Green grows the laurel, all sparkling with dew,
I'm lonely, my darling, since parting from you.
But by the next meeting I hope to prove true, And
change the green laurel for the red, white and blue.

XVI

Compromise and Calm

1846-1854

1. *The Wilmot Proviso*

JOHN C. CALHOUN well predicted that acquisition of new territory would reopen the question of slavery expansion. The man who opened the door was an obscure Democratic congressman from Pennsylvania named David Wilmot. On 8 August 1846, about twelve weeks after the war began, the President asked Congress for a secret appropriation of $2 million as a down payment to bribe Santa Anna into ceding California. Wilmot remarked that although it was all right with him to buy California, Mexican territory was free territory, and he did not think it compatible with democratic principles to extend slavery therein. He therefore proposed as an amendment to the $2 million bill that in any territory so acquired, "Neither slavery nor involuntary servitude shall ever exist." This phrase, copied from the Northwest Ordinance of 1787, became the famous "Wilmot Proviso."

The question of slavery extension was no abstraction. There was no climatic or other natural bar to slavery extension, or to the African race—a black accompanied Admiral Peary to the North Pole in 1909. If slavery could flourish in Texas, why not in New Mexico, Arizona, and points west? In the warm climate and rich soil of southern California, Negro slaves, if introduced, would undoubtedly have thrived and multiplied, as did the Chinese and Mexicans who later filled the demands of ranchers and fruit growers for cheap labor. The question was not immediately practical, to be sure; but principle was involved. Every Northern state legislature but one passed resolutions approving the Wilmot Proviso. To many Northerners it seemed monstrous for "the land of the free" to introduce slavery, even in principle, where it did not already exist. But to Southerners the Proviso seemed an insult to their "peculiar institution."

President Polk proposed that latitude 36° 30′ N (the old Missouri Compromise line of 1820) divide freedom and slavery in the new territories as in the old; but few favored this commonsense compromise. Southern Whigs who voted for the Proviso in the interest of peace were denounced as traitors to the South; Northern Democrats who voted the other way, for the same reason, were called "doughfaces" or "Northern men with Southern principles." The Wilmot Proviso did not pass, nor did any measure to organize the newly acquired territory. American settlers in the Far West went without law and government, because Congress could not decide whether or not they could have slaves. Oregon in 1848 was finally organized as a Territory without slavery because two Southern senators voted with their Northern colleagues; but Polk's presidential term ended on 4 March 1849 before anything had been done about California, New Mexico (including Arizona), or Utah.

Hitherto everyone assumed that Congress could legislate slavery in or out of territories, since the Constitution gave it the power to "make all needful rules and regulations respecting the territory or other property belonging to the United States." Congress had admitted slavery to some territories and banned it from others. Now, from the Wilmot Proviso debates new theories emerged: (1) Congress has the moral duty to prohibit slavery wheresoever its jurisdiction extends; freedom should be national, slavery sectional. Presently the Free-Soil and Republican parties would be founded to enforce this doctrine. (2) Congress has no power to prohibit slavery in the territories, but a duty to protect it there. Presently the South would insist on this doctrine, and the Supreme Court give it a supposedly final endorsement.

Calhoun was equal to the task of sustaining this extreme Southern view, upsetting a constitutional practice of sixty years. Territories, he argued, belonged to the States United, not to the United States. Congress was merely the attorney of a partnership, and every partner has an equal right to protection for his property anywhere in the United States. Slaves were common-law property like cattle; consequently Mexican laws against slavery ceased to have effect in Mexican territory annexed to the United States. Congress in 1820 had prohibited slavery in territories north of 36° 30′, but that act was unconstitutional and void. Slavery should follow the American flag, wherever firmly planted. Calhoun's doctrine, embodied in resolutions by the Virginia legislature in 1847, became the "platform of the South"; and in the Dred Scott case of 1857 it was read into the Federal Constitution. Only one more step, said many Northerners, and slave-owning would come to be regarded as a natural right which not even a state legislature could impair.

It is idle to debate whether Wilmot or Calhoun, North or South, was the aggressor in this matter. All depends on the moral standpoint. If slavery was a positive good or a practical necessity, any attempt to restrict or to pinch it out by degrees justified Southern opposition to the point of secession. If slavery was an evil and a curse, any attempt to establish it in virgin territory, even nominally, was an affront to the public opinion of the Western world. Motives on both sides were fundamentally defensive. Even when Calhoun wrote of forcing the slavery issue in the North, his motive was to protect the domestic institutions of the slave states. Even when Seward and Chase asserted that every inch of the new territory must be free soil, their object was to defend Northern farmers, wage-earners, and lovers of liberty against further wars and encroachments of the "slave power." To yield on this issue of the territories, it was feared, would encourage Southern extremists to demand protection for their property throughout the United States as their price for staying in it. It is just such matters of prestige and strategic advantage that bring on great wars.

The state of the American Union in 1848 may be compared with that of Europe in 1913 and 1938. Political and diplomatic moves become frequent and startling. Integrating forces win apparent victories, but in reality grow feebler. The tension increases until some event that, in ordinary times, would have little consequence, precipitates a bloody conflict.

2. *Gold Rush and Compromise*

President Polk, sick and exhausted by the labors of his eventful term, refused to stand for re-election in 1848. Lewis Cass of Michigan, an expansionist who had always tried to placate the South, received the Democratic nomination. The Whigs again passed over Henry Clay and, following the lucky precedent of Tippecanoe, nominated "Old Rough and Ready"

Taylor of Louisiana, hero of Buena Vista, with Millard Fillmore, a colorless lawyer of Buffalo who had played with splinter parties like the Anti-Masons, for second place. A third party, the Free-Soil, was formed in the North by a coalition of three hitherto separate and hostile elements—the abolitionist Liberty party, the radical "locofoco" or "barnburner" faction of the New York Democrats, and the "conscience" or anti-slavery Whigs of Northern states, especially New England. Their first object was to pass the Wilmot Proviso; their platform was comprised in the phrase "Free soil, free speech, free labor and free men." Martin Van Buren, snubbed in 1844 and convinced that only slavery restriction could save the Union, accepted the Free-Soil nomination for the presidency. He carried no state, but his personal popularity robbed Cass of so many votes in New York that the Whigs won that state; and as New York went, so went the election.

Nathaniel Hawthorne now lost his place in the Salem Custom House and proceeded to write *The Scarlet Letter*. Walt Whitman, through writing an editorial in favor of Van Buren, was fired from the Brooklyn *Eagle* and wrote *Leaves of Grass*. These were literary by-products of Zachary Taylor's election, and of the clean sweep that followed in the civil service. He was a simple, honest soldier who detested the sophistries of politicians and regarded the slavery question as an artificial abstraction. He was ready to sign any bill that Congress might pass for organizing the new territories; but before Congress could resolve the deadlock, California proposed to skip the territorial stage and become a free state of the Union.

On 24 January 1848, shortly before peace was concluded with Mexico, a workman in the Sacramento valley discovered gold in Sutter's mill-race. In a few weeks the news spread along the Pacific coast; and in a few months all America was repeating tales of fortunes made from the stream-beds of the Sierra Nevada merely by separating golden grains from the sand in a common washbowl. Farmers mortgaged their farms, pioneers deserted their clearings, workmen dropped their tools, clerks left their stools and even ministers their pulpits, for the California gold-washings. Young men organized companies with elaborate equipment and by-laws and were "grubstaked" by local capitalists. Any and every route was taken by the "forty-niners": around Cape Horn in the slowest and craziest vessels, across the continent by the Oregon or California trails; or, if pressed for time and well fixed for money, by the Isthmus of Panama. So, by the end of 1849, thousands of Argonauts from every region of Europe, North America and the antipodes were jumping each other's claims, drinking, gambling, and fighting in ramshackle mining villages such as Red Dog, Grub Gulch, and Poker Flat.

San Francisco rose in a few months from a squalid village to a city of 20,000 to 25,000 people, where eggs laid on the other side of Cape Horn sold for ten dollars a dozen, and a drink of whisky cost a pinch of gold; where Englishmen and Frenchmen, Yankees and Yorkers, Indiana "Hoosiers," Georgia "Crackers," Michigan "Wolverines," Illinois "Suckers," and Missouri "Pukes" rubbed shoulders with Indians, Mexicans, Sydney "Ducks," and the "Heathen Chinee." Fortunes were made in the gold-diggings, only to be lost overnight in a 'Frisco faro palace; even more was made by speculation in goods and land.

Owing to neglect by Congress, the government of California was still military in theory but impotent in fact; alcaldes appointed by the military governor administered any sort of law they pleased—the code of Mexico or of Napoleon, common law, or lynch law. So California went ahead and made herself a state, with the blessing of President Taylor. His military governor issued writs of election for a convention which met at Monterey in September 1849 and drafted a constitution prohibiting slavery. This was ratified by a popular vote of over 12,000 to 800. Without waiting for congressional sanction, the people chose a governor and legislature which began to function in 1850. Only formal admission to the Union was wanting.

This indecent haste shown in the admission of California balanced that of Texas. Besides the desire to establish law and order in a swarming country which had neither, there was the political motive of adding to the Whig contingent in the United States Senate. And California, like Texas, precipitated a crisis which almost split the Union.

Up to this time the most extreme Southerners had admitted the right of a state to prohibit slavery, slavery being a state matter. But if California were admitted to the Union with its "Wilmot Proviso" constitution, the most valuable American conquest from Mexico would be closed to slavery. During 1849 the temper of the South had been steadily rising. The governor and legislature of South Carolina hesitated from secession only because they hoped to persuade the rest of the South to go along. Calhoun wrote to his daughter, "I trust we shall persist in our resistance [to the admission of California] until the restoration of all our rights, or disunion, one or the other, is the consequence. We have borne the wrongs and insults of the North long enough." California's demand for admission to the Union when Congress convened in December 1849 started a movement for a Southern Convention. Like the Hartford Convention of 1814, this was intended by extremists to be a stepping-stone toward a new confederacy.

It is now difficult to grasp the real reason for all this sound and fury. After all, as Henry Clay pointed out, the Southern states had an equal vote in the Senate, a majority in the cabinet and the Supreme Court, and a President who was Virginia-born and Louisiana-bred. Since 1801 the South had obtained from the Union all that she really wanted—free trade (Polk's Congress had reduced the tariff again in 1846), protection to slavery in the national capital, vast theaters for slavery extension such as Louisiana, Florida, the Indian Territory, and Texas. Only extreme abolitionists threatened to interfere with slavery where it already existed, and Garrison had come out openly for separation of North from South—secession would be playing his game.

Probably we need a psychotherapist to unravel the Southern complexes of that day. "Cavaliers" were tired of hearing their form of society denounced by Northern "mongrels and mud-sills" who, according to popular Southern economics, fattened upon tribute forced from the South. From every side—England and New England, Jamaica and Mexico, Ohio and the Northwest, and now Oregon and California—abolition seemed to be pointing daggers at the South's heart. It is under circumstances such as these that fear, the worst of political counselors, supersedes thought. But there was a positive, almost a utopian aspect to secession. A vision of a great slaveholding republic stretching from the Potomac to the Pacific, governed by gentlemen and affording perfect security to their property in human beings, monopolizing the production of cotton and so dictating to the world, was beginning to lift up the hearts of the younger and more radical Southern leaders.

Zachary Taylor, the fourth distinguished soldier to be elected President of the United States, was the first to have had no political experience whatsoever; he had been in the army for over forty years, during which he had never cast his vote in a presidential election. His cabinet, with the exception of John M. Clayton of Delaware, secretary of state, was weak; he exerted no leadership, and had no knack for dealing with Congress. But he was straightforward, sincere, and although a large slaveholder, devoid of proslavery sentiment. He saw no reason why the South should be bribed to admit California as a free state if California rejected slavery.

The House of Representatives that met in December 1849 was so factional that 63 ballots were taken before it could elect a speaker, and even the opinions on slavery of candidates for the post of doorkeeper were subjected to careful scrutiny. President Taylor recommended the immediate admission of California with her free constitution, and the organization of New Mexico and Utah Territories without reference to slavery. To protesting senators from Georgia, the old soldier declared his determination to crush secession wherever and whenever it might appear, if he had to lead the army personally.

In the Senate, leaders of the new generation, such as Jefferson Davis, Stephen A. Douglas, William H. Seward, and Salmon P. Chase, sat with giants of other days, such as Webster, Clay, and Calhoun. It was Henry Clay who divined the high strategy of the moment. The Union was not ripe to meet the issue of secession. Concessions must be made to stop the movement now; time might be trusted to deal with it later. On 27 January 1850 he brought forward the compromise resolutions that kept an uneasy peace for eleven years. The gist of them was (1) immediate admission of California; (2) organization of territorial governments in New Mexico and Utah without mention of slavery; (3) a new and stringent fugitive slave law; (4) abolition of the domestic slave trade in the District of Columbia. Such was the Compromise of 1850.

These resolutions brought on one of those superb Senate debates that moulded public opinion. Clay defended them in a speech that lasted the better part of two days. Haggard in aspect and faltering in voice as he rose to speak, his passionate devotion to the Union seemed to bring back all the charm and fire of "Young Harry of the West," and to lift him and his audience to high levels. He appealed to the North for concession, and to the South for peace. He asked the North to accept the substance of the Wilmot Proviso without the principle, and honestly to fulfill her obligation to return fugitive slaves. He reminded the South of the great benefits she derived from the Union, and warned her against the delusion that secession was constitutional, or could be peaceful, or would be acquiesced in by the Middle West. For Clay was old enough to remember the excitement in Kentucky when Spain and France had threatened to close her outlet to the sea. "My life upon it," he declared, "that the vast population which has already concentrated . . . on the headwaters and the tributaries of the Mississippi, will never give their consent that the mouth of that river shall be held subject to the power of any foreign state."

Calhoun, grim and emaciated, his voice stifled by the catarrh that shortly led to his death, sat silent, glaring defiance from his hawk-like eyes, while his ultimatum was voiced for him by Senator Mason of Virginia (4 March 1850). "I have, Senators, believed from the first that the agitation of the subject of slavery would, if not prevented by some timely and effective measure, end in disunion. The cords that bind the States together" are snapping one by one. Three great evangelical churches are now divided. The Federal Union can be saved only by satisfying the South that she can remain within it in safety, that it is not "being permanently and hopelessly converted into the means of oppressing instead of protecting" her. The senator from Kentucky cannot save the Union with his compromise. The North must "do justice by conceding to the South an equal right in the acquired territory"—admitting slavery to California and New Mexico—by doing her duty as to fugitive slaves, by restoring to the South, through constitutional amendment, the equilibrium of power she once possessed in the federal government; and she must "cease the agitation of the slave question." Note well that imperative—silence on slavery.

Three days later Webster rose for his last great speech. His voice had lost its deep resonance, his massive frame was shrunk, and his face was lined with suffering and sorrow. But in his heart glowed the ancient love of country, and the spell of his personality fell on Senate and galleries with his opening words: "I speak to-day for the preservation of the Union. Hear me for my cause." Viewing the situation eye-to-eye with Clay, Webster merely restated in richer language the points made by his old-time rival. The North could never have been induced to swallow a new fugitive slave law, had not Webster held the spoon; and, even so, it gagged and vomited. Just as his reply to Hayne in 1830 stimulated the growth of Union sentiment, so the Seventh of March Speech of 1850 permitted that sentiment to ripen, until it became irresistible.

Senator Seward of New York, in opposing the compromise from the opposite angle, spoke for the yet unborn Republican party. He admitted that Congress had the constitutional power to establish slavery in the territories. "But there is a higher law than the Constitution which regulates our authority over the domain": the law of God, whence alone the laws of man can derive their sanction. The fugitive slave bill would endanger the Union far more than any antislavery measure. "All measures which fortify slavery or extend it, tend to the consummation of violence; all that check its extension and abate its strength, tend to its peaceful extirpation."

As the debate progressed, compromise sentiment developed.

The Nashville convention of delegates from nine Southern states adjourned in June after passing harmless resolutions. Yet much parliamentary maneuvering, and the steady support of Southern Whigs, both in and out of Congress, were necessary to get the compromise through. In early September 1850 the essential bills passed. Their passage was greased by Congress assuming the national debt of Texas. This obtained for Texas bondholders, mainly Northern bankers, 77 per cent of the par value of bonds that had cost them 5 to 15 per cent. Principal measures passed were the admission of California, a fugitive slave law, the organization of New Mexico and Utah as territories free to enter the Union without reference to slavery, and abolition of the domestic slave trade in Washington.

It was a fair compromise, this of 1850, for which Henry Clay deserves the chief credit; but he had powerful assistance from Stephen A. Douglas and other Democrats. Both North and South obtained something that they badly wanted, and the New Mexico-Utah bills avoided both the Wilmot Proviso "stigma" and the forcible introduction of slaves to regions which had none. Once more the Union was preserved by the same spirit of compromise that created it; but for the last time.

President Taylor did not like the compromise; he saw no reason why California should be included in a package deal. But he did not live long enough to be faced with the hard decision whether to sign or to veto the bills. "Old Rough and Ready," now sixty-five years old, succumbed to a combination of official scandals, Washington heat, and doctors. The scandal he knew nothing about until it broke, for like certain other military Presidents he trusted too many rascals. Governor G. W. Crawford of Georgia, Taylor's secretary of war, had taken over, on a fifty-fifty basis, the settlement of a pre-revolutionary claim which originally amounted to less than $45,000. With the help of friends he got a bill appropriating that amount through Congress. Then, by a smart triple play with the attorney general and secretary of the treasury, Crawford got an additional payment of $191,353 for 73 years' interest, the half of which made him a neat little fortune. As ventilated by Congress, this Galphin claim affair, as it was called, smelled worse than anything of the sort prior to the Credit Mobilier scandals in the administration of the next soldier president, U. S. Grant.

On 4 July 1850, already depressed by the Galphin revelations, the President was subjected to two hours' oratory by Senator Foote in the broiling sun, and then tried to cool off by consuming an excessive quantity of cucumbers, washed down with copious draughts of iced milk. Washington, with its open sewers and flies, was always unhealthy in the summer, and the President came down with acute gastroenteritis, then called cholera morbus. He would probably have recovered if left alone, but no President ever has that chance. The physicians of the capital, assisted by a quack from Baltimore, rallied around his bedside, drugged him with ipecac, calomel, opium, and quinine (at 40 grains a whack), and bled and blistered him too. On 9 July he gave up the ghost. Millard Fillmore now became President of the United States and signed all compromise acts before Congress adjourned on 30 September 1850, after a record session of 302 days.

In the North the Democrats accepted the Compromise. Free-Soilers and abolitionists denounced it in the most frenzied terms, Whigs were divided. The Fugitive Slave Act really stuck in Northern throats. The one hope for preserving slavery was to let the Northerners forget about it, instead of rubbing it in by hunting runaways in their streets and countryside. Even Emerson, the philosopher who had serenely advised the abolitionists to love their neighbors more and their colored brethren less, wrote in his journal, "This filthy enactment was made in the nineteenth century, by people who could read and write. I will not obey it, by God!" In the South, another year elapsed before it was certain that the secession movement could be halted. In state elections Whigs and Democrats disappeared; the contest was between a Union party and a Southern Rights or immediate secession party. The Unionists met the secessionists on their own ground, squarely denying the existence of a constitutional right of secession, and in every cotton state but South Carolina the unionists won.

Already two of the principal antagonists had passed away. Calhoun died 31 March 1850. His coffin made a triumphal progress through the Southern states to Charleston, where friends and followers pledged devotion to his principles by the marble tombstone over his grave in St. Philip's churchyard. His real monument, Walt Whitman heard a soldier say in 1865, was Southern society torn up by the roots, and servants become masters.

Andrew Jackson ended his long life of pain at the Hermitage in 1845; John Quincy Adams, stricken at his seat in the House, survived his old rival less than three years. "Old Bullion" Benton was defeated for re-election to the Senate in 1851; his sturdy nationalism had grown too old-fashioned for Missouri. Clay and Webster, the one denounced as traitor by Southern hotspurs, the other compared with Lucifer by New England reformers, had two years only to live; time enough to give them grave doubts whether their compromise could long be maintained. With their death the second generation of independent Americans may be said to have gone. Of all statesmen born during the last century and brought up in the generous atmosphere of the American Revolution and Jeffersonian Republicanism, only Van Buren was alive, fuming at home over the "half-baked politicians" of the 1850's; and the limp Buchanan. There seemed nobody left to lead the nation but weak, two-faced trimmers and angry young men, radical or reactionary.

3. *Prosperity, Pierce, and "Young America"*

The early 1850's shed a warm glow of hope and satisfaction over the American scene. A writer in the *United States Review* in 1853 predicted that electricity and automatic machinery would so transform life and relieve mankind of drudgery that, within half a century, "Machinery will perform all work—automata will direct them. The only task of the human race will be to make love, study and be happy."

Industrial development continued apace, railroads reached out into the West, supplanting the canals as freight carriers, immigration from Europe reached a new high level, yet wages rose, and in the labor movement talk gave way to action. Unions of the later American type were concluding trade agreements with their employers, federating nationally on craft lines, but avoiding politics. The National Typographic Union (1852), the United Hatters (1856), and the Iron Moulders' Union of North America (1859) were the first permanent federations. Marxian socialism arrived with the German immigrants, but the *Proletarierbund* that one of them founded soon expired; American workingmen discarded utopia for two dollars a day and roast beef. Neal Dow won an apparent victory for cold water with the Maine prohibition law; humanitarian reform and education marched hand in hand. Baseball first became popular, schooner yacht *America* won a race against all comers at Cowes in 1850 which gave a fillip to yacht racing. Intercollegiate rowing began, and the clipper ship gave the American eagle another exploit to scream about.

A promising beginning of orchestral music—which the Civil War diverted into brass bands—opened in 1853 when a Frenchman, Louis Jullien, started a school of music in New York. Theodore Thomas, the German-born boy wonder, became first violin of an orchestra that Jullien organized on the side. And when we consider the great American books of this decade, it is evident that culture was no laggard. In 1850–51 appeared Hawthorne's *Scarlet Letter* and *House of the Seven Gables,* Whittier's *Songs of Labor,* Melville's *White Jacket* and *Moby-Dick,* Emerson's *Representative Men* and *English Traits.* The following year Harriet Beecher Stowe's *Uncle Tom's Cabin* reminded the public that the slavery question could not be ignored. Thoreau's *Walden,* Whitman's *Leaves of Grass,* and Melville's *Piazza Tales* appeared in 1854–56. Elisha Kane, helped by the navy and a New York shipowner, completed his northern voyages and published his fascinating *Arctic Explorations* in 1856. The *Atlantic Monthly* was founded in 1857 with James Russell Lowell as editor, and Longfellow, Whittier, and Dr. Holmes (whose *Autocrat* appeared in 1858) as contributors. This was Longfellow's most productive decade, with *The Golden Legend, Hiawatha,* and *The Courtship of Miles Standish.* Parkman's *Conspiracy of Pontiac* (1851) opened a noble historical series that required 40 years to complete, and Prescott had almost finished his when he died in 1859.

All these were Northern writers. In the South, Poe was dead, John P. Kennedy had become President Fillmore's secretary of the navy; William Gilmore Simms, still writing historical novels, was still neglected in his native Charleston. Materially, however, the cotton kingdom was stronger and more self-conscious. Kentucky backwoodsmen who in the 1830's had taken up land in the black belts, were now gentlemen planters mingling on equal terms with the first families of Virginia in the thermal stations of the mountains. Their elder sons, after leading volunteers in the Mexican War, had become lawyers or planters; their younger sons were attending the newer colleges of the lower South, or the University of Virginia, with hounds and hunters and black servants. Dread of abolition, with its implication of black equality, was binding the yeomen and poor whites more closely to their slave-holding neighbors. There seemed to be no limit to cotton production. The annual crop rose from 1000 million to 2300 million pounds in this decade, but never wanted purchasers. De Bow's progressive *Review* was preaching the use of guano, conservation of soil, diversification of crops, and local manufactures; also, ominously, a revival of the African slave trade. If only the South had dared lift the ban on creative thought, the late 'fifties might well have brought an outburst of literature surpassing that of New England. Instead, she produced little but proslavery propaganda.

Another "might have been" is suggested by the progress of

manufactures in the South at this period, owing to the enterprise of William Gregg, a Charleston jeweler, and Edwin M. Holt of North Carolina. In the 1850's the value of the product of Southern cotton mills almost doubled. A good start; and had it continued without the interruption of war, it might have aligned the old South with the Northeastern states in favor of a protective tariff, as finally happened in the present century.

There was also progress in processing another raw material, tobacco. In 1860 Virginia and North Carolina factories were producing most of the chewing, smoking, and snuffing tobacco in the United States. Cigars, if not imported from Cuba, were made in Connecticut (out of cabbage leaves, the envious said); Cuban cigarettes had not yet invaded the North American market; but Richmond plug tobacco, especially a brand with the seductive name "Wedding Cake," was reaching even the California gold diggings. The Tredegar Iron Works of Richmond, employing slave labor, were doing well and would do better with war orders.

The Southern railway network, encouraged by financial aid from states, counties, and towns, was greatly extended. Georgia built a railroad across the southern end of the Appalachians, which helped to make Atlanta and Chattanooga great cities; Charleston planned a railway to the Ohio river to siphon off Western trade from New York, with a connecting steamship line to Europe; and by 1860 there was through rail connection between New York and New Orleans. Several other promising efforts were made toward bringing the South in line with dynamic America, but there was too little time. Southern liberals and industrialists for the most part were lonely individuals, socially looked down upon by aristocratic planters, neglected by politicians, and scolded by journalists.

Although extremists on both sides disliked the Compromise of 1850, the presidential election of 1852 proved that an overwhelming majority were disposed to regard it as final. As such it was proclaimed in the platform of the Democratic national convention at Baltimore. Owing to the operation of the two-thirds rule, all strong men of the party—Lewis Cass, Stephen A. Douglas, William L. Marcy, and Buchanan who, though a waverer, was a political veteran—killed each other off, so that on the forty-ninth ballot a dark horse won. This was Franklin Pierce of New Hampshire, whose only qualifications were a handsome face and figure, a creditable military record in the Mexican War, and an almost blank, hence blameless, political record. He was introduced to the public, who knew practically nothing about him, as "Young Hickory of the Granite State." It is a great pity that Cass, who had a touch of Old Hickory in him, or Douglas, the "Little Giant" of Illinois, was not nominated. What the presidential office then needed was backbone; and Pierce had the backbone of a jellyfish.

Any Democrat could have won in 1852. The New York "barnburners," starved by four lean years with the Free-Soil party, returned to their former allegiance; thousands of Southern Whigs, disgusted by the antislavery tendencies of Northern Whigs, went Democratic. General Winfield Scott, the Whig presidential candidate, made himself somewhat ridiculous in the campaign; and, although a Virginian by birth, that asset was canceled by a nationalist career. The result was a landslide for Pierce, 254 electoral votes to 42. Scott carried only Vermont, Massachusetts, Kentucky, and Tennessee.

The Whig party never recovered. Wanting organic unity, it had no chance when its rival undertook to maintain the great Compromise, and the great silence. The Democratic party, purged of democracy, became a national conservative party directed by Southern planters and maintained by Northern votes. It controlled the federal government for the next eight years.

A diversion of this period was the "Young America" movement, a grouping of the younger men in the Democratic party, originally intended to create new ideals of civic duty and to support democratic movements overseas. The first object faded out, and the second ended in loud talk and bad diplomatic maneuvers. The Young Americans in 1848 had talked wildly of annexing Ireland and Sicily, as certain revolutionists in those countries suggested; and when the news came that Hungary had fallen before a Russian invasion and had been forcibly incorporated with Austria, the legislatures of New York, Ohio, and Indiana called for action. Daniel Webster, as Fillmore's secretary of state, insulted the House of Hapsburg in a diplomatic note declaring, "The power of this republic at the present moment is spread over a region, one of the richest and most fertile on the globe, and of an extent in comparison with which the possessions of the House of Hapsburg are but as a patch on the earth's surface." Louis Kossuth, brought to New York as guest of the nation in 1851, was given an overwhelming ovation. "Europe is antiquated, decrepit, tottering on the verge of dissolution," declared Senator Douglas. "It is a vast graveyard." Young America wanted thirty-nine-year-old Stephen Douglas for President, but it got Pierce who, though at forty-eight the youngest man yet elected President, wanted no part of Young America, except the bad manners. He followed the Adams-Clay precedent (which continued to 1923) of appointing as secretary of state his chief rival for the nomination. This was William L. Marcy, the veteran New York spoilsman. Buchanan, who thought he should have had it, grudgingly accepted the London legation for which, since it spared him the contentions over Kansas, he later became very grateful.

Marcy, sixty-six years old when appointed, saw eye to eye with Young America in truculent diplomacy. Universally approved by the democracy was his circular on the official costume of American diplomats and consuls abroad. These had been accustomed to provide themselves with fancy uniforms covered with gold lace, a *chapeau-bras* (the "fore'n aft hat" recently discarded by the navy), knee breeches, and silver-buckled shoes. Secretary Marcy issued positive orders that members of the foreign service "appear in the simple dress of an American citizen." This created consternation, as no gentleman could attend a European official ball or reception except in court dress, complete with breeches and sword. James Buchanan after (fortunately) rejecting the notion that he dress like President Washington in Stuart's portrait, conformed by wearing the usual dark frock coat and trousers of that era with a black dress sword, which got by Queen Victoria's chamberlain. But John Y. Mason, minister to France, after ascertaining that the parvenu court of Napoleon III required more fixings, appeared in a fancy uniform which his envious first secretary described as having been designed by a Dutch tailor, following the livery of a minor German diplomat's lackey. For that, the minister received a strong reprimand from Marcy.

"Manifest destiny" under Pierce was directed by Southern gentlemen who wanted new slave territory as compensation for their "loss" of California. Cuba, during these eventful years, was in her normal state of unrest. There was fear lest the island fall to England or become a black republic like Haiti. President Polk proposed to buy Cuba in 1848 for $100 million, but Spain rejected the offer with contempt. There were filibustering expeditions, frowned upon by President Taylor, tolerated by Pierce, and consequent interference by Spanish authorities with suspicious-looking Yankee ships. One such case, that of the *Black Warrior* (1854), almost provoked Spain into war. The secretary of war, Jefferson Davis, egged President Pierce on; but Secretary Marcy kept his head, and Spain disappointed the annexationists by apologizing

The next move of the Pierce-Marcy team was exceedingly odd. At their suggestion the American ministers to Spain (Pierre Soulé of Louisiana), France (Mason), and Great Britain (Buchanan) met at Ostend and on 18 October 1854 drafted a pompous recommendation to Secretary Marcy of how to settle the Cuban question. "In the progress of human events," they observed, "the time has arrived when the vital interests of Spain are as seriously involved in the sale as those of the United States in the purchase of the island. . . . The Union can never enjoy repose, nor possess reliable security," as long as Cuba is not embraced within its boundaries. With the purchase money Spain might build railroads, "become a centre of attraction for the travelling world," and "her vineyards would bring forth a vastly increased quantity of choice wines." Should she refuse, then, "By every law, human and divine, we shall be justified in wresting it from Spain if we possess the power." The New York *Herald* obtained a "scoop" of this document—largely a product of Buchanan's muddled brain—and published it under the catchy title "The Ostend Manifesto," creating a furor at home and abroad. It seemed to indicate that the Pierce administration was ready to fight Spain to get Cuba, as a slave-state balance to California. Pierce had no intention of doing that, but he sent Soulé to Madrid with orders to buy Cuba. Democratic statesmen never seemed to learn that such offers were insulting. A Latin nation might cede to force, but it could not be bought.

4. Japan Opened

Not only trouble but much good flowed from the territorial acquisitions of 1846–48. The difficulty of communicating overland with Oregon and California led to the project of an interoceanic canal, the perfection of the sailing ship, and plans for transcontinental railways. And the United States, as a new Pacific Ocean power, was instrumental in ending the isolation of Japan. American diplomacy followed by almost fifty years the first American merchant ship to cross the Pacific. Caleb Cushing negotiated with China in 1844 a treaty by which American ships obtained access to ports already open to Europeans, and extraterritorial privileges for merchants. China for fifteen years was torn apart by the Taiping rebellion, and the China trade suffered. That was one reason for American interest in Japan, but not the only one.

Japan had been closed for two centuries to foreign intercourse except a strictly regulated trade with the Dutch and Chinese at Nagasaki. Foreign sailors wrecked on the shores of Japan were not allowed to leave, and Japanese sailors wrecked on the west coast of the United States were not permitted to return. U.S.S. *Preble*, Commander James Glynn, boldly entered Nagasaki harbor in 1849 and by a show of firmness recovered twelve American sailors. En route she called at Okinawa in the Ryukyus (then called the Great Lew Chew), where the crew "went ashore and rambled all about the country, visiting the king's palace, a privilege never before granted to any stranger." The same palace, at Shuri, was occupied by United States Marines in 1945.

After this knock at the outer door, President Fillmore decided to try the main entrance. He entrusted the mission to Commodore Matthew Calbraith Perry, brother of the hero of Lake Erie and commander of a squadron that had won two amphibious operations in the Mexican War. The Commodore was somewhat ostentatious, which helped him to deal with Orientals, but he had studied every available book on Japan. On 8 July 1853 his armed squadron, including steam frigates *Mississippi* and *Susquehanna*, anchored in the mouth of Tokyo Bay. Perry's orders forbade him to use force, except as a last resort; but the Kanagawa Shogun who then ruled Japan was so impressed by this display that, contrary to precedent, he accepted the President's letter in the name of the Emperor. Perry tactfully sailed away in order to give the elder statesmen time to make up their minds, and by the time he returned (February 1854) with an even more impressive squadron, they had decided to yield. Conferences were held at the little village of Yokohama where gifts were exchanged: lacquers and bronzes, porcelain and brocades, for a set of telegraph instruments, a quarter-size steam locomotive complete with track and cars, Audubon's *Birds* and *Quadrupeds of America*, an assortment of farming implements and firearms, a barrel of whisky, and several cases of champagne. Thus old Japan first tasted the blessings of Western civilization. Japanese progressives who wished to end isolation persuaded the Emperor to sign an agreement allowing the United States to establish a consulate, and permitting American vessels to visit certain Japanese ports for supplies and a limited trade.

Such was the famous "opening" of Japan. It was followed by an exploring expedition, successively under Commanders Ringgold and Rodgers, which in 1855 charted some of the Ryukyus, the east coast of Japan, and the Kamchatka peninsula. Next year, President Buchanan sent Townsend Harris, a New York merchant, to Japan as the first American consul and to negotiate a formal treaty. The fine character of Townsend Harris and his genuine appreciation of the Japanese founded that traditional friendship between the two countries, roughly but temporarily broken in the 1940's.

In the 1850's the Ryukyu and Bonin Islands were virtually

independent of Japan. Commodore Perry was eager to obtain a coaling station to serve the navy, which was being converted to steam, and merchant steamships, too. He bought land for one at Chichi Jima from a group of New Englanders and Hawaiians who had settled there many years earlier, and instructed them to set up a local government under American protection. But the navy department and Congress, unprepared for such "imperialism," disavowed both actions, and a few years later Japan formally annexed both island groups. Ninety years later, Okinawa and Iwo Jima were conquered by the United States after heavy loss of life.

5. *Isthmian Brawls*

For shortening travel time between the older states and those on the Pacific coast, an interoceanic canal was badly needed. Three different routes were considered: the Isthmus of Panama, the Isthmus of Tehuantepec, and the Nicaraguan. President Polk obtained right of transit across Panama in 1846 by treaty with Colombia, and in return guaranteed that republic her sovereignty over the Isthmus. American capital then built the Panama railway, completed in 1855. The Tehuantepec route was too long for a canal, but Mexico granted to the United States a right of way over it in 1855. Jockeying for control of the Nicaragua route brought on controversies with Central America and Great Britain.

At the time the Monroe Doctrine was declared, Britain had two bases in Central America: the old logwood establishment of Belize, the Bay Islands crown colony off Honduras, and a protectorate over the Miskito Indians along the coast of Nicaragua. Owing to the weakness of the Central American republics, the enterprise of British agents, and Washington's lack of interest in Latin America after the J. Q. Adams administration, British influence increased in Central America. "Mosquitia" became an Indian satellite state, with a flag incorporating the Union Jack; and Lord Palmerston, who believed it high time to check "manifest destiny" in that quarter, in 1848 declared the sovereignty of Mosquitia over Greytown or San Juan del Norte, eastern terminus of the proposed Nicaragua ship canal. A milestone in Isthmian diplomacy was planted when John Clayton, President Taylor's secretary of state, negotiated with Lytton Bulwer, British minister at Washington, the Clayton-Bulwer treaty of 15 April 1850. Therein it was agreed that neither government would fortify, or obtain exclusive control over, any Isthmian canal. Each guaranteed its neutrality, when and if built, and invited other nations to do likewise. This was a fair compromise of the responsibilities that Britain had undertaken in the political vacuum of Central America, and the new United States interest in Isthmian communication.

Unfortunately, like other Anglo-American treaties, the Clayton-Bulwer one was ambiguous. The United States assumed that it required the British to withdraw from the Bay Islands, Greytown, and the Miskito coast; the British government, insisting that it merely forbade future territorial acquisitions, held what it had. This dispute became acrid in 1854 when President Pierce and the Democrats were looking for an issue to distract the country from the slavery question, and virtual anarchy in Nicaragua led to dangerous jostling on the spot between rivals.

An incident at Greytown might have triggered off an Anglo-American war. Solon Borland, minister to Central America, when about to sail home from Greytown, got involved in a local political brawl and was hit on the head with a bottle. President Pierce sent U.S.S. *Cyane* to the scene to demand an apology; and, when none was forthcoming, her commander gave the population time to retire, bombarded Greytown 13 July 1854, and destroyed the town. The British government demanded reparation and didn't get it; the London press blustered and threatened war, but by this time England was involved in the Crimea and her government let the matter drop.

Incident followed incident in Nicaragua. During the California gold rush, "Commodore" Cornelius Vanderbilt of the Hudson river steamboat fleet organized a company to compete with the Panama railway. He ran steamers up the San Juan del Norte to Lake Nicaragua, whence freight was forwarded to the Pacific coast by muleback. Since Nicaragua was troubled by frequent revolutions as well as earthquakes, Vanderbilt hired William Walker, a professional filibuster, to set up a stable government. Walker, who had already tried to filibuster Lower California into a new slave state, succeeded in 1855 in making himself president of Nicaragua. "The grayeyed man of destiny," as his friends called him, was preparing, with the approval of Secretary Jefferson Davis, to re-establish slavery and to conquer the rest of Central America, when he had the bad judgment to quarrel with Vanderbilt. The Commodore then supported a Central American coalition that invaded Nicaragua, and threw Walker out. Walker tried twice again, finally meeting his death from a Honduran firing squad.

England's cession of the Bay Islands to Honduras and of Mosquitia to Nicaragua in 1859–60, ended this conflict in

Central America. But *Cyane*'s bombardment and Walker's filibustering left the Latins suspicious of and hostile to the United States.

6. *Relations with Canada*

The union of Ontario and Quebec as the Province of Canada, first fruit of Lord Durham's mission, did not work well. People of British stock mixed with the French habitants no better than oil with water. But the union did have a large degree of self-government: an elected assembly with a responsible ministry.

Hitherto, demands for the annexation of British North America to the United States had come from the southern side of the border, but now annexation propaganda came from Canada, even from Tories who hitherto had been vociferously loyal to the Queen. English merchants of Quebec were disgusted with the British government for repealing the corn laws, which had favored Canadian grain. So a group of leading Montrealers in 1849 issued the "Annexation Manifesto," pointing out advantages for Canada in joining the American Union. This movement fell flat. French Canadians would have none of it, knowing that their church could not maintain its special privileges under the American system; and the mass of British Canadians held loyalty to England above any economic advantage. The annexationists received no encouragement from the other side of the border, where the mere prospect of two or three more free states would have aroused Southern resentment.

The sensible alternative to annexation was reciprocity in customs duties, suggested in 1846 by William H. Merritt, promoter of the Welland Canal around Niagara Falls, first link in the St. Lawrence Seaway of a century later. But the moving factor was a dispute between the New England states and the Maritime provinces about fishing rights. Yankee fishermen claimed the right to pursue the sportive mackerel within the Canadian three-mile limit, which Newfoundland and Nova Scotia flatly denied. It was high time that such petty quarrels be composed.

The foreign office and the state department had no trouble in concluding a reciprocity treaty (5 June 1854), but this treaty required concurrent acts of Parliament and Congress, and of four Canadian provincial legislatures. Secretary Marcy is said to have greased the way at Halifax, Fredericton, and St. John; and Lord Elgin, a hardheaded but genial Scot, was accused of floating the treaty through the United States Senate on "oceans of champagne." If true, both men served their respective countries well. The treaty, renewable after ten years, opened the United States to Canadian coal, farm produce, lumber, and fish; and Canada to American turpentine, rice and tobacco, and Yankee fishermen. The navigation of the Lakes, the St. Lawrence, and their connecting canals became common to both nations. Thus Britain maintained her political dominion over Canada by sanctioning a partial economic union with the United States.

7. Noble Ships

While governments wrangled over future canals to the Pacific, the shipwrights of New York and New England were engaged in cutting down the time of ocean passage around Cape Horn. In one month of 1850, thirty-three sailing vessels from New York and Boston entered San Francisco Bay after an average passage of 159 days. Then there came booming through the Golden Gate the clipper ship *Sea Witch* of New York, 97 days out. At once the cry went up for more clippers.

This type of full-rigged sailing vessel was characterized by great length in proportion to breadth of beam, an enormous sail area, and long concave bows ending in a gracefully curved cutwater. *Sea Witch*, designed by John W. Griffith and built for the China-New York tea trade, now proved the new type's value for the California trade. Her record was broken by *Surprise*, designed by a twenty-three-year-old Bostonian, Samuel H. Pook. Well named was she, since her owners—the Lows of New York—cleared a profit of $650,000 over total cost from her first round voyage to California. Donald McKay of Boston now entered the scene as ship designer and builder. His *Flying Cloud* in 1851 made San Francisco in 89 days from New York, a record never surpassed, and only twice equaled, once by herself.

As California then afforded no return cargo except gold dust (the export of wheat did not begin before 1855), the Yankee clippers sailed in ballast from San Francisco to the treaty ports of China, where they came into competition with the British merchant marine; and the result was more impressive than *America*'s victory over the English yachting fleet. Crack British East Indiamen waited for a cargo weeks on end, while one American clipper after another sailed with a cargo of tea at double the ordinary freight. When the Lows' *Oriental* arrived in London 97 days from Hong Kong, crowds thronged the docks to admire her, and *The Times* challenged British shipbuilders to set their "long practised skill, steady industry, and dogged determination" against the "youth, ingenuity and ardour" of the United States.

In 1852 Donald McKay launched *Sovereign of the Seas,* largest merchant vessel yet built and the boldest in design; stately as a cathedral, beautiful as a terraced cloud. Lieutenant Matthew F. Maury USN having discovered that strong and steady westerly gales blew in the "roaring forties" south latitude, the *Sovereign* followed his sailing directions and on her homeward passage made a day's run of 411 nautical miles, surpassed only seven times in the history of sailing vessels, all but two of them by products of McKay's drafting board and shipyard.

Talk about races! The 15,000-mile course from New York or Boston to California, around Cape Horn, was the longest and toughest in the world, trying the skill and energy of navigator and crew to the utmost. Over it, McKay's *Flying Fish,* in the winter of 1851–52 raced *Sword Fish* of New York. They left their respective home ports the same day. The Bostonian led to the equator, the New Yorker caught up at lat. 50° S, and they raced around the Horn within sight of one another. *Sword Fish* drew steadily ahead and won, making San Francisco in less than 91 days from New York.

By this time the British Navigation Act had been repealed, and gold had been discovered in Australia. For that destination four clippers were ordered to be built by Donald McKay for the Australian Black Ball Line. These proved to be the world's fastest sailing ships. *James Baines,* with skysail, studdingsails, and main moonsail, established the record transatlantic sailing passage—12¼ days Boston to Liverpool—and another from Liverpool to Melbourne—63 days—that still holds. *Champion of the Seas,* combining the imposing majesty of a man-of-war with the airy grace of a yacht, from noon to noon, 11–12 December 1854, fulfilled the challenge of her name by hanging up the greatest day's run of all time made by a sailing vessel—465 nautical miles.

These clipper ships of the early 1850's were built of wood in shipyards from Rockland in Maine to Baltimore. Their architects, like poets who transmute nature's message into song, obeyed what wind and wave had taught them, to create the noblest of all sailing vessels, and the most beautiful creations of man in America. With no extraneous ornament except a figurehead, a bit of carving and a few lines of gold leaf, their one purpose of speed over the great ocean routes was achieved by perfect balance of spars and sails to the curving lines of the smooth black hull; and this harmony of mass, form and color was practiced to the music of dancing waves and of brave winds whistling in the rigging. These were our Gothic cathedrals, our Parthenon; but monuments carved from snow. For a few brief years they flashed their splendor around the world, then disappeared with the finality of the wild pigeon.

For the clipper ship fulfilled a very limited purpose: speed to the gold fields at any price or risk. When that was no longer an object, no more were built.

World-wide whaling out of Sag Harbor, New Bedford, and other New England ports reached its apogee in the 1850's; the discovery of oil in Pennsylvania in 1859 sounded its knell. The whale ships, mostly built locally, were low-bred compared with the clippers, as they had to be, in order to "try out" the blubber on board and bring home a cargo of full oil casks after a voyage lasting three years or more. Officers and petty officers were generally native New Bedfordites, Vineyarders, or Nantucketers. Gay Head Indians were preferred as har-

BLOW, YE WINDS

They send you to New Bed-ford, that fa-mous wha-ling port, And give you to some land-sharks for to board and fit you out,— sing-ing, Blow, ye winds in the morn-ing, And blow, ye winds, high-ol Clear a-way your run-ning gear, And blow, winds, blow!

pooners; the crews were of all races and colors—Yankee country boys lured to the sea for adventure; Portuguese from the Azores and Cape Verde Islands; Fijians like Melville's Queequeg. Although a green hand's "lay" or proportion of the catch (no wages were paid in the whaling industry) netted him little enough for a three-year voyage, there were other compensations—seeing the world, and the sport. *"Thar she blows!—thar she breaches!"* from a masthead lookout was the pistol shot that started an inspiring race to the quarry, each of the four mates exhorting his boat crew with slogans such as "Roar and pull, my thunderbolts! Lay me on—lay me on!" As the oarsmen's backs are to the whale, they know not how near they are until the mate shouts to the harpooner, "Stand up and let him have it!" A shock as bow grounds on blubber, a frantic "Starn all!" and the death duel begins. Anything may happen then. At best, a "Nantucket sleighride" as the harpooned whale tows the boat at tremendous speed, then slows down, exhausted, the crew closes, dispatches him with a few well-directed thrusts, and pulls quick out of his death-flurry. At worst, a canny old sperm whale sinks out of sight, rises with open jaws directly under the boat, and shoots with it twenty feet into the air, crushing its sides like an eggshell while the crew jump for their lives into seething, bloodstreaked foam.

Whalemen enjoyed a variety of adventures such as no other calling approached, such as no big-game hunter of today can command.

XVII

Kansas, Nebraska, and New Parties

1854-1859

1. *Prairie Settlement and Railroad Routes*

DOWN TO 1850, American agricultural settlement, owing to the pioneer's dependence on timber and running water, had been largely confined to woodland and to small prairies with oak groves. The vast, treeless prairies of Illinois and Iowa were not wanted, for lack of fuel. As late as 1849 one could look northward from a knoll near Peoria, Illinois, over an undulating plain unbroken by house or tree as far as the eye could reach. The earliest prairie settlers had to live in sod cabins and contend with wolves, fires, and locusts. Many of the old breed of pioneers preferred the long journey to Oregon, where they could renew the forest environment that they loved. But by the mid-1850's the typical American pioneer had become a prairie farmer, owing in part to new agricultural machinery:—Cyrus McCormick's mechanical reaper, Marsh's harvester, Appleby's self-knotting binder, the steel-toothed cultivator, an improved form of plow with a steel mould-board, steel wire fencing. Yet the greatest impetus to prairie farming came from the rising price of wheat—from 93 cents a bushel in 1851 to $2.50 in 1855—and a rapid building of railroads from lake and river ports like Chicago, Milwaukee, and St. Louis into the prairie country. Railroads had hardly pene-

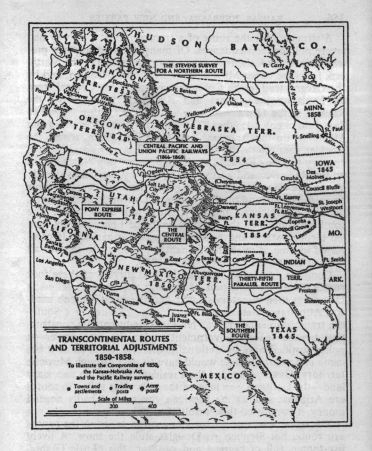

TRANSCONTINENTAL ROUTES
AND TERRITORIAL ADJUSTMENTS
1850-1858
To illustrate the Compromise of 1850,
the Kansas-Nebraska Act,
and the Pacific Railway surveys.

● Towns and settlements　★ Trading posts　▲ Army posts

Scale of Miles
0　　200　　400

trated the Middle West by 1850; in the next ten years it was covered by their network. The prairie farmer, hitherto dependent on long wagon hauls to a canal or river, was now able to market his grain and livestock. Most important of prairie railways was the Illinois Central, financed and managed by capitalists of New York and Boston, and endowed by Act of Congress with alternate sections (640 acres) of public land in a checkerboard pattern in a strip six miles wide on each side of its right of way. The completion of this line from Chicago to Cairo in 1856 opened the central prairies to profitable settlement.

A struggle over the route of a transcontinental railway had severe political consequences. Of many different schemes projected since 1845, the four most important were (1) the Northern, from the upper Mississippi to the upper Missouri, and by the Oregon trail to the Columbia river; (2) the Central from St. Louis up the Kansas and Arkansas rivers, across the Rockies to the Great Salt Lake and by the California trail to San Francisco; (3) the "Thirty-fifth Parallel" route from Memphis, up the Arkansas and Canadian rivers, across the Rockies near Santa Fe, and through the Apache and Mojave country to Los Angeles; (4) the Southern, from New Orleans up the Red river and across Texas, and by the Gila valley to Yuma and San Diego.[1] Either of the first two would follow an existing trail, and bind Oregon and California to the North, but the unorganized Indian country was an obstacle. The southern route was the shortest, with the best contours, and led through states and territories already organized. If completed in time, it might have enabled the South to recover all she had lost by the Compromise of 1850.

Congress, in March 1853, authorized surveys of these four routes under the direction of the war department. Jefferson Davis was then secretary of war and President Pierce's mentor. Although a state rights man, his keen desire for a Southern transcontinental railway led him to advocate its construction by the federal government under the war power—a policy justified only by nationalist theories. As soon as it became clear that this line would have to pass through Mexican territory, Davis persuaded the President to buy the necessary land—the Gadsden purchase of the Gila river valley in southern Arizona; and, as the Mexican government badly needed money, it swallowed this "insult" for $10 million.

The scene was now set for Congress to sanction the southern route, but Stephen A. Douglas stole the show. A lively five-footer, full of bounce and swagger, this "Little Giant," senior senator from Illinois, was the idol of the Northern Democracy. As a heavy speculator in Western lands and Chicago real estate, he wished the transcontinental railway to take the central route. In order to contest the southern route, law and government must be extended over, and settlers invited into, the region through which the central railroad would pass. Douglas, accordingly, reported a bill to organize the Great Plains as the Territory of Nebraska, in January 1854. Earlier bills of that nature had been defeated by opposition

---

[1] These worked out as (1) Northern Pacific, (2) Missouri Pacific, Denver & Rio Grande and Southern Pacific; (3) Rock Island and Santa Fe; (4) Texas & Pacific and Southern Pacific.

from Southern senators. So Douglas baited this one for their votes with a principle that he called "popular sovereignty." It would rest with the people of the new territory to decide whether or not they would have slavery, as soon as they obtained a territorial legislature.

Douglas's motives, and the forces behind a bill which caused the smoldering slavery-extension conflict to flare up again, have been discussed and analyzed ever since, and the "Little Giant" has been called everything from a reckless demagogue to the one great statesman who could have saved the Union. It is probable that his motives were not only economic but political. Old parties were breaking up, old issues were worn thin, politicians were feeling insecure and looking about for some powerful issue to keep themselves in power. Douglas and a group of Democratic politicians in Washington, known as the "F Street Mess" from the boardinghouse where they lived, were seeking an explosive political issue for 1856. The Kansas-Nebraska bill was their big idea. It was explosive enough to blow up the Union.

Popular sovereignty, or squatter sovereignty as it was contemptuously called, pleased nobody. As Nebraska lay north of 36° 30', slavery therein would be prohibited by the Missouri Compromise of 1820. Douglas's bill would have repealed that act implicitly; but Senator Dixon of Kentucky and Senator Atchison of Missouri insisted on repealing it explicitly. Douglas made a fatal mistake in consenting. He also agreed to divide the new territory into Kansas and Nebraska, so that the Missourians might secure the one and the Iowans the other. There was a touching scene when Senator Dixon told him, "Sir, I once recognized you as a demagogue, a mere manager, selfish and intriguing. I now find you a warm-hearted and sterling patriot."

2. Kansas-Nebraska Act and a Strange Interlude

The fat was in the fire. At this proposal to repeal the Missouri Compromise the angry passions of pro- and antislavery flared up; and there was no Henry Clay to quench them. Everyone forgot about the railroad. The South had not asked for Kansas, did not want Kansas; but "Southern rights" were involved. Few slaveholders planned to carry blacks further west, but Southern honor demanded that slavery follow the flag. Northerners, on the other hand, were alarmed at a proposed extension of slave territory, and the breach of a sectional compromise of over thirty years' standing. People could hardly have been more startled at a proposition to repeal habeas corpus and trial by jury. Stephen Douglas, morally obtuse, could not see that principles were involved; he never appreciated the strong sentiment in the North against opening virgin territory to the "peculiar institution." The North, in Lincoln's picturesque phrase, was determined to give her pioneers "a clean bed, with no snakes in it." Nor did he realize how passionate the South had become over prestige.

For three months the bitter debate dragged on. President Pierce tried to whip his party into line, and all but a few of the Northern Democrats obeyed. Old Sam Houston of Texas reminded the Senate in vain that by solemn treaties it had confirmed most of Kansas and Nebraska to the Indians "as long as grass shall grow and water run." Nobody else cared for the aborigines. Hordes of emigrants to Oregon and California had killed their game and thinned their numbers by spreading disease. Federal agents were already bullying them into selling their "perpetual" land titles. The once powerful Delaware or Leni-Lenape accepted a small reservation with an annual bounty. Others, like the Shawnee and the Miami, who had once terrorized the Old Northwest, were removed to the Indian Territory, which fortunately lay between the rival railway routes.

Democratic discipline triumphed. On 25 May 1854 the Kansas-Nebraska Bill passed the Senate by a comfortable majority and received President Pierce's signature.

As a sample of the effect on Northern opinion, one may quote the Reverend Francis Wayland, president of Brown University. He had always been a moderate antislavery man, declaring in 1844 that to terminate slavery "by violence, or without previous moral and social preparation," would be a calamity. But in 1854 he denounced this new extension of slave area as a violation of moral law, "giving just cause for a dissolution of the Union."

"If the Nebraska Bill should be passed, the Fugitive Slave Law is a dead letter throughout New England," wrote a Southerner from Boston. "As easily could a law prohibiting the eating of codfish and pumpkin pies be enforced." The day after it passed, a Boston mob led by a Unitarian minister tried to rescue a fugitive slave from the courthouse where he had been detained for examination. Anthony Burns, the slave, was identified by his master and escorted to the wharf by a battalion of United States artillery and four platoons of marines, through streets lined with hissing and groaning spectators who were kept back by twenty-two companies of state militia. It cost the United States about $40,000 to return that slave to his master; and he was the last returned from Massachusetts.

The Northwest, seething with indignation over the Kansas-Nebraska Act, was ripe to form a new antislavery party. A meeting in a little schoolhouse at Ripon, Wisconsin, on 28 February 1854 resolved to oppose the extension of slavery, and recommended that a new "Republican party" be formed to do it. Later in the year, similar meetings were held in other states, to the same purpose. Outside the Northwest the new party slowly gathered momentum. Seward sulked in his Whig tent; the "Anti-Nebraska Democrats" were loath to cut all connection with their party; the Free-Soilers could not see why a new party was needed; and the people were distracted by a new gospel of ignorance.

Know-Nothingism was a flare-up of the anti-Catholic and anti-foreign sentiment which had led to riots in the 1840's. The visit of a tactless papal nuncio appears to have convinced many that the Republic was in danger from Rome; and the activities of German radicals, who had begun to preach the gospel according to St. Marx, alarmed the pious. Accordingly a secret "Order of the Star-Spangled Banner," with elaborate ritual and rigid discipline, was formed by native-born Protestants. Members, when questioned by outsiders, answered, "I know nothing." Candidates secretly nominated developed surprising strength at the polls, and many minor politicians joined up, thinking that this was the wave of the future. In the state elections of 1854, the Know-Nothings almost won New York, and did win Massachusetts, electing a completely new legislature that passed some reform legislation but also conducted clownish investigations of Catholic schools and convents. At Baltimore they organized "plug-uglies," gangs of hoodlums who attended the polls armed with carpenters' awls, to "plug" voters who did not give the pass-word. In some Baltimore wards loaded swivel-guns were stationed at the polls to intimidate the Democrats, and bands of "native American" rowdies drove through the streets on election day, firing pistols and insulting women. St. Louis, in August 1854, was the scene of a series of pitched battles between native Americans and Irish Catholics—the Germans staying carefully aloof. Police and militia were helpless, eight lives were lost, and order was restored only after the mayor, Edward Bates (later Lincoln's attorney general) organized a force of 700 armed citizens to cow the rival mobs.

In the summer of 1855 the American party, as the Know-Nothings now called themselves, held a national convention at which the Southern members obtained control, passed pro-slavery resolutions, and nominated for the presidency old Millard Fillmore. The Northerners then lost interest; and ex-

cept in Maryland, which voted for Fillmore in 1856, the movement collapsed. Rufus Choate wrote their epitaph: "Any thing
more low, obscene, feculent the manifold heavings of history
have not cast up." He could not have said that a century later.

3. *Kansas and a New Party*

"Bleeding Kansas" soon diverted attention from the
"Popish Peril." Since popular sovereignty was to settle the
status of slavery in Kansas, pro- and antislavery people
scrambled to get there first. The federal government opened a
land office in Kansas in July 1854, before the Indian titles had
been extinguished; and even earlier, Missourians began to
flock across the border and stake out claims. In the meantime,
enterprising Yankees had formed a company to finance emigration to Kansas, as they already had to Oregon. This effort
aroused savage indignation among the Missourians, who proceeded to blockade the Missouri river against immigrants from
the Northeast, and to sack their first settlement at Lawrence.
The Emigrant Aid Company then decided to arm free-state
settlers with a new breechloading weapon of precision, the
Sharps rifle. These were merry times in Kansas for men who
enjoyed fighting. Parties of Northern "Jayhawkers" battled
"Kickapoo Rangers," "Doniphan Tigers," and other organizations from Missouri and points south, whom the Northerners
called "border ruffians." Senator Atchison of Missouri
boasted, "We had at least 7000 men in the Territory on the
day of the election, and one-third of them will remain there.
The proslavery ticket prevailed everywhere. Now let the
Southern men come on with their slaves. . . . We are playing
for a mighty stake; if we win, we carry slavery to the Pacific
Ocean."

Few Southerners, however, cared to risk valuable property
in such a region, and free-staters poured in with the spirit of
crusaders. One, a fanatic named John Brown, killed a number
of innocent people at the "Pottawotami massacre." Such were
the workings of Douglas's "popular sovereignty." Kansas had
become the theater of cold (and not so cold) war that led to
the Civil War. It was one of those contests preliminary to
major wars, like the Balkan Wars of 1912–13 to World War I,
and the Spanish Civil War to World War II.

Could nothing be done to prevent a head-on collision? The
abolitionists were no help. Garrison, who had long since denounced the Constitution as "a covenant with death and an
agreement with hell," accented this odd theory by publicly

burning a copy of it. The only constructive proposal came from the Sage of Concord. Before the Anti-Slavery Society of New York on 6 February 1855, Emerson proposed that slavery be extinguished by granting full compensation to the owners. He recognized that the slaveholder was caught in a trap from which emancipation on the British model offered the only peaceful escape. The federal government and the states could give the proceeds of public lands. "The churches will melt their plate," wealthy benefactors will give their thousands, and schoolchildren their pennies; "every man in the land would give a week's work to dig away this accursed mountain of sorrow once and forever out of the world."

Nobody seconded the motion. The South was determined not to give up slavery, and the North was unwilling to pay them to do it. Emerson's estimate of the cost, $2 billion, would have been cheap enough in comparison with that of the Civil War.

Charles Sumner, a scholar and a radical lawyer, senator from Massachusetts as the result of a political deal, had begun to rival William H. Seward as the spokesman of antislavery sentiment. His handsome features and oratorical talent caused him to be compared with Calhoun; but he had none of Calhoun's restraint. He was one of those fortunately rare and rarely fortunate persons who are not only thick-skinned themselves but assume that everyone else is. In a turgid oration on 19 May 1856, "The Crime against Kansas," he exhausted the vocabulary of vituperation. The elderly and moderate Senator Butler of South Carolina he described as a Don Quixote whose Dulcinea was "the harlot slavery," and Stephen A. Douglas as Sancho Panza, "the squire of slavery, ready to do its humiliating offices." The tone of this speech was so nasty that it would probably have ended Sumner's political career, had not "Southern chivalry" demanded physical chastisement. Three days after its delivery a South Carolina congressman, a distant cousin of Senator Butler, passed up the opportunity to attack Sumner on the steps of the Capitol when able to defend himself; then, with a stout stick, beat him senseless when sitting helplessly at his desk in the Senate chamber. The assailant was praised by the Southern press and presented by admirers with suitably inscribed sticks. Sumner, badly injured, returned to his seat only at intervals for the next three years; but he was now a hero and martyr in the North.

A few days after this disgraceful affair, the new Republican party held a national nominating convention at Philadelphia. It was a mass meeting of earnest men from all Northern states, who were convinced that the cause of freedom in self-defense must support the new party. The name of John C. Frémont, "The Pathfinder," whose career (except for a few months as senator from California) had been devoted to exploration of the Far West, stampeded the convention. Apparently the politicians thought that they needed a "glamour boy." The Republican platform took a swipe at the Mormons and the South by declaring it to be "both the right and the duty of Congress to prohibit in the Territories these twin relics of barbarism, polygamy and slavery."

Flabby James Buchanan, long an aspirant for the Democratic presidential nomination, now easily obtained it. The "Black Republicans," as their enemies called them, made a lively campaign. "Free soil, free speech, and Frémont" was the slogan, but slavery in the territories was the only real issue. Many Southern leaders warned the country that if Frémont were elected the South would secede; and when John M. Botts, an independent Virginia Whig, called this an idle threat, the Richmond *Enquirer* advised him to leave the state lest he "provoke the disgrace of lynching." A sectional showdown in 1856 was prevented by Buchanan's carrying every slave state except Maryland, together with Pennsylvania, Illinois, and Indiana, which gave him 174 electoral votes to Frémont's 114. But the "Pathfinder" polled an impressive popular vote, 1,340,000 to Buchanan's 1,838,000. Ominous figures, because all but 1200 of Frémont's votes came from the non-slaveholding states.

4. Dred Scott

Dred Scott was a slave who had been taken by his master, an army officer, to Illinois, thence to unorganized territory north of 36° 30′ where slavery had been forbidden by the Missouri Compromise, then back to Missouri, where he sued for his freedom as having been a resident of free soil. The case reached the Supreme Court, which published its decision on 6 March 1857.

Chief Justice Taney and the four Southerners among the associate justices saw in this case an opportunity to settle the question of slavery in the territories by extending it legally to all United States territory. President-elect Buchanan put them up to it, hoping thus to restore harmony to the Democratic party. Two justices tipped him off on the decision in advance. So Buchanan slipped a clause into his inaugural address declaring that the Supreme Court was about to decide "at what point of time" the people of a territory could decide for or against slavery. To their decision he pledged his support and urged "all good citizens" to do likewise.

Poor, foolish Buchanan! He had hoped for a peaceful term of office, but the Dred Scott case unleashed the worst passions of pro- and antislavery when his administration was less than a week old.

The opinion of the court decided against Scott's claim for freedom on three grounds: (1) as a black he could not be a citizen of the United States, and therefore had no right to sue in a federal court; (2) as a resident of Missouri the laws of Illinois had no longer any effect on his status; (3) as a resident of the territory north of 36° 30' he had not been emancipated because Congress had no right to deprive citizens of their property without due process of law. The Missouri Compromise of 1820, therefore, was unconstitutional and void.

None of the Chief Justice's opinion was *obiter dictum,* but only on the second point was it sound. As Justice Curtis proved in his vigorous dissenting opinion, blacks had been considered citizens in all Northern states, even though few had possessed the vote, and as citizens had frequently sued in federal courts. "Due process of law" in the Constitution referred to the method of a law's enforcement, not to the substance of a law itself. Only once before, in *Marbury* v. *Madison* had the Supreme Court declared an Act of Congress unconstitutional. In that case the law directly concerned the federal judiciary; but the Missouri Compromise was a general law which had been in force for 36 years, and had been regarded as hardly less sacred than the Constitution itself.

In this decision the Court sanctioned Calhoun's doctrine that slavery was national, freedom sectional. Oregon and Nebraska, as well as Kansas, were now opened to slavery. Squatter sovereignty thenceforth was no sovereignty; slavery was theoretically legal in every territory of the United States.

Federal troops were now keeping order in Kansas, but the free-state and proslavery men refused to co-operate. Each group held a convention, one at Topeka and one at Lecompton, drafted a state constitution and under it appealed to Washington for statehood. The anstislavery Topeka constitution was rejected by the Senate in 1856; the Lecompton constitution, an out-and-out proslavery charter, was accepted by the Senate. Douglas, however, insisted that the people of Kansas be allowed to vote, and they rejected it by an overwhelming majority. For his honest adherence to principle, and for standing by the result, Douglas was now denounced as a "traitor to the South," and lost his chance to be elected President in 1860.

5. *The Lincoln-Douglas Debate*

Abraham Lincoln, prior to the Kansas struggle, stood out from hundreds of Midwestern lawyer-politicians only by a reputation for complete honesty, and a habit of prolonged, abstracted contemplation. He had played the usual game of Illinois politics, and not too well. Elected to Congress as a Whig, he was defeated for a second term owing to his opposition to the Mexican War. Slavery he regarded as an evil thing from his first contact with it on a raft trip down the Mississippi; but the abolitionist agitation seemed to him mischievous and unrealistic. He was an antislavery man, but willing to let slavery alone where it was established.

About the time of the Kansas-Nebraska Act, some new force began to work in Lincoln's soul. He began to preach a new testament of antislavery, without malice or hatred toward the slave-owners.

> I surely will not blame them for not doing what I should not know how to do myself. If all earthly power were given me, I should not know what to do, as to the existing institution . . . When they remind us of their constitutional rights, I acknowledge them, not grudgingly, but fully, and fairly; and I would give them any legislation for the reclaiming of their fugitives, which should not, in its stringency, be more likely to carry a free man into slavery, than our ordinary criminal laws are to hang an innocent one. . . . But all this, to my judgment, furnishes no more excuse for permitting slavery to go into our own free territory, than it would for reviving the African slave trade by law.
>
> Slavery is founded in the selfishness of man's nature—opposition to it, in his love of justice. These principles are an eternal antagonism; and when brought into collision so fiercely, as slavery extension brings them, shocks, and throes, and convulsions must ceaselessly follow.

These quotations are from Lincoln's Peoria speech of 16 October 1854. It made him known throughout the Northwest. Four years later he became a rival candidate to Douglas for election as United States Senator from Illinois. The first paragraphs of his opening speech in the campaign (16 June 1858) gave the ripe conclusion to his meditations during the last four years; and struck the keynote of American history for the seven years to come:

We are now far into the *fifth* year, since a policy was initiated, with the *avowed* object, and *confident* promise, of putting an end to slavery agitation.

Under the operation of that policy, that agitation has not only, *not ceased,* but has *constantly augmented.*

In *my* opinion, it *will* not cease, until a crisis shall have been reached, and passed.

A house divided against itself cannot stand.

I believe this government cannot endure, permanently half *slave* and half *free.*

I do not expect the Union to be *dissolved*—I do not expect the house to *fall*—but I *do* expect it will cease to be divided.

It will become *all* one thing, or *all* the other.

Either the opponents of slavery, will arrest the further spread of it, and place it where the public mind shall rest in the belief that it is in the course of ultimate extinction; or its *advocates* will push it forward, till it shall become alike lawful in *all* the States, *old* as well as *new*—*North* as well as *South.*

William H. Seward echoed this sentiment in his speech of 25 October 1858. "It is an irrepressible conflict between opposing and enduring forces, and it means that the United States must and will, sooner or later, become either entirely a slaveholding nation, or entirely a free-labor nation."

Lincoln and Douglas engaged in a series of joint debates, covering every section of the state, through the summer and autumn of 1858. Imagine a parched little prairie town of central Illinois, set in fields of rustling corn; a dusty courthouse square, surrounded by low wooden houses and shops blistering in the August sunshine, decked with flags and party emblems; shirt-sleeved farmers and their families in wagons and buggies and on foot, brass bands blaring out "Hail! Columbia" and "Oh! Susanna"; wooden platform with railing, a perspiring semicircle of local dignitaries in black frock coats and immense beaver hats. The Douglas special train (provided by George B. McClellan, superintendent of the Illinois Central) pulls into the "deepo" and fires a salute from the twelve-pounder cannon bolted to a flatcar at the rear. Senator Douglas, escorted by the local Democratic club in columns of fours, drives up in an open carriage, and aggressively mounts the platform. His short, stocky figure is clothed in the best that Washington tailors can produce. Every feature of his face bespeaks confidence and mastery; every gesture of his body, vigor and combativeness. Abe Lincoln, having arrived by ordinary passenger train, approaches on foot, his furrowed face and long neck conspicuous above the crowd. Wearing a rusty frock coat, the sleeves of which stop several inches short of his wrists, and well-worn trousers that show similar reluctance to approach a pair of enormous feet, he shambles onto the platform. His face, as he turns to the crowd, has an air of settled melancholy. But no recorded debate in the English language has surpassed those between Lincoln and Douglas for keen give and take, crisp, sinewy language, and clear exposition of vital issues.

Although the Dred Scott decision was a stunning blow to the "gur-reat pur-rinciple of popular sovereignty," Douglas had stuck to it courageously, and defied Buchanan and the Southern Democrats when they attempted to impose the Lecompton constitution on Kansas. In the debate at Freeport, Lincoln attempted to place Douglas in a dilemma by asking whether the people of a territory could, in any lawful way, exclude slavery from their limits. Apparently, Douglas must either accept the Dred Scott decision and admit popular sovereignty to be a farce, or separate from his party by repudiating a dictum of the Supreme Court. Very neatly Douglas found a way out. "Slavery cannot exist a day or an hour anywhere, unless it is supported by local police regulations." If a territorial legislature fails to pass a black code, slavery will effectually be kept out. This "Freeport doctrine," as it was called, won Douglas his re-election to the Senate; and he deserved it. Kansas was safe for freedom; and if slavery were theoretically legal in the territories, there was slight chance of any except New Mexico and Arizona becoming slaveholding states. The main political justification for Lincoln's stand, forbidding slavery in the territories, was the extreme unlikelihood that the South would rest content with the Dred Scott principle, any more than she had rested content with the compromises of 1820 and 1850.

Lincoln furnished an even deeper justification in his Quincy speech of 13 October 1858. This controversy over strategic positions, he pointed out, was an effort to dominate the fundamental moral issue; it was

The difference between the men who think slavery a wrong and those who do not think it wrong. The Republican party think it wrong—we think it is a moral, a social and political wrong. We think it is a wrong not confining itself merely to the persons or the states where it exists, but that it is a wrong in its tendency, to say the least, that extends itself to the existence of the whole

nation. Because we think it wrong, we propose a course
of policy that shall deal with it as a wrong. We deal with
it as with any other wrong, in so far as we can prevent
its growing any larger, and so deal with it that in the run
of time there may be some promise of an end to it . . .

I will add this, that if there be any man who does not
believe that slavery is wrong in the three aspects which I
have mentioned, or in any one of them, that man is misplaced, and ought to leave us. While, on the other hand,
if there be any man in the Republican party who is impatient . . . of the constitutional guarantees thrown
around it, and would act in disregard of these, he too is
misplaced standing with us.

In his reply Douglas took the ground that the rights and
wrongs of slavery were nobody's business outside the slave
states. "If each state will only agree to mind its own business,
and let its neighbors alone, . . . this republic can exist forever
divided into free and slave states, as our fathers made it and
the people of each state have decided."

Lincoln, in rejoinder, thanked his opponent for the admission
that slavery must exist forever.

6. The African Slave Trade

Ominous was a growing insistence by spokesmen of the
lower South that new territory must be acquired for slavery,
no matter where, and that a fresh supply of Africans be imported to work it.

Laws of the United States and of almost every Western
nation declared the African slave trade to be piracy, punishable by death; but, prior to the Lincoln administration, no
American citizen was executed for this offense. Laws against
it either were not enforced, or were so construed that traffic
in human flesh was protected by the American flag. The British navy was the only force seriously trying to suppress the
trade; but successive presidential administrations, faithful to
the obsolete issue of visit and search, refused permission to the
British to search American vessels. A slave ship only had to
raise the "proud banner of freedom" to evade search, and
escape. Conversely an American slaver when sighted by a
United States warship could escape by displaying a foreign
flag.

A United States naval squadron was supposed to help the
Royal Navy police the African coast, but it consisted entirely
of sailing vessels, slower than most of the slavers, and accom-

plished very little. In 1849, for instance, the four American warships which were engaged in "suppressing the slave trade" spent most of their time at a temporary naval base in the Cape Verde Islands, 1000 miles from the nearest barracoon. "No one thinks of catching slavers," wrote a participant, "nor do I believe the officers of the squadron . . . wish to catch them." One reason for this attitude was the navy department's warning to these officers that they would be personally liable for damages if they made any mistakes. Several captured slavers sent into an American port for adjudication had been freed for "want of evidence" (chains and fetters on board being mere trade goods, apparently), and the officers who captured them were sued for damages by the shipowner. So it is not surprising that between 1843 and 1857 the United States Navy's score of captures was 19 slavers, only 6 of which were condemned; a period when the Royal Navy made almost 600 seizures and all but 38 were condemned. Even so, British cruisers were unable altogether to stop the trade. An estimated 440,000 slaves were illicitly exported from the West Coast of Africa in the years 1840–47 to the United States, Cuba, and Brazil, and the number rose annually; but only 31,180 were freed and returned to Africa. Of the residue, it is anyone's guess how many reached the United States. President Buchanan and navy secretary Toucey, ashamed of the monstrous proportions that the traffic had attained under their flag, really attempted to suppress it in 1858–60. Four steam warships were joined to the African squadron, the supply base was brought nearer to the coast, and in 1860 it captured seven slavers in addition to five taken by the home squadron off the coast of Cuba.

Ironically enough, profits of the trade in "black ivory" mostly went north. During eighteen months of 1859–60, some 85 slave ships were fitted out in New York City alone. Many, but not all, were owned by Cuban or Brazilian firms, and most of them carried slaves to the Latin American countries where slavery was still legal, rather than to the United States. Every Northern seaport, as well as Mobile, Charleston, and New Orleans, took part. Charles A. L. Lamar, scion of one of the first families of Georgia, was a leader in this inhuman traffic. He figured on a profit of 60 per cent per voyage, and another slave trader boasted that he had landed 1300 slaves in Cuba at $1000 a head. According to several estimates, the total number imported into the United States in the 1850's ran well into five figures and was greater than it had been half a century earlier when the trade was legal. In 1858, for instance, U.S.S. *Dolphin* captured off the coast of Cuba and sent into

Charleston slave ship *Echo,* with 300 Congo Africans on board. Charleston and Richmond papers then started an agitation to have "these useless barbarians" given "good masters" and put to work. They had reached the "threshold of civilization"; why return them to dark Africa? President Buchanan enforced the law and sent them to Liberia.

Open advertisements of fresh slave imports in Southern newspapers showed how the wind blew. At the annual Southern commercial conventions, speeches and resolutions favoring the legal reopening of the trade occupied much of the delegates' time after 1856. These conventions reflected the views of the Southern middle class, who could not afford to buy slaves at the prevailing high prices—more than $2000 for a prime field hand. They were commonly attended by radical "fire-eaters" who could not get elected to Congress or to state legislatures, and who stirred up this new issue just as rabble-rousers operate today on various "patriotic" conventions. A committee report of the Montgomery commercial convention of 1858 pointed out that the South could only regain power in the Union by obtaining more slaves to take into Kansas and other territories opened by the Dred Scott decision. Governor James H. Adams of South Carolina in 1856 recommended his legislature to press for a reopening. William L. Yancey declared that it was unjust for the North to enjoy free immigration of European labor while the South was forbidden access to the vast pool of African labor. "If it is right to buy slaves in Virginia and carry them to New Orleans," he said, "why is it not right to buy them in Cuba, Brazil, or Africa?" A Charleston gentleman named L. W. Spratt became a persistent advocate of reopening, and made a powerful speech in favor of it before the South Carolina legislature in 1858, painting an attractive picture of the "prosperity to be poured upon us by the teeming thousands from the plains of Africa," promising that every white man could then afford to own a slave. An "African Labor Supply Association" was formed at Vicksburg in 1859, and J. D. B. De Bow, whose *Review* supported the movement, was elected president.

Reopening the African slave trade was opposed in the border slave states, whose surplus blacks were exported southward; hence the lower South, needing their support in a crisis, refrained from pressing such proposals in Congress; and the Confederate Constitution, as a bait for the border states, forbade it. But Spratt promptly started a movement to have this prohibition removed by constitutional amendment. There was no denying Yancey's logic if it was right to buy slaves in Virginia, why was it wrong to buy them in Africa? This movement was growing, and reopening the African slave trade might well have become a Southern ultimatum if Douglas instead of Lincoln had been elected in 1860.

The African slave trade had always emitted a disagreeable odor; but no such stench emanated from Southern desire to acquire more slave territory at the expense of Spain or Mexico —a promising method to acquire new sources of "black ivory," and of political power.

President Buchanan, whose ministry in London had gained him valuable friendships there, conducted foreign relations himself, disregarding his aged and querulous secretary of state, Lewis Cass. A détente of all irritating questions between the two countries was signaled by a visit of the nineteen-year-old Prince of Wales (later Edward VII) to the United States. He was the first royal personage, except exiles, to visit this Republic. Balls in his honor were given in several Eastern cities; and the prince managed to pass through Baltimore without falling in love, like his grandson Edward VIII, with a local belle. His warm reception paid dividends later in the friendliness of his parents, Victoria and Albert, to the Union.

There were no filibustering expeditions against Cuba at this time because Narciso Lopez, leader of the *Cuba libre* rebels, was bent on abolishing slavery. But the hope of buying or conquering Cuba from Spain burned high in many a Southern breast, as well as in President Buchanan's. He urged measures to acquire Cuba in at least three of his annual messages, and both Democratic platforms of 1860 demanded that Cuba be annexed by fair means or foul.

Buchanan was equally zealous in trying to secure more Southern slave territory from distracted Mexico. During his administration Benito Juárez, a full-blooded Indian and by any standards a great statesman, was constitutional president of Mexico; but a reactionary regime ruled Mexico City and states bordering on the Rio Grande. Buchanan in messages of 1858–59 to Congress proposed that he be authorized to establish military posts in Sonora and Chihuahua to "restore order." He recognized the Juárez government, but attempted to extort from it, in return for paying several million dollars, the state of Baja California, obviously as a sop to the Southern expansionists who were still complaining of having been robbed by the State of California's outlawing slavery. That was a bit too much for Juárez to swallow, but he or his foreign minister did sign a draft treaty giving the United States a perpetual right of transit from the Gulf to the Pacific across the northern tier of Mexican states. Buchanan, who regarded this as a useful entering wedge for more annexation, submitted the treaty to the Senate in January 1860, but the Senate rejected it, hands down. Presently the American Civil War would give European powers an opportunity to intervene in Mexico far more deeply than Buchanan ever thought of doing; but in the meantime, the image of Uncle Sam as an intriguing imperialist had been created in Central America.

XVIII

The Approach to War

1859-1861

1. Booth, Brown, and the Election of 1860

NORTHERN AGGRESSIVENESS was not wanting. In 1859 came two startling portents of the irrepressible conflict. A certain Booth, convicted in a federal court of having forcibly rescued a runaway slave, was released by the supreme court of Wisconsin on the ground that the Fugitive Slave Act of 1850 was unconstitutional. After the Supreme Court of the United States had reversed this decision, the Wisconsin legislature, citing the Kentucky resolutions of 1798 which Southerners considered almost a part of the Constitution, declared "That this assumption of jurisdiction by the federal judiciary . . . is an act of undelegated power, void, and of no force." The federal government rearrested and imprisoned Booth; but that did not lessen the effect on Southern sentiment. The deeper significance lies in the fact that the slavery issue had transcended constitutional theory and each side turned to nationalism or state rights as best suited its supposed interest.

If the Booth case aroused bitterness, the next episode of 1859 brought the deep anger that comes from fear. John Brown, perpetrator of the Pottawatomi massacre in Kansas, was a belated Puritan who would have found congenial work in Cromwell's invasion of Ireland. A madman with a method, he formed a vague project to establish a republic of fugitive slaves in the Appalachians, whence to wage war on the slave states. From Canadian and New England abolitionists he obtained money and support, although none were informed as to his exact intentions, and he seems to have had no definite plan. On the night of 16 October 1859, leading an armed troop of thirteen white men and five blacks, John Brown seized the federal arsenal at Harper's Ferry, killed the mayor of the town, and took prisoner some of the leading people. By daybreak the telegraph was spreading consternation throughout the country.

Governor Wise called out the Virginia militia and implored the federal government for aid. John Brown retreated to a locomotive roundhouse, knocked portholes through the brick wall, and defended himself. Lewis Washington, one of his prisoners, has left us a graphic description of the scene: "Brown was the coolest and firmest man I ever saw in defying danger and death. With one son dead by his side, and another shot through, he felt the pulse of his dying son with one hand and held his rifle with the other, and commanded his men with the utmost composure, encouraging them to be firm and to sell their lives as dearly as they could." In the evening, when Colonel Robert E. Lee arrived with a company of marines from Washington, only Brown and four men were alive and unwounded. Next day the marines forced an entrance and took all five prisoner.

Eight days after his capture the trial of John Brown began in the courthouse of Charles Town, Virginia. From the pallet where he lay wounded the bearded old fighter rejected his counsel's plea of insanity. There could be no doubt of the result. On 31 October the jury brought in a verdict of murder, criminal conspiracy, and treason against Virginia. John Brown, content (as he wrote to his children) "to die for God's eternal truth on the scaffold as in any other way," was hanged on 2 December 1859.

He had played into the hands of extremists on both sides. Southern Unionists were silenced by secessionists saying, "There —you see? That's what the North wants to do to us!" Keenly the South watched for indications of Northern opinion. That almost every Northern newspaper, as well as Lincoln, Douglas, and Seward, condemned Brown they did not heed, so much as the admiration for a brave man that Northern opinion could not conceal. And the babble of shocked repudiation by politicians and public men was dimmed by one bell-like note from Emerson: "That new saint, than whom nothing purer or more brave was ever led by love of men into conflict and death . . . will make the gallows glorious like the cross."

The Republican party, having won the congressional elections of 1858, had good reason to hope for victory in 1860, although the leaders of the lower South let it clearly be understood that they would not submit to the rule of a "Black Republican" President. Only six years old, the new party was already more united than the Whigs had ever been; and the platform of its national nominating convention, adopted at Chicago on 18 May 1860, showed that it was no longer a party of one idea, but a Northern party. It had lost the first flush of radicalism, and was beginning that evolution to the right which made it eventually the party of big business and finance. In 1860 Republicanism combined the solid policies of Hamiltonian Federalism with the hopeful and humanitarian outlook of its namesake, the party of Jefferson.

On the slavery question the platform was clear enough, though less truculent than in 1856. No more slavery in the territories; but no interference with slavery in the states. So there was no place for abolitionists, who denounced the Republicans as no better than Cotton Whigs; Wendell Phillips called Lincoln "the slave-hound of Illinois." The Chicago platform repudiated John Brown, along with the border ruffians of Missouri, promised settlers a free quarter-section of public land, and revived Henry Clay's American system of internal improvements and protective tariff, Northern desires which had been balked by Southern interests. The tariff of 1857, passed by a Democratic congress and lowest since 1790, was blamed by Northern bankers and manufacturers for the short-lived panic of 1857, and for low prices that followed. Everything that the North had wanted in recent years—subsidies for transatlantic cables and steamship lines, dredging Western rivers, improvement of Great Lakes harbors, overland mail route, telegraph line to California—had been blocked by Southern votes or President Buchanan's vetoes.

Abraham Lincoln received the presidential nomination on the third ballot, not for his transcendent merits, which no one yet suspected, but as a matter of political strategy. His humble birth, homely wit, and skill in debate would attract the same sort of Northerner who had once voted for Andrew Jackson, and no one but he could carry Indiana and Illinois. William H. Seward, the most distinguished and experienced candidate, had too long and vulnerable a record; Salmon P. Chase was little known outside Ohio. As Lincoln's running mate the convention chose Senator Hannibal Hamlin of Maine, an old Jackson Democrat.

The Democratic nominating convention at Charleston split

on the issue of popular sovereignty in the territories. Southern Democrats believed that they had been duped by Douglas. They had "bought" popular sovereignty in 1854, expecting to get Kansas; but Kansas eluded them and its territorial legislature was now in the hands of antislavery men, encouraged by Douglas's Freeport Doctrine to flout the Dred Scott decision. Nothing less than active protection to slavery in every territory, present or future, would satisfy the Southerners. Jefferson Davis demanded a plank in the platform requiring Congress to apply a "black code" to all territories. William L. Yancey of Alabama insisted that the Democratic party declare flatly "that slavery was right." "Gentlemen of the South," replied Senator Pugh of Ohio, "you mistake us—you mistake us —we will not do it." Nor did they; and on 30 April 1860, after the convention had rejected an extreme proslavery platform with the Davis plank, the delegations of eight cotton states withdrew.

After this secession, since no candidate was able to win the two-thirds majority required by Democratic tradition, the convention adjourned to Baltimore, where in June it made Douglas the official nominee of the Democratic party. The seceders held a rival convention presided over by Caleb Cushing of Massachusetts, which nominated for the presidency the then Vice President, John C. Breckinridge of Kentucky, with Senator Joseph Lane of Oregon, and adopted the Charleston minority platform that the extremists wanted.

In retrospect, the symbolic secession at Charleston on an issue partly emotional, partly semantic, seems even more rash and foolish than the state secession which inevitably developed from it, like vinegar from cider. For the only possible way for the South to protect her "peculiar institution" was to elect a Democrat to the presidency, which this sectional split made impossible. Jefferson Davis, more than any other, was responsible for it. His object, apparently, was to throw the election of President, for want of a majority in the electoral college, into Congress. The House was then so evenly divided that it would have been deadlocked, but in the Senate the Democrats had a majority. They were expected to nominate Senator Joseph Lane of Oregon, who had proved himself a consistent proslavery man, Vice President; then, if the House could not agree, Lane would become President. Devious indeed, but legal.

John Bell of Tennessee and Edward Everett of Massachusetts were placed in nomination by the National Constitutional Union, a party freshly formed for this campaign, avowing no political principle other than the Constitution, the Union, and law enforcement. This was a praiseworthy attempt to build a middle-of-the-road party dedicated to solving the sectional issue by reason and compromise. Conservatives, North and South, declared it to be the only party "a gentleman could vote for." But passions had been too much aroused for a gentleman's party to win.

Although the Union was at stake, the campaign followed the pattern begun in 1840: torchlight parades, the Republicans carrying sections of rail fences, Bell-and-Everett processions featuring the ringing of a great bell as an alarm to the Union, fat boys recruited as "Little Giants" parading for Douglas; ballads, jokes, and songs, one of the most popular being a minstrel show "walkaround" called "Dixie's Land," which the Southern Confederacy later took over. There was plenty of serious argument, too. The Republicans managed to convince the plain people of the Northwest that if slavery extension continued, the Great Plains would be carved into slave plantations instead of free homesteads. Recent immigrants and native-born artisans disliked the Black, but were repelled by the sneers of Southern Democrats at wage earners, and by deadly quotations from Southern literature on the evils of a free society. Republican orators posed a rhetorical question: "Can a free laboring man expect to get two dollars a day when a slave costs his master but ten cents?" Or, as Senator Ben Wade put it when a Southern colleague called the Homestead Bill a sop to Northern paupers, "Is it to be lands for the landless, or niggers for the niggerless?" In some obscure way the Northern laborer had come to look upon slavery as an ally of the capitalists who were doing their best to exploit him. He wished to break up what Charles Sumner called the alliance between the "lords of the lash and the lords of the loom."

As Minnesota and Oregon had been admitted to the Union in 1858 and 1859, there were now eighteen free and fifteen slave states. Breckinridge carried every cotton state, together with North Carolina, Delaware, and Maryland. Douglas, though a close second to Lincoln in the popular vote, carried only Missouri. Virginia, Kentucky, and Tennessee went for Bell although his popular vote was the least. Lincoln carried every free state, and rolled up a large majority in the electoral college, although his combined opponents polled almost a million more votes than he. Here are the results:[1]

---

[1] These figures include no popular vote in South Carolina, where Breckinridge electors were chosen by the legislature.

	Popular Vote	Electoral Vote
Lincoln	1,866,452	180
Douglas	1,376,957	12
Breckinridge	849,781	72
Bell	588,879	39

Although it is difficult to argue that the election of Lincoln to the presidency was a mistake, it may well have been if one believes that postponement of the Civil War might have prevented it altogether. An examination of the election returns shows that moderate elements were still strong in the South, where important people were pointing out, as the Whigs had always done, that slavery extension into the territories was impractical, even if the Dred Scott case had made it legal; that there was no sense pressing for something which nobody really wanted. Even Breckinridge hoped that no slave-owners would go to the territories. But (one asks), if there was so much moderate sentiment in the South, why did it not rally to Douglas?

The answer is, politics. There had been a factional breach between the Douglas men and the Buchanan men. There was the feeling that Douglas was a fourflusher who had promised Kansas to the South and then let her down; and one of the politicians who did the most to foment that mischievous notion was Jefferson Davis. Douglas did his best to placate the South —he was the only candidate to go there on a speaking tour, but it was no use. The John Brown raid had jangled Southern nerves fatally. It started a chain of hysteria like the "great fear" of 1789 in the French Revolution. Rumors of slave insurrection popped up on every side; stories were spread of poisoned wells and the like, creating a feeling that nothing short of Breckinridge or secession could protect Southern society from subversion at the hands of vicious agitators.

Extremists on both sides whipped up hostile sentiment between the sections. Charles Sumner, returning to the Senate after a three-year attempt to cure the injuries inflicted by Preston Brooks, on 4 June 1860 delivered a four-hour oration on "The Barbarism of Slavery" which was no less offensive than the Kansas speech which provoked the beating. Southerners in general assumed that Sumner "spoke for the North"; they did not know that, for all his social graces and noble English friends, Sumner was ostracized by Boston society. Far closer to Northern sentiment was a letter of Francis Parkman the historian: "I would see every slave knocked on the head before I would see the Union go to pieces, and would include in the sacrifice as many abolitionists as could conveniently be brought together." That was pretty much Lincoln's feeling too.

On the other hand there were conciliatory pro-Union speeches by Senators Douglas, Crittenden, and many others. But Daniel C. DeJarnette, a "freshman" congressman from Caroline County, Virginia, countered Sumner with an extraordinary oration on the evils of free society and the beauties of slavery from which these are a few extracts:

> The free suffrage and free labor of the North . . . has so shattered the framework of society, that society itself exists only in an inverted order.
>
> African slavery furnishes the only basis upon which republican liberty can be preserved.
>
> There is more humanity, there is more unalloyed contentment and happiness, among the slaves of the South, than any laboring population on the globe.
>
> For every master who cruelly treats his slave, there are two white men at the North who torture and murder their wives.

More significant were the dithyrambic prophecies by Southern leaders of a Southern Confederacy's world prospects. Robert Barnwell Rhett, addressing the South Carolina assembly on 10 November 1860, predicted that historians in A.D. 2000 would praise the brave Southerners for "extending their Empire . . . down through Mexico to the other side of the great Gulf," establishing "a civilization teeming with orators, poets, philosophers, statesmen and historians, equal to those of Greece and Rome." Lucius H. Minor, a conservative Viginian, added that a Southern Confederacy, thus expanding, would command not only "the whole trade of South America with Europe," but the transit trade between Atlantic and Pacific. Henry Timrod, in his rapturous *Ethnogenesis*, predicted that a Southern Confederacy would not only extend from sea to sea, but would solve the problem of poverty throughout the world. This, he declared,

> Is one among the many ends for which
> God makes us great and rich!

Here indeed was the "purple dream," as Stephen Vincent Benét called it; the dream of a tropical empire based on African slavery. That enticing thought, recalling the wild ambitions of Hitler, permeated deeper than anyone in the North suspected. President Lincoln, in March 1861, sounded out James L. Petigru, a stout Unionist at the head of the South Carolina bar. Petigru told him that "no attachment to the Union" any longer existed there; Charleston merchants were looking forward to a "golden era" when their city would be the New York of a Southern empire. Foreign observers wondered at the landslide of secession, in contrast to the calm deliberations of the Continental Congress extending over a period of almost two years before cutting loose from Britain. Richard Cobden could not understand the "passionate haste and unreasoning arrogance of the secessionists." He had not heard of the purple dream. It had become so brilliant a dream that no possible concession from the North could have prevented an attempt to realize it. As the New Orleans *Bee* editorialized on 14 December 1860, the South could stay in the Union only after "a change of heart, radical and thorough" of Northern opinion "in relation to slavery." Or, as Lowell put it the following month, "What they demand of us is nothing less than that we should abolish the spirit of the age. Our very thoughts are a menace."

He did not exaggerate. South Carolina's Declaration of Independence, passed on Christmas Eve 1860, declared among the causes of her action, that the Northern states "have denounced as sinful the institution of Slavery," and that their public opinion had "invested a great political error with the sanctions of a more erroneous religious belief."

2. Secession Landslide in the Cotton States

The full-fledged secessionists chose South Carolina as their launching pad because of the prestige of Calhoun and the nullification tradition, and they chose well. Leaders of opinion in that state had long been waiting for an occasion to unite the South in a new confederacy. As soon as the election of Lincoln was certain, the South Carolina legislature summoned a state convention. On 20 December 1860 it met at Charleston and unanimously, after only a shadow of debate, declared "that the union now subsisting between South Carolina and other States, under the name of 'The United States of America' is hereby dissolved."

In other cotton states a strong Unionist party still existed. Men like Jefferson Davis, who had served in Washington and traveled in the North, wished to give Lincoln's administration a fair trial. Outside South Carolina, secession was largely the work of petty planters, provincial lawyer-politicians, journalists, and clergymen. Alexander H. Stephens waged a hopeless struggle in Georgia. "All efforts to save the Union will be unavailing," he predicted on 30 November 1860. "The truth is, our leaders and public men . . . do not desire to continue it on any terms. They do not wish any redress of wrongs; they are disunionists *per se*." And, on 3 December, "The people run mad. They are wild with passion and frenzy, doing they know not what." Howell Cobb of Georgia, who resigned as Buchanan's secretary of the treasury to agitate secession, convinced waverers with the meretricious argument "We can make better terms out of the Union than in it"; and Georgia took him at his word on 19 January 1861. Alabama, Florida, and Mississippi had already done so. Louisiana and Texas, where old Sam Houston the Jackson nationalist pled in vain for delay, were out of the Union by 1 February 1861. On the 8th, delegates from these seven states met at Montgomery, Alabama, and formed the Confederate States of America. Next day the congress elected Jefferson Davis president, and Alexander H. Stephens vice president of the Southern Confederacy.

Henry Timrod, unofficial laureate of the Confederacy, was there, and in honor of the occasion wrote one of his best poems:

> At last, we are
> A nation among nations; and the world
> Shall soon behold in many a distant port
>   Another flag unfurled!
> Now, come what may, whose favor need we court?
> And, under God, whose thunder need we fear?

The Constitution of the Confederate States of America, as Jefferson Davis said, differed from that of 1787 only insofar as it was "explanatory of their well known intent," as expounded in the South during the previous thirty years. It was based on the twin foundations of state rights and slavery. Congress was forbidden to grant bounties, pass protective tariffs, or appropriate money for internal improvements. No supreme court was provided and any federal judge could be impeached by the legislature of a state in which his functions were exercised. Congress could pass no law "denying or impairing the right of property in Negro slaves," and in any territory acquired by the Confederacy, or new state admitted to it, "the institution of Negro slavery, as it now exists in the Confederate States, shall be recognized and protected by Congress and by the territorial government." Vice President Stephens declared in a speech of 21 March 1861 on the new government, "Its foundations are laid, its cornerston: rests, upon the great truth that the Negro is not equal to the white man; that slavery . . . is his natural and moral condition." The fragile nature of the one foundation and the rottenness of the other doomed the Southern experiment to defeat. No federal government based on state rights could wage war efficiently; and the slavery underpinning lost the Confederacy all chance of winning a foreign ally.

It is true that many Southerners disliked slavery and believed it to be wrong; but they had to go along with their neighbors or fight them. And nobody who has read the letters, state papers, newspapers, and other surviving literature of the generation before 1861 can honestly deny that the one main, fundamental reason for secession of the original states which formed the Southern Confederacy was to protect, expand, and perpetuate slavery. In the official declarations by the seceding conventions in states which formed the Confederacy, there is no mention of any grievance unconnected with slavery. The tariff figured prominently as a cause in Confederate propaganda abroad, to win support in England and France; but most of the Southern congressmen, including the entire South Carolina delegation, had voted for the tariff of 1857, which the Confederate congress re-enacted.

After the war began, the higher motive of winning independence prevailed over the lower one of protecting slavery, and the white men who fought so gallantly for the Confederacy regarded their cause, as many a monument to the Confederate dead declares, as just and even holy.

3. The Contest for the Border States

When the Confederate States of America were organized, on 8 February 1861, the Democratic administration at Washington had almost a month more of life. President Buchanan possessed the same power that Jackson had asserted to enforce federal law, and General Winfield Scott begged him to exert it; but the seventy-year-old President, timid by nature and fearful of offending Virginia, prayed and twittered and did nothing. We shall be the more tolerant of him when we find his successor doing nothing for six weeks.

In the meantime, two sincere attempts were made to compromise. The essence of one, called after its principal proponent the Crittenden compromise was, by constitutional amendment, to declare slavery inviolate except by state law, to compensate owners for fugitive slaves not recovered, and extend to the Pacific the old Missouri Compromise 36° 30′ line between free and slave territories. Lincoln, when President-elect, promised to support the first two if Southern senators would issue an appeal against secession, which they refused to do; but on slavery extension he held "firm, as with a chain of steel." These measures were discussed in Congress, mostly in committee, for two months.

A second, eleventh-hour attempt to compromise was made by the Peace Convention of 133 delegates appointed by the legislatures of 21 states, which met in Washington for two weeks in February 1861. It had been initiated by the Virginia legislature in the hope of producing a set of constitutional amendments that would attract the seceding states back and satisfy the border slave states to stay in. Ex-President Tyler presided, and many distinguished men such as David Dudley Field of New York, James B. Clay of Kentucky, and Salmon P. Chase of Ohio took part. This convention adopted, and submitted to Congress, seven constitutional amendments similar to Senator Crittenden's, which were passed by narrow majorities. The most important was a "never-never" constitutional amendment on slavery, to the effect that Congress never by law, and the country never by further amendment, would presume to interfere with slavery in any state. That was passed by the House of Representatives on 27 February by a two-to-one majority, submitted to the states, and promptly ratified by Ohio. But this armor-plated assurance failed to budge the determination of the Confederate States to be independent, or to satisfy all the border slave states.

These were not the only evidences of the Republican and Northern desire to compromise. A Boston petition for the passage of the Crittenden compromise, with 22,313 signatures, was rolled into Congress on 12 February, and an equally imposing one followed from New York. Charles Francis Adams was working in Congress for the admission of New Mexico as a slave state if the people of that territory so chose. Wisconsin and other Northern states repealed their personal liberty laws favoring fugitive slaves. In Boston a well-dressed mob broke up an attempt to hold a memorial meeting in honor of John Brown, and howled Emerson down when he tried to speak. Nothing worked. The mind of the lower South was made up; the purple dream had now come too near reality to be abandoned. But the mind of Virginia was not yet made up.

On 4 March 1861, when Abraham Lincoln was inaugurated President of the United States, Washington nervously expected trouble. It was rumored that secessionists from Virginia or "plug-uglies" from Baltimore would raid the capital and prevent the inauguration. General Scott took every possible precaution, but the soldiers at his disposal were too few even to color the black-coated somberness of the crowd. The inaugural procession, as it moved up Pennsylvania Avenue under the harsh glare of a March sun, while a blustery wind blew the dust roof-high, might have been a funeral procession. The Capitol, with its uncompleted dome supporting an unkempt fringe of derricks, suggested a Piranesi engraving of Roman ruins. President Buchanan, urbane and white-haired, and old, bowed Chief Justice Taney, seemed symbols of a departed golden age of the Republic. President Lincoln, uncouth and ill at ease, inspired little confidence until his high-pitched, determined voice was heard delivering the solemn phrases of the inaugural address.

After a brief review of the constitutional issues involved in secession, Lincoln renewed the pledge of his party to respect slavery in the states, and to enforce any fugitive slave law that had proper safeguards for the colored people of the free states. But he made it perfectly clear that he was not going to acquiesce in secession.

> I hold that, in contemplation of the universal law and of the Constitution, the Union of these States is perpetual. ... No state, upon its own mere motion, can lawfully get out of the Union. ... I shall take care, as the Constitution itself expressly enjoins upon me, that the laws of the Union be faithfully executed in all the States. ... The power confided to me will be used to hold, occupy, and possess the property and places belonging to the government, and to collect the duties and imposts. ...
>
> In your hands, my dissatisfied fellow-countrymen, and not in mine, is the momentous issue of civil war. The government will not assail you. You can have no conflict without yourselves being the aggressors. You have no oath registered in heaven to destroy the government, while I shall have the most solemn one to "preserve, protect, and defend" it.

By this time, all forts and navy yards in the seceded states, except Fort Pickens at Pensacola and Fort Sumter at Charleston, had been seized by the Confederates. From the Southern point of view, jurisdiction over such places passed with secession to the states; their retention by the federal government was illegal. A few days after Lincoln's inauguration, Confederate commissioners came to Washington to treat for their surrender. Although Seward refused to receive the gentlemen, he assured them indirectly that no supplies or provisions would be sent to the forts without due notice, and led them to expect a speedy evacuation. Fumbling and bumbling on both sides in this unprecedented situation was natural. Secretary Welles on 28 March ordered U.S.S. *Powhatan,* just returned from sea, to be decommissioned, and her crew discharged from the navy! Four days later the President ordered her to be recommissioned as flagship of a relief expedition to the forts.

Lincoln had reached the conviction that to yield Forts Sumter and Pickens would bring no "wayward sisters" back, and that even though Virginia would probably secede the moment he struck a blow for the Union, strike he must. Against the advice of General Scott and of five out of seven members of the cabinet, he ordered a relief expedition to be prepared for Fort Sumter. Attempting to play fair with the Confederacy, he had a telegraphic warning sent to Montgomery that an attempt would be made "to supply Fort Sumter with provisions only."

The Confederate congress on 15 February had resolved "that immediate steps should be taken to obtain possession of Forts Sumter and Pickens, either by negotiation or force, as early as practicable." President Davis, having to do something, sent a group of staff officers to demand the surrender of Fort Sumter. Major Anderson, commander of the garrison, had no desire for the sort of fame that would come from starting a civil war. But, as no word got through to him of the relief expedition, he offered to surrender in two days' time, when his food supply would be exhausted. The Confederate staff officers refused to allow this slight delay, and on their own responsibility gave orders to the shore batteries that commanded the fort, to open fire. For, as one of them admitted in later life, they feared that Davis and Lincoln would shake hands and the chance of war would slip away forever.

On 12 April 1861, at 4:30 a.m., the first gun of the Civil War was fired against Fort Sumter. The relief expedition shortly appeared but was unable to get within range. All day Sumter replied to a concentric fire from four or five Confederate forts and batteries, while the beauty and fashion of Charleston flocked to the waterfront as to a gala. Next day, his ammunition exhausted, Major Anderson accepted terms of surrender and the garrison marched out with drums beating and colors flying.

Lincoln's patience during the first six weeks of his term was now rewarded. The rebels had fired on the flag; that was enough to arouse "a whirlwind of patriotism," as Emerson described it, in the Northern states. "Now we have a country again," he wrote. "Sometimes gunpowder smells good."

For a brief—too brief—time, until they realized what sacrifice a civil war would require, almost everyone in the North backed the President, and had only one word for the act of firing on the flag—treason.

Events now moved as swift as the telegraph. On 15 April Lincoln issued a call for 75,000 volunteers to put down combinations "too powerful to be suppressed by the ordinary course of judicial proceedings," and "to cause the laws to be duly executed." On the 17th the Virginia convention passed an ordinance of secession. On the same day Jefferson Davis invited ships in Southern ports to take out letters of marque and reprisal to prey on American commerce. Two days later Lincoln declared the ports of all seceded states under blockade. On the 20th, Virginia militia captured the important United States navy yard at Norfolk, which the navy department had neglected to reinforce for fear of offending that state.

Virginia alone of the Confederate states left the Union after due deliberation. In the state convention which met at Richmond on 13 February 1861 more than half the 158 delegates were sober and conservative men who had voted for Bell and Everett, and only about thirty were secessionists at the beginning; these decided to wait and see what Lincoln would do. But the President's call for volunteers—"coercion of a state"— fired latent localism in most of the Unionists' hearts. An ordinance of secession then passed by a vote of 88 to 53; and without waiting for popular ratification, Virginia organized for war and (25 April) joined the Confederacy. There then took place a secession from the seceders; the western delegates, long discontented with a state government that undertaxed slaveholders and denied them free public education, organized their trans-Appalachian region as a loyal Virginia, and in 1863 that part of the Old Dominion was admitted to the Union as the State of West Virginia.

The attitude of Maryland was crucial, for control of her by secessionists would have isolated Washington. The first Northern troops on their way to the capital were mobbed as they passed through Baltimore (19 April); and Lincoln wisely permitted the rest to be marched around the city until he could spare enough soldiers to occupy it and enforce martial law. The Maryland legislature protested against "coercion" of the Southern Confederacy but refused to summon a state convention. The government of Kentucky, where opinion was evenly divided, refused to obey the call for volunteers and endeavored in vain to remain neutral, but by the end of the year threw in its lot with the Union. Missouri was practically under a dual regime throughout the war; Delaware's loyalty never wavered.

In California there was a fierce struggle between Southern sympathizers and Unionists, which the latter won; but California was too remote to give the Union cause other than pecuniary aid, in which she was generous. Most of the five civilized tribes of the Indian Territory, many of them slaveholders, cast their lot with the South.

Undoubtedly the principle of state sovereignty strongly affected the attitude of Virginia, and of three more states (Arkansas, North Carolina, Tennessee) which elected to follow her out of the Union. If the states were sovereign, and the federal government a mere loose compact terminable at will by any member, a state had the right to secede; and any attempt to restore the Union by force was unjust and unconstitutional. This doctrine had been consistently drummed into the electorate for thirty years. Southerners, it is true, had been inconsistent in raising the nationalist banner to cover anything that their section wanted, such as the acquisition of new territory and the return of fugitive slaves. But the steady obbligato had been the Virginia and Kentucky resolutions of 1798, state sovereignty, and the writings of Calhoun. The bright flame of devotion to the Union, kindled in the North by the words and acts of men like Webster, Jackson, and Clay, had so little penetrated the South that hardly anyone there expected the North to fight for the Union, and everyone felt cheated when it did. The Northern states, too, had been inconsistent; they had tried by state action to defeat the annexation of Texas and the fugitive slave law; but in the North state rights were mere sticks in the woodpile to pull out occasionally and flourish, not a settled backlog of doctrine; and none had threatened secession since 1814.

The Union of twenty-three states and the Confederacy of eleven were now arrayed against each other. But the lines were not strictly drawn between the people of states that seceded and of those that did not. The majority went with their neighborhood leaders, as majorities usually do. But there were thousands who made their decision from high motives of sentiment and ideology. One might express the problem of "Which side shall I take?" in a pair of medieval dichotomies:

The Union must be preserved.
The Confederacy has a perfect right to
Independence.

Democracy cannot survive the breakup of the Union.
Democracy is played out; the Southern social system is
superior.

Thus, the Confederate army contained men from every Northern state who preferred the Southern type of civilization to their own; and the United States army and navy included men from every seceded state who felt that the breakup of the Union would be a fatal blow to self-government, republicanism, and democracy. Admiral Farragut was from Tennessee; Caleb Huse, the most efficient Confederate agent in Europe, was from Massachusetts; Samuel P. Lee commanded the Union naval forces in the James river while his cousin Robert E. Lee was resisting Grant in the Wilderness; two sons of Commodore Porter USN fought under Stonewall Jackson; Major General T. L. Crittenden USA was brother to Major General G. B. Crittenden CSA. Three grandsons of Henry Clay fought for the Union, and four for the Confederacy. Three brothers of Mrs. Lincoln died for the South; several kinsmen of Mrs. Davis were in the Union army. In a house in West 20th Street, New York, a little boy named Theodore Roosevelt prayed for the Union armies at the knee of his Georgian mother whose brothers were in the Confederate navy. At the same moment, in the Presbyterian parsonage of Augusta, Georgia, another little boy named Thomas Woodrow Wilson knelt in the family circle while his Ohio-born father invoked the God of Battles for the Southern cause.

Colonel Robert E. Lee USA was stationed at a frontier post near San Antonio in January 1861. To one of his sons he wrote that he could anticipate no greater calamity than a dissolution of the Union.

> Secession [he wrote] is nothing but revolution. The framers of our Constitution never exhausted so much labour, wisdom and forbearance in its formation, and surrounded it with so many guards and securities, if it was intended to be broken by any member of the Confederacy at will. . . . In 1808, when the New England States resisted Mr. Jefferson's Embargo law, and [when] the Hartford Convention assembled, secession was termed treason by Virginian statesmen; what can it be now? Still, a Union that can only be maintained by swords and bayonets, and in which strife and civil war are to take the place of brotherly love and kindness, has no charm for me. If the Union is dissolved, the government disrupted, I shall return to my native state and share the miseries of my people. Save in her defense, I will draw my sword no more.

Herein we see the distress of a noble mind. For such as he, and for thousands of others in Virginia, North Carolina, Kentucky, and Tennessee, making a decision was agonizing, as it had been for their grandfathers in 1775–76 to choose between king and congress, or for their remote ancestors in 1641 to choose between king and parliament. Two great Virginians in the United States Army, Generals Winfield Scott and George H. Thomas, remained loyal to the United States. For Thomas, "Whichever way he turned the matter over in his mind, his oath of allegiance always came uppermost." And to still another Virginian, Senator James M. Mason, we are indebted for the most accurate definition of the great struggle that was about to begin. "I look upon it then, Sir, as a war of sentiment and opinion by one form of society against another form of society."

Thus it was a true civil war,[1] as much ideological as sectional. By May 1861 everyone had taken his stand. Once having done so, everyone was steadfast in his loyalty; there was no switching sides in mid-war as had taken place in the American Revolution; no defection; but plenty of desertion by soldiers of both sides.

[1] The earlier official title, War of the Rebellion, has been dropped, out of deference to Southern wishes; and the cumbrous title "The War Between the States" is grossly inaccurate. "The War for Southern Independence" suggested by the historian Channing is well enough; but why change "The American Civil War," which it was? During the war it was generally called "The Second American Revolution" or "The War for Separation" in the South.

DIXIE'S LAND

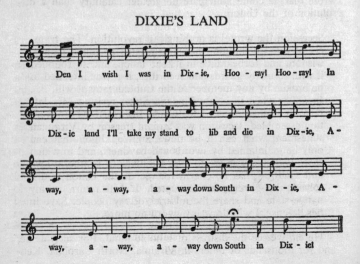

XIX

The War in 1861

1. *A Brothers' War*

So, THERE IT WAS. The "great tragic volume," of which John Quincy Adams had glimpsed the title page in 1820, now opened. As the philosopher William James put it, "What law and reason were unable to accomplish, had now to be done by that uncertain and dreadful dispenser of God's judgments, war. War, with its abominably casual, inaccurate methods of destroying good and bad together, but at last unquestionably able to hew a way out of intolerable situations, when through man's delusion or perversity every better way is blocked."

As always, one could have kept the peace, had one been willing to pay the price, which in this case would have been a permanent division of the Union and the prospect of an interminable series of internecine wars. Suppose Lincoln, on his accession, had recognized the Confederacy as of March 1861. The pulling and hauling of Virginia and the Border states would have gone on, the Confederacy would have insisted on a share of the territories and southern California, and dissension would have sprung up over fugitive slaves, reopening the African slave trade, the transit trade of the Mississippi, and aggression at the expense of Spain or Mexico. This war to preserve the Union, long and bloody though it was, prevented many more wars, and a probable fracturing of the United States into several confederacies, reducing North America to something approaching the present status of Central America.

The white South, almost unanimously, a strong minority in the Northern states, and almost every thinking European, expected the Confederacy to achieve independence. Numbers and wealth, to be sure, were against the South; comparison of her white population of 5.5 million with that of the nineteen free states, 18.9 million, is not entirely fair, since, with blacks to cultivate the soil, more white men could be spared to fight. The four non-seceding slave states (Delaware, Maryland, Kentucky, Missouri), with 2.6 million people, contributed about the same number of soldiers to each side. But determined secessions had generally been successful against even greater odds: the United Netherlands against Spain, the Thirteen Colonies against Britain, Latin America against Spain, the Italian states against Austria, Greece against Turkey. In the realm of high strategy, the Southern Confederacy, to win, needed only to defend her own territory long enough to weary the Northerners; but the United States, to win, had to conquer an empire and crush a people. Any less emphatic result than unconditional surrender of the Confederate armies and collapse of the government, would have been a Southern victory. Nor were material advantages all in favor of the Union. To offset Northern superiority in numbers, wealth, industry, and sea power, the Confederacy had the advantage of interior lines, and a social organization better fitted for creating an efficient fighting force. On the emotional scale, the Confederacy had a definite advantage, since the white Southerners, from their point of view, were fighting for everything that men hold most dear: liberty and self-government, hearth and home, racial superiority. But the Northern people could have stopped the war at any moment, at the mere cost of recognizing what to many seemed an accomplished fact, and without any sacrifice of the social and material factors that closely touch the life of the individual.

Every European military expert thought that Lincoln had taken on an impossible task to "conquer" the South, and two leading English military writers of the last generation, Fuller and Henderson, never seemed to understand how he did. But they ignored three vital factors:—sea power, Union sentiment, and the Emancipation Proclamation. Yet, in the first years of trial, the prospect of freeing slaves sent no blood leaping through Northern veins. It was the simple sentiment of "The Union forever!" Lincoln made this crystal clear in his famous Letter to Horace Greeley of 22 August 1862: "My paramount object in this struggle is to save the Union, and is not either to save or to destroy slavery."

Union sentiment alone made it possible for the superior

strength of the North to prevail. Even today one feels that there was something miraculous in the extent to which the common people came to share the vision of Abraham Lincoln, that the whole future of their country and of democracy everywhere was bound up with the Union of the States. Robert Frost has brought this out in his poem about the widow of one and the mother of two Union soldiers killed in this war:[1]

> One wan't long in learning that she thought
> Whatever else the Civil War was for,
> It wasn't just to keep the States together,
> Nor just to free the slaves, though it did both.
> She wouldn't have believed those ends enough
> To have given outright for them all she gave.
> Her giving somehow touched the principle
> That all men are created free and equal.
>
> *   *   *
>
> White was the only race she ever knew,
> Black she had scarcely seen, and yellow never.
> But how could they be made so very unlike
> By the same hand working in the same stuff?
> She had supposed the war decided that.

But it did not; and, as I write, white men in the states where the Confederacy was proclaimed, and in South Africa too, are desperately striving to hold back a rising tide of the race to which they so long have denied equality. Nevertheless, may not the future regard this American Civil War as a war of emancipation which brought a little nearer the realization of Jefferson's dream?

2. *The Presidents and Their Cabinets*

During the war both Davis and Lincoln were regarded by their enemies as fiends incarnate, and by many of their own people were accused of everything from incompetence to tyranny. In 1861 few on either side doubted that the Southerner was the abler, as he appeared more dignified. Successively lieutenant of dragoons, colonel of volunteers, congressman, senator, and secretary of war, Davis brought experience such as Lincoln had never had, and talents that he never claimed, to the Confederate presidency. Courage, sincerity, patience, and

---

[1] "The Black Cottage," *Complete Poems of Robert Frost*, Copyright 1930, 1939 by Holt, Rinehart and Winston, Inc. Reprinted by permission of the publishers.

integrity were his; only tact, perception, and inner harmony were wanting to make him a great man. He moved (said his wife) in an atmosphere of high thought and settled conviction, and "could not understand any other man coming to a different conclusion after his premises were stated." Isolated from the Southern democracy out of which he had sprung, Davis moved as to the manner born among the whispering aristocracy of Richmond; yet he had a perverse knack of infuriating the gentlemen who tried to work with him. In four years he had five secretaries of war, and he worked less in harmony with the Confederate congress than had any President of the United States with the federal Congress. Davis vetoed no fewer than 38 bills, all but one of which were passed over his veto; Lincoln exercised the veto power only thrice. Davis's military experience led to his cardinal error of attempting to direct military operations. His health and nerves gave way under self-assumed responsibilities, and his state papers show increasing querulousness and bitterness, in contrast to the sustained dignity and magnanimity of everything that Lincoln wrote.

Davis selected his cabinet for work, not for politics. It contained only two members of the governing class, Robert Toombs and Pope Walker, and they soon quarreled with him and resigned. The others exerted little political influence and inspired slight public confidence. Secretary Memminger of the treasury was a Charleston lawyer who knew nothing of public finance, and learned less. Judah P. Benjamin (successively war and state), of whom it has been said that no one served the Confederacy with better brain and less heart, was a British subject by birth and a Jew. Secretary Mallory of the navy, a West Indian, proved to be the ablest of the group, creating a navy from almost nothing. John H. Reagan, the Texan postmaster general, was so devoted to Davis as to put his face on Confederate postage stamps, which has never been done before or since for a living American.

Lincoln's cabinet carried more weight than that of Davis, but had even less cohesion. Not one member was a personal friend or follower of the President. William H. Seward as secretary of state brought the administration confidence, and eventually strength, but not until he had almost wrecked it by an over-aggressive foreign policy. Simon Cameron, secretary of war, a Pennsylvania manufacturer who proved to be criminally careless in the management of his department, had to resign under a cloud. Salmon P. Chase, an imposing college graduate, Cincinnati lawyer, antislavery leader, and governor of Ohio, received the treasury, for which he had no preparation; but the businessmen from whom the government had to borrow money trusted Chase, and he initiated the national banking system which lasted until 1917. Chase's aspirations were whetted by office, and he never really appreciated Lincoln, especially his sense of humor; once saying to a friend, "I can't treat this war as a joke." Gideon Welles, secretary of the navy, formerly a bureau chief in the navy department, latterly a small-town newspaper editor, was a recent convert from the Democratic party; he proved to be an excellent navy secretary. Edward Bates and Montgomery Blair, attorney general and postmaster general, were good sound men who represented the loyal states.

At the beginning of Lincoln's administration the cabinet members distrusted one another, Blair alone had much respect for the President, and several months elapsed before Lincoln was really master in his own house. The change of scene, the hurly-burly of war preparations, the pressure of patronage, seemed for a time to cut his contact with that unseen force which lifted him from the common herd. Yet his feeling for the democratic medium in which he had to work, for its possibilities, limitations, and imperfections, was akin to that of a great artist for the medium of sculpture or painting. He could capture the imagination of the common soldier and citizen, and at the same time make the outstanding quality of an ill-balanced character such as McClellan or Stanton the instrument of a great purpose. This railsplitter, this prairie lawyer with his droll stories and his few, crude social devices, had an innate tact and delicacy that carried conviction of his moral and intellectual greatness to all but the most obtuse, and a humanity that has opened the hearts of all men to him in the end.

If Lincoln was slow to direct the conduct of the war, he never faltered in his conception of the purpose of the war. From Sumter to Appomattox, it was for him a war to preserve the Union. The power that lay in that word came less from an instinct of nationality than from the passionate desire of a youthful people to prove its worth by the only test that the world accepted. The Union, which for Washington was a justification for the American Revolution, and for Hamilton a panoply of social order, had become, in the hands of Jackson, Clay, and Webster, a symbol of popular government. Lincoln drove home this conception in his every utterance, and gave it classical expression in the Gettysburg address. He made the average American feel that his dignity as citizen of the republic was bound up with the fate of the Union, whose destruction would be a victory for the enemies of freedom everywhere.

Lincoln could not bring everyone to this conception. Many

leaders of the Democratic party still looked upon the states as the guardians of democracy. The abolitionists would support the Union only on the condition of its serving their immediate purpose. Nor did Lincoln completely dominate his own group. Many Republicans regarded the war as a mere assertion of Northern superiority, for their party in 1861 was essentially a Northern party. Because Lincoln, ignoring every appeal to hatred, sectionalism, and humanitarianism, raised the standard of Union at the beginning and kept it paramount, the Union was preserved. Prominent Democrats such as Stephen Douglas rallied the best elements of their party to the colors; and in a few months the entire Ohio valley, half slaveholding in fact and largely proslavery in sentiment, was secure. His enemies sneered, "Lincoln would like to have God on his side, but he must have Kentucky." His friends doubted whether even God could preserve the Union without Kentucky. Nor did he ever forget that those whom he liked to call "our late friends, now adversaries" must, if his object were attained, become fellow citizens once more. The frantic appeals of Davis to class and sectional hatred found no answering echo in the words of Lincoln, who could never bring himself to contemplate the South with feeling other than regret for her rebellion and compassion for her plight.

3. The Two Armies

In military preparation the Confederacy had a start of several months over the United States. As early as 6 March 1861 President Davis called for and quickly obtained 100,000 volunteers for a year. Virginia's secession on 17 April gave the Confederacy many of the ablest officers of the United States Army; no new nation has ever had commanders of the caliber of Lee, both Johnstons, both Hills, Beauregard, and Jackson at its birth. The Union, on the contrary, found her proper military leaders only through the costly method of trial and error. McClellan, Grant, Sherman, indeed most of the West Pointers who rose to prominence in the Union army, were in civil life when war began. The regular army of the United States—16,257 officers and men—was kept intact instead of being broken up to leaven the volunteers; thus brilliant junior officers like Philip Sheridan were confined to small regular units until late in the war.

The forty United States naval vessels in commission were scattered over the seven seas. Until mid-April no attempt was made to enlarge or even to concentrate these slender forces, for fear of offending Virginia. In the meantime the Confederate States had seized upon the United States arsenals and navy yards within their limits and obtained munitions from the North and from Europe.

Winfield Scott, General in Chief of the United States Army, infirm in body but robust in mind, advised the President that at least 300,000 men, a first-rate general, and two or three years' time would be required to conquer even the lower South. No one else dared place the estimate so high; and Seward believed with the man in the street that one vigorous thrust would overthrow the Confederacy within 90 days. The President, in his proclamation of 15 April 1861, called for 75,000 volunteers, for three months. The response was heartening. Within two weeks 35,000 troops were in Washington or on their way thither, and 20,000 were waiting for transportation. The government should have taken advantage of this patriotic outburst to create a national army for the duration of the war. Instead, Lincoln on 3 May called for forty more volunteer regiments of an average of 1050 officers and men each, and 40,000 three-year enlistments in the regular army and navy, leaving the recruiting, organization and equipment of volunteer regiments to the states. Overzealous states were coldly admonished, "It is important to reduce rather than enlarge this number."

As a basis for the new army, every Northern state had a volunteer militia force, neither well officered nor properly drilled. Company officers were elected by the men, regimental and general officers were appointed by the state governor. There were also many semi-social, semi-military companies such as the Fire Zouaves,[1] the Garibaldi Guards with red shirts and *Bersaglieri* plumes, the New York Highlanders in kilt and sporran, and the Irish Sarsfield Guards. Many of these volunteered en masse and marched to glory without delay or change of uniform. But for the most part, the volunteer regiments that made up the bulk of the United States Army during the war, were regiments *ad hoc*. A patriotic citizen would receive a colonel's commission from his governor, then raise a regiment by his own efforts and those of men who expected majorities under him. Units of 50 to 100, recruited by some youth of local

---

[1] Zouaves were originally Moslem auxiliaries to the French army in Algeria. Their precise close-order drill, quick-step (preserved by the French *chasseurs alpins*), and showy uniforms, with baggy red breeches, red tasseled fez, and blue tunic, appealed to the urge for a little more color in life, North and South. The Louisiana "Tigers" and "Pelicans" were Zouave outfits. An entire regiment of New York Zouaves, red pants and all, was captured by Dick Taylor's Texans in the Battle of Pleasant Hill, April 1864. The Texans were disgusted—swore they hadn't enlisted to fight women!

popularity whom they would elect lieutenant or captain, were incorporated as companies. When the regiment was reasonably complete and at least partially equipped, it was forwarded to a training camp and placed under federal control. Examining boards were appointed to remove incompetent officers, but in practice the federal government had to respect state appointments until they were found wanting in action. And its own were scarcely better. Prominent politicians such as Frémont, Banks, and Butler received major generals' commissions from the President, outranking seasoned officers of the regular army. For giving the whole country a stake in the war, for using community pride and attracting to the colors the greatest number of men in the shortest possible time, no better method could then have been devised; but it was continued too long.

By much the same system was the first Southern army raised, but with less baneful results, and the Confederacy adopted conscription a year earlier than the Union did. Southern respect for rank and family meant prompt recognition of natural leaders. General Joseph E. Johnston CSA observed that familiarity with firearms, and zeal, gave the Confederates superiority in 1861, but that "the thorough system of instruction introduced into the United States army gradually established equality in the use of firearms; and our greater zeal finally encountered better discipline." Straggling and desertion impaired the strength of both armies, particularly the Confederate. "Stragglers cover the country, and Richmond is no doubt filled with the absent without leave," wrote General Johnston in the midst of the peninsular campaign. "The men are full of spirit when near the enemy, but at other times to avoid restraint leave their regiments in crowds."

If the Confederates won more battles, it was owing to better leadership, which gave them tactical superiority on the field of battle, against the superiority of their enemies on the field of operations. Frequently we shall find a numerically inferior Confederate force defeating its enemy in detail; or a Union commander failing to deploy superior forces to influence an action. Since the North had the greater immigrant population, it had a larger proportion of foreign-born soldiers; but the average Union soldier was a farmer's son. And there were considerable numbers of Irish, Germans, and foreign soldiers of fortune in the Confederate army.

Mostly boys fought this war. No age statistics are available, but it is certain that the majority on both sides were under twenty-one. Walt Whitman, who visited thousands of the wounded in hospitals and heard their stories, found many as young as fifteen. It was so, too, with the officers. Major

General S. D. Ramseur CSA, just out of West Point, won his first star at the age of twenty-five, and his second at twenty-seven. Francis Channing Barlow, who entered the war as a private, fought as a major general at Gettysburg, when he had just turned twenty-eight. His division was one of those driven from the knoll on the first day, and he fell, pierced by a minié bullet. General John B. Gordon CSA, seeing this youthful officer lying among the Union dead, dismounted, gave him water from his canteen and received a message to his wife, that his deepest regret was to be about to die without looking on her face again. But die he did not; carried to the Confederate rear, unconscious Barlow was viewed by General Early, who remarked that obviously nothing could be done to save his life. At which Barlow came to and responded, "General Early, I will live to whip you yet!" In a letter to his mother a week later, Barlow says, "Several Confederate officers were very kind and attentive." Abandoned when the Confederates retreated, Barlow fully recovered and distinguished himself in several later actions.

This is but one of many instances of humanity on both sides, which support the dictum of one who survived over half a century, Major Randolph Barton CSA: "This was the last gentlemen's war."

Throughout the war the "Federals," as the more polite Southerners called the Union army, were better equipped in shoes and clothing, and more abundantly supplied with rations and munitions. War department red tape, and the prejudice of elderly officers, prevented the adoption of the breech-loading rifle. Both in artillery and small arms it was largely a war of the muzzle-loader, and to a great extent, of the smooth-bore. Although the blockade stopped big shipments from Europe in 1862, the Confederate ordnance service, under a resourceful Pennsylvanian named Josiah Gorgas, was able to keep the army so well supplied that the South never lost a battle for want of ammunition. Richmond was one of the principal coal- and iron-producing centers in the United States, and her Tredegar Iron Works were well equipped for the manufacture of heavy castings and ordnance. It was there that the armor of C.S.S. *Virginia* (ex-*Merrimack*) was rolled and her rifled guns cast. These were the only works in the Confederacy so equipped until 1863, when a newly established plant at Selma, Alabama, began to turn out cannon. Great enterprise was also shown by the Confederate government in organizing woolen mills to weave cloth for uniforms, and the Confederate bluish-gray was less conspicuous than the Union dark blue. Southern regiments from frontier districts preferred homespun jackets and trousers dyed brown with the butternut or white walnut, and officers indulged them in that preference. The Confederate army was never properly supplied with shoes; many of those it did obtain came from Lynn, Massachusetts, via Bermuda and the blockade runners, or off Federal dead and wounded. And Confederate wants were often relieved by supplies abandoned by Union armies in their frequent retreats, or captured from wagon trains by cavalry raids.

Many of the general and flag officers of this war were "characters" who blazoned their individualities in diverse ways, especially tonsorially. Generals Pickett and Custer allowed their curly hair to grow long, and indulged in other sartorial whimsies suggesting the cavalier. Older officers who had served in the War of 1812, such as Admiral Farragut and Generals Scott and Wool, remained clean-shaven; but beards had returned to fashion during the Crimean War, and our Civil War heroes exhibited a greater luxuriance of whiskerage than any of their profession since Alexander the Great set the fashion of shaving. McClellan, Beauregard, and Joe Johnston, who fancied themselves successors to Napoleon, went in for the mustache and *impérial,* then fashionable in the Tuileries; Hooker, who probably had been told that he resembled Alexander, went clean-shaven; Don Carlos Buell trimmed his hair and beard to resemble portraits of Don Carlos I of Spain; Burnside cultivated a style of whisker extending from ear to ear which was named "burnsides" after him. Most of the others grew beards of varying lengths, but none could match those of John Pope, J. B. Hood, or Fitzhugh Lee, which extended well below the breastbone. Naval officers, not prevented (as their British compeers had been) by royal command from vying with the soldiers, matched the generals in whiskerage. Admiral Du Pont, in particular, grew a complete hairy frame for his face, in the style later associated with "Oom Paul" Kruger, the Boer president.

Leonidas Polk, who had left West Point to enter the church and served as bishop of Louisiana for the past twenty years, returned to his namesake's profession as major general CSA, but retained the hairdo of a Victorian bishop until his death in action. He was the most eminent man of God in either army; but there were many others of lesser rank, such as the Rev. Thomas Wentworth Higginson, colonel of the first Negro regiment in the federal service, and the Rev. William B. Greene, colonel of a coast artillery regiment that defended Washington, who posted a sign outside his headquarters tent, "Dogs and Congressmen Keep Out!"

Hardly less remarkable than the generals' whiskers was

their ill health, probably the result of constant exposure, lack of sleep, and bolted meals. George H. Thomas was the only general on either side who attempted to maintain a mess commensurate with his rank; but Thomas, like Jubal A. Early, suffered from arthritis, never mounted a horse without a wrench, and suffered agonies when riding rapidly. General Grant suffered from splitting headaches; D. H. Hill from dyspepsia and a spinal ailment; I. R. Trimble from erysipelas and osteomyelitis. Dick Ewell, described at the age of forty-six as an "old soldier with a bald head, a prominent nose and a haggard, sickly face," had only one leg, suffered from stomach ulcers and malaria, and lived largely on boiled rice and frumenty. A. P. Hill "took sick" on the first day of Gettysburg; Lee became very ill at a most critical time on the North Anna river. Braxton Bragg's chronic dyspepsia, coupled with a mean disposition, made him the most unpopular general in either army. After reading about the aches and pains of the Confederate generals, one feels that very few could have passed the "physical" for their rank in World War II.

Few generals on either side cared for guard mounts, dress parades, or other military pomp and circumstance. And, in contrast to the liberally decorated uniforms in the two world wars, those of the Civil War bore neither medals nor ribbons. Congress authorized the Medal of Honor in 1862, but it was awarded both sparingly and captiously, and the recipients do not appear to have worn it.[1] The Confederacy issued no medals. Judging from their photographs, the generals were averse to being buttoned up, and a wide variety in headgear was permitted. General "Jeb" Stuart, the dashing Confederate cavalryman, wore a plume in his felt hat to suggest that he belonged to the royal house of his name, and his chargers were frequently encumbered by floral decorations from admiring ladies.

Toward the end of the war the Union army, to ease the logistics problem involved in moving herds of live cattle and wagonloads of flour, tried canned rations on Sherman's army as it advanced into the Carolinas. The soldiers disliked them, and the general referred to the canned goods as "desecrated vegetables" and "consecrated milk."

Each army took an unprecedented amount of punishment; casualties in our Civil War were greater, in proportion to the population, than those even of the British and French in World

[1] After the war, distinguishing badges of the Army of the Cumberland, Army of the Potomac, etc., were informally adopted; these look like medals on the tunics of the officers but were really only badges, like those issued for marksmanship.

War I. The official Union casualties were 93,443 killed in action or died of wounds; 210,400 from disease—the latter being broken down into 29,336 from typhoid, 15,570 from other "fevers," 44,558 from dysentery, and 26,468 from pulmonary diseases, mainly tuberculosis. There are no statistics of Confederate losses, and estimates vary widely. Deaths from battle were probably around 80,000 or 90,000. If losses from disease ran proportionately as high as in the Union ranks—and there is no reason to suppose that they were any lower—they must have reached 160,000 to 180,000. We may safely say that at least 540,000 Americans, in a total population of over 31 million (1860), lost their lives in, or as a result of, this war. Yet, so fecund is nature that the population increased over eight million between 1860 and 1870.

The average soldier, whether in blue or in gray, was sick enough twice or thrice a year to be sent to a hospital, which often proved more dangerous than the battlefield. Poor sanitation, infected water, wretched cooking, dirt and sheer carelessness were largely responsible for this sad state of affairs, repeated in every war of the nineteenth century. Medical services were inadequate and inefficient, hospitals often primitive, care for the wounded haphazard and callous. Behind the lines, overworked doctors labored desperately in improvised field hospitals. Antisepsis was unknown, and anesthetics were not always available; abdominal wounds and major amputations meant probable death. Out of a total of 580 amputations in Richmond during two months of 1862, there were 245 deaths; no wonder a Confederate officer wrote that in every regiment, "There were not less than a dozen doctors from whom our men had as much to fear as from their Northern enemies."

It was still thought not quite respectable for women to nurse soldiers at the front, and the armies at first relied on untrained male nurses like Walt Whitman. Dorothea Dix was appointed superintendent of Union nurses at the beginning of the war, and over 3000 women volunteered to work in hospitals. Much of the medical care on both sides was voluntary. The United States Sanitary Commission inspected camps and hospitals and provided nursing and relief both at the front and behind the lines, combining the work which the Red Cross and the United Services Organization carried out in the two world wars. The Young Men's Christian Association did similar work in both North and South, but many of the Confederate sick and wounded were tenderly nursed in nearby homes. Confederate medical skill was no worse than that of the Union; but lack of drugs, anesthetics, and surgical instruments imposed heavy losses.

THE CIVIL WAR, 1861–1865

Boundary of Free Soil
Boundary of Confederate States
(Those between are loyal slave-holding states)

o Principal blockade-running ports
□ Union blockading bases
— Principal railways

Scale of Miles
0   100   200   300   400

4. *Geography, Strategy, and Bull Run*

Union strategy, aggressive by the nature of the Union cause, took a form dictated by geography and hydrography. The Appalachians and the Great River divided the Confederacy into three parts, nearly equal in area: the East, the West, and the Trans-Mississippi theaters of war. The first, Virginia and the Carolinas and Georgia east of the Blue Ridge, was the scene of the most spectacular campaigns and battles. Between the Blue Ridge and the Appalachians lay the Shenandoah-Cumberland valley, a natural military road leading north-easterly to Washington, or southwesterly to the heart of the Confederacy. Military operations west of the Mississippi were comparatively unimportant, but the area between the Appalachians and the Mississippi was of equal importance with the Eastern theater. Lee might perform miracles in Virginia; but after Grant, Farragut, and Porter had secured the Mississippi, and the Armies of the Tennessee and the Cumberland were ready to swing into Georgia, the Confederacy was doomed.

That it worked out this way was due primarily to a significant use of Union sea power. General Winfield Scott, though aged and infirm, had the right strategy of victory in mind—the "anaconda" it was called in derision. This meant constricting the Confederacy by control of the ocean and the Western waters, blockading it from the sea and splitting it along the Mississippi so that when the Union armies were ready to advance they would have to deal with a weakened enemy. Scott's "anaconda" is an interesting parallel to Winston Churchill's "closing the ring" in World War II, but it required too much patience on the part of the Northern public, which demanded swift, powerful jabs at the heart of the Confederacy to end the war quickly. Events proved the old veteran to have been right. In a series of costly campaigns covering more than two years, the South showed that she could take care of herself until starved by Union blockade and split by the Mississippi.

On both sides the best officers were graduates of West Point, where they had had a good military education. Their textbook *Advanced Guard . . . with the Essential Principles of Strategy and Grand Tactics* by Professor Dennis H. Mahan (father of Admiral A. T. Mahan) emphasized speed, surprise, and firepower; and they also read, in translation, the works of Jomini and Clausewitz. Blunders were made on both sides; but anyone who candidly compares the performance of our Civil War generals with that of the British in the Crimean War, the French in the war of 1870–71, or the British in the Boer War must conclude that the Americans of 1861–65 were relatively proficient in military art.

Abraham Lincoln, whose only military experience had been that of a company officer in the Black Hawk War, was the best of the Union strategists; fortunately so, since he had to perform many of the functions which in World War II were exercised by General Marshall and the Joint Chiefs of Staff. He, too, "boned up" on Jomini. Lincoln saw the whole strategic picture from the start, made very few mistakes, grasped immediately the advantages of superior numbers and sea power, and urged the generals to keep tightening the squeeze on the Confederacy until time and circumstance invited a breakthrough. And he saw that the main objective should be the surrender of the Confederate armies, rather than the occupation of territory. Clausewitz was right when he wrote that the best qualifications for a commander in chief, whether king, emperor, or president, were not military knowledge but "a remarkable, superior mind and strength of character." Lincoln had both. But Jefferson Davis, from supposedly expert knowledge, frequently overrode generals like Joseph Johnston and Lee, who were better strategists than he, and relied heavily on incompetents like Braxton Bragg, or blowhards like Beauregard.

Lincoln and Scott's plan of campaign for 1861 was to blockade the Southern coast and occupy strategic points both there and on Western rivers, while the big volunteer army was being trained. Since Kentucky had to be nursed out of neutrality, and Confederate sympathizers in Missouri threatened the Union right flank, and western Virginia was at stake, the first forward movements were diverted into those border states. George B. McClellan, commanding volunteers raised in Ohio, beat a small Confederate force, saving West Virginia for the Union and making himself the man of the hour. In Missouri, Nathaniel Lyon fought a skillful campaign against local Confederates, prevented the fall of Missouri into enemy control, and lost his life in action (10 August).[1] Kentucky was saved for the Union, largely through the energy of Ulysses S. Grant. The "sacred soil of Virginia" was first "polluted" by the "abolition hosts" of a "reckless and unprincipled tyrant" (so General

---

[1] In southern and western Missouri there was partisan warfare of the bitterest kind during almost the entire war. I once asked President Truman, whose forebears were on the Confederate side, to recommend an accurate and impartial history of the Civil War in Missouri. "There's no such thing;" he replied, "they're all liars!"

Beauregard declared) on 24 May 1861, when Union troops occupied the Lee mansion at Arlington Heights.

By July 1861 the Confederacy had almost 60,000 men under arms in Virginia, and 22,000 of them, commanded by General Beauregard, hero of the bloodless battle of Fort Sumter, concentrated near Centerville. There was another strong force at Harper's Ferry under General Joseph Johnston; and under him in the chain of command was Brigadier General Thomas J. Jackson, one of the most extraordinary characters of this or any other war. A thirty-seven-year-old West Pointer and Mexican War veteran, Jackson for the past nine years had been professor of mathematics and science at the Virginia Military Institute, which has educated more great soldiers than any other independent college. At "V.M.I.," recorded one of his pupils, "He was simply a silent, unobtrusive man, doing his duty, regarded as a quiet, harmless eccentric." Unknown to the boys, he was earnestly studying the art of war, and by 1861 probably knew more of strategy and tactics than any general on either side. In appearance he was unprepossessing. Colonel Dick Taylor, bringing up Louisiana troops to join Jackson's brigade in the Shenandoah valley, found the general seated on a rail fence sucking a lemon—his method of keeping healthy—and noted his "mangy cap with visor drawn low, a heavy, dark beard and weary eyes," and enormous hands and feet. Mounted, Jackson would usually be set on Little Sorrel, a short, thick-set, barrel-chested gelding of unknown ancestry, chosen from a load of captured Union army remounts. Little Sorrel had marvelous endurance, subsisted on corncobs if necessary, and could go without water like a camel.

The Confederate army was the most pious army since Cromwell's New Model, and Jackson's brigade was the "prayin'est" in the Confederacy. If possible, no day passed without divine service, and officers who visited Jackson's tent were apt to find the general on his knees "wrestling with the Lord." He wrestled to very good purpose in July 1861.

The United States Congress, convened in special session on 4 July, authorized the President to recruit half a million men for the duration of the war. Already there were some 25,000 three-month volunteers in Washington, spoiling for a fight. The Northern press and people were vociferous for action. Against General Scott's advice, Lincoln yielded to the cry, "On to Richmond!" So General McDowell crossed the Potomac to seek out Beauregard's army near Manassas Junction, Virginia. A throng of newspaper correspondents, sightseers on horse and foot, and congressmen in carriages with ladies and picnic hampers, came out to see the sport.

This was on 21 July, when the two armies clashed on a plateau behind a small stream called Bull Run. Troops on both sides were so ill trained, the officers so unused to handling large numbers, the opposing flags so similar, and the uniforms so varied, that a scene of extraordinary confusion took place. For hours it was anyone's battle. Union victory was averted by Johnston sending reinforcements by railroad in the nick of time, the "stone wall" stand of Jackson, and the charge of Colonel Arthur C. Cummings's 33rd Virginia Regiment. The Union lines began to retreat, and the retreat became a rout. All next day soldiers were straggling into Washington without order or formation, dropping down to sleep in the streets; rumors flying about that Beauregard was in hot pursuit, that the Capitol would be blown up if not abandoned. "One bitter, bitter hour—perhaps proud America will never again know such an hour," wrote Walt Whitman, who lived through it all. But Lincoln never flinched and Beauregard did not pursue; his army was more disorganized by victory than McDowell's by defeat. There was no more talk of a 90-day war. The Union was nerved to make adequate preparations for a long war; while the South, believing her proved superiority would dissolve the Northern "hordes" and procure foreign recognition, indulged in an orgy of self-applause.

Had the South but known it, the second half of 1861 gave her the best chance of victory. Cotton should have been rushed to Europe, arms and munitions imported, and Confederate finances put on a sound basis before the Union blockade closed in. Instead, the Southern states, faithful to the old Jefferson embargo theory, withheld cotton, fatuously believing that this would force Europe to break the blockade, and no taxes were levied by the Confederate congress in 1861! Joe Johnston urged an invasion of Pennsylvania before the Union had time to organize and train a great army, but Jefferson Davis thought he knew better; the South must stay on the defensive. Perhaps he was right, we never can know; but the folly of the cotton embargo, the tardy buildup in arms, and timid finance, are obvious.

5. Terrain and Tactics

Most actions of the Civil War were fought in rough, forested country with occasional clearings, and amid a scattered population. Antietam, Gettysburg, and Fredericksburg were the only important battles in open country. Standard tactics were, roughly, these: the defending infantry was drawn up in double line, the men firing erect or from a kneeling posture or from field entrenchments if there was time to dig them. The attacking force, also in two lines, moved forward by brigade units of 2000 to 2500 men,[1] covering a front of 800 to 1000 yards. Captains, and often colonels and majors, marched in front of their men, to encourage them with voice and sword; the other officers and non-coms were in the rear to discourage straggling. Normally the attacking troops moved forward in cadenced step to the beat of drum, halting at intervals to fire and reload. The defending force returned fire until one or the other gave ground. Occasionally the boys in blue, more often those in gray, advanced on the double, the former shouting a deep-chested *hurrah!*, the latter giving vent to their famous rebel yell, a shrill staccato yelp, derived perhaps from the view-halloo of the hunting field. As the two lines closed, swords flashed, colors glowed, bugles blew, drums beat, mounted aides dashed back and forth carrying messages. Since smokeless powder had not been invented, the battlefield soon became so thickly shrouded in smoke that the commanders had no idea of what was going on.

Standard books on tactics prescribed that an attack of this sort should be concluded with the bayonet, but that seldom happened because fire power had improved much faster than tactics. The conical minié bullet (invented by a French officer of that name in 1848) made infantry fire about twice as deadly as it had been in the Mexican War, and led to the earliest use of field entrenchments as the only way to prevent the defense being slaughtered. Fire directed from these improvised earth bulwarks, as at Fredericksburg and Kenesaw Mountain, made a shambles of the attack before it closed near enough to use bayonets. But Lee persistently underestimated the effect of rifle fire over open ground; that is why his attacks failed at Antietam and Gettysburg.

Not only in field entrenchments, but in skirmishing did the fighting in the Civil War foreshadow World War I. This description of General Barlow's skirmishers at Spottsylvania

[1] In general, 10 companies = 1 regiment; 4 regiments = 1 brigade; 4 brigades = 1 division, 2 or 3 divisions = 1 army corps. In six important battles, average regimental strength was only 500. The regiment at full strength numbered 1050 officers and men, but they were allowed to waste away to almost nothing; new regiments were organized, instead of providing replacements for the old ones.

might apply equally well to the standard tactics of an infantry attack on the western front in 1918; or in Sicily in 1943:

> To Barlow's brigades the very life of military service was a widely extended formation, flexible yet firm, where the soldiers were largely thrown on their individual resources, but remained in a high degree under the control of resolute, sagacious, keen-eyed officers, who urged them forward or drew them back as the exigency of the case required, where every advantage wàs taken of the nature of the ground, of fences, trees, stones, and prostrate logs; where manhood rose to its maximum and mechanism sank to its minimum, and where almost anything seemed possible to vigilance, audacity, and cool self-possession.

Although over 80 different types of shoulder arms were used in the Union army alone, the muzzle-loading .58 caliber rifle, 4 feet 8 inches long, weighing 9 pounds, and fired by a percussion cap, was standard. A trained infantryman could get off 3 rounds per minute, and with a minié-ball cartridge he could stop an attack at 200 to 250 yards, and kill at over half a mile. Good breech-loading repeating rifles were on the market, but the chief of Union ordnance James W. Ripley, (nicknamed "Ripley Van Winkle") disapproved of them—as did General Lee—and only by Lincoln's intervention were enough made for issue to Union cavalry. The mounted service, as of old, enjoyed top prestige. Cavalry in the Civil War was used mainly for reconnaissance or hit-and-run raids; not, as in Europe, for shock tactics. The romantic exploits of the great Confederate cavalrymen Stuart, Forrest, Morgan, and Shelby, contributed little to their cause; but Thomas and Sheridan, by turning troopers into dragoons (using horses to get there but fighting on foot), captured fortified lines at Nashville and cleared the Shenandoah valley of Confederate forces.

Union field artillery for the most part was muzzle-loading; either the "Napoleon" smooth-bore bronze cannon, firing a 12-pound ball, or the Parrott cast-iron 3-inch rifled cannon. The latter, an invention of Robert P. Parrott, a former United States Army officer, was guaranteed against bursting like the old "Peacemaker" by a wrought-iron hoop welded into the breech. Parrotts of larger caliber, firing projectiles up to 300 pounds' weight, were supplied in large numbers both to army and navy. Mortars up to 13-inch caliber were used in siege operations and on specially converted vessels; and Captain John A. Dahlgren USN invented a bottle-shaped 9-inch rifled cannon, which was also much in evidence. He also designed the 15-inch smooth-bores for the monitors. Confederate artillery, composed of a hodgepodge of imported and captured cannon, together with many pieces from the federal ordnance depots in the South, was well handled, especially in wooded terrain at very short range, to stop an infantry assault; but it was no match for the more powerful Union guns. This placed the Southern troops at no great disadvantage, because cannon fire never became an effective killer like the minié bullet; artillery then had neither the range nor the precision to give assaulting infantry valuable support. On the other hand, massed artillery as a defense, as on Malvern Hill in the peninsular campaign, could be decisive; and General O. O. Howard in the Atlanta campaign once held 12,000 Confederates at bay with 29 cannon.

Moments of actual combat were more deadly than modern battles to infantry officers and men, but as soon as contact was broken the men were comparatively safe, since there was no continued harassment by enemy artillery. A common feature of the Civil War was the fraternizing of picket guards, and even of whole units, during intervals between battles; the Southerners swapping tobacco, of which they had plenty, for coffee, of which they were always short.

Other important tactical innovations in the Civil War, on the naval side, were the armored ironclad, and the mine and submarine for defense in shoal waters; some 40 warships were sunk or badly damaged by mines during the war. On the land side, the extensive use of field entrenchments, railways and telegraph, and air observation from balloons, was new. An efficient field telegraph system would have been of great assistance to military commanders, enabling them to dispense with mounted messengers, as well as to keep distant commands promptly informed. But the Union telegraph service was controlled by a superintendent in Washington, who would allow no interference with his personnel by field commanders. General Grant was driven almost frantic by lazy, cowardly, or venal telegraphers who ran to the rear when most wanted, or let messages from speculators take precedence over military orders. General Schofield almost lost the Battle of Franklin, because his headquarters telegraph operator took fright and ran away with the code so that urgent messages to General Thomas had to be sent by messenger.

Exactly the contrary took place with the balloon corps; enthusiastic pioneer aviators were consistently snubbed by the military and their organizer was denied military rank. Balloons had been used for observation of enemy troop movements in

Europe as early as the French Revolution. A native of Jefferson Mills, New Hampshire, with the impressive name Thaddeus Sobieski Coulincourt Lowe, the leading American balloonist, obtained the support of Joseph Henry to investigate currents of the stratosphere, and made a record ascent of 23,000 feet in 1860. After war broke out he was allowed to organize and direct a civilian balloon corps attached to the army's signal corps. Lowe's organization at one time had six lighter-than-air ships costing only $1500 each. Two of them, with pongee silk envelopes, inflated with hydrogen gas from portable generators, were employed by the Army of the Potomac in the peninsular campaign. They were used both for observation and artillery spotting, and Lowe himself was in the balloon at Chancellorsville which reported Stonewall Jackson's flanking movement; but General Hooker was too stupid to profit by this intelligence. General Joe Johnston wanted balloons for his army, but apparently the technical difficulties were too much for the Confederates. So much friction was created by a civilian organization operating within the Union army, so many difficulties attended the inflating, launching and handling of these big gasbags with four-man baskets and mile-long manila cables in the wooded terrain of the Civil War, that the Union balloon corps was disbanded in June 1863.

6. *Europe, Canada, and the War*

Southern hopes of a quick victory were based on the expectation that the North would not fight, and the delusion that the Lord Chancellor of England sat on a cotton bale instead of a woolsack. Southerners were as certain that England would go to war, if need be, to get cotton, as they were of the justice of their cause. The European textile industry did largely depend on American cotton, but two important factors were overlooked by plantation economists. In April 1861 there was a 50 per cent oversupply both of the fiber and of cotton cloth in the English market; and the bumper cotton crop of 1860, largely exported before the blockade, added to the glut. The war enabled European cotton brokers to work off surplus stock at inflated prices, and later they found new sources of supply in Egypt and India.

Both North and South felt that they were entitled to the sympathy and support of the British and Canadian people, and were bitter when they didn't get it, as the British and Canadians were about American neutrality in 1914 and 1939. A chain of events threatened international complications. First, Jefferson Davis on 17 April 1861 invited Southern shipowners to take out letters of marque and prey on Northern merchant vessels. This forced Lincoln's hand, and two days later he declared a blockade of all ports and coasts of the seceded states. A blockade had to be publicly declared before neutral ships would submit to visit and search, but implicit in the proclamation was the recognition of the Confederacy as a belligerent. Hence it is not surprising that on 13 May Lord Palmerston's government, in recognizing the blockade and ordering British ships to respect it, declared England's "determination to maintain a strict and impartial neutrality in the contest . . . between the Government of the United States of America and certain States styling themselves the Confederate States of America." To the Northern people this seemed grossly unfriendly, and Seward took occasion to draft an intemperate protest which Lincoln toned down. In the excitement over this neutrality proclamation, almost everyone overlooked an order of 1 June forbidding British and imperial port authorities to admit prize ships. That British order killed Confederate privateering and resulted in the *Alabama* and her sister raiders having to destroy almost all the prizes that they captured. Thus, the British doctrine of naval warfare worked for the North. As Earl Russell, the foreign minister, observed, the Union blockade of Southern ports was a real blockade satisfying all the rules of international law, and in view of England's interest as the dominant sea power, he dared not insist on any stricter standard. The reiterated Southern complaints that the blockade was a mere "paper" one he shrewdly suspected to be indications to the contrary, as indeed they were.

Canada, Britain, and France were keenly interested in the Civil War. Opinions divided ideologically: restoration of the Union would mean a new triumph for democracy; destruction of the Union a possibly mortal wound to democracy. The United States had long been obnoxious to European ruling classes and to Canadian Tories for the encouragement that it afforded to liberal and radical elements. An "all-powerful and unconquerable" instinct, wrote the Comte de Montalembert, "at once arrayed on the side of the proslavery people all the open or secret partisans of the fanaticism and absolutism of Europe." Many liberals, however, could see no difference between the Southern struggle for independence and the nationalist movements in Europe which they had supported. Humanitarians, who would have welcomed a war against slavery, were put off by the repeated declarations of Lincoln and Seward that slavery was not an issue. The commercial classes marked the return of the United States in 1861 to a high protective tariff, which the Confederate constitution forbade, and Southern propaganda made much of the contrast. Shipping interests hoped for the ruin of their most formidable competitor, and approved a new cotton kingdom for which they might do the carrying trade Under the circumstances it is not surprising that the Union had few articulate partisans in the England of 1861. And there was grave danger lest some untoward incident precipitate hostilities between the Union and the Empire.

Such an incident was the *Trent* affair. A British mail steamer of that name was conveying from Havana to Southampton two Confederate diplomatic agents, Senators James M. Mason and John Slidell, when on 8 November 1861 she was boarded from U S S *San Jacinto,* Captain Charles Wilkes, and deprived of her two distinguished passengers and their secretaries, who were then confined in a federal fortress. Wilkes, who should have sent the *Trent* into port for adjudication instead of removing the two envoys, became a hero of the hour in the North and was promoted. But in England the incident was rightly considered an insult to the British flag—a reverse impressment, 1807 style. The London press shouted for apology or war, and Russell, for the cabinet, drafted a peremptory demand for apology and release of the envoys. Fortunately Prince Albert, Queen Victoria's ailing consort (he had only a fortnight to live), toned down the dispatch; and by a notable dispensation of Providence the Atlantic cable had ceased to function, so that mutual insults were not immediately reprinted in the newspapers. By 19 December, when Russell's dispatch reached Secretary Seward, the Northern public had begun to weigh the consequence of antagonizing England, but Lincoln feared the political effect of yielding to British menace. Senator Sumner argued before the cabinet for four hours on Christmas Day before the President yielded. Seward then told the British minister, "The four persons . . . will be cheerfully liberated." That was promptly done. In the end, the *Trent* episode cleared the air.

American-Canadian relations had been friendly since the adoption of the reciprocity treaty in 1854. The Rush-Bagot agreement was still in force, and the fresh-water navies hauled out in 1819 had rotted away. All phases of Canadian opinion, except for some descendants of 1776 Tories, were pro-Union at the start of the Civil War. Canada, having got rid of African slavery in 1833, had received some 20,000 fugitive slaves in the past decade. Friendliness quickly changed to resentment and apprehension in the latter half of 1861, owing to a number of factors. The British declaration of neutrality, and still more the *Trent* affair, unleashed a nasty jingoism in the Northern American press, with threats of invading Canada which recalled 1812.

During the *Trent* crisis, Britain strengthened her Canadian garrison of 6400 regulars by over 14,000 men. Many of these reinforcements were glad to avail themselves of Seward's tactful offer to be landed at Portland, Maine, instead of Halifax, and proceed to Quebec over the recently built Grand Trunk Railway. Thus the *Trent* affair cleared the air in Canada too.

THE BATTLE CRY OF FREEDOM

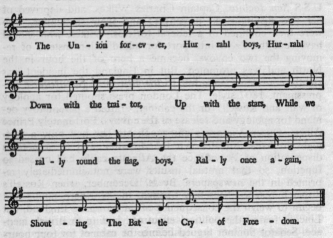

The Un - ion for - ev - er, Hur - rah! boys, Hur - rah!

Down with the trai - tor, Up with the stars, While we

ral - ly round the flag, boys, Ral - ly once a - gain,

Shout - ing The Bat - tle Cry · of Free - dom.

XX

Eighteen Sixty-two, the Crucial Year

1. McClellan, the Radicals, and Stanton

On 24 JULY 1861, three days after Bull Run, President Lincoln summoned General George B. McClellan to Washington and gave him command of the Army of the Potomac. McClellan was thirty-four years old. A graduate of West Point on the eve of the Mexican War, in which he performed distinguished service as a lieutenant of engineers, he later served as American military attaché to the allied armies in the Crimea and wrote a report that showed unusual powers of observation. Subsequent business experience accustomed him to deal with large affairs and won him the confidence of men of property; personal magnetism and success in West Virginia made him a popular idol. The Northern states provided him with plenty of three-year volunteers. Congress was generous with money and equipment, and the President gave him full support. No untried general in modern times has had such abundant means as McClellan enjoyed during the nine months that followed Bull Run.

This general proved to be a great organizer. His methodical mind, appetite for detail, vivid personality, and genuine interest in his men were exactly the qualities needed to form an army from a mob. But defects in conduct and character impaired his usefulness and weakened his support when the time came for action. There can no longer be any reasonable doubt of his technical military ability; General Lee, after the war, said that he was the ablest of his opponents. McClellan's position, however, required not only military ability but some perception of the democratic medium in which he must work; and that perception, which was given to Grant and Lincoln, he decidedly lacked. The note of self-laudation and contempt for the President that runs through McClellan's confidential letters, and his acceptance of the presidential nomination on a defeatist platform in 1864, make it difficult to do him justice today. Yet no Union general was so beloved as "Little Mac" was by the untrained volunteers whom he turned into a superb instrument of war, the Army of the Potomac.

McClellan's admirers called him, and he liked to be called, the "Young Napoleon," but apart from being adept at inspiring troops (even using Napoleon's own phrases, badly translated), his resemblance to the great Emperor was superficial. Napoleon was a master of audacity and celerity in maneuver, whilst McClellan excelled in careful preparation and methodical planning. So far as he resembled any French general, "Little Mac" may be compared with Bazaine or Pétain, who carried political ambitions in their marshal's batons and fancied that politicians were scheming against them. McClellan fully expected to "crush the rebels in one campaign," as he wrote to his adoring wife; he then would persuade the Confederate government to surrender by guaranteeing security to slavery. This arrangement, he expected, would be ratified by popular acclaim, and he would be elected to the presidency of a reunited country—still half slave and half free—in 1864.

Weeks stretched into months, and the newspapers had nothing to report but drills and reviews. "All quiet along the Potomac" appeared so often in the headlines as to become a jest.

Lincoln long resisted efforts of the politicians to worry him into forcing McClellan into action. When General Scott got in McClellan's way, the President allowed him to resign; and on 1 November 1861 he appointed McClellan general in chief of all the armies of the Republic. Yet the general persistently snubbed the President, and on one occasion—going to bed when Lincoln came to his headquarters for a conference—affronted him in a manner that no other head of state would have pardoned. "Never mind," said Lincoln, "I will hold McClellan's horse if he will only bring us success." December came, and the general began to play with plans for an oblique instead of a direct advance on Richmond. "If something is not done soon, the bottom will be out of the whole affair," said the President. "If General McClellan does not want to use the army I would like to *borrow* it." Lincoln knew what Churchill and Roosevelt learned in World War II, that the people and politicians in a democratic country will not stand for a "phony war," that they must have action. Yet McClellan's strategy of careful preparation and delay was correct. It was the true policy of the Union to postpone offensive movements until the blockade began to pinch, and superior Northern resources were organized for offensive war.

Walt Whitman shrewdly evaluated McClellan as a straddler, a soft hitter, one who "felt that the man who dealt the softest blows all around would be the great man, the general idol, the savior." The virtue of this defect was that McClellan kept the war clean; in Virginia he did his best to restrain soldiers from looting or committing outrages on civilians.

The new year 1862 opened gloomily in both capitals. President Davis was flattered by unanimous re-election to the presidency, but troubled by a new and factious Congress. The *Trent* affair had fizzled, the blockade was beginning to be felt, Confederate paper money had depreciated 50 per cent, and prices were soaring. But the Southern people still trusted in the potency of cotton and the impotence of Northern men.

In the North, McClellan's inaction enhanced Lincoln's political embarrassment. The unity forged by the guns that fired on Fort Sumter was falling to pieces; and from the Republican party a faction emerged to challenge Lincoln's leadership. This was led by "Bluff Ben" Wade, "Zach" Chandler, Western senators with a fine talent for politics, and "Thad" Stevens, a congressman from Pennsylvania. From their point of view the war was one of revenge on an insolent slave power; the policy they wished to force upon the President was immediate emancipation and arming of the slaves. That, if adopted in 1861, would have driven the border slave states into secession, alienated the Northern Democrats, and narrowed the war party to a faction.

Those violent elements which war inevitably releases were arousing a new and nasty temper in the Union, and to this temper the Radicals appealed by voice and pen during the recess of Congress, August–December 1861. To their standard surged the bitter-ender, unconditional-surrender sort of people, sincere in their desire to win the war yet certain to lose it for any government that yielded to their misguided zeal. In his first annual message to Congress Lincoln said, "I have been anxious and careful that the inevitable conflict . . . shall not degenerate into a violent and remorseless revolutionary struggle." To Radicals this was a sign of weakness.

The first product of this complex of hatred and zeal, suspicion and super-patriotism, was the appointment by Congress of a Joint Committee on the Conduct of the War, on 20

December 1861. Radical Republicans dominated this committee. Throughout the war their inquisitorial activities, *ex parte*
investigations, and missions to the front hampered the executive and the best generals—and undermined army discipline.
Frémont, Butler, Banks, and Hooker, four of the most incompetent generals on the Union side, were, in the opinion of
this committee, peerless leaders who could do no wrong.

Owing to the efforts of a House committee, corruption on a
gigantic scale was uncovered in the war department, and the
scandal smirched Secretary Cameron. Lincoln let him down
easily into the St. Petersburg legation and appointed a Democrat, Edwin M. Stanton, secretary of war. Gloomy, ill-man-
nered, and vituperative, Stanton was another cross for Lincoln
to bear. Intolerant of delay and harsh to subordinates, he was
hated by almost every officer with whom he came in contact,
and to several he did cruel injustice. Yet for all that, Stanton's
honesty, determination and system made him a fit instrument
for Lincoln's purpose. He stood for discipline against the
President's desire to pardon all deserters. He browbeat state
governors and other politicians and got things done. As Lincoln remarked at a dark period for the Union cause, "Folks
come up here and tell me that there are a great many men in
the country who have all Stanton's excellent qualities without his defects. All I have to say is, I haven't met 'em! I don't
know 'em! I wish I did!"

When Stanton took office (15 January 1862), McClellan
had already prepared, and the President approved, the general
outline of a plan of operations for 1862: (1) in the Eastern
theater of war, McClellan to advance against Richmond, but
by what route was still undecided. (2) In the Western theater
Don Carlos Buell, commanding the Union Army of the Ohio,
to rescue the beleaguered Unionists of eastern Tennessee and to
cut the Richmond-Memphis railway. Albert Sidney Johnston,
commanding the Confederate department of the West, was
there to prevent him. (3) In a military department which embraced both banks of the Mississippi, Henry W. Halleck, then
occupied with an isolated war in Missouri, was usefully constructing a fleet of armored river gunboats. This should support the army pushing down the Mississippi valley and join
with a naval expedition under Farragut, which would force a
passage from the Gulf to New Orleans and Vicksburg. The
Confederacy was improvising an armored naval force to repel
this invasion and break the blockade.

Action began in the Western theater. Colonel James A. Garfield marked a stage in his progress "from Log Cabin to White
House" by defeating a body of Confederate mountaineers at

Prestonburg in eastern Kentucky (10 January 1862), but went no farther. General George H. Thomas was attacked at Mill Springs on 19 January by General Zollicoffer, who lost both the battle and his life. Thick and sticky mud stopped a further advance, and almost smothered Thomas's communications. Lincoln, desperate for action, then issued (27 January) his pathetic General War Order No. 1, designating Washington's birthday as "the day for a general movement of all the land and naval force of the United States against the insurgent forces."

February 22 passed before even a definite plan for the Army of the Potomac had been agreed upon. The first substantial victory for the Union came in an unsuspected quarter by an almost unknown general.

2. Grant and Farragut

Captain Ulysses S. Grant, an officer who disliked war and loathed army routine, had fallen on evil days since his proud moment before Mexico City. He was forced to resign from the army to avoid a court-martial for drunkenness. Unable to extract a living from "Hardscrabble Farm" near St. Louis, he attempted to sell real estate, and failed again. His father bestowed a clerkship in the family leather store at Galena, Illinois. Brothers condescended, fellow townsmen sneered. Only his wife had faith; and the most ill-tempered horses were docile to his voice and hands.

Shortly after the war broke out Grant, now thirty-nine years old, obtained a colonelcy of volunteers. His regiment was promptly ordered into Missouri to dislodge a Confederate regiment under a Colonel Harris. Approaching the reported position, so Grant relates, fear gripped his heart; but he had not the moral courage to halt and consider what to do. Suddenly there opened a view of the enemy's encampment—abandoned! "It occurred to me at once that Harris had been as much afraid of me as I had been of him. This was a new view of the question I had never taken before; but it was one I never forgot afterwards."

This brief and bloodless engagement earned Grant a brigadier's commission. In the fall of 1861 he was assigned to Halleck's department and stationed at Cairo, the important junction of the Ohio with the Mississippi. In the summer of 1861 the Confederates began to throw up earthworks at various points along the Mississippi where the old Spanish forts used to choke down-river trade. In order to force a passage past them, J. B. Eads, an engineer of St. Louis, constructed a fleet of river gunboats, each with a partially armored casemate shaped like a mansard roof, and a flat-bottomed hull.

Less than 50 miles up the Ohio from Cairo the Tennessee and Cumberland rivers offered parallel routes into Tennessee, Alabama, and Mississippi. Grant observed that Forts Henry and Donelson, the Confederate earthworks which closed these rivers, were the twin keys to the rebel West. Their capture would open a navigable waterway into the enemy's center and drive in his flanks. On 30 January 1862 Grant, after consulting with Commodore Andrew H. Foote, commanding the gunboat flotilla, obtained Halleck's reluctant consent to try, and was furnished with the necessary transports and gunboats. On 6 February Fort Henry, feebly garrisoned, was reduced by the gunboats before Grant's army arrived. And a three-gunboat raid up the Tennessee river to Cerro Gordo near the Mississippi border, captured a big river steamer which the Confederates were converting to an ironclad.

Fifteen miles across country from Fort Henry, on the high left bank of the Cumberland, lay a much stronger entrenched camp, Fort Donelson. There Albert Sidney Johnston had stationed 20,000 men, over half his army. Grant, after a quick midwinter march, disposed his troops in a semicircle about this fort on the land side. Foote's gunboats steamed down the Tennessee, up the Cumberland, and on 13 February attacked the fort at a range of 200 yards. They were driven back, disabled. It seemed that a siege would be necessary. But General John B. Floyd (President Buchanan's secretary of war), commanding the Confederate garrison, decided to fight his way out, and almost did. Grant arrived in the thick of battle to find his right in disorder and his center in danger. Deducing from the three days' rations in a captured Confederate's haversack that the enemy was trying to escape, Grant made the right tactical dispositions to drive him back into the entrenchments. It was a fierce, blind battle in the forest but the result justified Grant in demanding and General Simon Bolivar Buckner (Floyd having escaped by boat) in consenting to "unconditional surrender" of garrison and fortress. The phrase gave new meaning to Grant's initials.

The results of this surrender were spectacular. Nashville was no longer tenable by the enemy, and A. S. Johnston retreated to the Memphis-Chattanooga Railway. Grant had practically restored Tennessee to the Union. Equally important was the moral gain to the then dispirited North. The prairie boys of the new Northwest had tested their mettle against rangy foresters of the old Southwest, and the legend of Southern invincibility began to fade.

Grant understood that momentum, keeping unremitting pressure on the enemy, is a first requisite in the art of war; but his jealous and pedantic superior, Halleck, instead of allowing him to pursue Johnston, diverted troops to attack the northernmost Confederate strongholds on the Mississippi. The capture of New Madrid and Island No. 10, with the aid of Foote's gunboats (7 April 1862), was a pretty operation, in which General John Pope unfortunately acquired fame; but it wasted time. Grant's way, up the Tennessee river, was the right method to open the Mississippi; Halleck's way gave Johnston time to concentrate some 50,000 men with Beauregard and Polk at Corinth.

Halleck, after subjecting Grant to unnecessary humiliation, finally ordered him, after waiting for Buell's Army of the Ohio to join, to lead against the enemy. Buell was a slow-motion general, and before he arrived Grant was caught napping. His Army of the Tennessee, encamped in an ill-chosen position at Pittsburg Landing, its front unprotected by entrenchments, was attacked on 6 April by Johnston and Beauregard. The Battle of Shiloh, or Pittsburg Landing, began. For twelve hours there was confused fighting between detached portions of the Union lines and the dashing Confederates, superbly led. Grant's steadfast coolness, the fiery valor of divisional commanders like William Tecumseh Sherman and B. M. Prentiss, and the pluck of individual soldiers, prevented a rout. By the end of that terrible Sunday the Confederates had captured the key position at Shiloh church, Union lines were dangerously near the river, and some 5000 refugees were cowering panic-stricken under the bluffs at Pittsburg Landing. It was a spectacle of complete defeat, and any ordinary general would have settled for saving the rest of his army by retreat. But Grant was no ordinary general. Reinforced by the van of Buell's Army of the Ohio and by Lew Wallace's division, he counterattacked Monday morning. Albert Sidney Johnston was killed, and Beauregard, after ten hours' desperate fighting, withdrew the Confederate army to Corinth. Grant hadn't the heart to call on his own exhausted troops to fight further, and Buell refused to move.

Shiloh was a Union victory at doleful cost. Out of 55,000 Union troops engaged the loss was over 13,000; the Confederates lost about 11,000 out of 42,000. A storm of controversy arose. Grant's lack of precaution was magnified by the newspapers into gross incompetence, even drunkennness. Buell's friends claimed all the credit for him. Political pressure was put upon the President to remove Grant, but Lincoln replied, "I can't spare this man; he fights."

Immediately after Shiloh, two Union jabs were made deep

into the Confederate West. Ormsby MacKnight Mitchel, America's leading astronomer, was now a divisional commander under Buell. On his own initiative he led his division in a rapid march from Shelbyville, Tennessee, to Huntsville, Alabama, captured the city, and would have captured Chattanooga, too, had the "Great Locomotive Chase" succeeded. James J. Andrews, a Union sympathizer, stole a railroad train near Marietta, Georgia, and with 20 soldier volunteers, started full speed for Chattanooga, hotly pursued by a Confederate train. The Southerners won, captured the locomotive crew, and executed them as spies.

Although Lincoln couldn't spare Grant, Halleck could and did, by personally taking over command of the Army of the Tennessee on 11 April. After assembling 100,000 men at Pittsburg Landing, Halleck took a month to cover 23 miles thence to Corinth, giving Beauregard plenty of time to withdraw the Confederate army intact.

Union gunboats continued their descent of the Mississippi, breaking up a Confederate flotilla off Memphis on 6 June, running up the White river into the heart of Arkansas, forcing the enemy to evacuate Missouri, and on 1 July 1862 joining Farragut's fleet above Vicksburg.

Commodore Farragut had to sail up the Mississippi from the Gulf without a single ironclad, but his old wooden walls were manned by stout hearts. At Plaquemines Bend, 90 miles below New Orleans, the river was protected by Forts Jackson and St. Philip, sunken hulks supporting a boom, a fleet of rams and armed steamers, and a 3- to 4-knot current. A flotilla of small Union mortar schooners fired continuously on Fort Jackson for three days, without much effect. In the small hours of 24 April, Farragut's fleet of eight steam sloops of war and fifteen wooden gunboats, with chain cables secured as a coat of mail abreast the engines, crashed the boom and ran the gantlet of armored rams, fire rafts, river-defense fleet, and the two forts.

In the gay creole city of New Orleans, largest and wealthiest of the Confederacy, there had been little business since the blockade closed down, and no laughter since the news of Shiloh. When Farragut's fleet anchored off the levee on 25 April, so near that the crowd could see the grinning Jack Tars as they fondled the breeches of their Dahlgren guns, New Orleans was already abandoned by Confederate armed forces and the United States took over. The Union troops of occupation were commanded by a tough character, General B. F. Butler. Repeated insults to his men by the creole wenches were put a stop to by his order of 15 May 1862, rendering such a person "liable to be treated as a woman of the town plying her avocation"; or in other words to be lodged in the common jail. Butler was declared a felon and an outlaw by President Davis, denounced in Parliament, and finally removed from his post in consequence of diplomatic protest. But, alas, this was not the end to his military career.

Farragut, after landing the army, proceeded upriver, received the surrender of Baton Rouge and Natchez and ran past Vicksburg to join the upstream gunboat fleet (1 July). But as General Halleck could not be induced to provide troops for a joint attack on Vicksburg, that "Gibraltar of the Mississippi" held out for a year longer, enabling the Confederacy to maintain communication with Arkansas, Missouri, and Texas. Thus the Union army and navy offensive in the West failed to attain its major objective, yet accomplished much. By July 1862 the enemy had been driven south of the Memphis-Chattanooga Railway, and the greater part of the Mississippi was under Union control. "Anaconda" tightly pinched the Confederacy along her waistline; but her blood still circulated.

3. Sea Power and the War

No big modern war has been won without preponderant sea power; and, conversely, very few rebellions of maritime provinces have succeeded without acquiring sea power. The Thirteen Colonies, as we have seen, could not have won independence but for the help of the French navy; the South American republics employed retired British naval officers to build up fleets which challenged Spain's; even the Dutch rebels of the sixteenth century had their "sea beggars" who played hob with Spanish communications. Similarly, in the Civil War, control of the sea was a priceless asset to the Union. The navy maintained communications with the outside world, severed those of the South, captured important points on the coast, and on the Western rivers cooperated with the army like the other blade to a pair of shears.

Gideon Welles's somewhat meager knowledge of the service was supplemented by a capable assistant secretary, Gustavus V. Fox. By them the navy was much more efficiently directed than the army, because Congress did not try to interfere or to make admirals out of politicians. But the problem of blockading 3350 miles of coastline from Washington to Matamoras, with the vessels and seamen available, seemed insoluble. The 42 ships of the navy in commission, mostly steam-propelled but none armored, could not cope with the problem. Only twelve ships were in the home squadron; the rest were dispersed among various foreign stations, and it took time to recall them

and refit for blockade duty. The American merchant marine
had a limited supply of screw steamers suitable for conversion
to men of war, and a few machine shops capable of turning out
good marine engines. But a large construction program was immediately undertaken—Ericsson's *Monitor* being the most spectacular example—and sidewheelers, clipper ships, tugboats, and
even ferry boats were purchased in wholesale quantities at re-
tail prices. Time and legislation were required to build ironclads, to retire aged officers, and to establish promotion by
merit.

The blockade was largely a "paper" one for about three
months, and did not become really effective until 1862. How
effective it ever became is still a matter of controversy. The
Richmond government declared loudly and frequently that it
never did, and that England should never have recognized it as
a proper blockade; but the scarcity of consumer goods in the
Confederacy, and soaring prices, proved the contrary. No ships
could cover so long a coastline without bases, which the Union
navy lost no time in obtaining.

Hatteras Inlet, back door to Virginia, was captured by a
small amphibious operation under General Burnside on 26 August 1861. Ship Island in the Gulf of Mexico, an important
staging point for Farragut's assault on New Orleans, was taken
on 17 September. An amphibious operation of 17,000 men,
under Commodore Samuel F. Du Pont, beat down the fort on
Hilton Head at the entrance to Port Royal Sound, South Carolina, on 7 November, forcing a gunboat flotilla under Commodore Tattnall CSN to retire. To these, by April 1862, were
added Roanoke Island (the site of the first Virginia colony),
New Bern, and Fort Macon, North Carolina, and Fort Pulaski
commanding the approaches to Savannah. The Confederate
commander in the South Carolina department, General Robert
E. Lee, here had his first experience of sea power. To his children, in December 1861, he wrote describing the "big black
ships like foul blots on the surface of the water miles from
shore," and the "Yankee gunboats" steaming up the Edisto
river and shelling the houses of prominent secessionists.

Once provided with these bases, the United States blockading
squadron put a tighter and tighter squeeze on the Confederacy
until it was practically eating its own tail. Few officers and still
fewer sailors who kept this ceaseless vigil became known to
fame. They deserve a tribute like that which Mahan paid to
Nelson's two-year blockade of the coast of France in the Napoleonic wars: "Those far distant, storm-beaten ships, upon
which the Grand Army never looked, stood between it and the
dominion of the world." The blockading squadrons under

Commodores Du Pont, Melancton Smith, John A. Dahlgren, and David D. Porter, a motley collection of sailing frigates, converted paddlewheel steamers, tugboats, ferry boats, and even stranger craft, which few leaders of the Confederacy even sighted, stood between them and the independence of the South.

Owing to the character of the Southern coast, it was impossible for blockading squadrons to close Confederate ports completely. Private firms in Nova Scotia and the British Isles built a fleet of low-freeboard blockade runners, powered by the best steam engines of the day and capable of turning up 14 knots' speed. Cargoes from Europe or Canada would be trans-shipped to the runners at St. George, Bermuda, from which it was only 674 miles to Wilmington, North Carolina; or at Nassau in the Bahamas whence it was 500 miles to Charleston; or at Havana, about the same distance to Mobile. Tampico and Vera Cruz were the jumping-off places for the Rio Grande. The runners, choosing the dark of the moon, would steal through a blockading squadron to a short distance off the coast, steam in shoal water at low speed, blacked-out, until off an inlet or harbor; then pile on coal and dash in, often under cover of a Confederate fort. If pursued and shelled, they could be run ashore and the cargo salvaged; for profits were so immense that one successful voyage paid for the ship. Bermuda and the Bahamas acquired an importance they had not known since the days of the buccaneers, and a prosperity they did not recover until they became winter playgrounds for the rich.

Richard King of Texas, who had founded the fabulous King Ranch in 1853, owned a fleet of river steamboats which he promptly put under the Mexican flag; and as both sides respected neutral flags in this war, the King fleet ferried thousands of bales of cotton to Tampico and Vera Cruz with impunity; for the Confederacy in 1862 changed its "hold back cotton" policy to an "export it all" policy. At times there were over 100 merchant ships in the roadstead off the mouth of the Rio Grande, waiting to land goods and load cotton, transported thither by ox wagon over distances as great as 500 miles. The Union did not even partly close this leak until November 1863 when General Banks, in his one successful military operation, landed 7000 troops at the mouth of the Rio Grande and forced the Mexico-Texas trade upriver to Laredo. By the end of 1863 the Union had occupied every principal Gulf port of Texas except Sabine City, an attack on which by Union gunboats was gallantly defeated by one company of Texas heavy artillery; and Galveston, where a small amphibious operation was similarly routed. This Texas-Mexico border would have been a very serious leak in the blockade, but for the insoluble problem of distributing goods imported there, and corruption in getting the cotton out; Texas profiteers were enriched, but the Confederate treasury profited very little.

Although blockade running gained the South both arms and consumer goods, it never did enough, as the runners had small cargo capacity, a large part of which was taken up by expensive luxuries which could stand the freights of $300 to $1000 a ton. A runner's life was gay but short; captains were paid up to $5000 in gold for a single round trip, but on an average only four and a half trips were made before capture or running aground. The Confederate treasury department issued some phony statistics—for instance, that half a million pounds of coffee were run into Wilmington in the last ten weeks of 1864 —to prove that the blockade was ineffective. Actually it was efficient enough to weaken the Southern will to victory. Almost 100 steamships were engaged in blockade running in 1864, but early next year the number dropped to 24. The Union navy captured or destroyed 295 steamers and about 1100 row- and sail-boats trying to run the blockade, and some 40 of the fast captured steamers were armed and converted to blockaders.

The Confederacy naturally had more difficulty in improvising a navy than building an army. Secession secured it about 20 per cent of the United States naval officers, but they couldn't bring their ships with them, and outside Norfolk, which she captured on 20 April 1861, the South had no great shipbuilding center. Secretary Mallory, who had been chairman of the naval affairs committee in the United States Senate, showed great energy and ingenuity, but could not get army-minded President Davis to support him in time to count. He did build a fleet of armored gunboats, but it took eleven months to get the first (*Virginia*, ex-*Merrimack*) to sea, and she fought her famous but inconclusive Battle of Hampton Roads with U.S.S. *Monitor* (9 March 1862) too late to influence the peninsular campaign. The Confederacy was energetic and ingenious in building armored rams and gunboats to defend Southern rivers and harbors, and produced the first submarine in history to make a kill. *R. L. Hunley*, a 35-foot boat built in Mobile and requiring eight men to turn the propeller shaft, poked her single torpedo's 95-pound warhead into U.S.S. *Housatonic* off Charleston after dark on 17 February 1864, and disappeared with all hands when the Union frigate blew up and sank. These suicide tactics were not repeated. The South never managed to create an oceanic fleet, or to break the Union blockade at any point.

Owing to negligence on the part of the British government

(for which it later paid dear), powerful steam raiders were built for the Confederacy in England and, manned largely by British crews, embarked on commerce-destroying cruises. C.S.S. *Alabama* and *Florida,* counterparts to Jones's *Ranger* and Barry's *Alliance* in the War of Independence, wrought relatively greater damage than those heroes did on enemy merchant vessels; but no more than Jones and Barry did they affect the outcome of a war. The Confederacy wanted what the infant United States had from 1778 on—an ally powerful on the ocean. That, she had high hopes of obtaining from England; but after the *Trent* crisis passed, the chance of the Royal Navy supporting the Confederacy became slim indeed.

The naval war on the Mississippi and its tributaries was as important as the maritime blockade in putting the squeeze on the Confederacy. Here, Gideon Welles put the Union fleet of river gunboats under the army, and the close co-operation between Grant and Foote won the important victory of Fort Donelson early in 1862. That same year the Union navy cooperated closely with General McClellan in the peninsular campaign and got his army out; after this campaign General Lee forced the Union armies to give battle well inland, where naval guns could not support them.

Naval blockade alone has never won a war; it was the armies of Grant, Sherman, and Thomas that delivered the knockout blows to the Confederacy. But they were only able to do that after the South had been materially weakened by the blockade. Again, the similarity to Winston Churchill's strategy for defeating Germany is striking. The Civil War well illustrated Mahan's dictum, "Not by rambling operations, or naval duels, are wars decided, but by force massed and handled in skillful combination."

4. *The Peninsular Campaign, March–July 1862*

We must now return to the biggest campaign of 1862, waged on the peninsula between the York and James rivers, between the Army of the Potomac (General McClellan) and the Army of Northern Virginia (Generals Joseph Johnston, Jackson, and Lee).

"In ten days I shall be in Richmond," boasted McClellan on 13 February. He was planning a frontal advance on the Confederate capital via Fredericksburg, but when Joe Johnston anticipated him by occupying that town, he demanded another delay. This was the last straw for Lincoln. He gave the general the choice between carrying out the frontal advance, and a wide flanking movement, supported by the Union navy, to the

James. McClellan wisely chose the latter, which *Monitor*'s victory in the Battle of Hampton Roads (9 March) made practicable, even though *Virginia* still closed the mouth of the James. The President then stripped McClellan of his supreme command over all armies of the Republic, leaving him only the Army of the Potomac; and within the next few weeks Lincoln detached McDowell's corps from that army to protect Washington, and gave Frémont more troops in West Virginia than he knew how to handle. Thus McClellan was no longer a theater commander.

The Army of the Potomac, 110,000 strong, clothed in dark-blue tunics, light-blue trousers, and blunted cloth kepis, was the most formidable military force yet seen on American soil. The men were well armed, equipped, and disciplined, eager for action, devoted to their glamorous commander. At the end of March they were floated down the Potomac in 100 or more transports and landed at or near Old Point Comfort, on the York peninsula. Here they were on a classic ground of American history: Jamestown, the Chickahominy river (first explored by Captain John Smith), Williamsburg, and Yorktown. The greater part of the peninsula had reverted to forest, and even the environs of Richmond were a wilderness, broken by occasional farms and clearings. Maps were unreliable, roads few. McClellan's best chance to win Richmond was to press forward at the best speed of marching men, before summer heat set in; audacity above all was wanted. Instead, he wasted a month on siege operations against Yorktown, where there were only 16,000 rebels.

That was exactly what Joe Johnston, a cautious thrust-and-parry, mine-and-sap strategist like McClellan, wanted the Union leader to do. General Lee, now "general in charge of military operations," liked it equally well, but for another reason—to gain time to build up the Confederate army by conscription, and to get Stonewall Jackson's army down from the Shenandoah. Johnston pulled his garrison secretly out of Yorktown 4 May, covering the retreat by a rear-guard action near the old capital of Williamsburg. And for the next three weeks he and "Little Mac" played classic tactics of maneuver on the peninsula while Stonewall Jackson executed a series of swift marches and smashing victories that have secured him a place among war's immortals. He beat Frémont at McDowell in Virginia on 8 May, and then sent Banks reeling back to Winchester. Secretary Stanton, in a blue funk, recalled General McDowell's corps to defend the capital; Jackson inflicted two more defeats on Frémont and Banks on 8 and 9 June, then hastened south to join Johnston and Lee before Richmond.

In the meantime the Army of the Potomac was proceeding slowly up the York river side of the peninsula, while the Union navy under Commodore Louis M. Goldsborough USN was seizing control of the James. On 10 May Goldsborough pinched the rebels out of Norfolk and forced Commodore Tattnall CSN to destroy ironclad *Virginia*. The *Monitor* and a second ironclad now steamed up the James but were rudely checked by a Confederate battery at Drewry's Bluff, eight miles below Richmond. Goldsborough begged McClellan to shift at least part of his army James-side to help the navy silence this battery, and open a water route to Richmond; but McClellan refused to alter his set plan.

On 31 May, Johnston had his first real clash with McClellan in the Battle of Fair Oaks. It was a drawn battle, and the Confederate commander, wounded, was relieved next day by Lee, who promptly and happily named his army the Army of Northern Virginia. McClellan, still cautious, took up a strong position and waited for fair weather to advance. In the meantime Jackson was sweeping down from the Shenandoah valley, threatening McClellan's York river base at White House. On 25 June, too late, the Union commander decided to accept Goldsborough's invitation to shift base to the James. Next day Lee took the initiative and the series of actions known as the Seven Days' Battles[1] began. Therein McClellan proved himself a tactical commander second to none. "Throughout this campaign we attacked just when and where the enemy wished us to attack," wrote General D. H. Hill CSA. McClellan, outnumbered after Jackson joined Lee, conducted his left-flank maneuver with the precision of a review, inflicted superior losses on the enemy (20,614 Confederates, 15,849 Federals killed, wounded or missing), and in a chosen position on Malvern Hill, stood at bay while Lee hurled his divisions one after another over wheatfields swept by artillery and fire from Union gunboats. By the close of 2 July, while Lee withdrew his decimated legions toward Richmond, the Army of the Potomac, with wagon trains intact and morale unimpaired, was safe under the guns of the Union navy in a fortified base at Harrison's Landing on the James.

It was magnificent, and not a retreat. The Army of the Potomac was still full of fight, ready to resume the advance on Richmond when and if reinforced. The Union navy in the James was now so formidable that Lee refused to attack McClellan at Harrison's Landing. The summer was still young.

[1] Mechanicsville (26 June), Gaines's Mill (27th), Savage Station (29th), Frayser's Farm (30th), Malvern Hill (1 July).

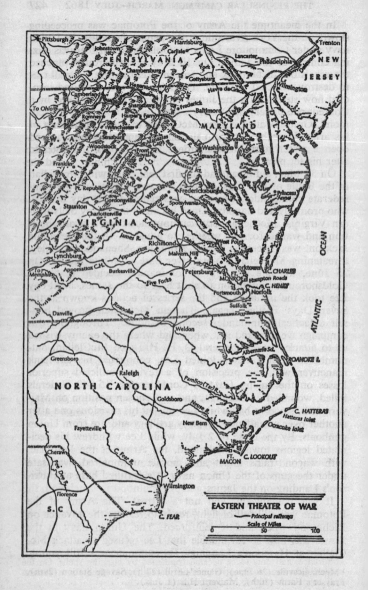

EASTERN THEATER OF WAR

— Principal railways

Scale of Miles

0   50   100

McClellan entreated Lincoln to give him an opportunity to attack Richmond via Petersburg. But General Halleck (who had replaced Stanton in control of operations) placed his clammy hand on this sound plan (which Grant adopted two years later), and Lincoln feared that the administration could no longer carry McClellan. It was not merely that performance had fallen short of promise; his dispatches during the campaign had been querulous, sometimes insolent, and once hysterical. The Committee on the Conduct of the War was clamoring for his scalp, and the autumn elections were coming up. Accordingly, on 3 August, Halleck ordered the Army of the Potomac by driblets back to its cantonments near Washington, and the navy covered and escorted its retirement by sea.

5. Interlude

The eight weeks that followed the Seven Days' Battles were pure gold for the Confederacy. Jefferson Davis and the people of Richmond enjoyed their last happy summer, confident that they had proved that the South could never be conquered. They had found a leader, Robert E. Lee—and what a leader! Fifty-five years old, tall, handsome, with graying hair and deep, expressive brown eyes which could convey with a glance a stronger reproof than any other general's oath-laden castigation; kind at heart and courteous even to those who failed him, he inspired and deserved confidence. No military leader since Napoleon has aroused such enthusiastic devotion among troops as did Lee when he reviewed them on his horse Traveller. And, what a horse!

—An iron-gray, sixteen hands high,
Short back, deep chest, strong haunch, flat legs, small head,
Delicate ear, quick eye, black mane and tail,
Wise brain, obedient mouth.[1]

Davis and Lee were masters of the situation. Thousands of replacements came pouring into Richmond. Although New Orleans was gone, Vicksburg kept Richmond in touch with the

---

[1] Stephen Vincent Benét, *John Brown's Body*, book 4, based on the general's own description. Traveller, foaled near Blue Sulphur in 1857, probably a descendant of the great Diomed, was purchased by Lee in 1861, and served as his principal mount throughout the war. He had amazing speed, frequently tiring out the horses of the staff, remarkable endurance, and only twice became frightened by bursting shells. On the second occasion, at Spotsylvania, he reared just in time for a cannon ball to pass harmlessly under his girth.

Far West; delegates from Arizona and the Indian Territory sat in the Confederate congress. Morgan's brilliant cavalry raid through Kentucky in July seemed to prove that state ripe for the plucking. There was that pesky blockade, to be sure, and prices rose daily, but four powerful ironclad rams were being built in Britain to break the blockade, and British-built C.S.S. *Alabama* now left port on a cruise that proved equally costly for the American merchant marine and the British taxpayer. The sunshine of victory was partly shaded by bickerings, characteristic of touchy "cavaliers." Robert Toombs challenged General D. H. Hill to a duel; A. P. Hill and Longstreet were not on speaking terms; there was even a cabal against Lee, who wrote to his wife before the end of July, "In the prospect before me I cannot see a single ray of pleasure during this war."

But the prospects for the Union being restored were really dim. "There is an all but unanimous belief that you *cannot* subject the South," Richard Cobden wrote to Senator Sumner when news of the Seven Days' Battles reached England. On 11 July an English M.P. introduced a motion for Franco-British mediation. It did not pass, but Napoleon III was ready to go along if Palmerston recognized the Confederacy. That summer there was a panic in Wall Street. The gold dollar reached a 17 per cent premium over paper when Congress authorized a second issue of $150 million in greenbacks. Lincoln called upon the states for 300,000 volunteers for nine months. There were patriotic rallies at which "John Brown's Body" was set to new words: "We are coming, Father Abraham, three hundred thousand more"; but fewer than 80,000 actually enlisted, and they were organized in new nine-months' regiments instead of being used like Confederate conscripts as permanent replacements.

"Old Brains" Halleck, now Lee's opposite number, decided to try the original plan for 1862, a frontal advance from Washington on Richmond. To execute this, General John Pope, hero of Island No. 10, was summoned from the West to command a new army, composed in part of the veterans of the peninsula. Pope, with a stern countenance and great black beard, looked more like a great general than anyone in either army, but had slight military ability and less common sense. His first act on taking command was to issue an extraordinary set of orders to his men, contrasting their lack of success with his in the West, "where we have always seen the backs of our enemies." To the press he proclaimed, "My headquarters will be in the saddle!" Lincoln, on reading this, remarked, "A better place for his hindquarters."

Pope in mid-August began to concentrate along the Rappahannock, covering both Washington and the point on the

Potomac to which McClellan's army was being rapidly transferred. Lee adopted a plan amazing in its audacity: to divide his army in the face of a far more numerous enemy, send Jackson by a circuitous route round Pope's right to attack the Union base at Manassas Junction, draw Pope away from his line of concentration, and fall upon him in the open.

On 26 August Jackson's "foot cavalry," having marched 50 miles in 36 hours, were between Pope and Washington, reveling in the Union stores at Manassas. Halleck and Pope, unprepared for this bold maneuver, made one blunder after another. Pope won the race with Lee to the old Bull Run battlefield, but, incapable of handling large numbers of men, and bewildered by attacks from unexpected quarters, was badly defeated in the Second Battle of Bull Run, or Manassas (29–30 August 1862). It was the neatest, cleanest piece of work that Lee and Jackson ever performed. Their irresistible combination of audacious strategy and perfect tactics had undone the Union gains of an entire year in the Virginia theater of the war. "Dark days are upon us. Pope, a lying braggart—has been driven into Washington. . . . The rebels again look upon the dome of the capitol," wrote Gustavus Fox at this crisis, "and the flag of disunion can be seen on the neighboring hills."

General Halleck, confounded by the rapid movements of the last few days, sat in the war department, perpetually rubbing his elbows and gazing with watery eyes at a mounting pile of dispatches. One bright thought came, to bring back McClellan, to his old command. On 1 September, as the news from the front became more and more alarming, McClellan conferred with Halleck and the President. Early next morning Lincoln, without consulting anyone, placed McClellan in "command of the fortifications of Washington, and of all the troops for the defense of the capital." The general at once rode out to meet Pope's retreating army, and to witness the wild enthusiasm that his presence always inspired among the troops.

In the meantime Lincoln had faced a tough cabinet meeting. Stanton and Chase vehemently opposed McClellan, and all but Seward and Blair concurred. Lincoln admitted most of their allegations but pointed out that no one else had the confidence of officers and men, or the ability to cope with so desperate a situation. "In stating what he had done," wrote Gideon Welles, "the President was deliberate, but firm and decisive. His language and manner were kind and affectionate, especially toward two of the members who were greatly disturbed; but every person present felt that he was truly the chief, and every one knew his decision, though mildly expressed, was as fixed and unalterable as if given out with the imperious command and determined will of Andrew Jackson."

Lincoln had attained new stature. Resolute in purpose and sure of vision he had always been; yet often vacillating and uncertain in performance. From those anxious vigils at the White House during the terrible summer of 1862 the perplexed, over-advised, and humble Lincoln emerged humble before God, but the master of men. He seemed to have captured all the greater qualities of the great Americans who preceded him, without their defects: the poise of Washington without his aloofness, the mental audacity of Hamilton without his insolence, the astuteness of Jefferson without his indirection, the conscience of John Quincy Adams without his harshness, the courage of Jackson without his irascibility, the magnetism of Clay without his vanity, the lucidity of Webster without his ponderousness; and fused them with a sincerity and magnanimity that were peculiarly his.

When, on 5 September, news reached Washington that Lee was crossing the Potomac at Sharpsburg above Harper's Ferry, Lincoln orally gave McClellan "command of the forces in the field."

6. Antietam and Emancipation

Of many crises for the Union, this was the most acute. General Lee, having persuaded President Davis to countenance a bold offensive, had decided to invade Maryland and Pennsylvania. If he could capture Harrisburg, there would be no railroad communication between Eastern cities and the West; he would cut the loyal states in two, as Burgoyne had attempted to do with the rebel states when he marched south from Canada in 1777. Additional objectives were food, shoes, clothing, of which northern Virginia had been swept clean, and to persuade Maryland, whose "dalliance does thee wrong," as the sentimental war song charged, to clothe her "beauteous limbs with steel" and "be the battle queen of yore."

Lee, counting on McClellan taking weeks to reorganize, ventured to divide the Army of Northern Virginia, sending Jackson to capture Harper's Ferry while he moved into Pennsylvania. But, within a week of Manassas, McClellan was marching on Frederick Town with 70,000 men, followed by frantic telegrams from Halleck to turn back and protect Washington. But McClellan kept on, reassured by picking up on 13 September a copy of Lee's plan of the campaign, dropped by some careless aide.

South Mountain, as the Blue Ridge is called where it crosses

Maryland, now separated the hostile armies. Sending his van to force the passes, McClellan sat his horse Dan as in review by the roadside, pointing to where clouds of smoke showed that the Battle of South Mountain had begun. Men and officers as they passed cheered themselves hoarse, falling out of ranks to touch his leg, pat his charger and cry, "God bless you, Little Mac!" That day (14 September) South Mountain was carried. "I thought I knew McClellan, but this movement of his puzzles me," exclaimed his West Point classmate, Stonewall Jackson. Lee knew exactly what it meant, and hastened south just in time to prevent McClellan's interposing between his great lieutenant and himself. They joined on 16 September, but even so the Army of Northern Virginia was not only outnumbered but caught in a cramped position between Antietam Creek and the Potomac, where Lee had no room to perform those brilliant maneuvers that were his delight and the enemy's confusion. He had no alternative but to fight or to retreat, and he chose to fight.

The Battle of the Antietam, or Sharpsburg (17 September 1862) was a series of desperate, uncoordinated attacks and equally desperate but skillful counterattacks that exhausted Lee's army but did not force it to retire. It was one of the bloodiest battles of the war. Of about 36,000 Confederates engaged, 10,700 were casualties, and three general officers were among the killed; of 87,000 troops under McClellan, only about half of whom were engaged, he lost 12,410. Although fresh reserves were available, McClellan refused to renew the battle next day, as Grant or Sherman would certainly have done. So Lee recrossed the Potomac into Virginia on the night of 18 September. The crisis was ended. Nevertheless, "Antietam's cannon long shall boom," as Herman Melville prophesied. The Union victory averted foreign recognition of Confederate independence; and by giving Lincoln the opportunity he sought to issue the Emancipation Proclamation, it brought the liberal opinion of the world to his side.

During the summer of 1862 the British government moved fast, impelled by many motives—desire to relieve unemployment before winter, a humane wish to stop the carnage, upper-class dislike of democracy, belief that the Confederacy was invincible. Napoleon III was eager to join. The British government's failure to prevent *Alabama* slipping out to sea from Liverpool in July was a hint of this change of policy. Palmerston wrote to his foreign minister on 14 September, "Washington or Baltimore may fall into the hands of the Confederates"; and Russell replied on the very day of Antietam, "I agree with you that the time is come for offering mediation to the United

States government with a view to the recognition of the independence of the Confederates. I agree, further, that in the case of failure, we ought ourselves to recognize the Southern States as an independent state."

The news of Antietam caused Palmerston to cool off; and although Gladstone, chancellor of the exchequer, in a speech on 7 October (which later he took great pains to explain away) declared that Jefferson Davis had "made a nation," and that the Northern people "have not yet drunk of the cup which the rest of the world sees they nevertheless must drink," Britain moved not.

On the heels of the news that Lee had retreated into Virginia came the Emancipation Proclamation. Lincoln, with his uncanny sense of timing, chose the week after Antietam to issue this famous document. His policy as to slavery had been stated in his famous Letter to Horace Greeley; but only a delicate perception of public opinion, and an accurate weighing of imponderabilia, could decide what action respecting the Negro would serve the Union best at a given time. Steps had been taken before Antietam. From the first advance into Confederate territory, slaves of rebel owners flocked into the Union lines, embarrassing both government and commanders, until the irrepressible Benjamin F. Butler declared them "contraband of war." The "contrabands" were then organized in labor battalions, and welfare workers were provided to look after them in the several occupied portions of the Southern coast where they congregated.

Loyal slave states had to be considered. Delaware, Maryland, Kentucky, West Virginia, and Missouri, sensitive on the subject, blocked proposals for compensated emancipation on which the President had set his heart. In April and June 1862 Congress carried out a Republican party pledge by abolishing slavery in the District of Columbia and the territories. Another long step was taken in the Confiscation Act of 12 July 1862 declaring "contrabands" and slaves of convicted rebels to be forever free, and authorizing the President to recruit blacks for the army. Lincoln signed this bill only after it had been so modified as to make its application discretionary with him; for the President's war powers were involved. Lincoln rightly insisted on his exclusive power, as commander in chief of the army and navy, to decree a general emancipation in enemy territory. If Congress were able to wrest this power from him it might also dictate his war policy, and—what he feared most of all—impose a vindictive peace.

An even larger question intruded: of what avail to restore the Union if slavery, the original cause of disruption, remained? "The moment came," said Lincoln, "when I felt that slavery must die that the nation might live," when he hearkened to "the groaning of the children of Israel, whom the Egyptians keep in bondage" (Exodus vi.5). In the cabinet meeting of 22 July he proposed to proclaim that on next New Year's Day all slaves in rebel territory would be free. Seward pointed out that such a declaration at that time would be interpreted as "our last shriek on the retreat" from Richmond. Lincoln saw the point, and put aside the proclamation, on which he had been working nights, to be a crown to the next Union victory. Then, on 22 September, five days after Antietam, Lincoln opened a cabinet meeting by reading a completely irrelevant passage from the humorist Artemus Ward—his method of putting the cabinet in a receptive mind. He then turned serious. He had not summoned them for their advice. He had made a covenant with God to free the slaves as soon as the rebels were driven out of Maryland; God had decided on the field of Antietam. His mind was fixed, his decision made. In the preliminary Emancipation Proclamation, published next day, the President, by virtue of his power as commander in chief of the army and navy, declared that upon 1 January 1863 all slaves within any state then in rebellion against the United States, "shall be, then, thenceforward, and forever free."

This proclamation, more revolutionary in human relationships than any event in American history since 1776, lifted the Civil War to the dignity of a crusade. Yet it actually freed not one slave, since it applied only to rebel states where it could not be enforced. The loyal slave states, occupied New Orleans, and occupied parts of Virginia were excepted.[1] The South, indignant at what she considered an invitation to the slaves to cut their masters' throats, was nerved to greater effort; for it meant that only a Southern victory would prevent unconditional surrender. The Northern armies received from it no new impetus. The Democratic party, presenting it to the Northern people as proof that abolitionists were responsible for the duration of the war, gained seats in the autumn elections. A large section of the press, in the United States and Canada, adopted a cynical and sneering attitude toward the Proclamation. It remained for Emerson, as usual, to strike the tuning fork of the future, when at a celebration in Boston of Emancipation Day he declaimed:

Today unbind the captive

[1] Slavery was abolished by state action in West Virginia in 1863, in Maryland in 1864, in Missouri and Tennessee in 1865, and in Delaware and Kentucky the same year by Amendment XIII to the Constitution.

> So only are ye unbound;
> Lift up a people from the dust,
> Trump of their rescue, sound!

In England and Europe generally, the Proclamation was hailed with joy by liberals and radicals. By degrees public opinion at home and abroad came to perceive that the Union cause had been definitely fused with that of human liberty. Pro-Union meetings were held in several English cities. One meeting of 6000 workingmen at Manchester resolved:

> The erasure of that foul blot upon civilization and Christianity—chattel slavery—during your Presidency will cause the name of Abraham Lincoln to be honoured and revered by posterity. Accept our high admiration of your firmness in upholding the proclamation of freedom.

To which Lincoln replied:

> I know and deeply deplore the sufferings which the working men at Manchester, and in all Europe are called to endure in this crisis. . . . I cannot but regard your decisive utterances upon the question as an instance of sublime Christian heroism which has not been surpassed in any age or in any country. . . . I hail this interchange of sentiment, therefore, as an augury that whatever else may happen, whatever misfortune may befall your country or my own, the peace and friendship which now exist between the two nations will be, as it shall be my desire to make them, perpetual.

Emancipation created so strong a feeling abroad in favor of the North that neither England nor France dared take a step toward recognizing Confederate independence; and those elements who dearly wished for it had to admit that Antietam rendered the winning of that independence very unlikely—unless (a big "if") the North grew tired of the struggle.

7. Fredericksburg

After the Battle of Antietam the Army of Northern Virginia retreated up the Shenandoah valley. "The absent are scattered broadcast over the land," Lee wrote to the secretary of war on 23 September. "Unless something is done, the army will melt away." And the invasion of Kentucky, too, had proved disappointing; "We must abandon the garden spot of Kentucky to its cupidity," wrote General Braxton Bragg on 25 September. Two weeks later, Don Carlos Buell won a Western Antietam, at Perryville, and Bragg abandoned not only Kentucky but most of Tennessee.

General McClellan now reverted to "the slows." Instead of pursuing Lee, or following Lincoln's good advice to try to beat Lee to Richmond "on the inside track," the general demanded more supplies, clothing, and remounts before he would move. The prospect of another winter of bickering and procrastination was more than Lincoln thought the Union cause could bear. He decided that if McClellan permitted Lee to get between himself and Richmond, McClellan must go. On 26 October the Army of the Potomac began to invade Virginia. Lee promptly moved Longstreet's corps athwart its path, and on 7 November the President relieved McClellan, this time for keeps. It may well be argued that this was a mistake; that "Young Napoleon" was growing up at last, that nothing could have been worse than sending the Army of the Potomac to fruitless sacrifice under its new commander, General Ambrose E. Burnside.

But nobody could have imagined how incompetent Burnside would prove to be. A handsome West Pointer and Mexican War veteran, he had handled the Hatteras Inlet invasion well, and his corps at Antietam had rushed the bloody "Burnside bridge" against Hill, one of the crucial attacks in that battle. It is not unusual in war for an officer competent on one echelon to be a failure on the one next higher. The captain of a battleship may prove to be incapable of handling a task force, a division commander may be no good when placed over an army corps, and so on. Burnside, to do him justice, didn't want the new command, felt inadequate; but he went in and did his best, which unfortunately was very bad indeed.

Burnside decided to mass his army behind the Rappahannock opposite Fredericksburg, and thence advance on Richmond. Lee and Jackson hastened across northern Virginia and had some 75,000 men posted on the south bank before Burnside had obtained pontoons to cross the river. "The luxurious Army of the Potomac, petted to bursting, is no match in celerity of movement to the famished freezing soldiers of Lee," wrote Gustavus V. Fox. Lee took his stand on the wooded heights above Fredericksburg. There, on 13 December, he met an attack by Burnside's army of 113,000 that presented the most inspiring spectacle and the most useless slaughter of the Civil War. With insane stupidity Burnside refused to make flank attacks through the forest, but delivered a frontal attack across open ground. Six times the Union infantry—long double lines of blue, bright national and regimental colors, bayonets gleaming in the sun—pressed on across a bare plain, completely swept by the Confederate artillery and entrenched infantry, to the stone wall at the foot of Marye's Heights. Six times the survivors were hurled back, leaving thousands of killed and wounded lying literally in heaps. "It is well that war is so terrible," said Lee as he watched the battle, "or we should grow too fond of it."

On 15 December Lee consented to a brief truce to bury the dead and relieve such wounded as had survived the day. Here the horror of the Brothers' War could be seen at its most horrible. According to an eye-witness, Randolph A. Shotwell:

> Eleven hundred dead bodies—perfectly naked—swollen to twice the natural size—black as Negroes in most cases—lying in every conceivable posture—some on their backs with gaping jaws—some with eyes large as walnuts, protruding with glassy stare—some doubled up like a contortionist—here one without a head—there one without legs—yonder a head and legs without a trunk—everywhere horrible expressions—fear, rage, agony, madness, torture—lying in pools of blood—lying with heads half buried in mud—with fragments of shell sticking in the oozing brain—with bullet holes all over the puffed limbs.

Four-fifths of them were victims of the deadly minié bullet; the rest, of the Confederate artillery. Total losses were 12,653 for the Union, 5309 for the Confederacy. On almost any other continent, to any European or Asiatic army, Fredericksburg would have been a knockout; but not here. Burnside retired beyond the Rappahannock and Lee wrote to his wife, "The battle did not go far enough to satisfy me. . . . The contest will have now to be renewed, but on what field I cannot say." That was the dispiriting thing about the Southern cause—no matter how often or how badly the Confederates whipped a Union army, Lincoln refused to admit defeat.

Walt Whitman, who too was there, recorded,

> That never did mortal man in an aggregate fight better than our troops at Fredericksburg. In the highest sense it was no failure. The main body troops descending the hills on the Falmouth side to cross the pontoon bridge could plainly see, over back of Fredericksburg, the Secesh batteries rising in tremendous force and plenty on the terrace required to our men's crossing . . . and also the flats thick with their rifle pits. . . . Nearer view on Saturday, the day

of the fight, made everything still more ominous to our side. But still the men advanced with unsurpassed gallantry —and would have gone further, if ordered.

Thus the year 1862 closed for the Union in gloom, and for thinking men in the Confederacy, without much hope. The Northern congressional elections increased the Democratic delegation; defeatist Democrats were elected governors of New York and Pennsylvania. Lincoln confided to a friend on 19 December, "We are now on the brink of destruction."

Yet, looking back, one can see that the Union cause had come out of its slough. The year 1862 in the Civil War corresponded to 1942 in World War II—"the end of the beginning," to use Winston Churchill's phrase. The danger of foreign intervention had passed; the Confederacy would never have a maritime ally; the anaconda squeezed ever tighter. Numbers, immigration (84,000 from Europe alone in 1862, double next year), industrial organization, were beginning to count. The Union army had been tried in battle and found not wanting in valor; only generals competent to match wits and skill with Lee and Jackson had not yet been found. Lincoln was master in his own house. If the Northern will to victory and devotion to union could endure, the end could not longer be in doubt. People might sneer at the Emancipation Proclamation, but it gave the cause the dignity of a crusade. Julia Ward Howe, in the darkness of her tent after viewing "the watchfires of a hundred circling camps," scribbled down the words in which she caught the new spirit, and which were to be sung to the stirring cadence of "John Brown's Body":

BATTLE HYMN OF THE REPUBLIC

He has sound - ed forth the trump - et that shall

nev - er call re - treat; He is sift - ing out the hearts of men be -

fore His Judge-ment Seat; Oh! be swift my soul to ans - wer Him, be -

ju - bi - lant my feet! Our God is march - ing on.

XXI

At Home and Abroad

1861-1865

1. *Internal Politics, North and South*

LINCOLN WIELDED a greater power throughout the war than any other President of the United States prior to Franklin D. Roosevelt; a wider authority than any British ruler between Cromwell and Churchill. Contemporary accusations against him of tyranny and despotism read strangely to those who know his character, but not to students of his administration. Lincoln came near to being the ideal tyrant of whom Plato dreamed, yet nonetheless he was a dictator from the standpoint of American constitutional law. Jefferson Davis is open to the same charge. And on both sides there were many men of high standing who preferred to risk defeat at the hands of the enemy rather than submit to arbitrary government.

At the beginning of the war, Lincoln as commander in chief of the army and navy called for enlistments not yet sanctioned by Congress, declared a blockade, and suspended the writ of habeas corpus in parts of Maryland. The first assumption of power was quickly made legal by Congress and the second by the Supreme Court; but Chief Justice Taney protested in vain against executive suspension of the famous writ (ex parte *Merryman*). Lincoln refused to indulge a meticulous reverence for the Constitution when the Union was crumbling. As he put it in his message of 4 July 1861, "Are all the laws but one to go unexecuted, and the government itself go to pieces, lest that one be violated?" But the power he asserted was grossly abused by some army officers. A loyal mayor of Baltimore, suspected of Southern sympathies, was arrested and confined in a fortress for over a year; a Maryland judge who had charged a grand jury to inquire into illegal acts of government officials was set upon by a provost marshal's guard while his court was in session, beaten, dragged bleeding from the bench, and imprisoned for six months; and there were many like incidents.

Simultaneously with the Emancipation Proclamation, Lincoln issued an order that seemed to deny white citizens the liberty that he proposed to accord to blacks. He proclaimed that all persons resisting the draft, discouraging enlistment, or "guilty of any disloyal practice affording aid and comfort to rebels" would be subject to martial law, tried by the military, and denied the writ of habeas corpus. Under this proclamation, over 13,000 persons were arrested and confined by military authority, for offenses ranging from theft of government property to treason. Earlier in 1862, and only a few days after he had denounced Lincoln's tyranny, President Davis obtained from his congress the power to suspend the writ of habeas corpus, and promptly did so in Richmond and other places, where equally arbitrary and unjust proceedings occurred.

Undoubtedly the provocation was great, especially in the North, where opposition to the war was open, organized, and active. For instance, the Laconia (New Hampshire) *Democrat* attacked Lincoln and the war with a virulence equal to that of the most rabid Southern newspaper. This journal urged that Democratic Northern states combine with the Southern, toss out Lincoln with the Constitution, and adopt that of the Confederacy, "rather than submit to have the country divided and ruined to carry out the . . . selfrighteous nigger abstractions of a set of ignorant and hypocritical fanatics of New England." A religious sect, the Osgoodites, regarded the Lincoln administration as the Beast of the Book of Revelation, and sang a hymn beginning, "The Lincoln party made the war, we know."

One of the most delicate and difficult subjects with which both presidents had to deal was the peace movement. Many sincere people on both sides believed that the Union could be restored, or Southern independence established, by negotiation; that only the obstinacy of Lincoln or the ambition of Davis stood in the way of peace. The "copperheads," as the Northern defeatists were called, held a mass meeting in Lincoln's home town on 17 June 1863, which resolved "that a further offensive prosecution of this war tends to subvert the Constitution and the Government." In North Carolina over 100 peace meetings were held within two months after Gettysburg, to promote negotiations for reunion. On both sides the defeatists organized secret societies. In the Middle West "Knights of the Golden Circle" harassed loyal households by midnight raids and barn-burnings; in the South "Heroes of America" gave aid and comfort to the Union. Neither government made any systematic effort to suppress these organizations: they were too formidable.

In Ohio, Indiana, and Illinois, where treason flourished side by side with the most stalwart loyalty, General Burnside attempted repression in 1863 with slight success. In a general order he declared, "The habit of declaring sympathy for the enemy will not be allowed in this department." For violating this order in a campaign speech, the most prominent copperhead, Clement L. Vallandigham, was arrested, tried by a military tribunal, and sentenced to confinement for the duration of the war. Lincoln humorously altered the sentence to banishment within the military lines of the Confederacy, whither Vallandigham was escorted in May 1863.[1] But it took more than that to silence Vallandigham. After assuring Jefferson Davis that if the South could hold out another year the Northern Democrats "would sweep the Lincoln dynasty out of political existence," he made his way to Canada, received *in absentia* the Democratic nomination for governor of Ohio, conducted a peace campaign from Canadian soil, and returned in time to draft the defeatist plank in the Democratic platform of 1864.

After the war was over the Supreme Court took cognizance of a case of arbitrary arrest and court-martial (ex parte *Milligan*), and declared that neither the Constitution nor any stretch of the President's war powers sanctioned the military trial of a civilian in districts where civil courts were open. This decision came too late to help anybody. Yet, on the whole, defeatists, conscientious objectors, the hostile press, and violent critics of the government, fared better under the Lincoln regime than under those of Woodrow Wilson and Franklin D. Roosevelt. Throughout the Civil War active disloyalty was effectively dealt with wherever it raised its head; but there was no general censorship of the press, no "relocation" of suspects; and discussion of leaders and war aims remained open, unrestrained and often ill-informed, libelous, and nasty. Sentences of courts-

---

[1] Vallandigham's declaration that "he did not want to belong to the United States" prompted Edward Everett Hale to write *The Man Without a Country*. This piece of fiction, which appeared in the *Atlantic* in December 1863, was widely republished, and did more to stimulate patriotism than any other wartime writing.

martial were comparatively mild, and offenders were pardoned with the coming of peace.

In the Confederacy there were no organized political parties, but Vice President Alexander H. Stephens of Georgia came very close to an opposition leader. Endowed with a superior mind, Stephens made several wise statements about the war; but in his loyalty to political abstractions he resembled John Randolph of Roanoke, and his thin body, falsetto voice, and waspish speech suggested that he suffered under a similar disability. Stephens hated the war, hated Davis, and hated Richmond, so much so that he absented himself for 18 months from his official post as president of the senate. Stephens conducted a campaign against the government for subverting the liberty it was supposed to protect, and encouraged state governors to resist conscription. This sniping campaign was directed by Linton Stephens, a member of the Georgia house of representatives, who went so far as to write to his brother in October 1863 that President Davis was "a little conceited, hypocritical, sniveling, canting, malicious, ambitious, dogged knave and fool." The Stephenses worked hand-in-glove with Governor Joseph E. Brown of Georgia, who obstructed the Confederate conscription laws in many ways and by 1864 had brought his state to a mental condition akin to open revolt. Barnwell Rhett of South Carolina, the original secessionist, even planned a convention of the states to depose Davis.

Governor Zebulon B. Vance of North Carolina was another sharp thorn in Davis's side. He not only withheld troops from the Confederate service but did his best to retain for the North Carolina regiments all the uniforms manufactured in his state, and to take the pick of all supplies that entered Wilmington through the blockade. He had a bitter controversy with Davis over C.S.S. *Tallahassee,* a converted blockade runner which slipped in and out of Wilmington in 1864 to destroy merchant vessels. On one of her visits to her home port, the captain of *Tallahassee* filled his bunkers with steam coal which Vance wanted for a state-owned blockade runner. Vance accused Davis of hamstringing operations which would have relieved his people of their misery, in order to fuel a Confederate raider that only destroyed "a few smacks." Davis, when the Confederacy was on its last legs, had to report this silly controversy to the Confederate congress, and explain that the "insignificant smacks" were forty-six ships, nineteen of them square-rigged.

General Bragg, a few other Confederate commanders, and the governor of Texas, declared martial law in 1862, but President Davis revoked these orders as unwarranted assumptions of power. Nevertheless provost marshals infested the South, demanding passports, credentials, and loyalty oaths from all who excited their attention or suspicion. A more general subject of Southern discontent was the impressment of supplies for the army by the commissary department, when farmers refused to sell for Confederate money. This practice stripped many a Southern farm of corn and livestock; then Sherman's "bummers" came along and took the poultry too.

In the face of frequent, acrid, and unreasonable attacks, Davis maintained an admirable patience. He could be acid and querulous when commenting on Union acts and policies; but to his own people, no matter how great the provocation, he was always the high-minded, courteous gentleman.

2. *Troubled Waters*

In Europe the movement for mediation in the Civil War, which implied recognition of the Confederacy, raised its head again in the first half of 1863, before Gettysburg and Vicksburg. Recognition of the Southern Confederacy would have made no practical difference, since all maritime powers respected the Union blockade. The United States and Great Britain in the last fifty years have recognized many small nations in Europe, Asia, and Africa, which have been snuffed out without either country doing anything to protect them. But a *de jure* recognition of Southern independence would have been a prestige victory of immense value, and the two principal Confederate agents in Europe, Mason and Slidell, pursued it vigorously by press subvention, personal interviews, and by selling Confederate bonds, which established a financial interest in Southern victory.[1] Mason, a provincial Virginian, made little headway in London, partly owing to his constant chewing of tobacco and letting the juice slobber over his chin and shirt. Slidell, a clever and subtle manipulator of men and money, found a sympathetic milieu in the somewhat raffish group which surrounded Napoleon III, and was even invited to dine at the Tuileries. But one needed a longer spoon than Slidell possessed to sup with "Napoleon the Little." He would gladly have recognized the South, but owing to many European commitments, and his wish to cultivate liberal opinion in France, he dared not do so without British support. And of that there was never a chance after the Emancipation Proclamation. So

[1] In Britain a Confederate loan of over £2 million, and in France an even bigger one, was floated, with cotton (to be delivered after the war) as security; and a large part of the domestic Confederate loan also was taken up by British investors.

the Emperor's note to his ambassador in London in June 1863, to the effect that the time had come to recognize the Confederacy if the Union refused mediation, fell on barren ground.

Napoleon's Mexican adventure dictated his favoring the Confederacy as much as he dared. This adventure stemmed from a joint British, French, and Spanish naval demonstration before Vera Cruz to force the Juárez government to pay its foreign debts. Britain and Spain withdrew in April 1862 after discovering that Napoleon III intended to make the debts an excuse for taking over the country. Napoleon then poured some 30,000 troops into Mexico, who entered Mexico City in June 1863 and set up a puppet government which chose Maximilian, a young Austrian archduke, as emperor.

Here was a new problem for Lincoln and Seward. Napoleon's intrusion of monarchy into Mexico was obnoxious in 1863 as, a century later, the intrusion of communism into Cuba, and equally a violation of the Monroe Doctrine; but they could do nothing about it but protest. Napoleon III was trying to do what Talleyrand and George Canning had attempted unsuccessfully, to extend the European balance-of-power system to America. Before Maximilian left Europe to assume his uneasy crown, he became the focus of a series of odd intrigues and shady deals. Napoleon persuaded him to turn over the Mexican states of Sonora and Lower California to France to exploit, retaining only nominal Mexican sovereignty, in return for more French aid; but Maximilian, after arriving in Mexico (May 1864), found this proposition so distasteful to his new subjects that he refused to honor it. Former Senator Gwin of California, who had defected to the South, tried to sell Napoleon a project to set up under his protection a colony of Confederate refugees and sympathizers in the states of Sonora, Chihuahua, Durango, and Taumalipas. The French emperor was favorable, but the Mexican emperor would have none of it. There is also a tradition (for which no substantial evidence can be found) that when the Confederacy was *in extremis* a Southern agent, claiming to act for President Davis, offered to cede Texas to France in return for recognition. However that may be, something equally crazy was seriously proposed to Jefferson Davis by the veteran journalist Francis Preston Blair in January 1865. He would reunite North and South on the basis of a joint crusade, spearheaded by the Confederate army under Davis's personal command, to overthrow Maximilian and restore the Republic to Mexico.

Spain's attitude, too, was important, as she still held Cuba and Puerto Rico, and had a respectable navy. The Spanish government at the outset of the Civil War was in the hands of an ambitious premier, General Don Leopold O'Donnell, duke of Tetuan. Although he followed England and France in declaring neutrality and closing Spanish ports to prize ships, O'Donnell did a little fishing for Spain in the troubled waters of the Caribbean. Shortly before the firing on Fort Sumter, General Don Pedro Santana of the Dominican Republic endeavored to end the civil war in that unhappy land by offering to return it to Spain; O'Donnell accepted for his queen (and mistress) Isabella II, who made Santana her viceroy and awarded him a Spanish marquisate. Here was an even more spectacular violation of the Monroe Doctrine, about which Lincoln's government was unable to do anything but protest. In Santo Domingo the harshness and stupidity of Spanish rule defeated itself, a republican rebellion against the Spaniards erupted in 1863, O'Donnell's ministry fell, Spain agreed to withdraw her garrison early in 1865, and by the time Lee surrendered the Dominican Republic was restored.

One curious semi-diplomatic incident of the war was the simultaneous appearance of two Imperial Russian fleets in New York and San Francisco. Northerners took this to be a pro-Union demonstration, earnest of the Czar's intention to fight on their side if England or France helped the South. The Russion naval officers (one of whom was the composer Rimsky-Korsakoff) were entertained to capacity; but all that this visit signified was the Russian government's desire to have fleets at sea in case England went to war to help Poland, then in the midst of one of her many tragic rebellions.

A far greater menace to the Union than recognition, or fishing in American waters, was the building of warships for the Confederacy in British and French ports. After James D. Bulloch, Confederate navy agent in England, had hoodwinked the British foreign office and got C.S.S. *Alabama* and *Florida* out to sea, he made contracts with the Laird shipyard at Liverpool for two powerful double-turret seagoing ironclads, which were to be hurled against the Union blockading fleet. Charles Francis Adams, American minister at the Court of St. James's, frequently called Lord Russell's attention to the unneutral destination of the Laird rams (as these vessels were called), but not until 3 September 1863, after the meaning of Gettysburg and Vicksburg had sunk in, were they detained. The Royal Navy subsequently purchased them, and they became H.M.S. *Scorpion* and *Wyvern*. Another ironclad fleet was being constructed for the Confederacy at Nantes and Bordeaux, Slidell having been given the official wink that Napoleon III would not interfere provided the destination were kept secret. A clerk whom the shipbuilders had fired tipped off the United States legation, which protested vehemently; and in February 1864, when the Emperor's confidence in Confederate victory had been shaken, he compelled the sale of these six ironclads to foreign powers. Bulloch succeeded in buying back one from Denmark, but as C.S.S *Stonewall* she had only reached Cuba when the war ended.

In the meantime, *Florida* and *Alabama* had been romping around the Atlantic destroying almost every American merchantman they encountered. *Alabama* (Captain Raphael Semmes), most famous and successful of the Confederate commerce destroyers, with Southern officers and a British crew, even made an incursion into the Indian Ocean and sank a number of American ships pursuing the India and China trade. Her total score was 64 vessels, all but ten burned. The Union navy finally caught up with her in the shape of U.S.S. *Kearsarge*, Captain John S. Winslow, who took station outside the port of Cherbourg, waiting for the raider to sortie, as Semmes had threatened to do. On a beautiful Sunday in June, as Captain Winslow was reading divine service on the quarterdeck, a lookout reported the *Alabama's* masts pricking up over the horizon. Winslow with prayerbook in hand ordered his men to battle stations, closed to half a mile, and opened fire. The two ships fought broadside to broadside for 90 minutes. They were evenly matched in weight of metal, but Winslow's superior gunnery sank the Confederate cruiser before *Kearsarge* was seriously damaged.

Florida (Captain J. N. Maffitt) managed to run the blockade in and out of Mobile, and converted a couple of her prizes to armed cruisers which, in June 1863, raised havoc among fishing vessels in the Gulf of Maine. They burned all their captures except the Gloucester fisherman *Archer*, to which Lieutenant C. W. Read CSN transferred his armament and crew. Entering Portland, Maine, at night, Read surprised, boarded, and captured U.S. revenue cutter *Caleb Cushing* and in her put to sea. Before the cutter had a chance to operate under the Stars and Bars, she was cornered by a couple of sidewheel passenger boats commanded by the mayor of Portland, with soldiers and fieldpieces on board. Read abandoned and burned *Caleb*, surrendering to the mayor in steamer *Chesapeake*, whose adventurous war career had just begun.

An Indiana copperhead named Braine, with about fifteen fellow conspirators, some of them Canadian, took passage in *Chesapeake* on her regular New York-Portland run in December 1863, overpowered the crew and captured the ship, intending to take her to Bermuda for conversion to a Confederate privateer. After a game of hide-and-seek with Union patrol vessels along the Nova Scotia coast, she was captured inside the three-mile limit and towed by U.S.S. *Dacotah* into Halifax harbor. This "Second *Chesapeake* Affair" (with reference to 1807) was potentially as explosive as the *Trent* business, but Secretary Seward and the British minister in Washington handled it admirably, and the steamer was awarded by the vice-admiralty court at Halifax to her proper owner. Braine tried several similar exploits in the Caribbean, and his career as an international pirate continued for another half-century.

As the destruction of fishing schooners by *Florida*'s prizes indicates, the Confederate navy had adopted a policy similar to Grossadmiral Doenitz's integral tonnage doctrine in World War II. It mattered not what enemy ships you destroyed or where, so long as you made a score; if pursuit became too hot in one area, you moved to another. In pursuance of this dubious naval strategy, C.S.S. *Florida* was ordered to the Pacific Ocean in 1864, to prey on American whale ships. When she was coaling at Bahia, that port was raided by U.S.S. *Wachusett* (Commander Napoleon Collins), who captured *Florida* and towed her to Hampton Roads. Brazil protested and Secretary Welles promised to return the raider; but before he could do so, she was "accidentally" rammed and sunk. C.S.S. *Shenandoah*, last of the raiders, now performed *Florida*'s original mission around Cape Horn, and continued (for want of orders to the contrary) to destroy defenseless whale ships for several months after the war was over.

The Confederate navy, with only a handful of commerce raiders, destroyed 257 vessels, about 5 per cent of the Union merchant fleet—only two of them steamers—but caused over 100 more to be transferred to neutral flags. It probably inflicted more relative damage than the German surface raiders in the two world wars. All this destruction, however, was senseless, and the Confederacy could have used its limited resources to better advantage elsewhere. There is no more striking example in history of the uselessness of a third-rate navy, and the folly of trying to beat a maritime nation by mere commerce destroying.

Relations between Canada and the United States became touchy again in 1863. "Skedadlers," as Union draft dodgers were called, took refuge in Canada, Confederate prisoners escaped thither from prisons along the northern border, and Davis sent several well-heeled Confederate agents to Montreal and Quebec, seeking opportunities for mischief. On the other hand, about 5000 Canadians were recruited for the Union army. With some 15,000 Confederates and active Southern sympathizers in Canada, a tense situation arose, the reverse of that during the Canadian rebellion of 1837. A Confederate plot to seize U.S.S. *Michigan*, the single-gun American warship on Lake Erie, and liberate Confederate prisoners in a camp on Johnson Island off Sandusky, was thwarted in November 1863 by the vigilance of the governor-general. But the most explosive incident in our Canadian relations came late in 1864.

During October a score of young Confederate soldiers, passing as Canadian sportsmen, infiltrated the town of St. Albans, Vermont, about fifty miles from Montreal. After their leader had announced the annexation of St. Albans to the Southern Confederacy, these merry raiders robbed the local banks of some $200,000 in greenbacks, attempted to burn the town, and retired to British territory where, hotly pursued by a sheriff's posse, all but five of them were captured and handed over to Canadian authorities. This comic affair came close to creating a serious breach, which perhaps was its real purpose; Senator Clement C. Clay of Alabama, a Confederate agent in Canada, was the organizer. If so, the United States very nearly fell into the trap. Abrogation of the Rush-Bagot agreement and a naval building program on the Lakes almost passed Congress. General John A. Dix USA, commanding the military district to which Vermont belonged, ordered his troops, in the event of another such raid, to pursue the culprits into Canada "and destroy them." Dix's order set Canadian nerves jangling, and indignation was aroused on the American side when the Montreal police magistrate before whom the captured raiders were arraigned, discharged them. In the end, Lincoln countermanded Dix, Canada stiffened her frontier guard, the complacent police magistrate was reproved, five of the raiders were rearrested (the rest escaped), and the incident caused a reaction in Canada in favor of the Union.

3. *Conscription, Commerce, and Culture*

During the winter of 1862–63 it became evident in Washington that unless old scruples against conscription were forgotten, the war would be lost. Congress on 3 March 1863 passed the first conscription act. It was a most imperfect law, a travesty of conscription. All men between the ages of twenty and forty-five had to register as liable to military service. As soldiers were needed, the number was divided among the states in proportion to their population, and subdivided among districts, giving credit for previous enlistments. In the first draft, credits wiped out the liability of most of the Western states, which had been forward in volunteering. Between each subsequent call and the actual draft, every state and district had fifty days' grace to reduce its quota by volunteering, after which the balance was obtained by drafting names by lot from the registered list. No attempt was made to levy first on younger men or bachelors; and instead of exempting specified classes such as ministers and heads of families, money payment was made the basis of exemption. One could commute service in a particular draft upon payment of $300, or evade service during the entire war by procuring a substitute to enlist for three years—no matter if the substitute died or deserted next day. The system was inequitable to the poor, and in the working-class quarters of New York the first drawing of names in 1863 was the signal for terrible riots.

The hatred of Irish-Americans for blacks, which we have already noted, broke out viciously. Archbishop John Hughes, who later visited Europe to argue the Union cause with leading Catholics, warned the war department in 1861 that his Roman Catholic flock was "willing to fight to the death for the support of the constitution, the government, and the laws of the country," but not "for the abolition of slavery." The Emancipation Proclamation and the importation of blacks to break a stevedores' strike caused Irish resentment to boil up into riot. On 13 July, while the names of draftees were being drawn from the urns, the provost marshal was driven from his office by a mob. Rioters controlled the streets during the better part of four days and nights, sacking shops and the homes of antislavery leaders, gutting saloons, lynching or torturing blacks who fell into their clutches, burning mansions and a colored orphan asylum. Only the pleas of Catholic priests dissuaded them from burning the presidential lodge and other buildings of Columbia College. When the mob could find no more blacks, they vented their rage on Chinese and Germans, or anyone who would not go along. Priests and the police (also mainly Irish) did their best, but it was not until troops were poured into the city that order was restored, after the loss of several hundred people killed and wounded, and a million dollars in property damage. This was equivalent to a Confederate victory, for Meade's army was so weakened by detachments for guard duty in Northern cities that he was unable to resume the offensive after Gettysburg.

Although there were three more drafts in 1864, a very small proportion of the Union army was furnished by direct conscription.[1] Every fresh draft began an ignoble competition be-

[1] From the draft of July 1863, and the three drafts of 1864, there were 776,829 names drawn; 402,723 were exempted for physical disability or paying the $300 commutation, 200,921 substitutes were bought, and the

tween districts to reduce their quotas by credits, and to fill the residue by bounty-bought volunteers. As recruits were credited to the district where they enlisted, and not to that of their residence, several wealthy communities escaped the draft altogether. State agents scoured occupied portions of the South for black soldiers and even obtained men from the poorhouses of Belgium and the slums of Europe. Federal officials were bribed to admit cripples, idiots, and criminals as recruits. One can easily imagine the effect on the morale of a veteran regiment which received replacements of this sort.

War was the Confederacy's only business. Fighting for independence and race supremacy, the Southerners gave their government more, and asked less, than did the Northern people. Yet the latest generation of Southern historians has proved that selfishness, indifference, and defeatism played a great part in losing the "lost cause." And there was a shrewd instinct on the part of poor whites that it was "a rich man's war and a poor man's fight."

Confederate conscription, adopted in April 1862, was in theory a mass levy of Southern manhood between the ages of 18 and 35. Yet, instead of promoting solidarity, it fomented class antagonism. Although the law exempted conscientious objectors, railway employees, teachers, and the like, South Carolina of her own "sovereign" authority proceeded to extend the privilege and to assert the right of nullification in 1862 as roundly as in 1832. Congress was frightened into adding to the already numerous exempts, editors, printers, and plantation overseers at the rate of one to every twenty slaves. This "twenty-nigger law" created a mighty clamor from the poorer whites. Buying a substitute was allowed, as in the North, until the close of 1863, when the price of a substitute had reached $600. Shortly thereafter the Congress cut down exemptions and extended the age bracket to 17–50 years.

In June 1863, when the proportion of absentees from the Confederate army was approaching one-third, President Davis proclaimed an amnesty to deserters who would return to the colors. So few came in that the offer was repeated shortly after Gettysburg. The president may well have been right in his contention that the South would have been invincible had every white man done his duty.

It was an article of faith in the Confederacy that Northern industry would collapse when cut off from its Southern mar-

---

quotas were further diminished by 834,692 voluntary enlistments, so that the net number of draftees obtained amounted to only 46,347. The principal effect of the draft was to stimulate volunteering, because volunteers got bounties and draftees did not.

kets and its supply of cotton. Northern industry, on the contrary, grew fat and saucy during the war. Union sea power, despite Confederate raiders, protected freight and passenger service to foreign markets. War's demands stimulated production: in Philadelphia alone 180 new factories were built during the years 1862–64. A government generous in contracts and lavish in expenditure helped to create a new aristocracy of profiteers, who became masters of capital after the war.[1] Paper money and the high protective tariff that Congress imposed as a counterweight to internal taxation brought a sharp rise of prices, which the government made no effort to control. Owing to the relatively slight development of labor unions, wages did not rise in the same proportion; average prices rose 117 per cent, average wages 43 per cent in 1860–65, and teachers' salaries even less. There was unemployment in cotton mills, but American factory operatives, more mobile and less dependent than their English fellows, returned to the farms whence many of them had come, or shifted into woolen and other industries; and after mid-1862 enough cotton was obtained from occupied parts of the South to reopen many closed cotton mills. The only important Northern industry that suffered permanently from the war was shipping, and during the war neutral shipping took its place.

In several ways the drain of men into the army and navy was compensated. Immigration during the five war years amounted to almost 800,000 people. Many labor-saving devices, invented earlier, were now generally applied. The Howe sewing machine proved a boon to clothing manufacturers, and a curse to poor seamstresses, whose wages dropped to eight cents an hour in 1864. The Gordon McKay shoe machine for sewing uppers to soles speeded up that process one hundredfold. Petroleum, discovered in Pennsylvania in 1859, was so rapidly extracted that production increased from 84,000 to 128 million gallons in three years, and exports of it to Great Britain in the year prior to October 1862 were valued at over £500,000. Refining methods were so rapidly improved that kerosene in cheap glass lamps began to replace candles and whale-oil lamps for lighting American farmhouses and English cottages.

Like causes speeded a revolution in Northern agriculture.

[1] The foundations of fortunes laid during the war were: Armour (meat packing), Havemeyer (sugar), Weyerhaeuser (lumber), Huntington (merchandise and railroads), Remington (guns), Rockefeller (oil), Carnegie (iron and steel), Borden (milk), Marshall Field (merchandise), and Stillman (contraband cotton). There were even a few such in the South—the King Ranch of Texas, for instance.

The mechanical reaper, hitherto confined to the better prairie farms, came into general use, giving every harvest hand five-fold his former capacity with scythe and cradle. Westward migration and the opening up of new prairie cornlands were greatly stimulated by the passage of the Homestead Act in 1862, after almost forty years' agitation by agrarians and pioneers. Under this law the federal government presented a quarter-section of public land (160 acres) to any bona fide settler for a nominal fee. Fifteen thousand homesteads,[1] including 25 million acres, were thus given away during the war. The annual pork-pack almost doubled, the annual wood-clip more than tripled between 1860 and 1865. Every autumn brought bumper crops of wheat and corn, and since England and Europe suffered a series of poor harvests, they turned to the United States, whence over 40 million bushels of wheat and flour were exported in 1862, as compared with less than 100,000 in 1859. Although the lack of cotton threw many English factory operatives out of work, it was evident that any attempt to break the blockade, and consequently fight the United States, would bring the British Isles face to face with famine. "Old King Cotton's dead and buried, brave young Corn is King" went the refrain of a popular song.

The Far West continued to grow throughout the Civil War. Colorado, the goal of "Pike's Peak or Bust" gold rush in 1859, was organized as a territory in 1861; Dakota and Nevada became territories the same year. Kansas became a state in 1861, as soon as Congress lost its Southern delegation; and Nevada was admitted prematurely in 1864 because the Republicans thought they needed her electoral vote. At least 300,000 emigrants crossed the plains to California, Oregon, and the new territories during the war—some to farm or dig gold, many to escape the draft. Mark Twain was one of those who went west after a few weeks' inglorious service in the Confederate army.

In the North generally, normal activities continued throughout the war. Social functions were held as usual in the cities in winter; in Newport, Long Island, and Saratoga Springs in summer. New York City in September 1862 was less interested in the Battle of Antietam than in the trotting match for a purse of $5000 at a Long Island racecourse between the thirteen-

---

[1] Over 10,000 were in Minnesota, although there was a serious outbreak of Sioux Indians there in 1862; 5000 in Wisconsin, Kansas, and Nebraska. In addition, these states sold hundreds of thousands of acres from their educational grants, and the Illinois Central Railroad sold in wartime almost one-third of the 2.6 million acres granted to it by the federal government.

year-old stallion Ethan Allen, great-grandson of Justin Morgan, and six-year-old George Wilkes, son of Hambletonian, who won. The Saratoga track opened in 1863; Kentucky gentlemen did not allow the war to interrupt their favorite sport, except in 1862 when General Kirby-Smith, with singular want of taste, encamped his Confederate army on the Lexington race-course.

One of P. T. Barnum's greatest triumphs was staged at Grace Church, New York, on 10 February 1863 when "General Tom Thumb," his two-foot-five-inch midget, married the equally tiny Mercy Lavinia Warren Bump. It took two hours for carriages to deliver guests, who were described by the New York *Times* as "the elite, the creme de la creme, the upper ten, the bonton, the select few, the very FF's of the City, nay of the Country."

Enrollment in Northern colleges and universities dropped slightly, and fifteen new colleges were established in wartime, including Vassar, the Massachusetts Institute of Technology, LaSalle, Bates, Swarthmore, Cornell, and the University of Maine. Many bequests were obtained by the older institutions; Louis Agassiz even got a generous grant from the Massachusetts legislature for his new museum of zoology. The Harvard-Yale boat races, interrupted in 1861, were resumed in 1864, while Grant was besieging Petersburg.

Most of the Northern authors who were active before the war continued to write. Henry Thoreau, after a valiant defense of John Brown, succumbed to tuberculosis, and prematurely ended his quest for the lost hound, the turtledove, and the bay horse. His *Cape Cod* was published posthumously in 1864. Hawthorne lived just long enough to salute Longfellow's *Tales of a Wayside Inn* (1863) "with great comfort and delight." Every Northern man of letters except George Ticknor supported the administration and the war, "infernal" though most of them thought war to be. One of the youngest and most promising, Theodore Winthrop, was killed at Big Bethel, first of many battles lost by Ben Butler. Longfellow sought shelter from his private griefs and "the tumult of the times disconsolate" by translating Dante and writing a superb sonnet sequence on *The Divine Comedy;* the first volume appeared a month before Lee's surrender. Emerson, suffering poverty from falling royalties and lecture fees, turned his "serene, unflinching look" on anyone who proposed "any peace restoring the old rottenness," and enjoyed serving on the visiting board of West Point, where he concluded that "war is not the greatest calamity." Charles Eliot Norton ran the Loyal Publication Society (precursor of the syndicated column), which printed poems, articles, and opinions on the war, and sent them to 1000 different newspapers in the North.

Thomas Ball, a New England-born sculptor trained in Florence, spent the entire war working in Boston on his spirited equestrian statue of Washington, which was erected in the Public Garden in 1869. George Perkins Marsh, Vermont lawyer, congressman, and diplomat, composed, while American minister to Italy, his *Man and Nature* (1864), the bible of the conservation movement, pointing out from his observations at home and abroad the wasteful folly of destroying forests, making "the face of the earth . . . no longer a sponge, but a dust heap."

Walt Whitman wrote his incomparable sketches of the war while in active service as an army nurse. James Russell Lowell's second series of *Biglow Papers* had the merit of making people laugh at themselves, at England, and at the Rebels. Bancroft went ahead with his *History of the United States;* and Parkman, deeply chagrined that bad eyesight kept him out of the army, struggled along with his series on New France. Whittier continued to write poetry and to do war work, such as collecting money to relieve the unemployed English workers who had so nobly supported the Union. His purely fictitious "Barbara Frietchie" created a kindly feeling in the North toward Stonewall Jackson, and he was invited to visit the Army of the Potomac early in 1864 since (in the words of his host, Brigadier General Rice), "Your loyal verse has made us all your friends, lightening the wearisomeness of our march, brightening our lonely campfires, and cheering our hearts in battle when 'the flags of war like storm-birds fly.' " When a fellow Quaker confessed qualms of conscience to Whittier about supplying timber for U.S.S. *Kearsarge,* then building at Kittery, the bard remarked, "My friend, if thee does furnish any of that timber thee spoke of, be sure that it is all sound!" Bryant, who sturdily and elegantly edited the New York *Evening Post* throughout the war, published another *Thirty Poems* in 1864, more than half a century after his first imprint. The Northern magazines, especially *The Atlantic Monthly* (edited by James T. Fields), *The North American Review* (edited by Lowell and Norton), *Scientific American, Harper's Monthly* and *Weekly* (edited by George William Curtis) maintained their already high standards, and before the war ended a fund of $100,000 was raised to start the weekly *Nation,* with Edwin L. Godkin as editor.

In the South the war effort absorbed everything, the only Confederate literature that has endured are a few poems by

Timrod, Sidney Lanier, and Paul Hamilton Hayne, and an excellent *Life of Stonewall Jackson* (Richmond, 1863) by John Esten Cooke. The one original novel of the Confederacy, by Augusta Jane Wilson, *Macaria, or Altars of Sacrifice* (Richmond, 1864), gives an idealized picture of Virginia society before the war; the hero, mortally wounded in the peninsular campaign, dies happy when he hears that McClellan is whipped. Numerous reprints of English novels, mostly of "high life" (*East Lynne, or the Earl's Daughter; Lady Audley's Secret*, etc.), were published, and a few translations of French works, notably Victor Hugo's *Les Misérables*, which became so popular that the soldiers of the Army of Northern Virginia jokingly called themselves "Lee's Miserables." Two periodicals lived a precarious existence. De Bow's *Commercial Review* catered to Southern self-esteem with articles on "The Puritan and the Cavalier," and Timrod's "There's Life in the Old Land Yet." *The Southern Literary Messenger* kept a fairly high standard in articles of a general nature, giving its readers an opportunity to escape from the war by reading on Life in Japan, and Faraday's Experiments in Science. Both expired in the summer of 1864. Confederate literary output consisted largely of sermons on the death in battle of sundry "Christian soldiers," and sentimental war poems and songs, paperback accounts of the war, and schoolbooks, largely reprints of those which Southern schools had been buying from Northern publishers. An original exception is *The New Texas Primary Reader* (Houston, 1863), which declares Texas to be "an empire of itself," has a table of pronunciation of difficult Spanish and Indian place names (Guadalupe = "Warloop"), and promises "little reader" that if he is a good boy he may some day be governor of Texas.

Texas could afford to be smug. Distant from the scene of conflict, uninvaded until 1865 (except by the Comanche on her western frontier), she always had plenty to eat, and many luxuries imported via Mexico. East of the Mississippi, and in Missouri where local vendettas were most vicious, the people began to feel the pinch of poverty and undernourishment in 1863–64. This requires explanation, since the Confederacy was primarily an agricultural country, food production rose as an increasing proportion of cotton fields were planted with corn and wheat, and there was no lack of labor. The slaves generally remained loyal and at work until a Union army appeared in the neighborhood.

But transportation was wanting. That was the weakest point in the Confederate economic organization; yet the South in 1860 was as well provided with railroads as the North. Through traffic encountered many bottlenecks and even breaks, where goods had to be transported by wagon from one station to another. Congress appropriated money to construct missing links, but little was accomplished, and the few rolling mills and foundries were too busy with government work to replace outworn railway equipment. Main lines could be kept going only by cannibalizing branch lines; junctions became congested with supplies, and breakdowns were frequent. That is why a women's bread riot occurred in Richmond in 1863 when the barns of the Shenandoah valley were bursting with wheat, and why government clerks had to pay $15 a bushel for corn that was bringing the farmer only a dollar in southwestern Georgia. Blockade-run coffee cost $5 a pound in Richmond.

As an example of plenty in parts of Virginia, one may recount the experience of young Randolph Barton, who enlisted in the Stonewall Brigade at the age of seventeen (bringing two horses and a black groom with him) and ended the war as a major. Furloughed after receiving his sixth wound, in the Wilderness campaign, he first convalesces with friends at Staunton; then, owing to Sheridan's advance up the valley, seeks refuge with Colonel Massie in the highlands of Albemarle County:

> This establishment was typical of Southern life. It had never been visited by either army. It was a beautiful farm just at the foot of the mountain, which rose with some grandeur back of it or to the west, protecting it from the cold blasts of winter. All varieties of cultivation were to be seen on the rolling hills and fertile meadow bottoms. . . . The Negroes were around in the usual large numbers, docile and attentive. Gardens, lawns and orchards surrounded the house, and on all sides were evidences of peace and plenty. And to crown all was the unbounded hospitality of Colonel and Mrs. Massie and their family, the chief ornament of which was their pretty daughter, Miss Florence. Think of a tiresome day's journey crowned by such a reception, a bountiful Virginia supper and a spotlessly clean and far-retired chamber, and one can understand into what luxurious oblivion I sank about nine o'clock. I remember so well the beauty of the next morning. Dew, sunlight, shadows, sparkling water, a full feeling of refreshment, safety, an incomparable breakfast and three exceedingly pretty girls all to myself; and the enjoyment of all justified by a painlessly-healing, honorable wound! I record these incidents to show that the dark

clouds of war sometimes lifted and we basked once in a while in glorious sunlight.

Nor was this the first, or the last, of such happy interludes enjoyed by this gallant youngster during the war.

At the end of the war General Johnston obtained ample supplies in the Carolinas and Georgia for his retreating army, and President and Mrs. Davis, on their pathetic retreat from Richmond south, never wanted food or hospitality in regions that Sherman had not ravaged. But Lee's army, on the eve of Appomattox, was at the point of starvation because a whole trainload of supplies never reached it. The general himself had meat only twice a week and lived largely on corn bread and cabbage. Once, having invited a number of his officers to dine, he ordered his cook to prepare the best meal he could. The pièce de résistance turned out to be a mess of cabbage, in the midst of which was a small piece of "middling," pork off the side of a hog. The guests, with noble self-restraint, declined the meat, so the general did too. Next day he ordered his man to produce it. The cook admitted, "Marse Robert, de fac' is, dat ar middlin' was borrowed middlin'. We-all didn't have none, and I done paid it back to de place where I got it!" So General Lee, with a sigh, pitched into another meal of cabbage.

The ruling class in the South, which had most at stake, gave all it had to the cause. In the North able-bodied young men of means and position could remain in civvies without incurring social stigma; in the South the women saw to it that there were no gentlemen slackers. The patriotism of the Southern ladies was only equaled by their devotion. Left in charge of plantations, they had to direct the necessary change from cotton-raising to food production, to revive household industries such as spinning, weaving, and dyeing, to extract nitrates from the earth of cellars and smokehouses, to care for wounded soldiers, and feed passing armies. Yet those who remained on their plantations fared well in comparison with refugees and government clerks at Richmond, where speculators and their wives, dressed in the latest Parisian fashions and drinking expensive wines imported in blockade runners, offered as great a contrast to their own penurious lives as the more bloated profiteers of New York did to the Northern wage-earner. For, as Rhett Butler remarked in *Gone With the Wind*, there is as much money to be made out of a losing cause as from a winning one.

Richmond society remained gay and hospitable despite high prices. "You can always buy an egg for a dollar," wrote the editor of the *Examiner*. Baron von Borcke, a volunteer on Jeb

Stuart's staff, introduced the German cotillion. Vizetelly, war correspondent for the *London Illustrated News,* helped the ladies plan charades and private theatricals; officers from the Army of Northern Virginia would gallop into town night after night, to attend dances and dinners, and get back to camp in time for reveille. General Lee encouraged all this: "Go on, look your prettiest," he wrote to a committee of Richmond ladies, "and be as nice to them as ever you can be."

Although many, many instances of selfishness, indifference, incompetence, and defeatism on both sides, can be quoted, one main fact stands out:—no earlier war in history drew out so much sacrifice, energy, and heroism as this. Vice President Stephens divined the situation at the beginning of 1863 when he wrote: "The great majority of the masses both North and South are true to the cause of their side. . . . A large majority on both sides are tired of the war; want peace. But as we do not want peace without independence, so they do not want peace without union." Remember, too, that the average American then, as now, loathed army life, and only accepted it because of social and patriotic compulsion. Both Union and Confederate soldiers sang, "When This Cruel War Is Over," and both rejected the "fighting" ballads printed by patriots behind the lines. Yet both fought vigorously to the end.

"War, when you are at it, is horrible and dull," wrote thrice-wounded Captain Oliver Wendell Holmes, Jr. "It is only when time has passed that you see that its message was divine. I hope it may be long before we are called again to sit at that master's feet. But some teacher of the kind we all need. In this snug, over-safe corner of the world we need it, that we may realize that our comfortable routine is no eternal necessity of things, but merely a little space of calm in the midst of a tempestuous untamed streaming of the world, and in order that we may be ready for danger." Of his generation he wrote, twenty years after the war, "Through our great good fortune, in our youth our hearts were touched with fire." Alas that for so many, many thousands on both sides that fire was snuffed out with life itself; but in Holmes it burned bright and high for a long lifetime, so that young men who went to war in 1917 and even in 1941, were able to catch the flame from this noble master.

4. The Negro and the War

The attitude both of the Union and the Confederacy toward blacks was ambiguous, inconsistent and even hypocritical, reflecting the unfortunate fact that the average Northern soldier, hardly less than the Southern, disliked any contact with a colored man which implied equality. Congress at first refused to allow free blacks of the North to enlist in the Union army, and the influx of fugitive slaves into Union lines was an embarrassment. Benjamin F. Butler returned runaways to their masters when he invaded Louisiana in 1862, provided the masters were loyal. An effort was made to settle the "contrabands" on land deserted by its owners, but little land was available under Union control. Many were organized as labor troops, but most were simply kept alive in concentration camps.

After the Emancipation Proclamation it was only logical to allow blacks to fight for their own freedom, and efforts were made to organize black regiments, not only from Northern freemen but from able-bodied contrabands. Butler mustered the first colored army corps in Louisiana in 1862; and, with the imagination that is a redeeming feature of that old rogue, called it *Le Corps d'Afrique*. This corps, with black officers, took part in the assaults on Port Hudson in 1863 and fought well. With incredible meanness, the Federal Congress for over a year set the colored private's pay at $7 per month, when white soldiers received $13.

One of the first states to organize colored regiments was Massachusetts; her 54th and 55th Infantry were recruited from all over New England, and in Philadelphia, and St. Louis. Longfellow found it an "imposing sight, with something wild and strange about it," to see the 54th swinging down the flag-decked streets of Boston on 28 May 1863, commanded by Colonel Robert Gould Shaw. They embarked for the South on the very wharf whence less than ten years earlier the fugitive Anthony Burns had been returned to slavery. Seven weeks later, while a foreign-born mob was lynching blacks in New York City, Colonel Shaw's regiment had the place of honor in the five-regiment assault on Fort Wagner near Charleston, losing its commander, two-thirds of the officers, and nearly half the men. "Together," as the inscription on St. Gaudens's monument to Colonel Shaw in Boston reads, "they gave . . . undying proof that Americans of African descent possess the pride, courage and devotion of the patriot soldier."

To the Confederates, the use of black troops by the Union was a crowning indignity. Congress, on 1 May 1863, resolved that any white officer of colored troops, if captured, should be executed. Threats of retaliation prevented this from being carried out. The Confederacy, however, was just as ambiguous in its attitude as the Union. From the beginning of the war, both slaves and free blacks were employed in the Southern army as cooks, body servants, teamsters, and labor troops, in war industries such as the Tredegar and Selma Iron Works. Many of these were enlisted in the army and drew army pay. (General Lee was much amused by an enlisted cook explaining his absence of wounds: " 'Cause I stays back wid de ginerals!") In 1862 several Southern states, and next year the Confederate government, authorized the impressment of slaves for war work; and in February 1865 Secretary Mallory reported to Congress that out of 2225 workers employed in the Confederate navy's shore establishments, 1143 were blacks. But the rulers of the South gagged at allowing blacks to bear arms for the Confederacy.

General Lee on 10 March 1865 wrote to the president urging the enlistment of slave soldiers, provided both slave and owner volunteered. Davis then signed a bill calling on the states to provide 300,000 more troops irrespective of color, but including a certain proportion of slaves between the ages of eighteen and forty-five. Even these were not to be emancipated; and, except for two companies organized in Richmond, none had been recruited before Lee's surrender.

As one of Davis's adoring biographers has admitted, he did everything too late. In 1865 he sent a special envoy to London with power to promise abolition in return for British recognition. An amazing offer, considering that the Confederate constitution embalmed slavery! Could even Davis have persuaded his people to give up the basis of their society? But he did not have to ask, since the British government never contemplated the recognition of a tottering Confederacy to further an emancipation which Lincoln had already announced, if not effected.

XXII

The Campaigns of 1863-1864

1. Chancellorsville and Gettysburg

AFTER FREDERICKSBURG, beaten Burnside was relieved as commander of the Army of the Potomac by "brave, handsome, vain, insubordinate, plausible, untrustworthy" General Joseph Hooker, another good corps commander who failed higher up. Plenty of valor had "Fighting Joe"—thrice promoted for bravery on the battlefield in the Mexican War. Since Fredericksburg he had been so outspoken in criticism of brother officers and the government that the President, upon appointing him to the new command, read him a little lecture on conduct: "I have heard of your recently saying that both the army and the government needed a dictator. Of course it was not for this but in spite of it that I have given you the command. Only those generals who gain successes can set up as dictators. What I ask of you is military success, and I will risk the dictatorship." Hooker took in good part this reproof, surely one of the most singular ever sent by a chief of state to a general. He did much to restore the morale and improve the organization of the Army of the Potomac, but he began boasting of what he would do to Lee. What Lee did to him is history.

This was at the Battle of Chancellorsville, scenario for Stephen Crane's *The Red Badge of Courage,* and subject of John Bigelow's great battle monograph. It was fought largely in a wilderness a few miles west of Fredericksburg. Hooker's sound plan for a double envelopment of Lee's army was checked by stout Confederate defense on 1 May, and this seemed to take all the wind out of his sails. While he reformed defensively, Lee adopted the brilliant strategy of dividing his army, inferior in numbers to Hooker's, and sending Stonewall Jackson, with more than half of it, by circuitous roads to attack General O. O. Howard's XI Corps on the Union right flank. Cavalry under the General's nephew Fitzhugh Lee had reconnoitered this flank and found it to be "hanging in the air," with no defenses or natural obstacles to the west or south. At 4:00 a.m., 2 May, this bold movement began, and it took all of a hot and dusty day to complete. Although observed by the Union balloonists and others, Hooker fatuously estimated it to be a retreat. At 4:00 p.m. Jackson's 25,000 men began to deploy in the forest within a mile, and across a clearing, from Howard's unsuspecting troops who were cooking supper, playing cards, or lounging.

General Jackson sat on Little Sorrel, watch in hand. At 6:00 p.m. he gave the word. The woods rang with bugle calls and the skirmishers in gray sprang forward, followed by the battle lines. So rapid was the advance, so complete the surprise, that the first intimation Howard's troops had of Stonewall's forward surge was a flurry of rabbits, foxes, and deer, driven from the forest ahead of the Confederates. In ten minutes' time the whole Union right was in panic-stricken rout. Earlier in the war, this would have led to complete disaster, and only individual valor now saved the Army of the Potomac. Hooker seemed to forget the very rudiments of strategy, while Lee chose time and place of attack. After two days of it, Hooker retreated across the Rappahannock with some 37,000 troops still uncommitted.

The Chancellorsville victory, however, was too dearly won. During the moonlit night that followed the surprise, Jackson and his staff, returning to their lines after a reconnaissance, were mistaken for Union cavalry by a trigger-happy regiment, and swept with a deadly volley. Jackson received two bullets in the left arm near the shoulder, crushing the main artery. In an improvised field hospital the arm was amputated, the general was removed to a house at Guiney's Station, attended by his wife and a Richmond surgeon, and prayed for by the entire army—General Lee "wrestled in prayer" all night for Jackson's life. But pneumonia set in, followed by pulmonary embolism, and the intrepid commander sank into death, and deathless fame. His last words were, "Let us cross over the river and rest under the shade of the trees."

Above the pompous official obituaries Jackson himself would probably have preferred the impromptu tribute by General

Grant when, a year later, he rested in the very house where Stonewall had died: "He was a gallant soldier, and a Christian gentleman."

Lee was soon ready for another spring at the Keystone State, Pennsylvania. Others high in Confederate councils doubted the wisdom of an offensive at that juncture, when Vicksburg and the entire West were hanging in the bight, but political considerations forced Davis's hand. Victory in Pennsylvania might undermine Union morale, encourage (as Lee wrote) "the rising peace party in the North," even gain European recognition. It was a bold game for the highest stake, but Davis was not a bold player. He could not make up his mind to weaken Bragg's or Johnston's armies, or to strip Richmond and the Carolinas. So Lee moved northward (3 June 1863) with only 76,000 men, while 190,000 Confederate troops were deployed between the Mississippi and the Rappahannock.

General Hooker on 28 June, the day after Lee had the entire Army of Northern Virginia in Pennsylvania, conferred a benefit on the Union cause by resigning. Lincoln turned over the army to another corps commander, General George Gordon Meade. For once, "swapping horses in midstream," as Lincoln called it, was justified. Meade was the very type of good workinghorse general, sound in judgment, realistic, certain to do nothing foolish if unlikely to perform anything brilliant. An irascible disciplinarian, he "made people jump around," recorded a member of his staff; and his good eye for terrain, and power to make a quick decision in a fluid tactical situation, saved the day at Gettysburg.

Davis may have hoped that the mere presence of Lee's army in Pennsylvania would force Lincoln to negotiate on the basis of independence; for Davis entertained some peculiar ideas at this time. He told a visiting guards officer from the British army, that "most of the intelligent people" in the State of Maine were planning to secede and join Canada, in order to get out from "under the thumb" of Massachusetts! But the North showed no sign of flinching. Democratic as well as Republican governors promoted volunteering; state militia and even civilians turned out in large numbers to protect the Pennsylvania cities. Grave anxiety was felt, but no panic; and Lincoln did not recall a single unit from the West.

On 29 June, when the Army of Northern Virginia was spread over a wide arc between Chambersburg and Harrisburg, Lee still had no clear idea of where his enemy was—"Jeb" Stuart having gone off on one of his stunt rides. So Lee ordered the Army of Northern Virginia to concentrate on the eastern slope of South Mountain, near Cashtown. There, in a strong defensive position, he proposed to await attack. Meade intended to take a defensive position and let Lee attack him. But chance placed the great battle where neither general wanted it. On 30 June a unit of A. P. Hill's corps, covering Lee's concentration, marched toward Gettysburg in search of shoes, of which the Confederate troops were always short. Boots and saddles were there—on one brigade of General John Buford's cavalry division, which held up the Confederates two miles outside the town. Gettysburg commanded important roads, and each army was so eager for action that this chance contact drew both as to a magnet, into the quiet little town. There, on 1 July, the great three-day battle began, each unit joining in the fray as it arrived.

The first day went ill for the Union. A. P. Hill and Ewell drove the Union I Corps, General Winfield Scott Hancock, through the town. In the nick of time, Hancock rallied the fugitives on Cemetery Hill, where Howard had had the foresight to plant his XI Corps. This position, with its like-named Ridge, proved to be admirable for defense: a limestone outcrop shaped like a fishhook, with the convex side turned west and north, toward the Confederates. Along it Meade placed the Union army as rapidly as it arrived from the south and east, while the Confederates took up an encircling position, the right on the partly wooded Seminary Ridge parallel to the Cemetery.

Lee decided to attack the following day, 2 July. His great opportunity for a double envelopment of the enemy came that morning. Before half the Union army was in position, Ewell captured a part of Culp's Hill, on the Union right—the barb of the hook—but Longstreet's corps arrived too late (it always did) to do much against the Union left. It drove in Sickles's III Corps which had incautiously occupied a knoll in advance of Cemetery Ridge, but III Corps retired to Little Round Top —the eye of the hook—possession of which would have enabled Confederate artillery to enfilade the entire Union position. The Union army lost heavily; but Meade determined to stand his ground and fight it out.

The third day of the battle and of July opened with a desperate struggle for Culp's Hill, from which Ewell's corps was finally dislodged. Silence fell over the field at noon. Meade guessed what was coming, and reinforced his center. At one o'clock there came a preparatory artillery fire from 172 Confederate guns, which did surprisingly little damage. Deep silence again. Lee, against Longstreet's protest, had ordered a direct attack across open country to break through the Union center.

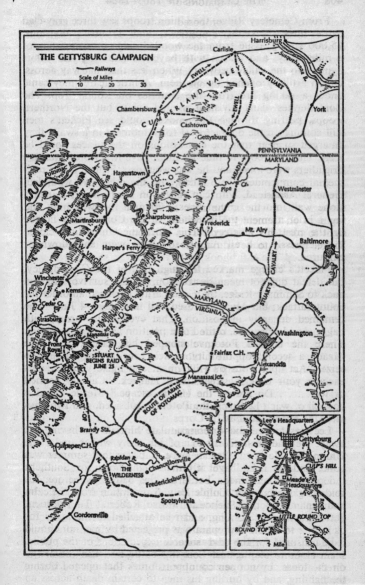

THE GETTYSBURG CAMPAIGN

Railways
Scale of Miles
0   10   20   30

Harrisburg

Carlisle

STUART

Susquehanna R.

EWELL

CUMBERLAND VALLEY

Chambersburg

LEE

Cashtown

Gettysburg

EWELL

York

MEADE

PENNSYLVANIA

MARYLAND

Hagerstown

SOUTH MTS

Pipe Cr.

Westminster

STUART'S CAVALRY

Potomac

Sharpsburg

Frederick

Mt. Airy

Baltimore

Martinsburg

W.VA. bounds

Harper's Ferry

BLUE RIDGE MTS

Winchester

SHENANDOAH R.

Kernstown

MARYLAND

Leesburg

HOOKER

VIRGINIA

Patuxent R.

Cedar Cr.

Strasburg

Manassas Gap

Washington

STUART
BEGINS RAID
JUNE 25

Front
Royal

Fairfax C.H.

Alexandria

Manassas Jct.

BULL RUN MTS

ROUTE OF ARMY
OF POTOMAC

Potomac

Brandy Sta.

Rappahannock

Aquia Cr.

Culpeper C.H.

Rapidan R.

THE
WILDERNESS

Chancellorsville

Fredericksburg

Spotsylvania

Gordonsville

Lee's Headquarters

Gettysburg

SEMINARY RIDGE

CEMETERY RIDGE

CULP'S HILL

Meade's
Headquarters

LITTLE ROUND TOP

ROUND TOP

0   ½   1 Mile

From Cemetery Ridge, the Union troops saw three gray-clad battle lines, Pickett's, Pettigrew's, and Trimble's divisions, 15,000 strong, issue from the wooded ridge three-quarters of a mile away, and march with bayonets glittering and colors flying into the valley between. When less than halfway across, Union artillery opened up on them. A little nearer they came under a raking fire from the batteries on Round Top. The Confederates' flank divisions melted away; but the Northern troops, peering through the smoke, could see Pickett's men still coming on the double. Lost for a moment in a swale, they emerged so near that the expressions on their faces could be seen. Then the boys in blue let them have it. Two of Pickett's brigadiers were killed and he was wounded. Fifteen of his regimental commanders were killed, and the other five wounded. General Armistead, with cap raised on sword-point, leaped a stone wall into the Union lines; 100 men followed him, and for a brief moment the battle flag of the Confederacy floated on the crest of Cemetery Ridge. Then the Union lines closed in relentlessly and all Armistead's men were shot down or captured.

Pickett's charge marked the high tide of the Confederacy, but defeat did not mean destruction. As the survivors limped back to Seminary Ridge, the Union army expected an order for counterattack; but Meade refused. All next day—4 July—Lee remained defiantly in position. That evening his army, with baggage and prisoners, retired to a position west of Sharpsburg. There the flooded Potomac stopped his retreat, and gave Meade a second opportunity, which Lincoln begged him to seize. "Act upon your own judgment and make your generals execute your orders," telegraphed Halleck. "Call no council of war. . . . Do not let the enemy escape." Meade called a council of war (12 July), the Potomac subsided, and two days later the enemy escaped.

Lee was too candid to congratulate himself for having got away. He had seen the flower of his army wither under the Union fire. He knew that all hope of peace that summer was gone, and he must have felt that slight hope for Southern independence remained. Yet after the battle, as before, his soldiers gathered only confidence and resolution from the calm countenance of their beloved "Marse Robert." To President Davis he wrote, "No blame can be attached to the army for its failure to accomplish what was projected by me, nor should it be censured for the unreasonable expectations of the public. I am alone to blame." Lee lost this battle by letting Stuart go on the loose, by not seizing opportunities that opened during the fighting, and by hurling his men to certain death across an open field covered by rifle and artillery fire. Burnside at Fredericksburg had not done much worse. Meade, placed in command of an army thrice whipped within a twelvemonth, on the eve of battle with the hitherto invincible Lee, fairly won the greatest battle of the war, even though he failed to deliver a knockout blow to a staggering enemy. And from the Wilderness to Appomattox he was the right arm of Grant.

On 19 November 1863, at the national cemetery on the battlefield of Gettysburg, Lincoln delivered his immortal address:

Fourscore and seven years ago our fathers brought forth on this continent a new nation, conceived in liberty, and dedicated to the proposition that all men are created equal.

Now we are engaged in a great civil war, testing whether that nation, or any nation so conceived and so dedicated, can long endure. We are met on a great battle-field of that war. We have come to dedicate a portion of that field as a final resting-place for those who here gave their lives that the nation might live. It is altogether fitting and proper that we should do this.

But, in a larger sense, we cannot dedicate—we cannot consecrate—we cannot hallow—this ground. The brave men, living and dead, who struggled here, have consecrated it far above our poor power to add or detract. The world will little note nor long remember what we say here, but it can never forget what they did here. It is for us, the living, rather, to be dedicated here to the unfinished work which they who fought here have thus far so nobly advanced. It is rather for us to be here dedicated to the great task remaining before us—that from these honored dead we take increased devotion to that cause for which they gave the last full measure of devotion; that we here highly resolve that these dead shall not have died in vain; that this nation, under God, shall have a new birth of freedom; and that government of the people, by the people, for the people, shall not perish from the earth.

2. *Vicksburg*

Let us now turn to great events in the Western theater of war, for these affected the eventual outcome even more than did the deadly battles in the East. Here was the situation on New Year's Day 1863: General Rosecrans's Army of the Cumberland had concluded the drawn battle of Murfreesboro or Stone River in middle Tennessee, with Braxton Bragg, after which both armies were too badly mauled to do anything for several months. Grant's Army of the Tennessee covered the important east-west railway from Memphis to a point beyond Corinth, Mississippi. His purpose was to open the Great River to New Orleans. Although both banks of it below Memphis were under Confederate control, there was nothing to oppose the passage of a Union fleet downstream until it reached Vicksburg, or upstream from New Orleans until it reached Port Hudson, Louisiana. At both points the line of bluffs that borders the valley touches the river itself. The Confederates fortified both ends of this natural defense which enabled troops and supplies from Arkansas, Louisiana, and Texas to cross the river.

Vicksburg was the most difficult nut to crack. Strongly fortified on a high bluff, the river front was impregnable to assault, and on the east the town was protected by the valley of the Yazoo river, intersected by countless backwaters and bayous. The Confederate commander here, with 56,000 troops at his disposal, was General John C. Pemberton, a Pennsylvania Quaker who unaccountably chose the United States Army for his career and, even less understandably, defected to the Confederacy, which he served very ill.

General Grant, after one check in December 1862, concentrated the Army of the Tennessee on the west bank of the Mississippi about twenty miles north of Vicksburg, and spent the wet months of the new year in fruitless attempts to outflank Pemberton in the slimy jungle of the lower Yazoo. There was no lack of amphibious activity, much of it of a confusing nature bordering on the burlesque—Confederates capturing ram *Queen of the West*, and Admiral Porter floating a dummy monitor past the Vicksburg batteries to draw their fire. Never a dull moment on the Western waters when Grant and Porter were in command!

Any other general would now have retired to Memphis with "baffled and defeated forces," as Jefferson Davis predicted Grant would do, but Grant was not that kind of general. In his judgment, "There was nothing left to be done but to go forward to a decisive victory." In order to advance he must cut loose from his base of supplies, march his army along the west bank of the Mississippi, cross over below Vicksburg to dry ground, and attack Pemberton from the rear. A bold plan, resembling Wolfe's strategy that won Quebec.

Grant's reputation was still under the cloud of Shiloh. He had failed to take Vicksburg. He was reported to be a drunkard. There was a vicious campaign against him in the Eastern press.

Owing to this controversy, important people and busybodies visited Grant's simple headquarters to size him up. Everyone was impressed by his rough natural dignity despite his sloppy military *tenue;* they noted his strong, quick eye, square jaw, and quiet way of handling men. The Army of the Tennessee worked in perfect concert with the fresh-water navy. "Grant and Sherman are on board almost every day. Dine and tea with me often; we agree in everything," wrote Porter.

Grant's plan was audacious as any of Lee's, and he had difficulties such as Lee never encountered. The Army of the Tennessee marched along the west bank of the Mississippi to Bruinsburg, south of Grand Gulf, where there was an easy crossing. Porter's gunboat fleet had to run the Vicksburg gantlet on the night of 16–17 April 1863, to support Grant's crossing. With lights dowsed and engines stopped, the gunboats floated downstream until discovered by a Confederate sentry. Then, what a torrent of shot and shell from the fortress, and what a cracking-on of steam in the fleet, and what a magnificent spectacle, lighted by flashing guns and burning cotton bales, as the casemated gunboats, turtlebacked rams, and river steamboats with tall flaring funnels, dashed by the batteries! "Their heavy shot walked right through us," wrote Porter; but all except one transport got by safely, and a week later twelve more river steamers, which Grant needed for his crossing, went through the same experience.

On 29 April, Porter's seven ironclads destroyed the Confederate batteries at Grand Gulf in a five-hour bombardment. That enabled the van of Grant's army, 20,000 strong, to cross to the east bank above Bruinsburg unopposed. William Tecumseh Sherman's XV Corps masked this movement by an attack on Haynes Bluff above Vicksburg, which completely fooled Pemberton. The XV Corps then marched south and, crossing at Grand Gulf 7 May, raised Grant's strength to 33,000 to face Pemberton's 56,000 Confederates, with a fair chance that Joe Johnston, over-all commander in that theater with at least 11,000 men in Mississippi, would pile in too.

There then followed one of the boldest campaigns of the war. Grant, leaving behind all his train except a few ambulances and vehicles crammed with ammunition, and with four days' rations in the soldiers' haversacks, struck across the state of Mississippi. It was a very difficult country—"stands on edge," as Grant put it:—rough, wooded, cross-hatched by deep gullies, the narrow tortuous roads following the crests of steep ridges lined by dense woods, all in sizzling heat and clouds of dust, except for two days when rain converted the roads into quagmires. Grant's purpose, to hurl a series of swift,

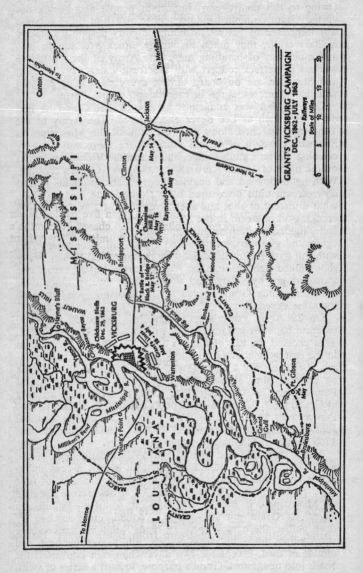

GRANT'S VICKSBURG CAMPAIGN
DEC. 1862 - JULY 1863
Railways
Scale of Miles
0   5   10   15   20

To Memphis
Canton
To Meridian
Jackson
Clinton
To New Orleans
Pearl R.
May 14
May 13
Raymond
Bolton
Champion
Hill
May 16
ADVANC
Bridgeport
MISSISSIPPI
Battle of
Black R. Bridge
May 17
Broken and thickly wooded country
GRANT'S
Big Black R.
Haynes' Bluff
WALNUT HILLS
Chickasaw Bayou
Chickasaw Bluffs
Dec. 29, 1862
VICKSBURG
Ass't
May 19
Grant 18
May
Warrenton
Pt. Gibson
May 1
Grand
Gulf
Bruinsburg
Mississippi R.
Milliken's Bend
Young's Point
GRANT'S
MARCH
To Monroe
LOUISIANA
Mississippi

lethal jabs at the enemy, was completely fulfilled. He had two excellent corps, Sherman's and McPherson's, besides the XIII Corps commanded by political General McClernand who always manged to be last to engage and first to call for help. Grant won easily the first battle, against the former Grand Gulf garrison near Port Gibson (1 May). On the 12th, McPherson's corps hit the enemy at Raymond, and the Confederates retreated. Two days later, Sherman's corps, having caught up, beat a portion of Joe Johnston's army near Jackson and occupied that state capital.

Johnston was now blocked off; and Grant, turning about-face toward Vicksburg, kept between him and the Vicksburg garrison. Pemberton lashed out vigorously at Champion Hill (16 May), but Grant sent him reeling. Sherman's corps, pursuing the fleeing Confederates, next day seized the bridge on Big Black river, last obstacle short of Vicksburg, then took positions around the city. In 18 days the Army of the Tennessee had marched 150 to 200 miles, won five battles, taken 8000 prisoners, checkmated Johnston, and chased Pemberton's army into Vicksburg. And, although outnumbered throughout the campaign, Grant always managed to have superior numbers at the point of impact, proof of his tactical genius. This campaign was as good as Stonewall Jackson's best, and Jackson's brilliant exploits were waged in home territory. Noteworthy, too, were Grant's dispositions to take care of both his own and the enemy's wounded, promptly forwarding them to field or floating hospitals where the major part were cured and rejoined the colors instead of being left to die of neglect as had happened to many in Virginia.

Grant now sent Sherman north to take Haynes Bluff and the enemy forts on the Yazoo from the rear. After a couple of probes at the defenses of Vicksburg, he sat down to besiege the city, with the help of Porter's fleet. Pemberton surrendered the city and his army, now reduced to 30,000 men, on 4 July 1863, the last day of Gettysburg, which made it "the best Fourth of July since 1776."

Lincoln, thanking Grant in a characteristic letter, did something which few politicians and still fewer Presidents ever do—he admitted a mistake. He had thought that when Grant crossed the Mississippi on 29 April he should have marched downstream to join General Banks. "I now wish to make the personal acknowledgment that you were right and I was wrong." Banks at that time was besieging Port Hudson on the east bank, about 24 miles upstream from Baton Rouge. He had naval gunfire support from Farragut's Gulf Squadron, and from Porter's gunboats. After two costly and fruitless attempts to take Port Hudson by assault, Banks sat down for a siege. But the Confederate commander there was so discouraged by the fall of Vicksburg that he, too, surrendered on 9 July with over 30,000 prisoners.

Lincoln could now announce, "The Father of Waters flows unvexed to the sea." The loss of Vicksburg and Port Hudson was a far more deadly blow to the Confederacy than Gettysburg. And a nasty, three-cornered controversy broke out between Jefferson Davis, Johnston, and Pemberton as to who was to blame. It never seemed to occur to them that Grant and his army were responsible.

3. *The Chattanooga, Red River, and Atlanta Campaigns*

"It was not until after both Gettysburg and Vicksburg that the war professionally began," wrote General Sherman, twenty years later. "Then our men had learned in the dearest school on earth the simple lessons of war. Then we had brigades, divisions and corps which could be handled professionally, and it was then that we as professional soldiers could rightly be held to a just responsibility."

Now that a watery ring, fresh and salt, had been flung around the Confederacy, the time was ripe for a lethal thrust from Tennessee to Savannah. Now began the campaign that led to Sherman's march to the sea. Initial target was Chattanooga, where the Tennessee river breaks through parallel ridges of the southern Appalachians, and an important junction on the Richmond-Knoxville-Memphis railway. Union armies, once in possession of Chattanooga, could swing round the Great Smoky Mountains and advance on Atlanta.

The opening phase of the Chattanooga campaign was conducted on both sides by second-raters; Rosecrans, who had most of McClellan's faults without his ability, and Braxton Bragg, a dyspeptic martinet whose actions were completely unpredictable. But from the first battle of the campaign, at Chickamauga (19 September), there emerged a great commander, the loyal Virginian George H. Thomas. After Bragg had swept the Union right and center into Chattanooga, General Thomas for six hours held his left against repeated assaults; and when nightfall found him stripped of ammunition, he retired unmolested to a safe position. "The *élan* of the Southern soldier was never seen after Chickamauga," wrote D. H. Hill. "That brilliant dash which had distinguished him was gone forever." It broke against the lines of Thomas, "the rock of Chickamauga."

Rosecrans now allowed his army to be penned up and besieged in Chattanooga. He was approaching a state of imbecility when Lincoln sent Grant to the rescue, as supreme commander in the West. Grant placed Thomas in command of the Army of the Cumberland, and ordered him to hold Chattanooga at all hazards. "I will hold the town till we starve," said Thomas.

There was no more accomplished horseman in either army than General Grant, but he had bad luck with his war horses. A handsome bay named Charlie shied at a locomotive's whistle in New Orleans and fell on Grant, causing him intense pain and confining him to bed for three weeks. He was still suffering from the effects when he received Lincoln's order; during the last part of the journey, over washouts and swollen creeks, he had sometimes to be lifted from his horse and carried in men's arms. Once in command, resolute and tireless, he ordered his army to take the offensive.

On 22–23 November opened the great battle for Chattanooga. Simultaneous attacks delivered by Hooker, Sherman, and Thomas drove the enemy from steep wooded ridges across the river. The capture of Missionary Ridge was the most gallant action of the war. As General H. V. Boynton, who was there, describes it:

Eighty-nine regiments rushed for the earthworks at the base of the ridge—every soldier like an arrow shot from a string which had been drawn to its full tension. . . . Riflemen in the Confederate earth-works and belching batteries above pelted them with the varied hail of battle. The sun swung low over the ridge. It never looked in all its shining over battle-fields upon a more imposing rush. Two miles and a half of gleaming rifle-barrels, line after line of them, and more than a hundred and fifty banners, state and national, blossoming along the advance. Not a straggler, only the killed and wounded, dropped from the ranks. They swept over the lower earthworks, capturing many prisoners, and . . . swarmed up the slopes. The colors rushed in advance, and the men crowded towards the banners. Each regiment became a wedge-shaped mass, the flags at the cutting edge cleaving the way to the summit. Without faltering, without a stay, the flags went on,— not long, it is sadly true, in the same hands, but always in willing hands, and in an hour from the sounding of the signal guns for starting, the crest for three miles was crowned with the stars and stripes, Bragg's whole centre was in flight, and forty of his guns and two thousand prisoners were in the hands of Thomas's victorious army.

This battle finished Bragg and placed the combined armies of the Tennessee and the Cumberland (Sherman and Thomas) in position to advance into Georgia in the early spring. The center of gravity had now shifted to the West. And the West had provided the Union with two great generals.

One more Union fiasco was yet to take place, the Red river campaign of the spring of 1864. After the fall of Vicksburg, all Confederate forces west of the Mississippi, including several thousand Indians, were under the command of General Edmund Kirby-Smith. Someone at Washington conceived the idea of using Porter's gunboat fleet to escort Banks's Army of the Mississippi, augmented by a corps from Sherman's army, up the Red river to Shreveport, whence the doughboys should be able to march into the heart of Texas. The gunboats did their part, but on 8 April 1864 Banks was jumped by Kirby-Smith at Pleasant Hill and badly defeated, leaving the fresh-water navy grounded and the river falling. Army engineers had to construct a dam to build up a head of water and float out the fleet.

Sherman's drive on Atlanta opened on 5 May, in accordance with typical orders from Grant: "You I propose to move against Johnston's army, to break it up and get into the interior of the enemy's country as far as you can, inflicting all the damage you can against their war resources." Sherman, the most trusted corps commander under Grant, resembled him physically—cropped rusty beard, disheveled appearance—and in an indomitable will to victory. But Sherman was loquacious when Grant was taciturn, and he loved dancing and pretty women. He proved himself even more skillful than the victor of Vicksburg, having learned from that campaign that surprise and mobility are the master keys to strategy. Sherman, too, glimpsed the concept of total war—war on the enemy's will to fight and capacity to support fighting men, as much as on the soldiers themselves. Robert E. Lee was the finest general of a Napoleonic age that was passing; Sherman was the first general of an age that was coming, and whose end we have not yet seen.

Sherman now commanded a group of three armies some 100,000 strong—the Cumberland (Thomas), Tennessee (McPherson), and Ohio (Schofield). Opposed to him was Joe Johnston with only 60,000 in his own Army of the Tennessee, but three excellent corps commanders—Hood, Hardee, and Bishop Polk—with the rich logistic resources of Georgia, and home-guard manpower and black labor troops to draw upon. Sherman jumped off from Chattanooga 5 May 1864, his army stripped to barest essentials in food and equipment; no tents even for senior officers. His base lay 150 miles north, at Nashville, over a one-track railroad that had to be protected from Confederate cavalry raids.

The four months' campaign for Atlanta that followed was professional war at its best. Johnston adopted Fabian strategy: to hold up Sherman by delaying actions, hoping to catch him "with his neck out" and, anyway, to produce war weariness in the North. "The whole country is one vast fort," wrote Sherman on 23 June. "As fast as we gain one position the enemy has another all ready." Sherman endeavored to outflank Johnston and get between him and Atlanta, but "Old Joe" showed as great skill and versatility in retiring actions as Marshal Kesselring was to exhibit in Italy some eighty years later, and the terrain was not dissimilar. On the 26th Sherman wrote, "We have devoured the land and our animals eat up the wheat and corn fields close. All the people retire before us and desolation is behind. To realize what war is one should follow our tracks." Next day Sherman, feeling that he had done enough marching and maneuvering, assaulted Johnston's entrenched line on Kenesaw Mountain, failed, and lost heavily; but this one mistake was followed by three weeks of brilliant maneuvering which took the Union army across the Chattahoochee river, eight miles from Atlanta. On that day (17 July) Jefferson Davis, in an insulting letter, relieved Johnston of his command and placed both theater and army under his impetuous corps commander, John B. Hood.

That was an ill-deserved cut to "Old Joe"; but retreats, however well conducted, do not win wars, and he had been outwitted. Again and again, in the 130-mile advance, Sherman lured the Confederates into vain attacks, and from each action gained a fresh vantage point. "To force an opponent acting on the strategic defensive into such a succession of costly tactical offensives was an example of strategic artistry rarely seen in history," writes Captain Liddell Hart.

Now, unwilling to decimate his army in frontal assaults on Atlanta's static defenses, Sherman tricked Hood into a series of reckless attacks. In one of these, at Allatoona Pass, Hood pushed some 1500 Union troops under General John M. Corse into earthworks at the crest of a hill. Here Corse, by flag signaling to Kenesaw Mountain, 20 miles away, asked for help; Sherman replied, "Hold the Fort. I am coming." Come

he did, in time to drive the Confederates off, and his cheery
signal became the theme of a popular hymn. Sherman now
maneuvered the greater part of his army in a wide wheel
about Atlanta and forced the Confederates to evacuate it on
1 September 1864.

"Atlanta is ours," reported Sherman. It had been a costly
campaign for both sides; but so firmly had Sherman guarded
communications, and so well had he been reinforced, that his
army, despite a loss of some 27,000 killed and wounded, was
stronger than it had been four months earlier. And the enemy's
loss, which could not be wholly replaced, was only about 1000
less.

4. The Wilderness Campaign

The first of January 1864 was the brightest New Year's day
for the Union since the war began. Volunteering was going on
rapidly, the danger of foreign intervention was over, the copperheads seemed cowed by recent victories, and nothing but
the armies of Lee and Johnston stood between the Union and
victory. A considerable "but." Lee's Wilderness campaign
came measurably close to destroying the Northern will to victory.

On 9 March 1864 Grant was appointed general in chief of
the armies of the United States. Summoned to Washington,
where he had never been, to confer with Lincoln, whom he
had never seen, the scrubby-looking general with his "slightly
seedy look" caused misgivings among those who were used
to the glittering commanders of the Army of the Potomac.
But Lincoln knew that now he had a general "who would take
the responsibility and act." And Grant never doubted the greatness and wisdom of his President.

Grant's plan for the Virginia campaign against Lee appeared
to be as inexorable as a nutcracker. With Meade commanding
the Army of the Potomac, he would move toward Richmond,
forcing the Confederates to give battle or abandon their capital.
General Franz Sigel (a veteran of the war of '48 in Germany
who had helped to save Missouri for the Union) now commanded the Army of the Shenandoah, whose mission was to
push up the valley to Lynchburg and prevent any Stonewall
Jackson shenanigans. That old rascal B. F. Butler was given
command of the Army of the James, apparently in order to
keep him out of politics. His mission was to march up the
south bank of the James, take Petersburg, and cut Lee's communications with the lower South. Both diversions miscarried.

Sigel, beaten by Breckenridge at Newmarket on 15 May, was superseded, and Jubal A. Early later drove his army across the Appalachians. The Army of the James, after being convoyed upriver by monitors and gunboats under Rear Admiral Samuel P. Lee, got itself, through Butler's fumbling ineptitude, "bottled up" (in Grant's words) by Beauregard in Bermuda Hundred at a loop of the river.

Thus, upon Grant fell the entire burden of the offensive. He chose the direct approach in which superior numbers would count, and he had as strong a will to victory as Marshal Foch, who employed similar strategy in 1918. "I determined," wrote Grant himself, "to hammer continuously against the armed force of the enemy and his resources, until by mere attrition, if in no other way, the military power of the rebellion was entirely broken."

On 4 May 1864 Grant crossed the Rapidan without opposition, and began to march his army of over 100,000 men through the same tangled Wilderness from which Jackson had fallen upon Hooker's flank at Chancellorsville. When he was halfway through, Lee repeated Jackson's maneuver. Grant accepted the challenge and promptly changed front, but his army maneuvered with great difficulty in that dense undergrowth, and in two days' fierce fighting he lost 17,700 men; Lee, less than half that number. A bad beginning for Grant; he now faced a general of different mettle from those whom he had beaten in the West.

Grant next tried to outflank the enemy. Clouds of dust from his marching columns warned Lee of his intention, and by the time his van had reached the crossroads at Spottsylvania Court House, the Army of Northern Virginia was there to check him. Both armies threw up field entrenchments, and the five days' battle that followed (Spottsylvania, 8–12 May, the battle of the "Bloody Angle") opened a long and terrible chapter of trench warfare, result of the increasing deadliness of firearms.

Having lost 12,227 more men at Spottsylvania, the indomitable Grant proposed "to fight it out on this line if it takes all summer." He moved by his left flank in the hope of outflanking Lee's right. Again the Army of Northern Virginia was there to receive him, and in a position so well chosen and entrenched that Grant needed all his adroitness to withdraw in safety and continue his flanking march (26 May). Lee swung with him to McClellan's old battlefield of Gaines's Mill. Both armies entrenched. Then came the Battle of Cold Harbor, costly and futile—an assault upon the entire line of

Lee's trenches with no adequate preparation to improve any temporary success. About 12,000 men were sacrificed, but hardly a dent was made on the Confederate lines.

During ten more days the armies faced one another. War had now acquired the horrors associated with World War I. The wounded, unattended between the lines, died of thirst and loss of blood. Corpses rotted on the ground. Sharpshooters kept up their deadly work. Officers and men fought mechanically, hopelessly. The war had begun so long ago that one could hardly remember a state of peace. Would it continue until everyone on both sides was dead?

In one month Grant had advanced to the Chickahominy, the exact spot where McClellan had stood two years before; and he had suffered severe losses, though no more, proportionally, than Lee.[1] But Grant never flinched. On 12 June he carried out McClellan's old plan—a change of base to the James, and an attempt to cut the communications of Richmond at Petersburg. The maneuver was skillfully executed, but an opportunity to push into undefended Petersburg was lost, owing to Butler's check on the James. Lee slipped into Petersburg, entrenched in time, and three general assaults of 15–18 June cost the Union 8000 more men.

A war of positions had arrived in the Virginia theater. Grant's army besieged Petersburg for nine months. He never had enough men or artillery to carry the enemy lines by assault, and one attempt to do so, by mining under them and blowing them up by dynamite—the Battle of the Crater—ended in costly defeat. But he was right in pinning Lee down while Sherman reduced the effective area of the Confederacy; for Lee unable to maneuver was not dangerous.

Such, in brief, was the most desperately fought campaign of the war. Lee, with inferior forces, had saved his army and saved Richmond. Grant, after making mistakes and suffering losses that would have broken any of his predecessors, was still indefatigable. But how long would the country suffer such stupendous losses, with no apparent result?

Lincoln, too, was indefatigable. In a speech on 16 June he said:

> We accepted this war for an object, a worthy object, and
> the war will end when that object is attained. Under God,
> I hope it never will end until that time. . . . This war has

[1] The oft-repeated statement (e.g. Freeman's *Lee*, III, p. 446) that Grant lost more men in this campaign than Lee's entire army at the outset, is shown by Channing, *United States*, VI, p. 571*n*. to be false. Actually, Lee's losses were proportionally greater than Grant's.

taken three years; it was begun or accepted upon the line of restoring the national authority over the whole national domain, and for the American people; as far as my knowledge enables me to speak, I say we are going through on this line if it takes three years more.

Within a month his fortitude would be severely tested by Early's raid and by peace intrigues.

TENTING TONIGHT

XXIII

Victory and Death

1864-1865

1. *Early's Raid and the Election of 1864*

JUBAL A. EARLY, "Old Jube" to his troops, was a snarling misanthrope, bent by arthritis contracted in the Mexican War, but eager and aggressive. He now pulled off a spectacular raid. On 2 July 1864 his 15,000 veterans were at Winchester, marching north by the classic valley route. A few days later he was across the Potomac, laying Hagerstown and Frederick under contribution, and at noon on 11 July his van passed through Silver Spring and reached Fort Stevens in the District of Columbia. Fortunately, his advance had been held up for two days at the Monocacy river by General Lew Wallace, so that on the same day that Early sighted the dome of the Capitol, a Union corps which Grant had hurriedly diverted from the Army of the Potomac, disembarked at Washington. It went right into action, President Lincoln watching the engagement from the parapet of Fort Stevens, rebel bullets whistling past his tall hat. The Confederates were driven back, and on 13 July made good their escape to the Shenandoah valley, gorged with loot and provisions.

Early's raid, in combination with Grant's check before Petersburg and Sherman's halt before Atlanta, provided fodder for the peace movement in the North; even for a change of administration. A considerable section of the public had lost confidence in Grant and in Lincoln. The appalling toll of casualties seemed to have brought the war no nearer conclusion. Paper dollars fell to one-third their value in gold on the day that Early appeared before Washington. And the cost of living had soared far beyond the rise of wages or salaries. Unable to look beyond their own troubles to the far greater ills of their enemy, many people in the North began to ask whether further prosecution of the war would profit anyone but the profiteers. This undercurrent of doubt and despair induced some strange developments in the presidential campaign that was already under way.

Alone of modern governments prior to World War II, the United States faced a general election in wartime. For, as Lincoln said, "We cannot have free government without elections; and if the rebellion could force us to forego or postpone a national election, it might fairly claim to have already conquered and ruined us." On 7 June 1864 Lincoln was renominated for the presidency by a National Union convention representing both Republicans and War Democrats, with Democrat Andrew Johnson, the stout Union war governor of Tennessee, for the vice presidency. The New York *World,* organ of "hightoned" Democrats, declared the nomination of these "two ignorant, boorish, third-rate backwoods lawyers" to be "an insult to the common sense of the people."

There now developed a movement against Lincoln within his own party. Salmon P. Chase, hoping to be President himself, resigned from the cabinet and struck an alliance with political adventurers and marplots such as General Butler, Roscoe Conkling a New York congressman, and Horace Greeley, editor of the New York *Tribune.* This noted journalist, suffering from one of his not infrequent brainstorms, believed that the Confederacy could be wheedled back into the Union by diplomacy, and that Lincoln was a liability. On the subject of peace, Lincoln wrote to Greeley on 9 July, "If you can find any person anywhere professing to have any proposition of Jefferson Davis, in writing, for peace, embracing the restoration of the Union and abandonment of slavery, say to him he may come to me." Greeley met on Canadian soil two men who claimed to have a peace offer, only to find that they were charlatans; but his ardor for negotiation was not dampened.

As if this were not enough, a breach opened between the President and the Radicals over reconstructing the Union after the war. When on 8 July Lincoln pocket-vetoed a bill embodying Radical views of reconstruction, Senator Ben Wade of Ohio and Representative Henry Winter Davis of Maryland issued a public manifesto accusing the President of a "studied outrage on the legislative authority of the people" from the basest motives of personal ambition. Greeley published this Wade-Davis Manifesto in the *Tribune* on 5 August; and two weeks later he and the Radicals began to circulate among other politicians a "call" for a new Republican convention to reconsider Lincoln and nominate General Butler, or anyone. Diehards and defeatists in alliance, to elevate to the presidency a general who had never won a battle! The executive committee of the Republican party even implored Lincoln to make peace overtures to Jefferson Davis, as a sop to defeatist sentiment.

This panic of the politicians—fortunately it went no further —was dangerous. What Lincoln really thought of the situation is clear from the paper he wrote and sealed on 23 August, to be opened only after the election: "It seems exceedingly probable that this administration will not be re-elected. Then it will be my duty to so co-operate with the President-elect as to save th Union between the election and the inauguration, as he will have secured his election on such ground that he cannot possibly save it afterward."

If Jefferson Davis had been adroit, he could have completed the distraction of Union councils by proposing an armistice or peace conference on any terms, For, had the fighting once been halted, it is doubtful whether it could ever have been renewed. But the Southern president was still living in a dream world, certain that his cause was invincible. "Say to Mr. Lincoln from me," he told a volunteer peacemaker, "that I shall at any time be pleased to receive proposals for peace on the basis of our Independence. It will be useless to approach me with any other."

In the face of this honest statement, published on 20 August 1864, the Democratic national convention on the 29th adopted a resolution drafted by the copperhead Vallandigham: "After four years of failure to restore the Union by the experiment of war . . . justice, humanity, liberty, and the public welfare demand that immediate efforts be made for a cessation of hostilities . . . to the end that, at the earliest practicable moment, peace may be restored on the basis of the federal Union of the States." General McClellan accepted the Democratic nomination for President; the vice-presidential nomination went to "Gentleman George" Pendleton, an Ohio congressman who had been vilifying the Lincoln administration throughout the war. McClellan repudiated the peace plank in the platform, but was not unwilling to ride on it to the White House.

Jefferson Davis by his frankness, the Democrats by their shameless defeatism, and Sherman by capturing Atlanta on 2 September, knocked the bottom out of this "reconsider Lincoln" conspiracy. On 6 September a new army draft went quietly into effect and, marvelous to relate, Wade and Chase took the stump for the President. A smashing military victory in an old theater of Union frustration undoubtedly helped.

Dashing, thirty-three-year-old, five-foot-two-inch Philip Sheridan, one of the heroes of Chickamauga and Lookout Mountain, had reorganized the mounted service of the Army of the Potomac so that it became tactically equal if not superior to the Southern *beaux-sabreurs*. In August 1864 Grant gave him command over the Army of the Shenandoah, with the objective of destroying the Shenandoah valley as a base of enemy opertions or supplies. After beating Early twice on 19 and 22 September, Sheridan began a systematic devastation of the valley. Leaving his army encamped at Cedar Creek near Strasburg, Sheridan, returning from a conference at Washington, had reached Winchester when he heard firing to the southward. Mounting his charger Rienzi, a magnificent jet-black Morgan gelding, Sheridan rode down the valley pike and presently met panic-stricken units of his army. Early had routed them in a brilliant surprise attack. Rallying the men and turning them right-about, Sheridan rode the 20 miles to Cedar Creek, galloped along the lines to hearten wavering troops who had not retreated, and did what few generals have done since Napoleon. He transformed a defeated, panic-stricken mob into an army again, and ended by completely routing Early's Confederates.[1]

Another victory that helped re-elect Lincoln was Admiral Farargut's at Mobile Bay. The Confederate navy there, under Admiral Buchanan, had constructed its most powerful ship, the 209-foot ironclad ram *Tennessee*, armed with 6- and 7-inch guns. Stupidly enough, she was given so much draught that she could not steam across the bar in normal tides to get at the blockading fleet; but she was strong enough to be a "fleet in being" that had to be eliminated. The Confederates had planted the channel into Mobile Bay with anchored mines (in that area called torpedoes), and the entrance was further protected by Fort Morgan. Admiral Farragut's seven wooden sloops-of-war, *Brooklyn* leading and flagship *Hartford* next,

---

[1] Rienzi is estimated to have covered 75 miles that day, and mostly on the gallop. The poem "Sheridan's Ride," a favorite subject of school declamations for half a century, was composed a few days after the event by the painter-poet Thomas B. Read, then a major on General Lew Wallace's staff.

with a parallel column of four monitors and ten gunboats in two groups, opened fire at 6:30 a.m. August 5. C.S.S. *Tennessee* and three gunboats steamed out to challenge. The lookouts in U.S.S. *Hartford* sighted what surely were mines, but Farragut the invincible, perched high in the rigging to get a better view, ordered, "Damn the torpedoes! Four bells! Captain Drayton, go ahead! Jouett, full speed!" He evaded *Tennessee*'s attempt to ram, but his round shot rolled off the rebel's six-inch armor like marbles off a tin roof. Buchanan's gunboats, however, were knocked off in one-two-three order. U.S.S. *Monongahela*, *Lackawanna*, and *Hartford* in succession rammed the rebel, scraping along her topsides so close that sailors could fight each other through the portholes. Finally the 11-inch bullets of U.S. monitor *Chickasaw*, by pounding on the after side of the casemate like a dentist's hammer on a sore tooth, made a breach and shot away the ram's tiller chains so that she became helpless. She surrendered at 10:00 a.m., and Admiral Buchanan with a broken leg became a prisoner of war. This was the greatest naval action of the Civil War. Fort Morgan surrendered 23 August to a troop assault, supported by a heavy naval bombardment. Mobile City was now sealed off, and the Union navy's control of the Gulf of Mexico became complete.

On 8 November 1864, the Northern voters chose 212 electors for Lincoln and Johnson, only 21 for McClellan and Pendleton, representing Delaware, Kentucky, and New Jersey. The popular vote was not so emphatic—roughly 2.2 million to 1.8 million, and in the three pivotal states of New York, Pennsylvania, and Ohio, Lincoln had a margin of only 86,400. This strong minority vote did not all represent defeatism; many thousands voted for McClellan because they regarded him as a possible Napoleon or De Gaulle who would save the country, and Lincoln as a country bumpkin who knew not how to end a war he had started. No presidential election better illustrated Lincoln's own adage that you can fool some of the people all the time, but not all of the people all the time.

2. *From Atlanta to Appomattox*

President Davis assured his people on 28 September that Sherman must sooner or later retreat from Atlanta, "and when that day comes the fate that befell the army of the French empire in its retreat from Moscow will be re-acted." On 17 October Sherman cut loose from Atlanta in the opposite direction, toward the sea. Abandoning his logistics line, and breaking all communications so he could not be recalled, he led 62,000 men and 2500 six-mule teams laden with supplies into enemy country, leaving two army corps to deal with Hood in Tennessee. Amazing as it seems, Washington had no news of Sherman's army for an entire month, except what it could glean from Richmond newspapers.

The march to the sea, like Sheridan's Shenandoah campaign, was one of deliberate destruction, in order to ruin a main source of provisions for Lee's and Hood's armies. Sherman cut a swath 60 miles wide through "the garden spot of the Confederacy," destroying stores of provisions, standing crops and cattle, cotton gins and mills, railways beyond possibility of repair; in fact, everything that could be useful to the Confederacy and much that was not. The indiscriminate looting of private houses, although forbidden by orders, was largely the work of the "bummers"—stragglers from both sides; and also of Joe Wheeler's Confederate cavalry which hung on the flanks. Outrages on persons were surprisingly few, and on women, none. It was the sort of campaign that soldiers love—maximum of looting and destruction, minimum of discipline and fighting: splendid weather, few impediments, plenty of broiled turkey and fried chicken and roast pork, swarms of blacks eager to pillage their former masters, tagging joyfully along. As Herman Melville wrote,

> It was glorious glad marching
> For every man was free;

and the song "Marching Through Georgia," composed shortly after by Henry C. Work, has become a part of black folklore, in the West Indies and even Africa. Sherman emerged at the seacoast near Savannah on 10 December, and was able to offer Lincoln the city as a Christmas present.

Sherman's ignoring Hood and going off in a contrary direction, perhaps the biggest gamble of the war, paid off handsomely. Hood, with 40,000 veterans, moved into central Tennessee, hoping to catch Thomas's and Schofield's corps and whip them separately. At the end of November he caught up with Schofield at Franklin, and sacrificed 6000 men in a series of gallant but futile attacks. Schofield slipped away to Nashville, where Thomas, "the rock of Chickamauga," was in command. Disregarding frantic telegrams from Stanton and Grant, Thomas bided his time, and on 16 December 1864 inflicted on Hood at Nashville the most smashing defeat of the war, capturing over 10,000 men and 72 guns. Grant made prompt amends to Thomas for his impatience; but this great Virginian, who had forsaken home and kindred out of loyalty to the Union, and to whom no military critic today would deny a place among the immortals was neglected in the distribution of postwar honors.

There were still leaks in the blockade that needed caulking, and the Confederate navy was constructing ironclads to bust through—notably *Albemarle,* built on the Roanoke river. Lieutenant William B. Cushing USN, a handsome, intrepid youth, commanding a 30-foot steam launch fitted with a torpedo at the end of a spar, sneaked upstream on the night of 27–28 October 1864 to find *Albemarle* moored to a wharf at Plymouth, N.C., and protected by a log boom. Cushing turned up full speed, crashed through the boom under hot fire from the ironclad, and poked his torpedo under her bottom just as one of her big guns opened on him at a range of 12 feet. The ironclad blew up and sank, and so did the launch; but Cushing and most of his crew escaped by swimming. Subsequent capture of Plymouth by Union gunboats stopped that leak in the blockade.

The biggest leak, through the Cape Fear river to Wilmington, whence a railway forwarded supplies to Richmond, was a difficult one to cork. The twin entrances to the river were dominated by forts; and one, 75-gun Fort Fisher, could only be taken by amphibious assault. Secretary Welles had been trying for over a year to get troops to do it, but the army insisted first on attacking Charleston, and wasted time and strength on that futile operation. General Grant, however, saw the strategic value of sealing off Richmond's back door, and provided a landing force. Unfortunately he placed these troops under General Butler, who here "goofed" for the last time. His big idea, to explode a dynamite-filled hulk under the sea face of the fort while he landed troops on a nearby beach, fizzled; Butler then quit cold, leaving the navy to extricate his men. Rear Admiral Porter, commanding the Union blockading squadron, begged Grant to let him try again, and Grant did. After the hottest naval bombardment of the war by Porter's 44 ships, on 13–14 January 1865, a landing force under General Alfred H. Terry attacked Fort Fisher from the rear, while 2000 bluejackets and marines of the fleet assaulted it directly from the sea. The sailors and leathernecks (Lieutenant Cushing leading) were driven back after heavy loss, but by throwing the defense off balance they enabled the doughboys to gain a foothold within the fort. The following night it surrendered, with 2100 Confederates. This, the most successful amphibious operation of the Civil War, ended blockade running.

Next day, in Washington, General Butler was testifying to his pals of the Congressional committee on the conduct of the war, that Fort Fisher was impregnable, when newsboys were heard shouting an extra—"Fort Fisher Surrendered!" Everyone, including Ben, roared with laughter.

Five days before the fall of Fort Fisher, Sherman's army broke loose from the sea and began marching into the Carolinas, as Cornwallis had done; but what a difference from 1780! Country from which the redcoats could not find food for one meal a day was now glutted with grain and livestock, and Sherman saw to it that only scorched earth was left. He had about 60,000 men at the start; Johnston (reluctantly restored by Davis to command over Hood on 23 February 1865) had about 40,000. Sherman adopted tactics which portended those of the German panzer forces that swarmed over northern France in 1940. Moving on a wide, irregular front in four to six columns, each one of which could push on if others were blocked, he kept the enemy guessing as to his next objective. Would it be Columbia or Charleston and, next, Charlotte or Fayetteville? and, after that, Raleigh or Goldsboro? Sherman himself never decided which it would be until his cavalry reported enemy dispositions. On 17 February he seized Columbia and pinched the Confederates out of Charleston. On 11 March he was in Fayetteville; on the 23rd, after pushing Johnston out of his way, Sherman arrived at Goldsboro, 425 miles from Savannah.

The sun of the Confederacy was setting fast, though gloriously; yet the civilian leaders looked the other way. Lee, they hoped, would break contact with Grant, unite with Johnston's 35,000 men, and pull off a counteroffensive against Sherman— like Rundstedt's Battle of the Bulge 80 years later. There were still enough white men of fighting age in the Confederacy to provide her army with half a million men.[1] The Confederate munitions service was now independent of foreign supplies; its producing center at Selma, Alabama, was not captured until 2 April. Despite Sherman, there was still plenty of cattle and corn in the Carolinas, and the latest Confederate war secretary, General John Breckenridge, reported 8 million rations to be en route from the deep South to Richmond. Every material factor seemed to justify protracted resistance; only morale was wanting. The re-election of Lincoln, the hopeless prospect of foreign aid, Union victories by land and sea, Grant's strategy of attrition, and the increasing pinch of the blockade, took the heart out of the South. "Two-thirds of our men are absent . . .

[1] Actually, 174,223 Confederate troops surrendered in April and May 1865. Comparing the number of desertions during the previous four months, and the white population of fighting age, the estimate of 500,000 possible fighting men is not excessive. But the Union armies on 1 May numbered 1,052,038 officers and men.

most of them absent without leave," admitted President Davis in September 1864. Joe Johnston wrote that he did not blame his men for going A.W.O.L.; they were getting letters from home telling how their farms had been stripped of food and animals by the Confederate commissary; they had to desert to save their families. Senator Benjamin H. Hill of Georgia, who wrote to President Davis on 25 March 1865, "We shall conquer all enemies yet," admitted nine years later, "All physical advantages are insufficient to account for our failure. The truth is, we failed because too many of our people were not determined to win."

Davis could see only the outer reality—so many men and rifles and cannon, so much food and gunpowder. To the deeper reality in the hearts of the people he was insensible as any European dictator. Pressure by some of his top advisers persuaded him to ask for a peace conference, in hope of obtaining from Lincoln a statement of Union war aims to "fire the Southern heart." The statement came out of a four-hour conference on board steamer *River Queen* in Hampton Roads, between President Lincoln and Vice President Stephens, who had been Lincoln's friend in Congress sixteen years earlier. Stephens had credentials to negotiate peace as the envoy of an independent republic. Lincoln patiently repeated his refusal to negotiate on that basis. Senator Hunter, who accompanied Stephens, alleged as precedent the negotiations during the English Civil War. Lincoln replied, "I do not profess to be posted in history. On all such matters I will turn you over to Seward. All I distinctly recollect about the case of Charles I is that he lost his head." But he added, "The war will cease on the part of the Government, whenever it shall have ceased on the part of those who began it." And that was that.

As Lincoln predicted, Davis "cannot voluntarily re-accept the Union; we cannot voluntarily yield it." Lee might with honor surrender his army to irresistible force; Davis could not with honor surrender his nation. The inherent dignity of his refusal was marred by a silly boast at a public meeting in Richmond that he would compel the Yankees in less than twelve months to petition him for peace on his own terms.

It was now the eighth day of February 1865, and the Confederacy was sinking fast. Even slavery was jettisoned in principle. Sherman, as he marched northward, was proving his sulphurous definition of war. Joe Johnston fought his last battle at Bentonville, North Carolina, on 19 March. On the 23rd Sherman marched into Goldsboro and made rendezvous with Thomas, the victor of Nashville. Reunited, this great Army of the West had 90,000 men; Johnston a scant 25,000. Sherman nevertheless passed some anxious hours when he learned that Lee and his grim veterans were on the loose again.

For nine months the two armies in Virginia had faced one another across long lines of entrenchment running through the suburbs of Petersburg. At the beginning of the siege their forces were not disparate; but by the middle of March 1865 Grant had 115,000 effectives to Lee's 54,000. If Lee did not move out of his trenches, Grant would envelop him; but if Petersburg were abandoned, Richmond must fall. Lee first tried moving forward, but his assault on the Union left was a costly failure. He must make up his mind to retreat, or it would soon be too late even for that. Sheridan, having disposed of Early, marched his Army of the Shenandoah across Virginia, thrust back Lee's right at the Battle of Five Forks (1 April), and next day Grant penetrated the center of the Confederate defenses. Lee's only hope was to retire and unite with Johnston.

On the night of 2–3 April, Lee's army slipped out of the Petersburg lines; next evening the Union forces entered Richmond. Without pause, Grant pursued. Rations failed to reach Lee, through fumbling at Richmond; his 30,000 men had to live on a thinly populated country in springtime. By 9 April Sheridan had closed the only avenues of retirement west or south. Possibly Lee could have cut his way through to the mountains and waged guerrilla warfare, but he had too great a sense of responsibility to take any such course, or to ride into a volley of Union bullets. So he ordered a white flag (the Confederates had no such thing, so used a towel) to be carried through the lines, to request an interview with General Grant.

The scene that followed, in the McLean house of the tiny village of Appomattox Court House, has become a part of American folklore: Lee, in a new full-dress uniform with sash and jewel-studded sword, Grant in his usual unbuttoned private's blouse, "his feelings sad and depressed at the downfall of a foe who had fought so long and valiantly." Small talk of other days, in the old army. Grant wrote the terms of surrender in his own hand. "Officers and men paroled . . . arms and matériel surrendered . . . officers to keep their side arms, and let all the men who claim to own a horse or mule take the animals home with them to work their little farms." "This will do much toward conciliating our people," said Lee. The conference over, the Confederate leader paused a moment in the doorway, looking out over a field blossoming with the Stars and Stripes. Thrice, and slowly, he struck a fist into the palm of his gauntleted hand. He mounted Traveller and returned to his field headquarters.

A sound of cheering spread along the Union lines. "The soldiers rushed, perfectly crazy, to the roadside, and shouted, screamed, yelled, threw up their hats and hopped madly up and down! The batteries were run out and began firing, the bands played, the flags waved." As soon as this clamor reached his ears, General Grant ordered it to cease, in these words: "The war is over; the rebels are our countrymen again."

"Over the carnage rose prophetic a voice," wrote Walt Whitman, catching the spirit of that great moment. "Affection shall solve the problems of freedom yet."

Could his prophecy have been fulfilled but for the insane assassination on 14 April? It certainly might have been, had things been left to the fighting officers and men. Commissioners appointed by Lee and Grant to arrange practical details of the surrender had no difficulty reaching an agreement. Grant not only rushed rations to the half-starved Confederates but allowed them free transportation home on government ships and railways. As General Gordon, one of the commissioners, said, courtesy and even deference was shown to the defeated officers; everyone looked forward to "a liberal, generous, magnanimous policy" toward the South. A Confederate cannoneer, who had expected to be "paraded through Northern cities for the benefit of jeering crowds" (as had been done to Union prisoners in Richmond), was relieved to learn that he could go home. There was good-humored chaffing between officers of both sides. General Meade, who had superbly commanded the Army of the Potomac through this last campaign, rode out to meet the Confederate commander, doffed his cap (the old-fashioned army salute), and said, "Good morning, General." Lee remarked, "What are you doing with all that gray in your beard?" To which Meade replied, "You have to answer for most of it!"

On 12 April came the formal laying down of arms. Two Union brigades were drawn up on each side of the road near Appomattox Court House. At the right of the line, mounted, was Major General Joshua L. Chamberlain, former colonel of the 20th Maine, chosen by Grant for this honorable post since he had fought nobly in the last campaign. At the head of the tattered, mud-caked Confederate column rode General Gordon, one of Jackson's old captains; and by his choice the Stonewall Brigade, now down to 210 officers and men, marched in the van. Then came the other regiments, now so decimated that their massed colors formed a ruddy crown to the marching men. As the column approached the Union lines, a bugle spoke; General Chamberlain had given the order "Carry Arms!"—the marching salute. General Gordon raised his downcast eyes when he heard the familiar snap and rattle of the muskets, gave Chamberlain the cavalryman's sword salute, and passed the word to his own men, "Carry *Arms!*" In complete, awed silence the Confederate column passed at the salute; then, in perfect order, the men stacked arms and cartridge boxes and laid down their flags. At that final symbol of defeat, many broke ranks, and, sobbing, pressed the beloved colors to their lips. General Gordon, with moist eyes, addressed the men from horseback, urging them to depart in peace to obey the laws and work for the future of a reunited nation.

The remaining history of the Confederacy is quickly told. President Davis slipped away from Richmond in a special train ahead of the Union troops on 2 April, together with several members of his cabinet and about $500,000 in specie. Davis did not feel that he was retreating, only looking for a new capital. On 4 April he issued a proclamation that the Southern people had "now entered upon a new phase of the struggle, the memory of which is to endure for all ages"; that nothing but "unquenchable resolve" was needed to make victory certain. Even the news of Lee's surrender affected Davis's resolve not a whit; he was still living in the purple dream, hero of an historic drama, blind to the raw fact of utter defeat. At Greensboro, North Carolina, he summoned General Johnston and Beauregard to attend a Confederate cabinet meeting and vainly endeavored to persuade them to continue the war. Secretaries Benjamin, Mallory, and Breckenridge urged Davis to throw in the sponge, but still he refused.

On 16 April the presidential party took to the road, with what was left of the treasury in a carriage. Ten days later, Johnston surrendered his army to Sherman. When Jefferson Davis reached Abbeville, South Carolina, on 3 May, he implored a group of faithful cavalry officers to stand firm:— "Three thousand brave men" he said, "are enough for a nucleus around which the whole people will rally." After the troopers had sadly told him the truth, he admitted "All is indeed lost." The cabinet ministers now took off to save themselves. On 10 May a troop of Union cavalry captured President and Mrs. Davis near Irwinsville, Georgia, and the Confederacy as a government flickered out.

General Richard Taylor had already surrendered all remaining Confederate forces east of the Mississippi; General Simon Bolivar Buckner, Kirby-Smith's chief of staff, negotiated at New Orleans on 26 May a surrender of all west of the Great River. While these negotiations were going on, the last land battle of the war was fought on 12–13 May at Palmetto Ranch

near the Rio Grande—and, ironically enough, it was a Confederate victory. The Confederacy's Indian allies held out a
month longer; Colonels Stand Watie of the Cherokee and Peter
B. Pitchlynn of the Chocktaw did not surrender their armed
men until 23 June. Most of the vessels of the Confederate navy
still in port were scuttled or burned, and their crews scattered.
One-sided hostilities continued in the Pacific Ocean, where
C.S.S. *Shenandoah* was engaged in destroying Yankee whale
ships. Her commander pursued this inglorious occupation into
August, then sailed back to England and surrendered his ship to
British authorities on 6 November 1865. Her ensign was the
last war flag of the Confederacy to be lowered.

3. The Last Days of Lincoln

With malice toward none; with charity for all; with
firmness in the right, as God gives us to see the right, let
us strive on to finish the work we are in; to bind up the
nation's wounds; to care for him who shall have borne
the battle, and for his widow, and his orphan—to do all
which may achieve and cherish a just and lasting peace
among ourselves, and with all nations.

Thus closed the second inaugural address of President Lincoln. The struggle over reconstruction was already on, but
when Congress next met in December, it might be confronted
with the established fact of a restored nation, if the South were
wise, and nothing happened to Lincoln.

Toward the end of March, the President and Mrs. Lincoln,
on steamer *River Queen*, visited General and Mrs. Grant at the
general's rear headquarters at City Point on the James. On
the 26th Lincoln accompanied Grant on an inspection of General Ord's division, and Grant paid the President a compliment
he had given to no other man, lending him his thoroughbred
Cincinnati. Lincoln rode Cincinnati, it is said, like a professional, although he presented a rather odd figure in his tall
stovepipe hat, flapping coattails, and trousers inching up toward
his knees. On 3 April Lincoln met Grant again in liberated
Petersburg, and next day, with a guard of under twenty officers
and men, he visited burned Richmond. Then back to City
Point. That evening a military band gave a concert on board
the *River Queen*, and at the President's request played "The
Marseillaise" in honor of Lafayette's grandson, the Marquis
de Chambrun, who was a guest; and "Dixie," which Lincoln

quaintly remarked, "is Federal property" now. On the 9th, as the party steamed up the Potomac to Washington, Lincoln read aloud passages from Shakespeare; and Chambrun later recalled with what solemnity he pronounced a passage from *Macbeth:*

> Duncan is in his grave;
> After life's fitful fever he sleeps well;
> Treason has done his worst: nor steel, nor poison,
> Malice domestic, foreign levy, nothing
> Can touch him further.

Driving from the Washington wharf to the White House, Mrs. Lincoln remarked, "That city is full of enemies," to which the President retorted with an impatient gesture, "Enemies—never again must we repeat that word!" Mary, alas, was right. An assassination plot was coming to a head.

Everywhere in Washington, wrote Chambrun, "the words peace, pardon and clemency can be heard." On 11 April, the day after Lee's surrender was announced, Lincoln delivered his last public address, from a window in the White House to a crowd on the lawn. After a brief allusion to Appomattox and the hope of a speedy peace, he unfolded his reconstruction policy—the most magnanimous terms toward a helpless opponent ever offered by a victor. For Lincoln did not consider himself a conqueror. He was, and had been since 1861, President of the United States. The rebellion must be forgotten; and every Southern state be readmitted to full privileges in the Union as soon as 10 per cent of its citizens had taken the oath of allegiance and organized a state government.

On Thursday night, 13 April, Washington was illuminated on account of Lee's surrender, and crowds paraded the streets. A general lightheartedness was in the air; everyone felt that the war was practically over. On Good Friday, the 14th, at breakfast Lincoln's son Robert showed the President a photograph of General Lee. "It is a good face," said the President. "I am glad the war is over at last." That morning he held his last cabinet meeting, with General Grant present. He had decided to lift the blockade. He urged his ministers to turn their thoughts to peace. There must be no more bloodshed, no persecution. Grant was asked for late news from Sherman, but had none. Lincoln remarked that it would come soon, and be favorable, for last night he had dreamed a familiar dream. In a strange, indescribable ship he seemed to be moving with great rapidity toward a far, indefinite shore. He had had this same dream before Antietam, Murfreesboro, Vicksburg, and Wilmington. Matter-of-fact Grant remarked that Murfreesboro was no victory; "a few such fights would have ruined us." Lincoln looked at him curiously and said, however that might be, his dream preceded that battle.

That evening Lincoln, who loved the theater, took his wife and two friends to Ford's Theater to see Laura Keene in a play called "Our American Cousin." This was exactly what the principal assassin wanted. As an actor, his face and presence were familiar to the theater employees, and he knew all the doors and passageways. The secret service man who should have guarded the entrance to the President's box moved to the balcony so he could follow the play better.

At about 10:13 p.m. a pistol shot rang out, the President slumped in his seat, Booth leaped from the box to the stage, paused a moment to brandish his gun and shout *Sic semper tyrannis!*, rushed through the rear exit, and was off and away on horseback.

Let Secretary Welles be our guide to the doleful events of that night. He had gone early to bed and was just falling asleep when someone shouted from the street that the President had been shot and the secretary of state and his son assassinated by another member of the murder gang. Welles dressed and crossed Lafayette Square to Seward's house on 15th Street. The lower hall was full of excited people. Welles rushed upstairs to a room where Seward was lying on a bed saturated with blood, his lower jaw sagging as if in death. In the next room lay Frederick Seward, unconscious from the injuries he had received while defending his father.

Welles, joined by Stanton, hurried downtown in a carriage. The President had been carried from Ford's Theater across 10th Street to a lodging-house, and laid on a bed in a narrow back room. He never recovered consciousness. "The giant sufferer," writes Welles, "lay extended diagonally across the bed, which was not long enough for him. . . . . His slow, full respiration lifted the clothes with each breath that he took. His features were calm and striking." It was a dark and gloomy night, and rain fell at dawn. Crowds remained in the street, looking in vain for hope from the watchers who came out for a breath of air. "About once an hour Mrs. Lincoln would repair to the bedside of her dying husband and with lamentation and tears remain until overcome by emotion." At 7:22 a.m. 15 April the President's breathing stopped and his heart ceased to beat. Dr. Gurley, the Lincolns' pastor, made a short prayer. Then silence, broken only by Stanton's calm sentence: "Now he belongs to the ages."

In a parlor of the lodging-house the cabinet assembled without Seward, and wrote a letter to Vice President Johnson, "informing him of the event, and that the government devolved upon him."

Welles continues, "I went after breakfast to the Executive Mansion. There was a cheerless cold rain and everything seemed gloomy. On the Avenue in front of the White House were several hundred colored people, mostly women and children, weeping and wailing their loss. This crowd did not appear to diminish through the whole of that cold, wet day; they seemed not to know what was to be their fate since their great benefactor was dead, and their hopeless grief affected me more than almost anything else, although strong and brave men wept when I met them."

XXIV

Reconstruction

1865-1877

1. *War's Aftermath*

TEN THOUSAND CURSES on the memory of that foulest of assassins, J. Wilkes Booth! Not only did he kill a great and good President; he gave fresh life to the very forces of hate and vengeance which Lincoln himself was trying to kill. Had Lincoln lived, there is every likelihood that his magnanimous policy toward the South would have prevailed; for, even after his death, it almost went through despite the Radicals. Never has a murderer wrought so much evil.

Lincoln himself had said, "Blood cannot restore blood, and government should not act for revenge." But for weeks after the assassination there was a petty reign of terror directed by Secretary Stanton. Only the stern intervention of General Grant prevented the arrest of Lee and other Confederate generals as "conspirators." Colossal rewards for Davis and his cabinet, as alleged promoters of the assassination, resulted in the capture of several, and "Hang Jeff Davis!" became a popular cry like "Hang the Kaiser!" after World War I. But the charge of official complicity in the crime was soon seen to be preposterous; and that of treason, though pressed for a time, was wisely directed to the circumlocution office. Almost every civil or military leader of the Confederacy expressed regret over the murder of Lincoln; the nastiest recorded remark about it was made by a mid-western copperhead journalist known as "Brick" Pomeroy: "The shameless tyrant, justly felled by an avenging hand, rots in his grave, while his soul is consumed by eternal fire at the bottom of the blackest hole in hell."

Popular thirst for revenge appeared to be slaked by shooting Lincoln's assassin and hanging three accomplices and the wretched woman who had harbored them, after trial by a military tribunal. Jefferson Davis was incarcerated in Fortress Monroe for two years and then released;[1] Stephens and a few members of the Confederate cabinet were confined for shorter periods. The only war criminal executed was Captain Henry Wirz for his cruelties to Union prisoners in the stockade at Andersonville. Many more Canadians were executed for their uprising of 1837 than were Confederates for a more costly rebellion.

European observers were astonished at the quick demobilization of the Union army and the almost universal acceptance of the war's verdict in the South. With a celerity that surprised everyone, the Union Army was reduced from a million men at the time of Appomattox to 183,000 on 10 November 1865, and by the end of 1866 to about 25,000, a number that remained constant for thirty years. Most of the navy's ships were sold; only a few wooden sloops-of-war and ironclad monitors were retained. Discharged soldiers and sailors were quickly absorbed into civilian life. Goldwin Smith, the British publicist, regarded American disarmament as "the most truly magnanimous and wisest thing in history." It was assumed in Europe that President Johnson, with a big army at his disposal, would grab Canada as "compensation" for war losses, or invade Mexico to oust Maximilian. But, beyond sending an army of observation to the Mexican border to give moral support to Juárez, he did nothing in either quarter; and a few years later, Congress refused to buy a naval base in the West Indies, indicating that "manifest destiny" had come to a full stop. The United States, to be sure, bought Alaska from Russia in 1867, but here the seller was more eager than the buyer, the transaction was denounced as "Seward's folly," and there is at least a strong suspicion that Russian gold eased the passage of the treaty through the Senate.

Equally astonishing to a Europe accustomed to persistence of Irish, Polish, and other national grievances was Southern ac-

[1] General Nelson A. Miles, governor of the fortress, put Davis in irons for five days because he hurled the first rations issued to him in the face of the corporal who brought them.

ceptance of the result. No guerrilla operations, no Confederate
"government in exile," but young Southerners entering West
Point and Annapolis to be trained as officers of the United
States. Lee, Johnston, and almost every Southern leader except
Davis advised their people to accept the verdict of battle and
endeavor to be good citizens in a reunited country. The great
majority did so, with important reservations on the freedom of
the black.

Of the several thousand who refused to return to their former
allegiance, a large proportion went to Texas, where this postwar ditty by Innes Randolf of Virginia was particularly popular:

> Oh, I'm a good old rebel, now that's just what I am;
> For this 'fair land of freedom' I do not care a damn;
> I'm glad I fit against it—I only wish we'd won,
> And I don't want no pardon for anything I've done.

A few hundred went abroad, where some of the leaders who
had built up bank accounts in Europe during the war—notably
Slidell, Toombs, Breckenridge, and Benjamin—lived in luxury.
A Confederate colony was planted in the state of São Paolo,
Brazil, where slavery still prevailed; but abolition eventually
caught up with it. General Jo Shelby, a dashing cavalry leader,
refused to surrender his Iron Brigade; with "Prince John"
Magruder and 1000 troopers he marched to Mexico City in
August 1865. Shelby offered to enroll them in the Mexican
foreign legion and to recruit 40,000 ex-Confederates to uphold
the empire. Maximilian declined; his throne already rested on
French bayonets and he did not propose to affront his subjects
further by shifting the support to *gringos.* The Emperor, however, encouraged immigration with generous land grants in a
fertile coastal plain near Vera Cruz. About 500 people, some
with faithful slaves, arrived within a year at Carlota, as Shelby
named the new town in honor of the beautiful Empress of
Mexico. But the French army evacuated, Indian soldiers of
Juárez moved in, and this last pathetic attempt to fulfill the
Confederacy's "purple dream" was rudely liquidated.

The vast majority of Southern white people returned to their
former allegiance, retaining only a nostalgic loyalty to the
Stars and Bars. Nevertheless, something much more powerful
and pervasive than a Confederate government in exile took
place. This was the firm and almost unanimous resolve by
Southerners of European descent to keep the South a "white
man's country." That conviction, observed a Southern historian, "whether expressed with the frenzy of a demagogue or

maintained with a patrician's quietude, is the cardinal test of a Southerner and the central theme of Southern history." It implied, primarily, keeping the emancipated black subservient, like the helots in ancient Sparta. This Confederate "underground," as we may call it, has been highly successful in a formally reunited country. In the British and French West Indies, descendants of black slaves now rule unchallenged; but the American South has remained "white man's country" to this day.

This deep determination and nourished resentment never exploded into violent nationalism, because the Southerner had a long training in representative government and democratic politics. He applied violence locally and sporadically to keep the black down, but in general he had the patience to wait, knowing that under a federal system he would eventually get his own way; no federal government could maintain a squad of soldiers on every plantation. The North may have won the war, but the white South won the peace. It preserved the essence of slavery: —a pool of cheap, subservient labor—but escaped the capital outlays and social obligations that slavery imposed on the masters. So, what difference did it make whether terms imposed on the defeated South, under the name reconstruction, were tender or severe? It made a vast deal of difference. Lincoln's plan for immediate re-entrance to the Union "as it was" would have made possible a policy of gradualism toward the black. It was wrecked by a combination of Southern folly and Radical malevolence.

The economic plight of the South in 1865 was deplorable; far worse than that of central Europe in 1919 or 1945. Unfortunately, the Southern sufferings of that era entered into the reconstruction myth as something deliberately imposed by the North, not the natural result of war and secession. The country had neither capital nor currency. Where Sherman and Sheridan had passed, almost the entire apparatus of civilized life had been destroyed. In many parts, the white rural underworld swarmed out of swamps and hills to loot the planters whom it envied, and kill the blacks whom it hated. These probably did as much damage as had the Union armies. No Southern bank was solvent, no shop had much to sell. Few schools were left for white children, and none for blacks. Young men of family, who had interrupted their education to fight for Southern independence, had to labor in the fields to keep their families from starving; and a planter's family which still had young men was deemed fortunate. "Pretty much the whole of life has been merely not dying," wrote the poet Sidney Lanier. But the landed basis of Southern wealth was still there, and in regions where the invading armies had not penetrated, blacks continued to work for their former masters and life went on as before the war. Texas, uninvaded by the Union army until the end of the war, and whose manpower losses had been relatively small, was back to normal by the fall of 1865, and her population increased 35 per cent in that decade. But the Carolinas, Georgia, and the Gulf states gained only 4.4 per cent between 1860 and 1870.

Adversity brought many fine qualities to the fore. One Confederate who refused to be defeated was Washington Duke, who returned from army service to his little farm near Durham Station, North Carolina, with total assets of one log cabin, two blind mules, half a dollar, and a barn full of local-grown bright tobacco. Sherman's army, quartered nearby while waiting for Joe Johnston to surrender, found this tobacco to its liking and carried a demand for it north. This encouraged Duke and his young sons to set up a small factory, whence "Bull Durham" in muslin bags began to furnish the "makings" for cigarettes all over the country. Similarly, the Reynolds family built up Winston, North Carolina, and pipe and cigarette smoking began to replace the traditional "chaw" as the favorite American method of taking tobacco.

Normal trading relations with the North and the world were promptly restored to the South; and the victorious Union, unlike the Germans and Russians after suppressing Polish, Hungarian, and other rebellions, did not systematically confiscate private property. All Confederate and state property—which amounted to very little—was confiscated, but President Johnson's attorney general ruled that peace turned wartime confiscation of personal property into mere sequestration until the owner established his claim and took the oath of allegiance. Lands abandoned in occupied parts of the South, such as Louisiana and the sea islands of South Carolina, were in many instances sold for unpaid taxes, bought in by the government and parceled out to freedmen, but the balance of the purchase price was paid to the original owners. General Lee was compensated for his Arlington estate being taken as a national cemetery; and Richard L. Cox, whose valuable estate in Georgetown, District of Columbia, was turned over to a colored orphans' home when he defected to the Confederacy, got it back after the war and the orphans were ousted.

A large segment of the Confederate officer class, especially in the upper South, sought better opportunities in the cities of the border states or in Philadelphia and New York. Baltimore for many years was jocosely nicknamed "the poorhouse of the Confederacy"; during the rest of the century many of Baltimore's prominent business and professional men were from Virginia and further south. Some of the most eminent Americans in arts and letters in the postwar generation were Southerners—Frederick Barnard, Joseph LeConte, H. H. Richardson, Basil Gildersleeve, George W. Cable, for example—but their careers were made outside the former Confederacy.

2. Presidential Reconstruction

Reconstruction is still a controversial subject in American history, distorted by emotion. A proud people led by a warrior caste who believed themselves to be invincible were badly whipped; and on top of the resulting emotional trauma, reconstruction was imposed by the victors. Naturally, a fabulous theory about the war and reconstruction was built up, as in Germany about World War I; and as Hitler used the Jews and the Allies as scapegoats, so the white South used blacks and Republicans. This Reconstruction stereotype, already generally accepted in 1890, was promoted by David W. Griffith's film *The Birth of a Nation* (1915), and reinforced by Margaret Mitchell's novel *Gone With the Wind* (1936). It has now taken so strong a hold on the American mind, North as well as South, that it seems hopeless for a mere historian to deflate it.

The accepted fable represents reconstruction as the ruthless attempt of Northern politicians to subject the white South, starving and helpless, to an abominable rule by ex-slaves which, as the Bible says, is a thing the earth cannot bear,[1] and from which it was rescued by white-hooded knights on horseback who put the Negro "back where he belonged." There is some truth in this, but it is far from being the whole truth; and only recently have Southern as well as Northern historians endeavored to bring out facts on the other side. Yet, even after that is known, reconstruction was a deplorable and tragic episode in our history.

One basic fact, ignored by the Griffith-Mitchell stereotype, is this: The white people of the former Confederacy were masters in their own states for a period of one to three years, when no compulsion was put upon them to enfranchise the Black. During that period, when no black was allowed to vote, nothing was done to prepare him for responsible citizenship; on the contrary, the whites did everything conceivable to humiliate him and keep him down. In the South there were half a million free Blacks—mechanics, truck farmers, barbers, small busi-

[1] Proverbs xxx.22. Compare Kipling's poem "The Servant When He Reigneth."

nessmen, and the like; the literate third-generation free colored of New Orleans collectively owned property worth $15 million. These could have been used as a nucleus to educate the ex-slaves; but the white South would have none of that, or of them. And no counsel was taken of Maryland and Kentucky, whose freed slave population quietly took its place in society without violence or repression.

Nor does the reconstruction stereotype mention the streams of private benevolence which poured in from the North immediately after the war. Hodding Carter has estimated that $4 million in food, besides what the government distributed, was donated by Northerners to relieve hunger by the end of 1867. George Peabody, a Massachusetts-born financier, set up a trust fund of $3.5 million to promote primary education in the "suffering South," and with no racial strings. Grant, Farragut, and Hamilton Fish were on the board of trustees, and Barnas Sears, a former president of Brown University who administered this and Peabody's other Southern charities, saw to it that the money was well spent.

General Samuel C. Armstrong, colonel of a black regiment in the war, was so moved by the plight of the freedmen at Hampton, Virginia, in 1886, that he raised funds to found the Hampton Normal and Industrial Institute. His object, which the Institute admirably served, was to afford the blacks both mental and manual training, to fit them for freedom. Booker T. Washington was an early alumnus. Other "damyankees" who helped the South to rise again were General Clinton B. Fisk who founded Fisk University at Nashville, in 1865; Paul Tulane who revived the moribund university in Louisiana which now bears his name; and Edward Atkinson, an economist who promoted diversified agriculture and cotton manufacture in the South. Massachusetts-born William Marsh Rice of Houston, a Texas Unionist, was so badly treated during the war that he left Texas never to return but, like Loyalist Count Rumford, he remembered his old home in his will and founded Rice Institute, now Rice University. In New York City in 1868 a financial drive headed by the Rev. Henry Ward Beecher and Bishop Potter was launched for support of Washington College in Lexington, Virginia, of which Robert E. Lee had become president. For the general had captured all well-disposed hearts in the North by his innate nobility and his advice to all Southerners to accept war's verdict.

The political aspects of reconstruction were discussed in Congress during the war. Were the seceded states to be considered in or out of the Union after the rebellion had been crushed? If secession was illegal, the Southern states would still be states of the Union. But if secession was constitutional, the Confederacy might consistently be treated as a conquered country. Yet each side adopted the proper deduction from the other's premise! Radical Republicans managed to prove to their satisfaction that the Southern states had forfeited their rights, whilst former secessionists clamored for privileges in the Union which they had made every effort to destroy.

Lincoln in his last speech, on 11 April 1865, declared that the question whether the Southern states were in or out of the Union was a "pernicious abstraction." Obviously they were not "in their proper practical relation with the Union"; hence everyone's object should be to restore that relation. The President himself had already pursued that policy, and at the time of his death loyal state governments, organized by virtue of his proclamation of 1863 that these could be organized as soon as 10 per cent of the 1860 voters had taken an oath of allegiance, controlled almost the whole of Tennessee, and a large part of Arkansas and Louisiana.

The Black was the central figure in reconstruction. Lincoln, who anticipated the difficulty of making large numbers of free blacks live amicably with whites, believed that colonization of that race offered the best solution, and made several fruitless efforts to start it. Lincoln was probably right; a wholesale colonization of the freedmen in, say, Arizona, as had been done with the five civilized Indian tribes in Oklahoma, might have solved the problem of fitting people of African origin into a predominantly European society without amalgamation. That, one must admit, has never been done anywhere, either in North or South Africa, Britain or the West Indies. And in many countries where blacks have won complete control, as in Haiti and the Congo, they have killed or expelled the whites. Colonization was impractical in postwar America because the black did not wish to leave and the Southern whites wanted him to stay and work for them. Thus the freedman became temporarily a ward of the Union with undetermined status and a dubious future. The Union victory and Amendment XIII to the Constitution set him free but made no provision for his livelihood. Many blacks, assuming that freedom meant leisure, took to the woods or clustered about army posts, living on doles and dying of camp diseases.

Congress recognized this new responsibility by creating the Freedmen's Bureau of the war department in March 1865, with general powers of relief and guardianship over all refugees. It performed wonders in relief but not in racial readjustment, largely because of Southern white obstruction to its efforts. Staffed largely by civilians and headed by General O. O. Howard, the Freedmen's Bureau issued emergency rations, established more than 40 hospitals, urged blacks to return to their former masters and work for agreed wages, restored thousands of white refugees to their homes, set up courts to adjust disputes between employers and employees, and founded the first schools that the Southern black ever had, besides helping to support four colleges for his higher education—Howard, Hampton, Atlanta, and Fisk. The Bureau's work was not confined to blacks; out of 21 million rations distributed in two years, 5.5 million were issued to white people. The usual mistakes were made that always occur when an army of "do-gooders" is turned loose; but the work of the Freedman's Bureau compares favorably with that of lush, overstaffed UNRRA in Europe after World War II.

Lincoln's reconstruction plan progressed smoothly during the year 1865. President Johnson appointed provisional civil governors in every former Confederate state where Lincoln had not already done so. Each governor summoned a state constitutional convention, elected by former citizens of the Confederacy who took the oath of allegiance to the United States. Fourteen specified classes, assumed to be impenitent rebels, were not allowed to vote: civil officials of the Confederacy, state governors, general officers of the Confederate army and senior officers of the navy, former U.S. Army or Navy officers or congressmen who had defected, and all other Confederates worth over $20,000. These, however, could be pardoned by the President if they asked for it and swore allegiance; and almost 14,000, starting with General Lee, did just that. Thus, there was no general proscription, but the immediate effect was to exclude many natural leaders and experienced statesmen from the new state governments. No blacks were allowed to vote for delegates to the conventions, or in the state governments that they set up. These conventions declared invalid the ordinances of secession, repudiated state war debts, admitted the abolition of slavery, and amended the state constitutions. Elections were promptly held, and by January 1866 civil administrations were functioning in every former Confederate state except Texas. President Johnson restored the writ of habeas corpus, and on 20 August 1866 declared the "insurrection" at an end, "and that peace, order, tranquility and civil authority now exist in and throughout the whole of the United States."

Such was the fact; yet within a few months this promising work was undone, and the former Confederate states were once more thrown into the melting pot. Radicals in Congress had vowed to do this even before Lincoln's death, but they never could have got away with it but for the provocation given by the restored state governments.

This provocation consisted, partly, in what seemed an excessive participation of former Confederate officers in the new governments, their occasional acts of defiance, such as the governor of Mississippi refusing to display the national flag on the state capitol, insulting speeches about "Yankee vandals," and the like. But mostly it was the new black codes, implementing a determination of middle- and lower-class whites to keep the black "in his place," that fed ammunition to the Radicals. Many leaders of the Confederacy such as Generals Lee and Wade Hampton, and Vice President Stephens, deplored this trend and even advised that respectable, property-owning blacks be given the vote on the same terms as white men; but their words of wisdom were not heeded. The white South felt that security required all blacks to be kept down. This was not all prejudice. No benefit was derived from British experience of emancipation because a revolt of landless blacks in Jamaica erupted in October 1865 and had to be violently suppressed. The only two nations that had long been controlled by blacks, Liberia and Haiti, did not offer promising examples of that race's capacity for self-government. In Haiti a burlesque imitation of Napoleon III, "L'Empereur Faustin I," had recently been overthrown by violence.

Every Southern state gave the freedmen essential rights to contract, sue and be sued, to own and inherit some forms of property. Their marriages, which under slavery had no more significance than the mating of cattle, were legalized. But in no instance were they accorded the vote or made eligible for juries; nor could they be witnesses in a lawsuit unless a black were involved, or possess firearms, bowie knives, or liquor. In some states the freedmen were forbidden to engage in any occupation other than domestic service or agriculture, or were required to pay prohibitive license fees to do anything else. Certain black children were forcibly bound out as apprentices to white people in Mississippi. That state even forbade blacks to own or lease rural real estate, and re-enacted the old slave code for cases not covered by the new laws. Municipal regulations were devised to impress inferiority on the black. Faulkner's Mayor Sartoris's forbidding a black woman to appear on the street without an apron may have been fiction, but in some places a black was forbidden to come to town without an employer's permission, or he was required to prove that he had some acceptable occupation as an alternative to being hired out to a white man. These black codes of 1865–66 in many ways resemble Hitler's laws against the Jews, but they were not conceived as a prelude to extermination. The white South wanted the black to stay, as a valuable worker; but he must be compelled to labor for a stable economy; and for social security he must be prevented from getting "uppity," a word still common in the South. Elsewhere in the United States it was deemed a virtue for a poor man to rise; in the South, for a black to better his condition aroused suspicion and invited violence from his poor white neighbors.

Southern whites, who had never dreamed it possible to live side by side with large numbers of free blacks, believed their new laws to be liberal and generous; they were passed by people who "understood the colored." But from the black and Radical point of view they were a palpable attempt to evade the Emancipation Proclamation. The more objectionable laws, nullified by the Freedmen's Bureau (which had power to regulate labor contracts and take jurisdiction over conflicts involving blacks) were both futile and injudicious; but equally futile in the long run was Northern opposition. The essential principle of the black codes, making the African a second-class citizen, is defiantly maintained by the white public of the lower South a century after the war ended.

Little was done by the new state governments to protect blacks from white hoodlums. Efforts of the Freedmen's Bureau to help the former slaves were bitterly resented as the "outside interference" of "nigger lovers" and were often nullified by violence such as burning schools set up by the Bureau, persecuting or running white teachers from the North out of town. The Southern white yeomanry firmly believed that education "spoiled" the black, that he must forever be required to be the hewer of wood and drawer of water for a superior race. The black codes, as Hodding Carter writes, were "a backward-looking effort to deal with a desperately new problem." And the sad thing is that they need never have been, had the old planter aristocracy not forfeited its leadership to "poor white trash."

3. Congress Takes a Hand, 1866–1868

That was the situation when the Congress elected in November 1864 assembled in December 1865. Lincoln and Johnson had refrained from calling a special session, hoping to carry out their reconstruction program without interference. Every former Confederate state except Texas now had a government elected under the presidential plan; the Freedmen's Bureau had successfully wrestled with black vagrancy and the destitution of both races, and agriculture was returning to normal; but black codes of varying severity were on the statute books. Reconstruction appeared to be an accomplished fact.

Accomplished facts, however, bore no terrors for the Radical leaders, who were determined to set up new state governments based on manhood (including black) suffrage, governments which they assumed would be run by the Republican party. Congress refused to allow any member-elect from the reconstructed states to take his seat, and set up a joint committee on reconstruction, a revival of that wartime pest, the committee on the conduct of the war. This committee promptly opened hearings on conditions in the Southern states, largely from witnesses who spread on the record tales of defiant rebels and oppressed blacks and Unionists.

Congressional opposition to the Lincoln-Johnson policy was due in large part to legislative *esprit de corps*. That has happened after each of our great wars; Congress feels frustrated by the executive calling the tunes and winning all the glory, and is mad to get back "into the act." Hatred engendered by the war and the assassination of Lincoln, and tales of horror spread about by the human wrecks released from Andersonville, also played their part. But the fundamental reason for the forthcoming appeal to passion seems to have been political. If the Southern states returned a solid Democratic contingent to Congress, the reunited Democratic party would have a majority in both houses and be able to repeal the fiscal, homestead, and other legislation passed by Republican congresses. As Thaddeus Stevens put it, the states of the South "ought never to be recognized as valid states, until the Constitution shall have been so amended . . . as to secure perpetual ascendancy" to the Republican party. The amendment that Stevens had in mind was Black suffrage. By this device, selfish and cynical politicians obtained the support of humanitarians an doctrinaires who believed the vote to be necessary to protect and uplift the Black.

Thaddeus Stevens, a sour and angry congressman, really loved Blacks; at least he lived with one, and had himself buried among them. The destruction of his property at Chambersburg by Lee's soldiers in 1863 had made him at the age of seventy-four harsh and bitter in his hatred, which now encompassed the memory of Lincoln with the living Johnson. Former slaves he would exalt to political and social equality; the former masters he would disfranchise and expropriate, distributing their landed property among the freedmen. Stevens was a finished parliamentarian, with a talent for controlled invective and devastating sarcasm. Charles Sumner, Republican leader in the Senate, vain, pedantic, and irritable, was a doctrinaire. Against the ex-Confederates he cherished no vindictive feelings; but, with little personal knowledge of former slaves, he believed that they only wanted the vote to prove themselves worthy of sharing the duties and privileges of citizenship. While Sumner, who loved the sound of his own voice, declaimed in polished periods on the rights and wrongs of the colored, Stevens played for time. It would not do to make an issue of Black suffrage on its merits, for few of the Northern states outside New England allowed their Blacks to vote; and the reaction of the average Union veteran to his contacts with the freedmen bordered on contempt.

In April 1866 the joint committee reported a congressional plan for reconstruction, in its essence a denial of the right of statehood to the South until black equality should be incorporated in their laws. Since even the Radicals doubted the constitutionality of any act of Congress to that effect, their plan was embodied in what subsequently became Amendments XIV and XV to the Constitution. These guaranteed to blacks civil rights and the vote, disqualified ex-confederates who had formerly held federal office, and forbade the states to pay Confederate war debts. Southern representatives would be admitted to Congress, it was announced, only on condition of their states ratifying the XIV Amendment. In July 1866 Congress passed over the President's veto an act giving the Freedmen's Bureau a new lease on life, at a time when its legitimate relief work was almost completed; and this worthy organization degenerated into a political machine.

The issue was now joined between President Johnson and the Radicals. Everything turned on the election of a new House of Representatives in November 1866. Politically astute Lincoln might have out-maneuvered the sharp-witted Radical leaders, but Johnson played into their hands. Of origin as humble as Lincoln's, in early life a tailor in a Tennessee mountain village and unable to write until taught by his wife, he had honesty and courage, but wanted tact and the art of winning men's minds and hearts. His policy was identical with Lincoln's, but he was unable to connect with Northern sentiment. And Johnson was in a far more difficult situation than Lincoln had been on the morrow of victory and the eve of death. He had taken over Lincoln's cabinet, and both Seward and Welles were loyal to him, but Stanton sneaked out cabinet secrets to the Radicals and they, including most of the professional Republican politicians, controlled the party machinery and the civil service. Johnson's pugnacious personality antagonized people, and by undignified acts and foolish speeches he lost the support of the Northern pulpit, press, and business.

In the congressional campaign of 1866, the most important off-presidential election in our history, the issue was clearly drawn; in most districts the voters had to choose between a Radical Republican and a Copperhead Democrat. Johnson openly supported the Democrats but managed the campaign very ill. Incapable of advocating a tolerant policy in a tolerant manner, his "swing around the circle," a stumping tour of the Middle West, became an undignified contest of vituperation. Instead of appealing to the memory of Lincoln, and to the Christian virtue of forgiveness, he called names and rattled the dry bones of state rights. The Radicals, on the other hand, soft-pedaling black suffrage, made the issue one of "patriotism" against "rebellion." Reiterated tales of Southern defiance and race riots at Memphis and New Orleans in which hundreds of blacks were murdered by white hoodlums, were played up for even more than they were worth. "Jefferson Davis is in the casemate at Fortress Monroe, but Andrew Johnson is doing his work," declared Sumner. "Witness Memphis, witness New Orleans." Under such circumstances it is not surprising that the Northern people returned a sufficient Republican majority to override any presidential veto.

The newly elected Congress met on 7 March 1867 in a vindictive temper. There is nothing to equal the kindness of the American heart when touched, except the bad judgment of Americans when irritated; and although the truth about the Southern states was enough to annoy men of good will, Radical propaganda had so enlarged on the facts as to make it seem that a defiantly disloyal South was planning to revive the Confederacy. One heard no more in Washington "the words peace, pardon and clemency" as Chambrun did in April 1865; now, barely eighteen months later, all one heard spoken of was armed force, punishment, retaliation. Photographs of the Radical leaders of this period, and of Johnson too, show visages glowering balefully like a Mussolini or a Hitler, in contrast to the calm and dignified war leaders, or the conventional smiles of latter-day politicians.

Lincoln had grasped a great truth which other Western statesmen never realized until 1945: that reconstruction of a shattered empire must be approached with wisdom rather than strict justice; the defeated foe must be helped to his feet and treated more like the prodigal son than a convicted felon. Lincoln and Johnson had tried this Christian policy on the South; the South (so it seemed) had contemptuously declined the friendly hand and defied the victors. Woe, then, to the South!

4. Reconstruction Reconstructed, 1867–1875

In March 1867 military rule by virtue of act of Congress replaced the civil administrations which had been operating in the South for one or two years. The first Reconstruction Act divided the South into five military districts under general officers who were to take orders from General Grant, not the President, and whose first duties were to protect persons and property, create a new electorate based on male suffrage, and supervise the election of conventions to draft new state constitutions on the same basis. They were also given the right to replace civil officials elected by fraud or violence, and to purge legislatures of "disloyal" members.

The five military governors, known in Southern literature as the "satraps" or "despots,"[1] ruled with a firm hand, though sometimes with flagrant disregard of civil rights. Confederate veterans' organizations, parades, and even historical societies were suppressed. Thousands of local officials and the governors of six states were removed. Civil courts were superseded by military tribunals, when the courts could not be depended on to punish violence against blacks. The legislatures of Georgia, Alabama, and Louisiana were purged in the Cromwellian sense; state laws were set aside or modified. An army of occupation, some 20,000 strong and aided by black militia, enforced this military rule, harsh indeed but with the merits of honesty and efficiency. Great efforts were made by the military to cope with economic disorganization and to regulate social life. Thus, in South Carolina General Dan Sickles, the most hated of the "satraps," stayed foreclosures on property, made the wages of farm laborers a first lien on crops, prohibited the manufacture of whisky, and forbade discrimination against Blacks. The troops were mostly confined in forts, army posts, and barracks; they were not quartered on the people in traditional army of occupation fashion, and not called out except to supervise elections and quell disorder.

In each of the ten states over which they had jurisdiction, the Union military enrolled a new electorate. In South Carolina, Alabama, Florida, Mississippi, and Louisiana the black voters outnumbered the white. This electorate chose in every state a

---

[1] The initial appointees were Generals Schofield, Thomas, Ord, Sickles, and Sheridan. The last two (and Pope who relieved Thomas) were replaced by President Grant after they had made themselves obnoxious to the white population through arbitrary acts.

constitutional convention which drafted a new constitution enfranchising the blacks, disqualifying former Confederate leaders, and guaranteeing civil and political equality to the freedmen.

The new constitutions were more democratic than those they superseded. South Carolina's, for example, abolished property qualifications for officeholding, drew up a new bill of rights, reformed local government and judicial administration, abolished imprisonment for debt, protected homesteads from foreclosure, enlarged the rights of women, and established the state's first system of universal public education. By the summer of 1868 reconstructed governments had been set up in eight of the Southern states; the other three—Mississippi, Texas, and Virginia—were reconstructed in 1870. After their legislatures had ratified Amendments XIV and XV, Congress formally readmitted them to the Union, seated their elected representatives and senators, and, as soon as the supremacy of the new governments appeared reasonably secure, withdrew or greatly diminished the army garrisons.

Both conventions and legislatures might have been of higher quality if thousands of whites had not boycotted the elections, or if they had condescended to organize the black vote and play on the African's basic trust in his old master class and not left that field to the "carpetbaggers" and "scalawags." President Johnson pardoned 13,500 Confederates excluded by earlier acts, and his "universal" proclamation at Christmastide 1868 left only 300 persons unpardoned and ineligible to vote, in the entire South. But congressional reconstruction acts annulled the benefits of executive clemency by denying political privileges to those pardoned by the two Presidents.

The "carpetbagger" was supposed to be a Northern adventurer who came South after the war with all his possessions in a carpetbag—a satchel made of two squares of carpeting held together by cloth or leather. A "scalawag" meant any Southern white who joined the Republican party or took a job under the Freedmen's Bureau. Some carpetbaggers were indeed adventurers—H. C. Warmouth, a notoriously corrupt governor of Louisiana, had been a Union officer with a bad war record —but many were Northerners who came South after the war to promote new industries. John T. Wilder and Willard Warner of Ohio, both Union general officers, were largely responsible for starting the iron works at Birmingham and Chattanooga. And some of the alleged scalawags, such as General Longstreet and Colonels J. A. Alcorn and R. W. Flournoy, were former Confederate officers who joined the Republican party in hope of moderating Radical zeal.

Although some illiterate blacks were elected to state conventions and legislatures, many of the colored leaders were men of education who showed ability equal to the ordinary run of state legislators anywhere. For instance, Jonathan J. Wright, state senator and associate justice of the supreme court of South Carolina, had been a member of the Pennsylvania bar before the war; Robert B. Elliott, member of the lower house of South Carolina and later representative in Congress, had been educated at Eton College in England. Hiram R. Revels, educated at Knox College, pastor of a Baltimore church before the war and chaplain to a black regiment, was elected in 1870 to Jefferson Davis's former seat in the United States Senate; John R. Lynch, a self-educated former slave of Louisiana, later a professional photographer, became speaker of his state house of representatives and a congressman. Of those whom he observed in Congress, Speaker Blaine wrote, "They were as a rule studious, earnest, ambitious men, whose public conduct . . . would be honorable to any race." Black faces in the newly elected legislatures were naturally conspicuous, and obnoxious to the average Southern white; but it is inaccurate to describe the state system under reconstruction as black rule. The colored controlled no state government at any time, and only in South Carolina did they ever have a majority in either house. Owing to their inexperience, they were manipulated by carpetbaggers and scalawags, on whom most of the blame for the corruption of these states should be placed, and who alone profited by it. Negroes did not attempt to domineer over or pass vindictive legislation against their former masters; in Mississippi the colored members of the legislature even petitioned Congress to restore the political abilities of former Confederates. Unlike the Congolese Africans who went on a vicious rampage in 1960 when Belgian rule was withdrawn, the Southern Black of 1865–75 behaved like a civilized and responsible citizen. He made no attempt to repeal laws against mixed marriages or to force his way into white society; on the contrary, he formed hundreds of "African" Methodist, Baptist, and other Protestant churches.

Although the white South was willing to tolerate colored clowns in office, it bitterly resented any black who showed political intelligence or ability, since he disproved the theory that his race was incapable of improvement. James Pike, on his way south in 1873, looked in at the lower house of the Virginia assembly where a "member three-quarters black" was speaking ably against a certain tax bill. He was "listened to with a good deal of interest after it was found that he could not be drowned out by rustlings and loud talk," although "the venerable old

Virginia gentlemen on the Democratic benches looked on with a mixture of surprise and chagrin at the spectacle." That was typical: surprise that the black could do it, chagrin that he was in a position to do it; and, had these been poor whites instead of gentlemen, there would have been a note of hatred.

Although the Radical governments that flourished for periods of two years (in North Carolina) to eight years (in Louisiana, Florida, and Texas) are famous for picturesque and flagrant forms of corruption, such as a free restaurant-bar for the Palmetto State "solons," and Governor Warmouth's stealing half a million dollars from Louisiana school funds, they were also responsible for much good legislation. War damage to public buildings, bridges, and roads was repaired; railroad building— a principal source of graft—was encouraged; efforts were made to obtain capital and settlers from the North and Europe, and, most of all, free public education for all children, although in racially separate schools, was established throughout the South by 1870. The black codes, naturally, were repealed, and laws against vagrancy were applied equally to both races. Penal systems were modified, though not always improved; public works were undertaken. All this cost money, still a scarce commodity in the South, and as the people could not bear heavy taxation, deficit financing was the order of the day. It may be said in excuse, though not in defense, of the reconstructed state governments, that their "lily-white" successors and many of their Northern contemporaries were no better; and that major operations such as those of the Whisky Ring and Boss Tweed's steal of over $100 million from New York City threw the operations of Southern carpetbaggers and scalawags into the shade.

A curious feature of reconstruction is the rival expectations that were built up. The former slaves believed that each Negro family was to be given "forty acres and a mule" by Uncle Sam; and Thaddeus Stevens, had he lived, would have pressed for just that, but nothing of the sort was attempted. Nor is it likely that giving land to former slaves would have helped them much. Attempts to set up peasant proprieties out of large landed estates, in Mexico and elsewhere, have mostly failed, as the small landowner cannot maintain himself without seed, stock, implements, and training to tide him over the first years of independence. And if he does not get these, as he certainly would not have done in the United States, he drifts back to serfdom.

On the other side, many Southern whites indulged the wild notion that if they could only elect a solid Democratic contingent to Congress, these would join with Northern Democrats to pay compensation for the freed slaves, and discharge the Confederate debt. A bill to indemnify former slaves for their years of servitude would have had a better chance in Congress.

After all that can be said in their favor, the congressionally reconstructed state governments were a disgrace, and in the end neither the freedmen nor the Republican party profited. The blacks, thrown into politics without preparation or experience, under conditions which would have tried the wisest statesmanship, were abandoned by the best men of the South and deceived by the worst; their innocence exposed them to temptation and their ignorance betrayed them into the hands of astute and mischievous spoilsmen. Some of the wisest men in the North predicted this. Even old abolitionist Garrison wished the Blacks to be given more education before they were accorded the vote.

Worse disgrace was to come—the impeachment of President Johnson and the hooded violence of the Ku Klux Klan.

5. Impeachment of Johnson and End of Reconstruction

The Radical leaders of the Republican party, not content with establishing party ascendancy in the South, aimed at capturing the federal government under guise of putting the presidency under wraps. By a series of usurpations they intended to make the majority in Congress the ultimate judge of its own powers, and the President a mere chairman of a cabinet responsible to Congress, as the British cabinet is to the House of Commons. An opening move in this game was the Tenure of Office Act of March 1867 which made it impossible for the President to control his administration, by requiring him to obtain the advice and consent of the Senate for removals as well as appointments to office. The next move was to dispose of Johnson by impeachment, so that Radical Ben Wade, president pro tem of the Senate, would succeed to his office and title.

Johnson, convinced that the Tenure of Office Act was unconstitutional—an attitude later vindicated by the Supreme Court in *Myers* v. *United States*—countered in August 1867 by ordering Secretary Stanton, who had long been playing with the Radicals, to resign. Stanton refused and barricaded himself in the war department. On 24 February 1868 the House of Representatives impeached the President before the Senate, "for high crimes and misdemeanors," as the Constitution provides. Ten of the eleven articles of impeachment rang changes on the removal of Stanton, the other consisted of garbled newspaper reports of the President's speeches.

Although a monstrous charge preferred by George S. Boutwell, that Johnson was accessory to the murder of Lincoln, was not included, the impeachment of Johnson was one of the most disgraceful episodes in our history. It was managed by a committee led by Benjamin F. Butler and Thaddeus Stevens, who exhausted every device, appealed to every prejudice and passion, and rode roughshod, when they could, over legal obstacles in their ruthless attempt to punish the President for his opposition to their plans. Ben Butler, now uglier and paunchier than ever, employed a device borrowed from Jenkins's ear in 1739; he illustrated an oration on the horrors of presidential reconstruction by waving a bloody shirt which allegedly belonged to an Ohio carpetbagger flogged by Klansmen in Mississippi.

Johnson was defended by able counsel including William Maxwell Evarts, leader of the American bar, and Benjamin R. Curtis, formerly a justice of the Supreme Court. They tore the prosecution's case to shreds. No valid grounds, legal or otherwise, existed for impeachment. Yet the Radicals would have succeeded in their object but for Chief Justice Chase's insistence on legal procedure, and for seven courageous Republican senators who sacrificed their political future by voting for acquittal: Grimes of Iowa, Trumbull of Illinois, Ross of Kansas, Fessenden of Maine, Van Winkle of West Virginia, Fowler of Tennessee, and Henderson of Missouri.[1] One more affirmative vote, and Ben Wade, president of the Senate, would have been installed in the White House. Then, in all probability, the Supreme Court would have been battered into submission and the Radicals would have triumphed over the Constitution as completely as over the South.

After the trial was over, President Johnson had less than ten months to serve, and the Republican national nominating convention met shortly after his acquittal. There was no longer any effective opposition to the Radicals within party ranks, and the reconstructed states gave them plenty of docile delegates. General Grant, who, to his discredit and subsequent sorrow, had been brought into the Radical camp by arousing an ambition to be President, obtained the nomination by acclamation, with Schuyler Colfax of Indiana for Vice President. The Democrats, regarding Johnson as a liability, nominated

[1] President Kennedy told the story of Senator Edmund G. Ross in his *Profiles in Courage*. All seven were denounced as Benedict Arnolds, Judas Iscariots, etc., and all but Grimes and Fessenden, who died shortly, were defeated when next they came up for election.

Horatio Seymour, the war governor of New York who had skated close to copperheadism. Grant won 214 electoral votes to Seymour's 80, but his plurality in the popular vote was only 300,000; three Southern states which would certainly have voted for Seymour took no part in the election. It would have been better for the country had that elderly lawyer and politician of the Jackson-Van Buren line been President for the next eight years, instead of General Grant.

Social revolutions such as Congress intended the reconstruction of the South to be, cannot be accomplished except by overwhelming force applied mercilessly and over a long period of time. That is how fascist and communist governments operate, but no Christian government could be merciless; and the South succeeded in wearing down Northern willingness to apply even limited force.

Thaddeus Stevens had the wit to see that political equality would avail the blacks little, as long as the whites owned the land. His death in 1868 cost Radicalism its fighting edge, and his program of confiscation was not carried out. Thenceforth congressional reconstruction was on the defensive. Of several attempts to hold ground already won, the most notable was Amendment XV to the Constitution, ratified in 1870, forbidding the states to deny anyone the vote "on account of race, color, or previous condition of servitude." To the time of writing, this has proved a mere paper guarantee.

Even if the congressionally reconstructed states had been as pure as Jeffersonian Virginia, the Southern whites would have overthrown them by fair means or foul, because of racial animosity and excessive taxation. Poor-white animosity was directed primarily against black schools and militia. Northern teachers who came South to teach the freedmen were ostracized, forced to board with colored families (and then accused of miscegenation), whipped, even murdered. The black militia companies organized by the carpetbag governors to preserve law and order were bitterly hated, and some of their officers were murdered. To the Southern gentry, the carpetbag governments were rendered intolerable by a crushing burden of taxation on real estate, forcing thousands of farms which the owners were painfully trying to bring back into production, to be sold for unpaid taxes. And the situation became worse after the panic of 1873, which depressed agricultural prices. The planter class was being strangled.

Even before Grant's election the white South was preparing to recover supremacy by the only means left: a combination of tomfoolery and terror. The methods of Radicals who had organized the black vote were turned against them and life became very uncomfortable for carpetbaggers, who were apt to find themselves "accidental" targets for the bullets of participants in a shooting affray. The blacks were dealt with largely by secret societies, of which the most famous, though not the most powerful, was the Ku Klux Klan. It began with a group of wild young men in Pulaski, Tennessee, who discovered that their initiation garb of sheets and pillowcases made them authentic spirits from another world to the superstitious. Realizing political possibilities, they formed other groups which in 1867 organized as "The Invisible Empire of the South." This was before congressional reconstruction began. When it did begin, this and other secret societies, such as the Knights of the White Camellia, became an "invisible empire," policing unruly or allegedly impudent blacks, delivering spectral warnings against using the ballot, and whipping or even murdering some of those who did. Thus Radical power was paralyzed at its source. Although apologists for the South decry the crimes of the K.K.K. (163 blacks murdered in one Florida county in 1871, 300 murdered in a few parishes outside New Orleans), they were led by "the flower of Southern manhood," who cannot escape responsibility for acts in the same class with those of Hitler's storm troopers. The "Grand Wizard" of the K.K.K. was General Nathaniel B. Forrest CSA; General Gordon was "Grand Dragon" for Georgia, and former Governor Vance had the same "exalted" rank in North Carolina. The Klan was formally disbanded in 1869 and the Knights the following year; but under one or another guise the intimidation of the blacks went on.

The Radical answer was renewed military occupation of districts formerly evacuated, and a new crop of supervisory acts of Congress authorizing the President to suspend the writ of habeas corpus and suppress disturbances by military force. Some 7400 indictments were found under these acts, but there were relatively few convictions, and only once did President Grant find it expedient to re-establish military rule on a large scale. And he withdrew all black units of the regular army.

Grant was re-elected in 1872, but two years later the Democrats captured the House of Representatives, marking Northern repudiation of Radicalism. In the meantime all Southern states had been "readmitted" to representation in Congress, and by the Amnesty Act of 1872 all white men still disfranchised were restored to full political privilege. An immense impact on Northern opinion was exerted through *The Prostrate State* (1873), by a former abolitionist, James S. Pike of Maine. This *Uncle Tom's Cabin* in reverse, an exaggerated description of conditions in South Carolina, has become a classic document

of the reconstruction stereotype. During the centennial cele-
brations of 1875–76 Southern orators like Henry W. Grady and
Lucius Quintus Cincinnatus Lamar played on the "mystic
chords of memory" to which Lincoln had vainly appealed in
1861, and paid moving tributes to the Great Emancipator
himself. In this sentimental meeting of hearts the cause of the
freedman was forgotten; and whatever solicitude for him survived in the North was conveniently overlaid by the picture of
the "happy darkey" presented by Joel Chandler Harris the
creator of Uncle Remus, and Thomas Nelson Page the creator of "Marse Chan's" Sam. In Congress, Ben Butler proposed
an amendment to a civil rights bill in 1875 which would have
compelled racial integration of all schools in the South, but
President Grant had the amendment stricken out on a plea
from Barnas Sears, Yankee almoner of the Peabody fund.

By this time the Radicals were in full retreat in the South.
Factional struggles between carpetbaggers and scalawags split
the Republican party; and the Blacks, finding that their vote
produced no "forty acres and a mule," began to desert the
Republicans and vote for members of the old master class in
whom they had confidence. It was becoming evident that Radical rule could only be maintained by a much stronger army of
occupation, but Congress was becoming so tired of reconstruction that the garrisons were progressively weakened. In state
after state the white people organized as "Conservatives" or
"Redeemers," and recaptured control of the political machinery. This occurred between 1869 and 1871 in Tennessee,
Virginia, North Carolina, and Georgia; in 1874–75 in Alabama, Arkansas, Texas, and Mississippi.

What happened in Mississippi is instructive. There the
carpetbag Republican governor was Adelbert Ames, a West
Pointer from Maine who had fought brilliantly in the Union
army and had come to Mississippi hoping to be a conciliator
But the conduct of white men toward blacks impelled him to
champion that race. Even Ames's enemies admitted him to
have been an honest and courteous gentleman who did his best
to build up the state's economy. Appointed provisional governor by General Grant in 1868 and elected United States
Senator in 1870, he resigned to be elected governor of Mississippi in 1873 for a four-year term. Unable to control his
more voracious supporters, he alienated some of the best, such
as Senator Revels. When elections for the state legislature were
coming up in 1875, Ames agreed with the Democratic leaders
to disband the black militia which, they claimed, were the
principal inciters of election riots, in return for a promise to
restrain white people from violence. This promise the local

Democrats either could not or would not keep, and they had as their leader L. Q. C. Lamar, the silver-tongued orator. Any meeting of black voters was apt to be set upon by armed white men; and in these clashes blacks, still timid and unresourceful, were invariably worsted. Governor Ames appealed to President Grant for federal troops, but was told by the attorney general, "The whole public are tired of these annual autumnal outbreaks in the South." With most of the Republicans intimidated from voting (only four Republican votes cast in one county where there was a black majority), the Democrats won a majority in both houses and threatened to impeach Ames. He resigned, since his position was hopeless, and the president of the newly elected senate became governor. A United States Senate committee which investigated this election reported it to be "one of the darkest chapters in American history," but nothing was done about it; the Northern public was sick of the subject.

By 4 March 1877, when Rutherford B. Hayes was inaugurated President, carpetbag regimes had been overthrown in every Southern state except South Carolina and Louisiana. In the Palmetto state two rival governors were elected: General Wade Hampton csa as champion of the Redeemers, and General Daniel H. Chamberlain usa as candidate of the Republicans. President Hayes broke this deadlock by withdrawing federal troops from Columbia on 10 April 1877, when the Redeemers peaceably took possession. Two weeks later, when the troops were evacuated from New Orleans, white rule was completely restored in Louisiana.

These Redeemer governments did not entirely undo the work of their predecessors. The most prominent and respected of the new governors, such as Wade Hampton and George F. Drew of Florida, had promised to respect the civil rights of the colored, and made their promises good. In every former Confederate state except Texas, which fell into the hands of spoilsmen and crooks, the government was now in the hands of the old officer class. For two decades, blacks continued to vote in large numbers, and a few were elected to state legislatures. Even more important than laws were good racial relations. Booker T. Washington, a former slave who founded Tuskegee Institute in Alabama, dedicated himself to making his people better farmers and artisans, and discouraged any effort toward political or social equality. Thomas Wentworth Higginson, former colonel of a black regiment, found race relations to be just and friendly when he revisited the South. The editor of a black newspaper in New York, who went South looking for trouble, found none. In general, white and colored mingled on railroad and street cars, at lunch counters, theaters, circuses, and public parks. But the disgruntled "white supremacists" had only gone underground, as numerous lynchings of blacks in rural districts indicated; and presently "Jim Crow" would emerge and the lot of the Southern black become worse than before.

Thus, by 1877 all former Confederate states were back in the Union and in charge of their domestic affairs, subject only to the requirements of two constitutional amendments to protect the freedmen's civil rights.

Looking back over the whole episode of reconstruction, one must regret that the magnanimous policy of Lincoln was not long followed. Yet, all in all, considering what it cost the Union to preserve itself, the victors treated the vanquished pretty well. A recent European historian of our Civil War remarked wryly that the Poles who were overrun in World War II, the central Europeans subjected to one totalitarian regime after another, the defeated Hungarian rebels of 1956, and the expropriated landowners and middle class in every communist state, including Cuba, would have considered the sufferings of the Southern white people a heavenly dispensation in comparison with theirs.

INDEX